COMPARATIVE CRIMINAL PROCEDURE

RESEARCH HANDBOOKS IN COMPARATIVE LAW

Series Editors: Francesco Parisi, *Oppenheimer Wolff and Donnelly Professor of Law, University of Minnesota, USA and Professor of Economics, University of Bologna, Italy* and Tom Ginsburg, *Professor of Law, University of Chicago, USA*

The volumes in this series offer high-level discussion and analysis on particular aspects of legal systems and the law. Well-known scholars edit each handbook and bring together accessible yet sophisticated contributions from an international cast of top researchers. The first series of its kind to cover a wide range of comparative issues so comprehensively, this is an indispensable resource for students and scholars alike.

Titles in this series include:

Comparative Administrative Law
Edited by Susan Rose-Ackerman and Peter L. Lindseth

Comparative Constitutional Law
Edited by Tom Ginsburg and Rosalind Dixon

Methods of Comparative Law
Edited by Pier Giuseppe Monateri

Comparative Law and Society
Edited by David S. Clark

Comparative Labor Law
Edited by Matthew W. Finkin and Guy Mundlak

Comparative Tort Law
Edited by Mauro Bussani and Anthony Sebok

Comparative Competition Law
Edited by John Duns, Arlen Duke and Brendan Sweeney

Comparative Law and Economics
Edited by Giovanni B. Ramello and Theodore Eisenberg

Comparative Criminal Procedure
Edited by Jacqueline E. Ross and Stephen C. Thaman

Comparative Criminal Procedure

Edited by

Jacqueline E. Ross

Professor of Law, University of Illinois College of Law, USA

Stephen C. Thaman

Professor of Law, Saint Louis University School of Law, USA

RESEARCH HANDBOOKS IN COMPARATIVE LAW

 Edward Elgar
PUBLISHING

Cheltenham, UK • Northampton, MA, USA

Published by
Edward Elgar Publishing Limited
The Lypiatts
15 Lansdown Road
Cheltenham
Glos GL50 2JA
UK

Edward Elgar Publishing, Inc.
William Pratt House
9 Dewey Court
Northampton
Massachusetts 01060
USA

A catalogue record for this book
is available from the British Library

Library of Congress Control Number: 2016931737

This book is available electronically in the **Elgar**online
Law subject collection
DOI 10.4337/9781781007198

ISBN 978 1 78100 718 1 (cased)
ISBN 978 1 78100 719 8 (eBook)

Typeset by Columns Design XML Ltd, Reading
Printed and bound in Great Britain by TJ International Ltd, Padstow

Stephen C. Thaman:
To my daughter, Raquella

Jacqueline E. Ross:
To my parents, Jana and Friedrich Katz

Contents

Contributors

Shawn Marie Boyne is Professor of Law at Indiana University's Robert H. McKinney School of Law, USA.

Mathilde Cohen is Associate Professor of Law at the University of Connecticut School of Law, USA.

Shahrzad Fouladvand is a Lecturer in Human Rights and Research Fellow at the Wilberforce Institute at the University of Hull, UK.

Elisabetta Grande is Full Professor of Comparative Law at East Piedmont University 'Amedeo Avogadro', Alessandria, Italy.

Jacqueline S. Hodgson is Professor of Law at the School of Law, University of Warwick, UK.

David T. Johnson is Professor of Sociology at the University of Hawaii, USA.

Vikramaditya S. Khanna is the William W. Cook Professor of Law at the University of Michigan Law School, USA.

Nikolai Kovalev is Associate Professor of Criminology at Wilfrid Laurier University, Canada.

Máximo Langer is Professor of Law at the UCLA School of Law, USA.

Andrew D. Leipold is the Edwin M. Adams Professor of Law at the University of Illinois College of Law, USA.

Kartikey Mahajan is an Advocate at the Supreme Court of India.

Jason Mazzone is Professor of Law and Co-Director of the Program in Constitutional Theory, History, and Law at the University of Illinois at Urbana-Champaign, USA.

Jacqueline E. Ross is Professor of Law at the University of Illinois College of Law, USA.

Christopher Slobogin is the Milton Underwood Chair at Vanderbilt University Law School, USA.

Stephen C. Thaman is Professor of Law at the St Louis University School of Law, USA.

Jenia Iontcheva Turner is Professor of Law at SMU Dedman School of Law in Dallas, Texas, USA.

Richard Vogler is Professor of Comparative Criminal Law and Justice at the University of Sussex, UK.

Tzu-te Wen is a Public Prosecutor at Taipei Prosecutors' Office and an Adjunct Assistant Professor at Ming Chuan University Law School, Taiwan.

PART I

INTRODUCTION

Introduction: mapping dialogue and change in comparative criminal procedure

Jacqueline E. Ross and Stephen C. Thaman

The study of comparative criminal procedure is not only a study of how national legal systems differ from each other but also a study of the dialogue between them, and between legal actors and interest groups across systems. Participants in this dialogue copy, criticize, or champion other systems. They seek to urge emulation of foreign models, or change their own. And they analyze processes and factors that bring legal systems closer or drive them apart or that create new hybrids out of elements of many different systems. Our volume seeks to track this dialogue and its evolution, mapping national changes over time in the influence of national models or of transplanted procedural devices, such as plea bargaining and the jury system, which have cross-pollinated multiple otherwise very different systems of criminal procedure. In particular, our volume tracks three shifts in the field of comparative criminal procedure.

These include, first, the way systems deal with error, and the recognition of their fallibility; a number of contributors to this volume track reform efforts that are meant to anticipate and correct errors. These reform efforts also seek to identify the vulnerabilities that contribute to mistakes and can lead to wrongful convictions, as well as acquittals against the evidence. Dialogue between systems often concerns the presumed promise or limitations of other systems' procedural devices for detecting and avoiding miscarriages of justice.

The second shift includes the rapid pace of legal change and increased borrowing and transplantation of procedural devices from the adversarial criminal process, including the jury system and plea bargaining. A number of chapters query the extent to which this represents an Americanization of criminal procedure, or instead a development of new hybrid and pluralistic models of adjudication. To the extent change is promoted by supranational bodies like the European Court of Human Rights and supranational norms like the European Convention of Human Rights, the contributors also debate the extent to which harmonization and convergence on minimalistic procedural safeguards tend to dilute the already strong protections in some countries as the price for raising the standards of others.

Third, our volume tracks a shift in the ways in which systems are compared. Though the contrast between adversarial and inquisitorial systems of criminal procedure retains considerable influence on the field of comparative criminal procedure – and perhaps too much, as Máximo Langer's conclusion suggests – legal reforms, transplantation, and borrowing have also suggested new dimensions along which systems may be compared. These include holistic criteria, which compare ways in which different systems anticipate error and compensate for the vulnerabilities of one part of the criminal process through advanced procedural safeguards; through the injection of lay-factfinders at trial; or through corrective mechanisms at the back end. But comparisons can also focus on fragments or segments of the criminal process, and on individual procedural devices and the ways in which transplantation transforms them. We note that many comparisons now focus on the legitimacy of the criminal process, variously evaluating the extent to which different procedural devices tend to promote or undermine the legitimacy of evidentiary inputs (which we call *input legitimacy*); the extent to which they promote or cast doubt on the ways these inputs are evaluated (which we call *process legitimacy*); and the extent to which they produce fair and reliable results (which we call *outcome legitimacy*).

And, finally, we note that many comparisons of legal systems now adopt either a diachronic approach, which organizes a comparison of legal systems around particular stages of the criminal process (comparing, for example, the standards for pretrial detention, or the evidentiary thresholds for invasive investigative procedures), or a synchronic, multi-track approach, which compares the various bypass mechanisms by which legal systems make it possible to avoid trial (for example, through quasi-consensual resolutions such as plea bargaining) or to opt out of the criminal process altogether, in the name of crime prevention and the pursuit of intelligence, mooting the question of individual guilt or innocence in favor of concern with risk management and the most efficient processing of bulk data about people, most of whom are assumed to be innocent.

1. THE PRESUMPTION OF INNOCENCE, THE SEARCH FOR TRUTH, AND THE PROBLEM OF WRONGFUL CONVICTIONS

In recent years, the comparative study of criminal procedure has come to be shaped by a variety of parallel developments worldwide. One of these is the recurrence of scandals that have exposed wrongful convictions and have renewed interest in the dynamics that may propel a rush to premature judgment. In the United States, for example, the Innocence Project has highlighted the disturbing number of cases in which innocent defendants have been convicted and sentenced to death for murders they did not commit. Increasingly sophisticated methods for retrieving and analyzing DNA have made it easier to detect such errors, which helps explain the rapid proliferation of cases in which demonstrably innocent defendants were convicted. At the same time, the high stakes for defendants charged with capital crimes have made the risk of error sufficiently salient, politically and legally, to attract legal talent and institutional resources to the task of identifying erroneous convictions and figuring out what went wrong. This has led to increased awareness of problems with eye-witness testimony; of the distorting impact of deceptive questioning; of the dynamics that lead innocent defendants to plead guilty to crimes they did not commit; and of the ways in which accurate adjudication can be undermined by moral panics surrounding particular types of offenses and by the cognitive biases of investigators and fact-finders.

While death penalty litigation has highlighted these concerns in the United States, there are few legal systems that have not been affected by disclosures of unjust convictions. In many modern legal systems, increased procedural protections for criminal defendants, along with scientific advances in testing forensic evidence, have made it easier to identify such cases, and therefore more politically and legally pressing to identify systemic flaws and institutional blind-spots that were at fault, and to improve the criminal process in ways that reduce the risk of error.

Concerns about unjust convictions have prompted many scholars of criminal procedure to adopt a tragic view of criminal procedure as inherently flawed. Such scholars are less interested in juxtaposing ideal-typical versions of how systems are designed to work and instead compare legal systems according to their characteristic weaknesses and vulnerabilities, as well as the fail-safe systems that have been put in place in order to deal with a system's inevitable failures. Chapters by Elisabetta Grande, David Johnson, and Stephen Thaman, for example, emphasize the extent to which Spanish, Japanese, and Russian reforms designate lay-people to serve as a corrective for and a counter-weight to the other, professional actors in the legal system. Contributors like Stephen Thaman and Shawn Boyne identify the tragic flaws and blind-spots of legal systems, which lead them to compare legal systems as error-prone ensembles. This holistic approach suggests ways in which different procedural mechanisms interact to compound or, alternatively, to prevent or to expose and to correct mistakes when they occur. David Johnson likewise points out that reforms to one part of the legal system may spur collateral improvements to other features of the system. He contends, for example, that Japan's introduction of lay judges into their trial process has prompted the inauguration of a new system of public defense for criminal defendants; a greater judicial willingness to release defendants on bail, so they can assist in their defense; the expansion of pretrial discovery rights for the defense; and the creation of a pretrial investigative stage designed to clarify the points of disagreement between the prosecution and the defendant, in order to allow compression of trials within the relatively brief time frame for which laypeople may reasonably be conscripted. In order for laypeople to evaluate the evidence, written dossiers were replaced, to a significant degree, by live testimony and more direct presentation of evidence at trial. And in order for juries to be able to evaluate confessions, interrogations needed to be made more transparent, which led the Japanese police to begin video-taping some confessions.

Thus, while the lay judge reform introduced a safeguard meant to correct or detect earlier errors by casting a critical external eye on the police and prosecutors' work, the introduction of this new check at the tail end of the criminal process stimulated the creation of new error-prevention mechanisms during the early stages of criminal cases. But Johnson also sees more diffuse systemic effects that may not be the product of design. These include greater caution by prosecutors in charging cases and a greater willingness by judges to scrutinize the government's evidence critically, as judges find themselves working closely with jurors, who are new to the criminal process and can look at criminal cases with fresh eyes.

Stephen Thaman highlights the risk of wrongful convictions when he analyzes the procedural dynamics that instill a confirmation bias into many legal systems, allowing initial suspicions to harden into an almost reflexive presumption of guilt. Shawn Boyne echoes these concerns when she highlights the traditions of deference that weaken judicial controls of prosecutorial charging decisions in Germany. Jenia Turner and Christopher Slobogin address different types of error in discussing the procedural devices (such as exclusionary rules) that derogate from truth more generally, for example by acquitting the guilty. In his normative evaluation of the exclusionary rule, Slobogin takes into account not only fairness to the defendant but how well that value is balanced against the 'substantive integrity' of the criminal law, in other words, how well the system does at producing outcomes that accurately reflect both guilt and innocence. Precisely because the exclusionary rule can lead to acquittals of the guilty – and because he thinks other remedies are more effective – he prefers liquidated damages as a remedy for many types of illegalities.

Nor do those concerned about error always focus on the outcomes of criminal cases; even when innocent defendants are likely to be acquitted, critics address the injustice of haling the innocent into court when a properly functioning screening process should have resulted in pretrial dismissal. Alarm at the difficulty of preventing unwarranted criminal prosecutions drives Tzu-te Wen's and Andrew Leipold's critique of pretrial screening in the United States and Taiwan. David Johnson likewise examines not only the extent to which Japan's introduction of a lay judge system has protected defendants from the risk of unjust convictions, but also the way in which the prospect of trying a case to a jury has disciplined prosecutors in deciding when to press charges. And when unfounded cases are brought primarily to harass or extort, great harm can be done simply by forcing the innocent to spend a night in jail before posting bond – even if the eventual dismissal of charges is a foregone conclusion. Accordingly, Vikramaditya Khanna and Kartikey Mahajan examine a unique system of anticipatory bail that India first developed informally and eventually codified, in order to protect the innocent from extortion or harassment by their enemies.

Richard Vogler and Shahrzad Fouladvand point to a global decrease of judicial control over the arrest power, and this may be one of the risk factors for erroneous outcomes and hasty charging decisions. Khanna and Mahajan certainly suggest the dangers of uncontrolled police discretion in this area, while highlighting an ingenious corrective mechanism that allows potential victims of abusive arrests to reclaim a right to judicial screening and control over the arrest power, and to do so *ex ante*, by seeking anticipatory relief from an impending arrest. Though potential arrestees can initiate the review *ex parte*, judges eventually summon police and prosecutors for a contested hearing that allows a preview of the concerns of the prospective defendants with respect to the underlying merits of the case, functioning much like a temporary restraining order in the realm of criminal procedure. The procedure secures many of the benefits of post-arrest bail hearings for the government, by allowing the court to insist on guarantees that the persons fearing arrest will appear in court when summoned and will cooperate with the police investigation – while protecting them from the dangers and indignities of an arrest. In a legal system in which the criminal process is notoriously slow, this anticipatory form of relief can play a crucial role in preventing or containing abuse of the criminal process.

Critical scrutiny of how well criminal procedure systems do at avoiding error motivates comparisons of how similar procedural safe-guards, like the right to counsel, are implemented across different systems. Such research frequently draws on law and society scholarship that uses empirical methods to contrast the 'law on the ground' with 'the law on the books', as Jacqueline Hodgson does in her empirical examination of the ways in which England, France, and the Netherlands implement the right to counsel during custodial questioning of criminal defendants. By examining the role defense attorneys actually play during police questioning of the accused, Hodgson brings into focus the highly variable extent to which formal recognition of the right to counsel really protects criminal defendants from pressures to make admissions that often become the primary evidence against them. Though Hodgson's methodology does not allow her to query the accuracy of such admis-sions, her work lays the groundwork for further research on the extent to which the right to counsel prevents false confessions or erroneous convictions, particularly since, as Jason Mazzone points out, confessions reduce investigators' incentives to search out other evidence, or pursue leads that point to other suspects.

Examining criminal procedure for the risk of error it carries with it thus attracts comparative law scholars' attention to how well different legal systems screen cases at intake; how well they guard against confirmation biases (by preserving the critical role of independent decision-makers); to what extent systems allow defense counsel as well as other system participants to challenge a dominant narrative or slow a rush to judgment; how heavily a criminal justice system relies on consensual resolutions that relieve the government of its burden of proof (allowing suspects to be punished based largely on suspicions coupled with negotiated admissions of guilt); and how well systems are designed to recognize and correct their mistakes.

To the list of procedural features that increase the risk of wrongful conviction one can add a system's twin tendencies to over-rely on evidence that is shaped by the interaction of suspects and investigators (through police interrogation or undercover stings) and to undervalue evidence that exists independently of the investigative mechanisms by which it is unearthed. As Christopher Slobogin makes clear in his comparative survey of how the exclusionary rule is used and justified across different jurisdictions worldwide, concern about the trustworthiness of evidence that the state has a hand in producing makes a number of legal systems more apt to exclude evidence shaped by police interaction with suspects (such as confessions) than 'pre-existing' physical evidence obtained through unlawful searches and seizures, even when the path used by investigative officials to discover such physical evidence was illegal. Because 'evidence obtained during an illegal search or seizure ... is almost always reliable proof of guilt', Slobogin contends, many legal systems take the position that any 'illegality connected with its seizure rarely rises to the level needed to mandate exclusion', preferring 'to reserve exclusion for cases where the police used the suspect as a means of obtaining evidence' or 'used coercive practices' to obtain statements.

Turner, likewise, contends that 'the differential treatment of tangible and testimonial evidence is due at least in part to a concern that tainted testimony is likely to be unreliable and to impair the search for truth'. Turner makes this point to demonstrate that the exclusionary rule is frequently applied in ways that limit its adverse impact on accuracy in fact-finding, so that the spread of safeguards for criminal defendants (for example, through the diffusion of exclusionary remedies) does not always come at the expense of the search for truth. Thus:

> while exclusionary rules can be seen as a triumph of individual rights over truth-seeking, such rules typically contain numerous qualifications to allow courts to minimize the burden on the search for truth. Even where exclusionary rules appear quite strict on paper, in practice, they frequently give way to a concern for accuracy.

Attentiveness to the vulnerabilities of different investigative mechanisms – such as the risk of contaminating the evidence through conscious or unconscious manipulation – leads criminal procedure scholars to focus on procedural reforms by which legal systems can prevent, expose and correct for various types of error – whether by insisting on live testimony by a defendant's accusers; requiring corroboration of confessions; or enhancing the role of defense counsel during questioning of the accused. Stephen Thaman, for example, favors a return to formal rules of evidence, like those which once constrained continental European judges, to protect defendants from conviction based on uncorroborated confessions, disputed eyewitness testimony, or the purchased testimony of informants or cooperating criminals. Because procedural safeguards often carry with them a pressure on defendants to waive trial, he also borrows from European constraints on plea bargaining to argue that consensual dispositions should not be available for more serious offenses.

For many commentators, however, the problem of wrongful convictions is related to the unavoidable compromises trading off the search for truth against other system values which are common to all criminal procedure systems, including respect for fundamental rights (in the case of the exclusionary rule), or efficiency (in the case of plea bargaining), or democratic participation (in the case of the lay judge or jury system). Jenia Turner explores all three types of compromises in her chapter, comparing the ways in which different systems of criminal procedure restrict the search for truth in pursuit of competing goals. Just as insufficient protection for certain rights can result in erroneous convictions of the innocent, Slobogin and Turner both argue that vigorous application of the exclusionary rule, coupled with broad protections for fundamental rights or procedural justice can also compromise truth-finding (Turner) or 'the substantive integrity of the criminal law' (Slobogin) by permitting the acquittal of the guilty. For Slobogin and Turner, this is not a bug of a poorly designed system of criminal procedure, but a feature of all systems. What differs is not the need to balance the search for truth against other system values, but the way in which the trade-off is made, and the nature of the competing goals a system embraces.

Boyne points out that many legal systems make these trade-offs in response to very similar pressures, such as increased resource constraints and caseloads for prosecutors, resulting in increased reliance on consensual dispositions like plea bargaining in the United States and confession bargaining in Germany. But the resulting trade-offs differ in ways that reflect the contrasting institutional roles, interactions, and professional identities of police, prosecutors, judges, and defense attorneys across disparate legal systems and procedural traditions. In the United States, caseload pressures coupled with prosecutors' tendency to view the criminal process as a contest that they must 'win' translate into coercive plea bargaining strategies, such as the practice of deliberately over-charging criminal cases and exacting a 'trial penalty' from defendants who exercise their right to contest the charges against them, thus creating a risk that innocent defendants may be induced to plead guilty to crimes they did not commit. In Germany, Boyne argues, pressure to dispose of cases efficiently leads many prosecutors to look for ways of closing out cases through dismissals, using prosecutors' increased discretionary powers to err on the side of not charging many cases that more probing investigations might otherwise have prompted them to charge.

Boyne's close empirical observations of German prosecutors enables her to illuminate these dynamics, by showing how time spent on file documentation can replace close teamwork with investigators or interviewing witnesses, leading to summary dispositions that survive supervisory scrutiny but do not necessarily reflect the underlying merits of the criminal case. As a result, Boyne concludes, '[t]he traditional vision of the prosecutor as the chief of the investigation process who marshals the resources of the state to find the truth today applies to a narrower range of cases'.

At the same time, however, Boyne identifies those special features of prosecutors' relationships both with judges and with their own administrative hierarchy that make these short-cuts possible – as well as those features that limit the extent to which prosecutors will be allowed to compromise accuracy of fact-finding for the sake of efficiency. Close collaboration between German judges and prosecutors, including regular *ex parte* contact to discuss cases and confession bargains, means that 'German prosecutors may lack the incentive to contradict the court' or to 'serve as a counterweight or an additional set of eyes' to weigh the evidence critically. On the other hand, internalized decision-making norms of the prosecution service itself – coupled with close hierarchical supervision – discourage the use of many investigative tactics that may derogate from the search for truth. Thus German prosecutors may not coach witnesses or ask leading questions, and they sometimes argue for acquittal at the close of a trial. And when German prosecutors do dispose of cases through confession bargains, 'the level of evidence required to support such agreements is higher than in the US', particularly since confessions do not relieve the court of the duty to hear other evidence.

For Thaman, as well as for Wen and Leipold, fairness to criminal defendants requires more than the avoidance of wrongful convictions or unwarranted prosecutions; it also commands respect for the presumption of innocence. In Thaman's view, the presumption of innocence entails limitations on the consensual resolution of criminal cases (since these make it possible to adjudicate a finding of guilt based on little more than probable cause) and acceptance of the finality of acquittals against the weight of the evidence. For Wen and Leipold, the presumption of innocence instead requires reforms that would force Taiwanese judges who screen initial charging decisions to hold prosecutors to a meaningful standard of proof and to dismiss weak cases, rather than sending such cases back to prosecutors with instructions to look for additional incriminating evidence. Taiwanese judges do this under the guise of enforcing a mandatory prosecution principle that undermines the judge's neutrality. Pursuant to this practice, judges highlight gaps in the prosecution's case and then suggest ways of filling them with additional evidence, thus making them play 'conflicting roles, as both an adviser to the prosecution as well as a neutral decision-maker'.

2.   LEGAL REFORM, TRANSPLANTS, AND PROLIFERATION OF PROCEDURAL MODELS: PLURALIST ALTERNATIVES TO THE DICHOTOMY BETWEEN ADVERSARIAL AND INQUISITORIAL CRIMINAL PROCEDURE

A second set of influences on comparative scholarship about criminal procedure can be traced to the astonishing acceleration of innovation and legal reform both of national legal systems and of international criminal tribunals. In this volume alone, contributors highlight the adoption of lay juries by legal systems as diverse as Spain, Russia, and Japan; the newly expanded role of defense counsel in France and the Netherlands; new legal requirements that juries give reasons for their verdicts; new surveillance powers in the United States, Germany, and Russia; and new procedures for plea or confession bargaining in much of Europe. In his seminal work at the intersection of comparative and international criminal procedure, Máximo Langer has drawn attention both to the transformation of criminal procedure in Chile and Argentina in the wake of their transitions to democracy and to the development of new hybrid forms of criminal procedure by international criminal tribunals (Langer, 2004; Langer and Doherty, 2011). And a growing body of literature on legal transfers and transitional justice documents the ways in which outside experts sought to transform legal institutions in Eastern Europe, Latin America, and South Africa, in the post-Cold War and post-Apartheid era (Damaska, 1997; de Brito et al., 2001; Delmas-Marty, 2003; Koreman, 1999; Kritz, 1995; Levinson, 2000; Linz and Stepan, 1996; McAdams, 1997; O'Donnell et al., 1986; Offe, 1997; Pogany 1997; Posner and Vermeule, 2004; Teitel, 2000).

Multiplying legal reforms have prompted a variety of scholarly concerns. How can the literature on legal transplants make sense of the international diffusion of the jury system and plea bargaining, which are both so controversial among American scholars? (Alschuler, 1981, 1986; Easterbrook, 1983; Langbein, 1978; Schulhofer, 1988, 1992; Scott and Stuntz, 1992). Is the diffusion of the jury and practices similar to plea bargaining evidence of a rampant Americanization of European, Asian, and Russian criminal procedure? Or is it, as Elisabetta Grande suggests, less an emulation of American institutions than the invention of a new, more pluralistic system populated by a more numerous and diverse ecology of legal actors? Should the transplant be thought of as the introduction of adversarial features into a hitherto inquisitorial criminal process? Or, following both Langer and Grande, should these reforms be understood to inaugurate new, hybrid, and eclectic forms, whose foreign features are transformed by the context and traditions of the systems into which they are transplanted?

Thus while the majority of criminal procedure scholars still use the adversarial-inquisitorial dichotomy as a heuristic tool for systemic comparison – as in the Tango-Rumba metaphor of Elisabetta Grande – it has become increasingly clear that it is difficult today to neatly classify systems as falling squarely in one camp or the other. For example, exclusionary rules, pioneered in the United States due to the influence of its Bill of Rights, cannot be seen as 'adversarial', as they have, until recently, been virtually non-existent in other common law countries without written constitutions. Moreover, inquisitorial countries very early on articulated the concept of 'nullities', which look very much like exclusionary rules – and did so at a time when English judges did not scrutinize the legality of the process by which evidence was collected, so long as the evidence proved relevant. As Slobogin makes clear, exclusionary rules now exist in some fashion in legal systems all across the spectrum, from fully adversarial to highly inquisitorial. What differs is not the willingness of legal systems to use the exclusionary rule but the types of violations for which legal systems are willing to implement this remedy; the scope of the underlying rights that the rule protects; as well as the rationales (such as protection for fundamental rights, deterrence, and concern for the reputation of the criminal justice system) which legal systems privilege.

Likewise, while plea bargaining has always been considered to be 'adversarial' and dependent on the unlimited discretion exercised by American prosecutors in (over)charging and dismissing criminal counts, plea- and confession-bargaining now thrive in inquisitorial legal systems in which, decades ago, such practices were considered anathema – and American-style plea bargaining has begun to look more and more like the primordial inquisitorial procedure of coercing admissions of guilt, as John Langbein has argued.

In addition, Article 6 of the ECHR – which in many respects resembles the Sixth Amendment of the US Constitution, albeit without the right to a jury trial – has expanded the traditionally more passive and restricted role of defense counsel and has gradually led to involvement of the defense and the prosecution in both the gathering and presentation of evidence in many continental European systems, so that trials in these countries look more and more like trials in the US and England. Even though the jury system has long been viewed as a key feature of the adversarial criminal process and has often been invoked to explain other characteristic features, such as the passive role of trial judges, the prominent role of the parties in presenting evidence, and the division of evidence into a 'prosecution case' and a 'defense case', lay juries have now been introduced into some systems which still have strong inquisitorial features.

The scholarship in this volume takes as its starting point the increasingly hybrid and diverse character of national systems of criminal procedure and notes that the tendency of formerly inquisitorial legal systems to borrow or emulate elements of adversarial procedure creates commonalities, while opening the transplant up to some of the same criticisms that are often leveled against adversarial legal systems. But many chapters – like those by Jason Mazzone, Elisabetta Grande, Shawn Boyne, David Johnson, Jacqueline Hodgson, and Jenia Turner – look more closely at the ways in which the new, hybrid systems have succeeded – or not – in importing some of the hoped-for benefits and in containing some of the problems hitherto associated with the transplanted feature in its home environment. If Grande sees the Spanish adoption of the jury system as an instance in which the adoption of a foreign model increases procedural safeguards by making decision-making more pluralistic, Mazzone cites Britain's dilution of protections during police interrogation as an instance in which 'dialogue among jurisdictions has ended up weakening these rights by comparison with their strong adversarial origins'.

Jason Mazzone's chapter thus highlights some of the dangers and limitations of efforts to increase protections for fundamental rights through supranational norms diffused by courts (like the European Court of Human Rights). The Court's jurisprudence on the right against compelled self-incrimination and the right to silence, he notes, risks reducing procedural safeguards to their lowest common denominator, to make them easier to implement across the procedural divide that continues to separate civil law countries from those with common law traditions.

To be sure, Mazzone concedes, some legal systems, like Germany's, 'might fully understand that global rules are merely a floor, and so stick to or pursue stronger rights domestically'. And in countries like France, where these rights have enjoyed very weak protection, the ECtHR jurisprudence has overcome domestic political resistance to reforms that have significantly improved protections for criminal defendants. But in places like the UK, where safeguards on police interrogations have traditionally been very substantial, Mazzone contends, universalist conceptions of rights 'can provide cover to local reformers interested in cutting back on pre-existing protections'. This dynamic has already weakened the right to silence, as courts in England and Wales may now draw adverse inferences from defendants' decisions to avail themselves of this right. As a result, '[r]eformers who speak the language of globalization can impose changes that actually leave localized rights worse off', lending legitimacy to cut-backs on the right to silence and privilege against self-incrimination simply because these reforms accord with the relatively more modest conception of these rights that the European Court of Human Rights has embraced as a minimum level of protection.

Jacqueline Hodgson's chapter suggests, however, that quasi-legislative mechanisms may be more effective at diffusing supranational procedural norms, 'not as a minimum threshold below which states should not fall', but as 'positive standards to apply in uniform and consistent ways'. An EU directive on how member states should interpret and implement the right to counsel not only allows EU citizens to enforce these safeguards in their national courts but goes into much greater detail than the ECtHR jurisprudence generally does on what new measures member states must adopt and how these provisions should work in practice. The directive also requires member states to incorporate the new standards into their national codes of criminal procedure.

Hodgson's empirical study concludes that constraints on defense rights come primarily from police resistance to the diffusion of pan-European norms in countries like France and the Netherlands, whose inquisitorial legal tradition assigns the protection of the criminal accused primarily to the judicial officers in charge of criminal investigations. Though France now permits defense counsel to sit in on their client's interrogation by the police, they are nonetheless 'not permitted to interrupt, to challenge police questions, or to ask questions or for clarification until the end of the interrogation'. And in the Netherlands, defense counsel are still not permitted to be present during police questioning, except when the defendants are juveniles, or when the police are investigating particularly serious crimes. In England and Wales, by contrast, where prosecutors do not supervise either the criminal investigation or the detention of suspects, defense counsel remains 'an important guarantor of due process rights as well as being responsible for investigating the defense case'.

Though Mazzone points out that England and Wales have reduced protections for the right to silence and the privilege against self-incrimination, the well-established role of defense counsel thus exerts countervailing pressures. This suggests that the adversarial procedural tradition and 'practical arrangements' in the provision of legal aid, which make the same defense counsel responsible for representing a criminal defendant throughout the criminal investigation, can counteract the tendency of less protective supranational norms to dilute other protections for criminal defendants.

Of course, national traditions can resist expansion as well as dilution of rights. Hodgson points out that there are relatively few French and Dutch lawyers who specialize in criminal defense. She argues that the protections called for by the EU directive are somewhat weakened, in the Netherlands and France, not only by the lack of a strong defense tradition in these two inquisitorial systems of criminal procedure, but also by the fact that custodial defendants must rely on different duty attorneys to represent them each time they appear in court after their initial arrest.

Although the dichotomy between civil law and common law retains its relevance for defense rights, rapid legal reforms do somewhat blur many of the systemic differences traditionally associated with the divide between inquisitorial and accusatorial models of criminal procedure. Thus Jenia Turner argues that inquisitorial legal systems, like the adversarial systems with which they are often contrasted, trade their truth-finding aims off against other system values by the use of exclusionary rules, plea bargaining, and lay juries, thereby making allowance for concerns with fairness, efficiency, and democratic decision-making as countervailing values. The focus of her comparison is on the ways in which these trade-offs differ across systems. What she rejects is the notion that the search for truth is a quest peculiar to the inquisitorial criminal process.

Shawn Boyne, too, notes that plea and confession bargaining has become increasingly common in Germany, and that in Germany, as in the United States, one can now observe a dynamic by which the increase in procedural safeguards for criminal trials heightens the incentives for prosecutors and judges to reduce at least some of the procedural complexities of criminal trials by negotiating for confessions that will allow them to shorten the duration of the trial. At the same time, however, Boyne notes that the context in which confession bargaining occurs is less coercive for criminal defendants than its American counterpart. Boyne explores the distinctive configuration of professional roles that can help to account for these differences. Though all legal systems sometimes trade the search for truth off against other system values, the respective roles of judges, defense counsel, and prosecutors help account for systemic differences between the ways these trade-offs are made and between the levels of effectiveness of procedural safeguards. National differences between these professional roles also help explain the particular ways as well as the extent to which the search for truth may be compromised.

Rapid transformation of national legal systems has in fact lent itself to multiple conflicting narratives about the prevailing direction of legal influence, including disagreements about whether criminal procedure systems are gradually converging or moving further apart. The Americanization thesis concerning criminal procedure runs directly counter to claims of American exceptionalism in the substantive criminal law (see for example, Dubber, 2004), particularly with regard to the harshness of American punishment, American commitment to the death penalty, and controversial doctrines of vicarious criminal liability, such as American conspiracy law, vicarious liability for the crimes of co-conspirators, and the felony murder doctrine as it applies to homicides that occur during crimes committed by co-felons. Procedural borrowing and innovation has likewise led to increased interest in the viability of legal transplants; in the dynamics of the legal reform of societies transitioning from dictatorships; and in the reciprocal procedural influences of national and supranational courts, including international criminal tribunals.

In this volume, Elisabetta Grande's chapter occupies intermediate ground between the proponents and critics of the Americanization thesis – that is, between those who highlight American influence and those who view American practices as increasingly isolated and exceptional – by highlighting the ways in which systems that transplant a foreign, seemingly American, legal institution, like the jury, transform and adapt the model while allowing the 'legal irritant' to transform the host system and to turn the jury system into something altogether unique. Khanna's and Mahajan's chapter on Indian provisions for anticipatory bail emphasizes the ways in which legal systems can generate and experiment with their own distinctive legal mechanisms, without recourse to foreign models.

Yet another view of legal reforms and borrowing dismisses the notion either of undue American influence (that is, the Americanization thesis) or of a collective recoil against the harsh example of American criminal justice (the thesis of American exceptionalism as a negative example for others). Instead, scholars who study the jurisprudence and influence of the European Court of Human Rights emphasize its influence as a third magnetic pole and the related emergence of uniform norms and baselines for what constitutes fair procedure (see for example, Amman, 2000; Stone Sweet, 2000). These harmonizing principles derive not only from the jurisprudence of the European Court of Human Rights but also from the legal directives issued by the European Union. Areas in which

European institutions have been active – through directives and jurisprudence – include reforms such as the increased investigative role of defense counsel (as explored by Jacqueline Hodgson's chapter), improved confrontation rights, an insistence that state surveillance be regulated by statute, and (as Mathilde Cohen and Elisabetta Grande point out) the ECtHR insistence, in *Taxquet*, that juries give reasons for their verdicts.

3. NEW WAYS OF COMPARING SYSTEMS

This diverse set of questions and theoretical preoccupations poses a daunting challenge of comparability. Along what axes should comparative scholars measure similarity and difference? What are the relevant yardsticks and normative frameworks within which systems may be compared with each other? Boyne and Hodgson both compare systems in institutional terms that emphasize the institutional and legal constraints on the roles of prosecutors, defense attorneys, and judges as explanatory variables. At the same time, supranational norms have thus turned protection for fundamental rights into the lingua franca of legal comparisons. For some scholars, like Jacqueline Hodgson, rights are themselves the subject of study, with empirical research making it possible to compare different ways in which these rights are understood and implemented. For others, like Jason Mazzone, differences between protection for fundamental rights like the right to silence and the right to counsel illuminate differences between investigative practices, and, specifically, between how far police across disparate legal systems can go in questioning custodial defendants, and how significantly the police find themselves constrained. Yet other contributors to this volume, like Jenia Turner, treat the protection of rights across different legal systems as one indicator among others of how systems strike a balance between competing values, such as the search for truth and efficiency (in the case of plea bargaining), democratic participation (in the case of the jury system), and the protection of fundamental rights (in the case of the exclusionary rule.)

Slobogin, too, studies trade-offs between accuracy and other system values. But his concern is specifically with the scope of the *remedy* for rights violations, not with the scope of the rights *per se*. Because the exclusionary rule now plays a role in both adversarial and inquisitorial systems of criminal procedure – and because there is considerable variation among the role of this remedy across countries within each of these traditions – the distinction between inquisitorial and accusatorial systems of criminal procedure is not very useful for explaining when and how legal systems use the exclusionary rule, that is to say, when and how legal systems are willing to 'depart from the search for truth' to remedy unlawful police tactics. Accordingly, Slobogin focuses on the policy reasons that ground different national approaches. His reconstructions of the competing rationales explain national differences in scope of the exclusionary remedy. He seeks primarily to understand legal systems' approaches on their own terms. Thaman's concern with wrongful convictions instead takes an externalist perspective to compare criminal procedure systems with regard to the effectiveness of each system's mechanisms for avoiding and correcting erroneous convictions or protecting the presumption of innocence.

Turner, too, measures legal systems against external benchmarks, examining empirical evidence about whether features like the jury trial, which serves policy reasons distinct from the search for truth, really compromise accuracy, as many critics have feared. Comparing plea bargaining, the exclusionary rule, and jury trials for their potential impact on accuracy in fact-finding, Turner points out that both the exclusionary rule and plea bargaining are sometimes used to promote rather than undermine the search for truth, as when the exclusionary rule is used to suppress unreliable confessions and when plea bargains are used to secure the cooperation of co-defendants in undercover operations. Turner compares different procedural devices for their tendency to undermine the search for truth and concludes that plea bargaining is perhaps the most problematic of the three procedures 'because its detrimental impact on truth-seeking in individual cases has proven the most difficult to mitigate'. Comparing criminal procedures according to the extent to which they derogate from the search for truth allows Turner to identify corrective mechanisms like reason-giving requirements that mitigate the error rates of certain procedural devices, like the jury system, which are often criticized for reducing the accuracy of fact-finding. At the same time, her juxtaposition of multiple types of procedural devices, all of which burden the search for truth, make it possible to compare different procedural devices with their counterparts in different legal systems with regard to their characteristic vulnerabilities (like lack of transparency) and their relative impact on the accuracy of fact-finding.

The contributors' comparative methodologies suggest yet another series of dimensions along which systems may be compared, namely, with respect to the input, process, and output legitimacy of procedural devices. Mathilde Cohen's chapter, for example, suggests that reason-giving requirements for mixed panels of lay and professional jurors can be viewed as efforts to reconcile a more democratic, participatory model of adjudication that enjoys significant process legitimacy (due to the

involvement of lay fact-finders who function as community representatives) with a commitment to accuracy in fact-finding and output legitimacy, as promoted by accountability through the giving of reasons. Cohen
argues that the reason-giving requirement serves as a device that makes
the professional judges who deliberate with lay assessors accountable for
jury verdicts by requiring them to draft a statement of reasons that can
serve both as a record on appeal and as a basis for scrutinizing the
verdicts rendered by mixed panels of lay and professional judges. The
French statute that followed on the heels of the ECtHR's newly enunciated reason-giving requirement created incentives for judges to draft
statements of reasons that anticipated and reconstructed the best justification for jurors' reasons, rather than simply tracking and recording the
process of decision-making that jurors actually followed. Though the
reason-giving required was hailed as a breakthrough for process legitimacy because it emphasized the moral project of making legal judgments
understandable to criminal defendants, Cohen suggests that the requirement may also promote the legitimacy of legal judgments by making
judges accountable for their role in guiding, reconstructing, and making
sense of jury deliberations.

Cohen links the reason-giving requirement to attempts to promote
judicial accountability by arguing that 'the reform is aimed as much at
keeping presidents [of tribunals] in check as at making verdicts understandable to defendants', particularly since 'some of the *cour d'assises'*
reasons are now more widely available to the general public through the
press than they are to defendants'. The absence of a harmless error rule
for poorly drafted reasons also suggests that the reason-giving requirement 'is meant as a check on judicial discretion', by showing 'the
relationship between the facts of the case and the verdict'. That the
reason-giving requirement is meant to discipline judges, Cohen argues, is
also reflected by the practice of remanding inadequate reasons directly to
them so as to '"punish" professional judges for unsatisfactory reason-
giving and force them to do their homework by sending the case back to
their court'. Judicial accountability thus promotes the legitimacy of jury
outputs – or verdicts – without compromising the process legitimacy that
inheres in lay participation.

An externalist perspective could reflect a concern with output legitimacy, which Thaman adopts in addressing the ways in which different
legal systems risk outcomes that are illegitimate because they convict the
innocent. Thaman and Turner offer complementary externalist critiques
of the jury system, with heavy emphasis on the accuracy of jury
decision-making, and, hence, on output legitimacy. Turner argues that
'[w]hile jurors do suffer from certain cognitive biases that affect all

humans, they are not less likely to produce accurate outcomes than professional judges'. Thus Turner defends juries as not much worse than judges, while Thaman criticizes judges as not much better than juries. Put differently, Turner seeks to explain why juries tend to get things right, while Thaman asks why judges sometimes get things wrong. Both of them are concerned with the legitimacy of outputs, or verdicts. But if Turner worries about how systems rank the search for truth in relation to other values, Thaman is less concerned with the ability of the legal process to get things right in the first place than with its failsafe mechanisms for correcting erroneous charging decisions and trial verdicts as well as coerced guilty pleas.

But an externalist perspective can just as well focus on input legitimacy, as Wen and Leipold do in comparing the Taiwanese and American screening procedures with regard to their ability to identify and dismiss weak cases before they go to trial, or with regard to their reliance on confessions obtained without adequate safeguards for a defendant's right to counsel.

An externalist perspective can also foreground process legitimacy, by evaluating legal systems according to external measures of fairness and respect for the dignity of the accused. Thus David Johnson argues that '[j]udging criminal trials solely in terms of their efficiency or effects on other parts of the criminal process makes no more sense than evaluating a wedding or funeral in terms of its accuracy (Kadri, 2005: 346)'. He contends that Japan's lay judge reforms may not only counteract the country's high conviction rate and the conviction mentality of a professional judiciary composed of repeat players who are highly deferential to prosecutors; the involvement of lay judges may prompt further reforms that improve safeguards for criminal defendants; and he hopes that these reforms can demonstrate the legal system's ability to 'treat[] its most despised enemies with respect, by presuming them innocent and by giving them a champion to argue their cause', so as to 'reinvigorate the ideals of democracy and reinforce the importance of dignity and other human values'.

4. DIACHRONIC COMPARISONS: COMPARING STAGES IN THE CRIMINAL PROCESS

Another way in which scholars can make systems comparable is by analyzing criminal procedure as a series of mini-trials which may be juxtaposed, across legal systems, according to the stage of the criminal process in which they intervene. Any criminal process organized around the handling of cases – that is, the processing of individual criminal prosecutions – can be grouped chronologically around investigation, adjudication, sentencing, and appeal. The chapters in this volume deal with criminal procedure as a crescendo of institutional responses to expanding levels of suspicion and as a process by which suspicions are tested and raw data gradually shaped into usable evidence. Comparing legal systems according to the way they process cases reveals the ways in which each tests evidence against burdens of proof whose thresholds increase from relatively low levels in the early screening stages of the criminal process to requirements of proof beyond a reasonable doubt at the stage of final adjudication. And it is not only the process of haling defendants into court that can be measured against an escalating series of evidentiary thresholds; governmental intrusions into protected interests, such as privacy and liberty, also require ever higher levels of factual predication to justify increasingly invasive investigative measures.

The contributors examine these parallel crescendos of invasive investigation and evidence-testing in an effort to compare the legal standards, across different systems, that justify this progression, from entering data into preliminary investigation case files, to processing evidence at trial, and, finally, to re-describing that evidence as factual findings that are transformed into judgment reasons by trial courts and appellate tribunals. These comparisons illuminate characteristic ways in which legal systems are vulnerable to error or protect against it. Thaman and Boyne, for example, closely examine the dynamics by which a failure to screen cases rigorously during the early investigative phase of the criminal process, coupled with traditions of collegial deference that link judges and prosecutors, can bias later proceedings against the defendant and reduce opportunities to detect and correct errors by weakening the presumption of innocence and subtly favoring a rush to premature judgment. Wen and Leipold closely examine some of the design flaws that exacerbate this risk in Taiwan, voicing their concern that Taiwanese courts are relatively less able than their American counterparts to screen out weak cases before they go to trial. In particular, they point out, screening is ineffective because the quantum of evidence needed for criminal charges to survive judicial screening once they are filed is actually lower than the amount of evidence needed to file such charges in the first place. And once charges are filed, the system makes it likely for errors or a rush to judgment in the pretrial phase to be locked in at trial, because the same three-judge panel that screens criminal charges in the pretrial stage of the criminal process will also preside over the trial. By contrast, David Johnson examines the ways in which the introduction of the lay jury into the Japanese criminal process may have improved prosecutorial screening decisions, arguably increasing critical scrutiny by prosecutors themselves.

Jacqueline Hodgson emphasizes structural flaws in the pretrial investigation rather than the screening process itself as a source of error early in the criminal process that tends to infect and bias later proceedings. She brings into focus how little the right to counsel, as implemented in France and the Netherlands, can protect defendants from pressures to make statements, potentially contributing to an over-reliance on confessions as a short-cut to obtaining convictions without much in the way of independent investigation to corroborate guilt.

A number of contributors also focus on legal reform efforts designed to make it easier to detect errors at later stages of the criminal process. Mathilde Cohen, Elisabetta Grande, Stephen Thaman, and Jenia Turner all discuss the way the European Court of Human Rights is transforming both lay and mixed jury systems through its recent decision in *Taxquet* requiring juries to give reasons for their verdicts. And Grande considers the introduction of the jury system in Spain in the context of a number of other reforms that have given new legal actors, including victims, a voice in the criminal process, as part of a concerted reform effort to multiply checks and balances, while also turning the trial itself into the main locus for testing the strength of the evidence against the defendant.

Organizing systemic comparisons by focusing on the particular stages of the criminal process can reveal the contrasting ways in which initial suspicions set the stage for more intrusive government action. Richard Vogler and Shahrzad Fouladvand, for example, plot the difference between the English standard of 'reasonable suspicion' and the American notion of 'probable cause', which govern when the police may intervene to detain or arrest a suspect on suspicion of having committed a crime. At the same time, they contrast both of these with the French notion of 'flagrant crime', which not only supports an immediate arrest but also allows the police to bypass the preliminary investigation and its attendant restrictions on residential searches. Investigations of 'flagrant crime' permit the French police to escalate to more invasive investigative tactics that do not require a suspect's consent or cooperation. Catching an offender in a flagrant violation also permits the police to set the case for immediate trial without supplemental investigation.

Vogler and Fouladvand's juxtaposition of evidentiary thresholds across different legal systems suggests that many European legal systems have 'a clear ladder of threshold tests' to track the progression of a criminal case through the investigative process, 'with "reasonable grounds to believe" for the issuing of arrest warrants, "substantial grounds to believe" for the confirmation of charges, and "beyond reasonable doubt" for a finding of guilt'. By contrast, the United States uses the same 'probable cause' standard to justify the arrest, to screen the charges at the preliminary hearing, and to vote a 'true bill' on an indictment confirming criminal charges. Instead of tracking the progress of the criminal investigation, American criminal procedure uses its ladder of threshold evidentiary requirements to test the legal validity of an escalating set of liberty deprivations along 'a continuum that begins with a hunch, then progresses to reasonable suspicion [justifying a "stop and frisk"], and then becomes probable cause' justifying an arrest. (Vogler and Fouladvand quoting Moak and Carlson, 2014: 41). And while American criminal procedure hinges the validity of an arrest primarily on the strength of the evidence against the defendant, English and Continental European criminal procedure supplement their evidentiary thresholds for making arrests or keeping someone in investigative detention with notions of necessity or proportionality which limit the exercise of the arrest power even in cases where there are good reasons to suspect someone of a crime.

At the same time, however, Vogler and Fouladvand point out that England, like other European jurisdictions, makes liberal use of pretrial detention to prevent future crimes 'in a way unconnected to the main proceedings', while the US, at least in theory, continues to use pretrial detention primarily to secure defendants' appearance at trial. This suggests that many of the necessity and proportionality considerations that act as brakes on European arrest powers, compared to their American counterparts, give way to an acceptance of preventive detention for serious offenses, 'mov[ing] dramatically away from a focus on the integrity of the trial process towards control and policing priorities'.

Higher standards for escalating liberty deprivations mirror the progression of the evidentiary thresholds needed to move a criminal case from the initial investigation to trial. But the ease with which government officials can fast-track a case for adjudication not only depends on the quantum of evidence that the state can mobilize but on whether and how courts distinguish between the types of evidence that support an initial inquiry and the types of evidence required to prove guilt. In the United States, search warrants may be issued based on second-hand information from anonymous sources, if they can be shown to be sufficiently reliable and have been sufficiently corroborated; but evidence at trial is subject to hearsay constraints that do not apply to the consideration of warrants, or to earlier screening procedures like preliminary hearings and grand jury proceedings.

The more exacting the evidentiary standards at trial, however, the more likely it is that defendants will face pressure to concede their guilt and thus avoid or at least shorten their trial, in exchange of lesser penalties. Boyne, Thaman, and Turner all explore the ways in which this pressure to waive a full trial, with its attendant safeguards, can lock in early factual errors (such as mistaken identifications), resulting in binding adjudication of guilt on little more than probable cause. These contributors worry that prosecutorial leverage can allow initial suspicions to harden into findings of guilt without independent verification.

Viewing criminal procedure through this sequential lens also makes it possible to compare systems according to how well they perform according to the chronologically more differentiated measures of legitimacy suggested above, namely, input legitimacy, process legitimacy, and outcome legitimacy. Roughly speaking, comparisons among jury systems and reason-giving requirements often examine the conditions that make legal systems' outputs legitimate, while comparisons among screening mechanisms to determine whether a case merits being held over for trial, and comparisons among investigative procedures, such as custodial interrogation, exclusionary rules, and the post-arrest right to counsel, focus on the legitimacy of inputs into the criminal justice system, for example, through efforts to avoid contaminating the legal system with evidence tainted by illegality. Comparisons among trial procedures and the role of plea bargaining or confession bargaining as alternatives to contested forms of adjudication seem to focus primarily on process legitimacy, in other words, the fairness of the procedures by which guilt is assessed.

But any stage of the criminal process can be assessed in terms of input, process, or output legitimacy. David Johnson's chapter on the Japanese jury system notes the extent to which introduction of the jury system has increased democratic participation in the criminal process – improving process legitimacy – and may have improved the care with which prosecutors screen cases, arguably making convictions a more reliable indicator of guilt and thereby improving output legitimacy as well. Turner and Cohen both discuss ways in which the *Taxquet* decision treats input and output legitimacy as acceptable alternatives for each other, noting that jury control through inputs such as jury instructions can substitute for reasoned opinions explaining jury verdicts, whose adequacy is otherwise necessary to lend jury outputs (or decisions) their legitimacy. And Thaman's concern with the problem of erroneous convictions captures a quintessential problem of output legitimacy.

Comparing criminal procedure systems as a series of escalating mini-trials allows the contributors to take into account how later stages of the criminal process may lock in biases and errors from lax screening at earlier stages of the criminal process, or the ways in which a requirement that juries give reasons for their verdicts can expose and allow appellate courts to correct errors in judgment or compensate for earlier system failures, such as weak screening systems. At the same time, attention to the criminal process as a series of opportunities to make up for earlier failings reveals the danger inherent in allowing courts to resolve even serious cases through plea bargains, as plea bargaining eliminates opportunities to correct errors made during the investigative stage or the pretrial screening process.

Thaman's, Johnson's, Grande's, Turner's, and Cohen's approaches to juries illustrate the ways in which different authors can approach the same issue from the vantage point of either input, process, or output legitimacy. Johnson's chapter focuses on all three issues, since he discusses the effect of the jury system on charging decisions (that is, inputs into the trial process); on the gains in process legitimacy that come about through democratic popular participation; and on the impact on the conviction rate, which remains so high as to cast doubt on output legitimacy for anyone who questions whether an acquittal rate that approaches zero can be accurate. Grande is concerned more specifically with process legitimacy, which, from her perspective, hinges less on inviting the public to participate in adjudication than on the pluralism of decision-making in a jury system that, like other reforms to the Spanish criminal process, multiplies and diversifies the array of institutional actors who take part in the criminal process, and accords each of them an increasingly significant role in a decision-making ensemble.

Turner, in turn, focuses primarily on the inputs – such as jury instructions – that ground the legitimacy of verdicts that are otherwise unsupported by reasons. Cohen discusses ways in which reasoned jury verdicts create output legitimacy, arguing that the reason-giving requirement is not there primarily to tame the process of democratic, participatory deliberation, but to control the judges who deliberate jointly with lay jurors, to ensure that their outputs accord with legal requirements. For Thaman, by contrast, output legitimacy depends on juries avoiding at all costs erroneous convictions, regardless of how they reason their way to a decision. Of course, concern with judicial accountability could be either a concern with process legitimacy or outcome legitimacy, depending on whether one is concerned with judges getting a wrong outcome or with a judicial process that fails to follow the rules. At the same time, output legitimacy, for Thaman, does not require that an acquittal signify the actual innocence of the accused, but, in due respect to the presumption of innocence, only that the evidence is insufficient to support a finding of guilt beyond a reasonable doubt. This requires, in his view, respecting acquittals, despite the presence of incriminating evidence, and making them final and not subject to appeal. From the externalist perspective of someone concerned more with accuracy of adjudication than with enforcing the presumption of innocence, by contrast, an acquittal against the weight of the evidence would lack output legitimacy.

5. SYNCHRONIC COMPARISONS: THE CRIMINAL PROCESS AND ITS ALTERNATIVES, IN A MULTI-TRACK SYSTEM OF THREAT REDUCTION AND RISK MANAGEMENT

Thinking about the ordinary criminal process in chronological terms, as the collection and testing of evidence against identified suspects, also makes it possible to distinguish it from alternatives that allow police, prosecutors, and intelligence agencies to bypass the criminal trial or indeed any form of criminal adjudication altogether, in the interest of efficiency, risk management, or national security. In many civil law systems, more elaborate trial safeguards and rights protection have increased case load pressures as well as resource constraints, resulting in new consensual mechanisms, akin to plea bargaining, for avoiding or shortening trials. Bypass mechanisms can include American-style plea bargaining, which avoids trial altogether, or German-style confession bargaining, which shortens and streamlines the criminal trial. Such mechanisms also include Italian-style 'procedure bargaining', which guarantees criminal defendants a lower sentence simply for agreeing to be tried on the basis of the evidentiary record compiled during the preliminary investigation, or for agreeing to forego the adversarial criminal trial, which features live testimony, in favor of adjudication based only on written evidence, including hearsay. The latter procedure essentially invites litigants to opt out of the adversarial process, in favor of the older, inquisitorial model that the 1988 Code of Criminal Procedure was intended to replace.

However, more radical bypass mechanisms can function as true alternatives to criminal prosecution. The chapter by Jacqueline Ross discusses American FISA investigations – which facilitate collection of bulk data without the individual showing of suspicion ordinarily required for criminal investigations – as alternatives to the criminal process, in contrast with German efforts to allow for limited use of data mining as part of the criminal process and to limit the collection of bulk data outside the criminal process. While German criminal procedure treats 'preventive' police operations as mere precursors to the criminal process, largely confining intelligence operations to intelligence agencies, foreign intelligence investigations function as true alternatives in the United States, even when conducted by law enforcement agencies. Nikolai Kovalev and Stephen Thaman, likewise, highlight what is at stake in the decisions many post-Soviet states have been facing about whether to codify special surveillance powers outside of the criminal process, as true alternatives, or to subject them to the procedural strictures of regular investigative powers that are governed by national Codes of Criminal Procedure.

Unlike the use of surveillance to pave the way for criminal prosecution, the use of surveillance as an alternative to the criminal process pursues intelligence rather than evidence. It does not ordinarily culminate in the bringing of criminal charges. It is not case-driven but focused on the analysis of data, which may never crystalize into a case. It is concerned with risks, not with crimes. And it often (but not always) centers on the identification of risk profiles and unusual behavior patterns rather than the investigation of particular suspects. It is not a chronological endeavor, as personal data are not organized around hypothesized wrongdoing by the people to whom they pertain. Indeed, almost all data collected together as bulk data are assumed to be about people who are wholly innocent of any wrongdoing and are simply assumed to provide the haystack within which an aspiring terrorist or spy may be hidden. One might contrast these two distinct bureaucratic repertoires for processing information about crime by describing the traditional criminal process as engaged, primarily, in the processing of cases, while intelligence operations that rely on data mining of vast databases focus primarily on narrowing the field of suspicion. The former tends to treat guilt as a foregone conclusion,[1] while the latter is arguably indifferent to guilt, in that those who are innocent do not disappear from the databases on account of their innocence. The risk in the case of the former is a rush to judgment; in the case of the latter, the risk is that of bypassing the need to pass judgment altogether and potentially assigning risk status to individuals whose guilt or innocence is never tested but who can find themselves in legal limbo simply by virtue of turning up on a list.

When data mining serves purely as a prelude to identifying particular persons of interest – as it may under Germany's police laws – the chronological logic of the criminal process dictates that the data set assembled for that purpose be destroyed once a suspect has been identified and his guilt tested in court. But when data is assembled purely for intelligence purposes, investigators are not limited to using it to generate and test hypotheses about possible wrongdoing by particular suspects – which means that the intelligence has no obvious time horizon beyond which it loses its relevance. The collection and analysis of intelligence is therefore ongoing; unlike the regular criminal process, it is not time-limited, linear and uni-directional.

As Kovalev and Thaman point out in their analysis of what it means for post-Soviet states to have legalized surveillance outside of their regular criminal process, the regulation of government surveillance can become a way of mapping the demarcation not only between the search for evidence and the pursuit of intelligence but also between a process that is designed to test a hypothesis of guilt and alternative procedures that are designed to maximize the collection of data about the innocent and guilty alike, in order to facilitate the search for patterns and to generate hypotheses, which investigators can later choose to test either through the intelligence system or through the regular criminal process. If the criminal process contemplates an escalating intrusion into the lives of a relatively limited number of people whom there is good reason to suspect of criminal wrongdoing, intelligence investigations contemplate relatively minor intrusions into the lives of massive numbers of people, almost all of whom are assumed to be innocent. If the criminal process is intended to culminate in a transparent judicial process, the alternative intelligence track is meant to remain secret, perhaps permanently, and to be subject to judicial review, if at all, only at the outset, when data is collected, and not later, when the data is combined, analyzed, disseminated, and used for intelligence operations.

More than the regular criminal process, intelligence operations are preventive and, especially, predictive, rather than reactive. People who attract the interest of intelligence analysts can remain in limbo – and in government records – indefinitely, without their guilt or innocence of any particular offenses ever being ascertained or even tested. Intelligence operations pose almost exactly the opposite epistemological and policy problem from that posed by criminal investigations. Of criminal investigations one might ask: how well do systems used to process the guilty do in detecting those who are actually innocent? And how well do such systems do in enforcing the presumption of innocence? By contrast, one might ask the opposite about intelligence investigations. How well do systems that process huge volumes of data about innocent or harmless people do at detecting the tiny number of guilty or at least dangerous people among them?

As the US and many European legal systems are creating legal regimes of exception for covert investigations of terrorism and organized crime, some of the post-Soviet republics, and reformers in many of the others, are trying to do the opposite, as Kovalev and Thaman document: at the urging of the European Court of Human Rights, which frequently criticizes the legal frameworks that govern post-Soviet covert practices, reformers wrestle with the legacy of the Soviet police state through efforts to fold formerly secret investigative tactics into criminal procedure; to require judicial oversight; to establish legal standards and evidentiary thresholds that must be met before the use of covert investigative tactics may be authorized; and to inaugurate a distinction between evidence and intelligence along with rules about when and how intelligence can be turned into evidence. The underlying principle is to separate the rules that govern true intelligence operations, whose aim is unconnected to the criminal process, from those that govern covert practices that were designed to create evidence that feeds back into the criminal process. The latter are increasingly subjected to rights-protective controls, such as: restricting particularly invasive covert tactics to the investigation of particularly serious offenses; imposing time limits on the duration of such tactics; and placing an outright ban on some tactics (such as secret searches) that can shelter corrupt practices like the planting of evidence. These reforms represent an effort to extend the rule of law to areas of covert investigation that have been inherited from the Soviet era and that reformers are attempting to tame.

Post-Soviet reforms thus represent an effort to limit the ability of the police to opt out of the strictures of the criminal process selectively, using the relatively unregulated powers of intelligence services to collect information that will ultimately feed back into the criminal process and be used to convict. These reforms represent an effort to draw a cleaner line between the powers of criminal investigators and the powers that these same investigators may possess when they conduct similar surveillance in their capacity as intelligence services. More generally, immigration investigations, *in rem* proceedings against the fruits or instrumentalities of crime, as well as administrative investigations by Customs and Revenue authorities, resemble intelligence investigations in their capacity to subject targets to state surveillance and sometimes to sanctions, without resort to the criminal process.

6.   LOCATING THE CRIMINAL PROCESS IN A LARGER CONTEXT

If diachronic comparisons make it possible to juxtapose and compare the way in which the criminal process unfolds over time, synchronic comparisons of 'multi-track' systems make it possible to link concerns about plea bargaining as a mechanism for bypassing trial to criticism of the lingering post-Soviet tendency to permit investigative short-cuts around the safeguards of the criminal process. Bypassing the criminal process altogether is merely a more extreme variant of such end-runs, as Ross contends in comparing American willingness to use intelligence operations as true alternatives to the criminal process with the German preference for using early-stage exploratory operations merely to generate testable hypotheses about criminal activity, for the criminal process to adjudicate. It remains a challenge for future scholarship to investigate the dynamics by which legal systems channel data inputs about suspects into the criminal track or into one of its alternatives, and to identify the institutional pressures, legal frameworks, and political power struggles that drive the competition between them.

NOTE

1. For a discussion of the epistemological and moral difficulties of processing criminal cases in a system which presumes innocence although most defendants are guilty, see Whitman, 'Presumption of Innocence or Presumption of Mercy? Weighing Two Western Modes of Justice', 94 *Texas L. Rev.* (forthcoming 2016).

REFERENCES

Alschuler, Albert. 1981. 'The Changing Plea Bargaining Debate', 69 *Cal. L. Rev.* 652.
Alschuler, Albert. 1986. 'The Prosecutor's Role in Plea Bargaining', 36 *Univ. Chicago. L. Rev.* 50.
Amman, Diane. 2000. 'Harmonic Convergence? Constitutional Criminal Procedure in an International Context', 75 *Indiana L.J.* 809.
Damaska, Mirjan. 1997. 'The Uncertain Fate of Evidentiary Transplants: Anglo-American and Continental Experiments', 45 *Am. J. Comp. L.* 839.
de Brito, Alexandra Barahona, Carmen Gonzalez-Enriquez, and Paloma Aguilar, eds. 2001. *The Politics of Memory: Transitional Justice in Democratizing Societies.* Oxford: Oxford University Press.
Delmas-Marty, Mireille. 2003. 'The Contribution of Comparative Law to a Pluralist Conception of International Criminal Law', 1 *J. Int'l Crim. Just.* 13.
Dubber, Markus Dirk. 2004. 'Toward a Constitutional Law of Crime and Punishment', 55 *Hastings L.J.* 509.
Easterbrook, Frank. 1983. 'Criminal Procedure as a Market System', 12 *Journal of Legal Studies* 289.
Kadri, Sadakat. 2005. *The Trial: Four Thousand Years of Courtroom Drama.* New York: Random House.
Koreman, Megan. 1999. *The Expectation of Justice: France 1944–1946.* Durham, NC: Duke University Press.
Kritz, Neil J., ed. 1995. *Transitional Justice: How Emerging Democracies Reckon with Former Regimes.* Washington, DC: United States Institute of Peace.
Langbein, John. 1978. 'Torture and Plea Bargaining', 46 *Univ. Chicago Law Rev.* 3.

Langer, Máximo. 2004. 'From Legal Transplants to Legal Translations: The Globalization of Plea Bargaining and the Americanization Thesis in Criminal Procedure', 45 *Harv. Int'l L.J.* 1.

Langer, Máximo and Joseph W. Doherty. 2011. 'Managerial Judging Goes International but Its Promise Remains Unfulfilled: An Empirical Assessment of the ICTY Reforms', 36 *Yale Journal of International Law* 241.

Levinson, Sanford. 2000. 'Trials, Commissions, and Investigating Committees: The Elusive Search for Norms of Due Process', in Robert I. Rotberg and Dennis Thompson, eds., *Truth v. Justice: The Morality of Truth Commissions*. Princeton, NJ: Princeton University Press, 211.

Linz, Juan J. and Alfred Stepan. 1996. *Problems of Democratic Transition and Consolidation: Southern Europe, South America, and Post-Communist Europe*. Baltimore, MD: The John Hopkins University Press.

McAdams, A. James, ed., 1997. *Transitional Justice and the Rule of Law in New Democracies*. Notre Dame, IN: University of Notre Dame Press.

Moak, Stacy and Ronald Carlson. 2014. *Criminal Justice Procedure* (8th edn). Hoboken: Taylor and Francis.

O'Donnell, Guillermo, Philippe C. Schmitter and Laurence Whitehead, eds. 1986. *Transitions from Authoritarian Rule: Comparative Perspectives*. Baltimore, MD: The John Hopkins University Press.

Offe, Claus. 1997. *Varieties of Transition: The East European and East German Experience*. Cambridge, MA: The MIT Press.

Pogany, Istvan. 1997. *Righting Wrongs in Eastern Europe*. Manchester: Manchester University Press.

Posner, Eric A. and Adrian Vermeule. 2004. 'Transitional Justice as Ordinary Justice', 117 *Harv. L. Rev. 761*.

Schulhofer, Stephen. 1988. 'Is Plea Bargaining Inevitable?' 97 *Harvard L. Rev.* 1037.

Schulhofer, Stephen. 1992. 'Plea Bargaining as a Disaster', 101 Yale Law J. 1979.

Scott, Robert E. and William J. Stuntz. 1992. 'Plea Bargaining as Contract', 101 *Yale L. J.* 1909, 1915.

Stone Sweet, Alec. 2000. *Governing With Judges: Constitutional Politics in Europe*. Oxford: Oxford University Press.

Teitel, Ruti G. 2000. *Transitional Justice* (2000). Oxford: Oxford University Press.

Whitman, James Q. forthcoming 2016. 'Presumption of Innocence or Presumption of Mercy? Weighing Two Western Modes of Justice', 94 *Texas L. Rev.* (forthcoming 2016).

PART II

HOLISTIC COMPARISONS

1. Limits on the search for truth in criminal procedure: a comparative view

Jenia Iontcheva Turner[1]

1. INTRODUCTION

Across diverse legal traditions, the search for truth is a basic function of the criminal process.[2] Uncovering the truth about the charged crime is regarded as an essential precondition to achieving justice, enforcing criminal law, and legitimating the verdict.[3] Yet while truth-seeking is a broadly accepted goal in the criminal process, no system seeks the truth at all costs. The search for truth must on occasion yield to considerations related to efficiency, democratic participation, and protection of individual rights.

Different jurisdictions around the world show different preferences with respect to the trade-offs between these values and the search for truth in criminal procedure. In an effort to promote efficiency, enhance democratic participation, or protect individual rights, legal systems tolerate certain procedures that are known to heighten the risk of inaccurate outcomes (Damaška, 1973; Dripps, 2011; LaFave et al., 2012; Laudan, 2006; Stamp, 1998; Weigend, 2003). Some of these procedural preferences can be explained with reference to the influence of the adversarial and inquisitorial traditions (Damaška, 1973; Grande, 2008; Laudan, 2006; Pizzi, 2000; Trüg and Kerner, 2007; Weigend, 2003). But the distinction between adversarial and inquisitorial systems on this point is not always clear. Great variation exists within these two traditions, and common approaches can be seen across the divide.

Some truth-limiting procedures, such as those related to the exclusionary rule and the protection of individual rights, have been widely adopted across the globe and have proven amenable to adjustments that accommodate the concern for truth. Other measures, such as lay participation in the criminal process, have retained their hold in some countries but have not spread to many others. Finally, one category of practices generally acknowledged to conflict with truth-seeking – plea bargaining and other methods of negotiated justice – have become increasingly prevalent, but have proven the most difficult to regulate and to align with the search for truth.

2. PROMOTING INDIVIDUAL RIGHTS: DOUBLE JEOPARDY AND EXCLUSIONARY RULES

Perhaps the most universally accepted reason for limiting the search for truth concerns the protection of individual rights such as dignity, privacy, and liberty. The willingness to compromise the search for truth in the service of individual rights influences a host of criminal procedures in both adversarial and inquisitorial jurisdictions – from heightened burdens of proof to witness privileges to exclusionary rules.

Since World War II and the rise of international human rights law, the protection of individual liberties has become a more central goal of criminal justice systems around the world. Many of the procedural rights that developed in the process – the right to counsel, to an impartial adjudicator, to confront adverse witnesses, and to receive notice of charges – are generally consistent with an emphasis on accuracy in criminal cases. But certain individual protections, including the privilege against self-incrimination, the ban on double jeopardy, and rules for excluding unlawfully obtained evidence, may impair the search for truth (Laudan, 2006; Stacy, 1991; Weigend, 2003). Under the influence of human rights ideals, countries around the world have come closer together in their willingness to adopt these protections and limit the search for truth when necessary to ensure fairness (Jung, 2004; Weigend, 2011). Nonetheless, there remain some perceptible differences in the way adversarial and inquisitorial systems balance these values.

One of the most powerful influences on the shape of adversarial criminal procedures has been the maxim that 'It is better that ten guilty persons escape than that one innocent suffer' (Blackstone, 1769).[4] Recognizing that errors are inevitable in any realm of human decision-making, this maxim suggests that we should opt for distributing errors away from wrongful convictions. Jurisdictions that take this 'innocence-weighted' approach thus aim to avoid mistaken convictions even when this diminishes accuracy overall and results in a greater number of wrongful acquittals (Laudan, 2006; Stacy, 1991).

Although the 'innocence-weighted' procedural preference has historically been more prominent in adversarial systems, it can be seen across the adversarial-inquisitorial spectrum and is enshrined in key provisions of international human rights conventions (International Covenant on Civil and Political Rights, 1976, art. 14; European Convention for the

Protection of Human Rights and Fundamental Freedoms, 1950). The reasonable doubt standard, for example, which sacrifices some accuracy for the sake of reducing wrongful convictions, is shared by a number of adversarial and inquisitorial systems, and now by international criminal courts (Rome Statute of the International Criminal Court, art. 66(3), 2002; ICTY R. Proc. & Evid. R. 87(A); General Comment No. 32, HRC, 2007; Acquaviva, 2013; Stacy, 1991). Likewise, the right to remain silent, which reduces the amount of information available to fact-finders, is now accepted widely at least in part in order to ensure that innocent persons do not falsely incriminate themselves (*Ohio v. Reiner*, 532 U.S. 17 (2001)).[5]

2.1 Double Jeopardy and the Ban on Appeals of Acquittals

The 'innocence-weighted' approach, however, remains somewhat more prominent in jurisdictions belonging to the adversarial tradition. One manifestation of this approach is the ban on appeals of acquittals. Adversarial systems typically prohibit the prosecution from appealing acquittals, while inquisitorial systems grant the prosecution and the defense equal rights to appeal, regardless of the verdict. The asymmetrical appeals mechanism in adversarial systems means that legal or factual errors which favor defendants may remain uncorrected. The willingness to adopt a procedure that hinders the ability of the legal system to correct mistakes can be explained at least in part by a desire to minimize the risk of false convictions.

The ban on appeals of acquittals is often traced back to the general restriction on *all* appeals of criminal judgments under the common law (Damaška, 1991; Law Reform Commission (Ireland), 2002). While neither defendants nor prosecutors had the ability to obtain review of most criminal judgments in the early days of the common law, by the late nineteenth and early twentieth centuries, concerns about false convictions led many common-law jurisdictions to create a system of appeals (Laudan, 2006; Law Reform Commission (Ireland), 2002). Yet courts and lawmakers believed that appeals of acquittals would violate the doctrine of double jeopardy, so the new appellate remedies applied only to convictions.[6]

The asymmetrical system of appeals has been defended on several policy grounds. First, the procedure is championed as necessary to protect innocent defendants from being overwhelmed by the pressures of an appeal and potential retrial (*Green v. United States*, 355 U.S. 184, 187 (1957); Rizzolli, 2010; Westen, 1980). Second, it is justified on the grounds that it reduces the risk that some acquittals might be erroneously reversed on appeal (Rizzolli, 2010; Westen, 1980). In cases decided by juries, it is also prized for protecting the jury's autonomy, and in particular, the jury's power to render a verdict against the evidence (Westen, 1980).

From a truth-seeking perspective, however, the ban on appeal of acquittals imposes significant costs as it precludes courts from correcting factual errors that favor defendants (Laudan, 2006). In a reflection of these concerns, inquisitorial countries and international criminal courts have rejected asymmetric appeals. The inquisitorial position – giving equal appellate rights to the defense and the prosecution – is formally rooted in a different understanding of double jeopardy (Jackson and Kovalev, 2006/2007). While adversarial systems generally consider a trial verdict to be a final judgment for purposes of double jeopardy (Jackson and Kovalev, 2006/2007; Rudstein, 2012),[7] inquisitorial systems deem criminal judgments to be final only after all appellate remedies have been exhausted (Jackson and Kovalev, 2006/2007; *Maresti v. Croatia* [2009] ECHR 981). But this different interpretation of double jeopardy is ultimately grounded in a stronger preference for procedures that assist the search for truth (Grande, 2008).

While the adversarial-inquisitorial split on appeals of acquittals remains clear, it has become narrower since the 1960s as concerns about accuracy have grown more dominant in certain common-law jurisdictions. Several common-law countries have allowed the prosecution to appeal questions of law even after acquittals (Crim. Code (Can.) § 676; Crimes Act (N.Z.) (1961) § 380; Crim. Proc. Act (S. Afr.) (1977) § 319). In a few of these, the appeal is 'with prejudice' – meaning that it may result in a reversal of the judgment (Crim. Code (Can.) § 676; Crimes Act (N.Z.) (1961) § 380; Crim. Proc. Act (S. Afr.) (1977) § 319). In others, the appeal is 'without prejudice', meaning that the appellate decision is merely declaratory (Crim. Just. Act (Eng.) (1972) §§ 36(1)– (3), (7); Crim. Proc. Act (Scot.) (1995) § 123(1); Crim. Proc. Act (Ireland) (1993) § 11).[8] In the United States, the law has also expanded the availability of prosecutorial appeals. Statutes and case law in a majority of states permit prosecutors to challenge dismissals of charges and the exclusion of evidence through interlocutory appeals at the pretrial stage.[9] Even after trial, prosecutors may now appeal a verdict favorable to the defendant where the defendant obtains a dismissal of the case 'on grounds unrelated to guilt or innocence' (*United States v. Scott*, 437 U.S. 82, 96 (1978))[10] or when a judge sets aside a jury conviction and acquits the defendant (*Smith v. Massachusetts*, 543 U.S. 462, 467 (2005) (citing *United States v. Wilson*, 420 U.S. 332, 352–353 (1975))).

Moving beyond appeals on legal issues, a few adversarial jurisdictions have introduced a more significant exception to double jeopardy principles, allowing re-prosecution on the grounds of newly discovered evidence. With the advent of DNA testing, England and several Australian provinces have provided for the reopening of proceedings in certain serious crimes cases where new and compelling evidence justifies it (Crim. Just. Act (Eng.) (2003) § 78; Crown Prosecution Service, Legal Guidance: Retrial of Serious Offences; Rudstein, 2007; Waye and Marcus, 2010).[11] US courts have also permitted successive prosecutions in certain limited cases of newly available evidence. Under the 'due diligence' exception to double jeopardy, a successive prosecution is not barred for a second offense when 'additional facts necessary to sustain that charge have not occurred or have not been discovered despite the exercise of due diligence'.[12] At least in the realm of appeals and retrials, therefore, we are seeing some rebalancing of priorities and a greater emphasis on the discovery of truth among several adversarial systems.

2.2 Excluding Unlawfully Obtained Evidence

In an effort to ensure a fair process and protect individual rights, criminal justice systems may also adopt rules that exclude unlawfully obtained evidence. Such exclusionary rules tend to conflict with the search for truth, as they remove probative evidence from consideration by the judge or jury, and, in some cases, entirely thwart the prosecution of guilty offenders.

Exclusionary rules are often associated with common-law jurisdictions, and the American rule in particular is frequently described as the strictest and broadest. Yet most contemporary civil-law jurisdictions also have rules that prohibit the use of unlawfully obtained evidence; in fact, some of these rules predate common-law exclusionary rules (Damaška, 1997; Thaman, 2011a). And while recent Supreme Court jurisprudence has continually narrowed the reach of the exclusionary rule in the United States, undermining the notion that the US rule is mandatory (*United States v. Leon*, 468 U.S. 897 (1984); *Hudson v. Michigan*, 547 U.S. 586, 591 (2006); *Herring v. United States*, 555 U.S. 135 (2009); Maclin, 2013), courts in a number of modern inquisitorial systems have begun taking a firmer approach to exclusion (Giannoulopoulos, 2007; Gruber et al., 2012; Sözüer and Sevdiren, 2013; Winter, 2013).

Categorization along adversarial and inquisitorial lines therefore does not appear useful with respect to the exclusionary rule – not only because of convergence among a number of adversarial and inquisitorial systems, but also because of significant divergence within each category.[13] Within the inquisitorial camp, countries such as Argentina, France, Italy, and Spain have maintained to some degree a tradition of procedural nullities. Under the nullity approach, when investigative action violates certain specified statutory rules, and when it has prejudiced the interests of the accused, the action is declared void and its evidentiary results may not be used (Illuminati, 2013; Pradel, 2013).[14] But with respect to evidence obtained as a result of other violations – to which nullities do not attach, but which affect fundamental rights – these countries take very different positions. Spain, Argentina, and Italy provide near-automatic exclusion, while France continues with a presumption of admissibility (Carrio and Garro, 2007; Frase, 2007; Gruber et al., 2012; Illuminati, 2013; Thaman, 2011a). Other countries, such as Greece, Turkey, and Russia, have recently adopted mandatory exclusionary rules under which unlawfully obtained evidence is generally inadmissible (Giannoulopoulos, 2007; Sözüer and Sevdiren, 2013; Triantafyllou, 2013). Finally, a number of jurisdictions, both adversarial and inquisitorial, use a balancing approach, as part of which they consider a host of factors related to the fairness of the process and the accuracy of the verdict (Evid. Act 2006 (N.Z.) § 30(3); Evid. Act 1995 (Cth) § 138(3); Evid. Act 1995 (NSW) § 38; *R v. Grant* [2009] 2 S.C.R. 353 (Can.); *Yissacharov v. Chief Military Prosecutor* [2006] (1) Isr. L.R. 320, ¶ 70; Beernaert and Traest, 2013). Contributing to this diversity, at least in Europe, is the reluctance of the European Court of Human Rights to lay down common rules pertaining to the admissibility of tainted evidence, except in certain extreme cases.[15]

If the adversarial-inquisitorial dichotomy appears outdated, perhaps a more useful classification would be based on the values that the exclusionary rule aims to promote.[16] One can distinguish four main categories here: (1) the reliability approach; (2) the vindication of rights approach; (3) the judicial integrity approach; and (4) the deterrence approach. Classification along these lines is not seamless, as the rules of many jurisdictions frequently aim to maximize more than one value at a time. But it has the advantage of reflecting more accurately how courts and lawmakers within different jurisdictions reason about the scope and function of their exclusionary rules. Furthermore, to the extent we are interested in understanding why different systems choose to depart from the search for truth, it is helpful to examine the policy reasons behind such departures.

Courts and commentators in both adversarial and inquisitorial systems occasionally justify exclusion on the grounds that it can help advance the search for truth. Under this approach, evidence is excluded when the methods used to obtain it have rendered it less reliable (Jackson and Summers, 2012). For example, courts may favor exclusion of testimonial evidence, which is more likely to be tainted by unlawful investigative tactics, but not of physical evidence (Stark and Leverick, 2013; *Yissacharov v. Chief Military Prosecutor* [2006] (1) Isr. L.R. 320, ¶ 71). The stricter treatment of testimonial evidence may be linked in part to the reprehensible nature of the methods typically used to obtain it (for example, torture, inhuman and degrading treatment, or deception). But a review of courts' decisions on these issues reveals that the differential treatment of tangible and testimonial evidence is due at least in part to a concern that tainted testimony is likely to be unreliable and to impair the search for truth (*R. v. Grant* [2009] 2 S.C.R. 353, ¶ 110 (Can.); *Chalmers v. H.M. Advocate*, 1954 JC 66, 83 (Scot.); *Yissacharov* [2006] (1) Isr. L.R. ¶ 71; Strafprozessordnung (Ger.) § 136a). While a focus on reliability can help explain certain features of exclusionary rules in some jurisdictions, it is not a satisfactory description of most modern exclusionary approaches, which sweep more broadly and often lead to the suppression of perfectly reliable evidence (Jackson and Summers, 2012).

In a number of jurisdictions, the exclusion of evidence is defended primarily on the grounds that it is necessary to vindicate fundamental rights. This theory is referred to alternatively as the 'rights theory', the 'remedial model', or the 'protective principle' (*Yissacharov* [2006] (1) Isr. L.R. 320, ¶ 60; Ashworth, 1977; Jackson and Summers, 2012), and it emphasizes the importance of providing an effective remedy to give meaning to individual rights. Without exclusion, provisions that protect fundamental rights are said to be reduced to 'a form of words' (*Silverthorne Lumber Co. v. United States*, 251 U.S. 385, 392 (1920)) such that they 'might as well be stricken from the Constitution' (*Weeks v. United States*, 232 U.S. 383, 393 (1914)). The US Supreme Court followed this approach in some of its earlier opinions on the exclusionary rule, though the Court has since abandoned it (Maclin, 2013). The 'protective principle' nonetheless remains important in a number of other jurisdictions.[17] As might be expected, in countries that follow this principle, the nature of the right breached is a critical factor in the decision whether to exclude. Some jurisdictions reserve mandatory exclusion only for violations of certain fundamental or constitutional rights (*Jalloh v. Germany*, 2006-IX Eur. Ct. H.R. 281, ¶ 105; *Harutyunyan v. Armenia*, 49 Eur. Ct. H.R. 9, ¶¶ 65–66 (2009); *Gäfgen v. Germany*, 52 Eur. Ct. H.R. 1, 42 (2011)).[18] Others place great weight on the type of right violated as part of a balancing test that determines whether exclusion is warranted (*People (A.G.) v. O'Brien* [1965] I.R. 142, 147, 170; Cras and Daly, 2013; Dellidou, 2007).[19]

Another justification for the exclusionary rule is that the rule helps preserve the integrity of the judicial system. Under this view, courts must exclude tainted evidence in order to avoid any perception that they are condoning illegal acts by government agents. As the US Supreme Court put it in one of its early decisions on the exclusionary rule, courts must not become 'accomplices in the willful disobedience of a Constitution they are sworn to uphold' (*Elkins v. United States*, 364 U.S. 206, 223 (1960)).[20] Instead, they must disown any evidence gathered through unlawful acts by government agents in order to ensure that the trial is fair and legitimate (Duff et al., 2007) and that the same standards of conduct apply to government actors and ordinary citizens.[21]

In American jurisprudence, the integrity rationale was prominent in the earlier days of the exclusionary rule (*Weeks v. United States*, 232 U.S. 383, 392 (1914); *Elkins*, 364 U.S. at 223), but has since been overtaken by a deterrence-oriented approach, at least at the federal level (Bloom and Fentin, 2010). It still remains salient in other national and international jurisdictions, however, as well as in the academic literature.[22] Under this approach, courts consider primarily the seriousness of the violation by law enforcement in deciding whether to exclude evidence (*Prosecutor v. Katanga*, Case No. ICC-01/04-01/07, Decision on the Prosecutor's Bar Table Motions ¶¶ 60, 62–63 (Dec. 17, 2010); *Prosecutor v. Lubanga*, Case No. ICC-01/04-01/06, Decision on the Admission of Material from the 'Bar Table' ¶¶ 42–46 (June 24, 2009)). Because courts focus on the damage to the integrity of the justice system as a whole, this approach often gives rise to multi-factor balancing tests. Such tests may consider whether exclusion, to the extent it thwarts the adjudication of a serious crime, might itself threaten judicial integrity in some cases.[23]

The preeminent justification for the exclusionary rule in contemporary US Supreme Court jurisprudence is the deterrence of official misconduct. Under this view, the exclusionary rule should be used only when it would effectively dissuade law enforcement officials from violating the law in the future (*United States v. Leon*, 468 U.S. 897, 918 (1984); *Hudson v. Michigan*, 547 U.S. 586, 591 (2006); *Herring v. United States*, 555 U.S. 135 (2009)). Even when exclusion does deter misconduct, courts may still decide not to impose it, if the social costs of exclusion outweigh the benefits of deterrence (*Leon*, 468 U.S. at 907; *Hudson*, 547 U.S. at 591, 599; *Herring*, 555 U.S. at 141). The cost-benefit analysis considers the availability of alternative sanctions, which may be able to discipline officers at a lesser cost to the administration of justice (*Hudson*, 547 U.S. at 591, 599). It also examines whether misconduct was an isolated occurrence or part of a pattern, under the theory that systemic abuses are in greater need of deterrence (*Herring*, 555 U.S. at 144). Finally, it considers officers' state of mind and reserves discipline only for reckless or deliberate violations of the law (*Herring*, 555 U.S. at 144). Although prominent in the United States, the deterrence approach has not been widely accepted elsewhere in the world.[24] Nonetheless, consistent with a focus on deterrence, a number of jurisdictions consider officers' state of mind, the systemic nature of the misconduct, and the availability of alternative remedies in deciding whether to exclude evidence (Evid. Act 2006 (N.Z.) § 30(3); Evid. Act 1995 (Cth) § 138(3); *R v. Grant* [2009] 2 S.C.R. 353 (Can.); *Yissacharov* [2006] (1) Isr. L.R. ¶ 70; Thaman, 2011a).

While the above discussion might suggest that jurisdictions choose one of the four competing rationales for exclusion, in practice, many justify exclusion by reference to multiple goals (*Yissacharov* [2006] (1) Isr. L.R. ¶ 60; Winter, 2013). Countries frequently adopt a discretionary approach, which tries

> to find the proper balance between the protection of the rights of the accused and safeguarding the fairness and integrity of the criminal process, on the one hand, and competing values and interests, including the value of discovering the truth, fighting increasing crime and protecting public safety and the rights of victims, on the other. (*Yissacharov* [2006] (1) Isr. L.R. 320, ¶ 62)[25]

Factors commonly considered in this balancing analysis include: (1) the importance of the right breached; (2) the seriousness of the violation (including whether the violation was deliberate or reckless; isolated or part of a pattern); (3) the probative value and importance of the improperly obtained evidence; (4) the seriousness of the offence with which the defendant is charged; and (5) whether alternative remedies could provide adequate redress to the defendant (Evid. Act 2006 (N.Z.) § 30(3); Evid. Act 1995 (Cth) § 138 (3); Evid. Act 1995 (NSW) § 38; *R. v. Grant* [2009] 2 S.C.R. 353; *Yissacharov* [2006] (1) Isr. L.R. ¶ 70; *Prosecutor v. Lubanga*, Case No. ICC-01/04-01/06, Decision on the Admission of Material from the 'Bar Table', ¶¶ 42–46 (June 24, 2009); *Prosecutor v. Brdjanin*, Case No. IT-99-36-T, Decision on the Defence 'Objection to Intercept Evidence', ¶ 63 (Int'l Crim. Trib. for the Former Yugoslavia Oct. 3, 2003); Bogers and Stevens, 2013; Gless, 2013; Groenhuijsen, 2008).

The various factors in the balancing analysis aim to address different concerns. An emphasis on the type of right violated is consistent with the 'protective principle'. Consideration of the gravity of the violation is linked to the systemic integrity rationale, while a few of the other factors reflect a concern for deterrence. Importantly, the third inquiry – how probative the evidence is – attempts to minimize the conflict between truth-seeking and the protection of individual rights. While the rest of the factors are not directly related to truth-seeking, they may nonetheless indirectly promote accuracy to the extent that they limit exclusion overall.

In addition to the diversity of formal rules of exclusion, considerable variation exists with respect to the rules' practical implementation (Lewis, 2011; Newcombe, 2007). Several factors may explain why the practice of exclusion often deviates from written rules. First, where exclusionary rules have been recently reformed, longstanding habits and traditional legal culture are likely to 'translate' new laws into a practice that is more consonant with preexisting value commitments of the legal system (particularly a commitment to the search for truth) (Jackson and Summers, 2012; Langer, 2004). Second, where courts follow a balancing test that is drafted in broad terms and considers multiple factors, judges can easily place more weight on factors that maximize accuracy instead of factors that serve other stated purposes of exclusion (Cho, 1998).[26] Deviation from exclusionary rules is likely to be easier in inquisitorial systems, where the same judge who rules on the admissibility of evidence then decides on the guilt or innocence of the defendant. In that situation, even under a mandatory rule, 'the taint from the forbidden but persuasive information cannot be avoided: it always affects the decision maker's thinking' (Damaška, 1997).[27] Although reasoned opinions and appellate review diminish the odds that excluded evidence influences the court's decision, judges trained to see their role above all as the elucidation of the truth are likely to find ways to conform the verdict to the true facts (Jackson and Summers, 2012). Even categorical rules of exclusion may therefore prove frail in systems with a strong preexisting commitment to the search for truth.

Finally, even when courts scrupulously apply mandatory exclusionary rules, a commitment to accuracy may produce some unanticipated adverse side effects. Judges concerned with truth-seeking may interpret the scope of individual rights more narrowly in order to minimize the risk that exclusion would be warranted (Calabresi, 2003; Starr, 2008). Once the underlying rights are weakened, exclusionary rules become less meaningful, regardless of their strictness.

The brief overview of exclusionary rules shows that they are an increasingly common feature of criminal justice systems around the world, although their scope and purpose differ significantly from jurisdiction to jurisdiction. While the adoption of exclusionary rules can be seen as a triumph of individual rights over truth-seeking, such rules typically contain numerous qualifications to allow courts to minimize the burden on the search for truth. Even where exclusionary rules appear quite strict on paper, in practice they frequently give way to a concern for accuracy.

3.   PROMOTING EFFICIENCY: PLEA BARGAINING

Around the world, efficiency fever has gripped criminal justice systems. Countries as varied as France, India, Nigeria, and Poland have increasingly sought to reform their procedures to expedite case flow (Langer, 2004; Rauxloh, 2012; Thaman, 2010; Turner, 2009). An array of different mechanisms has been introduced to accomplish these ends, ranging from diversion to penal orders to summary trials, and increasingly commonly, plea bargaining (Luna and Wade, 2011; Thaman, 2010).[28]

Plea bargaining has been at the forefront of the trend toward a more economical criminal process. In adversarial systems, plea bargaining has been practiced for decades and accepted by courts (at times begrudgingly) since at least the 1970s.[29] In inquisitorial systems, it has spread rapidly since the 1990s, overcoming longstanding resistance to 'trading with justice' (Thaman, 2010). Despite its global ascendance, plea bargaining remains deeply controversial in both adversarial and inquisitorial systems. The objections to the practice are manifold, but a central criticism is that it conflicts with the search for truth.[30]

That plea bargaining stands at odds with a quest for truth in criminal cases is commonly asserted, but less frequently explained.[31] The explanation is not as simple as it is for the exclusionary rule. The question is not simply how plea bargaining conflicts with truth-seeking, but rather whether it is worse than trials at uncovering the truth. Trials are also not perfectly accurate, so we must measure plea bargaining outcomes not simply in absolute terms, but also by how they compare with trial outcomes (Easterbrook, 1983).[32]

There are two principal ways in which plea bargaining – at least as practiced in the United States and a number of other adversarial jurisdictions – increases the risk of inaccurate verdicts. First, a sizeable plea discount can induce even some innocent defendants to waive their right to trial and plead guilty (Altenhain et al., 2007; Finkelstein, 1975; Gross et al., 2004; Wright, 2005). The even more common scenario is this: in exchange for sentencing or charge reductions, defendants who are guilty of some crime may agree to plead guilty to another crime (Bowers, 2008). This obviously does not accurately represent their conduct and thus impairs the search for truth.

The minimal judicial supervision of charging decisions and guilty pleas heightens the risk of inaccuracy. If prosecutors have exclusive authority over decisions to dismiss or reduce charges, with no meaningful oversight by the judiciary, they can negotiate charge bargains that significantly misrepresent the criminal conduct for which a defendant is responsible.[33] Particularly when judges' sentencing discretion is limited, prosecutors' charging choices also largely determine the punishment that a defendant is facing, which gives prosecutors enormous leverage during negotiations (Wright, 2005).[34]

In principle, judges can exercise some oversight over the product of plea negotiations when they examine whether a guilty plea is voluntary, knowing, and factually based (Fed. R. Crim. Proc. (U.S.) 11; Crim. Code (Can.) § 606; Crim. Proc. Act (S. Afr.) § 105A (6)(a)). Yet the pressure of heavy caseloads leads judges to conduct a cursory review, requiring little more than the defendant's confirmation that the allegations in the indictment are correct (Brown, 2005; Hodgson, 2012; Pizzi, 2000; Roach, 2013; Turner, 2006). Whereas at trial, a neutral judge or jury evaluates the evidence carefully and weighs the credibility of witnesses after cross-examination, at a plea hearing, judges test the facts only superficially, based on meager documentary evidence and a brief questioning of the defendant, but no other witnesses (Brown, 2005).

Once a plea agreement is negotiated, the parties themselves have no incentive to question its validity, so they commonly acquiesce to the *pro forma* review by the court. At the negotiation stage, when the prosecution and defense may benefit from greater access to information, such information may be unavailable or it may be too costly to obtain. In adversarial systems, the defense frequently lacks access to the prosecutor's evidence before negotiating a plea. At least in the United States, prosecutors need not disclose even certain evidence favorable to the defendant at that stage (*United States v. Ruiz*, 536 U.S. 622 (2002)).[35] While other adversarial jurisdictions tend to provide for more extensive pre-plea disclosure, it is still not as broad as the disclosure provided just before trial (Crim. Just. Act (Eng.) 2003, c.44 §§ 37; *R. v. Stinchcombe* [1991] 3 S.C.R. 326 (Can.); *R. v. Taillefer & R. v. Duguay* [2003] 3 S.C.R. 307 (Can.); Crim. Disclosure Act 2008 (N.Z.) §§ 12–13; Rofe, 1996); moreover, at least in some adversarial jurisdictions, plea bargaining is increasingly occurring before charges are filed and therefore before disclosure obligations attach (Sanders et al., 2010). Adequate investigation of the facts by the defense is further constrained by the short time limits on plea offers, the heavy caseloads carried by most defense attorneys, and the limited funding for defense investigations (Brown, 2005; McConville et al., 1994; Rauxloh, 2012).

Accuracy in plea bargaining is also impaired because prosecutors tend to negotiate deals early in their investigation, in order to conserve valuable investigative and trial preparation resources. They frequently offer greater concessions for early guilty pleas and, in some cases, leave plea agreements open for only a limited time before trial (Turner, 2006). The haste to conclude an agreement deprives prosecutors of useful information they could glean from a more thorough investigation, and it increases the risk of factual errors.

Finally, at least in adversarial systems, verdicts based on guilty pleas are typically not supported by a thorough reasoned judgment (or any reasoned judgment at all), and appeals of negotiated verdicts are more circumscribed than appeals from contested cases (Horne, 2013; Turner and Weigend, 2013). This arrangement reduces the system's ability to correct inaccuracies.

While many plea bargains conflict with truth-seeking for the reasons just discussed, some can also help uncover facts that would otherwise remain unknown to prosecutors. Cooperation agreements, under which the prosecution offers concessions to a defendant in exchange for his/her agreement to reveal information about other defendants or to participate in undercover investigations, can assist the search for truth, at least in some cases. But the precise extent to which cooperation agreements promote truth-seeking is subject to debate.

Some scholars have argued that cooperation agreements are less likely to implicate innocent defendants because such defendants are less likely to be useful as links to a criminal enterprise and 'are likely to redirect investigative efforts to the worthiest targets' (Ross, 2006). But others have raised serious concerns about the reliability of informants who receive concessions in exchange for cooperation (Natapoff, 2009). They have pointed out the risk that defendants may falsely accuse other persons in order to obtain a good bargain. Likewise, some have criticized the lenient treatment given to cooperating defendants who can provide valuable information only because of their deep involvement in a criminal enterprise.[36] Such defendants may help the search for truth with respect to other investigations, but to the extent their cooperation is rewarded with lesser charges, it could undermine accuracy in their own case. For these reasons and others, inquisitorial countries have been slower than their adversarial counterparts to embrace cooperation agreements (Turner, 2009).

In the final analysis, the principal defense of plea bargaining is that even if it deemphasizes the search for truth in particular cases, it yields a net benefit for truth-seeking across the board. By freeing up resources that prosecutors and courts can use to pursue more offenders, the argument goes, plea bargaining may help resolve more cases and thus achieve an overall gain in criminal law enforcement (Damaška, 1997– 1998).[37] Negotiated justice may be rough and in some sense more superficial, but its reach is far broader. At least for those who accept utilitarian principles, the overall gain in the enforcement of criminal law may be worth the risk that we will uncover fewer facts in individual cases.

There are several potential problems with this view, however. First, it is practically impossible to assess objectively whether the disadvantages of reduced accuracy in individual cases outweigh the benefit from the resolution of more cases. Second, plea bargaining seriously limits what we learn about individual cases, and this has consequences beyond the mere decrease in accuracy. The shallower resolution of cases may provide less solace to victims, hinder the system's ability to diagnose the causes underlying different crimes, and in the end undermine various goals of punishment. Finally, overuse of coercive tactics in plea bargaining means that a certain number of innocent persons plead guilty, which is a result no one interested in just and accurate outcomes should desire.[38]

While it may be difficult to calculate the precise effect of plea bargaining on the search for truth in the criminal justice system, it is clear that certain features of plea bargaining – sizeable plea discounts, minimal judicial supervision, lack of transparency and disclosure – are particularly likely to undermine truth-seeking in individual cases. Even if one is satisfied that plea bargaining is on the whole beneficial to the search for truth, it is still worth studying these procedures to see if their negative effects in individual cases can be minimized without significantly reducing efficiency. From a comparative perspective, it is notable that certain inquisitorial and international jurisdictions have made more serious attempts to limit these truth-impairing procedures.

In the first place, inquisitorial countries have reduced the likelihood that plea bargaining would conflict with the search for truth by imposing restrictions on charging and sentencing reductions that can be offered in exchange for a guilty plea. As noted earlier, this helps minimize the risk that innocent persons might plead guilty, as well as the risk that charges would misrepresent the defendant's conduct. In the United States, few jurisdictions regulate charge or sentence reductions or other concessions offered as part of a plea bargain. A few other adversarial jurisdictions have begun introducing presumptive plea discounts, although enforceable limits are still the exception rather than the norm in the common-law world.[39] More importantly, guidelines on plea discounts remain of little use, if, as is the case in most adversarial jurisdictions, charge bargaining remains common and largely unregulated (Leverick, 2010; Rauxloh, 2012; Waye and Marcus, 2010).

In inquisitorial systems, by contrast, prosecutors are more limited in their ability to negotiate over charges (Turner and Weigend, 2013). Many of these systems follow the principle of mandatory prosecutions, under which prosecutors are required (at least in more serious cases) to bring charges where sufficient evidence exists (Strafprozessordnung (Ger.) § 170(1); Thaman, 2010). Even in systems that do not follow the mandatory prosecution principle, charge bargaining is regarded as impermissible because of its conflict with the search for truth, a central principle of inquisitorial (and international) criminal procedure (*Prosecutor v. Momir Nikolić*, Case No. IT-02-60/1-S, Sentencing Judgment ¶ 65 (Int'l Crim. Trib. for the Former Yugoslavia Dec. 2, 2003); Gruber et al., 2012). Reflecting this preference for factual and legal accuracy, inquisitorial systems allow judges to modify the legal characterization of the facts alleged in the indictment. If judges believe the evidence warrants it, they may substitute more serious charges than those initially filed by the prosecution, as long as they give notice to the defendant and the opportunity to respond and adjust his defense (Strafprozessordnung (Ger.) § 265; Stahn, 2005).

Plea bargaining in inquisitorial systems is therefore typically restricted to bargaining about the sentence (Strafprozessordnung (Ger.) §257c; Thaman, 2010). Moreover, sentence discounts are often capped or presumptively set at around one-third (Thaman, 2010). The baseline sentences from which plea discounts are assessed are also significantly milder (Whitman, 2005). Finally, in a number of inquisitorial countries, plea bargaining is limited to only certain minor offenses which carry mild sanctions (Thaman, 2010). These three factors – particularly in combination – help reduce the pressure on defendants to plead guilty to crimes they did not commit.

Another way in which inquisitorial systems have reduced the truth-impairing nature of plea bargaining is by ensuring that bargains occur after a thorough inquiry into the facts by law enforcement and the prosecution. In adversarial systems guilty pleas are often sought early in the investigation, and early pleas are typically rewarded more generously.[40] By contrast, in inquisitorial systems, negotiations usually occur only after the completion of a thorough pretrial investigation (Langer, 2004; Thaman, 2010; Turner, 2006). The investigation is more thorough for various reasons, some of which are a function of professional culture and resource allocation, while others reflect formal legal requirements.[41] Although there is great variation across inquisitorial systems, in general, prosecutors tend to be more closely involved in the investigation than they are in adversarial systems (Hodgson, 2012).

Prosecutors also have a duty to uncover both exculpatory and inculpatory evidence in inquisitorial systems and at international criminal courts (Strafprozessordnung (Ger.) § 160; Rome Statute of the International Criminal Court, art. 54(1), 2002). While this requirement is not always sufficient to ensure a more thorough and objective investigation (Hodgson, 2006; Ostendorf, 1978), education, training, and professional culture help to reinforce the self-identification of prosecutors as neutral 'organs of justice' (Boyne, 2014; Whitman, 2009). Because many inquisitorial systems have traditionally measured prosecutors' performance along qualitative rather than quantitative lines, prosecutors tend to take the task of seeking evidence for both sides seriously.[42]

Even when prosecutors do not take the initiative to pursue exculpatory leads, at least in some inquisitorial jurisdictions, the defense has the right to request that they undertake specific investigative measures.[43] Moreover, defendants in inquisitorial jurisdictions typically cannot waive their right to an attorney in a plea bargained case, unlike their American counterparts (Hodgson, 2012; Weigend and Turner, 2014).

Another accuracy-enhancing feature of inquisitorial systems is that judges and defense attorneys have access to the investigative file before plea negotiations (Strafprozessordnung (Ger.) § 147 (1); Gilliéron, 2013; Hodgson, 2012). The prosecution can prevent the defense from seeing certain portions of the file while the investigation is still ongoing, but plea bargaining rarely occurs at that stage.[44] Unlike their American counterparts (Klein et al., 2015), prosecutors in inquisitorial systems and at the international criminal courts do not seek waivers of this right to review the investigative file; in any event, such waivers would likely be held unlawful in at least some inquisitorial jurisdictions (Judgment of the Federal Constitutional Court of March 19, 2013, BVerfG, 2 BvR 2628/10, BvR 2883/10, 2 BvR 2155/11).

Rules concerning judicial supervision of admissions of guilt also tend to be stricter in inquisitorial systems. Judges have an independent duty to establish the objective truth, and this duty implies a searching review of the facts supporting an admission of guilt (Hodgson, 2012; Weigend and Turner, 2014). In some inquisitorial countries, courts are constitutionally prohibited from relying solely on the defendant's confession as the basis for a verdict (Turner, 2009). Both legislation and court decisions across inquisitorial systems emphasize judges' duty to go beyond defendants' admissions of guilt to verify their accuracy. At a minimum, judges must examine the investigative file to determine if it contains independent

evidence corroborating the admissions (Judgment of the Federal Constitutional Court of March 19, 2013, BVerfG, 2 BvR 2628/10, BvR
2883/10, 2 BvR 2155/11; Hodgson, 2012). In many jurisdictions outside
the United States, judges are also not allowed to accept so-called *Alford*
pleas or equivocal pleas, in which the defendant protests his innocence
while entering a formal guilty plea.[45]

Finally, inquisitorial judges have the requisite tools to pursue the truth
independently of the parties. In most systems, they can and do consult
the investigative file before reviewing an admission of guilt (Strafprozessordnung (Ger.) § 147(1); Gilliéron, 2013; Hodgson, 2012). In some, they
also participate in the plea negotiations, and this gives them a fuller
picture of the facts of the case (Thaman, 2010; Turner and Weigend,
2013). Ultimately, judges can call and examine their own witnesses and
order further investigative measures to determine the true facts before
deciding whether to accept a plea agreement (Strafprozessordnung (Ger.)
§ 244; Rome Statute of the International Criminal Court, art. 65, 2002).

When plea negotiations do produce factual errors, these errors are
more likely to be caught and corrected in those systems that require a
reasoned judgment and provide for appellate review in negotiated cases.
In inquisitorial systems and at international criminal courts, unlike in
adversarial systems, reasons for the verdict tend to be required in
plea-bargained cases (Thaman, 2010; Turner, 2009). The reasoning is
typically shorter, however, as it relies significantly on the defendant's
admission of guilt. While a few inquisitorial countries limit appeals of
negotiated judgments, others make appeal available as broadly as in
contested cases; moreover, at least in some jurisdictions, a plea agreement may not include an appeals waiver (Strafprozessordnung (Ger.)
§ 302(1); Thaman, 2010).

The above overview may leave the impression that plea bargaining is
significantly less likely to deviate from the search for truth in inquisitorial and international criminal jurisdictions than in adversarial ones. This
would be a fair conclusion if one were to focus solely on the formal rules
that regulate plea bargaining. But a glance at the practice of plea
bargaining reveals a somewhat different picture.

Empirical studies of plea bargaining in Germany, for example, reveal a
wide gap between the law on the books and bargaining in practice
(Altenhain et al., 2007; Hassemer and Hippler, 1986; Turner, 2006). The
most recent survey, conducted in 2012, found the divergence persisting
even after the adoption of legislation to formalize and regulate the
practice.[46] A majority of judges surveyed admitted that they concluded
more than half of their negotiations 'informally', that is, without complying with the requirements of the legislation (Altenhain et al., 2013).[47] In

a significant percentage of cases, judges accepted a formal agreement of the prosecutor's factual allegations by the defendant as the sole basis for finding the defendant guilty, contrary to the law's demand of independently establishing the 'truth' (Altenhain et al., 2013). The study also found that the subject matter of bargains extended beyond that authorized in the Code. For example, many judges listed the contents of the charges as a frequent subject of bargaining (Altenhain et al., 2013).

Likewise, a study of plea bargaining at the ICTY and ICTR has shown that bargaining often involved charge and even fact bargaining, despite the tribunals' repeated pronouncements that such practices would conflict with the search for truth (Combs, 2007). When the Tribunals' judges attempted to counter such practices by ignoring charge reductions and departing from the prosecutors' recommended sentences, they effectively extinguished the interest of international defendants in guilty pleas (Combs, 2012).

In Russia, judges were found to depart frequently from the formal rules concerning plea bargaining. In some cases, they deviated from the rules in order to advance the search for truth (Semukhina and Reynolds, 2009).[48] But, more frequently, they ignored provisions of the law designed to protect the accuracy of plea bargains. In 16 out of 33 cases studied, judges relied only on the investigative file or on the agreement between the parties and did not inquire further whether the plea was voluntary or knowing (Semukhina and Reynolds, 2009).

In short, even in systems that have attempted to regulate plea bargaining and to align it more closely with the search for truth, informal practices may push in the opposite direction, in favor of a convenient and quick resolution of cases. Such practices are difficult to contain, as lawyers and judges have powerful economic and other incentives to resolve cases 'amicably' (Alschuler, 1968, 1975; Bibas, 2004; Schulhofer, 1988; Weigend, 2008). As long as certain structural features of the criminal justice system persist (expanding criminal codes; increasing numbers and complexity of cases, without a corresponding adjustment of human resources; outdated trial procedures; and evaluation of criminal justice professionals based on efficiency rather than quality), formal constraints on plea bargaining will have a more limited effect than expected.

4. PROMOTING DEMOCRATIC PARTICIPATION: UNREASONED AND UNREVIEWABLE JURY VERDICTS

Another hindrance to the search for truth in criminal cases may arise from certain evidentiary and procedural rules associated with jury trials. This section focuses on one such procedure – jury verdicts that contain no reasoning and are subject to limited appellate review. I discuss how unreasoned and unreviewable verdicts conflict with truth-seeking and why they nevertheless continue to be used in a number of jurisdictions around the world.

Trial by jury has often been introduced into criminal justice systems as an element of broader democratic reforms.[49] The French Revolution ushered in jury trials as a means of increasing popular participation in the criminal process (Vogler, 2005). Liberal thinkers in other European countries, influenced by the same democratic ideals, were likewise successful in introducing juries in the nineteenth century (Koch, 2001; Vidmar, 2000; Vogler, 2005). As authoritarian governments took power in several European countries in the early twentieth century, however, they limited or entirely abolished lay participation (Thaman, 2011b). The subsequent return of democracy did not always restore juries, although many jurisdictions reintroduced lay participation through mixed courts in which professional judges deliberate and decide alongside their lay counterparts.[50]

The association of juries with democracy can be found in a number of non-European countries as well. Most recently, South Korea and Japan launched mixed courts of judges and jurors in an effort to bolster the democratic legitimacy of their criminal justice systems (Park, 2010; Weber, 2009). Around the world today, laypersons participate in criminal trials in over fifty countries, all of which can be described as roughly democratic (Leib, 2008; Park, 2010). While most of these countries rely on mixed courts of professional judges and jurors, more than a dozen (typically common-law) countries employ all-lay juries (*Taxquet v. Belgium* [2010] Eur. Ct. H.R. 1806, ¶ 47; Vidmar, 2000).

In the academic literature and judicial opinions, juries have been defended on several different grounds. One justification is fully consistent with an emphasis on truth-seeking: it maintains that jurors, with their diverse perspectives and deliberative decision-making process, are more likely to reach accurate outcomes (Ellsworth, 1989; Goldbach and Hans, 2014; *A.K. v. Western Australia* [2008] HCA 8, 232 CLR 438, 492). Other rationales for jury trials are not linked to the jury's fact-finding abilities but instead emphasize the jury's democratic virtues. Jury trials are praised for giving ordinary citizens a say in the criminal process and for producing verdicts that are more consistent with community standards of justice (*A.K. v. Western Australia* [2008] HCA 8, 232 CLR 438, 492; *R. v. G. (R.M.)* [1996] 3 S.C.R. 362, ¶ 13 (S.C.C.)). These features are said to increase 'public confidence in the fairness of the criminal justice system' (*Taylor v. Louisiana*, 419 U.S. 522, 530 (1975)).

Juries are also prized as a symbol of rejecting authoritarian government and a means of controlling biased or corrupt judges.[51] As Patrick Devlin colorfully remarked, the jury is 'the lamp that shows that freedom lives' (Devlin, 1966, cited in *A.K. v. Western Australia* [2008] HCA 8, 232 CLR 438, 489). This association with democratic government and the protection of individual liberties is one of the main reasons why juries retain such a strong symbolic significance today, even as their practical influence has sharply decreased (Lloyd-Bostock and Thomas, 1999; Malsch, 2009).

One of the main reasons why juries are 'uncongenial to authoritarian rule' is that, in many systems, they can 'reach a verdict based on conscience, against the letter of the law, and occasionally in defiance of government' (Lloyd-Bostock and Thomas, 1999). The ability to render verdicts against the law rests on the unique procedural arrangement that is the subject of discussion in this chapter – the unreasoned, and in the case of acquittals, unreviewable jury verdict. While often extolled as a principal virtue of juries, it is also the subject of intense criticism.[52]

Critics of the jury target a variety of perceived flaws in the institution. For the purposes of this chapter, I address the critiques that concern the jury's ability to render truthful verdicts. These critiques take three main forms. Some commentators challenge the jury's capacity to discern facts accurately, particularly in more complex cases that involve scientific or statistical evidence.[53] Others focus on the jury's perceived weakness in understanding and following the law.[54] Finally, a number of critics focus not on the cognitive capacities of jurors, but rather on the truth-thwarting features of certain procedural and evidentiary rules associated with jury trials (Laudan, 2006; Weigend, 2003).

Empirical evidence does not bear out the first critique. While jurors do suffer from certain cognitive biases that affect all humans, they are not less likely to produce accurate outcomes than professional judges. On the whole, jurors do not appear to be worse at discerning facts than judges are, even in cases where the evidence is technical and complex.[55] A number of the studies that find difficulties in the comprehension or retention of certain facts trace the problem not to the cognitive capacities of jurors, but rather to rules that prohibit jurors from taking notes, asking questions of the witnesses or lawyers, and seeing certain relevant evidence (Ellsworth and Reifman, 2000; Vidmar and Hans, 2007).

A number of studies have also found that jurors have difficulty understanding certain aspects of the law and that they struggle to follow legal instructions.[56] Yet these difficulties diminish when clearer wording is used, when attorneys clarify the instructions, or when other preventive measures are taken (Seidman Diamond et al., 2012; Ellsworth and Reifman, 2000; Vidmar and Hans, 2007). Moreover, with respect to understanding certain limiting instructions (to disregard particular evidence or to consider it only for a limited purpose), judges appear to suffer from similar cognitive weaknesses (Vidmar and Hans, 2007).

Whatever difficulties juries may have in understanding the law, in the vast majority of criminal cases, they render the same verdicts that judges would have imposed.[57] In the few cases where judges and jurors disagree about the outcome of a case, this is typically the result of a reasonable difference in the interpretation of the law, not of misunderstanding by jurors (Eisenberg et al., 2005; Kalven and Zeisel, 1966; Vidmar and Hans, 2007).

While jurors do not appear to be less capable than judges in discovering the truth, certain procedural and evidentiary rules accompanying jury trials may interfere with truth-seeking. Section 2.2 discussed certain exclusionary rules that fall in that category. This section focuses on two other features, unreasoned jury verdicts and limited appellate review of such verdicts.

All-lay juries typically do not have to provide a reasoned judgment in support of their decisions. By contrast, most jurisdictions today require judges and mixed tribunals to submit written reasons for their judgments in criminal cases.[58] The lack of reasons for jury verdicts in common-law countries is justified on the grounds that it protects the confidentiality of jury deliberations and preserves the jury's ability to render a verdict of conscience.

Common-law systems attempt to make up for the lack of reasons for the jury verdict by requiring judges to give jurors elaborate instructions on the law and, in some countries, to summarize the evidence.[59] In recent years, some jurisdictions have also experimented with giving jurors decision 'flowcharts' and 'decision trees', in addition to judicial instructions, to help guide their deliberations (Marcus, 2013). A few countries – mostly in the civil-law tradition – also present jurors with specific questions that they must answer in support of their verdict.[60] These are all valuable efforts to reduce inaccurate verdicts, but it is not clear whether they go far enough 'to shore up … the legitimacy of inscrutable jury verdicts' (Damaška, 1997: 46). The lack of a reasoned decision is a major reason why many continental European countries disfavor the common-law jury trial. It is seen as inconsistent with statutory and in some cases constitutional requirements that a criminal verdict be based on factual evidence (Damaška, 1997).

From a truth-seeking perspective, the problem of inscrutable jury verdicts is compounded by the limited possibility of appeal. As discussed earlier, appeals of acquittals are generally prohibited in adversarial countries, where most all-lay juries are found. Although appeals from acquittals from bench trials are also often banned, 'protection afforded by the double jeopardy principle has been at its strongest where the accused has been acquitted by the jury, rather than where the acquittal is delivered as a result of a judicial direction' (Law Reform Commission (Ireland), 2002: ¶ 3.093).

The restrictions on appeals of jury verdicts of acquittal are often justified on the grounds that they safeguard the beyond a reasonable doubt standard, double jeopardy protections, and, more broadly, the innocence-weighted approach (Law Reform Commission (Ireland), 2002). But these rationales do not explain the disparate treatment of jury verdicts and court judgments in many jurisdictions. Likewise, they do not explain why *convictions* by juries, which do not implicate the double jeopardy and standard of proof concerns, are also given great deference by reviewing courts. Appellate review is typically more deferential to convictions by juries than by judges (Pizzi, 2000). In some countries, appeals of jury verdicts are limited to questions of law, while appeals from bench trials are de novo (Code de Procedure Penale § 572 (Fr.); *Taxquet v. Belgium* [2010] Eur. Ct. H.R. 1806, ¶ 99).

Limited appellate review has been explained in part on practical grounds: if the jury offers no justification for its decision, appellate courts have no way of discerning how the jury evaluated the evidence and applied the law (*R. v. Biniaris* [2000] 1 S.C.R. 381, ¶¶ 36–40 (Can.)). But this reasoning is somewhat circular, as it presumes that juries should provide no reasoning. Moreover, while the lack of reasoning makes appellate review more challenging, it does not entirely preclude such review. The court could examine the evidence in the case de novo, or it could assess whether the verdict was one that a reasonable jury could have reached (*R. v. Biniaris* [2000] 1 S.C.R. 381, ¶ 40 (Can.); Law Reform Commission (Ireland), 2002). It appears that a principal motivation for restricting appeals of jury verdicts, particularly of acquittals, is to preserve the autonomy of the jury to apply the 'sense of the community' and to protect individuals against official abuse of power (*People (Director of Public Prosecutions) v. O'Shea* [1982] IR 384, 438).

Even if one were to accept the value of a mechanism that permits jury nullification, however, the lack of reasoning for jury verdicts means that we cannot be certain whether an acquittal in a particular case reflects disagreement with the law or simply a legal or factual mistake by the jury. Studies of judge–jury disagreements suggest that nullification is rarely the motivation for jury acquittals (Kalven and Zeisel, 1966; Vidmar and Hans, 2007). Furthermore, because the lack of reasoning extends to convictions and acquittals alike, it makes appellate review difficult even when the jury returns a conviction (that is, when nullification is not implicated). Some commentators have therefore questioned whether the benefits of nullification are worth the costs of inscrutable and unreviewable verdicts (Jackson, 2002).

Reflecting this concern about unreviewable jury verdicts, countries that have adopted jury trials more recently have generally opted for more accountable juries.[61] In Spain and Russia, for example, all-lay juries must respond to specific questions concerning the verdict. Spanish juries must also provide reasons for their judgments by answering a detailed questionnaire to explain factual findings.[62] In both Spain and Russia, acquittals can also be reviewed on appeal, and review of both convictions and acquittals is said to be rather searching (Martín and Kaplan, 2006). Japan and South Korea adopted juries that fall closer to the mixed-court model than full-blown juries, in which professional judges (even when they do not participate fully in the deliberations) help produce reasoned judgments that can be reviewed on appeal (Park, 2010; Weber, 2009). Kazakhstan adopted the traditional mixed-court model, in which judges and jurors deliberate and reach a verdict together, and judges produce a reasoned judgment that is subject to review (Kovalev and Suleymenova, 2010). Belgium, which has long had trial by jury, has amended its criminal procedure to require juries to provide the 'main reasons' for their verdicts (*Taxquet v. Belgium* [2010] Eur. Ct. H.R. 1806, ¶ 60).

More significantly, the European Court of Human Rights recently rendered a judgment that may require European countries to devote greater attention to the problem of inscrutable and unreviewable jury verdicts. In *Taxquet v. Belgium*, the Court held that jury verdicts may comply with fair trial principles even if they do not provide reasons, but it emphasized that states must implement other measures to compensate for the brevity of jury verdicts (*Taxquet* [2010] Eur. Ct. H.R. 1806, ¶ 90). The Court suggested that several procedures, seemingly when used in combination, can make up for the lack of a reasoned judgment: 'directions or guidance provided by the presiding judge to the jurors on the legal issues arising or the evidence adduced', 'precise, unequivocal questions put to the jury by the judge, forming a framework on which the verdict is based or sufficiently offsetting the fact that no reasons are given for the jury's answers', and the defendant's recourse to appeal (*Taxquet* [2010] Eur. Ct. H.R. 1806, ¶ 92). National courts will therefore have to examine jury procedures against these benchmarks to determine whether they guard sufficiently against arbitrary verdicts.

The *Taxquet* judgment suggests that juries are increasingly expected to be accountable for their judgments. Countries that have recently expanded lay participation in criminal cases have taken measures to ensure that jury decisions are more transparent and reviewable. This emphasis on accountability – together with the limited diffusion of criminal jury trials around the world – shows that the democratic virtue of juries is less accepted today as a reason to depart from fair trial principles or an emphasis on truth-seeking.

5. CONCLUSION

Criminal justice systems around the globe profess a strong commitment to the discovery of truth in criminal cases. At the same time, courts and legislatures across the adversarial-inquisitorial spectrum increasingly concur that the truth should not be sought at any price. Competing values, such as individual rights, efficiency, and democratic participation have motivated the introduction of procedures that often depart from the singular quest for truth. As a result of a stronger commitment to individual rights, many systems today follow rules that exclude unlaw-fully obtained evidence and deprive fact-finders of probative evidence. Some also rely on juries to provide a democratic check on the criminal process, and, by making jury verdicts difficult to review and revise, privilege jury autonomy over truth-seeking. Finally, a growing number of jurisdictions have introduced abbreviated procedures such as plea bar-gaining, which help resolve criminal cases quickly and conveniently, but often less accurately. While the trend has not been exclusively in the direction of truth-impairing procedures (as reform of double jeopardy laws and requirements of reasoned decisions by juries indicate), on the whole, legal systems around the world continue to confirm that the search for truth does not trump all other concerns.

As these various reforms have occurred, the adversarial-inquisitorial dichotomy has become less relevant in determining the commitment of a criminal justice system to the discovery of truth. There is broad agree-ment across systems of both traditions that truth-seeking should be limited to some degree by the concern for individual rights and liberties. While the details differ on how the balance between these competing goals is struck, there is as much divergence within inquisitorial systems as across the adversarial-inquisitorial divide.

Among the procedures that rest in tension with truth-seeking, plea bargaining appears at once the most attractive and the most problematic. It is attractive due to its undeniable contribution to efficiency in crowded and overworked criminal justice systems; it is problematic because its detrimental impact on truth-seeking in individual cases has proven the most difficult to mitigate. Rules introduced to regulate plea bargaining often appear overly inconvenient to prosecutors, defense lawyers, and even judges. To a great degree, this is because shrinking resources and broad emphases on efficiency dominate criminal justice systems around the world today. As long as this is so, effective regulation of plea bargaining is likely to be challenging. The goal of greater alignment between plea bargaining and the search for truth, if it is to be reached, will demand tough and deep structural reform.

NOTES

1. I thank Darryl Brown, Claus Kress, Maximo Langer, Saira Mohamed, Meghan Ryan, Darryl Robinson, Sonja Starr, James Stewart, John Turner, Thomas Weigend, and participants in the Institute of Criminal Law and Criminal Procedure at the University of Cologne workshop, SMU Faculty Forum and the SMU Criminal Justice Colloquium for helpful comments on earlier drafts. Tom Kimbrough provided invaluable research assistance. I am also grateful to the Mike and Marla Boone Faculty Fund for a generous research grant in support of this project.
2. In this chapter, I use the terms accuracy and truth interchangeably, even though one could view accuracy as demanding greater detail and precision about what occurred. For decisions emphasizing the importance of truth-seeking in criminal cases, see *Rose v. Clark*, 478 U.S. 570, 577 (1986) ('The central purpose of a criminal trial is to decide the factual question of the defendant's guilt or innocence'); *Tehan v. United States*, 383 U.S. 406, 416 (1966) ('The basic purpose of a trial is the determination of the truth'); *R. v. Levogiannis* [1993] 4 S.C.R. 475; Judgment of the Federal Constitutional Court of March 19, 2013, BVerfG, 2 BvR 2628/10, BvR 2883/10, 2 BvR 2155/11.
3. On the link between truth and legitimacy in criminal cases, see, for example, Laudan (2006) 2; Stamp (1998: 22–23, 265) (observing that truthfulness is a necessary but not sufficient condition for a legitimate verdict); Thomas Weigend (2003: 157–158).
4. For variations on this formula, both before and after Blackstone, see Laudan (2006) at 63; Volokh (1997).
5. While the right to remain silent protects against some false self-incriminations, it also produces more false acquittals. See, for example, Laudan (2006: 150).
6. For the common law provenance, see Law Reform Commission (Ireland) (2002) ¶ 1.02 (citing *R. v. Tyrone County Justices* for the proposition that it was an 'elementary' and 'a broad principle of common law' that 'an acquittal made by a Court of competent jurisdiction and made within its jurisdiction, although erroneous in point of fact, cannot as a rule be questioned and brought before any other court'). For the link to double jeopardy, see *Kepner v. United States* 195 U.S. 100 (1904); see

also *Thompson v. Master-Touch TV Service Pty Ltd. (No.3)* (1978) 38 FLR 397, 403 (Fed. Ct. Austl.).

7. For an elaboration on how this fits with the 'horizontal' model of adjudication in common-law countries, see Damaška (1991: 59–60).

8. Ireland is currently reviewing proposals to further expand its system of appeals of acquittals. Law Reform Commission (Ireland) (2002).

9. This is a departure from the common-law position prohibiting government appeals (Miller and Wright, 2007: 751).

10. The Court in *Scott* clarified that appeal was permitted because the defendant had not in fact been acquitted: the proceedings had been terminated 'on a basis unrelated to factual guilt or innocence' (*United States v. Scott*, 437 U.S. 82, 99 (1978)).

11. In 2008, New Zealand had also introduced a provision allowing retrials after acquittals where 'new and compelling evidence' has been discovered, but this provision was repealed in 2013. Crimes Act (N.Z.) § 378D, *repealed by* Section 6 of the Crimes Amendment Act (No 4) 2011 (2011 No 85).

12. *Brown v. Ohio*, 432 U.S. 161, 169 n. 7 (1977). For a discussion of the due diligence exception, see Poulin (2004).

13. For an excellent analysis of exclusionary rules in different systems, see Thaman (2013). Cf. Nijboer (1993: 335) ('It is the lack of uniformity of the non-adversarial systems that causes the main difficulties in using the inquisitorial and the adversarial style or system or proceedings as basic models for comparison ...').

14. Certain nullities (so-called nullities of the 'general order') may even result in the dismissal of the prosecution. But the consequences of a violation – ranging from no nullity to exclusion of evidence to dismissal of the prosecution – do not necessarily track the seriousness of the violation. See, for example, Ryan (2014: 158–159) (noting that excessive pretrial detention does not typically result in a nullity); Pradel (2013) (discussing violations of the public order, which can result in the dismissal of the prosecution, as including 'judicial incompetence, the absence of a date on a document, [and] the failure of an expert witness to swear an oath or a failure to question the accused'); Thaman (2011a: 699) (discussing nullities of the 'general order').

15. *Khan v. United Kingdom*, App. No. 35394/97, 31 Eur. Ct. H.R. 45, ¶ 34 (2000): 'It is not the role of the Court to determine, as a matter of principle, whether particular types of evidence – for example, unlawfully obtained evidence – may be admissible or, indeed, whether the applicant was guilty or not. The question which must be answered is whether the proceedings as a whole, including the way in which the evidence was obtained, were fair. This involves an examination of the "unlawfulness" in question and, where violation of another Convention right is concerned, the nature of the violation found'. The Court has enforced an exclusionary rule only in cases where the evidence was obtained through torture or inhumane and degrading treatment. *Jalloh v. Germany*, 2006-IX Eur. Ct. H.R. 281,¶ 105; *Harutyunyan v. Armenia*, 49 Eur. Ct. H.R. 9, ¶¶ 65–66 (2009); *Gäfgen v. Germany*, 52 Eur. Ct. H.R. 1, 42 (2011).

16. For a similar approach, see Slobogin (forthcoming 2016).

17. See, for example, *D.P.P. v. Kenny* [1990] 2 I.R. 110, 134 (justifying exclusion with reference to the 'unambiguously expressed constitutional obligation 'as far as practicable to defend and vindicate the personal rights of the citizen'). See generally Slobogin (forthcoming 2016).

18. Consistent with the 'rights theory', there is growing consensus that evidence obtained through torture or inhumane and degrading treatment should be suppressed, regardless of its reliability (Jackson and Summers, 2012: 162).

19. The German approach to exclusion might also be characterized this way. See, for example, Weigend (2011: 401) (noting a 'growing tendency [among German courts]

toward rejecting evidence that was acquired in clear, conscious violation of a person's constitutional rights').

20. See also *United States v. Leon*, 468 U.S. 897, 978 (1984) (Stevens, J., dissenting) ('If such evidence is admitted, then the courts become not merely the final and necessary link in an unconstitutional chain of events, but its actual motivating force'); *A and Others v. Secretary of State for the Home Department (No. 2)* [2006] 2 AC 221, ¶ 87; *Levinta v. Moldova*, App. No. 17332/03, ¶ 100 (Eur. Ct. H.R. Dec. 16, 2008).

21. *Olmstead v. United States*, 277 U.S. 438, 485 (Brandeis, J., dissenting) ('Our government is the potent, the omnipresent teacher. For good or for ill, it teaches the whole people by its example ... If the government becomes a lawbreaker, it breeds contempt for law; it invites every man to become a law unto himself; it invites anarchy').

22. See, for example, Canadian Charter of Rights and Freedoms § 24(2) (1982) ('the evidence shall be excluded if it is established that, having regard to all the circumstances, the admission of it in the proceedings would bring the administration of justice into disrepute'); *R. v. Grant* [2009] 2 S.C.R. 353, ¶¶ 68–70 (Can.); *Prosecutor v. Lubanga*, Case No. ICC-01/04-01/06, Decision on the Admission of Material from the 'Bar Table' (June 24, 2009); Duff et al. (2007: 108–109); Bloom and Fentin (2010: 47–49); Slobogin (forthcoming 2016).

23. See, for example, *R v. Collins* [1987] 1 S.C.R. 265, 283 (Can.) (noting that administration of justice may be brought into disrepute if reliable evidence that is central to conviction is excluded because of a 'trivial' breach by law enforcement); *Lubanga*, Case No. ICC-01/04-01/06, Decision on the Admission of Material from the 'Bar Table', ¶¶ 42–46 (considering the gravity of the violation, the impact on the rights of the accused, the level of involvement by agents of the ICC prosecution, and whether the agents acted in good faith). See generally Slobogin (forthcoming 2016).

24. See, for example, *D.P.P. v. Kenny* [1990] 2 I.R. 110, 134 ('The detection of crime and the conviction of guilty persons, no matter how important they may be in relation to the ordering of society, cannot ... outweigh the unambiguously expressed constitutional obligation "as far as practicable to defend and vindicate the personal rights of the citizen"'); *R. v. Mason* [1988] 1 WLR 139, 144; *Yissacharov v. Chief Military Prosecutor* [2006] (1) Isr. L.R. 320, ¶ 60; Sangero and Merin (2013: 93, 97).

25. See also Constitution of South Africa § 35(5) (1996) (evidence obtained in violation of the Bill of Rights 'must be excluded if the admission of that evidence would render the trial unfair or otherwise be detrimental to the administration of justice'); *R. v. Grant* [2009] 2 S.C.R. 353, ¶¶ 68–71 (Can.); Police & Crim. Evid. Act (Eng.) 1984 § 78 (evidence would be excluded where it 'would have such an adverse effect on the fairness of the proceedings that the Court ought not to admit it'); *H.M. Advocate v. Higgins*, S.L.T. (2006), 946, 950, SC, 9.

26. Madden (2011: 237) (noting roughly a 70% rate of exclusion under the more concrete Canadian balancing test after *R. v. Grant*); Nadon (2011: 42) (finding a 64% post-*Grant* exclusion rate in Quebec).

27. For a discussion of empirical studies supporting this notion, see Jackson and Summers (2012: 72–73).

28. The term plea bargaining is not entirely accurate when applied to inquisitorial systems, which still do not accept formal guilty pleas, but instead require confessions or admissions of guilt. But for the sake of readability, I use it here to denote any 'process of negotiation and explicit agreement between the defendant, on one hand, and the prosecution, the court, or both, on the other, whereby the defendant confesses, pleads guilty, or provides other assistance to the government in exchange for more lenient treatment' (Turner, 2009: 1).

29. See *Brady v. United* States, 397 U.S. 742 (1970); see also *R. v. Winterflood* [1979] Crim. L.R. 263, cited in Rauxloh (2012: 26) (accepting charge bargaining under the

condition that it is practiced openly); Di Luca (2005: 41–46) (discussing the mixed reactions to plea bargaining in Canadian case law from the 1970s and 1980s). But see Rauxloh (2012: 29–31) (noting that in the 1970s, the English Court of Appeal attempted to discourage sentence bargaining, but after it was largely ignored by lower courts and practitioners, it eventually began accepting the practice in the mid-1980s).

30. See, for example, Fisher (2000: 859) ('In place of a noble clash for truth, plea bargaining gives us a skulking truce').

31. For a notable exception in the US literature, see Brown (2005: 1610–1612). The conflict between plea bargaining and truth-seeking is much more commonly discussed in German literature. See, for example, Stamp (1998: 149–151); Weigend (2008: 56–62).

32. The high burden of proof, the uncertain reliability of testimonial evidence, and exclusionary rules are examples of hindrances to the search for truth at trial. See, for example, Laudan (2006: *passim*); Simon, (2011).

33. In common-law jurisdictions, judges typically may not interfere with prosecutorial decisions to dismiss or reduce charges. See, for example, *Inmates of Attica Correctional Facility v. Rockefeller*, 477 F.2d 375, 379–81 (2d Cir. 1973); *United States v. Giannattasio*, 979 F.2d 98, 100 (7th Cir. 1992); *Vanscoy v. Ontario* [1999] O.J. No. 1661, 1999 CarswellOnt 1427, ¶ 38 (Ont. S.C.J.) (observing that the prosecution in Canada has 'complete discretion' in charge bargaining); Ashworth and Redmayne (2010: 80) ('In recent years there have been some cases of successful judicial review of certain policies for and against prosecution, but the prevailing attitude remains one of reluctance'); Waye and Marcus (2010: 348–349) (noting that in Australia, judicial review of prosecutorial decisions is limited and charge bargaining is well entrenched).

34. Mandatory minimum sentences and rigid sentencing guidelines are not used as broadly in other systems as they are in the United States. See, for example, Horne (2013); Waye and Marcus (2010: 377, 383).

35. Even when the defense has the right to access some of the prosecution's evidence, the waiver of that right is frequently an element of the negotiations. *United States v. Ruiz*, 536 U.S. 622 (2002); Brown (2005: 1612).

36. For example, *United States v. Griffin*, 17 F.3d 269, 274 (8th Cir. 1994) (J. Bright, dissenting).

37. See Easterbrook (1983: 297). Cf. Combs (2007: 5–6) (making this argument in the context of international criminal cases, where prosecution is the exception rather than the norm).

38. Although this is a question about the distribution of error and not simply about accuracy, it remains relevant as one considers whether mistakes in individual cases are worth a net gain in accuracy across the board.

39. For England, see Sentencing Guidelines Council, *Reduction in Sentence for a Guilty Plea: Definitive Guideline* (2007) (setting out discounts between one tenth and one third depending on the timeliness of the plea). The most recent government had proposed increasing the discount to 50% for early pleas, but this proposal was abandoned. *The Guardian* (2011); Lipscombe and Beard (2013). In New South Wales, Australia, plea discounts were regulated for several years, but the relevant legislation was recently repealed. Criminal Case Conferencing Trial Act, 2008 (NSW), *repealed by* Criminal Case Conferencing Trial Repeal Bill, 2012 (NSW).

40. Crim. Just. Act (Eng.) 2003 § 144(1) (a); Sentencing Guidelines Council, *Reduction in Sentence for a Guilty Plea: Definitive Guideline* ¶ 5.3 (2007); Turner (2006: 211) (discussing the United States). But cf. Di Luca (2005: 54, 64–65) (observing that, despite efforts to move plea bargaining earlier in the process, guilty pleas in Canada too often occur on the day of trial because the prosecution had not had an

opportunity to review the file in detail and the defense had not received the Crown briefs before then).

41. See, for example, Jackson and Summers (2012: 72; Gilliéron (2013: 237, 250). Cf. Goldstein (1971: 1021) ('The operation of any model and of the procedure reflecting it will depend upon the interaction of many factors: the normative content of the standards to be applied in making decisions, how the participants are perceived and trained, the controls introduced at strategic points, and the resources assigned to implement policies and controls').

42. Cf. Boyne (2014: 214 *passim*) (observing the continued influence of the norm of objectivity on German prosecutors, but noting how certain competing influences, including an increased focus on efficiency, at times interfere with prosecutors' commitment to objectivity).

43. See, for example, Kruszynski (2007: 196); Krey and Windgätter (2012: 586–592); see also Illuminati and Caianiello (2007: 142) (noting that Italian defense attorneys can conduct their own investigations and request the assistance of the prosecution with some of the investigations). But cf. Fermon et al. (2007: 55–56) (noting that defense attorneys have increasing ability to influence the pretrial investigation, at least in more serious cases, but that overall, they are still seen as obstacles, rather than contributors, to the search for truth in criminal cases); Hodgson (2012: 116, 129) (noting the difficulties experienced by French attorneys 'who sought to assert the rights of their clients to participate in the investigation, and to propose a line of inquiry that pointed away from the guilt of the suspect').

44. Strafprozessordnung (Ger.) § 147(2); see also ibid. § 68(4) (providing that a witness's name and address may be removed from the file as long as there exists a risk of harm to the witness from the disclosure of this information); Kruszynski (2007: 196) (noting similar limits to disclosure in Poland).

45. See *North Carolina v. Alford*, 400 U.S. 25, 28 (1970) (permitting such pleas); Thaman (2010: 297, 356) (listing inquisitorial jurisdictions that require an admission of guilt before accepting a plea agreement); *Prosecutor v. Erdemović*, Case No. IT-96-22-A, Joint Separate Opinion of Judge McDonald and Judge Vohrah ¶ 29 (Int'l Crim. Trib. for the former Yugoslavia, Oct. 7, 1997) (requiring that guilty pleas be unequivocal and listing national jurisdictions that follow the same rule). Some inquisitorial jurisdictions, such as Spain, Italy, and Russia, do not require an admission of guilt by the defendant. But even there, judges would likely not accept a plea agreement if the defendant actually asserts his innocence; this would be inconsistent with the requirement that the defendant accept the charges against him. See Thaman (2010), at 355–356.

46. The study was conducted in 2012 and surveyed 190 criminal court judges from the German state Nordrhein-Westfalen. The study also surveyed 68 prosecutors and 76 criminal defense attorneys. Altenhain et al. (2013: 18–24). The description of the study is adapted from Weigend and Turner (2014: 92–94).

47. The statute requires that the contents of the agreement be placed on the record, that the court and the parties do not bargain about the facts or the charges, that the court take into account 'all circumstances of the case as well as general sentencing considerations', which means that the sentence proposed must be proportional to the 'true' guilt of the defendant, that the court independently search for the truth, and that the court does not indicate that a specific sentence be imposed after contested proceedings or after a confession. Weigend and Turner (2014: 89–91) (discussing Strafprozessordnung (Ger.) § 257c).

48. For example, some judges refused to accept an agreement between the parties on the ground that 'the truth of the case cannot be discovered without full trial' even though such a ground for refusal is not available under the law. And some courts have mistakenly allowed appeals of plea-bargained cases based on a factual error, even

though such appeals are not allowed under the law. Apparently, the appeals were seen by judges as necessary to find the true facts of the case. Semukhina and Reynolds (2009: 412–414).

49. Jury trials have not always represented self-government. In some European countries, the jury was introduced as a result of Napoleonic conquest. Across a number of jurisdictions in Africa, Asia, and South America, it was installed as part of colonial rule and was used as a means of protecting the rights of colonists rather than as a guarantor of democracy. See, for example, Vidmar (2000: 422–431). Not surprisingly, a number of post-colonial governments abolished juries because of their affiliation with oppressive regimes (ibid.). Countries that follow the adversarial model but do not have jury trials include India, Pakistan, Nigeria, Tanzania, Kenya, Zimbabwe, and South Africa. Ibid.; see also Vogler (2005: 230); Ehighalua (2012). While in most of these countries, juries were abolished as a sign of rejection of the colonial legal system, in some cases the abolition of juries was also an effort by authoritarian governments to maintain control over the judiciary. Vidmar (2000: 424).

50. Several jurisdictions, including Spain, Russia, and Georgia, introduced all-lay-jury trials as part of their transition to democracy. Thaman (2011b: 619–620).

51. *Duncan v. Louisiana*, 391 U.S. 145, 155–156 (1968). Juries are said to 'support democratic forms of government, because they are uncongenial to authoritarian rule' (Lempert, 2007: 481).

52. For a review of some of the debates, see Brown (1997); Butler (1995: 700–703); Scheflin and Van Dyke (1980: 85–111).

53. Jurors are frequently 'thought to more easily believe lies, to evaluate expert testimony uncritically, and to insufficiently attend to relevant information' (Bliesener, 2006: 179, 186); Shuman and Champagne (1997: 249–256).

54. More specifically, jurors are blamed for failing to understand and follow jury instructions and for deciding cases based on innate notions of justice rather than the written law. For example, Vidmar and Hans (2007: 158–163); see also Damaška (1997: 29, n. 6) ('On the Continent, where the machinery of justice is dominated by professional civil servants, Hegel's lament – "the masses are miserable hands at judging" – has a very long history').

55. Shuman and Champagne (1997: 253–256); see also Guthrie et al. (2001: 826–827). Cf. Vidmar and Hans (2007: 188) (reporting studies where jurors appear to have some difficulty interpreting statistical evidence, but observing that judges experienced similar difficulties).

56. Hope and Memon (2006: 31, 38, citing Young et al., 1999) ('[T]hese basic misunderstandings persisted through, and significantly influenced, jury deliberations despite clarifications provided during the course of the judges' summary'); see also Goodman-Delahunty and Tait (2006: 61) ('In 1998, a study of 48 jury trials in New Zealand revealed that … in 35 of the 48 trials studied, some of the jurors misunderstood the law, especially the offense charged').

57. Kalven and Zeisel (1966: 56–58) (after excluding hung-jury cases, finding agreement in 75.4% of cases); Eisenberg et al. (2005: 182) (after excluding hung-jury cases, finding agreement in 70.5% of cases); Sangjoon Kim et al. (2013: 42) (reporting a 91.4% agreement rate).

58. The United States is unfortunately an exception to this rule. At the federal level, findings of fact are available, but only at the request of the party. Fed. R. Crim. Proc. (U.S.) 23(c). More troubling is the fact that many states do not require findings of fact in bench trials even upon request. Doran et al. (1995: 45–46).

59. In a number of common-law countries (but not the United States): '[A]t the conclusion of the evidence, the judge sums up the case to the jurors. He reminds them of the evidence they have heard. In doing so, the judge may give directions about the proper approach to take in respect of certain evidence. He also provides the

jurors with information and explanations about the applicable legal rules. In that context, the judge clarifies the elements of the offence and sets out the chain of reasoning that should be followed in order to reach a verdict based on the jury's findings of fact' (*Taxquet v. Belgium* [2010] Eur. Ct. H.R. 1806, ¶ 50); see also *Yager v. The Queen* [1977] W.A.R. 17, 11 A.L.R 646 (Austl.); *R. v. Krieger* [2006] 2 R.C.S. 501 (Can.); *R. v. Osolin* [1993] 4 S.C.R. 595, 683 (S.C.C.). See generally, Marcus (2013).

60. This is similar to the 'special verdict' questions common in civil-law trials in the United States. Within Europe, Austria, Belgium, Ireland, Norway, Russia, and Spain require jurors to answer such questions. *Taxquet* [2010] Eur. Ct. H.R. 1806, ¶ 49.

61. Only Georgia has adopted an essentially American-style jury whose acquittals cannot be reviewed. See Crim. Proc. Code § 231(4) (Georgia), cited in Thaman (2011b), at 619 and n. 40. Georgia introduced the criminal jury as part of a broader reform to introduce adversarial elements in its criminal procedure, and it was very heavily influenced by the US model, which may explain the ban on appeal of acquittals. See Criminal Justice Reform Strategy. It also appears that Georgia may have been trying to avoid some of the problems encountered in Russia, where appellate courts frequently reversed jury acquittals. See Lomsadze (2010).

62. Martín and Kaplan (2006: 71, 73) (noting that jurors must specifically note the evidence that led them to believe that a particular proposition was proved or not proved). As the European Court of Human Rights succinctly described the Spanish jury verdict: '[It] is made up of five distinct parts. The first lists the facts held to be established, the second lists the facts held to be not established, the third contains the jury's declaration as to whether the accused is guilty or not guilty, and the fourth provides a succinct statement of reasons for the verdict, indicating the evidence on which it is based and the reasons why particular facts have been held to be established or not. A fifth part contains a record of all the events that took place during the discussions, avoiding any identification that might infringe the secrecy of the deliberations' (*Taxquet v. Belgium* [2010] Eur. Ct. H.R. 1806, ¶ 57).

BIBLIOGRAPHY

A and Others v. Secretary of State for the Home Department (No. 2) [2006] 2 AC 221.

Acquaviva, Guido. 2013. 'Written and Oral Evidence', in Linda Carter and Fausto Pocar, eds., *International Criminal Procedure*. Cheltenham, UK and Northampton, MA, USA: Edward Elgar Publishing.

A.K. v. Western Australia [2008] HCA 8, 232 CLR 438.

Alschuler, Albert W. 1968. 'The Prosecutor's Role in Plea Bargaining', 36 *U. Chi. L. Rev.* 50.

Alschuler, Albert W. 1975. 'The Defense Attorney's Role in Plea Bargaining', 84 *Yale L.J.* 1179.

Alschuler, Albert W. 2013. '*Lafler* and *Frye*: Two Small Band-Aids for a Festering Wound', 51 *Duq. L. Rev.* 673.

Altenhain, Karsten, et al. 2007. *Die Praxis der Absprachen in Wirtschaftsstrafverfahren*. Baden-Baden: Nomos.

Altenhain, Karsten, et al. 2013. *Die Praxis der Absprachen in Strafverfahren*. Baden-Baden: Nomos.

Ashworth, Andrew. 1977. 'Excluding Evidence as Protecting Rights' [1977] *Crim. L. Rev.* 723.

Ashworth, Andrew and Mike Redmayne. 2010. *The Criminal Process* (4th edn). Oxford: Oxford University Press.

Beernaert, Marie-Aude and Philip Traest. 2013. 'Belgium: From Categorical Nullities to a Judicially Created Balancing Test', in Stephen C. Thaman, ed., *Exclusionary Rules in Comparative Law*. Dordrecht: Springer.

Bibas, Stephanos. 2004. 'Plea Bargaining Outside the Shadow of Trial', 117 *Harv. L. Rev.* 2463.

Blackstone, William. 1769. *Commentaries on the Laws of England*, Vol. 4. Oxford: Clarendon Press.

Bliesener, Thomas. 2006. 'Lay Judges in the German Criminal Court: Social-Psychological Aspects of the German Criminal Justice System', in Martin F. Kaplan and Ana M. Martin, eds., *Understanding World Jury Systems Through Social Psychological Research*. New York: Psychology Press.

Bloom, Robert M. and David H. Fentin. 2010. '"A More Majestic Conception": The Importance of Judicial Integrity in Preserving the Exclusionary Rule', 13 U. Pa. J. Const. L. 47.

Bogers, Matthias J. and Lonneke Stevens. 2013. 'The Netherlands: Statutory Balancing and a Choice of Remedies', in Stephen C. Thaman, ed., *Exclusionary Rules in Comparative Law*. Dordrecht: Springer.

Bowers, Josh. 2008. 'Punishing the Innocent', 156 *U. Pa. L. Rev.* 1117.

Boyne, Shawn Marie. 2014. *The German Prosecution Service: Guardians of the Law?* Dordrecht: Springer.

Brady v. United States, 397 U.S. 742 (1970).

Brown, Darryl K. 1997. 'Jury Nullification Within the Rule of Law', 81 *Minn. L. Rev.* 1149.

Brown, Darryl K. 2005. 'The Decline of Defense Counsel and the Rise of Accuracy in Criminal Adjudication', 93 *Cal. L. Rev.* 1585.

Brown, Darryl K. 2014. 'The Perverse Effects of Efficiency in Criminal Process', 100 *Va. L. Rev.* 101.

Brown v. Ohio, 432 U.S. 161 (1977).

Butler, Paul. 1995. 'Racially Based Jury Nullification: Black Power in the Criminal Justice System', 105 *Yale L.J.* 677.

Calabresi, Guido. 2003. 'The Exclusionary Rule', 26 *Harv. J.L. & Pub. Pol'y* 111.

Canadian Charter of Rights and Freedoms § 24(2) (1982).

Carrio, Alejandro D. and Alejandro M. Garro. 2007. 'Argentina', in Craig Bradley, ed., *Criminal Procedure: A Worldwide Study* (2nd edn). Durham, NC: Carolina Academic Press.

Chalmers v. H.M. Advocate, 1954 JC 66, 83 (Scot.).

Cho, Kuk. 1998. 'The Japanese "Prosecutorial Justice" and Its Limited Exclusionary Rule', 12 *Colum. J. Asian L.* 39.

Code de Procedure Penale § 572 (Fr.).

Combs, Nancy Amoury. 2007. *Guilty Pleas in International Criminal Law*. Stanford, CA: Stanford University Press.

Combs, Nancy Amoury. 2012. 'Obtaining Guilty Pleas for International Crimes: Prosecutorial Difficulties', in Erik Luna and Marianne Wade, eds., *The Prosecutor in Transnational Perspective*. Oxford: Oxford University Press.

Constitution of South Africa § 35(5) (1996).

Cras, Arnaud and Yvonne Marie Daly. 2013. 'Ireland: A Move to Categorical Exclusion?', in Stephen C. Thaman, ed., *Exclusionary Rules in Comparative Law*. Dordrecht: Springer.

Crim. Code (Can.).

Crim. Disclosure Act 2008 (N.Z.).

Crim. Just. Act (Eng.) (1972).

Crim. Just. Act (Eng.) (2003).

Crim. Proc. Act (Ireland) (1993).

Crim. Proc. Act (S. Afr.) (1977).
Crim. Proc. Act (Scot.) (1995).
Crim. Proc. Code § 231(4) (Georgia).
Crimes Act (N.Z.) (1961).
Crimes Act (N.Z.) § 378D, *repealed by* Section 6 of the Crimes Amendment Act (No 4) 2011 (2011 No 85).
Criminal Case Conferencing Trial Act 2008 (NSW), *repealed by* Criminal Case Conferencing Trial Repeal Bill 2012 (NSW).
Criminal Justice Reform Strategy, at http://www.cpt.coe.int/documents/geo/2011-19-appendix-I.pdf.
Crown Prosecution Service, Legal Guidance: Retrial of Serious Offences, at http://www.cps.gov.uk/legal/p_to_r/retrial_of_serious_offences.
D.P.P. v. Kenny [1990] 2 I.R. 110.
Damaška, Mirjan. 1973. 'Evidentiary Barriers to Conviction and Two Models of Criminal Procedure: A Comparative Study', 121 *U. Pa. L. Rev.* 506.
Damaška, Mirjan. 1991. *The Faces of Justice and State Authority: A Comparative Approach to the Legal Process*. New Haven, CT and London: Yale University Press.
Damaška, Mirjan. 1997. *Evidence Law Adrift*. New Haven, CT: Yale University Press.
Damaška, Mirjan. 1997–1998. 'Truth in Adjudication', 49 *Hastings L.J.* 289.
Dellidou, Zinovia. 2007. 'The Investigative Stage of the Criminal Process in Greece', in Ed Cape et al. eds. *Suspects in Europe*. Cambridge: Intersentia.
Devlin, Patrick. 1966. *Trial by Jury*. London: Stevens & Sons Ltd.
Di Luca, Joseph. 2005. 'Expedient McJustice or Principled Alternative Dispute Resolution? A Review of Plea Bargaining in Canada', 50 *Crim. L. Q.* 14.
Doran, Sean, John D. Jackson and Michael L. Seigel. 1995. 'Rethinking Adversariness in Nonjury Trials', 23 *Am. J. Crim. L.* 1.
Dripps, Donald A. 2011. 'The Substance-Procedure Relationship in Criminal Law', in R.A. Duff and Stuart Green eds. *Philosophical Foundations of Criminal Law*. Oxford: Oxford University Press.
Duff et al., Antony. 2007. *Towards a Normative Theory of the Criminal Trial*. Oxford: Hart.
Duncan v. Louisiana, 391 U.S. 145, 155–156 (1968).
Easterbrook, Frank H. 1983. 'Criminal Procedure as a Market System', 12 *J. Legal Studies* 289.
Ehighalua, Daniel. 2012. 'Trial by Jury: Is It About Time for Nigeria?', 17 February, at http://wrongfulconvictionsblog.org/2012/02/17/trial-by-jury-is-it-about-time-for-nigeria.
Eisenberg, Theodore, et al. 2005. 'Judge-Jury Agreement in Criminal Cases: A Partial Replication of Kalven & Zeisel's The American Jury', 2 *J. Emp. Leg. Studies* 173.
Elkins v. United States, 364 U.S. 206, 223 (1960).
Ellsworth, Phoebe C. 1989. 'Are Twelve Heads Better Than One?', 52 *L. & Contemp. Probs.* 205.
Ellsworth, Phoebe C. and Alan Reifman. 2000. 'Juror Comprehension and Public Policy: Perceived Problems and Proposed Solutions', 6 *Psychol. Pub. Pol'y & L.* 788.
European Convention for the Protection of Human Rights and Fundamental Freedoms, Nov. 4, 1950, 213 U.N.T.S. 221.
Evid. Act 1995 (Cth).
Evid. Act 1995 (NSW).
Evid. Act 2006 (N.Z.).
Fed. R. Crim. Proc. (U.S.).
Fermon, Jan, et al. 2007. 'The Investigative Stage of the Criminal Process in Belgium', in Ed Cape et al., eds., *Suspects in Europe*. Cambridge: Intersentia.
Finkelstein, Michael O. 1975. 'A Statistical Analysis of Guilty Plea Practices in the Federal Courts', 89 *Harv. L. Rev.* 293.

Fisher, George. 2000. 'Plea Bargaining's Triumph', 109 *Yale L.J.* 857.

Frase, Richard. 2007. 'France', in Craig Bradley, ed., *Criminal Procedure: A Worldwide Study* (2nd edn). Durham, NC: Carolina Academic Press.

Gäfgen v. Germany, 52 Eur. Ct. H.R. 1, 42 (2011).

General Comment No. 32, HRC, UN Doc. CCPR/C/GC/32, Aug. 23, 2007.

Giannoulopoulos, Dimitrios. 2007. 'The Exclusion of Improperly Obtained Evidence in Greece: Putting Constitutional Rights First', 11 *Int'l J. Evid. & Proof* 181.

Gilliéron, Gwladys. 2013. 'The Risks of Summary Proceedings, Plea Bargains, and Penal Orders in Producing Wrongful Convictions in the U.S. and Europe', in C. Ronald Huff and Martin Killias, eds., *Wrongful Convictions and Miscarriages of Justice*. New York: Routledge.

Gless, Sabine. 2013. 'Germany: Balancing Truth Against Protected Constitutional Interests', in Stephen C. Thaman, ed., *Exclusionary Rules in Comparative Law*. Dordrecht: Springer.

Goldbach, Toby S. and Valerie P. Hans. 2014. 'Juries, Lay Judges, and Trials', in Gerben Bruinsma and David Weisburd, eds., *Encyclopedia of Criminology and Criminal Justice*. Dordrecht: Springer.

Goldstein, Abraham. 1971. 'Reflections on Two Models: Inquisitorial Themes in American Criminal Procedure', 26 *Stan. L. Rev.* 1009.

Goodman-Delahunty, Jane and David Tait. 2006. 'Lay Participation in Legal Decision-Making in Australia and New Zealand: Jury Trials and Administrative Tribunals', in Martin F. Kaplan and Ana M. Martin, eds., *Understanding World Jury Systems Through Social Psychological Research*. New York: Psychology Press.

Grande, Elisabetta. 2008. 'Dances of Criminal Justice: Thoughts on Systemic Differences and the Search for the Truth', in John Jackson et al., eds., *Crime, Procedure and Evidence in a Comparative and International Context*. Oxford: Hart Publishing.

Green v. United States, 355 U.S. 184, 187 (1957).

Groenhuijsen, Marc. 2008. 'Illegally Obtained Evidence: An Analysis of New Trends in the Criminal Justice System of the Netherlands', in *The XIIIth World Congress of Procedural Law: The Belgian and Dutch Reports* (2008), available at https://pure.uvt.nl/ws/files/1070475/illegally.PDF.

Gross, Samuel, et al. 2004–2005. 'Exonerations in the United States, 1989 Through 2003', 95 *J. Crim. L. & Criminology* 523, 536.

Gruber, Aya, et al. 2012. *Practical Global Criminal Procedure*. Durham, NC: Carolina Academic Press.

The Guardian. 2011. 'Ken Clarke Forced to Abandon 50% Sentence Cuts for Guilty Pleas', *The Guardian*, 20 June, at http://www.theguardian.com/law/2011/jun/20/ken-clarke-abandon-sentence-cuts.

Guthrie, Chris, et al. 2001. 'Inside the Judicial Mind', 86 *Cornell L. Rev.* 777.

H.M. Advocate v. Higgins, S.L.T. (2006).

Harutyunyan v. Armenia, 49 Eur. Ct. H.R. 9 (2009).

Hassemer, Raimund and Gabriele Hippler. 1986. 'Informelle Absprachen in der Praxis des deutschen Strafverfahrens', 8 *Strafverteidiger* 360.

Herring v. United States, 555 U.S. 135 (2009).

Herzog, Sergio. 2003. 'The Relationship Between Public Perceptions of Crime Seriousness and Support for Plea-Bargaining Practices in Israel: A Factorial-Survey Approach', 94 *J. Crim. L. & Criminology* 103.

Hodgson, Jacqueline. 2006. 'The Role of the Criminal Defence Lawyer in an Inquisitorial Procedure: Legal and Ethical Constraints', 9 *Legal Ethics* 125.

Hodgson, Jacqueline. 2012. 'Guilty Pleas and the Changing Role of the Prosecutor in French Criminal Justice', in Erik Luna and Marianne L. Wade, eds., *The Prosecutor in Transnational Perspective*. Oxford: Oxford University Press.

Hope, Lorraine and Amina Memon. 2006. 'Cross-Border Diversity: Trial by Jury in England and Scotland', in Martin F. Kaplan and Ana M. Martin, eds., *Understanding World Jury Systems Through Social Psychological Research*. New York: Psychology Press.

Horne, Juliet. 2013. 'Plea Bargains, Guilty Pleas and the Consequences for Appeal in England and Wales', at http://papers.ssrn.com/sol3/papers.cfm?abstract_id=2286681.

Hudson v. Michigan, 547 U.S. 586, 591 (2006).

ICTY R. Proc. & Evid. R. 87(A).

Illuminati, Giulio. 2013. 'Italy: Statutory Nullities and Non-usability', in Stephen C. Thaman, ed., *Exclusionary Rules in Comparative Law*. Dordrecht: Springer.

Illuminati, Giulio and Michele Caianiello. 2007. 'The Investigative Stage of the Criminal Process in Italy', in Ed Cape et al., eds., *Suspects in Europe*. Cambridge: Intersentia.

Inmates of Attica Correctional Facility v. Rockefeller, 477 F.2d 375 (2d Cir. 1973).

International Covenant on Civil and Political Rights, G.A. Res. 2200A (XXI), U.N. Doc. A/RES/ (March 24, 1976).

Jackson, John D. 2002. 'Making Juries Accountable', 50 *Am. J. Comp. L.* 477.

Jackson, John D. and Nikolay P. Kovalev. 2006/2007. 'Lay Adjudication and Human Rights in Europe', 13 *Colum. J. Eur. L.* 83.

Jackson, John D. and Sarah J. Summers. 2012. *The Internationalisation of Criminal Evidence: Beyond the Common Law and Civil Law Traditions*. Cambridge: Cambridge University Press.

Jalloh v. Germany, 2006-IX Eur. Ct. H.R. 281.

Judgment of the Federal Constitutional Court of March 19, 2013, BVerfG, 2 BvR 2628/10, BvR 2883/10, 2 BvR 2155/11.

Jung, Heike. 2004. 'Nothing But the Truth? Facts, Impressions, and Confessions about Truth in Criminal Procedure', in Anthony Duff et al., eds., *Trial on Trial*. Oxford: Hart Publishing.

Kalven, Jr., Harry and Hans Zeisel. 1966. *The American Jury*. Boston and Toronto: Little, Brown and Company.

Kepner v. United States, 195 U.S. 100 (1904).

Khan v. United Kingdom, App. No. 35394/97, 31 Eur. Ct. H.R. 45 (2000).

Kim, Sangjoon, et al. 2013. 'Judge-Jury Agreement in Criminal Cases: The First Three Years of the Korean Jury System', 10 *J. Emp. Leg. Studies* 35.

Klein, Susan R. et al. 2015. 'Waiving the Criminal Justice System: An Empirical and Constitutional Analysis', 52 *Am. Crim. L. Rev.* 73, 83–85.

Koch, Arnd. 2001. 'C.J.A. Mittermaier and the 19th Century Debate About Juries and Mixed Courts', 72 *Revue Internationale de Droit Penal* 347.

Kovalev, Nikolai and Gulnar Suleymenova. 2010. 'New Kazakhstani Quasi-Jury System: Challenges, Trends and Reforms', 38 *Int'l J. L. Crime & Just.* 261.

Krey, Volker and Oliver Windgätter. 2012. 'The Untenable Situation of German Criminal Law: Against Quantitative Overloading, Qualitative Overcharging, and the Overexpansion of Criminal Justice', 13 *German L.J.* 579.

Kruszynski, Piotr. 2007. 'The Investigative Stage of the Criminal Process in Poland', in Ed Cape et al., eds., *Suspects in Europe*. Cambridge: Intersentia.

LaFave, Wayne R. et al. 2012. 'Implementing the Enforcement of the Substantive Law', 1 *Crim. Proc.* § 1.5(a).

Langer, Maximo. 2004. 'From Legal Transplants to Legal Translations: The Globalization of Plea Bargaining and the Americanization Thesis in Criminal Procedure', 45 *Harv. Int'l L.J.* 1.

Laudan, Larry. 2006. *Truth, Error, and Criminal Law: An Essay in Legal Epistemology*. Cambridge and New York: Cambridge University Press.

Law Reform Commission (Ireland). 2002. Consultation Paper on Prosecution Appeals in Cases Brought on Indictment, at http://www.lawreform.ie/_fileupload/consultation%20papers/cpProsecutionAppeals.htm.

Leib, Ethan J. 2008. 'A Comparison of Criminal Jury Decision Rules in Democratic Countries', 5 *Ohio St. J. Crim. L.* 629.

Lempert, Richard O. 2007. 'The Internationalization of Lay Decision-Making: Jury Resurgence and Jury Research', 40 *Cornell Int'l L.J.* 477.

Leverick, Fiona. 2010. 'Plea Bargaining in Scotland: The Rise of Managerialism and the Fall of Due Process', in Stephen C. Thaman, ed., *World Plea Bargaining*. Durham, NC: Carolina Academic Press.

Levinta v. Moldova, App. No. 17332/03 (Eur. Ct. H.R. Dec. 16, 2008).

Lewis, Margaret K. 2011. 'Controlling Abuse to Maintain Control: The Exclusionary Rule in China', 43 *NYU J. Int'l L. & Pol.* 629.

Lipscombe, Sally and Jacqueline Beard. 2013. 'Reduction in Sentence for a Guilty Plea', SN/HA/5974 (Feb. 5).

Lloyd-Bostock, Sally and Cheryl Thomas. 1999. 'Decline of the "Little Parliament": Juries and Jury Reform in England and Wales', 62 *L. & Contemp. Probs.* 7.

Lomsadze, Giorgi. 2010. 'Georgia: Jury Trials Aim to Bolster Public Confidence in Courts', 1 October, at http://www.eurasianet.org/node/62059.

Luna, Erik and Marianne Wade. 2011. 'Prosecutors as Judges', 67 *Wash. & Lee L. Rev.* 1413.

Maclin, Tracey. 2013. *The Supreme Court and the Fourth Amendment's Exclusionary Rule*. Oxford: Oxford University Press.

Madden, Mike. 2011. 'Marshalling the Data: An Empirical Analysis of Canada's Section 24(2) Case Law in the Wake of *R. v. Grant*', 15 *Can. Crim. L. Rev.* 229.

Malsch, Marijke. 2009. *Democracy in the Courts*. Farnham, UK: Ashgate Publishing.

Marcus, Paul. 2013. 'Judges Talking to Jurors in Criminal Cases: Why U.S. Judges Do It So Differently from Just About Everyone Else', 30 *Ariz. J. Int'l & Comp. L.* 1.

Maresti v. Croatia [2009] ECHR 981.

Martín, Ana M. and Martin F. Kaplan. 2006. 'Psychological Perspectives on Spanish and Russian Juries', in Martin F. Kaplan and Ana M. Martin, eds., *Understanding World Jury Systems Through Social Psychological Research*. New York: Psychology Press.

McConville, Mike, et al. 1994. *Standing Accused: The Organisation and Practices of Criminal Defence Lawyers in Britain*. Oxford: Clarendon Press.

Miller, Marc L. and Ronald F. Wright. 2007. *Criminal Procedures: Prosecution and Adjudication* (3rd edn). New York: Wolters Kluwer.

Nadon, Thierry. 2011. 'Le paragraphe 24(2) de la Charte au Québec depuis Grant: si la tendance se maintient!', (2011) 86 *C.R. (6th)* 33.

Natapoff, Alexandra. 2009. *Snitching: Criminal Informants and the Erosion of American Justice*. New York: New York University Press.

Newcombe, Catherine. 2007. 'Russia', in Craig Bradley, ed., *Criminal Procedure: A Worldwide Study* (2nd edn). Durham, NC: Carolina Academic Press.

Nijboer, J.F. 1993. 'Common Law Tradition in Evidence Scholarship Observed from a Continental Perspective', 41 *Am. J. Comp. L.* 299.

North Carolina v. Alford, 400 U.S. 25 (1970).

Ohio v. Reiner, 532 U.S. 17 (2001).

Olmstead v. United States, 277 U.S. 438 (1928).

Ostendorf, Heribert. 1978. 'Strafvereitelung durch Strafverteidigung', 28 *Neue Juristische Wochenschrift* 1345.

Park, Ryan. 2010. 'The Globalizing Jury Trial: Lessons and Insights From Korea', 58 *Am. J. Comp. L.* 525.

People (A.G.) v. O'Brien [1965] I.R 142.

People (Director of Public Prosecutions) v. O'Shea [1982] IR 384.

Pizzi, William. 2000. *Trials Without Truth*. New York: New York University Press.

Police & Crim. Evid. Act (Eng.) 1984.

Poulin, Anne Bowen. 2004. 'Double Jeopardy Protection from Successive Prosecution: A Proposed Approach', 92 Geo. L.J. 1183.

Pradel, Jean. 2013. 'France: Procedural Nullities and Exclusion', in Stephen C. Thaman, ed., *Exclusionary Rules in Comparative Law*. Dordrecht: Springer.

Prosecutor v. Brdjanin, Case No. IT-99-36-T, Decision on the Defence 'Objection to Intercept Evidence' (Int'l Crim. Trib. for the Former Yugoslavia Oct. 3, 2003).

Prosecutor v. Erdemović, Case No. IT-96-22-A, Joint Separate Opinion of Judge McDonald and Judge Vohrah (Int'l Crim. Trib. for the former Yugoslavia, Oct. 7, 1997).

Prosecutor v. Katanga, Case No. ICC-01/04-01/07, Decision on the Prosecutor's Bar Table Motions (Dec. 17, 2010).

Prosecutor v. Lubanga, Case No. ICC-01/04-01/06, Decision on the Admission of Material from the 'Bar Table' (June 24, 2009).

Prosecutor v. Momir Nikolić, Case No. IT-02-60/1-S, Sentencing Judgment (Int'l Crim. Trib. for the Former Yugoslavia Dec. 2, 2003).

R v. Biniaris [2000] 1 S.C.R. 381 (Can.).

R v. Collins [1987] 1 S.C.R. 265, 283 (Can.).

R. v. G. (R.M.) [1996] 3 S.C.R. 362 (S.C.C.).

R v. Grant [2009] 2 S.C.R. 353 (Can.).

R. v. Krieger [2006] 2 R.C.S. 501 (Can.).

R. v. Levogiannis [1993] 4 S.C.R. 475.

R. v. Mason [1988] 1 WLR 139.

R. v. Osolin [1993] 4 S.C.R. 595 (S.C.C.).

R. v. Stinchcombe [1991] 3 S.C.R. 326 (Can.).

R. v. Taillefer & R. v. Duguay [2003] 3 S.C.R. 307 (Can.).

R v. Tyrone County Justices (1906) 40 Ir LT 181, 182.

R. v. Winterflood [1979] Crim. L.R. 263.

Rauxloh, Regina. 2012. *Plea Bargaining in National and International Law*. Abingdon: Routledge.

Rizzolli, Matteo. 2010. 'Why Public Prosecutors Cannot Appeal Acquittals', XV *Studi e Note di Economia* 81.

Roach, Kent. 2013. 'Canada's Experience with Constitutionalism and Criminal Justice', 25 *Singapore Academy L. J.* 656.

Rofe, P.J.L. 1996. 'Disclosure by Both Sides', Australian Institute of Criminology, at http://www.aic.gov.au/media_library/conferences/prosecuting/rofe.pdf (last accessed 6 February 2014).

Rome Statute of the International Criminal Court, U.N. Doc. A/CONF. 183/9 (July 1, 2002).

Rose v. Clark, 478 U.S. 570 (1986).

Ross, Jacqueline. 2006. 'The Entrenched Position of Plea Bargaining in United States Legal Practice', 54 *Am. J. Comp. L.* 717.

Rudstein, David. 2007. 'Retrying the Acquitted in England, Part I: The Exception to the Rule Against Double Jeopardy for "New and Compelling Evidence"', 8 *San Diego Int'l L.J.* 387.

Rudstein, David. 2012. 'Prosecution Appeals of Court-Ordered Midtrial Acquittals: Permissible Under the Double Jeopardy Clause?' 62 *Cath. U. L. Rev.* 91.

Ryan, Andrea. 2014. *Towards a System of European Criminal Justice: The Problem of Admissibility of Evidence*. Abingdon: Routledge.

Sanders, Andrew, Richard Young and Mandy Burton. 2010. *Criminal Justice*. Oxford: Oxford University Press.

Sangero, Rinat Kitai and Yuval Merin. 2013. 'Israel: The Supreme Court's New, Cautious Exclusionary Rule', in Stephen C. Thaman, ed., *Exclusionary Rules in Comparative Law*. Dordrecht: Springer.

Scheflin, Alan W. and Jon Van Dyke. 1980. 'Jury Nullification: The Contours of a Controversy', 43 *Law & Contemp. Probs.* 51.

Schulhofer, Stephen J. 1988. 'Criminal Justice Discretion as a Regulatory System', 17 *J. Legal Stud.* 43.

Seidman Diamond, Shari, Beth Murphy and Mary R. Rose. 2012. 'The "Kettleful of Law" in Real Jury Deliberations: Successes, Failures, and Next Steps', 106 *Nw. U. L. Rev.* 1537.

Semukhina, Olga B. and K. Michael Reynolds. 2009. 'Plea Bargaining Implementation and Acceptance in Modern Russia: A Disconnect Between the Legal Institutions and the Citizens', 19 *Int'l Crim. Just. Rev.* 400.

Sentencing Guidelines Council. 2007. *Reduction in Sentence for a Guilty Plea: Definitive Guideline*. Sentencing Guidelines Council.

Shuman, Daniel and Anthony Champagne. 1997. 'Removing the People from the Legal Process – The Rhetoric and Research on Judicial Selection and Juries', 3 *Psychol. Pub. Pol'y & L.* 242.

Silverthome Lumber Co. v. United States, 251 U.S. 385 (1920).

Simon, Dan. 2011. 'Limited Diagnosticity of Criminal Trials', 64 *Vand. L. Rev.* 143.

Slobogin, Christopher. Forthcoming 2016. 'A Comparative Perspective on the Exclusionary Rule in Search and Seizure Cases', in Jacqueline Ross and Stephen Thaman, eds., *Research Handbook on Comparative Criminal Procedure*. Cheltenham, UK and Northampton, MA, USA: Edward Elgar Publishing.

Smith v. Massachusetts, 543 U.S. 462 (2005).

Sözüer, Adem and Öznur Sevdiren. 2013. 'Turkey: The Move to Categorical Exclusion of Illegally Gathered Evidence', in Stephen C. Thaman, ed., *Exclusionary Rules in Comparative Law*. Dordrecht: Springer.

Stacy, Tom. 1991. 'The Search for the Truth in Constitutional Criminal Procedure', 91 *Colum. L. Rev.* 1369.

Stahn, Carsten. 2005. 'Modification of the Legal Characterization of Facts in the ICC System: A Portrayal of Regulation 55', 16 *Crim. L. F.* 1.

Stamp, Frauke. 1998. *Die Wahrheit im Strafverfahren*. Baden-Baden: Nomos.

Stark, Findlay and Fiona Leverick. 2013. 'Scotland: A Plea for Consistency', in Stephen C. Thaman, ed., *Exclusionary Rules in Comparative Law*. Dordrecht: Springer.

Starr, Sonja. 2008. 'Rethinking "Effective Remedies": Remedial Deterrence in International Courts', 83 N.Y.U. L. Rev. 693.

Strafprozessordnung (StPO) [German Criminal Procedure Code].

Taxquet v. Belgium [2010] Eur. Ct. H.R. 1806.

Taylor v. Louisiana, 419 U.S. 522 (1975).

Tehan v. United States, 383 U.S. 406 (1966).

Thaman, Stephen C. 2010. 'A Typology of Consensual Criminal Procedures: An Historical and Comparative Perspective on the Theory and Practice of Avoiding the Full Criminal Trial', in Stephen C. Thaman, ed., *World Plea Bargaining*. Durham, NC: Carolina Academic Press.

Thaman, Stephen C. 2011a. 'Constitutional Rights in the Balance: Modern Exclusionary Rules and the Toleration of Police Lawlessness in the Search for Truth', 61 *U. Toronto L.J.* 691.

Thaman, Stephen C. 2011b. 'Should Criminal Juries Give Reasons for Their Verdicts? The Spanish Experience and the Implications of the European Court of Human Rights Decision in *Taxquet v. Belgium*', 86 *Chi.-Kent L. Rev.* 613.

Thaman, Stephen C., ed. 2013. *Exclusionary Rules in Comparative Law*. Dordrecht: Springer.

Thompson v. Master-Touch TV Service Pty Ltd (No. 3) (1978) 38 FLR 397 (Fed. Ct. Austl.).

Triantafyllou, Georgios. 2013. 'Greece: From Statutory Nullities to a Categorical Statutory Exclusionary Rule', in Stephen C. Thaman, ed., *Exclusionary Rules in Comparative Law*. Dordrecht: Springer.

Trüg, Gerson and Hans-Jürgen Kerner. 2007. 'Formalisierung der Wahrheitsfindung im (reformiert-) inquisitorischen Strafverfahren? Betrachtungen unter rechtsvergleichender Perspektive', in Heinz Schöch et al., eds., *Recht Gestalten – Dem Recht Dienen, Festschrift für Reinhard Böttcher*. Berlin: De Gruyter Recht.

Turner, Jenia Iontcheva. 2006. 'Judicial Participation in Plea Negotiation: A Comparative View', 54 *Am. J. Comp. L.* 199.

Turner, Jenia Iontcheva. 2009. *Plea Bargaining Across Borders*. New York: Wolters Kluwer.

Turner, Jenia Iontcheva and Thomas Weigend. 2013. 'Negotiated Justice', in Göran Sluiter et al., eds., *International Criminal Procedure: Principles and Rules*. Oxford: Oxford University Press.

United States v. Giannattasio, 979 F.2d 98 (7th Cir. 1992).

United States v. Griffin, 17 F.3d 269 (8th Cir. 1994).

United States v. Leon, 468 U.S. 897 (1984).

United States v. Ruiz, 536 U.S. 622 (2002).

United States v. Scott, 437 U.S. 82 (1978).

United States v. Wilson, 420 U.S. 332 (1975).

Vanscoy v. Ontario [1999] O.J. No. 1661, 1999 CarswellOnt 1427 (Ont. S.C.J.).

Vidmar, Neil. 2000. 'The Jury Elsewhere in the World', in Neil Vidmar, ed., *World Jury Systems*. Oxford: Oxford University Press.

Vidmar, Neil and Valerie Hans. 2007. *American Juries: The Verdict*. Amherst, NY: Prometheus Books.

Vogler, Richard. 2005. *A World View of Criminal Justice*. Aldershot, UK: Ashgate Publishing.

Volokh, Alexander. 1997. 'N Guilty Men', 146 *U. Pa. L. Rev.* 173.

Waye, Vicki and Paul Marcus. 2010. 'Australia and the United States: Two Common Criminal Justice Systems Uncommonly at Odds, Part 2', 18 *Tul. J. Int'l & Comp. L.* 335.

Weber, Ingram. 2009. 'The New Japanese Jury System: Empowering the Public, Preserving Continental Justice', 4 *E. Asia L. Rev.* 125.

Weeks v. United States, 232 U.S. 383 (1914).

Weigend, Thomas. 2003. 'Is the Criminal Process About Truth? A German Perspective', 26 *Harv. J.L. & Pub. Pol'y* 157.

Weigend, Thomas. 2008. 'The Decay of the Inquisitorial Ideal: Plea Bargaining Invades Criminal Procedure', in John Jackson et al., eds., *Crime, Procedure and Evidence in a Comparative and International Context*. Oxford: Hart Publishing.

Weigend, Thomas. 2011. 'Should We Search for the Truth, and Who Should Do It?', 36 *N.C. J. Int'l L. & Com. Reg.* 389.

Weigend, Thomas and Jenia Turner. 2014. 'The Constitutionality of Negotiated Criminal Judgments in Germany', 15 *German L.J.* 81.

Westen, Peter. 1980. 'The Three Faces of Double Jeopardy: Reflections on Government Appeals of Criminal Sentences', 78 *Mich. L. Rev.* 1001.

Whitman, James. 2005. *Harsh Justice*. Oxford: Oxford University Press.

Whitman, James Q. 2009. 'Equality in Criminal Law: The Two Divergent Western Roads', 1 *J. Legal Analysis* 119.

Winter, Lorena Bachmaier. 2013. 'Spain: The Constitutional Court's Move from Categorical Exclusion to Limited Balancing', in Stephen C. Thaman, ed., *Exclusionary Rules in Comparative Law*. Dordrecht: Springer.

Wright, Ronald F. 2005. 'Trial Distortion and the End of Innocence in Federal Criminal Justice', 154 *U. Pa. L. Rev.* 79.

Yager v. The Queen [1977] W.A.R. 17, 11 A.L.R 646 (Austl.).

Yissacharov v. Chief Military Prosecutor [2006] (1) Isr. L.R. 320.

Young, Warren, et al. 1999. Juries in Criminal Trials: A Summary of the Research Findings, at http://www.nzlii.org/nz/other/nzlc/pp/PP37/PP37.pdf.

2. Ensuring the factual reliability of criminal convictions: reasoned judgments or a return to formal rules of evidence?

Stephen C. Thaman

1. INTRODUCTION: REASONED JUDGMENTS AND THE PROTECTION OF THE INNOCENT

Since 1989 in the United States (US), at least 337 innocent persons have been exonerated based on DNA tests after having been convicted, nearly always by juries,[1] in trials which were otherwise 'fair' in the sense that the judgments were not overturned on any legal grounds, nor due to insufficiency of the evidence (Innocence Project, 2016). Since 1976, more than 150 persons sentenced to death for murder have been exonerated through DNA testing and other means (Death Penalty Information Center, 2016). The greatest percentage of wrongful convictions are due to erroneous eyewitness identification, but some 25–30 percent are due in part to false confessions or admissions and 15 percent of the wrongful convictions involved false testimony of an informant. Bad lawyering and negligent or outright dishonest practices of police, prosecutors, and forensic experts were also significant causes of these miscarriages of justice (Illinois, 2002; Innocence Project, 2016).

In relation to all of these convictions of the innocent, we can presume the trial judge denied a motion for a directed verdict of acquittal based on insufficiency of the evidence,[2] and that appellate panels implicitly found sufficient incriminating evidence for a reasonable jury to convict. In other words, the American rules of evidence allowed juries to decide the fates of people charged with capital and other serious felonies based on either weak or fabricated evidence in each of these cases.

It is easy to blame these shocking miscarriages of justice on the fact that the jury's decision finding 'proof beyond a reasonable doubt', remains, for all practical purposes, a purely subjective internal one, 'according to conscience' or as the French said, after importing trial by jury after the French Revolution, based in *intime conviction*.

Continental European legal systems have, however, gradually departed from a purely subjective assessment of the magnitude of proof and have required the trier of fact to objectify its reasons for finding the facts, which underlie a finding of guilt. *Intime conviction* has given way to *conviction raisonnée*. I have argued, in the past, that the extra layer of protection inherent in judgment reasons perhaps should be required in American jury trials, in order to reduce the number of wrongful convictions (Thaman, 2011: 660–661).

The requirement of reasoned criminal judgments has become a recognized facet of the right to a fair trial or due process in the civil law world.[3] In the landmark case of *Taxquet v. Belgium* (GC), App. No. 926/05 (Eur. Ct. HR, Nov. 16, 2010, the European Court of Human Rights (ECtHR)) reconfirmed earlier case law that:

> [i]n proceedings conducted before professional judges, the accused's understanding of his conviction stems primarily from the reasons given in judicial decisions. In such cases, the national courts must indicate with sufficient clarity the grounds on which they base their decisions ... Reasoned decisions also serve the purpose of demonstrating to the parties that they have been heard, thereby contributing to a more willing acceptance of the decision on their part. In addition, they oblige judges to base their reasoning on objective arguments, and also preserve the rights of the defence (§ 91).

In *Taxquet*, the ECtHR held for the first time, that an unreasoned conviction by a jury could violate the right to a fair trial guaranteed by Article 6 of the European Convention of Human Rights (ECHR). The upshot was that juries, in the future, might have to give reasons for their verdicts,[4] and Belgium and France have now amended their laws to require their *jurés* to give reasoned decisions.[5]

In this chapter, however, I go further and argue that European systems also have inherent flaws which contribute to convicting the innocent, and that the judicial practice of writing judgment reasons has become so routinized that it is inadequate to guarantee a solid factual foundation for judgments of guilt. I believe that, both in the common-law US and civil-law European jurisdictions, procedural rules should require a minimum amount of solid evidence of guilt in order to rebut the presumption of innocence and send a case to a trier of fact for its subjective assessment of proof beyond a reasonable doubt.

The comparison of US and European law in this context is difficult, because of the vast procedural differences between jury trial, with its general verdicts and laconic, reasonless judgments, and the reasoned judgments of professional and mixed courts in Europe. However, when one focuses on why and how innocent persons are convicted, the excellent investigations and scholarship in the US have been able to pinpoint factors, many of which are equally applicable in a European context. Nearly every major case of wrongful conviction in the US involves a violent felony against the person such as murder, rape, or robbery (Gould et al., 2014: 483). Especially in cases of rape-murder, child-murder, murders of police officers, serial killings and particularly brutal rapes, there is great pressure on police and prosecutors to arrest and convict someone (often the 'usual suspects') and this pressure is exacerbated by the press coverage which further alarms the public. This leads to prosecutions based on weak evidence, and even the occasional concoction of false evidence to facilitate the prosecution (Gould et al., 2014: 505–506). I will discuss cases in Europe that also fit this model.

The requirement of reasoned judgments should also be analyzed in its contemporary context, where, due to plea bargaining and other methods of inducing guilty pleas or stipulations, full trials on the merits, in which all due process guarantees for the suspect-accused are respected, are becoming rare. In such consensual or simplified procedures, there is usually no proof beyond a reasonable doubt, indeed, no attempt to ascertain the truth of the charges, much less to give reasons justifying the results. The canon of judgment reasons is greatly relaxed in most systems when these simplified procedures are utilized (Thaman, 2010: 368–369).

One could say that, in practice, nearly all criminal justice systems which encourage the use of trial-sparing mechanisms based on what is tantamount to an admission of guilt, actually presume the guilt and not the innocence of the accused. The overwhelming majority of cases, are thus decided based on, at most, *probable cause of guilt* – all that is required to arrest and charge someone. Then comes plea bargaining, penal orders, dismissals with conditions (diversion), abbreviated trials, and stipulations to the charges which resolve the great majority of all cases in bouts of 'efficiency fever'.[6] In the absence of proof beyond a reasonable doubt, defendants accept punishment based on suspicion alone, or what the Germans call *Verdachtsstrafen*, which have a long history to which I will later allude.

In the US 95 percent or more of all criminal cases, which are not dismissed in the exercise of prosecutorial discretion, are resolved through what I and others believe is an inherently coercive system of plea bargains (Thaman, 2010: 344). The numbers in the United Kingdom are nearly as high as in the US, whereas continental European countries tend to limit the use of their consensual procedural forms to low or mid-level offenses, leading to a higher percentage of cases going to trial (Thaman, 2010: 377–380). Although German *Absprachen* (confession bargains) only take place during the trial (Altenhain, 2010), trial is avoided in Germany in an increasing number of cases through the use of diversion and penal orders.[7]

The defendant who confesses or otherwise agrees to be sentenced based on probable cause without a trial gets mitigation for sparing law enforcement organs and courts their purported truth-finding tasks.[8] The few defendants who refuse to admit guilt, either because they are innocent, or the crime is so grave that bargaining is eschewed, actually get their day in court and supposedly benefit from the presumption of innocence and the standard of proof beyond a reasonable doubt before their liberty (or in the US, their life) may be taken.

Those who take advantage of their trial rights, however, are treated more harshly if they are convicted, for wasting the court's time and sometimes for 'perjuring themselves' by claiming innocence. In practice, asserting one's innocence is thus treated as an aggravating factor in most criminal justice systems. It is, thus, no surprise that so many innocent people are caught up in this Catch 22 system and convicted of the most serious crimes of violence.

Although the majority of guilty defendants in Europe likely take advantage of the expedited, abbreviated, or consensual forms of disposition, these are usually not as coercive as America's plea bargaining system. The guilty thieves, burglars, drunk drivers, and white collar criminals can and do benefit from consensual justice. But such consensual arrangements do not take place against the background threat of artificially inflated sanctions for those who exercise their right to trial. There is also no community or media pressure to proceed with ambiguous evidence as there is in the high-profile rape and rape-murder cases and the like. They are given a lesser sentence, without proof beyond a reasonable doubt, or a rigorous reasoned judgment. There is a kind of proportionality in this set-up.

Since 'suspicion punishments' are today the typical currency of our criminal justice systems, it is not surprising that there is 'system creep' in the sense that judges in the first and second instances appear to validate convictions based on evidence which at most indicates a strong suspicion of guilt. Because of the flimsiness of evidence which satisfies American courts of appeal and the canon of reasoned judgments in Europe, it must ultimately be asked whether we should return to 'formal rules of evidence' of the type which governed in criminal justice systems up until the early 19th century.

In this chapter, I will give a brief history of the standards of proof as they developed on the European continent from formal rules of evidence to an adoption of the subjective standard employed by English juries in the form of *intime conviction*, and finally to the canon of judgment reasons which has gradually gained supremacy in Europe. I will then show why both the subjective standard of inner conviction and the more objective canon of judgment reasons allow convictions without solid evidentiary foundations.

The shared failures of modern American and European systems are facilitated by the practical inefficacy of the presumption of innocence, innate pro-prosecutorial leanings of trial and appellate judges, and the vagueness of the canon of judgment reasons which allow appellate courts to arbitrarily change judgments with which they do not agree. In making my argument, I will concentrate on the types of cases which tend to produce the majority of wrongful convictions: (1) cases based on questionable circumstantial evidence without eyewitnesses or hard scientific evidence of guilt; (2) cases based on uncorroborated eyewitness identification; (3) cases based on uncorroborated confessions or admissions by the defendant; and (4) cases in which one witness is pitted against another and the resolution of the case depends on the relative credibility of the two.[9]

Finally, since nearly all countries today already have a two-level system of criminal adjudication, which allows punishment to be imposed based on probable cause, if the defendant agrees to consensual resolution of the case, and a trial system, which lacks formal rules to ensure that evidence is scientifically and logically actually capable of ensuring factual accuracy, we could adapt this model to prevent the conviction of the innocent in grave felony cases. I will suggest, that plea-bargaining and other consensual forms of trial, which skirt the standard of proof beyond a reasonable doubt, be limited to cases where the punishment may not exceed, say, six or eight years.[10] If the prosecution wants to impose a grave felony sanction in excess of that, then formal rules of evidence, of the kind I will suggest, should be met before a jury, mixed court, or professional panel would be allowed to decide the case according to *intime conviction* or *conviction raisonée*. If a defendant insists on being tried on a charge punishable by less than six or eight years, which would normally be a case in which the pressures on law enforcement to find a suspect at all costs would be absent, then the current canon of judgment reasons, without formal rules of evidence, could continue to be applied in continental European systems, and common law juries could find guilt beyond a reasonable doubt. In close cases, I would still give a convicted defendant, however, the right to request reasons from the jury (Thaman, 2011: 665).

2. FROM FORMAL RULES OF EVIDENCE TO *INTIME CONVICTION* AND REASONED JUDGMENTS

The kind of circumstantial evidence which has led to many of the documented wrongful convictions would have been patently insufficient for a conviction in many traditional legal systems. It is worth quoting at length the great Jewish philosopher, Maimonides (b. 1135? d. 1204) in this respect:

> We are forbidden to punish one on the basis of strong or even virtually conclusive circumstantial evidence. Thus if A pursues B with intent to kill and B takes refuge in a house into which the pursuer follows, and we enter after them and find B in his last gasp and his pursuing enemy, A, standing over him with a knife in his hand, and both of them are covered with blood, the Sanhedrin may not find A liable to capital punishment, since there are no eyewitnesses to the actual murder. ...

> The Almighty has therefore foreclosed this possibility, ordaining that no punishment may be imposed unless there are witnesses who testify that they have clear and indubitable knowledge of the occurrence and it is impossible to explain the occurrence in any other way. If we do not impose punishment even on the basis of a very strong probability, the worst that can happen is that a transgressor will go free; but if we punish on the strength of probabilities and suppositions, it may be that one day we shall put an innocent person to death, and it is better and more desirable that a thousand guilty persons go free than that a single innocent person be put to death. (Elon et al., 1999: 201)

Around the time in which Maimonides wrote, two radically different systems developed in Europe, the common-law system in Great Britain, which relied on public trial by jury based on the oral testimony of witnesses, and the continental European inquisitorial system, in which judges decided cases without lay participation based on a secret investigation, written evidence, and the use of torture.

The jury had an inherent popular and political legitimacy as the 'conscience' of the community. Its decisions literally 'spoke the truth' in the *verdict*, which needed no other justification. In common-law systems, the jury verdict, whether of conviction or acquittal, was final and guilty verdicts were not subject to appeal in the US until the US Supreme Court allowed them in 1899 (*United States v. Scott*, 437 U.S. 82, 88 (1978)). Historically unanimous in the common-law world, the verdict possessed a legitimacy akin to that of a democratic election[11] or parliamentary vote – even when the results appeared, on occasion, to be irrational. Although rules prevented the use of hearsay in the oral, public jury trials, juries were free to convict on circumstantial evidence to an extent which would have alarmed Maimonides. However, juries were free to acquit, and often did (around two-thirds of the time in the 13th century), even in the face of strong evidence, if they felt the Draconian English punishments were disproportionate to the crime, and these acquittals could not be overturned by appellate judges (Green, 1985: 31, 61).

In inquisitorial Europe, although professional judges were in firm command of the criminal investigation and the ultimate guilt and punishment decision, they were not allowed to judge freely, according to conscience, as would a jury. They were bound by formal rules of evidence, excellent examples of which can be found in the German *Constitituo Criminalis Carolina* of 1532. Paragraph 64 of the *Carolina*, for instance, would allow conviction and a possible death sentence only upon 'full proof', which required at least two or three 'believable' and 'good' eyewitnesses to the crime. If only one such witness was available, then torture was permitted. But if two 'good' witnesses could testify to circumstantial evidence pointing to a particular suspect, then the judge, according to § 23 *Carolina*, had the equivalent of 'probable cause' (*gnugsame anzeygung*), to administer torture if the suspect would not voluntarily confess. Further, §§ 25–26 *Carolina* list the types of circumstantial evidence accepted by the code, among which were: that the suspect was a 'criminal type' who had committed similar crimes in the past; that he was caught near the scene of the crime or possessed evidence related to the crime; that he lived with persons who committed similar crimes; that he had a motive to commit the crime; that he was accused by a victim in a dying declaration; or that he was seen fleeing from the scene of the crime.

Although the existence of 'full proof' according to the formal rules of evidence led to automatic conviction in Italy, even if the judge himself harbored doubts as to guilt, this was not the case under the rules of the *Carolina*, according to which the judge still had discretion to acquit (Küper, 1967: 129–130, 131, 140–141). Although the great Italian jurist Gaetano Filangieri (1752–1788) also promoted the idea of 'negative rules of evidence', which would allow a judge to convict but not bind him to do so, the notion of 'negative' formal rules was forgotten by later scholars until the idea reemerged in the early 19th century (Küper, 1967: 131, 140–141).

Since 'full proof' was extremely difficult to come by, coerced and tortured confessions became the 'queen of evidence' and the lynchpin of the overwhelming number of criminal convictions (Deppenkemper, 2004: 171–181). But, even if a tortured person refused to confess, making 'full proof' and a death penalty impossible, the judge could still impose a *poena extraordinaria*, a form of *Verdachtsstrafe*, which would allow a lesser penalty of imprisonment (Langbein, 1977: 45–52).

Only with the French Revolution and the Enlightenment critique of the brutality of confession-based inquisitorial procedure did the English common-law approach gain a foothold on the continent. The French introduced trial by jury and abolished the formal rules of evidence, allowing the jury to decide based on its inner conviction (*intime conviction*) alone, and these reforms made the jury's decision final, in cases of acquittal (Esmein, 1913: 409–419, 516). Most other European countries followed the French lead. But the new continental jury did not return a simple, unanimous general verdict of 'guilty' or 'not guilty', as is the case today in England and the US, but an itemized special verdict in the form of responses to a 'question list'. These questions addressed the basic elements of the charged crimes and any possible excuses or justifications in separate propositions, requiring only a majority vote as to each question (Thaman, 2011: 615). By taking the jury through the elements of crimes, excuses, justifications, etc., a well-drafted question list reveals the logic of the jury's decision and enables the court to determine the legal qualification of the jury's factual findings.[12]

In France, juries and distrust of judges went hand in hand. The same Enlightenment thinkers who supported the jury and free evaluation of the evidence were just as adamantly against professional judges doing anything but subsuming the law from the jury-determined facts. As Montesequieu famously wrote: 'the judges of the nation are nothing, as we have said, but the mouth which pronounces the words of the law; inanimate beings who can moderate neither its force, nor its rigor' (Montesequieu, 1979: 301).

The subjective standard of *intime conviction* was originally adopted, consistent with the strong French mistrust of judges, only for jury trials; professional judges, on the other hand, should still have been subject to formal evidence rules. But gradually, by the late 1840s, professional judges were freed up to rule according to their inner conviction, as would a juror (Küper, 1967: 217–219).

In Germany, however, there remained a reluctance to allow professional judges to decide cases freely, without being bound by strictures of some kind. Many of the most prominent 19th-century legal thinkers in Germany, including Mittermaier and Zachariä, pushed for some kind of negative evidentiary rules to provide a more solid evidentiary basis for the exercise of *intime conviction* (Küper, 1967: 222–230). In 1846, the great German jurist Savigny suggested that judges should be bound in their evaluation of the facts by the 'laws of thought, experience and human knowledge' (Geipel, 2008: 11). A Berlin ordinance of the same year required the trial judge to decide 'based on a careful appraisal of all evidence for the prosecution and the defense according to his free conviction, resulting from the essence of the trial held in his presence. He is, however, obligated to give the reasons, which guided him, in the judgment' (Deppenkemper, 2004: 209–210).

Although § 261 CCP-Germany (1877), still exhorts the trial judge to rule based on his 'free conviction derived from the content of the trial', or 'free evaluation of the evidence', the German approach has been characterized as 'reasoned conviction' (*conviction raisonée*) (Deppenkemper, 2004: 208). Damaška has characterized the French notion of *intime conviction* as 'romantic' and compared it with the German approach whereby the judge no longer had the 'license to disregard the extralegal canons of valid inference' (Damaška, 1997: 21).

Jury courts were never the default jurisdiction for criminal cases on the European continent as they were in England and the US. They were usually reserved for charges of murder and other serious felonies, and sometimes political or press crimes (Thaman, 1998: 246–248, 259–260, with reference to Spain). Under the 1877 German CCP, jury trial was reserved for felonies punishable by more than five years' imprisonment, or the death penalty, and a panel of five professional judges heard cases punishable by up to five years' deprivation of liberty, with a mixed court or *Schöffengericht*, made up of one professional judge and two lay assessors, hearing only minor misdemeanors or infractions punishable by no more than three months' deprivation of liberty (Dubber, 1995: 235).

Many German jurists pushed to replace the jury court with the mixed court, because the jury was perceived to be unable to give reasons for its decisions, whereas the professional judge rapporteur could perform this function for the mixed court, and thus leave a record for review by the higher courts. The professional component of the mixed court, however, could and usually did control the deliberations due to the passivity of the lay judges (Rennig, 1993: 272–273). Eventually the classic jury was swept from most of Europe, falling prey especially to totalitarian and Fascist regimes, and ceded to the mixed court (Italy, France, Soviet Union, Germany) or to professional courts (Spain, Portugal) (Thaman, 2011: 618–619). With the demise of the jury, the canon of reasoned judgments became part and parcel of nearly all civil law justice systems, even attaining constitutional status in Italy (Art. 111 (para. 6) Const.-Italy), Spain (Art. 120(3) Const.-Spain) and Belgium (Art. 149 Const.-Belgium).

3. THE PRESUMPTION OF INNOCENCE AND THE INDEPENDENCE OF THE TRIER OF FACT

3.1   Presumption of Innocence and Proof Beyond a Reasonable Doubt at Trial

According to Iacoviello, it is difficult to transplant proof beyond a reasonable doubt (and the presumption of innocence) into a system of reasoned judgments (Iacoviello, 2006: 3874). Ideally, the judge should subject the prosecution's hypothesis of guilt to systematic rebuttal using the 'instrument of doubt'. He contrasts this 'falsificationist' epistemology, derived from the writings of Karl Popper (Fallone, 2012: 79–88) with what he calls the 'verificationist' epistemology usually employed by continental European judges, which merely tests the logical coherence of the prosecutorial hypothesis and its compatibility with the facts. 'Doubt' can be internal or external to the prosecutorial hypothesis. The internal doubt is that which reveals the '*self-contradictoriness* of the hypothesis or its *explicatory incapacity*'. External doubt is that which counterposes the prosecutorial hypothesis with an alternative hypothesis, reasonable enough so that one can say: 'it is possible that things happened in this way'. For Iacoviello, a doubt for which one cannot give reasons is 'irrelevant' and 'procedurally inert' (Andrés Ibáñez, 2005: 173; Iacoviello, 2006: 3876). An example of 'explicatory incapacity', which is not 'self-contradictory' is presented:

> [i]f the accused was the last person with the victim and had a motive to kill, that is not enough. Even if one cannot imagine alternative hypotheses, this is not enough to convict. The thesis is logical, but improbable in the etymological sense. A judgment which organizes in a logical manner little probative evidence will not be *illogical*, but foments *reasonable doubt*. (Iacoviello, 2006: 3877)

Although the presumption of innocence was proclaimed in Art. 9 of the French Declaration of the Rights of Man, is included in the notion of due process in the US (*In re Winship*, 397 U.S. 358, 364 (1970)), and is guaranteed by Art. 6(2) of the ECHR, many continental European criminal justice systems have had, and still have, an ambiguous attitude towards this important principle. To my knowledge it is not mentioned in either the German constitution or code of criminal procedure, and the formulation which found its way into Art. 27 of the Italian constitution of 1949, whereby the 'defendant is considered not guilty until there is a final judgment' is ambiguous.[13] Soviet criminal law theorists rejected the presumption of innocence as 'bourgeois nonsense' (Thaman, 2002: 212) and *Garofalo* of the Italian school of criminology called it an 'empty and absurd phrase' (Illuminati, 1984: 16).

The presumption of innocence means different things in different countries. In the US it serves primarily as a mechanism at trial to enforce the prosecutor's burden of proof beyond a reasonable doubt, and to validate findings of 'not guilty' when there is a failure of proof. Twenty years ago, California juries were told that they must acquit if they do not have an 'abiding conviction to a moral certainty' of the truth of the charges. Today the term 'moral certainty' has been dropped. Juries are still told that the 'evidence need not eliminate all possible doubt because everything in life is open to some possible or imaginary doubt' (CALJIC 1.03). The Massachusetts Supreme Judicial Court, however, recently decided to maintain the 'abiding conviction to a moral certainty' language and added: 'When we refer to moral certainty, we mean the highest degree of certainty possible in matters relating to human affairs – based solely on the evidence that has been put before you in this case' (*Commonwealth v. Russell*, 470 Mass. 464, 477 (2015)).

In Europe, the presumption of innocence is usually treated as being more embedded in the substantive criminal law (Mayer, 1989: 67), in that it requires actual production of a certain amount of evidence before the trier of fact will be allowed to assess guilt. In Spain, whether or not the 'minimal evidentiary activity' required to rebut the presumption had been presented was traditionally subject to appellate review. On the other hand, the principle of *in dubio pro reo* (all doubts in favor of the defendant) was deemed to be a subjective decision by the trier of fact, which, before the 1978 Constitution required reasoned judgments, was not subject to review by the higher courts (De Paúl Velasco, 2004: 522).

This approach, which sees the presumption of innocence as an objective, evidence-based hurdle which must be transcended, before a trier of fact may engage in the subjective assessment of proof beyond a reasonable doubt, will be useful in a new system of formal rules of evidence.

3.2   The Problem of the Trial Judge with a Prosecutorial Bias

3.2.1   The relative disappearance of acquittals

If there is indeed a presumption of innocence, and a high burden of proof, why are acquittals such rarities in so many countries? In Japan the acquittal rate approximates 'absolute zero' (Johnson, 2002: 215). The same is true in China where acquittals are virtually unheard of (McConville, 2011: 376). The near impossibility of being acquitted in the

Soviet-Russian courts and notorious convictions of the innocent were reasons for Russia's re-introduction of trial by jury in 1993–2001. Death sentences against completely innocent persons in Japan also led to introducing a large mixed court of six jurors and two judges in 2009.[14]

Juries traditionally acquitted at a higher rate than did mixed or purely professional courts. A possible exception can be found in Spain, where both juries and courts staffed with professional judges acquit about 19 percent of the time (Consejo General del Poder Judicial, 1998: 28). But even in the US, those few cases which do go to trial end in convictions more often than they did in the past, and the near disappearance of jury trials has resulted in a miserly overall acquittal rate.[15] The acquittal rates in Russia and other post-Soviet republics are also under 1 percent, even if, in Russia, one includes a near 15 percent acquittal rate in jury trials (Thaman, 2008b: 108). The number of acquittals has also fallen in Germany, from around 8 percent in 1958, to around 3 percent in 2006 (Geipel, 2008: 151).

It is customary to attribute the low acquittal rates in the US federal courts, Japan and Germany, *inter alia*, to the professionalism of the prosecutor's office, which filters out all weak cases, either by dismissing them, diverting them, resolving them with penal orders, or offering irresistible plea bargains. But the relative absence of acquittals can, in part, be explained by the fact that the judges who decide guilt are often biased towards the prosecution and, in effect, presume the guilt of the defendant before the trial commences.[16]

3.2.2   The file-prejudiced judge

The continental European and Soviet trial judge traditionally received the investigative file of the investigating magistrate or prosecutor, and thoroughly reviewed the evidence before setting the case for trial. Still today, in Germany and some other countries, the first decision of the trial judge, who in non-jury systems is always a trier of fact and will eventually formulate the judgment reasons, is to review the state's evidence and determine whether the defendant is 'sufficiently guilty' for trial to be set (Schünemann, 2000: 159). I agree with Mirjan Damaška that systems in which the judge has already pre-judged the case to the detriment of the defendant before the trial begins, take the presumption of innocence 'somewhat less seriously' (Damaška, 2001: 491). This decision on whether to hold the defendant to answer has been called 'an anticipatory step towards conviction' (Küper, 1967: 207). The principle of mandatory prosecution, called the 'legality principle' in Europe, which reigns especially strongly in Germany and Italy, might also contribute to judges too quickly affirming the charging decisions of prosecutors.

Professor Bernd Schünemann conducted a study which clearly confirmed the perceptions of practitioners that German trial judges act in a community of interests with the public prosecutor, or literally, in a 'shoulder embrace' (*Schulterschluss*) with them, and will nearly always consciously or unconsciously view the evidence at trial in conformity with the prosecutor's initial assessment in the file. The study involved judges and prosecutors reading a 'file' constructed so that the evidence of guilt was not clearly sufficient to support a criminal prosecution, and then participating in a mock trial based on the evidence. Evidence contradicting the prosecutor's version of events was consciously or unconsciously rejected (*cognitive dissonance*) and that confirming it was noted and emphasized in the judgment reasons (Schünemann, 2000: 160). This phenomenon is similar to that of 'tunnel vision', a recognized reason for wrongful convictions in the US, which has been defined as: 'the social, organizational, and psychological tendencies that lead actors in the criminal justice system to focus on a suspect, select and filter the evidence that will build a case for conviction, while ignoring or suppressing evidence that points away from guilt' (Gould et al., 2014: 503–504).

Schünemann's study also showed that judges who had no knowledge of the contents of the investigative file were substantially less likely to convict based on the same evidence, and that if they also had the power to question witnesses, their questions were more probing than those of file-prejudiced judges (Schünemann, 2000: 161–162).

The *Schulterschluss* between prosecutor and judge in today's democratic Germany leads to similar results as those once obtained from Soviet criminal procedure, where the trial judge officially saw himself as an ally of the prosecutor in ensuring conviction in all cases. There is also still evidence in some countries, Spain for one, that trial judges just download the conclusions of the prosecutor expressed in the accusatory pleadings and reproduce them in the judgment reasons at the conclusion of the trial (Andrés Ibáñez, 2005: 147).

The active procedural role of the victim or aggrieved party in some European jurisdictions complicates the dynamics of any possible *Schulterschluss*. Although the role of the victim is relatively weak in Germany, Shawn Boyne has described some rape cases where victims play a role as 'auxiliary prosecutors' or *Nebenklägerinnen*, being represented by counsel, and the relationship between judge and prosecutor becomes more complex. In one case, the prosecutor was leaning towards dismissing the charge, but the judge convinced him to accept a confession bargain (*Absprache*) with a reduced sentence to resolve the case (Boyne, 2014: 168–174). In addition, the relationship between judges and prosecutors is affected by the very strong role of the victim in Spain, who may independently charge any case and plead it alongside, but independently of, the public prosecutor. The victim often pleads for conviction for a more serious crime and the imposition of a significantly higher punishment and amounts of civil restitution than does the public prosecutor. This makes the public prosecutor seem like a more moderate neutral party in the eyes of the judge.[17] The fact that judges acquit about as often as juries in Spain has been attributed both to a lesser influence of the prosecutor, due to the fact that the most serious cases are actually investigated and charged by the investigating magistrate and not the prosecutor, and to the fact that victims often push factually weak cases to trial.[18]

Even in systems without a procedurally enforced *Schulterschluss*, the rules of evidence tend to prevent a 'falsificationist' stance of the trier of fact, which is essential in enforcing the presumption of innocence. In many countries, reports prepared by state investigative officials and even police reports are admissible hearsay and are presumed to reflect truly the acts conducted by those officials. This is especially true in Russia and other former Soviet republics (Thaman, 2008b: 105–106). Although the French *juge d'instruction* is not a trial judge, Jacqueline Hodgson has shown how excessive reliance on police testimony skews the investigating magistrate's interpretation of the facts in a pro-prosecution manner (Hodgson, 2005: 223–226).

In some countries where investigative officials or even expert witnesses testify in court, they are also presumed to be telling the truth. The astonishing number of convictions of the innocent in the US based in part on dishonest police, prosecutors, and even expert witnesses have shown that these old presumptions of official integrity are misplaced, particularly in the especially grave felony cases which are most prone to error.[19]

3.2.3   The problem of the judge as investigator

The old written inquisitorial model was scuttled in large part because it was determined that the official who directed the investigation could not simultaneously be an impartial judge of the truth of the charges he himself had brought. Because the trial judge in Germany also has the inquisitorial duty to ascertain the truth, the preliminary reading and approval of the prosecutor's hypothesis of the case makes him/her a biased 'truth-finder', with, according to some, a psychological 'over-burdening of roles' that is difficult to manage (Schünemann, 2000: 159) and can also lead to 'falsification of the decision on the facts' (Küper, 1967: 204–205).

The inquisitorial duty to ascertain the truth in the Soviet Union led the trial judge, when faced with insufficient evidence to convict, to return the case to the pretrial stage for further investigation. One spoke of an 'insufficiency of evidence to acquit' (Thaman, 2008b: 106–107). Naturally, as soon as the inquisitorial judge feels compelled to look for further incriminating evidence, she tacitly admits that the extant incriminating evidence is insufficient. If she feels compelled to search for exculpatory evidence, then she already has reasonable doubt as to guilt. Under both scenarios, an acquittal would be compelled in a system which takes the presumption of innocence seriously. The power of the judge to interrupt the trial and initiate new investigative measures still exists in France and the Netherlands (Thaman, 2008a: 189), as well as in Germany, where this mindset goes back to the *Inquisitionsverfahren*, where the insufficiency of the evidence in the dossier was seen only as a failure of the investigating magistrate to bring the trial judges 'closer to the facts' (Küper, 1967: 117). Based on this same principle, an appeal in cassation in Germany can claim that the trial judge violated his or her duty to investigate the truth (*Aufklärungspflicht*) per § 261 CCP-Germany by not pursuing leads that were indicated in the prosecutor's file (Deppenkemper, 2004: 350–352).

The same is true in France, where the Court of Cassation reverses acquittals if the trial judge failed to order measures of investigation that 'would be useful in ascertaining the truth' because the court would 'not legally have had a foundation for acquitting the defendant due to the lack of certitude which seemed to exist in favor of him' (Cass. crim. (19 March 1975); Cass. crim. No. 318, (23 Nov. 1971), 805).

3.2.4 The problematic nature of reasons in collegial courts

Whereas a single judge may decide a case based on his or her individual psychological orientation to the case, in collegial courts, whether mixed or purely professional, the individuality of the judge is submerged, becoming part of an 'anonymous collective will'. This can lead to 'decisions, which, while derived from the deliberation and voting of individual judicial personalities, are supported by only a minority, for perhaps not a single judge was truly convinced or would claim responsibility for them' (Küper, 1967: 309–310). As with juries, the strong and convincing judicial personality may control the proceedings and even decide the case alone (Küper, 1967: 312–313).

In Germany, the code does not lay out how collegial courts must vote, yet it does require that judges, who were outvoted as to preliminary issues, continue to vote and accept as true, in subsequent votes, those questions as to which they were outvoted. In a sense, the judge must accept that he or she was 'wrong' in not going along with the majority. Despite the lack of a unified opinion, the judge-rapporteur is adept at presenting logical judgment reasons which feign a unity which did not exist. Collegiality becomes a pure fiction, for a single judge becomes the mouthpiece of the court and sets forth the reasons and their interrelationship (Küper, 1967: 320–323).

Judgment reasons are even more problematic, when, for instance, the lay assessors outvote the professional judge. Here the judge-rapporteur is giving reasons for a judgment with which he does not agree. He or she may thus intentionally sow the seeds of reversal by constructing a judgment which does not comport with the canon of judgment reasons.

4. THE EFFICACY OF THE CASSATIONAL COURTS IN PROTECTING THE PRESUMPTION OF INNOCENCE AND DISCOVERING POTENTIAL WRONGFUL CONVICTIONS

4.1   Technical Aspects of Review of Factual Findings in the First Instance

4.1.1   The right to appeal, and the difference between 'appeal' and 'cassation'

Appellate courts have traditionally been reluctant to review the factual assessments made by the trial court during an oral, public trial in which the court of first instance has observed the testimony and conduct of the witnesses. After all, traditional review was by cassation, in which the court heard no testimony and checked for *legal* error solely in the record presented to it. It was thus presumed to be incapable of second-guessing the decision of the trial court, which often contained lay judges, on the *facts*, and these had to be accepted as true for the purpose of review (Deppenkemper, 2004: 339–341). Thus, the cassational court would typically review only the reasons why the trial court decided to qualify the settled facts as constitutive of a particular criminal offense rather than another, or decided to impose a particular sentence rather than another. In Spain, this approach is gradually ceding to a firm requirement that reasons also be given for the *factual* finding of the judge (Andrés Ibáñez, 2005: 82).

Today, many legal systems provide for a second trial on the facts, called an 'appeal',[20] in which the court can re-hear the testimony and call new witnesses. These 'appeals' courts do not *per se* violate the principles of orality and immediacy in evaluating the evidence and they sometimes are staffed with lay judges. For instance, in Italy and France judgments of the large mixed court, the *cour d'assises*, which only hears very serious felonies, may be 'appealed' to another assizes court composed of professional and lay judges. The judgment of the appeals court may then be appealed in cassation. When 'appeals' courts re-hear cases, however, they sometimes overturn an acquittal based on the transcripts of the trial testimony, without even deigning to hear the witnesses who failed to convince the trial court (for example, *Destrehem v. France*, ECtHR, No. 56651/00 (May 18, 2004); *Mischie v. Romania*, ECtHR, No. 50224/07 (Sept. 16, 2014)).[21]

The role of the courts of cassation has changed, however, because the canon of judgment reasons now allows them to re-open the trial court's evaluation of the facts by labeling the trial court's purportedly faulty reasons as an 'error of law' rendering it subject to review in cassation.

In the US, the appellate courts function more or less like cassational courts, yet do engage in a limited review of the sufficiency of evidence produced at trial. According to the modern approach, the relevant question is whether 'after viewing the evidence in the light most favorable to the prosecution, *any* rational trier of fact could have found the essential elements of the crime beyond a reasonable doubt' (*Jackson v. Virginia*, 443 U.S. 307, 319 (1979)). In addition, the prosecution need not rule out 'every hypothesis except that of guilt' (*Wright v. West*, 505 U.S. 277, 296 (1992)). It is thus extremely difficult for a defendant to get a conviction reversed based on insufficiency of the evidence.

While the German Supreme Court used to deem the evidence sufficient to convict 'if the conclusions of the trier of fact were possible based on life-experience', now a judgment of guilt must be 'built on an evidentiary basis which can support it, which reveals an objectively high probability of the correctness of the evidentiary results' (BVerfG, 2 BVR 2045, 2003 StV 293 (April 30, 2003), paras 34–52). Despite such reassuring formulations, the canon of judgment reasons in most European countries has by and large not included formal rules of minimal sufficiency of evidence as part of its 'axioms of reason' or 'laws of thought', especially in the area of eyewitness identification or cases which are based on 'witness against witness' credibility battles.[22]

4.1.2 Selective review procedures
Many courts of cassation can decide a case without publishing an opinion. 'Postcard' denials were common, for instance, in California. The German Supreme Court also hears anywhere from 3,000 to 3,500 cases each year, but the amount of reasoned judgments in cassation has fallen from around 38.2 percent in the 1950s, to 25 percent in the 1960s, and 70s and down to a mere 6.6 percent in the 1990s (Geipel, 2008: 47). In

Italy, in the period from 1989 to 1995, the Court of Cassation rejected around 48.5 percent of all appeals without issuing a reasoned judgment, although the court reversed the judgment in 50 percent of those cases in which it issued a reasoned judgment and sent the case back for retrial (Carnevale and Orlandi, 2000: 141). In France, in 2013, the criminal panel of the Court of Cassation summarily rejected, without an opinion, 68.4 percent of all appeals in cassation, but if one separates out the appeals which are prepared with the aid of a lawyer, the percentage falls to 34.3 percent (Cour de Cassation, 2013: 649).

For example, Horst Arnold, a school teacher with no criminal record, was wrongfully convicted of rape and served 13 years in prison based on an utterly fantastic uncorroborated claim by a fellow teacher that he had raped and sodomized her between classes in the lunchroom. Long after the trial, it was learned that the complaining witness had accused other men of rape and was a pathological liar. The German Supreme Court affirmed the trial court's judgment without issuing an opinion, saying the 'review of the judgment … reveals no legal errors to the detriment of the defendant'. It then ordered the innocent man to pay all costs of the trial, including those of the perjurous complaining witness (BGH, 2 StR 444/02 (Dec. 13, 2002); Friedrichsen, 2012: 47).

4.1.3   The appellate record on which the decision is based

Appellate courts in the US have a full verbatim transcript of the trial available for them in conducting their review. Naturally it is a laborious task for the second instance court to read such voluminous material, but if a claim of insufficiency of evidence is made, the court can at least assess the totality of the evidence. This is not, however, the case in many countries.

In Russia and Germany, the only record of the case is a summary of the evidence created by the clerk of the court, with little or no input from the parties. Although audio recordings are provided for in § 308 CCP-France and also in Spain, Portugal, and elsewhere, they are seldom used by the higher courts. Efforts to require a verbatim record of trials have continually been defeated in Germany and are opposed by the courts (Geipel, 2008: 42–43).

In practice, the only record reviewed by cassational panels in Germany and Spain is the reasoned judgment written by the presiding judge. Judges will punctiliously describe important facts, circumstantial evidence, and statements which fit in with their conclusions, but avoid controversial and doubtful points. Possible erroneous interpretations, twisting, or conscious falsifications are very difficult then to uncover (Geipel, 2008: 40).

In Germany, one of the main causes for reversals of judgments by the courts of cassation is the inadequate rendition or description of the facts in the judgment reasons (*Darstellungsrüge*) (Deppenkemper, 2004: 364–365). In the words of the German Supreme Court:

> [T]he judgment reasons must reveal that the trier of fact took account of all circumstances which influenced its decision and included them in its considerations. The cassational court can only review the decision, if the testimony of the incriminating witness is reproduced and discussed, in order for it to judge the development of the testimony and its consistency. (BGH 5 StR 63/12, StV 2013, 7 (14 March 2012))

The stubborn refusal of the German courts to require a verbatim record of trials makes it all the more important for the judgment reasons to give a restatement of the facts which were crucial to its decision.

4.1.4 The dynamics of deliberations in the cassational court

How a case will come out on appeal, in Germany, depends to a large extent on the personality of the reporting judge. According to German Supreme Court judge Thomas Fischer, two similar cases which reached the Supreme Court, both murders, resulted in the reversal of one and the affirmation of the other, explicable only due to the relative liberality or strictness of the reporting judge. Although decisions are supposed to be decided by five judges, according to Fischer the reporting judge is the only judge to read the file and it is usually his or her personality which determines the outcome of the appeal. The first penal senate is called the 'Olli-Kahn-Senat', named after a famous German soccer goalkeeper, because it rejected all but 7 percent of appeals in the years 2008 to 2012. The third penal senate, on the other hand granted around 26 percent of all appeals (Hipp, 2013: 44–45).

Writing about the United States, Gould et al. have found that it is the punitive culture in the state or judicial district where a case is heard which is often crucial to whether an innocent charged person will be convicted or will, through dismissal or acquittal, escape as a 'near miss'. They found that officials in the more punitive states, such as those with high-levels of imposition of the death penalty 'may be more likely to assume the defendant's guilt' and 'overlook or undervalue evidence that contradicts the assumption of guilt'. On the other hand, 'defendants in less punitive jurisdictions might benefit from a law enforcement or legal community willing to consider exculpatory theories or evidence' (Gould et al., 2014: 492, 497).

5. AN ANALYSIS OF THE PRACTICE OF JUDGMENT REASONS AND THEIR UTILITY IN PREVENTING THE CONVICTION OF THE INNOCENT

5.1 Justifying Judgments of Guilt: *Intime Conviction* Plus Reasons

Many of the older codes still speak of *intime conviction*, or decisions based on 'free conviction' or 'free evaluation of the evidence', which on first blush smacks of a very personal, even psychological approach to evaluating the evidence. In France § 427 CCP provides that 'offenses may be established by any type of evidence and the judge decides according to his inner conviction'. In Spain § 741 CCP allows judges to 'appreciate the evidence admitted at trial according to their conscience'. In Germany § 261 CCP allows the judge to decide according to his or her 'free conviction derived from the content of the trial'.

Although the older codes require 'reasons' (§ 267 CCP-Germany; § 485 CCP-France; § 741 CCP-Spain), they give no clear direction to the court for the decision as to the *facts*, in other words, why it believed one witness over another, drew certain conclusions from circumstantial evidence and not others, felt the defendant's confession was credible, etc. The court normally only had to lay out the evidence which it found to be true and then give reasons for its legal qualification of those facts.

Stricter requirements, however, have been enforced through the jurisprudence of the high courts. The Spanish Constitutional Court held in a judgment of July 4, 2001, that: 'Every judgment of conviction must, in addition to indicating the evidence upon which it is based, also evaluate the evidence and give sufficient reasons subject to the rules of logic and experience' (STC 49/1966, 180 BJC 133, 137–38 (2001)). The German Constitutional Court in 2003 wrote about the quality of reasons required in a case based on eyewitness identification. The Court required

> a comprehensive evaluation of the evidence as to all evidentiary questions, which, according to material law, are critical to the decision … Not only the direct evidence must be presented, but also the circumstances essential to its evaluation (i.e., as to the credibility of witnesses and the believability of their statements) must be clarified within the framework of the evidence-taking and be made an object of the subsequent evaluation. (BVerfG, 2 BVR 2045, 2003 StV 293 (April 30, 2003), para. 35)

In Italy § 546(e) CCP, enacted in 1988, requires that the judgment of conviction contain the charges and 'a concise exposition of the factual and legal reasons upon which the decision is based, with an indication of the evidence which forms the basis of the decision itself and an enunciation of the reasons why the judge held the contrary evidence to be not reliable'. In a similar fashion, § 307(1, 2) CCP-Russia, enacted in 2001, requires that the judgment include a 'description of the criminal act, proclaimed by the court to have been proved' and the 'evidence, upon which the arguments of the court in relation to the accused are based and reasons why the court rejected other evidence'.

5.2 Justifying Judgments of Guilt: *Intime Conviction*, Special Verdicts on the Facts, Reasons, and Instructions to the Lay Members of the Panel

All courts which must provide reasons first lay out the facts they have determined to be true, which constitute the elements of the charged crime, or which might trigger an excuse, justification, or aggravating or mitigating circumstances. In the traditional European jury courts, the special verdict, or question list, contained factual assertions corresponding to these key juridical facts, which the juries answered either in the affirmative or negative. Juries did not have to give additional reasons for why they made these findings of fact – their *intime conviction* was sufficient. It was up to the professional bench then to more or less 'automatically' apply the *nomen iuris* to the facts found proved, and give reasons for this legal subsumption and for its choice of sentence. The professional bench was not allowed to question the jury's findings on the facts.

France's first instance jury court, the *cour d'assises*, which was converted into a mixed court in 1941, and is today composed of six lay and three professional judges (§ 296(1) CCP-France), still uses this form of question list (§§ 348–51 CCP-France). The new Russian and Spanish jury courts also re-adopted the special question-list verdicts, which were used in their 19th-century jury courts, and Austria, Belgium, Ireland, and Norway, additionally use them, (*Taxquet v. Belgium*, ECHR-GC, No. 926/05, 16 Nov. 2010, § 49).

The court in § 92 of *Taxquet* made it clear that well-formulated question lists and good targeted instructions to the jury would obviate the necessity of supplying additional reasons. Since the *Taxquet* decision, the Norwegian Supreme Court has ruled that its system of question lists and instructions is sufficient so as to not require its juries to give separate reasons, whereas the Belgian jury and the French *cour d'assises* must now give reasons along with their verdicts (Thaman, 2011: 663–664).

Pursuant to § 347 CCP-France, and in Belgium as well, the judge was not allowed to comment on the evidence or give the jury any public instructions, other than the admonition to decide according to *intime conviction* without being bound by any rules of evidence.

The new Russian and Spanish laws do, however, require jury instructions. In Spain, the judge may not summarize the evidence, but is allowed to explain the substantive criminal law to the jurors and how it applies to the questions they must answer. There are, however, no instructions as to how certain types of evidence should be weighed and many judges do not effectively explain the substantive criminal law to the jurors (Thaman, 1998: 353–356). In Russia, the judge is required to summarize the evidence in a neutral fashion, and also instructs as to the substantive criminal law applicable in the case, and as to the presumption of innocence and the burden of proof (Thaman, 1995: 123–124).

In England and Wales the judge summarizes the evidence and can also give his or her view on its strength, which can greatly influence the jury's decision. He or she also instructs the jury on the applicable law and on rules of evidence that may apply to the case, including the need to prove guilt beyond a reasonable doubt (Sprack, 2011: 345–347). In the US judges seldom summarize the evidence, but they do give detailed pattern jury instructions explaining the elements of the charged offenses and any pleaded excuses or justifications as well as the presumption of innocence and proof beyond a reasonable doubt. Jury instructions also advise juries on how to evaluate certain kinds of evidence.

In Italian and German mixed courts, however, there are no question lists and no special formalities for instructing the lay assessors on the law. There is no public instruction on the law to be applied. One never knows whether the judge's discussion of the law was correct, whether the decision was unanimous, or whether the lay judges outvoted the professional judges, due to the strict confidentiality of deliberations. Thus, this type of European mixed court is as much a 'procedural Sphinx' as the American jury (Damaška, 1997: 44).

The most innovative aspect of the new Spanish jury law is the requirement that the jury articulate a 'succinct explanation of the reasons why they have declared, or refused to declare, certain facts as having been proved' (Thaman, 1998: 364).

5.3   Justifying Judgments of Acquittal

If the defendant is acquitted, § 267(5) CCP-Germany provides that the 'judgment reasons must reveal, whether it was not proved that the accused was the person who committed the crime, or for what reasons the act, which was deemed to have been proved, was considered not to be punishable'. In Russia § 305 CCP requires that the judgment includes, *inter alia*, the 'reasons for acquitting the defendant and the evidence, supporting them' as well as 'the reasons, why the judge rejected the evidence presented by the prosecution'.

From the time of the passage of the Spanish jury law, many commentators maintained that requiring juries to give reasons for their acquittal verdicts would violate the presumption of innocence. A well-conceived question list and the answers of the jurors in rejecting the proof of the constituent elements of the charged crimes would, in their opinions, sufficiently reveal the jurors' reasoning process. Some courts, in the first years of the new Spanish jury system, considered it enough for the jury to express their doubt as to the convincing nature of the evidence because the presumption of innocence did not require proof of innocence (Thaman, 2011: 655–656).

However, this 'flexible' approach in cases of acquittal was rejected by the Spanish Constitutional Court in 2004. In the case of *Moisés Macía Vega*, the court maintained that reasons for convictions had to be 'more rigorous' than those for acquittals, because 'when other fundamental rights are at play – and, among those, when the right to liberty and the presumption of innocence are implicated – the requirement of reasons acquires particular intensity and thus we have reinforced the required canon'.

Nonetheless, the court stressed that an acquittal cannot be a result of 'pure decisionism', without 'taking account of the *why* of it'. Otherwise there would be a violation of the 'general principle of the prevention of arbitrariness'. The court held that 'the new law requires more than just a clearly formulated and answered special verdict'.

[It] remains absolutely necessary to explain, even if in an elemental and succinct manner, why one accepts some declarations and rejects others, why one attributes greater credibility to some over others, why one prefers one statement made in the police station to others made at trial, and that a part or parts of different contradictory declarations of the defendants should prevail, and why, over the rest. (STC 169/2004, §§ 6, 8 Fundamentos jurídicos)

The President of the Constitutional Court, María Emilia Casas Baamonde, joined by two other justices, dissented, arguing that to apply the canon of judgment reasons to the jury would denature the institution. With regard to the presumption of innocence, she wrote:

When one is dealing with judgments of acquittal, to demand an exteriorization of the reasons for finding the existence of evidence sufficient to declare innocence presupposes an inversion of the understanding of the fundamental right to a presumption of innocence. It is guilt which must be proved, not innocence, and when it is not done, the defendant is presumed innocent, it being the constitutional burden of the prosecution to present evidence of the guilt of the accused and it is sufficient for the trier of fact to acquit based on reasonable doubt as to the sufficiency of the incriminating evidence necessary for a conviction. Neither the Constitution nor the Jury Law require the existence of sufficient evidence to justify the innocence of the defendant. (STC 169/2004, §§ 1, 3, voto particular)

In the notorious Spanish jury case of *Otegi*, the only issue was the mental state of the defendant when he shot two Basque policemen to death. The jury, in answering the long special verdict consisting of 98 questions, clearly adopted by majority vote the theory of the defense that Otegi was drunk (his blood alcohol content upon arrest was .15), and that this, combined with psychological features of his personality, completely negated his capacity to formulate the intent to kill (Thaman, 2011: 636–639). The Spanish Constitutional Court, however, reversed the acquittal saying that the 'proof of facts cannot be supplemented by the logical force of the connection of the answers which only affirm or negate the historical reality of the evidence, for it is necessary to add the reasons which explain the development or consolidation of the jury's decision' (Thaman, 2011: 660).

When proof of guilt depends on an inference as to the defendant's mental state, such as knowledge that he is transporting controlled substances, or intent, rather than negligence or accident in a homicide case, triers of fact may of course rely on the testimony of the defendant, if offered, to acquit in the exercise of 'free evaluation of the evidence'. The Spanish Constitutional Court, in my opinion, was correct when it stated:

> It can happen that the same facts proved can permit of hypotheses as to diverse conclusions or different interpretations can be offered at the trial as to the same facts. In light of these same criteria one must examine the version which the accused offers in relation to the facts. Certainly, he need not demonstrate his innocence and even the fact that his version of what occurred is not convincing or is contradicted by the evidence is not enough to consider him to be guilty. But his version constitutes a fact which the judge must accept or reject with reasons. (STC 174/1985 of Dec. 27, 1985, BJC (1986-57), RA-415, at 53, 59)

The German doctrine, however, appears to require the trier of fact to prove in the reasons that the defendant's rendition of events was true, to justify an acquittal. I believe this approach ignores the presumption of innocence.

For instance, in a decision of January 18, 2011, the German Supreme Court overturned the acquittal of a driver, who had claimed he did not know the contents of four large bags of marijuana he had transported. The Supreme Court held that the trier of fact may not simply acquit based on exculpatory testimony of the accused, only because there is no direct evidence which contradicts it. It must, 'based on an evaluation of the totality of the evidence, come to its judgment as to the correctness or incorrectness of the defense [lack of knowledge]. This is even more so the case, when there is objective evidence which weighs against the correctness of the accused's defense' (BGH, 1 StR 600/10, NStZ 5 (2011), 302–303).

The German Supreme Court on March 11, 2010, also overturned the acquittal of a woman for having intentionally inflicted injuries on her four-year-old son. The trial court had a reasonable doubt as to guilt based on her testimony that the injuries occurred from a fall in the bathtub and her clumsy attempt to remove him from the tub and the testimony of an expert medical witness that the injuries could have been caused in the way described by the defendant. The child relied on familial privilege and did not testify. The Supreme Court said that the reasons given by the trial court were sufficient on their face, but nonetheless found error because the trial court in its reasons failed to investigate the 'history and personality of the defendant', although it recognized, as is the case in the US, that such information is mainly relevant for sentencing after a finding of guilt (BGH 4 Str 22/10, 10 NStZ 2010, 529). In other words, the court, using its inquisitorial powers, should have probed the character of the defendant in search of a motive for guilt, a seeming violation of the presumption of innocence.

I also disagree that acquittals should be accompanied by reasons so that the judgment will be comprehensible to the general public, the victim, or the public prosecutor – an argument made in Spain based on Art. 120(3) of the Constitution which requires reasoned judgments. This would imply that the prosecutor, victim, and even the public, have protected rights to due process in criminal cases similar to those enjoyed by defendants, a view shared by some voices in the European literature (Moos, 2010: 77). If an acquittal in a criminal case can be overturned because of a violation of the victim's due process right to adequate reasons, prosecutors and judges can exploit this situation to invalidate decisions with which they do not agree, and even collude to violate the rights of victims to achieve this purpose, a practice which is not uncommon in the Russian jury courts (Thaman, 2007: 370–375).

5.4   The Inadequacy of Judgment Reasons and the Need for Formal Rules of Evidence

5.4.1   Introduction

It has been said that 'free evaluation of the evidence', not to speak of *intime conviction*, had to give way to formal rules of evidence in order to avoid arbitrariness (Geipel, 2008: 58). The German Constitutional Court has intimated as well that rules should be developed for particularly troublesome types of evidence:

> Although the evaluation of the evidence is, according to the law, 'free', that is, not subject to rules of evidence …, the case law of the high court has developed principles for the evaluation of the evidence and its formulation in the judgment reasons out of scientific rules of experience, especially derived from criminalistic, forensic and psychological investigations, which if not followed will have, as a consequence, reversal in cassation. This is true especially for evidentiary situations which – constitutionally – present heightened demands on the evaluation of the evidence, such as, *inter alia*, judging a hearsay declarant …, cases in which the testimony of one witness is contradicted by that of another … as well as cases of identification. (BVerfG, 2 BVR 2045, 2003 StV 293 (April 30, 2003), para. 37)

Yet the 'scientific rules of experience' derived from 'criminalistic, forensic and psychological investigations' have not led, as one might have thought, to rules requiring significant corroboration for some of the most questionable forms of evidence.

5.4.2   Cases without confessions in which identity is proved based on circumstantial evidence

Although the formal rules in the *Carolina* and other ancient codes are no longer acceptable, the rule requiring at least two credible eyewitnesses to prove a circumstance from which guilt may be inferred contains a seed of truth. Today courts are too quick to allow inferences of guilt from pieces of circumstantial evidence which are of themselves ambiguous or shaky, if not fabricated by investigative officials or others.

In the *Wanninkhof* case, the Spanish Supreme Court overturned the conviction of Dolores Vásquez for the murder of 19-year-old Rocío Wanninkhof, because the jury provided no coherent reasons for a guilty verdict based on the flimsiest of circumstantial evidence following a merciless media campaign which stressed the defendant's lesbian relationship with the victim's mother. After the reversal of her conviction, the real culprit murdered another girl and was linked by DNA to the murder of Wanninkhof (Thaman, 2011: 639–643). Spanish Supreme Court judge

Perfecto Andrés Ibáñez found that the jury, by just listing the evidence they relied on in convicting the innocent Dolores Vásquez, committed reversible error. He noted that 'there being no eyewitnesses to the death of the victim nor of the subsequent manipulation of the body, the testimonies heard by the jury have no direct relation to these facts'. Thus, the jury should have 'concretized the *what* of what was said for each of the witnesses and experts which it used to, in a reasoned fashion, place the criminal action on the shoulders of the defendant and *why*' (STS 279/2003; Thaman, 2011: 653).

The Spanish Constitutional Court, in a case predating the jury law, also made it clear that 'in order to trace the distinction between one hypothesis and another, that is, between the existence of a true piece of circumstantial evidence capable of rebutting the presumption of innocence and the presence of simple suspicions', the circumstances, from which one may deduce guilt, must be 'completely proved' (that is, beyond a reasonable doubt), because 'no certainties may be constructed on the basis of simple probabilities' (STC 174/1985 of Dec. 27, 1985).

The law in California is similar to that in Spain. In cases based on circumstantial evidence, the jury is instructed that each piece of circumstantial evidence that is necessary to prove guilt must be proved beyond a reasonable doubt and that if the circumstantial evidence gives rise to two reasonable inferences, one of guilt and the other of innocence, then the inference of innocence must be adopted and the defendant acquitted (CALJIC, No. 2.01).

The Supreme Court of Germany, in a decision of December 6, 1998, set aside the decision of a mixed court to acquit *Monika Weimar* of the murder of her two children. The acquittal had been based on the fact that the circumstantial evidence failed to convince the fact-finders that the defendant, and not her husband, killed the children. This case attracted great media attention in Germany and it was quite clearly a case where the lay assessors prevailed in the vote over the professional judges. An alleged early morning identification of the children by a married couple was crucial for the Supreme Court in placing guilt on the defendant rather than her husband, because it would have undermined the defendant's contention that the husband had killed the children during the night. The trial court's doubts as to guilt were based, not only in the inadequate lighting and brevity of the observation by the married couple, which tended to undermine the accuracy of the identification, but also on the absence of a plausible motive for the defendant to kill her children. Yet the opinion of the trial court, written most likely by a dissenting judge, said that it was 'scarcely imaginable' that the couple could have been mistaken or could have lied about the identification.

The Supreme Court, while recognizing that '[i]f the court acquits a defendant because it cannot overcome doubts as to his identity as the perpetrator, then this must be accepted as a rule by the court of cassation', explained when faulty judgment reasons can constitute 'legal error':

> This is the case in a substantive legal sense if the evaluation of the evidence is contradictory, unclear, or fraught with gaps or violates laws of thought or secure axioms of experience. Evidentiary conclusions of the trier of fact are also subject to attack if they reveal that the court placed over-stretched demands on the formation of the inner conviction necessary to convict and thereby fails to recognize that an absolute certainty, which of necessity compels the intellect to exclude the opposite and is doubted by no one, is not required; rather a measure of confidence suffices which is sufficient according to life experience and excludes only reasonable doubt and not doubt based on conceptual theoretical possibilities ... (Thaman, 2008a: 209–213)

Since the reporting judge had said the identification was more than likely credible, then the decision to acquit was contradictory. There was, of course, no verbatim record of the trial, which might have allowed the court of cassation itself to evaluate the strength of the identification.

In a more recent case, the German Supreme Court also proffered what could be called the 'mega-evaluation' model for giving reasons in circumstantial evidence cases:

> If there are several sources of evidence, it does not suffice to deal with them individually. The individual piece of evidence must rather be placed in a mega-evaluation with all other circumstantial evidence. Only the evaluation of the totality of the evidentiary material will indicate whether the judge arrived at his conviction as to the guilt of the accused and the fact determinations which support it in an error-free manner. Even when none of the circumstantial evidence, by itself, would suffice to prove that the accused was the perpetrator, there is a possibility, that it, when viewed in its totality, could lead the trier of fact to the corresponding conviction. (BGH, 1 Str 114, NStZ 2012, 112)

The problem with the 'mega-evaluation' approach is that there does not seem to be a requirement that each piece of the circumstantial evidence be proved beyond a reasonable doubt, before it can be a source of a guilt inference. A similar approach was also applied in the notorious case of Amanda Knox and Rafaele Sollecito, who were charged with the murder of an English student, Meredith Kercher, while she was studying in Perugia, Italy. As in the German *Weimar* case, this was a case based on purely circumstantial evidence, where there was an alternative suspect for the court to consider, and no clear motive for the killing.

Knox was an American student who shared an apartment with the victim, and Sollecito was her boyfriend. A third suspect, Rudi Guede, was also charged and was convicted of the murder, after he stipulated that he be tried pursuant to an abbreviated procedure based on the investigative file of the case. Biological traces from Guede were found at the crime scene and on the body of the victim. Knox and Sollecito, who always denied their guilt, were first convicted by the Italian mixed court, the *corte di assisi*, but they appealed and won a new trial before the *corte di assisi di appello*, also a mixed court, which then acquitted them. But on March 26, 2013, the Italian cassational court, in a 74-page opinion, overturned the acquittal based on faulty judgment reasons.

The guilty judgment in the first trial was based on the totality of the circumstantial evidence, *inter alia*: that Knox had a key to the crime scene (she lived there); that she provided a false alibi when interrogated by the police; that someone faked a burglary of the crime scene; that Knox and Sollecito left biological traces at the crime scene; that a drug addict testified he saw Knox and Sollecito near the crime scene around the time of the crime; that Knox in the early morning after the crime perhaps bought detergent in a market near her boyfriend's home (perhaps to wash bloodstained clothing); that their alibi, that they were in Sollecito's home the entire night of the crime, was discounted by the testimony of the drug addict and the store owner; that a trace from Sollecito was found on the bra of the victim; that the blood of Knox was found on a knife in the home of Sollecito; and, finally, that Guede reportedly told his cellmate that Knox killed the victim during sexual games.

The appeals court called new expert witnesses and evaluated their testimony. By the time of the second trial, the cellmate of Guede had withdrawn his testimony. The appeals court rejected the statements of the drug addict and the store owner on grounds of credibility, *inter alia*, because they were offered to the authorities long after the crime occurred. The appeals court also had doubts as to the biological traces because of the possibility of contamination as the knife and the bra of the victim were only found 40 days after the crime and thus were not credible pieces of evidence.

The Court of Cassation criticized the appeals court due to its 'parcellized and atomistic evaluation of the circumstantial evidence', because it considered them 'one at a time and discarded them based on their demonstrative potential, without a broader and completer evaluation' (Cass. Pen., sez. un., 26 marzo 2013, n. 422/13, 40).

In overturning the acquittal, the Court of Cassation instructed the court on remand on page 73 of the opinion to conduct: 'a global and unitary examination of the circumstantial evidence', through which it should be ascertained 'whether the relative ambiguity of each piece of evidence can be resolved, for in a comprehensive evaluation each piece of circumstantial evidence is added to, and integrates itself with the others. The result of such an osmotic evaluation will be decisive, not only to demonstrate the presence of the two defendants at the scene of the crime, but also to eventually delineate the subjective position of the accomplices of Guede'. The court then suggests that this would show that the victim was 'forced into an erotic game by a group, which went out of control'.

The Court of Cassation, at page 41 of the opinion, seems to argue that a totality of weak circumstantial evidence, the kind which has contributed to the conviction of innocents in the US (statements of unreliable informants, or admissions by the defendant arguably induced by coercive or deceptive police tactics, etc.), could still lead to a finding of guilt, using the Latin saying 'quae singula non probant, simul unita probant'.

As in the *Weimar* case in Germany, the third mixed court convicted Knox and Sollecito based on the same questionable circumstantial evidence, but then, oddly, proffered an entirely new motive for the killing which had nothing to do with erotic group sex. Knox now supposedly killed Amanda Kercher with the help of Sollecito and Guede after an argument (Povoledo, 2014). In late March 2015 the Italian Court of Cassation reversed the convictions of Knox and Sollecito and entered final judgments of acquittal (Povoledo, 2015). The Court of Cassation (5th Section) pointed to 'clamorous breakdowns or investigative "amnesia" and culpable lapses in investigative activity' which led to a record which could not constitute proof beyond a reasonable doubt (Cass. Penale, No. 36080/2015, para. 4)

In both the *Weimar* and the *Knox* cases the courts of cassation would not let acquittals stand, despite the lack of a clear motive for attributing guilt to the defendants, and despite the existence of an alternative suspect. In my opinion, the 'mega-evaluation' approach to circumstantial evidence is too fuzzy a doctrine to use to squash an acquittal, especially when the jurisprudence is unclear on the standard for proving the circumstances from which guilt might be inferred. Yes, Amanda Knox and Monika Weimar might very well have killed the young victims – but they just as well may not have!

5.4.3   Rules relating to credibility: witness against witness

'Witness against witness' cases often are cases of acquaintance rape and provide great challenges to judges and juries alike. Proof beyond a reasonable doubt is often difficult to achieve and convincingly justify in a reasoned opinion.

On March 14, 2012, the German Supreme Court reversed a defendant's conviction for anal rape and infliction of serious bodily injury against his former girlfriend, a drug addict. The defendant claimed consent.

The Court, referring to settled doctrine, wrote:

> In cases in which testimony of one witness conflicts against testimony of another witness, the trier of fact must realize that the testimony of the single prosecution witness must be subject to a special credibility testing, because the accused in such cases has few avenues of defense through his own statements. ... [T]he judgment reasons must reveal, that the trier of fact took account of all circumstances which influenced its decision and included them in its considerations.

The Court then reversed the conviction, finding that the trial court 'did not illustrate and discuss the reasons why the aggrieved party was unable to give a more exact temporal sequence of the acts', finding the explanation in the reasons 'too superficial ...' (BGH 5 StR 63/12, StV 2013, 7).

The case of *Horst Arnold* was an acquaintance rape case based on 'witness against witness' testimony without any corroboration, where the defendant denied the act ever took place and the Supreme Court rubber-stamped the wrongful conviction without as much as an opinion. One can see that, in such cases, the absence of a rule requiring corroboration is a green light to wrongful convictions.

American law once had a corroboration requirement in rape cases, which, embedded in a series of other procedural hurdles to rape prosecutions, was rightly attacked by feminists and has, in all but perhaps two States, disappeared from American law (Denno, 2003: 214).

The Model Penal Code (1962) § 213.6(5) incorporated such a rule:

> No person shall be convicted of any felony under this Article upon the uncorroborated testimony of the alleged victim. Corroboration may be circumstantial. In any prosecution before a jury for an offense under this Article, the jury shall be instructed to evaluate the testimony of a victim or complaining witness with special care in view of the emotional involvement of the witness and the difficulty of determining the truth with respect to alleged sexual activities carried out in private.

I believe the error of the Model Penal Code was to have limited corroboration requirements to rape cases, rather than all 'witness against witness' felonies. It should also be noted, that the corroboration rule only related to felony rape, which in several states at the time was still a capital offense and, at the time, that ultimate punishment was effectively reserved for African-Americans accused of raping white women.

Although the Supreme Court declared that rape was no longer a capital offense in *Coker v. Georgia*, 433 U.S. 584, 592 (1977), the punishments for rape have skyrocketed in the US since the 1960s and forcible rape is punishable by life imprisonment in some states, for instance Missouri (V.A.M.S. § 566.030(1, 2)).

5.4.4 Rules relating to eyewitness identification

The US Supreme Court cited Justice Frankfurter in the landmark case of *United States v. Wade*, 388 U.S. 218, 228 (1967): 'What is the worth of identification testimony even when uncontradicted? The identification of strangers is proverbially untrustworthy. The hazards of such testimony are established by a formidable number of instances in the records of English and American trials'. Seventy-two percent of the wrongful convictions discovered by DNA analysis since 1989 were due in whole or in part to erroneous eyewitness testimony (Innocence Project, 2016). Yet despite the scientifically verified untrustworthiness of such evidence, in most if not all US states a conviction may stand even if based on uncorroborated eyewitness testimony. Many states still do not allow expert testimony regarding the dangers of eyewitness testimony or jury instructions informing the jury of its inherent unreliability (Thompson, 2008: 1514). For decades, however, the landmark decision of *Regina v. Turnbull* [1977] 1 Q.B. 224, 228–231 has required such instructions in England and Wales.

Spanish courts have generally required less rigorous reasons for guilt decisions in cases based on direct evidence, but one must also ask, as does Perfecto Andrés Ibáñez, whether identification testimony by alleged eyewitnesses is not really circumstantial evidence, because it is based on a conclusion deduced from factors such as the memory of a person's appearance, the time elapsed between crime and identification, the emotional distortions of the crime, etc. (Andrés Ibáñez, 2009: 50). Rafael Ricardi served 13 years after being wrongfully convicted in Cádiz of rape due to mistaken identification and a false DNA comparison (Espinosa, 2014). In the judgment reasons of the trial court, one reads that the identity of Ricardi as the rapist was proved by the 'statements of the victim' which were 'so clear, emphatic and errorless' that they 'leave no room for doubt'. For the judge, the identifications by voice and sight, were, even without the spurious corroboration given by the bad DNA evidence, 'such direct evidence which alone destroyed the presumption of innocence' and were sufficient for a conviction (Sentencia No. 125/96, Fundamentos de Derecho, ¶ 2, Audiencia Provincial de Cádiz, October 21, 1996).

It has been recently suggested that a rule requiring corroboration of eyewitness identification testimony in robbery cases should be introduced (Thompson, 2008: 1524–1526). There is, however, no reason to limit a corroboration rule to robberies. If a type of evidence is inherently suspect, it should not, without corroboration, be sufficient for proof beyond a reasonable doubt, even if the trier of fact, in its *intime conviction* harbors no subjective doubts.

5.4.5 Rules relating to corroboration of confessions or admissions of the defendant

Even after the official abolition of torture, most criminal justice systems still rely on inducing confessions and other incriminating admissions in order to prove guilt in the first instance – either through police interrogation or sophisticated plea bargaining or confession bargaining systems. Police-generated confessions are not *per se* solid evidence. Some 27 percent of those who have been exonerated in the last years through DNA analysis have confessed or pleaded guilty at some time during the proceedings (Innocence Project, 2016). Police-induced false confessions to murder have recently led to convictions of innocent persons in the Netherlands in the 'Schiedam Park Murder Case', where the victim was a 10-year-old girl and in the 'Hilversum Showbiz Murder Case',[23] and in Germany in the case of Franz-Josef Sträter (Ulrich, 2000: 72–74). False confessions, even when uncorroborated, are a juggernaut which usually leads to conviction. An innocent person who makes incriminating statements or confessions stands an 88 percent chance of being convicted if he or she takes the case to trial (Gould et al., 2014: 495).

So, should a confession given to the police ever be sufficient for conviction without independent corroboration? Should a confession to the police given in the absence of counsel even be admissible? In Russia, if a defendant retracts a confession or admission given in the absence of counsel, it is categorically inadmissible at trial (§ 75(2)(1) CCP-Russia). Similar rules are recognized in Spain and Italy (§§ 178(1)(c), 350(6) CCP-Italy) (Thaman, 2013: 423–424). Against such strong exclusionary rules one should compare the wide-open approach of the US Supreme Court in *Illinois v. Perkins*, 496 U.S. 292, 298 (1990), which freely permits the use of questionable unrecorded admissions allegedly given by confined suspects to jailhouse informants, the kind of evidence which often appears in convictions of the innocent.

The American common law used to have a rule that a defendant's confession or admission was inadmissible unless the prosecutor had already proved the *corpus delicti* of the offense independent of the confession. The federal courts have moved, however, to a 'trustworthiness' approach, according to which 'proof of any corroborating circumstances is adequate which goes to fortify the truth of the confession or tends to prove facts embraced in the confession' (*Opper v. United States*, 348 U.S. 84, 92–93 (1954); Thompson, 2008: 1536–1537).

Even before secret judge-driven 'confession bargaining' (*Absprachen*) was revealed in 1984 to astonished members of the public and academia (Thaman, 2010: 387), German judges, who were convinced of the guilt of suspects at the beginning of the trial, used their power as fact-finders and sentencers to induce suspects to admit guilt in order to have a chance at a reduced sentence. As early as 1960, a judge who told a rape defendant who was claiming his innocence that if he didn't confess he had no chance at anything less than the maximum punishment, was challenged in cassation for violating the prohibition against extorting confessions. The defendant had, indeed, confessed in court but was nonetheless sentenced to the statutory maximum. The German Supreme Court rejected the appeal, claiming that the judge only held out a possibility of a sentence less than the maximum, but did not specifically promise it (BGHSt 14, 189, 190 (1960))! The practice of confession bargaining, codified in 2009 as § 257c CCP-Germany, leads to an abbreviation of the trial and a reduction of the evidence upon which the judge must base her judgment reasons. Practice has shown that, even in Germany, judges will accept even threadbare confessions as a basis for guilt and that these judgments will usually be upheld on appeal (Geipel, 2008, 43; Malek, 2011: 565–566).

6.   RETURN TO FORMAL RULES OF EVIDENCE?

Although higher courts do occasionally overturn convictions based on unconvincing judgment reasons, and, as in the *Wanninkhof* case, have occasionally saved an actually innocent person, innocent persons still slip through the cracks due to the arbitrary way the canon is applied and the weakness of the presumption of innocence both in the trial courts and in cassation.

I believe that protections in all systems, civil law and common law alike, must be stronger, and be centered in the substantive law and the law of evidence. Overcoming the presumption of innocence should require more than just 'some evidence of guilt', even if an able judge rapporteur can make a cogent argument why this evidence convinced him/her of the guilt of the defendant, or a jury in its *intime conviction* was convinced beyond a reasonable doubt. We should return to a modern equivalent of negative formal rules of evidence, which will at least prevent convictions for capital crimes and grave felonies based on weak (and perhaps falsified) circumstantial evidence, uncorroborated eye-witness testimony, uncorroborated admissions or confessions of the defendant, or uncorroborated assertions of the complaining witness, for instance, in sexual assault cases. Such evidentiary constellations should be insufficient for proof beyond a reasonable doubt and the imposition of long prison sentences, not to speak of death penalties.

Corroboration should be something more than just indicia of credibility of a witness, untethered from any physical or situational evidence. In the *Horst Arnold* case, for instance, there should have been at least some physical evidence that the complaining witness had been anally pen-etrated by someone, in addition to evidence linking the crime to the defendant. In a witness-against-witness case where consent is alleged as a defense, the issue of corroboration is more complex, but if punishments can be for decades or life, the trier of fact's subjective beliefs should not be enough.

In cases based on such unreliable forms of uncorroborated evidence, which amount to 'probable cause' but cannot of themselves undermine the presumption of innocence, the prosecutor, if personally convinced of guilt, could try to resolve the case with a plea bargain or consensual stipulation to a sentence of less than, say, six or eight years. If the defendant, however, demands a trial, then the prosecutor can try to prove guilt beyond a reasonable doubt based on traditional procedural arrange-ments in the respective jurisdiction: a mixed or professional court would have to find guilt beyond a reasonable doubt and give cogent reasons for the decision, or a jury would have to do the same in its general or special verdict, and perhaps also have to give some 'succinct' reasons for having done so. But even where a trial ensues, the maximum period of imprisonment should never exceed six, or perhaps eight years, where my proposed negative formal rules of evidence have not been met.

Before sending the case to a jury, trial judges in the US should be required themselves to act as gatekeepers and assess the strength of the evidence in all serious felony cases, whether or not a motion for a directed verdict of acquittal has been made by the defense, and this decision, as I have argued in the past (Thaman, 2011: 661–662), should be subject to appeal in the higher courts. This would force trial and appellate judges to look long and hard at the evidence and to develop more stringent criteria for what kinds of evidence are legally sufficient. The opinion of the trial judge would then also aid the appellate courts in marshaling the sometimes voluminous evidence present in verbatim transcripts when reviewing the sufficiency of the evidence before confirming a felony conviction.

NOTES

1. According to a recent study of 260 wrongful convictions, 87% of them were following jury trials, 5% following bench trials, and 7% following guilty pleas (Gould et al., 2014: 485).
2. I believe all states have provisions similar to F.R.Crim. P. 29, which provide for motions for a directed verdict of acquittal upon motion of the defense, or in the absence of competent defense counsel, even upon a *sua sponte* decision of the judge.
3. For a classic comparison of the civil law system, based in Roman law, Catholic canon law, French codified law, and the common-law systems, based in English law, see Merryman and Pérez-Perdomo (2007).
4. The Spanish jury law of 1995, anticipating *Taxquet*, required that juries give concise reasons for their verdicts. For a discussion of *Taxquet* case and the Spanish experience with reasoned jury verdicts, see Thaman (2011).
5. For an analysis of the post-*Taxquet* French experience with reasoned jury judgments, and whether common law juries may have to consider requiring jury reasons, see the chapter in this book by Mathilde Cohen.
6. A phrase used by Jenia Iontcheva Turner in her chapter in this book.
7. In 1997, only around 5.4% of German criminal cases were decided without *Absprachen* in a court which included lay participation (Dubber, 1997: 563). For more on penal orders, see Thaman (2012).
8. On the various statutory discounts allowed in modern plea bargaining laws, and the non-statutory court 'tariffs', see Thaman (2010: 350–355).
9. A recent study which compared known wrongful convictions with 'near misses', that is, cases in which innocent persons were charged but escaped punishment either through dismissals or acquittals, pinpointed eight reasons which contribute to wrongful convictions: (1) mistaken eyewitness identification; (2) false incriminating statements or confessions; (3) tunnel vision; (4) perjured informant testimony; (5) forensic error; (6) police error; (7) prosecutorial error; and (8) inadequate defense representation. Factors 4 through 7 all occur frequently as pieces of false circumstantial evidence which are used to bolster weak direct evidence (Gould et al., 2014: 479, 502).
10. This is more or less the maximum sentence allowed in most European and Latin American countries which have adopted guilty plea procedures (Thaman, 2010: 347–350).
11. Thus Thomas Jefferson remarked once in a letter to a friend: 'Were I called upon to decide, whether the people had best be omitted in the legislative or judiciary department, I would say it is better to leave them out of the legislative. The execution of the laws is more important than the making of them' (Abramson, 2000: 30).
12. On the question lists used in Russia and Spain, both in the 19th century and in their modern jury systems, see Thaman (1998: 321–353; 2007: 379–399).
13. Many commentators disputed whether this was even an attempt to incorporate the presumption of innocence, and in the first 30 years after the promulgation of the 1949 constitution, the section was never even mentioned by the Italian Constitutional Court (Illuminati, 1984: 11–12). As in English, the Italian language differentiates between *innocenza* and 'not guilty' (*non-colpevole*). In German, the word *unschuldig* applies to both.

14. See for example, 'New Evidence Wins Retrial for Inmate on Death Row 33 Years', *Japan Times*, April 6, 2005. http://www.japantimes.co.jp/news/2005/04/06/national/new-evidence-wins-retrial-for-inmate-on-death-row-33-years/#.VrSHCNErGrF.

15. In 2009, there were acquittals in only 0.5% of all cases, if one includes guilty pleas and dismissals; 2.8% of those charged were convicted after a full trial. *Federal Justice Statistics*, 2009, table 7, S. 9, http://www.bjs.gov/content/pub/pdf/fjs09.pdf.

16. It must be determined, whether the high acquittal rate in Italy can be explained by the fact that the trial judge, following the enactment of the 1988 CCP, is no longer 'file-prejudiced' (see next section) or whether the acquittals are due to procedural reasons, such as failure to bring the case to trial within the statutory time limits.

17. On the role of victims as private prosecutors and the role of popular prosecutors representing NGOs and other popular interests in the first year of Spanish jury trials, see Thaman (1998: 397–401).

18. Discussions with Supreme Court judge Perfecto Andrés Ibañez and Madrid Provincial Court judge Juan-José López Ortega in Madrid, June, 2014.

19. Generally on police lying in the US, see Slobogin (1996). On a series of wrongful convictions, including the notorious 'Guildford Four' and the 'Birmingham Six', which involved police fabrications and bogus expert testimony, see Mark Oliver, 'Miscarriages of Justice', *The Guardian*, Jan. 15, 2002, at http://www.theguardian.com/uk/2002/jan/15/ukcrime.markoliver.

20. *Appellazione* in Italian, *apelación* in Spain, *appellation* in France, *appeliatsiia* in Russian, *Berufung* in German.

21. The appeals court in the Amanda Knox case in Italy also re-convicted her without hearing much of the evidence. (Povoledo, 2014). This case will be discussed in more detail later in this chapter.

22. We will discuss, *infra*, the rather weak rules relating to corroboration of confessions. Many European systems will also not allow a conviction based primarily on hearsay testimony in violation of the right to confrontation, although the case law of the ECtHR is weak in this area. *Al-Kawaja & Tabery v. United Kingdom*, ECHR (GC), Nos. 26766/05, 22228/06, 15 Dec. 2011, § 146. If the 'sole' or 'decisive' evidence of guilt is provided by undercover informants or police officers whom the defendant has been unable to cross-examine, the ECtHR also requires corroboration. *Papadakis v. Former Yugoslav Republic of Macedonia*, ECHR, No.50254/07, 26 Feb. 2013, § 88.

23. On the 'Schiedam Park Murder': http://nl.wikipedia.org/wiki/Schiedammer_parkmoord. On the 'Hilversum showbiz' murder: http://wrongfulconvictionsblog.org/2013/04/10/update-on-knoops-innocence-project-the-netherlands/.

REFERENCES

Abramson, Jeffrey. 2000. *We, the Jury, the Jury System and the Ideal of Democracy.* Cambridge, MA: Harvard University Press.

Altenhain, Karsten. 2010. 'Absprachen in German Criminal Trials', in Stephen C. Thaman, ed., *World Plea Bargaining: Consensual Procedures and the Avoidance of the Full Criminal Trial.* Durham, NC: Carolina Academic Press, 157–179.

Andrés Ibáñez, Perfecto. 2005. *Los 'Hechos' en la Sentencia Penal* 173. Mexico City: Fontamara.

Andrés Ibáñez, Perfecto. 2009. *Prueba y convicción judicial en el proceso penal.* Buenos Aires: Hammurabi.

Boyne, Shawn Marie. 2014. *The German Prosecution Service. Guardians of the Law?* Heidelberg, New York, Dordrecht, London: Springer.

Carnevale, Stefania and Renzo Orlandi. 2000. 'Italien', in Monica Becker and Jörg Kinzig, eds., *Rechtsmittel im Strafrecht. Eine internationale vergleichende Untersuchung zur Rechtswirklichkeit und Effizienz von Rechtsmitteln*. Freiburg im Breisgau: Edition Iuscrim, 85–150.

Consejo General del Poder Judicial. 1998. *Informe del Consejo General del Poder Judicial sobre la Experiencia de la Aplicación de la vigente Ley Orgánica del Tribunal del Jurado*. Madrid: Consejo General del Poder Judicial.

Cour de Cassation. 2013. *Rapport annuel*, 649, https://www.courdecassation.fr/IMG/pdf/cour_de_cassation_rapport_2013.pdf.

Damaška, Mirjan R. 1997. *Evidence Law Adrift*. New Haven: Yale University Press.

Damaška, Mirjan R. 2001. 'Models of Criminal Procedure', 51 *Zbornik (collected papers of Zagreb Law School)* 477–516.

Death Penalty Information Center. 2016. 'Documents', http://www.deathpenaltyinfo.org/documents/FactSheet.pdf (last accessed February 13, 2016).

Denno, Deborah W. 2003. 'Why the Model Penal Code's Sexual Offense Provisions Should Be Pulled and Replaced', 1 *Ohio State Journal of Criminal Law* 207–218.

De Paúl Velasco, José Manuel. 2004. 'Presunción de inocencia e in dubio pro reo en el juicio ante el tribunal del jurado', in Luis Aguiar de Luque and Luciano Varela Castro, eds., *La Ley del Jurado: Problemas de Aplicación Práctica*. Madrid: Consejo General del Poder Judicial, 473–546.

Deppenkemper, Gunter. 2004. *Beweiswürdigung als Mittel prozessualer Wahrheitserkenntnis: Eine dogmengeschichtliche Studie zu Freiheit, Grenzen und revisionsgerichtlicher Kontrolle tatrichterlicher Überzeugungsbildung*. Göttingen: V & R Unipress.

Dubber, Markus Dirk. 1995. 'The German Jury and the Metaphysical Volk: From Romantic Idealism to Nazi Ideology', 43 *American Journal of Comparative Law* 227–271.

Dubber, Markus Dirk. 1997. 'American Plea Bargains, German Lay Judges and the Crisis of Criminal Procedure', 49 *Stanford Law Review* 547–605.

Elon, Menachem, Bernard Auerbach, Daniel D. Chazin and Melvin J. Sykes. 1999. *Jewish Law (Mishpat Ivri): Cases and Materials*. New York and San Francisco: Matthew Bender.

Esmein, A. 1913. *History of Continental Criminal Procedure with Special Reference to France*. Boston: Little, Brown & Co.

Espinosa, Pedro. 2014. 'Rafael Ricardi, el inocente que pasó 13 años en prisión', *El País*, June 6, 52.

Fallone, Antonio. 2012. *Il processo aperto: il prinzipio di falsificazione oltre ogni ragionevole dubbio nel processo penale*. Milan: Giuffrè.

Friedrichsen, Gisela. 2012. 'Ohne moralische Skrupel', *Der Spiegel*, July 16, 46–47.

Geipel, Andreas. 2008. *Handuch der Beweiswürdigung* 11. Münster: ZAP-Verlag.

Gould, Jon B., Julia Carrano, Richard A. Leo and Katie Hail-Jares. 2014. 'Predicting Erroneous Convictions', 99 *Iowa Law Review* 471–522.

Green, Thomas Andrew. 1985. *Verdict According to Conscience: Perspectives on the English Criminal Trial Jury, 1200–1800*. Chicago and London: University of Chicago Press.

Hipp, Ditmar. 2013. 'Karlsruher Lotterie', *Der Spiegel*, July 29, 44–45.

Hodgson, Jacqueline. 2005. *French Criminal Justice: A Comparative Account of the Investigation and Prosecution of Crime in France*. Oxford and Portland, OR: Hart Publishing.

Iacoviello, Francesco Mauro. 2006. 'Lo standard probatorio dell'al di là di ogni ragionevole dubbio e il suo controllo in cassazione', *Cassazione penale*, No. 1591, 3869–3884.

Illinois, State of. 2002. 'Commission on Capital Punishment Report', http://chicagojustice.org/foi/relevant-documents-of-interest/illinois-govenor-george-ryans-commission-on-capital-punishment/report_of_the_commission_on_capital_punishment_rec.

Illuminati, Giulio. 1984. *La presunzione d'innocenza dell'imputato* (6th edn). Bologna: Nicola Zanichelli.

Innocence Project. 2016. 'DNA Exonerations Nationwide' (last accessed February 13, 2016). http://www.innocenceproject.org/free-innocent/improve-the-law/fact-sheets/dna-exonerations-nationwide.

Johnson, David T. 2002. *The Japanese Way of Justice: Prosecuting Crime in Japan.* Oxford and New York: Oxford University Press.

Küper, Wilfried. 1967. *Die Richteridee der Strafprozeßordnung und ihre geschichtlichen Grundlagen.* Berlin: DeGruyter.

Langbein, John H. 1977. *Torture and the Law of Proof in Europe and England in the Ancien Régime.* Chicago and London: University of Chicago Press.

Malek, Klaus. 2011. 'Abschied von der Wahrheitssuche', 9 *Der Strafverteidiger* 559–567.

Mayer, Karlheinz. 1989. 'Grenzen der Unschuldsvermutung', in Hans-Heinrich Jescheck and Theo Vogler, eds., *Festschrift für Herbert Tröndle zum 70. Geburtstag am 24 August 1989.* Berlin and New York: Walter de Gruyter, 61–75.

McConville, Michael. 2011. *Criminal Justice in China. An Empirical Inquiry.* Cheltenham, UK and Northampton, MA, USA: Edward Elgar.

Merryman, John Henry and Rogelio Pérez-Perdomo. 2007. *The Civil Law Tradition: An Introduction to the Legal Systems of Western Europe and Latin America* (3rd edn). Stanford, CA: Stanford University Press.

Montesequieu. 1979. *De L'Esprit des Lois* (1757). Vol. 1. Paris: GF-Flammarion.

Moos, Reinhard. 2010. 'Die Begründung der Geschworenengerichtsurteile', 132 *Juristische Blätter* 73–87.

Povoledo, Elisabetta. 2014. 'Amanda Knox is Re-Convicted of Murder in Italy', *New York Times*, January 30, A9, http://www.nytimes.com/2014/01/31/world/europe/amanda-knox-trial-in-italy.html.

Povoledo, Elisabetta. 2015. 'Amanda Knox Acquitted of 2007 Murder by Italy's Highest Court', *New York Times*, March 28, A4, http://www.nytimes.com/2015/03/28/world/europe/amanda-knox-trial.html?rcf=world.

Rennig, Christoph. 1993. *Die Entscheidungsfindung durch Schöffen und Berufsrichter in rechtlicher und psychologischer Sicht.* Marburg: N.G. Elwert.

Schünemann, Bernd. 2000. 'Der Richter im Strafverfahren als manipulierter Dritter? Zur empirischen Bestätigung von Perseveranz- und Schulterschlußeffekt', 3 *Der Strafverteidiger* 159–165.

Slobogin, Christopher. 1996. 'Testilying: Police Perjury and What To Do About It', 67 *University of Colorado Law Review* 1037–1060.

Sprack, John. 2011. *A Practical Approach to Criminal Procedure* (13th edn). Oxford: Oxford University Press.

Thaman, Stephen C. 1995. 'The Resurrection of Trial by Jury in Russia', 31 *Stanford Journal of International Law* 61–274.

Thaman, Stephen C. 1998. 'Spain Returns to Trial by Jury', 21 *Hastings International & Comparative Law Review* 241–537.

Thaman, Stephen C. 2002. 'Comparative Criminal Law Enforcement: Russia', in Joshua Dressler, ed., *Encyclopedia of Crime and Justice*, Vol. I. New York: Macmillan Reference, 207–218.

Thaman, Stephen C. 2007. 'The Nullification of the Russian Jury: Jury-Inspired Reform in Eurasia and Beyond', 40 *Cornell International Law Journal* 357–428.

Thaman, Stephen C. 2008a. *Comparative Criminal Procedure: A Casebook Approach* (2nd edn). Durham, NC: Carolina Academic Press.

Thaman, Stephen C. 2008b. 'The Two Faces of Justice in the Post-Soviet Legal Sphere: Adversarial Procedure, Jury Trial, Plea-Bargaining and the Inquisitorial Legacy', in John Jackson, Máximo Langer and Peter Tillers, eds., *Crime, Procedure and Evidence in a Comparative and International Context: Essays in Honour of Professor Mirjan Damaška*. Oxford: Hart Publishing, 99–118.

Thaman, Stephen C. 2010. 'A Typology of Consensual Criminal Procedures: An Historical and Comparative Perspective on the Theory and Practice of Avoiding the Full-Blown Criminal Trial', in Stephen C. Thaman, ed., *World Plea Bargaining: Consensual Procedures and the Avoidance of the Full Criminal Trial*. Durham, NC: Carolina Academic Press, 297–399.

Thaman, Stephen C. 2011. 'Should Criminal Juries Give Reasons for their Verdicts? The Spanish Experience and the Implications of the European Court of Human Rights Decision in *Taxquet v. Belgium*', 86 *Chicago-Kent Law Review* 613–668.

Thaman, Stephen C. 2012. 'The Penal Order: Prosecutorial Sentencing as a Model for Criminal Justice Reform?', in Erik Luna and Marianne L. Wade, eds., *The Prosecutor in Transnational Perspective*. New York: Oxford University Press, 156–175.

Thaman, Stephen C. 2013. 'Balancing Truth Against Human Rights: A Theory of Modern Exclusionary Rules', in Stephen C. Thaman, ed., *Exclusionary Rules in Comparative Law*. Dordrecht, Heidelberg, New York and London: Springer, 403–446.

Thompson, Sandra Guerra. 2008. 'Beyond a Reasonable Doubt? Reconsidering Uncorroborated Eyewitness Testimony', 41 *U. C. Davis Law Review* 1487–1545.

Ulrich, Andreas. 2000. 'Wer tötete Johanna Schenuit?', *Der Spiegel*, June 19, 72–74.

STATUTES, ETC.

California Jury Instructions. Criminal (CALJIC), http://www.courts.ca.gov/partners/documents/calcrim_juryins.pdf.

Constitutio Criminalis Carolina. 1532. https://login.gmg.biz/earchivmanagement/projekt daten/earchiv/Media/1532_peinliche_halsgerichtsordnung.pdf.

PART III

DIACHRONIC COMPARISONS

A. Screening mechanisms

3. Anticipatory bail in India: addressing misuse of the criminal justice process?

Vikramaditya S. Khanna and Kartikey Mahajan[*]

1. INTRODUCTION

The Indian criminal justice system allows for the granting of bail to a person in anticipation of arrest (generally referred to as 'anticipatory bail').[1] In essence, a court can issue an order, prior to an arrest, stating that a person is to be immediately released on bail should that person be arrested for the offenses listed, or related to those listed, in the order.[2] This prevents a person from being taken into police custody, even for a few moments, while allowing a criminal investigation to continue. This unique concept is used with some regularity in India, but is rarely found, if at all, outside of South Asia.[3] Nonetheless, anticipatory bail's ubiquity and importance in India is highlighted by the number of Government reports, reform proposals, and Supreme Court of India decisions on it, which in turn suggests that this humble provision has greater impact than might appear at first blush. This chapter explores the development and operation of anticipatory bail in India in order to gain a deeper understanding of it and to provide a window into the investigative and adjudicative processes of the Indian criminal justice system.

Before embarking on that journey it may prove useful to highlight some fairly typical examples of when anticipatory bail is requested and to discuss, in a thumbnail manner, some of the key institutional features of the Indian civil and criminal justice systems that led to its development. We examine these in more detail in the chapter, but for now a quick overview provides a taste of when anticipatory bail is sought and how it fits within the architecture of the Indian criminal justice system.

Some of the earliest instances in which parties sought anticipatory bail arose during the British Raj in civil lawsuits involving inheritance or contract disputes. One of the civil parties would file a complaint with the police alleging criminal wrongdoing.[4] If the authorities decided to pursue the matter, this could lead to an arrest and criminal proceedings. The complaining party could then offer to drop the complaint in exchange for a favorable outcome in the civil matter. Of course, one need not have a prior civil suit in order for the criminal system to be misused. For example, a putative defendant may be concerned that the police might arrest him because they were being encouraged, or paid, to do so by a political rival. Such an arrest – for example, on corruption charges – would serve to embarrass and politically weaken him (for example, in advance of an election).[5] Similarly, the police might initiate an arrest and criminal investigation on their own, or at another person's behest, in order to extort something of value from the putative defendant.[6]

However, for these scenarios to present systemic problems, the police must (i) be willing and able to easily arrest someone and (ii) suffer few negative consequences for dropping a criminal matter, or failing to obtain a conviction, once the desired ulterior outcome (for example, settling a suit, embarrassing a rival or extorting money) has been achieved. As we shall see, the institutional landscape in India fostered both of these conditions.

Indeed, a number of factors favored such abuses. First, police arrest powers were not seriously constrained in India. The institutional design of the Indian Police, devised during the British Raj and largely in place today, led to the police being subject to political influence, while possessing wide discretionary arrest powers. Although perhaps effective in maintaining British control over India, this structure led to a lack of accountability, corruption, and mistrust of the police, coupled with a very weak standard of review for arrests. It also meant that there were few negative repercussions for the police if a criminal matter was dropped or otherwise failed.

Second, although the examples noted above suggest substantial private involvement in prosecutions, these were not private prosecutions of the kind seen in England.[7] Rather these were officially public prosecutions. Nonetheless, even though it was up to the police to decide whether to pursue a criminal allegation, private parties played an important and, at times, corrupting role.

Third, in theory, abuses of the arrest power and the criminal process could generate tort actions – such as malicious prosecution – which, if effective, could reduce the incentives to use the arrest power in these ways. However, these torts were (and remain) under-developed in India and the endemic delays in the Indian civil litigation process make tort actions largely unappealing as a way to curtail police abuse.

Against this institutional milieu (and malaise), the examples noted above could become frequent occurrences. This problem was exacerbated by the length of time – between 24 to 48 hours after an arrest – that it took to secure bail. This increased the cost and inconvenience to the arrested individual and heightened the potential for harassment and abuse. In light of these considerations, if the likely arrestee suspected a criminal complaint had been (or would be) filed against her, she might ask the court for anticipatory bail in order to avoid the embarrassment, delays and detention an arrest would otherwise bring with it.

In spite of this, courts were quite unlikely, prior to 1973, to grant anticipatory bail because there was no explicit statutory authority for it. However, in 1973 the Indian Code of Criminal Procedure was substantially amended and a new Section 438 was enacted allowing individuals to seek bail prior to arrest for more serious offenses (referred to as 'non-bailable' offenses). It was enacted primarily in response to concerns, as noted above, that the arrest power was being misused in India by politically connected individuals to target their rivals or as a method to extort money from others. Although there were conditions on the grant of anticipatory bail under Section 438, its enactment ushered in a new era in deterring the misuse of the arrest power and reducing its costs.

Under Section 438 the process of applying for anticipatory bail typically begins with the potential accused (the applicant) and her attorney approaching the appropriate court for an order. The court then decides, at its discretion, whether to have a full hearing and issue a final order (with both the applicant and law enforcement making their arguments) or bifurcate the proceedings into two steps – an interim order followed by a final order. A bifurcation might occur for a variety of reasons, such as the court wishing to have some additional time to consider whether to grant the final order. Although it is possible for the interim order stage to be *ex parte* (that is, without law enforcement being heard), that is not common as the courts would typically seek law enforcement's views even at the interim stage. If an *ex parte* interim order is granted, the court issues a notice to the prosecutor and the police to appear for a final order hearing shortly thereafter. For a final order the hearings are required to include both the applicant and law enforcement regardless of whether there was an interim order or not. The burdens of proof and evidentiary requirements for the hearings are largely up to the discretion of the court, but often focus on the likely merits of the case, the potential for misuse of the arrest power, whether the applicant is a serious flight risk, concerns about evidence tampering, and other matters that we discuss in greater depth later in this chapter. Generally, the court will require the applicant to cooperate with law enforcement as the investigation proceeds (at the interim and final order stages and thereafter) and to provide some assurance that she will not abscond (for example, by depositing her passport). If the applicant fails to meet these conditions, the anticipatory bail order may be rescinded by the court.

Anticipatory bail thus differs in important ways from the methods of regulating arrest powers in key Anglo-American jurisdictions. Although we discuss these later in the chapter, it may be useful to note some of these differences now. For example, anticipatory bail combines pre-arrest judicial oversight with the courts typically receiving information from both parties. Other Anglo-American jurisdictions usually do not combine these – they may have pre-arrest hearings, but those are usually *ex parte* with only law enforcement being heard, or they may have hearings where both sides are heard, but that is usually post-arrest. Examining these differences, and others, forms one of the key areas of discussion in this chapter.

In light of this, our chapter aims to explore the operation and effects of this unique method of curtailing abuses of the arrest power. We contextualize our inquiry by examining the historical development of the regulation of arrest powers in India and its impact on anticipatory bail.[8] We also contrast anticipatory bail with the ways in which other jurisdictions address abuse of the arrest power. Through this analysis valuable insights are gained into many aspects of India's criminal justice system and, in particular, the ways in which India balances the investigation of important crimes with the protection of an individual's liberty. Both of these concerns animate the regulation of arrest powers in India.[9]

Section 2 begins by describing the historical context leading to the enactment of anticipatory bail. In particular, this section stresses the role of the broad, and weakly constrained, arrest power in India and its misuse for political gain and extortion as the background against which anticipatory bail would come into existence. Section 3 examines how anticipatory bail is currently administered in India and the kinds of issues this has raised. Section 4 takes a comparative turn and discusses how India's regulation of arrest powers, and use of anticipatory bail, compares with the regulation of the arrest power in other jurisdictions. This section also discusses when anticipatory bail's combination of features may be useful to have and examines some other, potentially complementary, methods of reducing misuse of the arrest power that have been utilized in other jurisdictions. It suggests that even if India's legal standards for arrest were to become more aligned with global standards, there would probably still be some value in anticipatory bail in the Indian institutional context.

2. HISTORICAL BACKGROUND TO THE DEVELOPMENT OF ANTICIPATORY BAIL

Although the statutory provision authorizing anticipatory bail (AB) did not exist until 1973, the debate about whether pre-arrest bail should be available in India predates India's Independence in 1947. To explore the development of AB we divide our discussion into three time periods: (i) enactment of the Indian Police Act 1861 to Independence in 1947; (ii) Independence to the enactment of Section 438 of the Code of Criminal Procedure 1973 (CCP); and (iii) the developments from 1973 until now.

2.1 The Indian Police Act 1861 to Independence in 1947

The critical starting point for the debate on pre-arrest bail was the enactment of the Indian Police Act in 1861 after the defeat of the Indian Mutiny in 1857. The Police Act was promulgated not so much as a method to provide security to citizens and reduce crime, but rather as a method to secure British control over India (Arnold, 1976, 1992; Bayley, 1969; Verma, 2005). This was achieved in two broad steps – first, subjecting the police to political (that is, British) control and, second, granting the police broad discretionary powers, similar to those granted to paramilitary forces, with respect to the citizens of India. These police prerogatives included the arrest power (Arnold, 1976; Bayley, 1969; Law Commission of India (LCI), 2001).[10]

Political control was achieved in a number of ways, but perhaps most importantly by erecting a system of dual control: the Indian police not only reported to their own senior police officers, but also were under the general control of the District Magistrate/Collector of the province, who was a member of the Indian Administrative Service (IAS) (Verma, 2005). In this system greater control rested with the more politically attuned officer (the IAS officer) who had the ability to influence the career prospects of police officers and to order their transfer to different (and perhaps less pleasant) parts of India (Verma, 2005).

Wide discretionary powers were granted both by statute and by a fairly weak standard of judicial oversight of these powers. This was highly visible with respect to the arrest powers enumerated in Sections 41 to 60 and Sections 149 to 153 of the Code of Criminal Procedure 1898 (the predecessor to the CCP 1973). These provisions are striking in their breadth. In particular, the police could arrest, without a judicial warrant, any individual: (i) for allegedly committing a 'cognizable' offense; (ii) to prevent the commission of a cognizable offense; (iii) for possessing an implement of house-breaking; (iv) for being reasonably suspected of being in possession of stolen property; (v) for being in exigent circumstances, among other reasons.[11] An offense was 'cognizable' if it was listed in the First Schedule to the Code of Criminal Procedure. Commentary suggests that the basis for categorizing an offense as 'cognizable' was whether there was a

> need to arrest someone immediately ... in order to prevent the person from committing further offenses, the need to reassure the public ... about the effectiveness of the law and order machinery, the need of investigation and [it] may be, in some instances, the need to protect the offender from the wrath of the public and so on. (LCI, 2001: 23–24)

The need for immediate arrest also arose when a suspect was considered likely to abscond. Cognizability and arrest were thus intimately related with each other. Examples of cognizable offenses included being a member of an unlawful assembly, promoting enmity between classes, impersonating a public servant, and murder, amongst others (Goel, 1981).

These wide arrest powers were not, however, accompanied by much serious scrutiny, judicial or otherwise. For example, although early cases held that the arrest power was not to be used capriciously or unreasonably, it appears these cases only required the police officer to be *subjectively* satisfied that the arrest power was being used as intended (LCI, 2001). This was not difficult to satisfy. Moreover, even if the requirements for arrest were more objective, it seems unlikely that the police would suffer any serious sanction for making arbitrary arrests. First, bringing a criminal charge against a police officer generally requires prior government approval, which was highly unlikely to be forthcoming (LCI, 2001).[12] Second, bringing a civil action against a police officer may take quite some time in India's much delayed civil litigation system and still yield little given their relatively paltry pay in comparison to a potential damages award (Khanna, 2015; Verma, 2005). Third, bringing suit against the state, which has deeper pockets than a police officer, is likely to run into sovereign immunity claims (LCI, 2001). Fourth, although internal police department proceedings against an officer are plausible, they are exceedingly unlikely to produce sanctions (LCI, 2001; Verma, 2005). Finally, even the tort of malicious prosecution might be of little avail given the relatively under-developed state of tort law in India, the difficulty of succeeding on such a case, and the delays accompanying civil litigation in India (Balganesh, 2016; Khanna, 2015).[13] Thus, combining the subjective standard, the paucity of effective remedies, and the broad arrest powers granted to the police, the ground reality became a 'conferment of a vast, sometimes absolute and on some other occasions, an unguided and arbitrary power of arrest upon police officers' (LCI, 2001: 24).

Indeed, serious judicial oversight of arrest and custody was hardly expected for cognizable offenses unless the police considered it necessary to detain an arrested individual beyond 24 hours and then a Magistrate would need to be approached and would have to decide whether to authorize continued detention for up to 15 days.[14] Even then, if the magistrate did not approve of further detention the individual would be released and the criminal case would continue – much the same as if the court were to somehow find the arrest was illegal.[15] Thus, there did not appear to be much scope for monetary or other liability against the police.

The situation was hardly better for non-cognizable offenses, for which the police are supposed to obtain a judicial warrant before arresting an individual. For these offenses it is up to the Magistrate to determine whether to issue a summons for an individual to appear before it. This is typically done if the Magistrate finds that there is a *prima facie* case.[16] There is no additional arrest standard (for example, probable cause or reasonable suspicion) that needs to be met and in the end it is the Magistrate's discretion to issue a summons. Arrest warrants may also be issued, but for non-cognizable offenses the common practice is that summons are issued first and warrants may be issued if the non-cognizable offense carries a term of imprisonment exceeding two years and if the accused has not appeared after receiving a summons, or if there is reason to think the accused may abscond. Again these decisions are not required to meet a probable cause or reasonable suspicion standard.[17]

The weak oversight of the police was also one of the contributing factors to the police bearing few negative consequences for dropping criminal matters or failing to obtain convictions. Indeed, it has never been clear that low conviction rates lead to negative employment effects on police. This is due in part to the structure of the Indian Police and to the delays in the court system as well as the low conviction rate – hovering around 38 percent in 2012 for crimes under the Indian Penal Code 1860 (National Crime Records Bureau, 2012). Although scholars are exploring reasons for this (Khanna, 2015), for our purposes this means that a failure to obtain a conviction (or dropping a case) was unlikely to be as salient in India as compared to other countries with substantially higher conviction rates, and therefore was less likely to attract scrutiny.

Thus, combining broad arrest powers, little judicial oversight, political control and few negative effects of dropping (or losing) criminal cases, we have an environment ripe for greater misuse of the arrest power. Unsurprisingly, there were many complaints about the arrest power and some aggrieved individuals brought suit in the higher courts asking them to intervene and prevent detention or confinement by the police by granting anticipatory bail (AB).

For example, one case involved a dispute over how to divide the estate of an individual who died without a will. Although the estate was put into receivership one of the potential heirs filed a criminal complaint (alleging fraud amongst other things) that could have led to the arrest of the receiver and caused substantial harm to him. The receiver approached the court for AB hoping to avoid arrest. The court, although very skeptical of the complainant's charges, was in a difficult position because the Code of Criminal Procedure at that time (enacted in 1898) did not specifically authorize the granting of AB, which meant the courts had to decide whether they could grant it from their inherent powers. Although the various High Courts did not all agree, the majority view was that the courts did not have such powers.[18] The Privy Council settled the issue in 1945 and held:

> In India ... there is a statutory right on the part of the police to investigate the circumstances of an alleged cognizable crime without requiring any authority from the judicial authorities, and it would, as their Lordships think, be an unfortunate result if it should be held possible to interfere with those statutory rights by an exercise of the inherent jurisdiction of the Court. The functions of the judiciary and the police are complementary, not overlapping, and the combination of individual liberty with a due observance of law and order is only to be obtained by leaving each to exercise its own function, always, of course, subject to the right of the Court to intervene in an appropriate case when moved under Section 491, Criminal Procedure Code, to give directions in the nature of habeas corpus.[19]

Thus, prior to Independence, India had a police system subject to political influence, with broad discretionary arrest powers and little judicial oversight, leading to many complaints about its arbitrary and perhaps corrupt misuse (LCI, 2001).

2.2   Independence to Section 438 and Anticipatory Bail

In the first two decades after Independence, the Government of India made little change to the arrest powers of the police (indeed the Police Act 1861 is still the law, with some amendments, regulating the police). Thus, the institutional design issues – substantial political control, wide discretionary powers and little penalty for low conviction rates – persisted through Independence. Moreover, reform recommendations to require a judicial officer to review the grounds of arrest and for the police to record the reasons for the arrest were essentially rejected (LCI, 1967).[20] One commentator suggested that it may not have been thought practical to require a written warrant to arrest people accused of cognizable crimes (or to record the reasons for the arrest) in a country as large as India, which has substantial areas with relatively weak communications and transportation systems (Goel, 1981).

Although there have been substantial improvements in communications and transportation systems over the years, little changed in the regulation of arrest powers until the late 1960s when the Law Commission of India (LCI) – an entity created by the Government whose primary function is to work for law reform – began exploring the misuse of the arrest power (LCI, 1969).[21] One of the key concerns emanated from a perception that the arrest power was being used by politically connected individuals to target their rivals. This problem became more prominent in the late 1960s when the Congress party, which had ruled both centrally and in most states in India since Independence, lost power in several states leading to several coalition governments. Commentators note that the jostling to obtain, maintain, or regain power often led to increased political interference in institutions such as the police (Verma, 2005).[22] Indeed, the National Police Commission's second report in 1979 explicitly recognized the increasing politicization of the police and how this was corroding the faith of the public in the police and distorting basic police operations (National Police Commission (NPC), 1979).

In light of this, the LCI produced its 41st Report, which suggested the creation of a process of AB by statute. This was largely because:

> [S]ometimes influential persons try to implicate their rivals in false cases for the purpose of disgracing them or for other purposes by getting them detained in jail for some days. In recent times, with the accentuation of political rivalry, this tendency is showing signs of steady increase. Apart from false cases, where there are reasonable grounds for holding that a person accused of an offence is not likely to abscond, or otherwise misuse his liberty while on bail, there seems no justification to require him first to submit to custody, remain in prison for some days and then apply for bail.[23]

It is noteworthy that the recommendation is not targeted to just suspected false cases, but also other cases in which it appears reasonable to think the accused would not abscond or otherwise interfere in the investigation. This suggests the LCI was most concerned with the abuse of arrest powers and its deleterious effects on liberty interests, rather than simply reducing false cases. It is also interesting to note that, in spite of this focus on abuse, the LCI does not explicitly consider strengthening the tort of malicious prosecution, given that it seems more targeted to addressing abuses of the criminal system. As noted earlier, this was likely due in part to the state of tort law in India and because of the endemic delays in civil litigation, which would have made reforms to these torts perhaps not worth the candle without broader reforms to speed up litigation.

The concerns motivating the LCI report can, however, be broken down further. The first concern – which we call *political targeting* – arises when influential individuals orchestrate the arrest of their political rivals either to embarrass them or to keep them confined for a few days (an arrested individual can usually obtain bail in short order and hence the confinement may last only a few days).[24] However, even when the confinement is short, it could still cause considerable harm if inflicted at an untimely moment (for example, near an election or an important rally) and it can subject the accused to substantial stigma or to abuse while in police custody (a common concern in India).[25]

A second concern surrounds the misuse of the arrest power by the police or other third parties (even non-influential individuals) in order to intimidate or abuse a regular person for a few days so that corrupt payments or extortion can be collected. For example, an individual might encourage the police to arrest, confine, and 'rough up' Mr. X for a few days because that will lead to X paying a form of ransom to the individual who may share it with the police. One can refer to these as *extortion* or *corruption* concerns.[26] Alarm about political targeting and extortion provided the momentum for the introduction of AB.

The LCI's report then focused on providing a draft of what AB might look like. We note that the cases motivating the LCI report were all cases of public prosecutions, and AB is tailored to such actions. These were not private prosecutions of the kind that might be seen in England (where the private party is the person bringing the prosecution). Thus, when we discuss the role of private parties in influencing a prosecution, our concerns focus on the parties' influence of *public* prosecutions, as run by law enforcement authorities.[27]

By 1970, a new Code of Criminal Procedure Bill provided for courts to grant bail to individuals who feared they were going to be arrested (implementing a reform proposed in the 41st Report of the LCI (LCI, 1969)). The LCI in its 48th Report supported the new provision in the Bill, but went on to state that:

The Bill introduces a provision for the grant of anticipatory bail ... We agree that this would be a useful addition, though we must add that it is in very exceptional cases that such a power should be exercised.

We are further of the view that in order to ensure that the provision is not put to abuse at the instance of unscrupulous petitioners, the final order should be made only after notice to the Public Prosecutor. The initial order should only be an interim one. Further, the relevant section should make it clear that the direction can be issued only for reasons to be recorded, and if the court is satisfied that such a direction is necessary in the interests of justice.[28]

Here the LCI expressed concerns about the potential for misuse of the opportunity to obtain AB. The suggestion appears to be that if it is easy to obtain bail prior to arrest then that may give influential individuals greater opportunity to engage in misbehavior or to cover up wrongdoing after misbehavior.[29] With these admonitions in mind, the Indian Parliament enacted the Code of Criminal Procedure 1973, bringing into effect the power of the courts under a new Section 438, to grant AB.[30]

Now it was the turn of the courts to operationalize this provision and strike a balance between the ability of authorities to investigate serious crimes and the need to provide effective checks against the often complained about misuse of the arrest power which deprived individuals of their liberty.[31] The Indian judiciary, which is a unitary one, with the Supreme Court sitting as the apex court followed by the various High Courts and then the lower District and Magisterial courts, has been active in defining the relevant standards. Indeed, a number of Supreme Court decisions have held that striking this balance is critical and a matter of Constitutional importance in light of Article 21 of the Constitution which views the right to liberty to be a fundamental right.[32]

Although we discuss the operation of Section 438 in part 3, we think it useful to note that the debate over arrest powers did not end with the enactment of a provision authorizing AB. Indeed, the debate only seemed to intensify as both the judiciary and the LCI continued to discuss arrest powers and put forward recommendations for reform. We discuss these proposals in the next section because there is a direct and palpable connection between AB and efforts to inhibit the misuse of arrest powers.

2.3 Developments Since 1973 in Regulating Arrest Powers

Soon after the enactment of Section 438, India was thrown into political turmoil with the declaration of a state of emergency from 1975 to 1977, in which elections were suspended, civil liberties constrained, and the Prime Minister (Indira Gandhi at the time) had the authority to rule by decree (Guha, 2008; Jalal, 1995). Along with many other matters of concern, there were rampant allegations of police abuse (Guha, 2008; Mehta, 2007). From that time on, the debate about police powers took on ever greater fervor, as the National Police Commission (NPC) was formed in 1977 and issued an important report in 1979 that criticized the increasing politicization of the police (NPC, 1979). This debate was matched by complaints about police abuse that often became the basis for lawsuits. This eventually led to a pair of very important Supreme Court cases that provided guidelines for the exercise of the arrest power, until legislation was enacted that codified these guidelines.

The first case – *Joginder Kumar v. State of U.P.* – concerned a petitioner who had been detained by the police for roughly five days without notification to his relatives and with little information provided about the reason for his arrest and detention.[33] The Supreme Court began its analysis by noting that the crime rate in India was rising just as complaints were growing about human rights abuses related to misuse of the arrest power. The Court asked '[h]ow are we to strike a balance between the two? ... The law of arrest is one of balancing individual rights, liberties and privileges, on the one hand, and individual duties, obligations and responsibilities on the other'. After discussing developments in a number of other countries, including the United States and England, the Court held that:

> No arrest can be made in a routine manner on a mere allegation of commission of an offense against a person. It would be prudent for a Police Officer in the interest of protection of the constitutional rights of a citizen and perhaps in his own interest that no arrest should be made without a reasonable satisfaction reached after some investigation as to the genuineness and bona fides of a complaint and a reasonable belief both as to the person's complicity and even so as to the need to effect arrest ... There must be some reasonable justification in the opinion of the officer effecting the arrest that such arrest is necessary and justified.[34]

This standard was meant to uphold the fundamental right of liberty enshrined in Article 21 of the Indian Constitution. The Court approvingly cited the section devoted to arrests in the UK's Royal Commission Report on Criminal Procedure (Philips Commission) (1981) and stressed both the need for reasonable belief in the accused's complicity and the need for a finding that it was actually necessary to arrest the accused. Thus, if the accused was unlikely to abscond, interfere with the investigation, or commit another crime there might be little need to effect an arrest even if there was a reasonable belief that the accused was guilty. In order to implement these standards, the Court laid out guidelines that police officers were to follow (although it was not entirely clear what violation of these guidelines would mean for those police officers). According to these guidelines: (i) the arrestee has a right, if he requests, to have a friend, relative or another person of his choosing informed about his arrest and whereabouts; (ii) the police must inform the arrestee of this right when he is first brought to the police station; (iii) the police must record in the police diary who was informed of the arrest; and (iv) the police department must instruct police to record the reasons for the arrest.

The *Joginder Kumar* case attracted great attention to the issue of arrest and was quickly followed three years later by another seminal Supreme Court decision on arrest – *D.K. Basu v. State of West Bengal.*[35] This case began as a writ petition filed by the Legal Aid Services of West Bengal due to concerns raised by the alleged increasing frequency of injuries and deaths occurring in police custody. This decision reinforced the guidelines from *Joginder Kumar* and added a few of its own. The additional requirements were: (i) the police involved must have visible and accurate identification and name tags and their names must be recorded in a register as the arresting officers; (ii) the police must prepare an arrest memo at the time of an arrest; (iii) the memo must be signed by the arrestee, contain the time and date of arrest, and be attested to by at least one respectable member of the locality or a relative of the arrestee; (iv) the arrestee, upon his request, should be physically examined at the time of his arrest and any injuries recorded at that time (with both the arrestee and police officer signing it and a copy of it being given to the arrestee); (v) there must be further medical examinations every 48 hours while the arrestee is detained with proper recording of the findings; (vi) the arrestee should be able to meet his lawyer during interrogation; and (vii) all documents should be sent to the appropriate magistrate for her records.[36]

Failure to comply with these requirements could trigger both departmental proceedings and contempt of court proceedings against the arresting officer. Further, the Court required these guidelines to be forwarded to relevant police officials across the country and suggested broadcasting these requirements across all important media (radio, television and print) in order to disseminate it within the general populace so they too would be aware of these safeguards.

Clearly, the regulation of arrest power had become an important topic in India. However, it was not clear that these guidelines were followed immediately, that much had changed in terms of actual practice (beyond paper compliance), or that police officers were sanctioned for failing to meet these guidelines. In light of this, the LCI considered reform of the arrest power in its 177th Report issued in 2001.

The LCI began with a generally depressing account of the current state of arrests in India. It noted that, based on information obtained from police departments across the country, the vast majority of arrests appeared to take place without a warrant and that, in a number of states, arrests meant to *prevent* the commission of offenses (preventive detention) exceeded arrests for offenses that had already been committed. The overall picture was that a majority of arrests were made for minor matters and were not necessary to reduce or prevent crime. Indeed, the LCI quotes from a National Police Commission report saying that 'The power of arrest is the most important source of corruption and extortion by police officers' (LCI, 2001). This was only compounded by the findings of the courts and the National Police Commission that the majority of people in jails were 'undertrials' (those awaiting trial who did not seek or obtain bail) rather than people convicted of crimes (LCI, 2001). Further, it was already well known that the general conviction rate in India was quite low.

After an exhaustive review of available evidence, case law, developments in other jurisdictions and consultations with interested parties, the LCI recommended changes to the Code of Criminal Procedure designed to curtail abuses of the arrest power. The LCI adopted the guidelines put forward in the *Joginder Kumar* and *D.K. Basu* decisions, but it also made a few additional recommendations. First, it detailed in a new Section 41 'the three types of defendants whom police officers may arrest without a warrant for cognizable offenses: (i) those who have committed cognizable offenses in front of the police officer; (ii) those charged, on the basis of credible information with the commission of a cognizable offense, even when not committed in front of the police, if the offense carries a sentence of no more than seven years (subject, however, to heightened procedural safeguards); and (iii) those charged, on the basis of credible information, with the commission of a cognizable offense, even when not committed in front of the police, which carries a sentence that could extend beyond seven years (LCI, 2001).

For the second category of arrests, which are the most common, the special safeguards took the form of two additional requirements. First, the police officer must have credible information leading him to believe that the individual has committed the offense. Second, the police officer must be satisfied that the arrest is necessary according to the criteria suggested by the Philips Commission Report (Royal Commission, 1981). The grounds of necessity are limited to: (i) preventing further offenses; (ii) aiding proper investigation or for the accused's safety; (iii) preventing tampering with evidence or other steps to obstruct justice; or (iv) obtaining the presence of the accused for court when that cannot be otherwise ensured. It also requires the police to record the reason for the arrest and make that known to the accused (LCI, 2001).

One additional important recommendation was the creation of Section 41A, which applies when an arrest is not required under Section 41. This provision requires the police to issue a notice informing a person accused of a cognizable offense that he must appear before the police (or the court) when summoned (LCI, 2001). Thus, the individual receives some notice that he is potentially under suspicion for a cognizable offense, which was not the case before the new Section 41A was enacted. Failure to comply with the notice might provide another ground for arrest.[37]

Although the LCI report came out in 2001, its recommendations did not become law until 2009 when the CCP was amended and Section 41 took shape in its current form. The reforms enacted in 2009 might have led one to believe that the long struggle to regulate arrest powers was now entering a new era, but these new standards did not appear to specify the consequences for failing to meet their strictures, as they did not specifically address or resolve the questions raised in *D.K. Basu* about the potential consequences of violating Section 41 (for example, whether such violations would lead to contempt of court proceedings or internal department proceedings against police officers). For that one had to wait until 2014 when the Supreme Court again intervened to clarify some of the potential consequences for violating the new rules on the arrest power.

In *Arnesh Kumar v. State of Bihar & Anr.*, the lower court had denied a petition for AB where the petitioner was concerned that he might be arrested on suspicion of violating Section 498A of the Indian Penal Code 1860 (which is a cognizable offense).[38] This provision makes it a crime to subject a wife to cruelty, for example by harassing her with dowry demands. The petitioner was concerned that his wife might file a complaint (which he alleged was false) and thereby trigger his and his elderly parents' arrest. His request for AB was rejected by the lower court and he appealed all the way to the Supreme Court. The Court took the opportunity to both discuss its views on cases under Section 498A (which it considered a widely misused provision) and to reiterate that the arrest power was not to be used lightly, especially after the 2009 reforms and because it involved restricting an individual's liberty – a fundamental Constitutional right. The Court also underscored the statements from *D.K. Basu* that violation of the requirements for Section 41 could lead to internal department proceedings against the police and potential contempt of court proceedings.

Soon thereafter, cases arose in which penalties were imposed for violations of Section 41. One of the more interesting is *Satish Vasant Salvi v. The State of Maharashtra and Anr.*, which again involved a Section 498A harassment claim (alleging dowry demands).[39] This time the husband was arrested (and hence this was not an AB petition) and required to undergo a humiliating medical examination against his wishes. The Bombay High Court found the arrest and compelled medical examination (ostensibly to test whether he was impotent) to be illegal under Section 41 and its accompanying sections, and concluded that the arrest and compelled examination had also violated the petitioner's fundamental Constitutional right to liberty under Article 21. For these violations, the court imposed costs *on the state* in the amount of Indian Rupees (INR) 20,000 (approximately USD 320) and further compensatory costs of INR 200,000 (approximately USD 3,200). This, however, did not end the matter. The court further held that the state was to conduct an inquiry, and if it found that the woman's (wife's) father (a police inspector) was responsible for these violations, he would be made to reimburse the state INR 200,000 for its losses. Further, these orders did not preclude the petitioner from pursuing a civil suit against the appropriate parties (for example, the police, his father-in-law) as well as contempt of court proceedings.

This decision is unusual because it allows for sanctions to be imposed on *the police inspector* in addition to the state. Given that this decision was issued in June 2015, it is perhaps too soon to know whether other courts will also allow for the imposition of direct sanctions on the police, but it is potentially an important marker of a changing attitude towards misuse of arrest powers.

The overall impression one obtains from the historical development of the regulation of arrest powers in India is that until very recently – despite judicial pronouncements, public condemnations, LCI reports, and draft bills – little has changed on the ground. Indeed, things may have become worse as more and more people attempt to influence the criminal process to settle scores, to extort cash, or to extract a settlement of a civil dispute that has likely been pending for quite some time in the Indian courts. This seems consistent with the increasing number of reports and cases dealing with the arrest power. Although the last 18 months have witnessed some greater efforts to impose penalties on the state and police for violations of the new rules on arrest powers, it appears that the arrest power is still quite frequently misused.

3. ANTICIPATORY BAIL AS ADMINISTERED IN INDIA

Although Section 438 is the critical provision on AB, a number of key steps in the criminal investigative process surround an application for AB. The criminal process often begins when a complaining witness registers the First Information Report (FIR) with the police, thereby triggering the start of the investigative process for cognizable offenses.[40] Following this, the police conduct their official investigation and begin to gather evidence. At some point in the process they may decide that it is appropriate to arrest an individual. If someone is arrested, he can seek bail, usually within a day or two, under Section 437 of the CCP. Whether or not bail is granted, the next step would be the production of a charge-sheet (the primary charging document) by law enforcement (that is, police and prosecutors).[41] Sections 173, 211–218 and 240 of the CCP detail the requirements and steps in the charging process. In essence, the charge-sheet must contain clear details of the individuals implicated, the events in question, and all other information in the investigation, along with supporting documents and descriptions of the alleged offense (which must not be vague).[42] Once produced, the charge-sheet is then submitted to a judicial officer (usually a magistrate) who can accept, reject or order amendment of the charge-sheet and frame the charges.[43] The court must decide whether there is sufficient *prima facie* evidence against any of the accused to proceed to trial (in other words, mere suspicions or presumptions are insufficient). This is largely a decision the court comes to after reviewing the charge-sheet and supporting documentation. Once that phase has been completed, and if the court has decided that at least some of the accused should be tried, the matter is scheduled for hearing in front of the trial court.

If a potential accused is interested in seeking AB, she should petition the court *before an arrest*. This naturally raises a question about how a potential accused may know whether she is likely to be arrested. This can happen in various ways, but we briefly mention a few typical scenarios. If a private party files a criminal complaint in order to extort money or help settle a pending civil matter, then it is not uncommon for the potential accused to be made aware of this possibility by the private party as a step towards extracting a settlement. The private party may prefer to use the credible threat of arrest, rather than actual arrest, to extract a settlement because effecting an arrest has its own costs. Sometimes an arrest ruptures a pre-existing and on-going relationship between the parties or it may involve having to pay (that is bribe) the police to make the arrest. In other cases, the investigation and questioning associated with it tip off the accused to a pending investigation and complaint against him, before the arrest can take place. Other scenarios may involve 'leaks' from the police (deliberate or otherwise) or a general suspicion by the likely accused that someone may file an arrest based on her experience with how things work in that locale (for example, neighborhood disputes might commonly escalate to criminal charges in some areas). Alternatively, if the accused is actually involved with a crime, he may anticipate a future arrest.

With these points in mind, let us begin to explore AB, which can only be granted if a court is satisfied that the requirements of Section 438 have been met. Because of the centrality of Section 438 we reproduce it in important parts below with the full version provided in the Appendix.[44]

438. Direction for grant of bail to person apprehending arrest.

(1) When any person has reason to believe that he may be arrested on an accusation of having committed a non-bailable offence, he may apply to the High Court or the Court of Session for a direction under this Section; and that Court may, if it thinks fit, direct that in the event of such arrest, he shall be released on bail.

(2) When the High Court or the Court of Session makes a direction under sub-section (1), it may include such conditions in such directions in the light of the facts of the particular case, as it may think fit, including –
  (i)   a condition that the person shall make himself available for interrogation by a police officer as and when required;
  (ii) a condition that the person shall not, directly or indirectly, make any inducement, threat or promise to any person acquainted with the facts of the case so as to dissuade him from disclosing such facts to the court or to any police officer;
  (iii) a condition that the person shall not leave India without the previous permission of the court;
  (iv) Such other condition as may be imposed under sub-section (3) of section 437, as if the bail were granted under that section.

Section 438(1) contains the grant of power to the courts to award bail pre-arrest, while 438(2) allows the court to craft conditions on to that bail. Because Section 438(1) is the provision of greatest interest we examine its details and evidentiary requirements most closely in the following sections.

However, before doing that there are three noteworthy operational points. First, Section 438 decisions can, at the discretion of the court, occur in two steps – an interim order and a final order – or just one step (the final order). A court may decide on the two-step approach for a number of reasons, including that it wishes to have more time to consider the arguments. If the two-step approach is chosen, it is possible for the interim order hearing to be *ex parte* – in other words, the State is not heard – but that is not very common as courts may be interested in hearing the views of law enforcement even at the interim-order stage. If the interim order was granted in an *ex parte* hearing then that order is forwarded to the police and prosecutor in order to provide them with an opportunity to be heard before issuing a final order where both sides are required to be heard.[45] Second, if an interim (or final) order is granted in favor of AB, it is often worded so as to come into play only when, and if, the potential accused is arrested. For example, an AB order may state that if the police decide to arrest the potential accused, the police must release him immediately on bail in the amount set in the AB order and on the conditions placed in the AB order.[46] Thus, no bail is paid until the accused is arrested, although lawyers' fees are paid in the hearing to obtain AB. Third, Section 438(2) allows courts to impose conditions on AB that include requiring the individual to cooperate in or join the investigation and not to tamper with witnesses. Moreover, the court can rescind the grant of AB in certain situations, including if it appears the accused has violated any of the conditions in the AB order.[47] This underscores that an AB order does not limit the police in pursuing its investigation and framing charges. An order granting AB only prevents the detention or confinement of the individual, but does not *per se* end the investigation.[48]

3.1 The Key Features of Section 438(1)

Section 438(1) has four key features: (i) an individual must apply to the court for AB – it would not arise independently otherwise; (ii) the applicant must have a 'reason to believe' he will be arrested; (iii) the impending arrest must be for a non-bailable offense (as further defined below); and finally (iv) the court must decide whether it thinks it is appropriate to order this kind of bail.[49] The first feature is self-explanatory, but the remaining features merit greater discussion.

3.1.1 Applicant must have 'reason to believe'
The applicant must have a 'reason to believe' he will be arrested. The Supreme Court in *Adri Dharan Das v. State of W.B.*[50] held that a reason to believe must be based on reasonable grounds and not simply any sense by the applicant that he may be arrested. The Court went further and stated that the grounds for the belief must be capable of being examined by the Court. This in turn involves specifying the type of allegation that might be, or has been, made against the applicant.[51] The Court's concerns

in this context revolve around AB being granted too easily for 'whichever offence whatsoever'.[52] The Court elaborated that one must be cognizant of the fact that the Indian Judicial System is subject to lengthy delays in adjudication.[53] If an individual could obtain a very general AB order in her favor then she could commit crimes with little fear of being arrested and, given the delays in the judicial system, face a relatively small chance of being convicted (although no examples were provided).[54] To avoid this situation the Court was keen to require something more than an individual's general fear of arrest before granting anticipatory bail.

Other cases have provided further indicia about what the 'reason to believe' standard means. For example, in *Thayyanbadi Meethal Kunhiraman v. S.I. of Police, Panoor*,[55] the court held that an application under Section 438 must be based on a reasonable apprehension of being arrested for *past behavior*. In this case, the applicant had been in a property dispute with another person and was arrested when he entered the disputed land to pick coconuts. He obtained bail and soon thereafter applied for AB on the grounds that he would like to return to the disputed property in the future and pick more coconuts and thought he may as well seek bail in advance. The Kerala High Court rejected the application stating that AB was for accusations of existing alleged violations not for potential alleged future violations. The court would not grant AB if it served to make it easier for an applicant to engage in future offenses.

Similarly, the Supreme Court in *Jaswantbhai M. Sheth v. Anand V. Nagarsheth*[56] held that AB cannot be granted if there are insufficient grounds for the applicant to reasonably believe he is going to be arrested. In that case the applicant was concerned that he might be arrested on murder charges. The Court held that the applicant was not named in the First Information Report (FIR) and had not yet been accused. It was premature to grant AB, but the applicant was permitted to apply again if the facts changed. This, however, did not mean that it was necessary for the applicant to be named in an FIR before a court would find a 'reason to believe',[57] but the absence of being considered an accused was one factor to be considered among the totality of the circumstances and could support denial of AB.

3.1.2 Only for non-bailable offenses
The next important feature is that AB can only be granted for non-bailable offenses. As mentioned earlier, non-bailable offenses are generally the more serious offenses and a list of them is contained in the First Schedule to the CCP 1973. But the term non-bailable is somewhat misleading – it refers to offenses for which the *police* cannot simply grant bail on their own, but for which a *court* can, if it chooses to do so.[58]

Bailable offenses, on the other hand, refer to offenses for which an individual can obtain bail by simply requesting it of the *arresting police officer* and providing the necessary sureties or personal bond.[59] Because bailable offenses allow an individual to avoid confinement by obtaining bail from an officer directly, there is less need for AB for such offenses.

Thus, as a practical matter, AB is most common for individuals charged with cognizable offenses (where no warrant is needed before an arrest) that are also non-bailable offenses (to fit within section 438(1)). It is possible for someone to seek AB even for non-cognizable offenses, because Section 438(1) does not exclude such offenses.

3.1.3   Factors courts consider in deciding whether to grant anticipatory bail

The final feature of great importance is what factors a court may consider in deciding whether to grant AB.[60] In *State of Rajasthan v. Bal Chand*, Justice Krishna Iyer of the Supreme Court noted that bail should be granted unless there are 'circumstances suggestive of fleeing from justice or thwarting the course of justice or creating other troubles in the shape of repeating offences or intimidating witnesses and the like by the petitioner'.[61] Thus, the risk of recidivism, witness tampering, or flight might deter a court from granting AB.

Later cases have further elaborated what courts can consider in exercising their discretion. Perhaps the most detailed recitation of factors is in the Supreme Court's decision in *Siddharam Satlingappa Mhetre v. State of Maharashtra*.[62] In this case the appellant (a member of the Indian National Congress (INC) political party) was accused of having incited his party workers to beat anyone from the opposing party who came to speak with people in that constituency. Some days later, members of the opposing party (the BJP) were assaulted and shot at (with one dying) after coming out of a temple in that constituency, where INC party workers appeared to have gathered. The appellant sought AB, apprehending a likely arrest based on information suggesting a criminal case would be filed against him. His application was denied in the High Court and he appealed to the Supreme Court where the appeal was allowed. The Supreme Court provided a non-exhaustive list of considerations, building on those in Section 438(1), relevant to determining whether to grant anticipatory bail. These are:

i.   The nature and gravity of the accusation and the exact role of the accused must be properly comprehended before arrest is made;

ii. The antecedents of the applicant including the fact as to whether the accused has previously undergone imprisonment on conviction by a Court in respect of any cognizable offence;

iii. The possibility of the applicant to flee from justice;

iv. The possibility of the accused's likelihood to repeat similar or the other offences.

v. Where the accusations have been made only with the object of injuring or humiliating the applicant by arresting him or her.

vi. Impact of grant of anticipatory bail particularly in cases of large magnitude affecting a very large number of people.

vii. The courts must evaluate the entire available material against the accused very carefully. The court must also clearly comprehend the exact role of the accused in the case. The cases in which accused is implicated with the help of sections 34 and 149 of the Indian Penal Code,[63] the court should consider with even greater care and caution because over implication in the cases is a matter of common knowledge and concern;

viii. While considering the prayer for grant of anticipatory bail, a balance has to be struck between two factors[,] namely, no prejudice should be caused to the free, fair and full investigation and there should be prevention of harassment, humiliation and unjustified detention of the accused;

ix. The court to consider reasonable apprehension of tampering of the witness or apprehension of threat to the complainant;

x. Frivolity in prosecution should always be considered and it is only the element of genuineness that shall have to be considered in the matter of grant of bail and in the event of there being some doubt as to the genuineness of the prosecution, in the normal course of events, the accused is entitled to an order of bail.[64]

This long list is very similar to a list produced by the Soli Sorabjee Committee, which drafted a new Police Bill in 2006 that has not yet been enacted.[65] Thus, in addition to the risk of flight, witness tampering, and recidivism, the courts are to consider the risk of other evidence tampering, prior convictions, the genuineness of the prosecution and how the charges are framed (for example, use of provisions known to be suspect or misused frequently) along with both liberty concerns and a desire to ensure proper investigation of crimes. Further, the Court held that courts must carefully examine all the allegations and the record to note where there is corroborating evidence.[66] Simply put, an individual's liberty is an important fundamental right under Article 21 of the Indian Constitution and should not be easily set aside. Thus, the clear message from the Court's analysis is that 'arrest should be the last option and it should be restricted to those exceptional cases where arresting the accused is imperative in the facts and circumstances of that case'.[67] This does not mean that the charges against the accused need to be false to grant AB, just that proof that the prosecution was pretextual and meant to harass would be factors to consider. Indeed, AB is targeted to preventing abuses of the criminal justice system and that does not require the charges to be false.[68] The *Siddharam* Court's approach has been cited with approval by the Supreme Court as recently as this year in *Teesta Atul Setalvad & Ors. v. State of Gujarat.*[69]

Before leaving the factors considered in an AB application, it may be useful to note that the evidence and arguments provided by either side in an AB hearing do not necessarily prevent a party from taking a different position in later criminal proceedings. If the police have not produced a charge sheet by the time of the AB hearing (which they generally have not), they may deviate from their AB statements in the later criminal trial (for example, if their investigation after the AB hearings led to a change in their views). If a charge sheet has been filed, it is difficult for the police to take a position at odds with the allegations made in the charge sheet. For the applicant, much of what she presents in the AB hearings is not under oath or in the form of an affidavit, which implies that in potential later criminal proceedings the applicant may argue a different position than that taken in the AB hearings.[70] This suggests that there are few, if any, official penalties, including for perjury, on either side for taking different positions in later criminal proceedings. However, if a court discovers misrepresentations in the AB hearings (even before a criminal trial), it can rescind the anticipatory bail order.

3.2 Implications of Decisions on Anticipatory Bail Applications

There are many questions arising from the decision to grant or deny AB. In this section we examine the questions that have been most frequently addressed by the courts: How often is AB granted? How long does it last if granted? What offenses are covered by it? Must the police arrest the applicant if AB is denied? And, can an applicant try more than once for AB if her first application is denied? For expositional ease the first three concerns are discussed in section 3.2.1 and the last two in section 3.2.2, which discusses the consequences of a denial of an AB application. As a general matter, the trend has been to grant AB more liberally, which in turn has led to the recent push to reform AB, as discussed in section 3.4.

3.2.1 Implications of granting an application for anticipatory bail
Our starting point is how often one might expect AB to be granted if sought. There has been considerable judicial discussion of this issue. A number of Supreme Court decisions have held that AB should be granted only in exceptional circumstances, such as when a person might be

falsely implicated or if there are reasonable grounds for thinking that the person is not likely to misuse his liberty.[71] This approach is countered by a series of Constitutional Bench judgments of the Supreme Court (which carry greater precedential value) preferring a broader approach to AB and granting it more generally.[72] The Court has held that limiting Section 438 to exceptional circumstances would effectively make it of little to no value.[73] This divergence of approaches was recently addressed by the Supreme Court in *Siddharam* where it held that AB should be granted more generally and liberally.[74]

Another issue that has attracted judicial attention is how long a grant of AB lasts. Section 438 says little about the duration of an AB order. Clearly, AB only starts once the accused is actually arrested.[75] But, how long should AB be operational? Some courts desired a limited period of time for which AB might apply; after it lapses, these courts would require an individual to apply for bail through the regular process, if and when he is arrested.[76] This approach has been jettisoned in favor of having AB continue until the end of trial unless the Court decides to cancel it earlier.[77] This outcome is considered more in line with the motivation behind Section 438 and the desire to protect an individual's liberty.[78]

Finally, commentators debate how to determine the proper scope of a decision granting AB. What offenses will be covered? And over how wide a range? To better grasp this concern let us recall that Section 438 was meant to reduce the misuse of the criminal process and arrest power and that this misuse might not be confined to any particular charge. For example, let us assume that someone (A) plans to bribe the police to arrest another individual (B) for a particular alleged offense, in order to extort money from B. Let us further assume that B somehow suspects this and petitions the court for AB, receiving it for any arrest predicated on charges relating to the alleged crime. Once A and the police become aware of this, can they simply charge a different offense and arrest B for that? If so, then the protection afforded by AB is quite weak. Indeed, this is similar to concerns voiced in the US over how tightly the courts define the protection available against double jeopardy.[79] However, at the other extreme, if an AB order does cover all crimes, then the person granted AB has less to fear from the criminal justice system and thus may have less reason not to engage in criminal behavior.[80] The question of how many offenses an AB order covers is thus a critical issue.

Indian jurisprudence has vacillated on this point. The Supreme Court has held that the court granting AB needs to precisely describe the charges for which it is being granted in order to avoid giving the applicant a *carte blanche* AB.[81] The Court's decision seems to suggest that if AB is granted for a lesser offense, then that AB can be effectively ignored if a more serious offense charge is added after further investigation.[82] This is similar to courts' treatment of regular bail applications.[83]

However, recent High Court decisions seem to adopt a broader approach. In 2001, the Delhi High Court held that the police cannot avoid an AB order for one set of charges by making trivial changes to those charges.[84] The police in such a situation must still approach the courts to have the AB cancelled.[85] Interestingly, some other High Courts have gone further and have held that the filing of serious charges does not, by itself, allow the police to avoid an AB order for a lesser offense.[86] Rather, the Rajasthan High Court has held that the grounds for cancelling AB should be something more akin to whether the accused is likely to obstruct justice in some manner (for example, tamper with evidence or abscond) or otherwise misuse his liberty, rather than whether the new charges resemble the old ones.[87]

3.2.2 Implications of denying an application for anticipatory bail

The discussion has thus far assumed that AB is granted to the applicant. However, what are the consequences if AB is denied? A common concern is whether the police are required to arrest, or are prohibited from arresting, an individual to whom AB is denied. The law does not compel either outcome and the standard for arresting someone does not change because of a failure to obtain AB.[88] However, the common practice is that police routinely attempt to arrest someone who has failed to obtain AB. There could be many reasons for this, but this routine police practice may respond, at least in part, to the perceived affront of seeking AB.

It is also uncertain whether, if an application for AB is denied, the courts must entertain a renewed application for AB by the same person. Section 438 says nothing about subsequent applications and the Supreme Court has not opined on the issue. High Courts have largely allowed for second applications in certain situations. The Full Bench of the Calcutta High Court allowed for a second application only if there had been a substantial change in the facts or circumstances.[89] The Madhya Pradesh High Court has held that a second application is not prohibited and is to be decided on its own merits.[90] Finally, the Rajasthan High Court allows for second applications if there is a change in the facts or the law or if the earlier decision has become obsolete.[91] Thus, many High Courts allow for second applications in some circumstances.

3.3   Anticipatory Bail – Only Available for the Well Off?

To obtain AB, an individual must apply to the court before being arrested by the police. This suggests that the individual must have some inkling that an arrest is likely and the financial and other wherewithal to hire attorneys to file an application for AB prior to that. This has led some to be concerned that AB may be, or may become, an instrument only used by the rich and influential, leaving the rest of India to its own devices.[92]

In light of this, the question whether less well-off individuals might be able to rely on the right to counsel to apply for AB takes on some salience. The general right to counsel for indigent individuals has been recognized multiple times in India. This is both due to a specific provision in the CCP providing for the right to free legal counsel for accused individuals who are charged with crimes that may involve the risk of imprisonment,[93] and Supreme Court case law holding that the Indian Constitution entitles those who are in custody to counsel.[94]

Because the right to counsel is generally available *after* someone has been charged with, or accused of, a crime,[95] one would not expect a right to counsel for AB where no charges have yet been filed. However, denying indigent individuals the right to counsel for AB (when they have evidence that would lead to the grant of it) might be seen as discriminating against the less well off. Although the Supreme Court has not ruled on this issue, the Kerala High Court has held that AB may be sought by someone seeking legal aid under Indian Law.[96]

3.4   Current Concerns and Stalled Reforms

The current approach is to grant AB broadly. When combined with the well-known delays in the Indian justice system, this has raised concerns about whether the frequent grant of AB might allow the accused who obtains it to have the time and freedom to tamper with evidence, influence witnesses and thereby evade conviction.[97] This concern and the sense that AB was being granted to the rich and influential have led to calls to repeal Section 438 and to proposals by the LCI to impose limits on AB (LCI, 2007).[98]

Although these reforms had substantial support in the Indian Parliament, they have been stymied by the protests of lawyers groups in various parts of India (LCI, 2007). This ongoing controversy underscores the continuing importance of AB in the Indian criminal justice system.

In spite of these controversies, we think the concerns voiced in the debate over AB are not about AB *per se*. Much of the concern stems from the long delays in India's judicial system that then allow the accused, who is not in jail, more time to tamper with evidence, influence witnesses or abscond. Although these concerns are real, it is noteworthy that the same concerns arise with grants of bail *after an arrest*. Given that bail is often granted (and on standards similar to those for AB), the accused is likely to be free for quite some time while waiting to have the criminal case adjudicated. As long as the likely accused can obtain bail, she would have essentially the same freedom to tamper with evidence, with or without anticipatory bail. Further, if AB is granted before a regular bail application could be brought and decided, it might afford the likely accused a few more days or weeks of freedom, but this pales in comparison to the likely delays in adjudication (for example, four to five years for criminal cases). In light of this, we are inclined to think that the concerns voiced about AB are more about lengthy delays between arrest and final adjudication rather than about the unfairness or unreliability of anticipatory bail in comparison to the regular bail process.[99]

However, the debates about reforms to AB are instructive for a somewhat different reason – they indicate active discussion in India about how to respond to the concerns of misuse of arrest power in creative and potentially effective ways. It is to that question we now turn.

4. COMPARATIVE ANALYSES AND REFORMS?

India's reliance on AB to curtail misuse of the arrest power reflects many of its unique institutional and historical characteristics: police with broad and weakly constrained arrest powers, political interference with police operations, slow courts, and weak tort remedies, amongst others. However, some of these background features (such as constraints on arrest powers) are beginning to change, raising the question of whether there may be worthy alternatives to AB. To explore this more fully, we briefly lay out the approaches of the US and England and discuss how their experiences might prove useful for India.

Perhaps the first thing to note is that AB is a rarity outside of India. Jurisdictions such as the US and England do not possess the concept of AB, although individuals have at times sought, unsuccessfully, to have something like AB granted to them.[100] For example, *In re the Matter of Sturman*, a potential accused had received information that he might be indicted on tax charges (although no arrest warrant had been issued.) He filed for anticipatory bail in the Northern District of Ohio.[101] The court rejected the motion, noting that bail is not meant for avoiding arrest but for ensuring that the accused appears for trial. In American constitutional terms, the defendant's liberty interest would not be considered ripe for adjudication until it was actually infringed or threatened through an arrest or some other invasive form of state action.

Instead of anticipatory bail, the US and England primarily rely on stronger judicial and legislative oversight of the arrest power via arrest standards and tort claims, amongst others, to curtail misuses of the arrest power. Richard Vogler and Shahrzad Fouladvand's chapter in this volume describes the standards of England and Wales, of the United States, and of Continental Europe for making factual determinations about arrest and pre-trial detention. They detail how judicial and legislative standards vary across these jurisdictions – England relying on reasonable suspicion, the US on probable cause and some Continental European jurisdictions on 'flagrancy' – and how these standards are used to assess both whether to grant a warrant pre-arrest and how to assess the legality of a warrantless arrest afterwards (Vogler and Fouladvand, 2016).[102] Although hardly perfect, these standards are likely to constrain the arrest power of the police more than the general approach in India. In addition to arrest standards, the US and England both have the tort of malicious prosecution (as does India),[103] but the relative speed of their judiciaries and their more detailed tort law make this tort cause of action – even though not particularly easy to satisfy – more of a potential constraint on arrest powers in the United States and England than in India.

Nonetheless, we note that – at least on paper – India's judicial and legislative standards for reviewing the validity of arrests are getting closer to the emerging international norm of reasonable suspicion discussed in Vogler and Fouladvand (2016). This raises the question of whether AB would serve much purpose if India's *de facto* standards also moved toward these global norms.

Although we do not provide a definitive and comprehensive answer to this question, we do begin to explore the contours of an answer here. As a starting point it is helpful to note the features of AB that in combination may distinguish it from other methods of curtailing abuse of the arrest power. These appear to be:

1. AB occurs before an arrest.
2. AB allows both sides – law enforcement and the applicant – to present information to the court.
3. AB hearings tend to favor granting AB to the applicant.
4. AB hearings occur only if the potential accused files an application, and thus AB hearings arise in only a subset of likely arrests.

The US and English approaches have some of these features, but not all in combination. For example, arrest warrants, like anticipatory bail orders, are issued before an arrest, but they do not make it possible for both sides to present evidence to a judge. Instead, law enforcement provides its information *ex parte*. Bail hearings in the US and England allow both sides to present evidence, but not before an arrest. Further, anticipatory bail may be more effective in preventing or deterring false arrests than the English and American warrant requirement. The English reasonable suspicion standard will deter some false arrests, but will allow some as well (since the reasonable suspicion standard is not difficult to manipulate). These remaining false arrests also generate costs and would be problematic in India, where the abuse of the arrest power for political, puerile or extortionary purposes are more salient concerns than in the United States and England. AB hearings may be less likely to allow as many false arrests (or may deter more of them) because anticipatory bail is granted fairly liberally (except perhaps in cases alleging particularly heinous crimes), and this reduces the incentive to bring criminal accusations for political or extortionary reasons. Thus, the number of false arrests may decline, but there may also be an increase in the number of cases in which the police fail to arrest someone who then attempts to manipulate the investigative processes or tamper with witnesses.[104]

This suggests that AB is likely to be a valuable supplement when these four features together are desirable. Let us begin with the first and third features. When would having a pre-arrest hearing that tends to bias against false arrests be useful? This is more likely when the costs of false arrest are high and difficult to compensate.[105] An example might be politically motivated arrests where the harm caused might be a loss in an election – how might one compensate for that and would the police and related parties have the assets to pay for it? In such situations prevention is likely to be better than cure and thus pre-arrest hearings and the bias against false arrests in AB hearings seem valuable.

Further, AB is likely to be desirable where there would be value in hearing both sides before an arrest. This seems more likely when the costs of false arrest are high (because hearing both sides would increase accuracy and thus reduce erroneous decisions) as well as when a court may not have great faith in law enforcement's information.[106] Low reliability of law enforcement tends to occur when law enforcement is perceived to be politicized and corrupt.

Finally, AB is more desirable if potential arrestees are likely to suspect an arrest before it happens and file an application for AB. Without this there would be few AB hearings and few potential benefits. Potential arrestees may be more likely to suspect an arrest when they believe the background level of misuse of arrest power is high or that the police are

highly politicized or otherwise easily instrumentalized for private ven-
dettas, extortion, and the like.

Taking these considerations together, an AB system may well be a
desirable supplement when corruption and political manipulation of law
enforcement are major concerns. This suggests that even if stronger
standards of judicial and legislative oversight of arrests were implemented in India, but the police were still thought to be corrupt and
subject to political control, there may be some value in having AB as a
supplement. Given the discussion in section 2 about the institutional
structure of the police in India and that little major reform has happened
to it in over 150 years, one expects that AB – perhaps in a more targeted
and limited form – will continue to be useful even as both *de jure* and *de
facto* arrest standards become stronger.

The primary disadvantage of using AB as a supplement is that the
administrative costs of AB hearings are likely to be higher than those of
a system that only allowed post-arrest review. AB hearings could also add
to the long delays in the Indian courts. Although we think these concerns
are important, when viewed from a broader perspective, AB is still likely
to be useful for India.

For example, the LCI has reported that over 60 percent of arrests in
India should not have been undertaken in the first place or were
unnecessary.[107] If better screening of arrests had removed even half of
these then the benefits to the judicial system in having fewer cases to
handle would have resulted in fewer delays. Indeed, given that roughly
two-thirds of the cases pending in Indian courts are criminal, such
screening could easily have had a large impact on delays. Second, many
of the arrests that should not have occurred would probably have led to
acquittals, which reduces the conviction rate (and India's conviction rate
is fairly low), thereby undermining the deterrent effect of the law. If these
likely acquittals were removed from the queue of cases to be heard then
conviction rates would be higher and deterrence enhanced. Deterring
false arrests reduces criminal caseloads and shortens delays. Thus, the
potential short run increase in costs and delays of an AB supplement are
likely to provide medium- to longer-run gains that could outstrip those
costs.[108]

Although we do not develop the details of a system that combines
stronger *de jure* and *de facto* arrest standards with AB as a supplement in
this paper, we think that the analysis provided here suggests that it will
be well worth the efforts of those interested in the criminal justice system
to consider it. We leave that for future work.

5. CONCLUSION

Anticipatory bail is one of the most hotly debated topics in India's criminal justice system. The numerous Supreme Court cases and Government reports on this topic underscore the importance of this unusual procedural device. Indeed, there is no shortage of attempts to reform both the rules governing anticipatory bail and their implementation. Yet this controversial area of criminal procedure is not to be found outside of South Asia. This raises intriguing and important questions about why anticipatory bail came into existence, whether it is the best way to achieve its purposes, and what it tells us about India's criminal justice system. Our analysis in this chapter suggests anticipatory bail arose to meet a combination of institutional problems such as broad discretionary arrest powers, weak standards of judicial and legislative review of the arrest power, political control of the police, and tort remedies that are both weak and slow. Indeed, the ways in which anticipatory bail has been adapted and interpreted suggest that these considerations were paramount for lawmakers and courts alike. However, the judicial and legislative standards for reviewing arrests in India are gradually becoming more aligned with the more exacting standards seen in England and the US. This suggests there may be something to be gained from re-examining whether anticipatory bail may be useful in this changing context. We suggest that it still is likely to retain a valuable supplementary role in the Indian institutional context.

We began by examining the historical development of anticipatory bail and arrest powers in India. The Indian Police Act 1861, enacted primarily to strengthen British control over the Subcontinent, granted broad powers to the police to arrest individuals (with weak judicial oversight) while subjecting the police to political control. This in turn generated debate about the prospects for abuse. After Independence in 1947, the Government of India did little to change the institutional characteristics of the police. As the political structure within India became more competitive, concerns mounted that the broad arrest powers and greater political interference with the police would lead to misuse of arrest powers by politically influential individuals wishing to target their rivals or by the police and private parties seeking to extort money or legal settlements from others. These concerns led to the creation of Section 438 of the CCP in 1973, providing courts with the power to grant bail in anticipation of a person's arrest. This prevented the person from being detained by the police, even for a short period of time, while allowing a criminal investigation to continue.

Although Section 438 was intended to be used sparingly, the courts have over time opted for a broader and more generous approach to anticipatory bail. This is in part due to increasing concern about the misuse of arrest powers and because there was little implementation of stronger arrest standards.

The breadth of these protections has generated considerable controversy and raises questions about whether the problems that led to the AB system should lead to more sweeping reforms of arrest powers. Reliance on anticipatory bail to address the concerns noted above stands in stark contrast to the approaches utilized in other Anglo-American jurisdictions where reliance on stronger judicial and legislative oversight standards (both pre- and post-arrest) is the norm. A variety of reform proposals have captured the attention of India's legal and political elites, but so long as the police themselves remain corrupt, politicized, and unreliable, some of these may be viewed as promising supplements to the AB system but not as substitutes.

However, we are quick to note that many of the concerns noted in this paper are not simply driven by arrest powers but by the institutional context in which police enjoy broad discretion in exercising their powers, against the further background of a slow adjudicatory system that is itself subject to significant political distortion, corruption and misuse. These interrelated problems need to be addressed for India's criminal justice system to function better. Reforms to anticipatory bail are a small palliative and should not be mistaken for a cure to the larger ills of the criminal justice system.

NOTES

*   The authors would like to thank the editors – Jacqueline Ross and Steven Thaman – for their valuable insights and suggestions, and the participants at the University of Michigan Law School Faculty Brown Bag Lunch for comments and suggestions. We would also like to express our gratitude to Neal Patel for excellent research assistance.

1.   Neither the section permitting this kind of bail nor its marginal note so describes it, but the expression 'anticipatory bail' is a convenient mode of conveying that it is possible to apply for bail in anticipation of arrest.
2.   See *Balchand Jain v. State of Madhya Pradesh* 1977 AIR 366; *Savitri Agrawal and Ors v. State of Maharashtra and Anr.* 8 SCC 325.
3.   Anticipatory bail is available in Pakistan under Section 498 of the Pakistan Code of Criminal Procedure 2001, but the wording of that section suggests its availability is more restricted than in India. It appears that Kenya may, in limited circumstances allow for anticipatory bail via the inherent powers of their courts when a Constitutional provision is violated. See *Eric Mailu v. Republic & 2 others* [2013] eKLR, available at: http://kenyalaw.org/caselaw/cases/view/87371/.

4. See *Jairam Das v. Emperor*, AIR 1945 PC 94.
5. See *Shri Gurbaksh Singh Sibbia Etc v. State of Punjab*, 1980 AIR 1632 [*hereinafter Sibbia*].
6. See *Arnesh Kumar v. State of Bihar* (2014) 8 SCC 273 [*hereinafter Arnesh Kumar*].
7. See Section 6(1) of the Prosecution of Offences Act 1985; Friedman (1995); Klerman (2001).
8. Section 41, Code of Criminal Procedure India, 1973.
9. See *Arnesh Kumar, supra* note 6 for a Supreme Court decision discussing such balancing.
10. It appears the Indian Police have for a very long time kept detailed information or databases (often called 'history sheets') on various groups such as 'criminal tribes', 'goondas' and those considered to have 'bad character' (Satish, 2011).
11. See Sections 41 and 149 of the Code of Criminal Procedure 1898. The other provisions in the text also govern specific aspects of arrest powers (sometime referring to those of citizens' arrests and so forth) – we do not discuss them for reasons of expositional brevity. It is also interesting that the law appears to expect police constables and functionaries to make fairly nuanced subjective judgments that do not seem to match with the typical police constables' training and education. Finally, police are supposed to seek an arrest warrant for those offenses not covered by the sections granting police the power to arrest without a warrant. However, the LCI (2001) found that even for these crimes the police frequently arrest without a warrant.
12. See Section 197 CCP.
13. Khanna (2015) discusses the issue of judicial delays in India in greater detail and the many LCI reports on judicial delays (numbering at least 13 now), as well as numerous Supreme Court decisions and law reform proposals targeted to this issue.
14. See Article 22 of the Constitution of India and Section 50 of the CCP. See also Goel (1981).
15. The court could in theory quash the case (in other words, effectively dismiss it), but this power is not used lightly. See Section 482 of the CCP and *Nikhil Merchant v. Central Bureau of Investigation & Anr.* (2008) 9 SCC 677.
16. *See State of Punjab v. Ajaib Singh*, AIR 1953 SC 10 (stating that the standard for the magistrate to take cognizance of the matter is whether the 'person arrested has committed the offense or is likely to have or is suspected to have committed it').
17. Generally speaking, the accused may challenge a warrant before he is arrested. Thus, before he is arrested (but after a warrant is issued) the accused may seek to have the warrant cancelled, which usually happens when the warrant was issued because of the accused's non-appearance in court on a particular date.
18. Two cases are instructive: *Hidayat Ullah v. The Crown*, AIR 1949 Lah 77, in which the court held it could grant bail to an individual prior to his arrest on an offense he was suspected of committing; and *Amirchand v. The Crown*, AIR 1950 East Punj 53, where the Full Bench of the East Punjab High Court held that bail could not be granted unless a person was already under restraint. See also *Varkey Paily Madthikudiyil v. State of Kerela*, AIR 1967 Ker 189, ¶ 4 (tracking the decision in *Amirchand*); *Sibbia, supra* note 5.
19. *Emperor v. Khwaja Nazir Ahmed*, AIR 1945 PC 18.
20. LCI (1967) did, however, recommend that the arrested individual be told the reason for the arrest. The LCI relied upon English case law, holding the same and stating that a constable who fails to inform the arrested individual of the reason for the arrest could be liable for false imprisonment.
21. The Law Commission of India was established for the first time in 1955. See http://www.lawcommissionofindia.nic.in/main.htm#a1.

22. Although the police had been under political control since the time of the British Raj, we see increasing politicization from the 1960s onwards because single party rule (first the British Raj and then the Congress party via elections) became less stable and the resulting contestation seemed to lead to parties using the police more frequently in political ways (Verma, 2005).

23. LCI (1969) at ¶ 39.9.

24. Concerns about the stigmatic and embarassing effects of arrest have been noted as recently as 2014 in the Supreme Court's decision in *Arnesh Kumar, supra* note 6: 'Arrest brings humiliation, curtails freedom and casts scars forever. Lawmakers know it so also the police. There is a battle between the lawmakers and the police and it seems that the police has not learnt its lesson: the lesson implicit and embodied in the [Criminal Procedure Code]. It has not come out of its colonial image despite six decades of Independence, it is largely considered as a tool of harassment, oppression and surely not considered a friend of [the] public. The need for caution in exercising the drastic power of arrest has been emphasised time and again by the courts but has not yielded [the] desired result. Power to arrest greatly contributes to its arrogance so also the failure of the Magistracy to check it'.

25. *See People's Union for Civil Liberties and Anr. v. State of Maharashtra and Ors* (2014) 10 SCC 635.

26. This concern has also been noticed by the Supreme Court in *Arnesh Kumar, supra* note 6, where it states: 'the power of arrest is one of the lucrative sources of police corruption. The attitude to arrest first and then proceed with the rest is despicable. It has become a handy tool to the police officers who lack sensitivity or act with oblique motive'. The poor opinion of the police this view suggests has been common in India (see the Supreme Court's decision in *Prakash Singh v. Union of India* (2006) 8 SCC 1, ¶¶ 8–9). It has also been connected to the arrest power in LCI (2001) at 27–28, 48–50. This view finds further implicit support in the Indian Evidence Act 1872 Sections 25 and 26 (along with sections 162 and 164 of the Code of Criminal Procedure), which do not allow statements or confessions obtained in police custody to count as evidence on the matters noted in the statements or confessions. Khanna and Hylton (2007) provide a discussion of how some criminal procedure doctrines might reduce corruption.

27. Private parties can make complaints to a Magistrate under Section 190(1)(a) or (c) of the CCP and the Magistrate can then decide whether to take cognizance of it and order the police to investigate under Section 156 of the CCP. Because these cases are quite infrequent and represent few, if any, of the anticipatory bail cases we address we do not discuss this any further.

28. LCI (1972) at ¶ 31.

29. See *Durga Prasad v. State of Bihar*, 1987 Cri. L.J. 1200. Indeed, as we shall discuss shortly, this is a concern currently animating efforts to reform AB.

30. Perhaps another way to explain what Section 438 provides is to look at Section 46(1) of the Code of Criminal Procedure 1973, which states that a police officer making an arrest 'shall actually touch or confine the body of the person to be arrested, unless there be a submission to the custody by word or action'. A decision to grant bail under Section 438 grants conditional immunity from such a 'touch' or confinement. See *Sibbia, supra* note 5, at ¶ 7 (stating that '[a]n order of anticipatory bail, constitutes, so to say, an insurance against police custody following upon arrest for offence or offences in respect of which the order is issued. In other words, unlike a post-arrest order of bail, it is a pre-arrest legal process which directs that if the person in whose favour it is issued is thereafter arrested on the accusation in respect of which the direction is issued, he shall be released on bail').

31. The Police Commission of India (1974) at ¶ 61.44; LCI (2001) at 23–24. See also the recent decision of the Supreme Court in *Arnesh Kumar, supra* note 6, where it

states: 'Law Commissions, Police Commissions and this Court in a large number of judgments emphasised the need to maintain a balance between individual liberty and societal order while exercising the power of arrest. ... We believe that no arrest should be made only because the offence is non-bailable and cognizable and therefore, lawful for the police officers to do so. The existence of the power to arrest is one thing, the justification for the exercise of it is quite another. Apart from the power to arrest, the police officers must be able to justify the reasons thereof. ... It would be prudent and wise for a police officer that no arrest is made without a reasonable satisfaction reached after some investigation as to the genuineness of the allegation'.

32.   In particular, Article 21 of the Indian Constitution grants individuals the right to liberty, which then needs to be balanced against the societal right to maintain public order. Case law has held that when an arrest is made in compliance with legally required procedural and substantive protections, the State can curtail the liberty of the person arrested and not violate Article 21. *See Ambikesh Mahapatra and Ors. v. The State of West Bengal and Ors.* (10.03.2015 – CALHC); *Sibbia, supra* note 5, at ¶ 31; *Sumit Mehta v. State of N.C.T. of Delhi*, 2013 (11) SCALE 374, ¶ 9; *Siddharam Satlingappa Mhetre v. State of Maharashtra*, AIR 2011 SC 312, ¶ 17; *State of M.P. v. Ram Kishan Balothia* (1995) 3 SCC 221, ¶ 11.

33.   AIR 1994 SC 1349.

34.   See ibid. at 1356.

35.   AIR 1997 SC 610.

36.   The Court also held that if the chosen friend or relative of the arrestee was not living in the locality they were to be identified telegraphically within 8 to 12 hours.

37.   The LCI also recommended that if the police decided not to arrest someone they should record the reasons for that.

38.   (2014) 8 SCC 273.

39.   (2015) Cri.W.P. No. 725/14.

40.   See Section 154, CCP 1973. It is noteworthy that once the FIR is registered the contents cannot be changed without explicit approval from the Supreme Court or the High Court (which is one level below the Supreme Court). See Sections 173 and 482, CCP 1973. If the police do not file an FIR, the complaining party can file a complaint (see Sections 190 and 200–204 of the CCP 1973). We do not discuss the process for a complaint under these sections as they are not that common and have not materially influenced the anticipatory bail cases.

41.   See Section 173(2) CCP 1973.

42.   See Sections 211–218 CCP 1973.

43.   See Sections 211–218 and 240 CCP 1973.

44.   It is noteworthy that, under India's Constitutional scheme, states can deviate from this provision of the CCP. Some states have done this over time (for example, Maharashtra, see Maharashtra Act 24 of 1993, Sec. 2) and at least one state (Uttar Pradesh) has even removed the provision for AB for their state. See U.P. Act 16 of 1976, Sec. 9.

45.   See *State of Assam and Another v. R.K. Krishnan Kumar and Others*, AIR 1998 SC 144, cited from LCI (2007) at 35. See also *Sibbia, supra* note 5, at 591, where the court says: 'Can an order of bail be passed under the Section without notice to the Public Prosecutor? It can be. But notice should issue to the Public Prosecutor or the Government Advocate forthwith and the question of bail should be re-examined in the light of the respective contentions of the parties. The ad interim order too must conform to the requirements of the Section and suitable conditions should be imposed on the applicant even at that stage.

46.   For a recent example see *State of Gujarat v. Unknown* (2015) R/Cr.Ma/11926/2015 (7 July 2015).

47. See *Mahant Chand Nath Yogi v. State of Haryana*, AIR 2003 SC 18.
48. There are some crimes for which anticipatory bail is not available. See, for example, Section 18, Scheduled Castes and Scheduled Tribes (Prevention of Atrocities) Act 1989. It is noteworthy that AB is available for crimes punishable by death or life imprisonment, but to grant AB for these offenses (for example, murder), there must be some very compelling circumstance or likelihood that the charges are false. See *Pokar Ram v. State of Rajasthan and Anr.*, 1985 AIR 969.
49. The *Sibbia* case held that there is no reason for reading the limitations in Section 437 and 439 (the general bail sections) into Section 438. See *Sibbia, supra* note 5, ¶ 21; *Siddharam, supra* note 32, ¶ 98.
50. (2005) 4 SCC 303.
51. The phrasing of Section 438 assumes the allegations the applicant is concerned about are based on events that have allegedly occurred already rather than things that might happen in the future.
52. (2005) 4 SCC 303.
53. See Khanna (2015) for more discussion on the delays.
54. See LCI (2007).
55. 1985 Cri. LJ 1111 (Ker). A similar decision was made in *B.V. Seetharama v. State of Karnataka*, 2007 Cri. LJ 3503. After the applicants sought AB for all future cases that might be brought against them for offenses related to publication of articles on the Jain religion, the Karnataka High Court required the applicants to show imminence of a likely arrest based on reasonable belief.
56. (2000) 10 SCC 7.
57. See *Sibbia, supra* note 5.
58. See LCI (2001).
59. See LCI (2001) at 20–26.
60. When Section 438(1) was first enacted it did not specify many factors to consider, although the amendments in 2005 provide a list that is detailed in the Appendix.
61. AIR 1977 SC 2447.
62. AIR 2011 SC 312, ¶ 122.
63. Section 34 of the Indian Penal Code 1860 relates to what might be termed group or conspiracy-based liability and Section 149 relates to group liability for individuals who knew an unlawful act was being committed.
64. *Siddharam, supra* note 32, ¶ 122.
65. See Model Police Act, Soli Sorabjee Committee (2006).
66. See *Siddharam, supra* note 32, ¶ 124, cited with approval in *Teesta Atul Setalvad and Ors. v. State of Gujarat*, Criminal Misc. Application (For Anticipatory Bail) Nos. 4677, 4679 and 4680 of 2014, MANU/GJ/0051/2015 at Para 57.
67. *Siddharam, supra* note 32, ¶ 123, cited with approval in *Teesta, supra* note 66.
68. See *Pokar Ram, supra* note 48.
69. Criminal Misc. Application (For Anticipatory Bail) Nos. 4677, 4679 and 4680 of 2014, MANU/GJ/0051/2015 at Para 57.
70. It is also noteworthy that it is not common practice for the court reporter to note down everything said in court verbatim, but rather to note down what the court requests that the reporter note down. This results in trial records that do not include every word or argument made in the proceedings and usually reflect only the orders of the Court and statements that the courts or the parties specifically want to include (subject to the court's discretion).
71. See *Naresh Kumar Yadav v. Ravindra Kumar* (2008) 1 SCC 632, ¶ 6. See also, *Salauddin Abdulsamad Shaikh v. State of Maharashtra*, AIR 1996 SC 1042; *K.L. Verma v. State and Anr.* (1998) 9 SCC 348; *Adri Dharan Das v. State of West Bengal* (2005) 4 SCC 303; *Sunita Devi v. State of Bihar and Anr.* (2005) 1 SCC

608. In these decisions, the Supreme Court largely adopts the approach of the LCI in its 48th report. See LCI (1972), ¶ 31.

72. See *Sibbia, supra* note 5; *Joginder Kumar v. State of U.P. and Ors.* (1994) 4 SCC 260.

73. *See Sibbia, supra* note 5.

74. The Court observed that '[w]e do not see why the provisions of Section 438 Code of Criminal Procedure should be suspected as containing something volatile or incendiary, which needs to be handled with the greatest care and caution imaginable', *Siddharam supra* note 32, ¶ 98.

75. Anticipatory bail can be granted even prior to the lodging of a First Information Report or registration of a crime. See *Sibbia, supra* note 5, ¶ 38.

76. Earlier, there was a slew of cases which held that after the order of anticipatory bail, the accused has to surrender before the trial court and after that he can request bail by the trial court (which would release the accused only after he has surrendered). This practice had been endorsed in *Salauddin Abdulsamad Shaikh v. State of Maharashtra* (1996) 1 SCC 667, *K.L. Verma v. State and Anr.* MANU/SC/ 1493/1998: (1998) 9 SCC 348; *Adri Dharan Das v. State of West Bengal* (2005) 4 SCC 303, and *Sunita Devi v. State of Bihar and Anr.* (2005) 1 SCC 608.

77. See *Siddharam, supra* note 32, at ¶¶ 105, 106; *Sibbia, supra* note 5. The court that grants bail, which is an interim order, also has the power to cancel it. The court can always review its decision based on subsequent facts, circumstances and new material. It is noteworthy that the applicant's reluctance in fully cooperating could result in cancellation of bail.

78. See *Siddharam, supra* note 32, at ¶¶ 105, 106.

79. See Khanna (2002); Westen and Drubel (1978).

80. See LCI (2007).

81. In *Sibbia, supra* note 5, at ¶ 47, the Court expressed concern that a blanket order of anticipatory bail (covering all offenses) could interfere with police investigations even in cases where the individual commits a crime (for example, murder) in front of the public. In light of this, a court granting anticipatory bail must carefully delineate the specific offenses with respect to which the order is granted.

82. See *Prahlad Singh Bhati v. N.C.T. Delhi & Anr.* (2001) 4 SCC 280, ¶ 9. Simply put, the liberty granted to the accused via anticipatory bail is with respect to a minor offence, not a more serious one.

83. See *Hamida v. Rashid and Ors.* (2008) 1 SCC 474 at ¶¶ 2 and 12. This has been followed in a number of other decisions. See generally, *Prahlad, supra* note 82; *Abhay Singh Yadav v. The State (Govt. of NCT of Delhi)*, 217 (2015) DLT 695. This would not apply if the other offence is added with a *mala fide* intention. See *Manjit Kaur v. State of Punjab*, 2014(1) Crimes 504 (P&H), ¶¶ 10–16.

84. *See Jagbir Singh v. State*, 90 (2001) DLT 16, at ¶ 7.

85. See ibid.

86. See *Shukpal v. State of Rajasthan*, RLW 1988 (1) 283, followed in *Chandra Pal Singh Choudhary v. Vijit Singh and Anr.*, 2009 Cri LJ 3416.

87. See *Shukpal, supra* note 86; *Chandra Pal, supra* note 86; and *Gheesya and Ors. v. State of Rajasthan*, RLW 1988(2) 307.

88. See *M.C. Abraham and Another v. State of Maharashtra and Others* (2003) 2 SCC 649.

89. See *Sudip Sen v. State of West Bengal*, 2010 Cri LJ 4628 (Cal). However, the applicant will not be permitted to succeed on a second application if his only argument is that the earlier court did not consider some part of the record that was available then or if the applicant tries to raise a point that could have been raised earlier, but was not.

90. See *Imratlal Vishwakarma v. State of Madhya Pradesh*, 1997 (1) Crimes 289 (MP).

91. See *Ganesh Raj v. State of Rajasthan*, 2005 Cri LJ 2086 (Raj).
92. See LCI (2007), at 22–23.
93. See § 304(1) CCP 1973; *Shrichand v. State of Madhya Pradesh*, 1992 (1) Crimes 362, 364, ¶¶ 6–7; Manohar and Singh (2011), at 1192.
94. See Constitution of India, 1950 Art. 21 and 22(1); *Janardhan Reddy v. State of Hyderabad*, AIR 1951 SC 217, ¶ 5. Courts have held that this right applies when someone is in custody (see *Directorate of Enforcement v. Deepak Mahajan*, AIR 1994 SC 1775, ¶¶ 85–86) and is only violated if a request for counsel is denied. See *Ramaswarup v. Union of India*, AIR 1965 SC 247, ¶ 5. The Supreme Court has held that counsel must be provided to all unrepresented individuals accused of a crime because indigence should not be a ground for denying someone a fair trial or equal justice. See *Ranchod Mathur Wasawa v. State of Gujarat*, 1974 SCR (2) 72. Many cases have extended the right to people not in custody but who are accused of crimes. See *Mohd. Hussain v. Government of NCT*, AIR 2012 SC 75, ¶ 17; *Suk Das v. Union Territory of Arunachal Pradesh*, AIR 1986 SC 991, ¶ 5; *Habu v. State of Rajasthan*, AIR 1987 Raj 83, ¶ 5; *Sanjay Khanderao Deore v. State of Maharashtra*, AIR 2006 Bom (4) 544, ¶ 13; Manohar and Singh (2011), at 1189.
95. See *Poolpandi v. Superintendent, Central Excise* (1992) 3 SCC 259, ¶¶ 6–10; Aiyer (2010), at 90–91.
96. See *Sreedharan T. and Ors. v. Sub Inspector of Police and Anr.*, 2009 CRI LJ 1249, ¶¶ 28–39; Legal Services Authorities Act, 1987 cited in LCI (2007), at 22–23.
97. See LCI (2007), at 22–23.
98. See ibid. at 25.
99. Of course, both AB and bail can be cancelled by the courts if the accused is engaging in this behavior. For AB see *Mahant, supra* note 47, and for regular bail see Section 439 of the CCP. The political implications of the interaction between AB, arrest standards and police regulation and the impact that has had on the Indian criminal justice (for good or bad) is being pursued by one of us in separate research.
100. See Devine (1990).
101. 1984, 604 F. Supp. 278.
102. Other jurisdictions have similar requirements for obtaining arrest warrants except in exigent, or otherwise limited, circumstances. For Canada, see Section 29 of the Criminal Code of Canada and for the European Union, see the discussion on European Arrest Warrants, which must be issued by a judicial authority. See Article 8, *EU Council Framework Decision of 13 June 2002 on the European Arrest Warrant* (2002/584/JHA). Some courts have held that 'judicial authority' can include public prosecutors. See *Assange v. The Swedish Prosecution Authority* [2011] EWHC 2849 (Admin) and *Assange v. The Swedish Prosecution Authority* [2012] UKSC 22.
103. For the US see Prosser, Keeton, Dobbs, Keeton, and Owen (1984). For the UK see Deakin, Johnston, and Markesinis (2007). For India see *West Bengal State Electricity v. Dilip Kumar Ray* (2007) 14 SCC 568.
104. This largely encapsulates the concerns in India about the broader granting of AB. This concern might be somewhat assuaged by the way in which AB orders are granted. For example, if the potential accused is required to identify himself, commit to making himself available for trial (often accompanied by handing over his passport), and commit to not interfering in the investigation, then concerns – although not eliminated – might be somewhat reduced. Indeed, these are frequently the conditions attached to AB and their violation can lead to revocation of bail. Nonetheless, the risk of false non-arrests increases to some extent.
105. See Shavell (1993).
106. The concern with accuracy is similar to that discussed in Kaplow (1994).

107. See LCI (2001) at 50.
108. There may also be ways to reduce the cost and delay of having AB as a supplement. For example, one might expect senior police officers to be less likely to initiate arrests for smaller-scale extortion and harassment (for example, alleged false dowry cases under Section 498A). In light of that, one could imagine requiring arrests for certain crimes (for example, Section 498A cases) to be approved by a senior police officer, in writing, prior to any arrest (unless the prohibited activity is occurring in front of the police officer).
109. See Appendix at the end of this chapter. Inserted in substitution of pre-existing Section 438(1) by Act 25 of 2005, sec. 38.

REFERENCES

Aiyer, P. Ramanathan. 2010. *The Major Law Lexicon*, Vol. 1 (4th edn). Mumbai: LexisNexis.

Arnold, David. 1976. 'The Police and Colonial Control in South India', 4 *Social Scientist* 3–16.

Arnold, David. 1992. 'Police Power and the Demise of British Rule in India, 1930–47', in David Anderson and David Killingray, eds., *Policing and Decolonisation: Politics, Nationalism, and the Police, 1917–65*. New York: Manchester University Press.

Balganesh, Shyamkrishna. 2016. 'The Constitutionalization of Indian Private Law', in Sujit Chaudhry, Madhav Khosla and Pratap Bhanu Mehta, eds., *Oxford Handbook of the Indian Constitution*. Oxford: Oxford University Press.

Bayley, David H. 1969. *The Police and Political Development in India*. Princeton, NJ: Princeton University Press.

Deakin, Simon, Angus Johnston, and Basil Markesinis. 2007. *Markesinis and Deakin's Tort Law* (6th edn). Oxford: Oxford University Press.

Devine, F.E. 1990. 'Anticipatory Bail: An Indian Civil Liberties Innovation', 14 *International Journal of Comparative and Applied Criminal Justice* 107–114.

Friedman, David D. 1995. 'Making Sense of English Law Enforcement in the Eighteenth Century', 2 *University of Chicago Law School Roundtable* 475–505.

Goel, Hukum Chand. 1981. 'Anticipatory Bail – A New Experiment in India', in Minoru Shikita, ed., 19 *UNAFEI Resource Material Series* 48–52.

Guha, Ramachandra. 2008. *India After Gandhi: The History of the World's Largest Democracy*. New York: Harper Collins.

Jalal, Ayesha. 1995. *Democracy and Authoritarianism in South Asia: A Comparative and Historical Perspective*. New York: Cambridge University Press.

Kaplow, Louis. 1994. 'The Value of Accuracy in Adjudication', 23 *Journal of Legal Studies* 307–401.

Khanna, Vikramaditya. 2002. 'Double Jeopardy's Asymmetric Appeal Rights: What Purpose Do They Serve?', 82 *Boston University Law Review* 341–404.

Khanna, Vikramaditya. 2015. 'An Analysis of the Indian Judicial System', Draft.

Khanna, Vikramaditya and Keith Hylton. 2007. 'A Public Choice Theory of Criminal Procedure', 15 *Supreme Court Economic Review* 61–118.

Klerman, Daniel M. 2001. 'Settlement and the Decline of Private Prosecution in Thirteenth-Century England', 19 *Law and History Review* 1–65.

Law Commission of India. 1967. *37th Report on the Code of Criminal Procedure 1898 (Sections 1 to 176)*.

Law Commission of India. 1969. *41st Report on the Code of Criminal Procedure 1898 (Volume 1)*.

Law Commission of India. 1972. *48th Report on Some Questions under the Code of Criminal Procedure Bill, 1970.*

Law Commission of India. 2001. *177th Report on Law Relating to Arrest.*

Law Commission of India. 2007. *203rd Report on Section 438 of the Code of Criminal Procedure, 1973 as Amended by the Code of Criminal Procedure (Amendment) Act, 2005 (Anticipatory Bail).*

Manohar, V.R. and Avtar Singh. 2011. *Ratanlal and Dhirajlal: The Code of Criminal Procedure* (19th edn). Mumbai: LexisNexis.

Mehta, Pratap Bhanu. 2007. 'The Rise of Judicial Sovereignty', 18 *Journal of Democracy* 70–83.

Model Police Act, Soli Sorabjee Committee. 2006. Available at: http://www.vifindia.org/sites/default/files/Draft%20Police%20Act%20%28submitted%20by%20the%20Soli%20Sorabjee%20Committee%29,%202006.pdf.

National Crime Records Bureau. 2012. Available at: http://ncrb.gov.in/.

National Police Commission of India. 1979. *2nd Report.*

National Police Commission of India. 1980. *3rd Report.*

The Police Commission of India. 1974. *8th Report.*

Prosser, William Lloyd, W. Page Keeton, Dan B. Dobbs, Robert E. Keeton, and David G. Owen. 1984. *Prosser and Keeton on Torts* (5th edn). Eagan, MN: West Group.

Royal Commission Report on Criminal Procedure (Philips Commission). 1981.

Satish, Mrinal. 2011. *'Bad Characters, History Sheeters, Budding Goondas and Rowdies: Police Surveillance Files and Intelligence Databases in India'*, 23 *National Law School of India Review* 133–154.

Shavell, Steven M. 1993. 'The Optimal Structure of Law Enforcement', 36 *Journal of Law and Economics* 255–288.

Verma, Arvind. 2005. 'The Police in India: Design, Performance and Adaptability', in Devesh Kapur and Pratap Bhanu Mehta, eds., *Public Institutions in India: Performance and Design*. New Delhi: Oxford University Press.

Vogler, Richard and Shahrzad Fouladvand. 2016. 'Standards for Making Factual Determinations in Arrest and Pretrial Detention: A Comparative Analysis of Law and Practice', in Jacqueline Ross and Steven Thaman, eds., *Comparative Criminal Procedure*. Cheltenham, UK and Northampton, MA, USA: Edward Elgar Publishing.

Westen, Peter and Richard Drubel. 1978. 'Toward a General Theory of Double Jeopardy', 1978 *Supreme Court Review* 81–169.

APPENDIX: SECTION 438 OF THE CODE OF CRIMINAL PROCEDURE 1973

438. Direction for grant of bail to person apprehending arrest.
[(1) Where any person has reason to believe that he may be arrested on accusation of having committed a non-bailable offence, he may apply to the High Court or the Court of Session for a direction under this section that in the event of such arrest he shall be released on bail; and that Court may, after taking into consideration, inter alia, the following factors, namely:–

(i)   the nature and gravity of the accusation;
(ii) the antecedents of the applicant including the fact as to whether he has previously undergone imprisonment on conviction by a Court in respect of any cognizable offence;
(iii) the possibility of the applicant to flee from justice; and
(iv) where the accusation has been made with the object of injuring or humiliating the applicant by having him so arrested,

either reject the application forthwith or issue an interim order for the grant of anticipatory bail:

Provided that, where the High Court or, as the case may be, the Court of Session, has not passed any interim order under this sub-section or has rejected the application for grant of anticipatory bail, it shall be open to an officer in-charge of a police station to arrest, without warrant the applicant on the basis of the accusation apprehended in such application.

(1A) Where the Court grants an interim order under sub-section (1), it shall forthwith cause a notice being not less than seven days notice, together with a copy of such order to be served on the Public Prosecutor and the Superintendent of Police, with a view to give the Public Prosecutor a reasonable opportunity of being heard when the application shall be finally heard by the Court.

(1B) The presence of the applicant seeking anticipatory bail shall be obligatory at the time of final hearing of the application and passing of final order by the Court, if on an application made to it by the Public Prosecutor, the Court considers such presence necessary in the interest of justice.][109]

(2) When the High Court or the Court of Session makes a direction under sub-section (1), it may include such conditions in such directions in the light of the facts of the particular case, as it may think fit, including –

(i)   a condition that the person shall make himself available for interrogation by a police officer as and when required;

(ii) a condition that the person shall not, directly or indirectly, make any inducement, threat or promise to any person acquainted with the facts of the case so as to dissuade him from disclosing such facts to the court or to any police officer;

(iii) a condition that the person shall not leave India without the previous permission of the court;

(iv) such other condition as may be imposed under sub-section (3) of section 437, as if the bail were granted under that section.

(3) If such person is thereafter arrested without warrant by an officer in charge of a police station on such accusation, and is prepared either at the time of arrest or at any time while in the custody of such officer to give bail, he shall be released on bail, and if a Magistrate taking cognizance of such offence decides that a warrant should issue in the first instance against that person, he shall issue a bailable warrant in conformity with the direction of the court under sub-section (1).

4. Mechanisms for screening prosecutorial charging decisions in the United States and Taiwan

Tzu-te Wen and Andrew D. Leipold

1. INTRODUCTION

No one would deny the importance or scope of prosecutorial charging authority in the modern world, regardless of whether the prosecutor is operating in an adversarial or a continental criminal justice system. Along with law enforcement, prosecutors are the gatekeepers of the criminal system, deciding whether a person should be criminally charged, diverted, left to non-criminal sanctions, or ignored. Once a person is committed to the criminal process, the prosecutor has enormous discretion to decide what charge to set, and whether to offer a deal in return for a guilty plea. And in many cases, a prosecutor has the ability to influence the sentence that follows a conviction, either directly through bargaining or through a recommendation to the court.

All observers agree that the prosecutorial power is vast (Allen et al., 2011; Davis, 1978), and in the United States there is theoretical agreement that vast power creates a large potential for abuse (Davis, 2001),[1] but little agreement on the amount of actual abuse. Likewise, prosecutors in Taiwan have been criticized by scholars, lawyers, and judges for bringing criminal charges where there is insufficient evidence to indict, or where there is an ill or unjustified motivation or influence behind the charge (Wang, 2010).[2]

If the prosecutor employs her authority too aggressively, the result can be unfounded or overzealous charging – accusations that are not supported by sufficient evidence to convict. In such a case there are three possible outcomes, ranging from the unfortunate to the intolerable: the suspect (who may be innocent or guilty) is set free after a long, embarrassing, and expensive process; or, a factually guilty defendant is convicted by a process that has failed to operate as it should; or, a factually innocent person is wrongfully convicted. Each of these outcomes – particularly the third – imposes large costs on the accused, inflates the system's caseload, and breeds public mistrust of the system.

Some number of charging errors, whether caused by mistakes, misjudgments, excessive zeal, or corruption, are inevitable in any system, regardless of its structure. But other errors are avoidable. Many of the costs imposed by improper charges flow from a pervasive feature of all modern criminal processes that are based on the rule of law – the final resolution of criminal charges takes time, often a great deal of time. It can take weeks, months, or occasionally years to bring a case to conclusion, and although this delay is often for prudent reasons,[3] the resulting costs are still significant. Even if the eventual outcome of the case is an acquittal, the expense and stigma can be life-altering for the accused and corrosive to a just society (Leipold, 2000).

As a result, one of the primary goals of the pretrial process should be to ensure that there is an effective screening mechanism in place, one that will scrutinize prosecutorial charging decisions and ensure that inadequate or ill-motivated charges are eliminated from the process at the earliest realistic time. The purpose of this chapter is to examine and evaluate the screening mechanisms now in place in the United States and Taiwan.[4] In particular, it asks how likely it is that under the current processes a weak charge will be eliminated from the system. It also asks the related question: How does the presence of the screening mechanisms influence the prosecutor's charging decision?

Section 2 briefly describes the prosecutorial system in the United States and Taiwan, while section 3 articulates the screening mechanisms and their current norms in both countries. Section 4 concludes by examining a few implications of the hypothesis that the current screening function does not operate as effectively as it should, and is in need of reform. In addition, we offer some ideas of what the potential normative design of a screening mechanism should be.

2.   THE PROSECUTORIAL SYSTEMS

2.1   The United States

The United States Constitution makes the prosecutor part of the executive branch, not of the judiciary. Criminal charges may be filed by federal prosecutors or by state prosecutors, who have independent but overlapping jurisdictions. Although federal cases play a distinctive and critical role in the prosecution of interstate and international crimes, the vast majority of crimes, including the bulk of all violent and property crimes, are prosecuted by the states.

The federal prosecutorial power is under the direction of the US Attorney General, who serves as the head of the Department of Justice (DOJ) and is answerable to the President of the United States. Although the DOJ sets broad enforcement priorities, the actual prosecution decisions are delegated to the 93 US Attorneys, who are the chief federal law enforcement officers in each federal judicial district.[5] Working for each US Attorney are Assistants, in whom much of the day-to-day prosecution power rests. Neither the Attorney General, the US Attorneys, nor the Assistant US Attorneys are elected. They are thus insulated from direct public pressure. In contrast, the primary prosecutorial power in the states typically resides in an elected prosecutor for a subdivision of the state, although her assistants normally are not subject to electoral control.

American prosecutors possess a wide range of discretionary powers, including the authority to establish priorities among offenders, offenses, and law enforcement strategies; as a result, prosecution offices are able to manage heavy caseloads with relatively limited resources (Goldstein and Marcus, 1977). Decisions on whether or not to charge, what to charge, and whether to bargain, have been left in the prosecutors' hands with very few limitations (Vorenberg, 1981). Most importantly, these decisions are normally not subject to judicial review.[6] The US Supreme Court has observed that 'prosecutorial decisions necessarily involve both judgmental and factual decisions that vary from case to case ... It is difficult to imagine guidelines that would produce the predictability sought by ... [those who favor judicial review] without sacrificing the discretion essential to a humane and fair system of criminal justice'.[7]

The impact of this broad range of discretion is two-fold. First, decisions to charge (or not to charge) are made exclusively by a member of the executive branch, whose duties include law enforcement and serving as an advocate for conviction once the charges are brought. Second, the tension between the pressure to capture and punish criminals and the need to make objectively fair charging decisions creates an unavoidable risk that unfounded charges will work their way into the criminal system.

2.2 Taiwan

Taiwan has no federal and state jurisdictions; instead, it has a unitary centralized prosecutorial system which directs various levels of prosecutors' offices. Structurally, the prosecutor is subordinated to the Ministry of Justice, a department subordinate to the Executive Yuan (Execution branch). However, the prosecutor is not a pure executive officer as is her counterpart in the United States.

The continental origins of the prosecutorial structure can be traced from the Japanese system, one that adopted the French semi-inquisitorial system, which was imposed through Japanese colonization of Taiwan. By the first half of the twentieth century, Taiwanese judges were active at trial, including extracting confessions from the accused, and the prosecutor wielded magistrate-like authority to detain suspects to secure their appearance at trial (Wang, 2002). After World War II, the Taiwanese criminal justice system remained consistent with the Continental legal system, maintaining the structure, organization and personnel of the system, and grouping judges and prosecutors together as part of the magistracy. Later on, the Taiwanese prosecutorial system was more heavily influenced by German criminal procedure than that of any other country, until the Taiwanese justice system began its transformation towards the adversarial system at the turn of the twenty-first century. Several features typical of the Continental system can be identified in Taiwan's prosecutorial structure.

First, the prosecutorial system is centralized and subject to strong hierarchical control. Second, Taiwan's prosecutors are recruited, trained, and selected much in the same way as their European counterparts. Unlike prosecutors in the United States, prosecutors in Taiwan are neither elected nor appointed; they are governmental officials who pass the annual National Judiciary Examination, the most competitive judicial examination in Taiwan.[8] They are not 'attorneys' as are their counterparts in the United States; instead, they are a type of civil servant or government official (Pizzi, 1993), although they are still part of the judiciary. The promotion of prosecutors is based in part on conviction rates, dismissal rates, and the ability to handle high-profile cases successfully. Climbing up the career ladder requires prosecutors to pursue criminal cases aggressively.

As in many inquisitorial systems, the prosecutorial system places heavy emphasis on centripetal and uniform decision-making. In theory, top-down hierarchical control and a unitary structure enhance the uniform application and interpretation of law (Damaška, 1974: 484–485). This system is designed to avoid prosecutorial charging discretion and favor consistent charging practices. Both of these are important goals because Taiwan, like Germany, mandates the investigation and prosecution of all provable criminal offenses. The hierarchical command structure of Taiwan's prosecution service is also intended to ensure uniform compliance with general policies and specific orders (Lin, 2000). Prosecutors are supposed to base their decisions solely on the evidence and the law. If an investigation provides 'evidence obtained by a public prosecutor in the course of investigation [which] is sufficient to show that an accused is suspected of having committed an offense', the principle of mandatory prosecution obligates the prosecutor to charge the offense.[9] This rule is meant to forestall arbitrary decision-making and to protect charging decisions from being influenced by political pressures or other external considerations.

In theory, then, the prosecution has no leeway in deciding whether a criminal charge should be brought, unless she ignores, misjudges, or intentionally abuses the scope of her mandatory authority. Nonetheless, prosecutors retain a large measure of informal discretion that permits abusive or erroneous charges to be filed, because whether the evidence meets the mandatory prosecution standard is itself a decision that requires the exercise of discretionary judgment. Stated differently, prosecutors still have the ability to charge a case that should not be brought if they misjudge the strength of the case, or let impermissible factors influence their evaluation of whether the mandatory prosecution standard has been met. Whether the prosecutor abuses the prosecution or merely misjudges the evidence, there should be a gatekeeper for the protection of the innocent, to screen out unwarranted prosecutions.

3. SCREENING MECHANISMS

In adversarial and inquisitorial legal systems alike, prosecutorial charging decisions remain mysterious to the public at large. Despite Taiwan's commitment to the principle of mandatory prosecution, the process remains opaque. Mandatory prosecution makes direct corruption of prosecutors less likely and decision-making more uniform. However, not all cases that prosecutors must bring under application of the principle of mandatory prosecution are appropriate for a full trial. Even if prosecutors correctly evaluate the evidence, the mandatory prosecution standard is set at a level that provides no assurance of conviction. Evidence that is 'sufficient to show that an accused is suspected of having committed an offense' provides some protection against wholly fictitious charges, but falls short of requiring evidence that will ensure a conviction.

By contrast, the accepted role of discretion in American charging decisions inherently makes such decision-making processes more complex, less predictable, less understandable to outsiders, and less uniform across jurisdictions. As a consequence, the implementation of screening mechanisms prior to trial is critically important, not only to counteract the various costs imposed by the mere fact of a prosecution, but also to shield the innocent from unfounded charges. This section compares the current screening mechanisms in the United States, consisting of the preliminary hearing and grand jury investigations, with their counterpart in Taiwan, which consists of judicial review of the case file.

3.1   The United States

3.1.1   Preliminary hearing

The initial appearance of an arrestee before a judicial officer presumptively occurs within 48 hours of the arrest. At this initial appearance, the magistrate will advise the arrestee of charges, appoint counsel, and set bail if appropriate. An additional goal of this hearing is to determine whether there is probable cause for arrest (assuming, as is usually true, that the arrest is made without an arrest warrant).[10] In the federal system, this showing is typically made when a federal prosecutor drafts a criminal complaint and a federal agent swears out a supporting affidavit, based on which the magistrate must determine whether the arrest was supported by probable cause. In the case of a warrantless arrest, these documents are drafted and presented to the magistrate after the arrest but prior to the initial appearance. This procedure serves as a first-level screening of the arrest decision, and undoubtedly discourages some arbitrary arrests. But the finding of probable cause is often made quickly, on limited information, and is not subject to adversarial testing.

Thereafter, in a federal case the magistrate-judge will schedule the preliminary hearing. The preliminary hearing is to be held within two weeks of the first appearance if the suspect is in custody, and within three weeks if he is not in custody. The purpose of the preliminary hearing is to check whether there is sufficient evidence to proceed to trial. The magistrate judge will determine whether there is 'probable cause' to believe 'the crime' has been committed and the 'defendant' committed the crime (Wright and Leipold, 2008). If there is no probable cause, the defendant is discharged and the case is dismissed.

While the goal of the preliminary hearing is to conduct another layer of screening, the level of proof needed to survive the screening (probable cause) is curiously identical to the level needed for an arrest warrant or to survive an initial appearance (Wright and Leipold, 2008).[11] In fact, however, there are additional features of the preliminary hearing that are designed to advance the screening function.

First, the preliminary hearing is conducted in an adversarial process so that the defendant may test the prosecutor's evidence (Wright and Leipold, 2008).[12] The burden is on the prosecutor to establish probable cause, and she must present the evidence through witnesses, who are then subject to cross-examination by the defense. The defendant is entitled to put on an affirmative case to show that probable cause does not exist, although, as discussed below, he often will not do so.

Second, the defendant is entitled to the assistance of counsel at the preliminary hearing. Unlike the *ex parte* process in obtaining a warrant, the defendant now has the benefit of an experienced player in the system who can more properly evaluate the strength and weaknesses of the government's case. The fact that some time has passed since the arrest also means there has been the chance for a preliminary investigation of the facts by the defense.

Third, the preliminary hearing adds another layer of review before trial to ensure the continued detention of the suspect is warranted. Not only has the magistrate now heard the government's theory of what happened in a case, the magistrate and the defendant have both obtained a preview of the evidence that is likely to be presented at trial. Collectively, these features should ensure that the probable cause determination by the neutral magistrate in an open hearing meets the minimum requirements of reliability (Arenella, 1980). This also ensures that the screening is not entirely controlled by law enforcement and that the defendant has had an opportunity to test the strength of the government's evidence through cross-examination and to offer evidence of its own.

If the prosecution establishes probable cause, the case is bound over to the grand jury in federal jurisdictions and in those state jurisdictions that adopt the grand jury mechanism. In state jurisdictions that proceed by an 'information' (a formal charge prepared by the prosecutor that is not subject to grand jury review), the case is bound over to the trial court. Critically, once the case has passed through the preliminary hearing and been sent on to the grand jury or the trial court, no further judicial review of the prosecution's case will occur before formal charges are filed. (Before trial, the defendant will nonetheless have the opportunity to bring pretrial motions to challenge the constitutionality of the government's investigative tactics or the admissibility of evidence at trial.)

The preliminary hearing thus can be a critical moment in the pretrial process, because it is the only meaningful stage at which the defendant can challenge the government's evidence and at which judicial screening of the prosecutor's charging decision takes place. Nonetheless, preliminary hearings are not mandated by the US Constitution;[13] only grand jury review (discussed below) is constitutionally compelled. As a result, if the prosecution has obtained an indictment before the scheduled date of preliminary hearing, the preliminary hearing is mooted. In fact, once the grand jury has reviewed the government's case – a process that involves no judicial oversight – no further review by *any* entity is required before trial.

The right to have the state's case screened can be important to the defense, but there are also strategic considerations that both sides must consider that can alter the degree of screening that takes place. For the defense, a preliminary hearing can serve as an informal means of discovery.[14] In the federal system and in some states, the pretrial exchange of evidence can be quite limited, and by requiring the prosecution to convince a judge of the validity of the charges, the preliminary hearing can provide valuable insight into the prosecution's theory of the case, the names of key witnesses, and the substance of their testimony. Of course, the prosecution may not want to reveal important evidence too early in the process, especially if she has enough other evidence to establish probable cause, so disclosure is by no means certain (Leipold, 2002).

A similar benefit may flow to the government. If the defense tests a government witness at a preliminary hearing by cross-examination, this could afford the prosecutor a chance to discover the potential defects of her case, including problems with her theory of the case, while revealing to the prosecutor the defense version of events (Leipold, 2002). Although the scope of cross-examination is circumscribed by the testimony under direct-examination, as it will be at trial (Wright and Leipold, 2008), a complete cross-examination of a witness can provide both parties' with vital impeachment materials for use at the trial. In addition, a transcript of a witness's prior statement – that is, the testimony given at the preliminary hearing – could be admissible as substantive evidence against the accused in a later trial if that witness for some reason becomes unavailable to testify, but only if the defendant has the opportunity to cross-examine the witness during the preliminary hearing.[15] These considerations will affect the scope of the evidence presented at the preliminary hearing, and thus will affect the judge's ability to evaluate the prosecutor's case.

The extent to which the preliminary hearing serves as a screening mechanism is also significantly affected by the quality of the evidence presented. The normal rules of evidence at trial do not apply in a preliminary hearing, which means that hearsay and illegally obtained evidence can be offered by the prosecution to support a finding of probable cause (Wright et al., 2007).[16] The impact of this rule can be significant: a magistrate judge at a preliminary hearing may be deciding whether to send the case forward on the basis of evidence that will never be heard by a trial jury. Whatever screening the preliminary hearing otherwise provides, it is unavoidably diminished by this mismatch between the evidence considered at the hearing and the evidence eventually considered at trial.

The other feature of the preliminary hearing that affects its screening function is the standard of proof required to bind a case over. The federal system requires a finding of probable cause, meaning that there must be evidence sufficient to cause a person of ordinary prudence and caution to conscientiously entertain a reasonable belief of the accused's guilt.[17] There are, however, alternative standards used by some state courts. One common alternative is the *prima facie* case standard, which requires that at least some credible evidence be presented for each element of the crime charged.[18] For example, in Pennsylvania, the court held that the *prima facie* standard was established by viewing the evidence presented by the Commonwealth in the light most favorable to the prosecution and with respect to 'all reasonable inferences based on that evidence which could support a guilty verdict'.[19] In no instance, however, does the screening standard of proof approximate the standard of proof required at trial, namely proof beyond a reasonable doubt.

In sum, preliminary hearings in the United States accentuate the defense role and allow the defense to review the basis of the prosecution. The screening achieved by the adversarial process is enhanced by the right to counsel, since the hearing relies on professional lawyers to counterbalance the power of the government. Although there are significant limits on the amount of screening that can be achieved, notably the low standard of proof and the court's ability to consider otherwise inadmissible evidence, the fact that the government is required to present its case to a neutral decision-maker helps remove weak cases from the criminal process.

3.1.1.1 Grand jury review   The Fifth Amendment of the US Constitution provides 'No person shall be held to answer for a capital, or otherwise infamous crime, unless on presentment or indictment of a Grand Jury, except in cases arising in the land or naval forces, or in the Militia, when in actual service in time of War or public danger'. This has come to mean that before a person can be charged with a federal felony (a crime punishable by more than one year in prison), he is entitled to have a panel of citizens chosen from the community review the prosecutor's evidence and decide if there is enough evidence to warrant a formal criminal charge.

Unlike a preliminary hearing, the grand jury's review of the prosecutor's case is not conducted in public – grand jury hearings are secret, and are closed to all except the prosecutor, the jurors, a court reporter, and the witness who is presenting evidence. Neither the person being investigated, nor his lawyer, nor the public, is permitted to see the government's case. The prosecutor simply presents the witnesses, documents, and physical evidence that she has gathered to the jurors and encourages the grand jury to approve the criminal charges that the prosecutor suggests (Holderman and Redfern, 2006). The prosecutor then leaves the room, the jury deliberates, and if 12 or more of the 23 jurors agree that the prosecutor has presented sufficient evidence, the jury approves the formal charge, which is called an indictment.

In this way, screening is entrusted to laypeople, not to a legally trained judicial officer like those who preside at a preliminary hearing. This has both advantages and disadvantages. The jurors are drawn at random, which ensures that they are independent from both the prosecution and the judiciary. On the other hand, the jurors will rarely have the training or experience to determine whether the prosecutor has 'sufficient' evidence to call for a trial, and because this is largely a legal determination, it will be natural for the jurors to defer to the prosecutor's conclusion that the evidence is adequate (Leipold, 1995).

Since its inception in Britain centuries ago (Leipold, 1995),[20] the grand jury has at times provided critical protections against some political and vindictive prosecutions. It was instituted to reflect the will of the community, thereby integrating an element of democracy into the screening process (Washburn, 2008). It provides an opportunity for the community to express local views, even in cases involving national law (Washburn, 2008). In the United States, it was also intended that the grand jury serve as a check on federal power.

Although courts today still occasionally speak of the grand juries in glowing terms, modern views diverge somewhat from their historical antecedents. Scholars have recognized that, however the grand jury was intended to work in theory, in practice it does little screening (Campbell, 1973; Leipold, 1995; Morris, 1978). Federal prosecutors obtain indictments from the grand jury in virtually every case where they seek one, and the rules governing the grand jury give little reason to think that weak cases will be identified and eliminated.

The standard of proof that the prosecutor has to meet is, once again, 'probable cause' to believe that the suspect committed the crime. In contrast, some states require prosecutors to present a *prima facie* case that a potential defendant has committed a crime (LaFave et al., 2004). Although the *prima facie* standard brings more confidence to the screening process, it is debatable whether such a standard requires a much more vigorous evaluation of the quality of the government's cases. As with the preliminary hearing, however, it is generally true that the higher the burden on the government, the more reliable and useful the screening will be.

In addition, the rules of evidence once again do not apply, which means that hearsay and illegally obtained evidence may be presented by the prosecutor and considered by the grand jury (Bernstein, 1994).[21] As with preliminary hearings, this means that the jury's decision whether to send the case to trial may be based on evidence that may not be admissible at the trial itself. Notice, however, that while many of the states follow a similar rule, there are exceptions. New York, for example, bars the use of inadmissible evidence in support of the indictment, and provides an ideal model for grand jury practice by requiring that the evidence presented to the grand jury be admissible and competent; otherwise, an indictment may be dismissed (Arenella, 1980).[22]

Just as importantly, the grand jury's screening function has been criticized as being completely within the control of the prosecution. In theory the grand jurors themselves have the power to call and question witnesses, but in practice this task is handled by the prosecutor. She decides what witnesses to call, what evidence to present, and what charges to recommend. The prosecutor *may* call witnesses that are favorable to the defense, and present evidence that is inconsistent with the government's theory, but is not constitutionally required to do so (Leipold, 1995). When prosecutors do present witnesses favorable to the defense, they often do so in order to learn more about – or foreclose – possible avenues of defense and in order to 'lock in' the witness's version of events. Given this, it is not surprising that grand jurors very rarely reject a government request to return a formal criminal charge.

Indeed, when the grand jury returns a 'no bill', rather than an indictment, it is possible that the prosecutor has acquiesced in the decision. It has been argued that when faced with high-profile, controversial cases where the prosecutor would prefer not to bring criminal charges, prosecutors will sometimes present the matter to the grand jury, recommend against (or not push for) an indictment, then when the grand jury declines to indict, shift the focus of the unpopular decision not to charge to the grand jury, as if that were the real source of the decision.

Put differently, this can also enable prosecutors who are under political pressure to charge a high-profile case, but who fear that the evidence will be insufficient to sustain a conviction, to counteract the political pressure by unveiling the evidentiary weaknesses of their cases to a politically more insulated cadre of lay fact-finders, in the context of a secret evidentiary hearing in which their concerns can be aired without generating a publicity backlash, allowing representatives of the community to play a more neutral role in assessing the weight of the evidence. Under either characterization, however, it remains true that the grand jury will hear only the evidence the prosecutor chooses to present and evaluate only those charges the prosecutor allows them to consider.

In sum, it is not hard to conclude that defects are embedded in the grand jury's procedures and that 'the flaw is structural' (Leipold, 1995), making effective screening difficult or impossible. Many critics are also skeptical of the grand jury's supposed independence, given how much of the process is controlled by the prosecutor. Without a dramatic, or at the very least, a meaningful reform of the grand jury, the operation of the grand jury and its associated cost cannot serve as a consistent or effective screening mechanism. Despite the grand jury's image as a buffer between citizens and the state, the limited safeguards afforded by the grand jury process mean that any screening that occurs is quite limited.

3.2   Taiwan

As noted, prosecutors in Taiwan wield no discretionary power in the charging of felony cases. They may, however, still abuse their powers, for example by charging a defendant with a crime without sufficient evidence to meet the required charging threshold. Conceptually, this is not an abuse of discretionary power, as prosecutors do not have the discretion to charge without sufficient evidence; instead this is an abuse of the charging authority. Other than this type of abuse, charging decisions may also be erroneous because there has been a factual mistake about the existence of sufficient evidence, a mistake in judging mandatory offense elements, or a legal error in evaluating the threshold requirements.

In 2002 and 2003, Taiwan reformed its Code of Criminal Procedure. The goals were to permit more party involvement in the criminal trial process, to reinforce defendants' rights, and to re-establish citizens' trust in the system. In crafting these changes, reformers looked to the adversarial style of the United States for insights. One of the critical characteristics of the newly enacted system is the enhanced state burden to prove a criminal charge beyond a reasonable doubt, a clearer and higher threshold for reaching a conviction. Additionally, the presumption of innocence was codified for the first time, although it had already been previously announced many times by the Constitutional Court. Since the law clarifies that the prosecutor bears the burden of proof, the judge plays a neutral role at trial except in limited situations.[23]

In order to review prosecutors' charging decisions and monitor compliance with the requirements of mandatory prosecution, Taiwan enacted a screening mechanism for prosecutors' charging decisions in the Code of Criminal Procedure Article 161,[24] to afford judges the power to prevent cases that fail to satisfy the requirement of mandatory prosecution from proceeding to trial, and also to afford the accused another opportunity to challenge the prosecution (Lin, 2005). The next sections set forth the goals of the screening mechanism as well as its procedures, evidentiary rules, standard of proof, and the drawbacks of the design.

3.2.1   Purpose of the screening

Under the principle of mandatory prosecution, once there is sufficient suspicion to believe the accused has committed the crime, the prosecutor is obligated to prosecute. Theoretically speaking, there is no abuse of such a decision as long as the prosecutor adheres to the mandatory requirement. But, how can we be sure that the mandatory prosecution requirement is not being abused or misused? If the prosecutor misjudges or violates the requirement of mandatory prosecution and charges the accused, that is, if there is an insufficient basis for believing that the accused has committed the crime, what prevents the case from proceeding to trial?

In the United States, the goal of screening is not to decide whether the accused is guilty of the crime; instead it is to check whether 'sufficient evidence' exists to proceed to trial. Likewise, the first goal of screening in Taiwan is to justify proceeding to trial. When the prosecutor submits insufficient evidence to justify a charge, the judge should have some mechanism to prevent the case from moving forward. In short, the screening mechanism should enable judges to scrutinize the prosecutor's decision to formally accuse the suspect.

A second goal of screening, some commentators claim, is to ensure that the prosecutor carries the burden of proof at trial.[25] One of the major reasons for revising the criminal procedures was to fortify the prosecutor's burden of proof (Lin, 2005; Peng, 2003; Wu, 2006), and some scholars have promoted additional screening as a means of ensuring that the burden stays with the prosecutor throughout the process (Tsai, 2002). These reformers contend that Taiwan's screening mechanism is designed to alter the traditional civil law practice of allowing both judges and prosecutors to play an active role in investigating and gathering the evidence. After the recent reforms, the judge does not play a role in gathering evidence. Instead, the judge determines whether the information gathered crosses a 'sufficient evidence threshold to establish the possibility that the accused is guilty' and whether the prosecution is able to carry its burden of proof at trial.

As worthy as this goal is, the arguments are ultimately misguided because the screening mechanism has nothing to do with the burden of proof prosecutors must meet at trial. Taiwan's legislative intent seems to conflate the prosecutor's initial burden of proof for screening purposes with the standard of proof required at trial. As critics have noted, the screening process is not meant to ensure that the prosecutor's proof justifies a conviction, but rather to prevent abusive or unfounded prosecution in the pretrial stage (Hwang, 2009). The legislative rationale seems to blend the two separate notions into one idea, inserting the ultimate burden of proof at trial into the wrong phase of criminal procedure.

A third goal of the screening procedure is to protect the innocent, a principle at the core of the ethical integrity of the criminal process. Regardless of its other features, a proper criminal system should prevent wrongful conviction, incarceration, and harassment of innocent people (*Yale Law Journal* (Notes), 1974). If the prosecutor is allowed to charge the accused without proper pretrial screening, this may result in many malicious prosecutions and may cause many losses and costs to the accused. In the absence of credible, admissible evidence, the accused should be protected from harassment and should not be subjected to trial, or even to a continuation of the pretrial process. Indeed, the goal of protecting the innocent is actually the most critical one of all, because wrongful prosecutions contribute to wrongful convictions and wrongful imprisonments.

A final goal of the screening process is that of preserving limited resources. The criminal process can be long and complex, consuming enormous financial and manpower resources that could be better used elsewhere. From investigation to conviction and sentencing, the prosecution propels the case forward and triggers the associated costs. A properly functioning system should seek ways to minimize these costs associated with weak cases and divert resources to the most deserving prosecutions.

3.2.2 Screening after prosecution

Unlike the screening or review process that takes place between an arrest and the bringing of formal charges in the United States, Taiwan's screening mechanism intervenes after the prosecution has been initiated. Naturally, increasing the difficulties of obtaining an indictment would enhance the quality of prosecution and decrease the number of weak cases because the prosecutor will present the best evidence and choose cases that can withstand critical scrutiny. If it takes real effort from the prosecutor to convince external screening institutions that there is sufficient evidence to justify her charge, then the prosecutor has every incentive to build a strong case at the earliest stage. Accordingly, critics have argued that the screening is best achieved before the charging decision is made (Wang, 2003).

In contrast, Taiwan's screening point is established 'prior to the first trial date', which means that the prosecutor has obtained an indictment before the screening takes place. At that point the charges have been internally reviewed by the prosecutor's chain of command. Formally, supervisors examine prosecutorial recommendations and exercise administrative control if they disagree with a decision. For example, a supervisor may demand further investigation before formal charges are brought. But in reality, the care with which the cases are scrutinized is an empirical question that has not been researched. The extent and degree to which an internal screening takes place depends on many variables that are not found in the rules of procedure.

Even assuming careful supervisory review, prosecutors need to submit charges only to one layer of administrative review prior to indictment. Supervisors review the dossier prepared by the prosecutor to decide whether the evidence supports the charging decision. And supervisors will also carry out the wishes of the chief prosecutor if she has specific directives. Once charges have been approved, the case is transferred to the court without any screening by any entity outside the prosecutor's office. After the accused is indicted, the case goes public, bringing with it many of the costs and disadvantages to the accused discussed above.

The screening procedure itself is a pure dossier review by a three-judge panel. The procedure takes place inside judicial chambers, without the parties present. Because it occurs before trial, this review process does not afford the accused a right to participate; hence, the accused is not entitled to challenge the indictment or to question whether the requirements of mandatory prosecution were satisfied, or whether the evidentiary rules and law were properly applied. Only when the judges decide that the case may proceed to trial will the panel set the trial date and inform the parties. By contrast, if the panel decides the case is too weak, the judges will issue a ruling to ask the prosecutor to support the charge with more specific evidence within a specific period of time, and if the prosecutor fails to do so, the judges are entitled to dismiss the case by written ruling.

To be sure, the system is better off with the current screening device than without it, and the existing practice may deter the abuse of authority under current law (Wang, 2003). However, an external pre-indictment screening mechanism that reviews the case before trial would offer many of the benefits of screening without significantly increasing the costs. Even if the judge eventually dismisses an indictment before trial, much of the potential harm caused by the indictment will already have reached fruition and remains irreversible.[26] By comparison, American screening procedures directly interpose an outside perspective, and do so at an earlier point in the process.

In addition, the Taiwanese screening procedure may be mistakenly thought of as an integral part of pretrial case preparation[27] because the only restriction on the timing of the review is that it take place 'prior to the first trial date'. The risk is that the screening process might overlap with the trial preparation phase and the review of pretrial motions. This concern with trial preparation also dominates the pretrial session (conference), in which judges address a wide variety of issues, all of which assume the case is sufficient to proceed to trial. The pretrial session can include such matters as whether the defendant pleads guilty, the nature of her defense, whether certain evidence and confessions will be admissible or not, a presentation of witness lists, as well as other evidentiary issues of the case.

In the United States, by contrast, independent screening procedures are stand-alone procedures unless waived and focus exclusively on the sufficiency of the government's case. The judicial officer who conducts the preliminary hearing may have no role in the trial itself, and the grand jury will never have later dealings with the case. Since the goals of the screening procedure and pretrial 'preparation of trial' are distinguished from each other, the screening ought to be carried out before the preparation of trial to avoid a confusion of roles and ensure an independent review.

3.2.3   The screener

The internal review by the prosecutor's office is an opaque process that does little to sustain public confidence. As one scholar has noted, the public has distrusted prosecutorial bureaucratic monitoring in the past, even if the internal review was held to a high standard (Wang, 2003). To impose external supervision is a much more convincing method of supervision and screening, at least from a public perspective.

Once the case is in court, screening is conducted by a three-judge panel that will preside over the subsequent trial. The panel is authorized to review the dossier (the case file and the evidence) to determine whether there is sufficient evidence to warrant further proceedings. This means that no independent screening procedure is contemplated except by those who will eventually consider the merits of the case at trial. As noted above, the United States often relies on the grand jury or on the magistrate, other than the trial judge to conduct the screening, which, despite its other shortcomings, is normatively preferable. These decision-makers probably command more public confidence because of their independence from the related but distinct decision of whether the prosecution has proved the charges beyond a reasonable doubt.

Having the same judges preside at both the trial and in the screening process can affect the proceedings in different ways. Judges may short change or rush through the preliminary question of whether there should be a trial at all. This risk is especially present when the screening is carried out before the pretrial session during which other decisions will be made, all of which assume that a case will continue. In addition, judges may be more likely to convict if they have already been exposed to the prosecutor's (unchallenged) case and have already concluded that the case is strong. Particularly if the dossier contains damaging evidence that is later found inadmissible at trial, a question also arises as to whether the judge who has just found sufficient evidence to send the case forward is in the best position to adjudicate guilt impartially. Some critics have thus claimed that installation of the independent screening judge is necessary to safeguard the impartial role of the trial judge (Lin, 2002).

3.2.4 Screening procedures

Taiwan's screening procedure consists of an *ex parte* dossier review at the pretrial stage. It therefore has two distinctive characteristics. One is that it does not afford the accused a right to participate. The other is that the accused has no legal right to an independent screening. Hence, the accused is not entitled to challenge the indictment or to question whether the requirements of mandatory prosecution were satisfied, or whether the evidentiary rules and law were properly applied. We analyze both of these features below.

First, in the United States, the preliminary hearing gives the accused the right to challenge the government's case through cross-examination, and to present an affirmative defense if he wishes to do so. Even if the defendant is denied a preliminary hearing because the prosecutor presents the case directly to the grand jury, the accused still has an affirmative right to have the case screened, and some of the grand jury testimony may eventually be discoverable. Given that it is purely a dossier-review process in Taiwan, it is not possible to know whether judges do in fact exercise their screening power and to what degree they use their powers. Since the law affords no legal right to pretrial review of the charges, there is thus no basis for the defendant to challenge any decision that is made about the sufficiency of the evidence. Instead the accused must passively wait to see how the judges decide. As a consequence, there is no way for the accused to know whether her charge was warranted, and no means to check whether the judiciary has properly exercised its authority.

Second, the screening in Taiwan is performed without the participation of the parties. The indictment lists a written 'method of proof', which describes the evidence the government has gathered, and from this the court makes its finding of the sufficiency of the evidence. The accused is not entitled to take part in the screening or to challenge the indictment. In the United States, by contrast, the preliminary hearing allows for input from the accused and an adversarial testing of the government's case through cross-examination. Reforming Taiwan's screening procedure to allow the accused to challenge the indictment is an intuitively appealing and workable blueprint to make the screening function more effective.

Third, when the court finds that the evidence is 'obviously insufficient' to establish the possibility that the accused is guilty,[28] the court now permits the prosecutor to present additional evidence to pass the 'obviously insufficient' threshold. The decision to allow the prosecutor to supplement the additional evidence is not subject to challenge by the defense, nor is it a proper subject for interlocutory appeal (Peng, 2003). Indeed, such a procedure is required before the court dismisses a case for insufficiency of evidence. Only when the prosecutor fails to comply with the court ruling could the court dismiss the case. Such a dismissal may be appealed by the government pursuant to Code of Criminal Procedure article 161 section (5).

Critics have argued that it is inconsistent with a presumption of innocence for the trial court to assist the prosecutor in preparing the case by pointing out what evidence is lacking.[29] The screening mechanism aims to check whether the prosecution has abused or violated the requirement of mandatory prosecution. Since it is clear that the judge must maintain an unbiased role in reviewing the prosecution, the judge should only inform the prosecutor of the 'insufficiency' of the evidence, and should not instruct the prosecutor to supplement specific evidence or even regarding which evidence should be used to prove the charged offense. She should retain her impartial role and only inform the prosecutor of which part of the evidence in the dossier is insufficient. Otherwise, to teach and to inform the prosecutor of specific additional evidence inevitably places the judge in conflicting roles, as both an advisor to the prosecution as well as a neutral decision-maker.

Some scholars have responded that, from the outsider's perspective, the judge and the prosecutor are allied in combating the crime (Lin, 2005; Wu, 2006). But the judges are not part of the prosecution team, and are not the prosecutor's superiors (Lin, 2005). Allowing judges to find errors in the prosecutor's case and suggest ways to correct them creates the impression that the prosecutor is subordinate to the judge, and the image of collaborators combating crime also seems inconsistent with an independent judicial role (Hwang, 2009).

3.2.5 Evidentiary rules

Evidentiary rules determine the kind of information upon which an adjudicator can reliably base her decision. According to the Taiwanese criminal procedure,[30] hearsay evidence is admissible in the screening procedure, and the law is silent on whether illegally obtained evidence can be considered. Scholars argue that the evidentiary rules that apply at trial should not apply to the screening stage for several reasons. First, there are different goals at the trial and the screening stages: the trial is to determine guilt by applying stringent evidentiary rules, while the screening is to decide whether or not the prosecution is justified (Wang, 2003). Second, they claim that more relaxed evidence rules avoid unfair outcomes (Wang, 2003). The exclusion of all hearsay evidence is burdensome to witnesses who have to appear in person and to prosecutors who understandably do not have their cases prepared to the same extent that they will at trial. It is also burdensome to society because it makes the hearing slower and more cumbersome. Third, the exclusion of illegally obtained evidence from the screening process is not necessary to deter police misconduct – preventing the use of illegally obtained evidence and adopting an exclusionary rule at trial is sufficient to discourage illegal police behavior (Wang, 2003).

Similarly, in US federal cases, the rules of evidence do not apply at either type of screening proceeding. Federal courts refrain from applying them pretrial because of the administrative burdens and costs associated with resolving fact-specific evidence questions at an early stage in the process. The evidence rules are also designed to shield juries from improper and unreliable evidence, but there is of course no jury at a preliminary hearing. In some states, nonetheless, rules of evidence do apply at the preliminary hearing. The decision about whether to apply evidence rules or not reflects a policy choice about the importance of the screening process and how best to balance the costs of pretrial review with the benefits of enhanced scrutiny of the charges. Adopting stringent evidentiary rules approximating those that apply at trial is surely the better way to protect the innocent and to anticipate the likely outcome at trial. If evidence that will be excluded at trial is admissible during screening, weak cases with little chance of success will more easily find their way to trial, thus inflicting the very harms that screening is designed to avoid.

3.2.6 Charging thresholds and screening thresholds

A threshold strategic issue for the prosecution is to determine the degree to which a case should be prepared before it is sent to the trial court. The current charging threshold requires evidence to establish merely that the accused is 'suspected' of having committed the offense. Consider the following example: the accused was seen leaving the victim's residence with blood stains on his clothing and his departure was caught on video camera, while one neighbor heard loud quarrelling inside the house an hour before the accused rushed to leave. If the prosecutor had gathered all of this evidence, then a court would likely say that there is sufficient evidence to suspect the defendant of homicide, warranting criminal charges. Standing alone, however, the same evidence might not suffice to convict after a trial.[31]

There are different views on how high or low the charging threshold is, and how high it should be. In one empirical study, a scholar interviewed 11 judges, six prosecutors, and 21 defense attorneys, and asked them to describe the charging threshold to institute a prosecution under existing law. With the exception of six interviewees who believed that quantification of the threshold is not possible, all other interviewees believed that the threshold required more than fifty percent certainty that the accused is guilty (Wang, 2003; Wang and Wu, 2001). But there were also interviewees who believed that, descriptively, prosecutors are one hundred percent certain before bringing charges (Wang, 2003). In other words, the charging threshold is uncertain and different prosecutors will very likely set it at different levels. Currently, neither law nor regulation establishes the degree of certainty required before a charge may be brought.

At the same time, the case may be dismissed for insufficiency of the evidence only if the prosecutor's evidence is 'obviously insufficient' to establish the possibility that the accused is guilty. According to the Code of Criminal Procedure, article 161, if the court finds that 'the method of proof indicated by the public prosecutor is obviously insufficient to establish the possibility that the accused is guilty', the court shall order the prosecutor to present additional evidence to pass the 'obviously insufficient' threshold within a specified time period. The 'obviously insufficient' threshold that governs pretrial screening once charges have been brought is set by a statute that does not precisely define what it means, but this screening standard appears to be highly deferential, suggesting that dismissal of charges is warranted only when the evidence clearly fails to meet the threshold needed to press charges in the first place.

This creates an apparent gap between the evidence prosecutors must possess in order to bring charges and the evidence they will need to survive pretrial screening, with the screening standard setting the evidentiary bar rather lower than the initial standard required to charge the offense in the first place. Because the terms are not precisely defined, the size of the gap is unclear. Professor Wang Jaw-Perng (2003) has argued that the screening threshold is identical to the *prima facie* standard that applies to preliminary hearings in some US jurisdictions. He also claims that the *prima facie* threshold is more predictable in context than the standard of 'obviously insufficiency' (Wang, 2003). The Judicial Yuan issued a guideline and adopted an objective standard to help judges evaluate whether the evidence is obviously insufficient to establish possible guilt.[32] This guideline, however, is itself vague, and, as a result, different cases screened by different judges may well result in different fates.

In one case, for example, the government prosecuted a sexual offense case on the basis of the victim's testimony, pictures of the wounds, and the medical report regarding the wounds. A district court dismissed the charge.[33] It is unclear whether such prosecution would be obviously insufficient to establish the possibility that the accused is guilty in the eye of different judges. Certainly, a judge cannot draw any conclusion from the guideline of the Judicial Yuan. In another example, the defendant was prosecuted for taking drugs, and the prosecutor presented evidence of a confession without the defendant's urine laboratory report. Usually the judge will dismiss this type of charge, since there is no corroborating evidence outside of the confession to prove the defendant was taking drugs. But while this result is not directed by the guideline, it is not precluded by it either.

A higher screening threshold brings more confidence that both factually and legally innocent defendants are being removed from the process, and, importantly, ensures that a prosecution is more likely to lead to a future conviction. But under the current system, the screening threshold in Taiwan is not only lower than the charging threshold; the screening threshold employed might be too low to reach any of the goals – to justify proceeding to trial, to protect the innocent, to ensure that the prosecutor carries the burden of proof at trial, and to preserve limited resources – that a screening mechanism is designed to achieve, which is to weed out weak cases.

There are two additional defects in the Taiwan process that require only brief mention. The first involves the right of the accused to the assistance of counsel in the screening process. Because the defendant has no right to participate, he has no right to have his arguments made by a trained and effective advocate. The second defect is the lack of discovery of the prosecution's evidence. The current norm provides for full disclosure of the evidence once the formal charges have been presented to the court. But this will be inadequate if the current screening mechanism is reformed to provide for an independent procedure and an adversarial process. An independent screening mechanism, imitating the preliminary hearing in the United States, adopts an adversarial screening process, and allows the defendant to challenge the prosecution and sufficiency of evidence.

4.   CONCLUSIONS AND IMPLICATIONS

The criminal justice system should focus on more than crime control and more than obtaining the maximum number of convictions; the legitimacy of the criminal process should depend to a large degree on the extent to which it prevents the conviction, incarceration, and harassment of innocent people (*Yale Law Journal* (Notes), 1974). As US Supreme Court Justice Harlan noted, a fundamental belief of the American criminal justice system is that 'it is far worse to convict an innocent man than to let a guilty man go free'.[34] It is the prosecutor who shoulders the responsibility for both the initiation of the criminal trial and the potential error of convicting the innocent. Correspondingly, prosecution and screening should be of similar significance in any criminal justice system. Since the goals of any screening mechanism – to prevent hardship to the defendant, to protect the rights of the innocent, and to preserve the limited resources – are so important, it is worth asking whether the current screening mechanisms in both countries function as well as they should.

There are reasons to be discouraged about the effectiveness of screening in both the United States and Taiwan. In the US, with only limited statistical information available, it appears that very few cases are in fact filtered out of the system. The US federal grand jury annual dismissal rate is less than 1 percent (Simmons, 2004; U.S. Department of Justice, 1984),[35] and the experience in many states is similar (although in New York State, the grand jury dismissed the cases or reduced offenses to misdemeanors in 5.9 percent of the felony cases in 1999) (Fairfax, 2010; Simmons, 2004). While these statistics do not tell us how many times a prosecutor is deterred from bringing a weak charge because of the *presence* of a screening mechanism, there is reason to be skeptical that this happens very often. The primary deterrent to bringing unfounded prosecution remains the risk of losing at trial, but this is undercut by the relative ease with which prosecutors can use the so-called trial penalty – the threat of a harsher sentence for defendants who opt for a trial – to leverage a guilty plea in weak cases. Particularly with respect to grand juries, the prosecutor's dominance of the process means that she will rarely be deterred by the difficulties of obtaining an indictment, a point noted by many scholars and practitioners.

Preliminary hearings are more promising because they add the adversarial feature that the American system finds so useful in uncovering the truth in other settings. The public nature of the proceeding, the presence of an experienced but neutral decision-maker, the right of cross-examination, the burden on the government, and the presence of defense counsel all suggest a more robust screening is likely, one that better tests the validity of the government's accusation (Leipold, 1995).[36] There remain problems, however, most notably the relaxed standards of evidence and the prosecutor's ability to avoid the preliminary hearing by first obtaining an indictment. Another problem may arise when the prosecutor seeks an indictment even if the court finds no probable cause at the preliminary hearing.

In Taiwan, prosecutors have been criticized for abuses and errors in charging unfounded cases, either because there was not sufficient evidence to indict a case or unjustified motivations or considerations led to the charge. At the same time, the evidence suggests that the screening function is not as effective as it should be.

First, one may infer that the system seldom results in a rejection of the prosecutor's charging decision. The overall offense dismissal rates are far below 1 percent, ranging from 0.0025 percent to 0.03 percent (Judicial Yuan, 2011: tbl62 and tbl64). Of course, the dismissal rate might be this low because the prosecution decisions are themselves of extraordinarily high quality. Perhaps prosecutions in Taiwan are rarely dismissed because prosecutors know their decisions will be screened, or are afraid of losing at trial, and therefore, only bring charges that are very strong. In such a case, we would expect the final conviction rate for these charges to be quite high.

If we examine the overall conviction rate throughout these years, we see that it is in fact quite high;[37] however, if we break down the conviction rate into distinct felonies, a different picture emerges. For example, the conviction rates for corruption offenses, including facilitation payment and favoritism, from May 2001 to 2012 averages only 59.48 percent, and ranges from a low of 49 percent to a high of 68 percent.[38] When this modest conviction rate is compared to the dismissal rates for corruption offenses in the same year, we see that the dismissal rates are mostly zero (Judicial Yuan, 2011: tbl64).

These statistics are not determinative, but they still suggest that the screening mechanism is under-employed. Although cases fail to end in conviction for a variety of reasons, one reasonable inference is that some of the non-conviction cases should never have been brought in the first instance, and also that the screening mechanism currently in place failed to detect these cases.

A second reason to doubt the effectiveness of the Taiwan screening procedure concerns the structure of the process. When compared to American preliminary hearings, the defects of the Taiwan system become obvious: the lack of an adversarial process to truly test the government's case; the lack of a separate procedure to evaluate the sufficiency of evidence; and the low threshold the prosecution needs to attain all indicate a system that is not fully committed to the values that the screening process can promote. By the same token, a greater commitment by the United States to the preliminary hearing and a lesser emphasis on the grand jury would strengthen the American effort to accomplish the removal of unfounded charges early in the process.

Structural reforms that added an adversarial component would greatly improve the screening process in Taiwan. A process that engages both parties is more trusted than an inquisitorial or government-dominated screening process. In the end, we can conclude that Taiwan's screening mechanism is much in need of reform if it is to achieve the important goals of the screening process.

NOTES

1. Harsh critics will even emphasize the arbitrary part of the decision-making process and call it arbitrary justice.
2. Cai Tuan Fa Ren Min Jian Si Fa Gai Ge JiJin Hui [Judicial Reform Foundation], Jian Zuo Ni Lei Le Ma? Zhui Qi E Jian Xi Lie JiZhe Hui Zhi Yi ZhiZhiSi [The Prosecutor, Are You Tired? In the Pursuit of Evil Prosecutor Conference I to IV] (Taiwan), Nov. 29, 2011, Dec. 8, 2011, Mar. 29, 2012, Jun.11, 2012, available at http://www.jrf.org.tw/newjrf/RTE/myform_detail.asp?offset=20&id=3629 (last accessed Aug. 12, 2012).
3. Some delay is necessary to allow the defense to investigate and prepare its case, and to prevent the rush to judgment that often characterized criminal cases at an earlier period in history. Thus, for example, although the American Speedy Trial Act ensures that the defendant's trial is not unnecessarily delayed, the Act also ensures that the trial is not *too* speedy, by guaranteeing that, absent a waiver, the trial cannot start until at least 30 days after the accused appears in court with a lawyer. See 18 U.S.C. §3161(c)(2).
4. In focusing on the US and Taiwan, we realize that an evaluation of these systems is illustrative, not exhaustive.
5. See Office of United States Attorneys, available at: http://www.justice.gov/usao/about/mission.html (last accessed Sept. 6, 2013). (Each United States Attorney is assigned to a judicial district, with the exception of Guam and the Northern Mariana Islands, where a single United States Attorney serves both districts. United States Attorneys have three statutory responsibilities under Title 28, Section 547 of the United States Code: 1. the prosecution of criminal cases brought by the Federal Government; 2. the prosecution and defense of civil cases in which the United States

is a party; and 3. the collection of debts owed the Federal Government which are administratively uncollectible.)

6. As discussed below, whether a criminal charge is supported by adequate evidence *is* subject to judicial oversight, and a weak charge may be dismissed by a judge or prevented by a grand jury. But the initial decision whether to institute charges or not is free from judicial review.

7. *McCleskey v. Kemp*, 481 U.S. 279, 313, 314 n 37 (1987).

8. Kao Xuan Bu [Ministry of Examination], Kao Xuan Tong JiNianBao [Examination Statistics] (Taiwan), available at http://wwwc.moex.gov.tw/main/content/wfrm ContentLink.aspx?menu_id=268 (last accessed Oct. 12, 2012) (The pass rate of the judiciary exam ranges from 0.99% to 4% for the past decade).

9. Code of Criminal Procedure, article 251(Taiwan). There is a discretionary power to charge regarding non-felonious offenses.

10. An arrest warrant is a judicial authorization for the police to make an arrest, and is obtained by making a showing by law enforcement to a judge of 'probable cause' to believe that the person named committed a crime. Here the judge has made a probable cause finding prior to the arrest, so an additional showing at the initial appearance is not required after the arrest.

11. The preliminary hearing is regulated by Rule 5.1, Federal Rules of Criminal Procedure, and initial appearance is regulated by Rule 5, Federal Rules of Criminal Procedure. The latter is a non-adversarial proceeding that occurs within 48 hours after the arrest.

12. Testing for probable cause is the only official function of the preliminary hearing, and discovery is the by-product.

13. *Gerstein v. Pugh*, 420 U.S. 103 (1975).

14. See *U.S. v. Hinkle*, 307 F. Supp. 121 (D.D.C., 1969) (noting the hearing affords 'the defendant not only the opportunity to contest the issue of probable cause, but also to use the preliminary hearing as a discovery vehicle for production of the government's case').

15. *Crawford v. Washington*, 541 U.S. 36(2004).

16. See Fed. R. Crim. P. 5.1(e), Fed. R. Ev. 1101(d)(3). See also Wright et al. (2007: Vol 3, p. 73) (noting the law is supported by many Supreme Court decisions).

17. *Beck v. Ohio*, 379U.S. 89, 91 (1964); *Brinegar v. U.S.*, 338 U.S. 160, 175–176 (1949).

18. See, for example, *Commonwealth v. Lutz*, 661 A. 2d. 405, 408 (Pa. Super. 1995).

19. See *Commonwealth v. Williams*, 911 A. 2d. 548, 549, 550, 553 (Pa. Super. 2006) (noting the government presented sufficient evidence required to establish the *prima facie* case that the accused unlawfully possessed a firearm).

20. The use of an accusing body of jurors in Anglo-American law is believed to have begun in the twelfth century, but the use of a citizen jury to protect the accused from the government is often dated to the late seventeenth century.

21. In some simple cases, the prosecutor may only call one witness, namely the law enforcement agent who is managing the case, to brief facts and to summarize other witnesses' testimonies, which is presented through hearsay evidence.

22. N.Y. Crim. Proc. Law § 190.65(1) provides that '[s]ubject to the rules prescribing the kinds of offenses which may be charged in an indictment, a grand jury may indict a person for an offense when (a) the evidence before it is legally sufficient to establish that such person committed such offense provided, however, such evidence is not legally sufficient when corroboration that would be required, as a matter of law, to sustain a conviction for such offense is absent, and (b) competent and admissible evidence before it provides reasonable cause to believe that such person committed such offense'. N.Y. Crim. Proc. Law § 210.30(4) further provides, 'If the court determines that there is not reasonable cause to believe that the evidence before the

grand jury may have been legally insufficient, it may in its discretion either (a) deny both the motion to inspect and the motion to dismiss or reduce, or (b) grant the motion to inspect notwithstanding and proceed to examine the minutes and to determine the motion to dismiss or reduce'. N.Y. Crim. Proc. Law § 70.10(1) defines 'legally sufficient evidence' as 'competent evidence which, if accepted as true, would establish every element of an offense charged and the defendant's commission thereof; except that such evidence is not legally sufficient when corroboration required by law is absent'.

23. See Zui Gao Fa Yuan [The Supreme Court], Zui Gao Fa Yuan Yi Bai Ling Yi Nian Du Di Er Ci XingShiTing Hui Yi JiLu [The 2th Supreme Court Criminal Divisions' Conference Transcript 2012] (Taiwan), Jan. 17, 2012, available at http://tps.judicial.gov.tw/faq/index.php?parent_id=589 (noting that the obligation of the prosecutor to bear the burden of proof ought to be disentangled from the fact-finding obligations of judges, to reflect the judicial duty of impartiality).

24. Code of Criminal Procedure, article 161 (Taiwan) (providing 'Prior to the first trial date, if it appears to the court that the method of proof indicated by the public prosecutor is obviously insufficient to establish the possibility that the accused is guilty, the court shall rule to the public prosecutor to supply additional evidence within a specified time period; if additional evidence is not presented within the specified time period, the court may rule to dismiss the prosecution. Once the ruling on dismissing the prosecution becomes final, no prosecution can be initiated for the same case, unless one of the conditions specified in Article 260 exists').

25. Code of Criminal Procedure, article 163 II (Taiwan).

26. There are a few cases in which defendants committed suicide after being indicted, suggesting that the harms that flow from being charged with a crime may sometimes be irreversible. In one case, a suspect committed suicide while being investigated, due at least in part to the media attention and attendant embarrassment that the investigation generated. The wrongful charge itself does bring irreparable harm to the defendant; see for example, Bai Wen Zheng Shen Wang Bei Xin Zui Shi Dao Huo Xian? ZiSha Biao Qing Bai? [Wen-Cheng Bai Passed Away, the Offense of Breach of Trust is the Fuse? Committing Suicide to Demonstrate Innocence?], JinRiXing Wen Wang [Nownews] (Taiwan), July 4, 2008, available at http://diary.blog.yam.com/qqaa3456/article/5723379 (noting that Yuan ta Securities ex-president Bai Wen Zheng committed suicide while being investigated for breach of trust; he was alleged to have sold his stock shares at a high price to Yuan ta Securities).

27. See, for example, Code of Criminal Procedure, article 273 (Taiwan) ('The court may summon the accused or his agent and notify the public prosecutor, defense attorney, assistant to be present in the preliminary proceeding before the first trial date to arrange the following matters: (1) The effect of the prosecution and its scope and any circumstance that might change the article of law charged with as cited by the public prosecutor; (2) Asking the accused, agent, or defense attorney whether to plead guilty to the crime charged by the public prosecutor, and determining whether to apply summary trial procedure or summary procedure; (3) Main issues of the case and evidence; (4) The opinion regarding the admissibility of the evidence; (5) Informing the parties to motion for investigation of evidence; (6) The scope, order and methods of investigation of evidence; (7) Ordering the presentation of exhibits or evidential documents; (8) Other trial related matters. If the court determines, in accordance with the provisions of this code, that the evidence referred to in Item IV of the preceding section shall not be admitted, then, the said evidence shall not be presented at the trial date. The provision of the preceding article shall apply mutatis mutandis to preliminary proceeding. Records shall be taken by the clerk regarding the matters being arranged in the proceeding as specified in section I of this article,

then the persons at the hearing shall sign his name, affix his seal, or affix his fingerprint on the space next to the last line of the contents of the records. The court may still make arrangements with those attending the preliminary procedure if the person, referred to in section I of this article, fails to appear in the hearing, after being summoned or notified, without good reasons. If lack of required legal formality exists in initiation of prosecution or other litigation related acts but such defect can be cured, the court shall by a ruling order that the same be cured within the period granted').

28. See for example, Xing Shi Su Song Fa [The Code of Criminal Procedure] art. 161(2013) (Taiwan) (stating that, before the first trial date, if the court finds that the method of proof indicated by the public prosecutor is obviously insufficient to establish the possibility that the accused is guilty, the court shall order the public prosecutor to supply additional evidence within a specified time period; if additional evidence is not provided within the specified time, the court may dismiss the prosecution. Once the ruling to dismiss the prosecution becomes final, no prosecution can be reinitiated for the same case, unless specified conditions in the article 260 exist).

29. See Li Fa Yuan Di Si Jie Di Liu Qi Si Fa Wei Yuan Hui Xin Shi Su Song Fa Di Yi Bai Liu Shi Yi TiaoJi Di Yi Bai Liu Shi SanTiaoXiu Zheng An Zeng Qiang Dang Shi Ren Jing Xing Zhu Yi JiCai Xing Xin Zheng Gong Kai Zhi Du ZhiKe Xing Xing Gong Ting Hui Wei Yuan Hui Ji Lu [Legis. Yuan, 4th Term, 6th Sess., Judicial Comm. Public Hearing], 90 LiFa Yuan Gong Bao [LEGIS. YUAN GAZ.] (No. 56) (Taiwan), 169–170 (2001) (Professor Ke Yaw-Cheng of National Chung-Cheng University contends that the revision violates the principle of presumption of innocence and asks the judge to prejudge the case in violation of the protection of human rights).

30. See, for example, Code of Criminal Procedure, art. 159 (Taiwan) (2013) (which states 'Unless otherwise provided by law, oral or written statements made out of trial by a person other than the accused, shall not be admitted as evidence. The provision of the preceding section shall not apply to the circumstances specified in section II of Article 161, nor to the case in a summary trial proceeding or where sentencing is ordered by a summary judgment; the same rule shall apply to the review of the application for detention, search, detention for expert examination, permission for expert examination, perpetuation of evidence and other compulsive measures').

31. The evidence at trial may reveal that the accused just went to the victim's house to pay a short visit and found his friend dead, and that the shocked suspect simply turned and ran away. Because the accused checked his friend for signs of life, he had the victim's blood on his shirt. And since the argument overheard by the neighbor occurred while the defendant can show that he was at work, the evidence turns out to have much less probative value than it first appears. And while no screening procedure should replicate the trial itself, a more vigorous screening mechanism, one that required a higher standard of certainty, as well as one that allowed the defendant to participate and offer counter evidence, might lead to a different result in this hypothetical case.

32. Fa Yuan Ban Li Xing Shi Su Song Ying Xing Zhu Yi Shi Xiang Di Jiu Shi Wu Dian [Guidelines to the Criminal Court in Handling Criminal Procedure], art. 95 (Taiwan) (The guideline indicates that judges, should apply objective and logical rules, based on their experience, in evaluating whether the evidence is obviously insufficient to establish possible guilt).

33. Ping Dong Di Fang Fa Yuan [Ping Dong Dist. Ct.], Criminal Division, 91SuZiDi [No.] 251(2002) (Taiwan).

34. *In Re Winship*, 397, U.S. 371–372 (1969) (Harlan, J., concurring) (noting that the harm of convicting an innocent is far greater than that of acquitting one who is guilty).
35. Statistical report, United States Attorney's Office fiscal year 1984, gave the dismissal rate as 0.4 percent in 1984.
36. 'Unless there is a clash of adversaries, grand juries composed of non-lawyers will be left to make a foregone legal conclusion, and thus will be a shield in name only' (Leipold, 1995: 313).
37. From May 2008 to June 2012, the overall offenses conviction rates are 95.7%, 95.4%, 95.6%, 96.1%, and 96.1%. See Ministry of Justice, Statistics of Justice, available at http://www.moj.gov.tw/public/Attachment/273111445976.pdf (last accessed Aug. 30, 2013).
38. See Ge di fang fa yuan jian cha shu tan du an jian 97 nian 5 yue qi jinjiquan ban xian an ding zuilugenian du tong jibiao [Corruption and overall criminal cases conviction rate of national prosecutors office from May, 2008 to 2012] in Ministry of Justice, Statistics of Justice, available at http://www.moj.gov.tw/public/Attachment/273111445976.pdf (last accessed Aug. 21, 2013). From May, 2008 to May, 2012, the average conviction rate of corruption offense was 63.1% while the overall offense conviction rate was 95.7%, see also Ministry of Justice, Statistics of Justice, available at: http://www.moj.gov.tw/public/Attachment/9221455414.pdf (last accessed Aug. 30, 2013).

BIBLIOGRAPHY

Allen, Ronald Jay, William J. Stuntz, Joseph L. Hoffmann, Debra A. Livingston, and Andrew D. Leipold. 2011. *Criminal Procedure-Adjudication, and Right to Counsel.* New York: Wolters Kluwer Law & Business.
Arenella, Peter. 1980. 'Reforming the Federal Grand Jury and the State Preliminary Hearing to Prevent Conviction Without Adjudication', 78 *Michigan. Law Review* 463–585.
Bai Wen Zheng Shen Wang Bei Xin Zui Shi Dao Huo Xian? ZiSha Biao Qing Bai? [Wen-Cheng Bai Passed Away, the Offense of Breach of Trust is the Fuse? Committing Suicide to Demonstrate Innocence?], JinRi Xing Wen Wang [Nownews] (Taiwan), July 4, 2008, http://diary.blog.yam.com/qqaa3456/article/5723379.
Bernstein, Fred A. 1994. 'Behind the Grey Door: Williams, Secrecy, and the Federal Grand Jury', 69 *New York University Law Review* 563–623.
Cai Tuan Fa Ren Min Jian Si Fa Gai Ge JiJin Hui [Judicial Reform Foundation], Jian Zuo Ni Lei Le Ma? Zhui Qi E Jian Xi Lie JiZhe Hui Zhi Yi ZhiZhiSi [The Prosecutor, Are You Tired? In the Pursuit of Evil Prosecutor Conference I to IV] (Taiwan), Nov. 29, 2011, Dec. 8, 2011, Mar. 29, 2012, Jun.11, 2012, available at http://www.jrf.org.tw/newjrf/RTE/myform_detail.asp?offset=20&id=3629 (last accessed Aug. 12, 2012).
Campbell, William J. 1973. 'Eliminate the Grand Jury', 64 *Journal of Crime & Criminology* 174–182.
Damaška, Mirjan. 1974. 'Structures of Authority and Comparative Criminal Procedure', 84 *Yale Law Journal* 480–544.
Davis, Angela J. 2001. 'The American Prosecutor: Independence, Power, and the Threat of Tyranny', 86 *Iowa Law Review* 393–466.
Davis, Kenneth Culp. 1978. 'Confining, Structuring, and Checking Prosecuting Power', in Burton Atkins and Mark Pogrebin, eds., *The Invisible Justice System, Discretion and the Law.* Cincinnati: Anderson Publishing Co.

Fairfax, Jr., Roger A. 2010. 'Grand Jury Innovation: Toward a Functional Makeover of the Ancient Bulwark of Liberty', 19 *William & Mary Bill of Rights Journal* 339–368.

Frase, Richard S. 1990. 'Comparative Criminal Justice as a Guide to American Law Reform: How Do the French Do It, How Can We Find Out, and Why Should We Care?' 78 *California Law Review* 539–683.

Ge di fang fa yuan jian cha shu tan du an jian 97 nian 5 yue qi jinjiquan ban xian an ding zuilugenian du tong jibiao [Corruption and overall criminal cases conviction rate of national prosecutors office from May 2008 to 2012] in Ministry of Justice, Statistics of Justice, available at http://www.moj.gov.tw/public/Attachment/273111445976.pdf (last accessed Aug. 21, 2013).

Goldstein, Abraham S. and Martin Marcus. 1977. 'The Myth of Judicial Supervision in Three "Inquisitorial" Systems: France, Italy, and Germany', 87 *Yale Law Journal* 240–283.

Holderman, James F. and Charles B. Redfern. 2006. 'Preindictment Prosecutorial Conduct in the Federal System Revisited', 96 *Journal of Crime & Criminology* 527–578.

Hwang, Jau-Yih. 2009. *Xing Shi Su Song Fa [Criminal Procedure]*. Taipei: New Sharing Publishing (Taiwan).

Judicial Yuan. 2011. *Judicial Statistics Yearbook*. Taipei: Judicial Yuan (Taiwan).

Kao Xuan Bu [Ministry of Examination], Kao Xuan Tong JiNianBao [Examination Statistics] (Taiwan), available at http://wwwc.moex.gov.tw/main/content/wfrm ContentLink.aspx?menu_id=268 (last accessed Oct. 12, 2012).

LaFave, Wayne R., Jerold H. Israel, and Nancy J. King. 2004. *Principles of Criminal Procedure: Post-investigation*. St Paul, MN: West.

Leipold, Andrew D. 1995. 'Why Grand Juries Do Not (and Cannot) Protect the Accused', 80 *Cornell Law Review* 260–324.

Leipold, Andrew D. 2000. 'The Problem of the Innocent, Acquitted Defendant', 94 *Northwestern University Law Review* 1297–1356.

Leipold, Andrew D. 2002. 'Preliminary Hearing', *Encyclopedia of Crime and Justice*, available at http://www.encyclopedia.com/doc/1G2-3403000193.html.

Li Fa Yuan Di Si Jie Di Liu Qi Si Fa Wei Yuan Hui Xin Shi Su Song Fa Di Yi Bai Liu Shi Yi TiaoJi Di Yi Bai Liu Shi SanTiaoXiu Zheng An Zeng Qiang Dang Shi Ren Jing Xing Zhu Yi JiCai Xing Xin Zheng Gong Kai Zhi Du ZhiKe Xing Xing Gong Ting Hui Wei Yuan Hui Ji Lu [Legis. Yuan, 4th Term, 6th Sess., Judicial Comm. Public Hearing], 90 Li Fa Yuan Gong Bao [Legis. Yuan Gaz.] (No. 56) (Taiwan), 169–170 (2001).

Lin, Yu-Xiong. 1999. *Jian Cha Guan Lun [The Prosecutor]*. Taipei: Sharing Publishing (Taiwan).

Lin, Yu-Xiong. 2000. *Xing Shi Su Song Fa [Criminal Procedure]*, 2nd edn. Taipei: Lin, Yu-hsiung.

Lin, Yu-Xiong. 2002. 'LunZhong Jian Cheng Xu-De GuoQi Su Shen Cha Zhi De MuDi, Yun ZuoJi Li Fa Lun' [The Intermediate Stage Procedure: The Goal, Exercise and Legislative Perspective of Screening Mechanism in German]', 88 *Taiwan Ben Tu Fa Xue [The Taiwan Law Review]* 69–84.

Lin, Yu Xiong. 2005. *Xing Shi Su Song Fa Xia Ce Ge LunPian [Criminal Procedure: Specific Provisions]*. Taipei: Angle Publishing Co. (Taiwan).

Morris, Norval. 1978. 'A Plea for Reform, Book Reviews', 87 *Yale Law Journal* 680–684.

Office of United States Attorneys, available at: http://www.justice.gov/usao/about/mission.html (last accessed Sept. 6, 2013).

Peng, Kuo-Shu. 2003. *The Research of the Prosecuting Supervision System in Criminal Procedure*. Unpublished Masters thesis, National Taipei University, Taiwan.

Pizzi, William T. 1993. 'Understanding Prosecutorial Discretion in the United States: The Limits of Comparative Criminal Procedure as an Instrument of Reform', 54 *Ohio State Law Journal* 1325–1373.

Simmons, Ric 2004. 'Re-Examining the Grand Jury: Is There Room for Democracy in the Criminal Justice System?' 82 *Boston University Law Review* 1–76.

Tsai, Ching-You. 2002. 'Xing Shi Su Song Fa Di Yi Liu Yi, Di Yi Liu San TiaoXiu Zheng HouZhi Xin Si Wei, Xin Zuo Wei [New Concept and Exercise of the Revised Code of Criminal Procedure Article 161 and 163]', 1067 *Si Fa Zhou Kan* [*Judicial Weekly*] 2–3.

U.S. Department of Justice. 1984. Executive Office for United States Attorney, Statistical Report, United States Attorney's Office, Fiscal Year 1984.

Vorenberg, James. 1981. 'Decent Restraint of Prosecutorial Power', 94 *Harvard Law Review* 1521–1573.

Wang, Jaw-Perng. 2003. *Xing Shi Su Song Jiang Yi (Er)* [*Criminal Procedure II*]. Taipei: Angle Publishing Co. (Taiwan).

Wang, Jaw-Perng. 2010. 'Yin Yan Ti Yao Yi Xing Shi Zhen Cha Ren QuanZhiBaoZhang [Synopsis of the Reform of Criminal Procedure (3) Human Rights Protection in Criminal Investigations]', in Dennis Te-Chung Tang and Kuo-Chang Huang, eds., *The Tenth Anniversary of the National Conference on Judicial Reform: Retrospect and Prospect (Symposium Records)*. Taipei: Academia SinicaInstitum Jurisprudentiae (Taiwan).

Wang, Jaw-Perng and Chung-Jau Wu. 2001. 'Banqiao Di Fang Fa Yuan Shi Yan Dang Shi Ren Jin Xing Zhu Yi Zhi Shi Zheng Yan Jiu [Empirical Study of the Banqiao District Court's Experimental Use of an Adversarial System]', 30 *Guo Li Taiwan Da Xue Fa XueLun Yi* [*National Taiwan University Law Journal*] 57–132.

Wang, Tey-Sheng. 2002. 'The Legal Development of Taiwan in the 20th Century: Towards a Liberal Democratic Country', 5 *Waseda Proceedings Comparative Law* 304–337.

Washburn, Kevin K. 2008. 'Restoring the Grand Jury', 76 *Fordham Law Review* 2333–2388.

Wright, Charles Alan and Andrew D. Leipold. 2008. *Federal Practice and Procedure*. Thomson/West.

Wright, Charles Alan, Peter J. Henning, Nancy J. King, Susan R. Klein, Andrew D. Leipold, and Sarah N. Welling. 2007. *Federal Practice and Procedure. Appendices–Tables–Index.* St Paul, MN: West/Thomas Reuters Business.

Wu, Guan-Ting. 2006. 'Wo Guo Qi Su Shen Cha Zhi Du Zhi Jian Tao [Examination of Screening Mechanism in Taiwan]', 50 *Xing Shi Fa ZaZhi* [*Criminal Law Journal*] 42–81 (Taiwan).

Yale Law Journal (Notes). 1974. 'The Function of the Preliminary Hearing in Federal Pretrial Procedure', 83 *Yale Law Journal* 771–805.

5. Standards for making factual determinations in arrest and pre-trial detention: a comparative analysis of law and practice

Richard Vogler and Shahrzad Fouladvand

1. INTRODUCTION

Arrest and pre-trial detention represent two of the most dangerous and widely abused aspects of the criminal justice process. They both embody threats to the right to liberty, which is central to international human rights jurisprudence, but their modalities and operation are very different. The right of arrest emphasises the power of the state to exercise authority over individuals in the interests of the forensic investigation of crime, whereas pre-trial detention, in theory at least, is directed towards the integrity of the trial process itself. One engages discretion over capture and the other, discretion over release. Both practices are important at the very outset of the criminal process and both exercise a profound influence over the eventual outcome.

Although arrest must be considered one of the most significant, intrusive and personally intimidating procedural acts in criminal justice practice, it is very little examined or theorised in comparative studies. National approaches differ considerably and the guidance on arrest rights and procedures in international conventions is, for the most part, vague and unspecific. This is particularly unfortunate given that arrest is, by its nature, also the most unobserved and clandestine aspect of decision-making in criminal procedure, taking place in a variety of different locations, often under dangerous and threatening conditions. It remains associated in many jurisdictions with unregulated violence and the 'disappearance' of suspects, and everywhere represents the main portal into criminal justice and a crucial change of status for the citizen who is confronted directly and overwhelmingly with the coercive power of the state. It is a mass process. For example, 11.2 million arrests took place in the United States alone in 2014.[1]

Pre-trial detention and the right to release have enjoyed considerably more comparative attention (see for example, Charret-Del Bove and Mourlon, 2014; Hafetz, 2003; Morgenstern, 2009; Ruggeri, 2012; van Kalmthout, Knapen, and Morgenstern, 2009; van Kempen, 2012). Nevertheless, despite the continuing evolution of international standards, and the striking similarity of national approaches to factual determinations, which will be discussed below, pre-trial detention remains an area of urgent concern, while the percentages of unconvicted persons within prison populations worldwide vary dramatically.[2] Not only is excessive pre-trial detention strongly associated with the use of torture (Open Society Justice Initiative, 2011a), corruption (Open Society Initiative, 2011) and ethnic discrimination,[3] but it has the gravest possible health-care implications, providing the bridge over which infections such as HIV or tuberculosis can be spread to the general population. Hammett (2006: 976) has estimated that 'in a given year, about 25% of all people who have HIV disease, about 33% who have HIV infection, and more than 40% who have tuberculosis disease will pass through a correctional facility'. Putting aside the financial costs of maintaining large remand facilities, the socio-economic implications of the excessive use of pre-trial detention are well known (HM Inspectorate of Prisons for England and Wales, 2000; Open Society Justice Initiative, 2011b), and there is overwhelming evidence that it disproportionately affects the poorest individuals in society. Worse still, from the jurisprudential perspective, it is clear that pre-trial incarceration has a direct impact on the outcome of the trial and sentencing (Sacks and Ackerman, 2014). In South Africa, for example, people held in custody before their trials were six times more likely to be sentenced to imprisonment than those released on bail (Karth, 2008), and it will be argued here that pre-trial detention has an impact on the outcome of the proceedings which goes well beyond any predictable correlation between the bail and sentencing decisions. The United Nations Commission on Human Rights noted in 2006 that empirical research showed clearly that those in pre-trial detention had a significantly lower likelihood of obtaining an acquittal than those who remained at liberty before trial and that this 'deepens further the disadvantages that the poor and marginalized face in the enjoyment of the right to a fair trial on an equal footing' (paragraph 66).

This chapter will examine the factual determinations on which decisions about arrest and detention are based from a comparative perspective, and will focus necessarily on the legal provisions which underpin these decisions. It has been widely suggested in the sociological literature that the police and courts in fact pay very little attention to formal legal standards when making arrests or deciding on detention, but rely instead on stereotyping, perceived lack of deference or other undisclosed criteria (Piliavin and Briar, 1964; Skolnick, 1966). In this interactionist analysis, legal rules are dismissed as 'empty' or merely 'rhetorical' (McBarnett, 1978). Whilst there may be some force in these observations, nevertheless it is argued here that the character of the legal rules can make a significant difference to the nature of the decision-making and can protect individuals against abuse.

2. COMPARATIVE STANDARDS FOR FACTUAL DETERMINATIONS ON ARREST

Given the immediate historical context of the 1948 Universal Declaration of Human Rights, it is hardly surprising that freedom from 'arbitrary arrest'[4] should rank very highly amongst the protected rights (Morsink, 1999: 49). The same wording, was adopted by Article 9 of the International Covenant on Civil and Procedural Rights, which went on to assert, albeit without reference to any specific thresholds, that '[n]o one shall be deprived of his liberty except on such grounds and in accordance with such procedure as are established by law'. The American Convention on Human Rights has followed this abstentionist approach with regard to criteria for arrest,[5] but the 1950 European Convention on Human Rights (ECHR), reflecting its British draftsmanship, offered more detail and in Art. 5(1) set out explicit 'necessity' and 'reasonable suspicion' tests for the deprivation of liberty by arrest. In 2014 the European Court of Human Rights (ECtHR) emphasised that the reasonable suspicion requirement could now be considered as nothing less than 'an essential part of the safeguard against arbitrary arrest and detention'.[6] This approach has clearly had a significant impact on attitudes towards arrest, not only in the Council of Europe area but in other jurisdictions around the world and in international criminal law.

It is evident from the ECtHR case law that the test of reasonable suspicion under the ECHR is to be considered as primarily an objective one. In the 1990 case of *Fox, Campbell and Hartley v. the United Kingdom* the court held that 'having a "reasonable suspicion" presupposes the existence of facts or information which would satisfy on objective observer that the person concerned may have committed the offence. What may be regarded as "reasonable" will however depend upon all the circumstances ...'.[7] Subsequent decisions have re-emphasised the objective character of reasonable suspicion under the ECHR and the mere fact that a suspicion is held by the officer concerned in good faith is insufficient.[8] The suspicion must be based on relevant facts or information. The court has also emphasised that facts which raise suspicion need not satisfy as high a standard of proof as those necessary to justify a conviction or even the bringing of a charge, since these come at later stages of the process of criminal investigation.[9]

Article 58 of the Rome Statute of the International Criminal Court also adopts the 'necessity' and 'reasonable grounds' threshold for issuing an arrest warrant. In their interpretation of this Article, the ICC judges have relied specifically on 'the reasonable suspicion' standard under Article 5(1) of the ECHR as well as the more limited jurisprudence on the subject of the Inter-American Court of Human Rights (Scheffer, 2009: 163). Art. 91(4) requires that local provisions on arrest apply to arrests as they would to extradition. The approach of the court has been to establish a clear ladder of threshold tests starting with 'reasonable grounds to believe' for the issuing of arrest warrants, 'substantial grounds to believe' for the confirmation of charges, and 'beyond reasonable doubt' for a finding of guilt.[10]

The adoption of a 'reasonable suspicion' model for arrest by some of these international instruments does not reflect the very diverse approaches to arrest standards implemented around the world. Although some universal global developments are evident, such as the move from judicially-determined procedure to autonomous police-determined procedure, nevertheless diversity in arrest practice is very marked.

Many of the controversies over the legal standards on which factual determinations on arrest are grounded raise questions about whether the seizure of an individual should be based on the subjective/objective perceptions of the arresting officer ('reasonable suspicion'), or his or her purely objective perceptions on a probability standard ('probable cause'), or on assumed public perceptions of overt criminality ('flagrancy'). These also represent three very different approaches to decision-making which have been developed in different historical contexts. In the case of a 'reasonable suspicion' standard, some balancing of the interests of the individual against the rights of the community is implied, whereas probable cause requires a qualitative assessment of likelihood. Flagrancy, on the other hand, obligates state officials to respond to the immediate and destabilising effect of public outrage arising from crime by apprehending the perpetrators. It also gives them greater investigative powers in the immediate aftermath of the crime, implicating privacy as well as liberty interests and affording the police some measure of investigative autonomy from supervising magistrates. These three approaches will be explored in turn in the context of their English, North American and continental European homelands respectively.

2.1 The Concept of 'Reasonable Suspicion' in England and Wales

The move to autonomous, police-determined arrest occurred earlier in England and Wales than in many other countries. In 1827 Lord Tenterden established the basis for autonomous police arrest, subject to a reasonable suspicion test in the case of *Beckwith v. Philby*, in which a constable 'having reasonable ground to suspect that a felony has been committed' was empowered 'to detain the party suspected until inquiry can be made by the proper authorities'.[11] With the creation of a professional police force, a new and informal procedure was developed to engage the defendant directly with the investigation process without the need for formal arrest. This was described as 'helping the police with their enquiries' and involved the quasi-voluntary, quasi-lawful attendance of the suspect at the police station for interrogation (Sanders and Young, 2007: 118). It wasn't until 1967 that the role of arrest in the investigation process was formalised by the Criminal Law Act of that year. This legislation created a category of 'arrestable offences' (generally, serious offences) in respect of which the police could arrest on their own authority and without recourse to a magistrate's warrant. Effectively, it introduced the modern English concept of arrest and subsequent interrogation as a necessary part of the investigation process.

Following a series of spectacular miscarriage of justice cases in the 1970s, the whole process of arrest, investigation and interrogation was formalised by the Police and Criminal Evidence Act 1984 (PACE), which established a rigorous and rights-based procedure throughout the pre-trial stage of the criminal process. In many ways, PACE remains a model of good pre-trial practice which is amongst the most effective and rights-protective in the world. Nevertheless it closed off the possibility of informal contact between the police and a suspected person and elevated arrest to a crucial and seemingly indispensable first stage in the process, triggering an array of subsequent procedures. Arrest, henceforth, was to be subject to a 'necessity principle'. As anticipated, the number of arrests began to climb significantly and it is only in recent years that this rate has begun to decline. The total number of arrests in England and Wales has been falling for the last eight years to 2015 and currently stands at 1 million a year, down by 7 per cent on the previous year and the lowest number since data collection began.[12] There is considerable evidence that arrest practices remain discriminatory with respect to ethnic minorities (Phillips et al., 1998). For example, per 1,000 of the population aged 10 or older, a black person is nearly three times more likely to be arrested than a white person (Ministry of Justice, 2013: 37), and these figures rise to six times in respect of drug offences.[13] In neither case is this disparity reflective of the ultimate conviction rate.

The arrest provisions for England and Wales are set out in Section 24 of the Police and Criminal Evidence Act 1984 (PACE),[14] which now provides, after subsequent amendments, that a police constable may arrest without a warrant for all offences, not just (as before 2005) 'arrestable' ones. Guidance on practice is given by Code G, which is published under the Act.[15] The essential principle is that a constable with reasonable grounds for suspecting that an offence has been committed may arrest without a warrant anyone whom he or she has reasonable grounds to suspect of being guilty of committing it. In addition, the constable must have reasonable grounds for believing that it is *necessary* to arrest the person in question. The potential grounds for such a belief include the need, for example, to ascertain the name and address of the person in question[16] or to allow the prompt and effective investigation of the offence, or to prevent any prosecution for the offence from being hindered by the disappearance of the person in question, etc.[17] As a matter of principle, therefore, it can never be necessary to arrest a person unless there are reasonable grounds to do so, but there is no specific proportionality requirement with regard to arrest.[18]

The first and most important questions are always whether the officer actually believed that there were grounds for the arrest and whether that belief was objectively reasonable. In the 1997 Northern Irish case of *O'Hara v. Chief Constable of the Royal Ulster Constabulary*,[19] the issue was whether a reasonable person would hold that opinion, having regard to the information known to the arresting officer at the time. It was the account of what the arresting officer actually had in his mind that really mattered. The information on which the opinion was based did not have to derive from the officer's own observations, as he or she was entitled to form a suspicion based on information which had been given anonymously or perhaps in the course of an emergency, even if this later turned out to be mistaken. However, if a physical restraint on a person was applied before the constable had formed a settled intention to arrest, based on the above grounds, this would be an unlawful assault.[20]

Similarly, with regard to the second limb, the 'necessity' requirement, the court in the 2011 case of *Hayes v. Chief Constable of Merseyside Police*[21] held that an arrest would be 'necessary' only where (i) the arresting officer actually believed it to be so under the criteria contained in s. 24(5) of PACE (the subjective element) and (ii) where that belief was objectively reasonable (the objective element). Two years later this was confirmed in the case of *Lord Hanningfield of Chelmsford v. Chief Constable of Essex Police*,[22] where it was argued that an arrest had been carried out solely for the purpose of enabling a search of Lord Hanning-field's property and that there were other, less intrusive ways, which didn't involve an arrest, to carry on the 'prompt and effective investigation of the offence' under s. 24(5)(e) of PACE.

The result is that factual determination on arrest in England and Wales is based on a hybrid concept of reasonable suspicion which must be both subjective (the officer must actually have the relevant suspicion) and objective (a reasonable officer in his or her position would also have such a suspicion). Both tests are subject to a necessity condition which relies on much wider community standards than those which are engaged merely by the interests of the police in successful prosecution.

2.2 The Concept of 'Probable Cause' in the United States of America

In sharp contrast to English practice, arrest in the United States is dependent on a fully objective standard, and the threshold test of 'reasonable suspicion' has been decisively rejected in favour of 'probable cause'. The concept of probable cause has been celebrated by some authors as the 'glory of American legal history' (Weber, 1982: 166) and a 'universal standard' (Oliver, 2010: 429), while at the same time it has been derided by others as 'a hopelessly indeterminate constitutional standard' (Lerner, 2003: 953). Its continuing attraction as a test for the lawfulness of an arrest lies in the apparent straightforwardness and clarity of its approach compared to the moral uncertainties occasioned by the balancing of different interests inherent in the 'reasonable suspicion' approach. Unfortunately, the history of its operation in relation to the law of arrest in the United States has shown how the concept of probability can itself become a deceptive and slippery slope.

Probable cause owes its first modern incarnation to the Fourth Amendment to the United States' Constitution which holds that:

> The right of the people to be secure in their persons, houses, papers, and effects, against unreasonable searches and seizures, shall not be violated, and no Warrants shall issue, but upon probable cause, supported by Oath or affirmation, and particularly describing the place to be searched, and the persons or things to be seized.

Recent scholarship has demonstrated that the adoption of the probable cause wording in the Fourth Amendment had nothing whatsoever to do with the regulation of criminal arrests. On the contrary, it was largely an attempt to restrict excise searches, which were much resented since they were initiated for alleged violations of customs and excise regulations without the safeguard of a deposition from a victim-complainant. According to Davies (2010: 40), 'there is not a shred of historical support for the modern myth that the Framers intended for the Fourth Amendment to create any overall "reasonableness" standard for assessing all government intrusions' (Davies, 2010: 40). In fact, criminal procedure at this period, as in England, was largely victim-driven, and in order to procure an arrest, the complainant had to swear before a magistrate that a crime had been committed and that he or she had 'probable cause' to believe that the named suspect was the perpetrator (Arcila, 2007; Oliver, 2010: 384). The creation of publicly-funded police services revolutionised criminal procedure and the new forces were almost immediately given powers to carry out warrantless arrests on suspicion only and without any firm evidence that an offence had actually occurred (Davies, 2010: 42–57; Oliver, 2010: 419–428). Whereas the 1827 English test referred to above required a reasonable basis,[23] in the United States, two decades later, a similar intention was generally expressed – in an explicit reference to the now largely defunct warrant procedure, sanctified by the Constitutional Amendment – as a requirement of 'probable cause' (Oliver, 2010: 421).

The contemporary concept of 'probable cause' in the United States was famously, if elusively, defined by Justice Stewart in *Beck v. Ohio*, a 1964 case in which the petitioner, Beck, was arrested on the basis of unspecified 'information' and 'reports' but in the absence of any objective facts, known to the officer at the time, that could justify his detention. Such an arrest was held to be in breach of Beck's Fourth Amendment rights and the question to be asked in each case was '… whether at that moment the facts and circumstances within their knowledge and of which they had reasonably trustworthy information were sufficient to warrant a prudent man in believing that the petitioner had committed or was committing an offense'.[24]

The decision was part of the Warren Court's historic and much celebrated attempt to extend the protections of the Fourth Amendment to pre-trial criminal proceedings (Kamisar, 1995: Miller, 2010). In a very different political environment some years later, the whole project, so it has been argued, was 'eviscerated' by the Burger, Rehnquist and Roberts Courts, which sought to provide more practical support to the policing agencies (Davies, 2010: 59–67). Subsequent decisions have therefore proposed a more flexible and a pragmatic approach to probable cause, suggesting in one case that '[a]n officer need not be astronomically precise before making an arrest'.[25] In 1983, in the case of *Illinois v. Gates*, the Supreme Court went even further to dilute the stringency of the probable cause test. In order to legitimise arrests prompted by anonymous or poorly corroborated tip-offs, Justice Rehnquist made it clear that the probable cause requirement was satisfied if the police had information merely indicating a 'fair probability' or 'substantial chance' of criminal activity.[26] Such a test clearly departed considerably from the rigorous *Beck v. Ohio* standard of 'reasonably trustworthy information ... sufficient to warrant a prudent man in believing that the petitioner had committed or was committing an offense' (Kamisar, 1983).

As a result, the current test for the existence of probable cause in the United States must be seen as located on a broad sliding scale between 'beyond reasonable doubt'[27] and a mere suspicion.[28] Police expertise acquired through experience, may have a role to play in establishing probable cause in the mind of the arresting officer (Kinports, 2009), just as may information received from a third party, such as a police bulletin or computer database. However, reliance upon such information cannot make an arrest lawful where the original author of the bulletin or database could not have made the arrest himself because, for example, of illegality in the issuance of the warrant.[29] In short, the probable cause rule means that no arrest will be lawful unless the police are in possession of information which indicates, on an objective view, that it is more probable than not that the individual concerned has committed a crime.[30] The subjective views or motives of the police officers themselves are irrelevant. All that matters is whether a prudent, reasonable, cautious police officer on the scene at the time of the arrest and guided by his experience and training would have concluded that there was probable cause for suspicion.[31]

'Reasonable suspicion' in the United States' context has been relegated to a test for the less intrusive 'stop and frisk' procedure in circumstances where the available evidence would not justify an arrest.[32] This suggests that it is regarded in the United States as an easier standard to satisfy than probable cause and the conventional wisdom is that there exists '... a continuum that begins with a hunch, then progresses to reasonable suspicion, and then becomes probable cause' (Moak and Carlson, 2014: 41). The diversity of these tests and the procedural acts which they permit is perhaps attributable to the prevalence of firearms in the United States and the consequent special dangers to American police officers in making arrests. Therefore, the two elements of stop and frisk began to be treated in practice as separable. A reasonable suspicion of criminal conduct could give rise of itself to an investigative stop whereas a subsequent reasonable suspicion that the person concerned was armed and dangerous could lead to a frisk of the individual who had been stopped.[33] Stop and frisk, based on such fragile foundations, has played a crucial role in the 'zero-tolerance' policing policies of the 1990s and remains a potent source of resentment, particularly in Black and Latino communities where this procedure is often viewed as thinly disguised racial harassment (Rengifo and Fratello, 2014).

The extent to which this complex hierarchy of conceptually distinct tests for stop, frisk and arrest represents a pragmatic solution to the challenge of protecting the public from excessive and abusive policing is open to question. The approach in the US differs starkly from the English procedure by insisting on the fully objective character of both probable cause and reasonable suspicion (Kinports, 2009; Lerner, 2005) and in refusing to regard the latter (at least in its domestic American incarnation) as a sufficient justification for the detention of a suspect.[34]

2.3 The Concept of 'Flagrancy' in Continental Europe

In contrast to the individual police officer's 'reasonable suspicion/ probable cause' approach taken by Anglo-American criminal justice, the continental model has always depended on the notion of public 'flagrancy'. The original concept of 'flagrancy' was derived from the Roman Law notion of *flagrans crimen*, or the existence of an evident and visible offence that ignited immediate public outrage. Such an obvious demonstration of culpability dispensed with the complexities of evidence collection and examination and was always used as a procedural means of short-circuiting investigation on the basis of the public's awareness of guilt.[35] It was adopted, without definition in the very authoritarian Code Louis of 1670[36] and retained in the revolutionary codes (Béchéraoui, 1997: 198–199). The concept of flagrancy has spread around the world, not only to former European colonies (Béchéraoui, 1997) but also to countries such as China[37] and Japan (Terrill, 2014: 144). Art. 53 of the current French *Code de Procédure Pénale* (*CPP*) explains that:

> [a] grave or serious offence is described as being flagrant if it is actually in the process of being committed or has just been committed. It is also considered flagrant when, in the period immediately following the act, the suspected person is pursued by public clamour, or is found in possession of objects, or presents traces or indications, leading to the belief that he has participated in a grave or serious offence.

The two types of flagrancy are therefore 'true flagrancy',[38] where the offence is committed immediately under the eyes of the investigators, or in the immediate past (for example, up to 48 hours beforehand), and 'presumed flagrancy',[39] where secondary sources of evidence only are required. Such sources could include the direct accusation of the victim[40] or the smell of cannabis emerging from a vehicle involved in a roadside stop.[41] The significance of the existence of flagrancy is that it permits the adoption of expedited procedures or the use of coercive measures such as search and arrest without the immediate participation of a judge.

French criminal law has long maintained the fiction of 'judicial control' over police action, which has inhibited the development of a culture of rights for the arrested person in favour of the supposedly benevolent supervision of the judicial authorities (which, in France, include the state prosecutor) (Hodgson, 2004). Two consequences flow from this tradition of judicial control of the pre-trial investigation. First, it has created a very significant obstacle to the creation of specific arrest rights for the suspect. Despite significant reforms in 1993 and 2000, the arrested defendant in France is still disadvantaged in comparison with those elsewhere (Hodgson, 2004), and it was only after January 2015, in a very reluctant and long-delayed response to a European Union Directive of 2012,[42] that he or she was to be notified of a full set of rights (including the right of silence) and allowed free access to a lawyer and the details of the prosecution file on arrest.[43] These rights have very much been grafted on to a procedure which is primarily bureaucratic and authoritarian.

The second consequence is that there is no separate and specific phase of 'arrest' which is identified in the *CPP* and hence no specific statutory regulations governing police conduct at this crucial point. Essentially, the concept of 'arrest' in the Anglo-American sense, is unknown to French criminal practice and, instead, the notion of being placed under detention at a police station ('*garde à vue*') takes precedence. What is important here is the technical classification of the enquiry under which such detention has been ordered and the consequent level of judicial supervision. The relatively informal 'preliminary enquiry' (*enquête préliminaire*) is initiated without notification to the judicial authorities and is generally less coercive than an enquiry which is launched in respect of 'flagrant' serious and middle-range offences, which must be authorised by and conducted under the nominal authority of the prosecutor. In both cases, however, the apprehension of suspects for the purposes of detention at the police station and the 'discovery of the truth'[44] is possible.

The *CPP*, which has not been reformed in its basic structure since 1957, refers merely to the passive state of being apprehended but not the process by which this is achieved, and the focus on police requirements is relentless. For example, according to Article 62.2 of the *CPP*:

> custody is a coercive measure ordered by a police officer under the control of the judiciary, by which a person against whom there are one or more plausible reasons to suspect that he has committed or has attempted to commit a crime

or an offence punishable by a term of imprisonment, is kept at the disposal of investigators.

In addition, the Article holds that custody is allowable provided it is the only way to achieve at least one of a number of objectives, including the facilitation of 'investigations involving the presence or participation of the person' or ensuring 'the implementation of measures to prevent crime'. The rights provisions which have been introduced into this scheme tend to be general and abstract in character. For example, although all coercive actions authorised by the *CPP* are subject to the overriding principles of 'necessity', 'proportionality' and respect for human dignity which were introduced into the preamble to the *CPP* text in 2000, there are no provisions which provide specific requirements about the actual mode of arrest.

Germany, by contrast, does provides some specific provisions on arrest, but these are rather limited and are not qualified by any statutory requirements about the reasonableness of the suspicion. They rely, again, on a 'flagrancy' perspective. Article 2(2) of the German Constitution guarantees the freedom of the person, and the longstanding jurisprudence of the Constitutional Court has established that such rights can be infringed only where such interference is necessary to secure a legitimate object and is carried out by the least intrusive means and in a way that is proportionate to the objective.[45] The ECHR has been directly incorporated into German domestic law.

Article 127 of the *Strafprozessordnung* (*StPO*) allows arrest without a warrant by any private citizen (*Flagranzfestnahme*) or by the police or prosecution, of a person who is either caught in the act of committing a criminal offence or immediately after having done so. The second part of Art. 127(I) empowers the police to hold (but not arrest!) a person suspected of a criminal offence (but not necessarily caught in the act) for up to 12 hours for the purpose merely of ascertaining their identity under the provisions of Art. 163(b) and (c). This very wide power may even apply to persons not suspected of any offence where it is 'necessary to clear up any criminal offence'. Equally, powers of arrest are available under Art. 127(b) in respect of a person caught in the act who is likely to be subject to the fast-track criminal procedure but who is unlikely to attend court of his or her own free will (Bohlander, 2012: 71–73).

Moreover, as Weigend and Salditt put it, '... the arrest of the suspect (ie the seizing and taking of the suspect to the police station or courthouse) is not the normal method of initiating the criminal process' (2007: 82). As frequently occurs in European jurisprudence, the concept of arrest is elided with that of pre-trial detention, and the police and prosecution have a further power to arrest under Art. 127(II) 'in exigent circumstances' if the requirements of a pre-trial detention order are met. These include where, on the basis of certain facts, it is established that the accused has fled or is hiding or there is a risk that the accused will evade the criminal proceedings. Alternatively, detention can be ordered where the danger exists that establishment of the truth will be made more difficult and the accused's conduct gives rise to the strong suspicion that he will (a) destroy, alter, remove, suppress or falsify evidence, (b) improperly influence the co-accused, witnesses or experts, or (c) cause others to do so (*StPO*, Art. 112).

There are no specific provisions in the *StPO* requiring officers to notify the suspect of his rights or of the nature of the allegation at the point of arrest. Moreover, as Bohlander (2012: 73–74) points out, there is a practice in some police forces of inviting suspects to voluntarily attend the police station in order to 'help the police with their enquiries' and delaying the actual arrest for as long as possible in order to provide the maximum time for interrogation.

'Flagrancy' provisions are common elsewhere in Europe. In the Netherlands only a person who is caught in the act of committing a criminal act, or who is suspected of committing an offence for which preventative custody is available or a suspect who has previously given false personal details to the police, can be arrested and brought to the police station.[46] Arrest by any person in Spain is possible when it is necessary to prevent the commission of a crime, or in cases of *delincuente in fraganti* that are actually being committed or have just been committed.[47] Additionally, an officer must make an arrest when there are sufficient reasonable indications of the commission of a crime and of the participation of the arrested person in it.[48] These reasonableness criteria apply only to arrests by public officials and agents of the judicial police. A power of arrest is not available for minor offences as this would be considered disproportionate,[49] but an officer is empowered to require identity details of an individual in such cases (Bachmeier and del Moral Garcia, 2010: 253). In Italy, police may arrest anyone caught *in flagranza* after a non-negligent completed crime or an attempted crime punishable with a penalty exceeding five years.[50] In the same way, flagrancy is central to the arrest provisions in Belgium[51] and Greece.[52]

It is evident however, that the importance of 'flagrancy' is slowly giving way in continental Europe to the 'reasonable suspicion' arrest standard promoted by the ECtHR, since the ECHR has been directly incorporated into the domestic legislation of most states. Reasonable suspicion, for example, has appeared as the standard for arrests in a number of states, including Poland (Kruszynski, 2007: 184). Moreover, initiatives such as the Stockholm Process, which have aimed to establish a standard notification of a 'letter of rights' (Spronken, 2010) to arrested persons throughout the European Area of Freedom, Security and Justice (Guild and Carrera, 2009), depend upon a formal process of arrest reflecting the Anglo-American model. With the increasing importance of mutual arrest protocols such as the European Arrest Warrant, the growth of common evidentiary standards for arrest, inevitably based on the developing international approaches, are likely to assume even greater significance.

3.   COMPARATIVE STANDARDS FOR FACTUAL DETERMINATIONS IN PRE-TRIAL DETENTION

For the reasons outlined above, the international community has developed a strong and relatively consistent approach to the question of pre-trial detention. The United Nations, for example, have emphasised the very severe threat which it presents to the rights of individuals, the successful administration of criminal justice and, above all, to the principle of the presumption of innocence, set out in Article 11 of the Universal Declaration of Human Rights 1948. This was made abundantly clear in Article 9 of the International Convention on Civil and Political Rights (ICCPR) which insists, that '[i]t shall not be the general rule that persons awaiting trial shall be detained in custody ...'. In 1988, this negative prohibition on the general use of pre-trial custody was converted into a positive requirement of release in the UN Body of Principles of 1988 which held that:

> Except in special cases provided for by law, a person detained on a criminal charge shall be entitled, unless a judicial or other authority decides otherwise in the interest of the administration of justice, to release pending trial subject to the conditions that may be imposed in accordance with the law.[53]

The Bangkok and Salvador Declarations of 2005[54] and 2010,[55] respectively, reiterated the principles outlined above, emphasising the centrality of pre-trial release to the achievement of a fair and effective criminal justice process.

The European Convention on Human Rights provides no positive right of pre-trial release and in 2006 the Council of Ministers re-emphasised the existing, negative approach by asserting merely that there should 'not be a mandatory requirement that persons suspected of an offence (or particular classes of such persons) be remanded in custody'.[56] However, the ECtHR have gone to some lengths to strengthen the requirements to release defendants on bail. In *Saadi v. the United Kingdom*[57] the Grand Chamber held that the detention of an individual was such a serious measure that it was justified only as a last resort where other, less severe, measures have been considered and found to be insufficient to safeguard the individual or public interest. The detention had to be lawful (within the prescribed grounds) but also reasonable and proportionate,[58] and it has repeatedly been emphasised that the gravity of the charge alone cannot justify a remand in custody.[59] This approach reflected that of the UN Human Rights Commission.[60]

These concerns argue powerfully for the use of rigorous and enforceable national standards for factual determinations in custodial remand cases. Two issues have emerged as central to the nature of these determinations. These are the question of the existence or otherwise of a presumption in favour of release and the growing use of pre-trial detention for preventative and policing strategies.

3.1 Bail and the Presumption in Favour of Release

The gradual emergence of a presumption in favour of pre-trial release is intimately connected with the difficulties inherent in the characteristically Anglo-American institution of 'bail'. Because of the presence of the jury in English procedure, the trial itself was central and there was no pre-trial process of any kind until 1554,[61] and therefore no need to detain defendants for interrogation and confrontation, as was common in the continental European Roman-Canon practice (Langbein, 1977). The idea of bail was developed as a contractual relationship between the court and the accused for the payment of a money bond or security which would be forfeited in the event of non-appearance. The principle of a 'right' to bail, although clearly discriminatory towards the poor, was nevertheless described by Sir James Stephen 'as old as the law of England itself and … explicitly recognised by our earliest writers' (Stephen, 1883: vol. 1, 233). Politically-motivated bail refusal became a matter of the greatest importance in the constitutional struggles of the seventeenth century, and the resulting legislation ensured that a refusal of bail or a delay in granting bail by a judge was a criminal offence under the Habeas Corpus Act 1679[62] and the Bill of Rights 1688.[63] Moreover, the same Bill of Rights enacted the rule that 'excessive bail ought not to be required',[64] a provision of such fundamental importance for political freedom that it was reproduced verbatim in the Eighth Amendment to the United States Constitution.

The drawbacks of such a 'free market' right to release are obvious and were widely criticised in England and elsewhere (see for example, Wiseman, 2014: 1358–1363), particularly outside the common-law world, where money bail has always been regarded with deep suspicion. First, it permitted draconian and extra-judicial powers to anyone standing as contractual security for a bailed defendant (particularly, commercial bail-bondsmen), to use force if necessary to bring him or her to court. Second, although the amount of bail was set in accordance with a defendant's financial means, the system was inevitably unfair to the impecunious defendant and, in its most extreme American manifestation was '… at best a system of chequebook justice [and] at worst a highly commercialized racket' (Goldfarb, 1965: ix).

Three potential solutions have been attempted. The first, promoted originally in the United States, was to establish support mechanisms for indigent defendants to allow them to present convincing arguments for bail in court. The second, adopted in England, was to abolish money bail completely. Finally, many jurisdictions around the world have attempted, with varying degrees of success, to establish a statutory presumption in favour of bail.

In the United States, the 1961 Manhattan Bail Project, organised by the Vera Institute of Justice, sought to provide information for decision-makers and to post bail itself for indigent defendants with strong community ties, thereby demonstrating that they would attend court on their own recognizance. Following a conference convened by the US Attorney General, Robert Kennedy, the Bail Reform Act 1966 created a structured bail process and a presumption of own-recognizance release, reforms consolidated in the 1984 Bail Reform Act (Metzmeier, 1996: 407–409; Woodruff, 2013: 251–253). In England, a 1974 Working Party Report (Graham-Harrison, 1974), which was highly critical of the money bail system, recommended its abolition and the Bail Act 1976 was introduced as a means of 'enabling courts to release more persons on bail without diminishing the protection of the public'.[65] It ended the historic procedure of money bail and personal sureties offered by the defendant and for the first time created a criminal offence of 'failing to answer bail'. A free-market contractual relationship between state and bailee was replaced by a penal relationship and its most radical provision created a statutory presumption in favour of release on bail for almost all offenders.[66]

While not all common-law jurisdictions abolished money bail, presumptions in favour of release on bail were introduced widely in the 1970s. For example, following the Bail Reform Act 1972 in Canada, the 1981 Charter of Rights and Freedoms introduced a negative provision that any person charged with an offense 'has a right not to be denied bail without just cause'.[67] Positive provisions were established in the New South Wales Bail Act 1978 and exist in a number of Australian jurisdictions (King et al., 2009: 29). In New Zealand, the Bill of Rights Act 1990 guaranteed that persons charged with an offence be released on 'reasonable terms and conditions unless there is just cause for continued detention'.[68] It is not only common-law jurisdictions which have sought to establish a positive right to release. French law, for example, insists that '(t)he defendant, presumed innocent, remains free'.[69]

From the 1990s onwards, however, there has been a worldwide reactive tendency to establish reverse-onus provisions in specific categories of offenders (King et al., 2009: 25). In England, for example, those defendants charged with a serious offence which was allegedly committed while on bail for another serious offence cannot be granted bail at all unless the court believes that there is no significant risk of offences being committed on bail.[70] European defendants in Germany, Italy (Illuminati and Caianiello, 2007: 140), Poland (Kruszynski, 2007: 186) and elsewhere enjoy no statutory presumption in favour of release.

3.2 Pre-trial Preventative Detention

Pre-trial custodial detention represents a significant exception to the universal right to freedom enjoyed by unconvicted persons and can be justified therefore only by the imperative necessities of the trial process. In theory, therefore, process-related considerations such as the prevention of absconding or the interference with evidence should be regarded as the only acceptable criteria for the refusal of pre-trial release. However, the second half of the twentieth century has seen the rise of a new and potentially illegitimate ground for pre-trial custody: 'preventative detention'.

The pre-existing position was summarised by Lord Russell in 1898: 'It cannot be too strongly impressed on the magistracy that bail is not to be withheld as a punishment but that the requirements of bail are merely to secure the attendance of the prisoner at his trial'.[71] The same principle operated in the US, and the Supreme Court, in *Stack v. Boyle* in 1951, reaffirmed the doctrine that risk of flight was the sole legitimate justification for pre-trial remand. They pointed out that 'unless the right to bail is preserved, the presumption of innocence, secured after centuries of struggle, would lose its meaning'.[72] The pre-trial precautionary measures of this period were accordingly entirely determined (in law at least) by the requirements of the main proceedings. It is worth noting that, despite the impact of the Federal Bail Reform Act 1984 (Metzmeier, 1996: 409–410; Wiseman, 2009), the US has continued to emphasise, at least in theory, the subservience of the bail decision to the main proceedings. Although Metzmeier (1996: 412) has asserted that the United States remains 'unique among common law nations in the primacy it still places on appearance at trial as the basis of bail' it is clear that preventative detention plays a major role in bail decisions (Wiseman, 2014: 1351; Woodruff, 2013).

In England the law remained settled for nearly a century until Lord Goddard introduced an entirely new and unprecedented ground for the refusal of bail. In his view, bail could in future be refused solely to prevent a defendant 'having the opportunity of committing further offences'.[73] For the first time, in England, detention was to be used systematically to prevent future crime in a way unconnected with the main proceedings. It was argued forcefully at the time that the proper means of deterring crime was the threat of trial and punishment, not prior imprisonment. Nevertheless this justification for the refusal of bail was enshrined in law by the Bail Act 1976.

Under Schedule 1, Part 1, paragraph 2 of the Act, a defendant charged with an imprisonable (for example, serious) offence *must* be granted unconditional bail unless the court is satisfied that there are substantial grounds for believing that one of the three rebutting conditions apply. These are that the defendant, if released on bail (whether subject to conditions or not) would (a) fail to surrender to custody, or (b) commit an offence while on bail, or (c) interfere with witnesses or otherwise obstruct the course of justice, whether in relation to himself or any other person. Since condition (b) rapidly came to represent the single most likely ground for the refusal of bail (Vogler, 1982: 11), the major importance of the bail/custody decision has clearly shifted from judicial to policing objectives. The use of bail for 'preventative detention' was adopted in New Zealand in the 1950s and in Canada and some Australian states in the 1960s, while in Ireland it was introduced by Constitutional amendment after a referendum in 1996 (King et al., 2009: 28).

Unfortunately, this approach has also been promoted in international conventions. In Europe, Art. 5(1) of the ECHR permits an exception to the right to liberty for the purpose of bringing a person 'before the competent legal authority on reasonable suspicion of having committed an offence or when it is reasonably considered necessary to prevent his committing an offence or fleeing after having done so'. This wording was unfortunate in relation to pre-trial release in a number of respects. Not only did it elide arrest and pre-trial detention, but it could be seen as positive justification for the use of bail refusal as preventative detention.

Preventative detention is almost universal in legislation governing pre-trial remand in European jurisdictions. According to Art. 144 of the

French *CPP* '[r]emand cannot be ordered or extended unless it is shown by precise and substantiated evidence ... that this is the only way to achieve one or more of the following objectives and that these cannot be achieved through judicial control or house arrest with electronic monitoring'. These objectives include the prevention of interference with evidence, ensuring that the person concerned remains 'at the disposition of justice', preventing the current offence and preventing its repetition or, in the case of serious offences, in the interests of 'public order'. This last concept, well-known for its elasticity, has been much abused, and it has been convincingly argued that these provisions in practice represent a reversal of the presumption of innocence (Chassang, 2014).

In Germany a defendant who is 'strongly suspected' of an offence can be remanded provided the applicable 'grounds' exist. These include the risk of absconding (the justification for 90 per cent of all detention orders) (Huber, 2008: 305) and tampering with evidence in a way which will interfere with the establishment of the truth.[74] There is no presumption in favour of release but there is a proportionality requirement, and the Federal Constitutional Court has decided that no offenders are excluded from consideration for release on grounds of seriousness alone (Bohlander, 2012: 22). Art. 112a provides a further ground for remand in custody where a defendant has committed repeated criminal offences which 'seriously undermine the legal order' and there is a substantiated risk of reoffending. Article 116 of the *StPO* authorises a judge to 'suspend' a detention warrant which is based wholly on flight risk if the aims of the order can be achieved by less severe measures, such as a reporting condition or monetary bail, although this provision is rarely used (Huber, 2008: 306). Spain has no overarching right to release nor a specific proportionality requirement, but Art. 503 of the *LEC* provides the usual three 'requirements' justifying remand. Each of the different grounds have different time limits ascribed to the duration of custody (Gascón Inchausti and Villamarin López, 2008: 586). The use of pre-trial detention for preventative purposes is a truly international phenomenon, and can be observed in countries as distinct as China (Yi, 2008) and Canada (Metzmeier, 1996: 417–423).

4. CONCLUSION

Arrest and pre-trial detention might be seen together as part of a continuum of control over the suspect throughout the criminal process. The material presented here suggests that this is far from the case and that these two decision-making processes are based on very different factual determinations governed by very different criteria. The decision on arrest is now predominantly a police competency, requiring a street-level analysis regulated by different national templates often based on objective (probable cause) principles or public order (flagrancy) criteria. International regulation is permissive of these different approaches, generally approving of action which is not merely 'arbitrary'. However, the increasing need to co-ordinate arrest between different jurisdictions is encouraging attempts to provide specific, internationally agreed criteria, and the likelihood is that the growing international acceptance of a 'reasonable suspicion' approach, stripped of the subjective elements adopted in English practice, will prove to be persuasive. Pre-trial detention has also been the subject of a transition which has been prompted by policing requirements. The widespread use of reverse-onus decision-making and the global shift towards preventative detention all suggest that the developing standards for factual determinations in this area have moved dramatically away from a focus on the integrity of the trial process towards control and policing priorities.

The problem with 'factual' determinations in both these areas is simply the absence of facts. Arrest decisions must rely in many cases on suspicion, probability or public awareness rather than hard evidence, whereas the decision on pre-trial detention is essentially a speculation about future conduct. Such high levels of contingency and indeterminacy make these two decision-making processes uniquely vulnerable to subjective bias and demand that the criteria for regulation be much more tightly drawn than many of those described above.

NOTES

1. FBI Uniform Crime reports 2014, https://www.fbi.gov/about-us/cjis/ucr/crime-in-the-u.s/2014/crime-in-the-u.s.-2014/persons-arrested/main (accessed 13 February 2016).
2. From 90% in Libya, to 26% in France, 22% in the United States, 14% in England and 8% in Poland. World Prison Brief, http://www.prisonstudies.org/highest-to-lowest/pre-trial-detainees?field_region_taxonomy_tid=All (accessed 3 January 2015).
3. United Nations Committee on the Elimination of Racial Discrimination, General Comment 31 on the Prevention of Racial Discrimination in the Administration and Functioning of the Criminal Justice System. Preamble and Paragraph 1.III.2.
4. Art. 9 Universal Declaration of Human Rights.
5. Art. 7.
6. *Ilgar Mammadov v. Azerbaijan*, no. 15172/13, May 22, 2014 §88.
7. *Fox, Campbell and Hartley v. the United Kingdom*, nos. 12244/86, 12245/86 and 12383/86, August 30, 1990, §32.
8. *Ilgar Mammadov v. Azerbaijan*, op. cit., §88.
9. *Erdagöz v. Turkey*, no. 127/1996/945/746, October 22, 1997, §51.

10. United Nations Committee on the Elimination of Racial Discrimination, General Comment 31 on the Prevention of Racial Discrimination in the Administration and Functioning of the Criminal Justice System. Preamble and Paragraph 1.III.2; Ventura, 2013.

11. *Beckwith v. Philby* [1827] 6 B & C 635 at 636.

12. See Home Office 'Police Powers and Procedures. England and Wales 2012 to 2013', at https://www.gov.uk/government/publications/police-powers-and-procedures-england-and-wales-2012-to-2013/police-powers-and-procedures-england-and-wales-2012-to-2013. See https://www.gov.uk/government/publications/police-powers-and-procedures-england-and-wales-year-ending-31-march-2015/police-powers-and-procedures-england-and-wales-year-ending-31-march-2015 (accessed 13 February 2016).

13. Release: http://www.release.org.uk/press-release-racial-disparities-drug-policing.

14. As substituted by s. 110 of the Serious Organised Crime and Police Act 2005.

15. https://www.gov.uk/government/uploads/system/uploads/attachment_data/file/117583/pace-code-g-2012.pdf.

16. Ss. 24(5)(a) and (b) of PACE.

17. Ss. 24(5)(e) and (f) of PACE. All these provisions are elaborated in paragraph 2.9 of the Code G.

18. Gibson-Morgan, 2014. Where there is no necessity for arrest, proceedings are initiated by Summons.

19. [1997] 1 All ER 129.

20. *Elkington v. Director of Public Prosecutions* [2012] EWHC 3398 (Admin).

21. [2011] EWCA 911 (Civ).

22. [2013] EWHC 243 (QB).

23. *Beckwith v. Philby, op cit.*

24. 379 U.S. 89 (1964).

25. *Lathers v. United States*, 396 F.2d 524, 531 (5th Cir. Miss. 1968).

26. *Illinois v. Gates,* 462 U.S. at 236 (1983).

27. *Henry v. United States* (1959) 361 US 98, 102, 4 L Ed 2d 134, 80 S Ct 168.

28. *People v. Medley*, 23 Misc. 3d 25, 878 N.Y.S.2d 570, 572 (App. Term 2009).

29. *Whiteley v. Warden, Wyoming State Penitentiary*, 401 U.S. 560, 28 L. Ed. 2d 306, 91 S. Ct. 1031, 58 Ohio Op. 2d 434 (1971).

30. *Brinegar v. U.S.*, 338 U.S. 160, 176, 69 S. Ct. 1302, 93 L. Ed. 1879 (1949).

31. *U.S. v. Davis*, 458 F.2d 819, 821 (D.C. Cir. 1972).

32. *Terry v. Ohio*, 392 U.S. 1 (1968).

33. *Adams v. Williams*, 407 U.S. 143, 92 S. Ct. 1921, 32 L. Ed. 2d 612 (1972).

34. The ascending ladder of proof-standards which is to be expected during the criminal process is also compromised to some extent in the United States by the use of probable cause as a test for the Grand Jury in determining whether a prosecution should be brought forward. See, for example, Fairfax, 2008.

35. Article 16 of the 1532 German Imperial Code, the *Constitutio Criminalis Carolina*, permits the immediate torture of an individual caught in the act who nevertheless denies the offence.

36. Title II, Art. 6.

37. Chinese Criminal Procedure Code, Art. 61.

38. 'La flagrance proprement dite'.

39. 'La flagrance par présomption'.

40. Judgement of the Criminal Chamber, April 22, 1992.

41. Judgement of the Criminal Chamber, November 4, 1999.

42. 22nd May 2012.

43. *Statut de Personne Soupçonnée, Parlement de France*, Paris, 15th May 2014.

44. Article 53.

45. Bohlander (2012: 80).
46. *Wetboek van Strafvordering* (Netherlands Code of Criminal Procedure), Arts 53–54. See Groenhuijsen and Simmelink, 2008.
47. *Ley de Enjuiciamento Criminal* (Spanish Code of Criminal Procedure) (*LEC*), Art. 490.
48. Ibid., Art. 492. See Gascón Inchausti and Villamarin López, 2008, 418–424.
49. Art. 495, *LEC*.
50. *Codice de Procedura* Penale, Art. 381(1). See Illuminati and Caianiello, 2007, 134).
51. Art. 41 of the *Code d'Instruction Criminelle*.
52. Art. 276.1 of the Criminal Procedure Code of Greece.
53. United Nations (1988) UN Body of Principles for the Protection of All Persons under Any Form of Detention or Imprisonment Adopted by General Assembly resolution 43/173 of 9 December 1988. Principle 39.
54. United Nations (2005) Bangkok Declaration. Synergies and Responses: Strategic Alliances in Crime Prevention and Criminal Justice. Resolution 60/177 of 16 December 2005. Paragraph 8.
55. United Nations (2010) Salvador Declaration on Comprehensive Strategies for Global Challenges: Crime Prevention and Criminal Justice Systems and Their Development in a Changing World. Resolution 65/230 of 21 December 2010. Paragraph 52.
56. Council of Europe Recommendation Rec (2006)13 of the Committee of Ministers of the Council of Europe on the Use of Remand in Custody etc. Adopted by the Committee of Ministers on 27 September 2006, Article 2[2].
57. No. 13229/03, January 29, 2008, §§ 67–72.
58. *Ladent v. Poland*, no. 11036/03, March 18 2008, §§ 55–56.
59. See, for example, *Petkov v. Bulgaria*, no. 32130/03, January 7, 2010.
60. *H. van Alphen v. the Netherlands* (Views adopted on 23 July 1990), in UN doc. GAOR, A/45/40 (vol. II), p. 115, para. 5.8.
61. Bail Statute of 1554, 1 and 2 Philip and Mary, c.13.
62. 31 Car. 2, ch. 2, (1679).
63. 1 W. & M. (2d. Sess.) (1688).
64. Ch. 2, s.10.
65. House of Commons Debates, Vol. 912, 25th June 1976, 475ff. See also Graham-Harrison (1974: para. 6).
66. S. 4(1).
67. Art. 11(e).
68. S. 24(b).
69. Art. 137 of the CPP.
70. S. 25 of the Criminal Justice and Public Order Act 1994 as amended by the Criminal Justice Act 2003.
71. In *R v. Rose* (1898) 78 LT 119.
72. 342 U.S. 1 (1951) at 4.
73. *R v. Wharton* [1955] CLR 565.
74. Art. 112 of the StPO.

REFERENCES

Arcila, Jr, Fabio. 2007. 'In the Trenches: Searches and the Misunderstood Common-Law History of Suspicion and Probable Case', 10 *University of Pennsylvania Journal of Constitutional Law* 1–63.
Bachmeier, Lorena and Antonio del Moral Garcia. 2010. *Criminal Law in Spain*. Alphen aan den Rijn: Kluwer.

Béchéraoui, Doreid. 1997. 'La Notion de Flagrance en Droits Français, Libanais et Egyptien', 5 *Revue Juridique de l'USEK* 197–232.

Bohlander, Michael. 2012. *Principles of German Criminal Procedure*. Oxford: Hart.

Charret-Del Bove, Marion and Fabrice Mourlon, eds. 2014. *Pre-trial Detention in 20th and 21st Century Common Law and Civil Law Systems*. Cambridge: Cambridge Scholars.

Chassang, Céline. 2014. 'Detention on Remand and the Presumption of Innocence Principle: The French Pattern of a Tricky Conciliation', in Marion Charret-Del Bove and Fabrice Mourlon, eds., *Pre-trial Detention in 20th and 21st Century Common Law and Civil Law Systems*. Cambridge: Cambridge Scholars.

Davies, Thomas. 2010. 'How the Post-Framing Adoption of the Bare-Probable-Cause Standard Drastically Expanded Government Arrest and Search Power', 73 *Law & Contemporary Problems* 1–67.

Fairfax, Roger. 2008. 'Grand Jury Discretion and Constitutional Design', 93 *Cornell Law Review* 703–764.

Gascón Inchausti, Fernando and Maria Luisa Villamarin López. 2008. 'Spain', in Richard Vogler and Barbara Huber, eds., *Criminal Procedure in Europe*. Berlin: Duncker & Humblot.

Gibson-Morgan, Elizabeth. 2014. 'Police Custody in England and France: A Lawful Deprivation of Liberty?', in Marion Charret-Del Bove and Fabrice Mourlon, eds., *Pre-trial Detention in 20th and 21st Century Common Law and Civil Law Systems*. Cambridge: Cambridge Scholars.

Goldfarb, Ronald. 1965. *Ransom: A Critique of the American Bail System*. New York: Harper & Row.

Graham-Harrison, Francis. 1974. *Bail Procedures in Magistrates' Courts: Report of a Working Party*. HMSO: London.

Groenhuijsen, Marc and Joep Simmelink. 2008. 'The Netherlands', in Richard Vogler and Barbara Huber, eds., *Criminal Procedure in Europe*. Berlin: Duncker & Humblot.

Guild, Elspeth and Sergio Carrera. 2009. 'Towards the Next Phase of the EU's Area of Freedom, Security and Justice: The European Commission's Proposals for the Stockholm Programme. CEPS Policy Brief No. 196', Centre for European Policy Studies 1–11.

Hafetz, Jonathon. 2003. 'Views on Contemporary Issues in the Region: Pretrial Detention, Human Rights, and Judicial Reform in Latin America', 26 *Fordham International Law Journal* 1754–1777.

Hammett, Theodore. 2006. 'HIV/AIDS and Other Infectious Diseases among Correctional Inmates: Transmission, Burden and an Appropriate Response', 96 *American Journal of Public Health* 974–978.

HM Inspectorate of Prisons for England and Wales. 2000. *Unjust Deserts: A Thematic Review by HM Chief Inspector of Prisons of the Treatment and Conditions for Unsentenced Prisoners in England and Wales*. London: Home Office.

Hodgson, Jacqueline. 2004. 'The Detention and Interrogation of Suspects in Police Custody in France: A Comparative Account', 1 *European Journal of Criminology* 163–199.

Huber, B. (2008). 'Germany', in R. Vogler and B. Huber, eds., *Criminal Procedure in Europe*. Berlin: Duncker & Humblot.

Illuminati, Giulio and Michele Caianiello. 2007. 'The Investigation Stage of the Criminal Process in Italy', in Edward Cape, Jacqueline Hodgson, Ties Prakken, and Taru Spronken, eds., *Suspects in Europe: Procedural Rights at the Invesigation Stage of the Criminal Process in the European Union*. Antwerp: Intersentia.

Kamisar, Yale. 1983. 'Gates, Probable Cause, Good Faith, and Beyond', 69 *Iowa Law Review* 551–615.

Kamisar, Yale. 1995. 'The Warren Court and Criminal Justice: A Quarter-Century Retrospective', 31 *Tulsa Law Journal* 1–56.

Karth, Vanja. 2008. *'Between a Rock and a Hard Place': Bail Decisions in Three South African Courts*. Johannesburg: Open Society Foundation for South Africa.

King, Sue, David Bamford, and Rick Sarre. 2009. 'Discretionary Decision-Making in a Dynamic Context: The Influences on Remand Decision-Makers in Two Australian Jurisdictions', 21 *Current Issues in Criminal Justice* 24–40.

Kinports, Kit. 2009. 'Veteran Police Officers and Three-Dollar Steaks: The Subjective/ Objective Dimensions of Probable Cause and Reasonable Suspicion', 12 *University of Pennsylvania Journal of Constitutional Law* 751–784.

Kruszynski, Piotr. 2007. 'The investigation Stage of the Criminal Process in Poland', in Edward Cape, Jacqueline Hodgson, Ties Prakken, and Taru Spronken, eds., *Suspects in Europe: Procedural Rights at the Invesigation Stage of the Criminal Process in the European Union*. Antwerp: Intersentia.

Langbein, John. 1977. *Torture and the Law of Proof: Europe and England in the Ancien Régime*. Chicago: University of Chicago Press.

Lerner, Craig S. 2003. 'The Reasonableness of Probable Cause', 81 *Texas Law Review* 951–1029.

Lerner, Craig S. 2005. *Reasonable Suspicion and Mere Hunches*. Fairfax: George Mason University School of Law Working Paper Series, Volume 36.

McBarnett, Doreen. 1978. 'The Police and the State: Arrest, Legality and the Law', in G. Littlejohn, B. Smart, J. Wakeford, and N. Yuval-Davis, eds., *Power and the State*. London: Croome Helm.

Metzmeier, Kurt. 1996. 'Preventive Detention: A Comparison of Bail Refusal Practices in the United States, England, Canada and Other Common Law Nations', 8 *Pace International Law Review* 399–438.

Miller, Eric. 2010. 'The Warren Court's Regulatory Revolution in Criminal Procedure', 43 *Connecticut Law Review* 1–82.

Ministry of Justice. 2013. *Statistics on Race and the Criminal Justice System 2012*. London: HMSO.

Moak, Stacy and Ronald Carlson. 2014. *Criminal Justice Procedure* (8th edn). Hoboken: Taylor and Francis.

Morgenstern, Christine. 2009. 'Pre-Trial/Remand Detention in Europe: Facts and Figures and the Need for Common Minimum Standards', 9 *Era Forum* 527–542.

Morsink, Johannes. 1999. *The Universal Declaration of Human Rights: Origins, Drafting, and Intent*. Philadelphia: University of Pennsylvania Press.

Oliver, Wesley MacNeil. 2010. 'The Modern History of Probable Cause', 78 *Tennessee Law Review* 377–429.

Open Society Initiative. 2011. *Pretrial Detention and Corruption*. New York: Open Society Foundations.

Open Society Justice Initiative. 2011a. *Pretrial Detention and Torture: Why Pretrial Detainees Face the Greatest Risk*. New York: Open Society Foundations.

Open Society Justice Initiative. 2011b. *The Socioeconomic Impact of Pretrial Detention*. New York: Open Society Foundations.

Phillips, C., D. Brown, Z. James, and P. Goodrich. 1998. *Entry into the Criminal Justice System: A Survey of Police Arrests and their Outcomes*. London: Home Office.

Piliavin, Irving and Scott Briar. 1964. 'Police Encounters with Juveniles', 70 *American Journal of Sociology* 206–214.

Rengifo, Andres and Jennifer Fratello. 2014. 'Perceptions of the Police by Immigrant Youth Looking at Stop-and-Frisk and Beyond Using a New York City Sample', *Youth Violence and Juvenile Justice* 1–19.

Ruggeri, Stefano. 2012. *Liberty and Security in Europe: A Comparative Analysis of Pre-Trial Precautionary Measures in Criminal Proceedings*. Osnabruck: V & R Unipress.

Sacks, Meghan and Alissa Ackerman. 2014. 'Bail and Sentencing: Does Pretrial Detention Lead to Harsher Punishment?', 25 *Criminal Justice Policy Review* 59–77.

Sanders, Andrew and Richard Young. 2007. *Criminal Justice*. Oxford: Oxford University Press.

Scheffer, David. 2009. 'A Review of the Experiences of the Pre-Trial and Appeals Chambers of the International Criminal Court Regarding the Disclosure of Evidence', 21 *Leiden Journal of International Law* 151–163.

Skolnick, Jerome. 1966. *Justice Without Trial*. London: Wiley.

Spronken, Taru. 2010. *EU-Wide Letter of Rights in Criminal Proceedings: Towards Best Practice*. Maastricht: University of Maastricht.

Stephen, James Fitzjames. 1883. *A History of the Criminal Law of England*. London: Macmillan.

Terrill, Richard. 2014. *World Criminal Justice Systems: A Comparative Survey* (8th edn). Hoboken: Taylor and Francis.

van Kalmthout, Anton, Marije Knapen, and Christine Morgenstern. 2009. *Pre-trial Detention in the European Union: An Analysis of Minimum Standards in Pre-trial Detention and the Grounds for Regular Review in the Member States of the EU*. Tilburg: Wolf Publishers.

van Kempen, Piet Hein. 2012. *Pre-trial Detention – Détention Avant Jugement*. Mortsel: Intersentia.

Ventura, Manuel. 2013. 'The "Reasonable Basis to Proceed" Threshold in the Kenya and Côte d'Ivoire Proprio Motu Investigation Decisions: The International Criminal Court's Lowest Evidentiary Standard?', *The Law and Practice of International Courts and Tribunals* 49–80.

Vogler, Richard. 1982. 'The Changing Nature of Bail', *Legal Action Group Bulletin* 11–12, 15.

Weber, Jack K. 1982. 'The Birth of Probable Cause', 11 *Anglo-American Law Review* 155–167.

Weigend, Thomas and Franz Salditt. 2007. 'The Investigative Stage of the Criminal Process in Germany', in E. Cape, J. Hodgson, T. Prakken, and T. Spronken, eds., *Suspects in Europe*. Antwerp: Intersentia.

Wiseman, Samuel. 2009. 'Discrimination, Coercion, and the Bail Reform Act of 1984: The Loss of the Core Constitutional Protections of the Excessive Bail Clause', 36 *Fordham Urban Law Journal* 121–157.

Wiseman, Samuel. 2014. 'Pretrial Detention and the Right to Be Monitored', 123 *Yale Law Journal* 1344–1404.

Woodruff, Michael. 2013. 'The Excessive Bail Clause: Achieving Pretrial Justice Reform through Incorporation', 66 *Rutgers Law Review* 241–297.

Yi, Yanyou. 2008. 'Arrest as Punishment: The Abuse of Arrest in the People's Republic of China', 10 *Punishment & Society* 9–24.

B. Pre-trial investigation

6. Procedural economy in pre-trial procedure: developments in Germany and the United States

Shawn Marie Boyne

> Almost from the adoption of the Constitution, it has been apparent that the provisions dealing with criminal procedure represented a set of ideals rather than a code of practice. (Goldstein, 1974: 1009)

1. INTRODUCTION

For decades, comparative law scholarship that focused on Western criminal justice systems regularly viewed national legal systems through what A. Esin Örücü calls a '[t]raditional black-letter law-oriented (rule-based)' framework that was 'normative, structural, institutional, and positivistic' (Örücü, 2006: 449). Seen through this lens, scholars categorized most of the world's criminal justice systems as adversarial, inquisitorial, or mixed systems. According to conventional scholarship, these two alternative models captured the essential structural differences that reflected competing visions of criminal law and procedure (Van Koppen and Penrod, 2003: 2). As the field of comparative law has continued to develop, theorists such as Mauro Cappelletti (1989), Mirjan Damaška (1986), and John Merryman (Merryman and Perez-Perdomo, 2007) proposed alternative frameworks employing concepts such as legal culture, legal families, and contrasting models of governmental authority to categorize legal systems. However, when we shift the focus away from contrasting the normative theories that underlie the criminal justice systems and seek to understand how institutional actors operate within the framework of the law, the utility of these models wanes. Although the traditional dichotomy between adversarial and inquisitorial systems often reflected an analysis of criminal procedure as it existed in statutory and case law, the law's impact is mediated by institutional interactions. The implementation of law is thus a dynamic process that includes not only judicial or legislative interpretations of statutes, but also workplace routines and the relational interactions between legal actors (Liu and Halliday, 2009: 214). Given the complexity, variability, and malleability of the criminal process, when we compare pre-trial practices in Germany and the US, we can no longer limit our comparison to a framework which contrasts a system that features a battle between two parties with one that pursues a unified objective investigation (Langer, 2014). To do so, we will miss evolving changes in practice.

Although models never precisely mirror reality, over the past three decades, socio-legal scholars have argued that a myriad of exogenous forces beyond the law, as well as the law itself, influence the decision-making practices of legal actors. This development is particularly important in the field of criminal procedure where a global financial crisis and shifting political priorities have imposed resource constraints on the truth-finding process in both countries. Indeed, as prosecutors, judges, and defense attorneys in both states work to move case files through the system, concerns about efficiency and limited resources have skewed the shape and goals of the truth-finding process. Although there will always be a gap between practice on the ground and the law's normative aspirations, in this era of world-wide economic stagnation and shifting fiscal priorities, resource limits have significantly widened that gap.

In this chapter, using the US system as a point of comparison, I examine the ongoing changes which have been occurring in German pre-trial practice. The daily practice of the key players in the criminal justice systems of both countries continues to shift in response to ever-increasing resource constraints and varied organizational incentives. These shifts have created areas of both convergence and divergence. Faced with heavy caseloads, prosecutors in both countries have increasingly utilized settlement mechanisms that resolve cases short of a full-fledged public trial. As a result, the course of pre-trial practice has become more outcome-determinative. While plea bargaining in the US came to play a dominant role several decades ago, its use in Germany is a more recent and controversial development. Although German prosecutors have had the power to dismiss or defer prosecutions of minor cases for several decades, it is only recently that the judicial and legislative branches have sanctioned the practice. Although American judges have long accepted the practice, German courts have imposed strict limits on deal-making – most notably demanding that the facts uncovered during the investigation substantiate the level of guilt referenced in the confession agreement (BVerfG, 2013).

The shortened investigation process in both countries raises questions about whether these abbreviated process outcomes fulfill the objectives of the criminal law. A key question in both countries is the extent to which the shortened process may embolden or undermine prosecutorial power vis-à-vis the judiciary. Additionally, this shift towards efficiency challenges the traditional 'storyline' about the path to truth in both adversarial and inquisitorial systems. By highlighting these two developments, this chapter will examine how the organization of the German prosecution function has reshaped the truth-finding process and altered the relationship between the prosecution service and the judiciary.

2. COMPARING NORMATIVE ASSUMPTIONS

2.1 Introduction

On paper, the structure of criminal justice in the United States and Germany reflects divergent assumptions about the path to truth as well as the degree of public confidence in government's role in the truth-finding process. Rather than place the adjudication function in the hands of the judiciary, the founding fathers' distrust of the king's authority led the colonists to rely on citizen juries to weigh the facts and the law (Rapping, 2012: 538). Seen from perspective of state authority, according to Damaška (1986: 222–225), the purpose of the adversarial process is to legitimate the resolution of a single dispute between identifiable parties (Twinning, 1990: 181). In contrast to inquisitorial systems, which vest their faith in the scientific nature of the law and judicial expertise, adversarial systems reflect the belief that, if the contest is structured fairly, the truth will emerge out of the battle between the parties (Weisbord and Smith, 2001: 256). In theory, American prosecutors are not merely adversaries committed to winning. In fact, American prosecutors are bound by an ethical duty to seek justice and not merely to seek to convict (New York Lawyer's Code of Professional Responsibility, 2013: 7–13). Although American prosecutors are required to disclose exculpatory evidence, German prosecutors possess a more robust duty to function objectively as they are required to investigate the facts both for and against the defendant (StPO § 60(2)).

In theory, since colonial times Americans have distrusted the government's ability to be objective. For this reason, the American system entrusts ordinary citizens with the role of ascertaining the relevant facts in a case and applying the law to reach a verdict. Ironically, the shift away from trials has not only usurped the jury's role, but it has also emboldened prosecutors. This development is noteworthy because, for the past two decades, scholars have not only questioned whether the 'contest' between the parties is a fair one, but they have also debated whether prosecutors possess a 'conviction mentality' that undermines their duty to pursue justice.

For several reasons, prosecutorial behavior in the US is often uncon-strained. Because state and federal legislatures inadequately fund indigent defense services (Uphoff, 2010), most defendants are represented by appointed counsel who are underfunded, unprepared, and overburdened (Mosteller, 2011: 325). In 2004, the American Bar Association noted that 'this underfunding places poor persons at constant risk for wrongful conviction' (2004: v). The minute the criminal process commences, the scales of justice are tipped in prosecutors' favor. Whatever 'battle' occurs is often one-sided. Absent a well-funded opponent, prosecutors, who are often embedded in organizations that reward conviction rates and stiff sentences, find few institutional incentives to protect defendants' rights and achieve fairness. While prosecutors are in principle bound to play fair, they are seldom disciplined for violating their ethical duties (Keenan et al., 2011: 203).

Even though the percentage of cases that culminate in a jury trial has dwindled, an adversarial outlook may shape the parties' behavior during the pre-trial process. Indeed, neither a prosecutor's refusal to disclose exculpatory evidence, nor a defense counsel's search for 'dirt' to damage witnesses, is likely to bring the investigation closer to the 'truth'. In both cases, the rules that exist to curb the parties' out-of-bounds behavior sometimes fail to guarantee that the process will serve the ends of justice. Despite the fact that defense counsel have a right to access whatever exculpatory evidence the prosecution team has in its possession, prosecu-tors' failure to disclose exculpatory evidence has been a significant factor in many wrongful conviction cases (Joy, 2013: 44).[1]

The final reason why the adversarial system falls short of its normative goal to find the truth is that most cases are resolved through a plea agreement. Although both parties are free to negotiate the outcome of a plea, the prosecutor typically has the upper hand in the negotiation because the specter of harsh penalties imposed by stiff mandatory minimum sentences increases the risk to the defendant of going to trial. Even before negotiations begin, prosecutors may increase the number or seriousness of the charges filed against a defendant simply to strengthen their bargaining position (Meares, 1995: 868). Without deep pockets to fund their own investigations, overworked and underfunded public defenders lack the time and resources necessary to challenge a prosecu-tor's case. Given this resource disparity, defense counsel themselves may strongly encourage their clients to accept a plea during the pre-trial phase.

It is not only underfunding that puts defense counsel at a disadvantage in the pre-trial phase of the proceedings. Weak discovery rights, espe-cially in federal courts, compromise the defendant's ability to uncover information which may undermine the state's case. Indeed, in federal courts prosecutors possess limited discovery obligations which may not come into play until just before or immediately after a witness testifies. As a result, a defendant may be forced to accept a guilty plea without full disclosure of the state's evidence. Thus, the combination of inadequate representation, limited discovery rights, and prosecutors' over-charging practices increase a prosecutor's leverage to force a plea. In a world of bargained justice, it is prosecutors, rather than judges, who most frequently engineer the system's results. On the surface, the portrait of pre-trial practice in America, at least for indigent defendants, looks more like the inquisitorial model, in which the 'truth' reflects the government's theory of the case – but without the more even-handed approach to fact-finding to which prosecutors and investigative judges in civil law systems are (supposed to be) committed.

2.2 Germany's Inquisitorial System

The German model reflects the inquisitorial model's conviction that a neutral fact-finder can objectively discover the 'truth'. Charged with leading the search for truth during the investigation process, prosecutors are entrusted, not with spearheading the effort to convict a suspect, but rather with uncovering all of the facts that are relevant for determining a suspect's guilt or innocence. One key difference between German and American prosecutors is that, while political pressures may drive American prosecutors to be tough on crime, German prosecutors are typically more insulated from public pressure. Moreover, German lawyers are trained not to view the law as a contest, nor are they evaluated on the basis of conviction rates.

In contrast to the American system, 'truth' in the German system is discovered through the state's objective investigation of the facts. To find that 'truth', the state directs career bureaucrats, not to function as parties, but rather to serve in a quasi-judicial role, investigating the facts for and against the defendant. Indeed, this vision of the law is introduced and reinforced in law school, where law faculties instruct students that an objective truth exists and most legal problems have only one 'solution'. Because the law is not perceived as a contest, prosecutors are free to dismiss cases which are unsupported by evidence and to ask the court to acquit a suspect. (The compulsory prosecution principle, even in its present diluted form, may facilitate this less conviction-minded ethos, since prosecutors in such a system will be expected to bring cases they probably won't 'win'.)

While the large majority of prosecution offices in the US are headed by an elected public prosecutor, the political accountability of German prosecutors is less direct. Except for a small number of federal prosecutors, all prosecution offices are subsumed under the Ministries of Justice on the 'Land' or state level. Both the law and the prosecution service's sense of institutional identity block most efforts made by the Ministry to influence case outcomes. However, the Ministries do influence prosecutorial practice as they determine staffing levels, create organizational incentives, and set overall priorities. Still, prosecution priorities are more reflective of the bureaucratic will rather than the politics of the District Attorney. Critically, individual German prosecutors do not view cases as an opportunity to 'win' in the courtroom.

The structure of practice is determined not only by prosecutors' institutional role, but also by the state's larger vision of the purpose of the criminal justice system. Rather than branding criminals as dangerous offenders who must be separated from society, the German justice system views offenders as individuals who have fallen out of compliance with community norms. Instead of relying heavily on incarceration and long minimum sentences, the German system relies extensively on fines and conditional dismissals. Even when an offender commits a serious crime, the system of justice often acts in a paternalistic manner, not to punish and isolate offenders, but rather to reintegrate offenders back into the society. This vision contrasts with that of the US system of justice – as reinforced by heightened security concerns after the 9/11 attacks – that increasingly privileges the goal of crime control over the protection of due process rights.[2] Thus, while American prosecutors' thirst to convict may translate into a desire to seek stiff punishments, German prosecutors' fidelity to less politicized norms and a tradition of tailoring punishment to the individual defendant tend to encourage a more tempered approach to punishment.

Although German prosecutors possess a near-monopoly on the state's charging power, the discretion that they possess has historically been more circumscribed than that of their American counterparts (Packer, 1968: 509). The Code of Criminal Procedure aims to limit discretion through the Principle of Legality (*Legalitätsprinzip*) which requires prosecutors to initiate proceedings in all cases where there is sufficient factual basis to believe that a criminal offense has been committed. It also dictates selection among overlapping offense definitions, to reduce redundancy and accumulation of punishment (Jescheck, 1970: 509). However, in practice, prosecutors possess substantial discretion in low-level criminal cases which include many white-collar crimes (Boyne, 2014: 65–72). In contrast to the US, German prosecutors often use this discretion to dismiss or defer cases where the state's interest in prosecution is low or the defendant's culpability is limited (StPO § 153(1) and (2)). In the case of more serious crimes, prosecutors are bound to the key pillars of the *Rechtsstaat* – fidelity to the principle of legality and adherence to rules for selecting among overlapping offense definitions. The widening discretion enjoyed by German prosecutors in the pre-trial stage contradicts a key pillar of the civil law tradition which has historically aimed to ensure that prosecutors and judges function as legal scientists and steer clear of discretionary and interpretive decision-making.

To ensure that prosecutors conduct an objective investigation, the Code of Criminal Procedure mandates that prosecutors investigate the facts 'for' and 'against' a suspect (StPO § 160(1) and (2)). In theory, the inquisitorial truth-finding process demands that prosecutors view the 'facts' through an objective lens. By eliminating prosecutors' ability to decline to press charges in serious cases and requiring prosecutors to function as neutral investigators, the Code aims to achieve an even-handed system of justice. Although prosecutors may decline cases for lack of evidence, to some extent, the Code even provides victims with the right to appeal a prosecutor's decision not to prosecute a case (StPO § 172).

While inequalities between the power of prosecutors and defense attorneys in the United States have challenged the assumption that the battle will be fought even-handedly, German practice has also fallen short of the system's normative goals. In particular, increasingly severe funding shortages have led to manpower shortages and undermined the system's ability to produce the 'truth'. Over the past three decades, budget constraints and personnel shortages have dramatically eroded the efficacy of the principle of mandatory prosecution. Frequently, German prosecutors now lack the time to thoroughly investigate every case with an objective eye. High caseloads force prosecutors to dismiss or short-cut investigations and move on to other cases (Prosecutor Interview [12CJ], November 12, 2005).[3]

Prosecutors' workload pressures derive from multiple sources. First, as 'security' concerns have trumped the cause of 'justice' in Land- and national-level budget battles, the budgets and manpower of police agencies have grown faster than the resource levels of prosecution offices and the courts. In many prosecution districts, the growth in police departments has enabled police departments to assume more responsibility for case investigation. While that shift may have little effect in many cases, it does create a risk that investigations will be captured by the investigator's single-minded quest to establish the suspect's culpability.

Second, the development of globalized markets, coupled with weak international oversight mechanisms, has led multi-national criminal enterprises to use sophisticated methods to move capital illegally across national borders. Because state-level prosecution offices, rather than the Federal Prosecutors Office, bear the primary responsibility for investigating complex crimes, many prosecution offices are ill-equipped to investigate many serious economic crimes ('Die Beschlüsse', 1990: 2992). In addition, in some Länder, the police themselves lack the training and staffing to conduct the investigations (Prosecutor Interview [19BN], May 14, 2008). As a result of resource constraints, prosecutors either fail to investigate complex crimes or settle serious cases with a German analogue to plea bargaining known as confession bargaining (Feeney and Hermann, 2005: 380). Because the courts are also backlogged, when a defendant is charged with an economic crimes case, the case can take a year to resolve.

Finally, the land-level Ministries of Justice have shifted the focus of their oversight of case-handling practices from the use of quality-based assessments to quantitative metrics that emphasize efficiency. In the past, individuals from the Ministries of Justice would visit prosecution offices and review random case files. Those field visits now occur rarely. Instead, management uses metrics to track the number of cases a prosecutor has open, investigation length, and case-closure rates. The shift in performance evaluation methods to metrics that privilege efficiency may undermine prosecutors' commitment to neutrality and objectivity. According to one prosecutor that I interviewed, 'in determining who will be promoted, it is more important that the person has been productive, rather than that they do good work' (Prosecutor Interview [12FG], April 24, 2006). While the statistics have grown in importance, other department managers described a more time-intensive evaluation system to me. As one manager explained:

> In order to determine whether a prosecutor has done a good job during the investigation stage of a case, I must read through the entire file ... Then I must think how I would have handled the investigation and whether or not the decisions made by a prosecutor on the case can be justified. There are some decisions that may reflect differences of opinion. Then there are [other] things that are naturally not so favorable – how a prosecutor prepares a charging document for example. Some prosecutors prepare great charging documents and then others make mistakes when preparing the documents that one will naturally notice. (Senior Prosecutor Interview [19BS], May 14, 2008)

As a result of growing resource pressures, a gap has emerged between the German system's faithfulness to the principle of legality and pre-trial practice. As this gap developed, the German legislature has led from behind reforming the Code of Criminal Procedure to bridge the gap between practice and the law. In a growing number of cases, these changes give prosecutors the power to short-circuit the truth-finding process. As an example, in the mid-1970s, the legislature introduced statutory provisions that were intended to give prosecutors limited discretion to dismiss low-level crimes short of a full adjudicatory process (Feeney and Hermann, 2005: 380). Although the law permits prosecutors to depart from the norm of mandatory prosecution when handling low-level crimes and juvenile offenses under Section 152 of the Criminal Procedure Code (StPO), during the past twenty years, prosecutors have nearly doubled the rate of discretionary non-prosecution cases (Oberwittler and Höfer, 2005: 472–473). As a result, the principle of mandatory prosecution is now counterbalanced by the 'opportunity principle', which allows a prosecutor to consider the public's interest in prosecuting a particular case. The economic pressures facing Germany today, and the resulting resource constraints on the judicial system, have brought concerns for efficiency to the fore.

By the mid-1980s, prosecutors had begun to short-circuit investigations and negotiate 'confession agreements' with an increasing number of defendants (Hermann, 1992: 756). Ironically, while the use of 'confession agreements' blossomed in practice for a long time, scholars and practitioners minimized its scope and took care to distinguish 'confession agreements' from American plea bargains. While the legal academy continued to profess its faith in the principle of mandatory prosecution, a distinct gap between the Code and actual practice developed as courts began to use settlement practices not found in the statute books. As increasingly severe resource constraints continued to fuel the growth of these informal bargaining practices, it was not until 1997 that the Federal Court of Justice (BGH) acknowledged and attempted to regulate the practice (BGHSt, Aug. 28, 1997, p. 206).

While the Court attempted to prevent 'procedural deals' that short-circuited the truth-finding process, bargaining practices encouraged courts and prosecutors to short-circuit case investigations (Schemmel et al., 2014). Finally, in 2013, Germany's Federal Constitutional Court (BVerG) handed down a landmark decision that placed strong restrictions on case negotiation practices (BVerG Mar. 19, 2013, 2 BvR 2628/10). The decision appears to have cooled prosecutors' willingness to engage in deal-making prior to the opening of the main proceeding (Prosecutor Interview [5PA], July 10, 2014). Because a sentence must now conform to the state's evidence of an individual's level of guilt, some prosecution offices are now reluctant to agree to a deal in a case's investigation stage

(Prosecutor Interview [5PA], July 10, 2014). Still, the rise of confession bargaining, coupled with the increase in discretion that German prosecutors enjoy, represents a sharp departure from the criminal justice system's normative claims (Weigend, 1990: 774).

3. PRE-TRIAL INVESTIGATION PRACTICES

3.1 Introduction

In both Germany and the United States, tight resource constraints have fueled the use of procedures that short-circuit the production of evidence necessary to allow the fact-finder to weigh the facts and the law. The full factual and legal inquiry anticipated by the drafters of the codes of criminal procedure is in decline in both countries. In the United States, these changes have expanded prosecutorial discretion and increased prosecutors' power. In Germany, prosecutors look for ways to dismiss, rather than investigate, minor cases – while judges look to confession agreements to manage their caseloads. Although resource constraints have curtailed the truth-finding process in both systems, the nature of the impact caused by these constraints differs, because of the contrasting roles of the players in the two systems, and because organizational incentives affect prosecutorial decision-making in rather distinct ways.

A key point of comparison between both systems is the process that governs how criminal charges are filed as well as the relative roles that the police and prosecutors play in the case investigation. A prosecutor's initial decision to file charges against an individual is one of the most important and consequential decisions made by public officials (Secunda, 1997: 1267). It is important to acknowledge that prosecutors in both systems lack the resources necessary to prosecute all cases in which a suspicion exists that a crime has been committed.[4] Thus, one of the most important functions that prosecutors play is their gate-keeping role as they decide which cases will be dismissed, investigated, or proceed to trial. While prosecutors in both systems possess discretion, the law is not the only structure that mediates how prosecutors exercise that discretion. Indeed, organizational controls help to shape prosecutors' investigation and charging decisions, and the diversity of those controls within both countries makes it harder to compare the ways the two systems actually function.

3.2 United States

Although the evidentiary rules that structure the presentation of evidence at trial are complex, relatively few rules govern prosecutorial behavior during the investigation process (Brown, 2005: 1585). Ironically, the Supreme Court's reluctance to regulate the pre-trial process is premised on assumptions about the adversarial system which, in many cases, no longer apply. Most critically, the judiciary's hands-off approach assumes that the adversarial structure of the trial will encourage both parties to conduct a thorough investigation to obtain any evidence necessary to present their 'side' of the facts in the courtroom (Brown, 2005: 1588). Since the burden of proof lies with the state, in some cases, the defense investigation may aim to generate facts designed to undermine the credibility of the state's witnesses. To this end, the system presumes that defense counsel will highlight any missteps made by the state at trial. However, if the defense lacks the resources to investigate the state's case and the defendant feels pressured to accept a plea, a jury will never judge the comprehensiveness of the state's investigation.

3.2.1 An uneven playing field

A second point of comparison is the role and stance that the police take during the investigation stage. During the pre-arraignment period, the police may function as adversaries against an undefended suspect (*Brewer v. Williams*), because indigent defendants in the US enjoy a right to counsel only after adversarial criminal proceedings commence. As a result, even after the police have acquired probable cause to believe that an individual has committed a crime, officers may employ a variety of tactics designed to continue to gather incriminating information.

Although a suspect has a right to an attorney when the police commence a custodial interrogation, the state need not provide indigent suspects with an attorney until formal charges are filed. While the Bill of Rights grants suspects the right to remain silent, it is difficult for unrepresented suspects to maintain silence in the face of a strong pressure to confess. From the start, police officers do not enter interrogation rooms with a neutral attitude towards the suspect as the police primarily use interrogations to confirm their initial suspicion of guilt (Kassin et al., 2009). Indeed, recent research on criminal investigation processes in general suggests that an investigator's pre-existing beliefs regarding a particular suspect's guilt may create a 'confirmation bias'. According to this research, individuals do not process new information in an objective manner, but rather in a manner that is consistent with their prior beliefs. As Ask, Rebelius and Granhag (2008: 1246) state:

Interrogators with high, as opposed to low, expectations of guilt selected more guilt-presumptive questions, used more manipulative interrogation techniques and pressed suspects harder for a confession, particularly when questioning an innocent suspect. In other words, there was a tendency to primarily seek information that confirmed interrogators' expectations. In addition, regardless of suspects' actual guilt, highly suspicious interrogators judged suspects' behaviour during the interrogation as more guilty than did interrogators with low levels of suspicion.

Even more troubling, in recent years the Supreme Court has drastically rolled back the scope of constitutional protections that regulate pre-trial procedures. According to current case law, the police may lie to a suspect (*Frazier v. Cupp*), mislead a suspect about the strength of the state's case (*Frazier v. Cupp*), and even employ a question first, and give Miranda warnings later interrogation protocol, in order to increase the probability of a subsequent, usable confession (*Missouri v. Seibert*). Although it is impossible to document the percentage of suspects who confess to crimes that they did not commit, forced confessions are a leading cause of wrongful convictions (Massie, 2015).

In theory, prosecutors' duty to fairness and justice should check police officers' confirmation bias. Indeed, in many cases, fair-minded prosecutors have disclosed exculpatory evidence to the defense. However, recent scholarship has detailed patterns of widespread prosecutorial misconduct that are: 'largely the result of three institutional conditions: vague ethics rules that provide ambiguous guidance to prosecutors; vast discretionary authority with little or no transparency; and inadequate remedies for prosecutorial misconduct, which create perverse incentives for prosecutors to engage in, rather than refrain from, prosecutorial misconduct' (Joy, 2006: 400).

The fact that a case is likely to end in a plea may compound the problems created during the investigation process. In order to gain the upper hand in the negotiation process, prosecutors may try and gain the plea bargaining process by over-charging a case (Nagle and Schulhofer, 1992: 548) to gain leverage in the subsequent negotiations (Goldstein and Marcus, 1977). Although the Rules of Professional Conduct state that 'the prosecutor in a criminal case [shall] … refrain from prosecuting a charge that the prosecutor knows is not supported by probable cause', the probable cause standard is a relatively low evidentiary standard (Mosteller, 2011: 336). Not only it is easy to meet this evidentiary bar, but prosecutors possess no affirmative duty to probe the sufficiency of the police investigation (Mosteller, 2011: 336). In addition, the standard's low threshold of factual sufficiency allows prosecutors to press cumulative charges to increase the sentence a defendant will face if she loses at trial.

The advent of high mandatory minimum sentences at the federal and state levels further heightens prosecutors' ability to penalize defendants who choose to go to trial, as prosecutors can determine whether a mandatory minimum will be triggered by the way they frame the charges, as the availability of mandatory minimum penalties often depends on the quantities of narcotics for which the prosecutor seeks to hold a defendant accountable, or on the prosecutor's decision about whether to charge the defendant with using a weapon during the commission of another offense (Opel, 2011). As Michelle Alexander (2012: 87) writes:

> The practice of encouraging defendants to plead guilty to crimes, rather than affording them the benefit of a full trial, has always carried its risks and downsides. Never before in our history, though, have such an extraordinary number of people felt compelled to plead guilty, even if they are innocent, simply because the punishment for the minor, nonviolent offense with which they have been charged is so unbelievably severe. When prosecutors offer 'only' three years in prison when the penalties defendants could receive if they took their case to trial would be five, ten, or twenty years – or life imprisonment – only extremely courageous (or foolish) defendants turn the offer down.

3.2.2   Unchecked power

In both inquisitorial and accusatorial legal systems, the pre-trial process is meant to redress any prosecutorial or police misconduct that may have occurred. The adversarial process supposedly allows police tactics to be brought out and tested at trial, where a jury of the defendants' peers can acquit against the weight of the evidence if it abhors the means by which evidence was obtained. In general, however, constitutionality of police tactics is tested in pretrial motions and hearings, not at trial. However, because few cases now culminate in a jury trial, defense counsel must rely on pre-trial motions to counter unconstitutional tactics. In theory, defense counsel may also raise discovery issues during the pre-trial phase. However, absent egregious behavior from the prosecutor's office, judges grant prosecutors wide discretion at the discovery stage (Barkow, 2006: 997). Though defense attorneys may move to suppress unconstitutionally seized evidence, at least on the federal level, the Supreme Court has continued to narrow the scope of the exclusionary rule (Slobogin, 2013: 348).

A key area of recent contention is whether or not prosecutors are complying with their duty to disclose exculpatory evidence. While Model Rules 3.8(d) and Supreme Court decisions (for example, *Brady v.*

Maryland) require prosecutors to provide the defense with exculpatory evidence, the reluctance of both courts and disciplinary authorities to sanction prosecutorial misconduct undercuts the effectiveness of these mandates.[5]

A key reason why prosecutorial power has grown is that judges, concerned with respecting the separation between judicial and executive powers, have traditionally been reluctant to challenge prosecutors' exercise of discretion. In some cases, the judicial branch is powerless to force a prosecutor's hand. For example, a judge cannot compel a prosecutor to file charges that the judge believes to be supported by sufficient probable cause (Krug, 2002: 647). In other cases, judges are often reluctant to challenge cases based on 'questionable police testimony' or to intervene on behalf of an overburdened public defender (Roberts, 2013: 1093). In a system where trials are uncommon, a prosecutor's unparalleled discretion and power ensures that most indigent defendants never confront the state on even terms (Krug, 2002: 648–649). As a result, the 'truth' that emerges bears the imprint of the state's power to coerce a defendant to accept a plea.

Many scholars have argued that the system's truth-finding compass is currently skewed. As Robert Mosteller has written, 'the prosecutor has effectively become not only an advocate but also the adjudicator in determining the resolution of the case through the omnipresent practice of plea bargaining as a substitute for trial' (Mosteller, 2011: 324). However, the problem of resource constraints is not restricted to public defender offices, as both prosecutors and police investigators also do not possess unlimited resources. In addition, while battles over serious felony cases occur, prosecutors and defenders are often engaged in compromise.

3.2.3   Resource constraints and case screening practices

While the desire to keep cases moving may drive prosecutorial decision-making in American misdemeanor cases, where a 'conviction mentality' shapes decision routines that mentality may also color screening decisions. As Professor Peter Joy has written:

> Practically speaking, the prosecutor is the first line of defense against many of the common factors that lead to wrongful convictions. The prosecutor's supervisory authority to evaluate the quality and quantity of evidence holds the potential for assuring the accused both procedural and, when the accused is actually innocent, substantive justice. When prosecutors do not critically examine the evidence against the accused to ensure its trustworthiness, or fail to comply with discovery and other obligations to the accused, rather than act as ministers of justice, they administer injustice. (Joy, 2006: 406)

A prosecutor's initial case-screening decisions play a critical role in determining a case's final outcome. Office policies, resource limitations, and the prosecutor's initial evaluation of the strength of the evidence influence a prosecutor's initial decisions on how to handle a case (Frederick and Stemen, 2012: 15). While portrayals of prosecutorial zeal may be commonplace, resource constraints at the courtroom level may actually lead prosecutors to undercharge cases.

> Shortages of courtrooms, judges, clerks, court reporters, and scheduled court hours – and especially unscheduled reductions in court hours – posed persistent difficulties for prosecutors. According to Southern County prosecutors, the lack of courtroom space and the consequent continuance of cases caused prosecutors to undercharge cases, continually re-evaluate plea offers, and dismiss cases they otherwise 'should prosecute'. They described a process of ranking cases, based on evidence, offense seriousness, victim cooperation, and time since initial filing. The effect was to change the threshold of what prosecutors were willing to accept or dismiss and often resulted in decisions the prosecutors considered less than ideal. Moreover, these decisions were often beyond the control of an individual prosecutor; when resource constraints required a re-evaluation of cases, some units determined case priorities and dispositions by group consensus.

> According to the district attorney in Northern County, constraints on court resources freed up prosecutors to do more work on cases at the front end. As a result, the prosecutor's office worked harder to evaluate cases for declination and deferral, effectively restructuring the process to remove people from the system early. (Frederick and Stemen, 2012: 15)

3.2.4 Summary

Without a doubt prosecutorial power in the US has grown dramatically. It is also true that public pressure may fuel a 'conviction mentality' that narrows prosecutors' objectivity. Where prosecutors are beholden to a conviction mentality, they may suppress exculpatory evidence, overcharge a suspect, and use their leverage to make it too risky for defendants to proceed to trial. At the same time, prosecutors themselves are not immune from the impact caused by resource constraints. The presence of limited courtroom resources and high caseloads may make prosecutors more amenable to dismissing or undercharging a case. At both ends of the spectrum, imbalances in power or resources may undermine the robustness of the truth-finding process.

3.3   Germany

For decades, the primary difference between the scope of a prosecutor's power in Germany and the United States was that American prosecutors had more authority to decline prosecution than German prosecutors. In the wake of the changes mentioned earlier, the discretion of German prosecutors has increased dramatically. Despite recent changes in German law, on paper, American prosecutors still possess greater authority to decline cases than German prosecutors, as German prosecutors' discretion is by law limited to minor criminal cases (StPO § 152(2)). Still, at least one empirical study calls into question the significance of these differences in the scope of discretion. Feeney's (1998) study found that the percentage of cases actually charged by German and American prosecutors was strikingly similar for most offenses examined in the report. While empirical research on this question is lacking, this study suggests that German prosecutors, like their American counterparts, may fail to prosecute primarily those cases they view as weak.

3.3.1   The quest for objectivity
Despite this statistical congruence between the two systems' charging practices, the structure of pre-trial practice in Germany and the United States mirrors each system's differing assumptions about the path to truth. While the adversarial model treats the pre-trial process as another stage in a competitive process, German prosecutors are supposed to function as 'second judges' rather than as parties. German prosecutors are mandated to maintain 'absolute objectivity' from the start to the finish of the criminal process (Siegismund, 2001: 58). Underpinning the German belief in this objective outlook is the system's faith that prosecutors function as legal scientists who classify facts within the correct legal categories. Both the charging decision and the final verdict function as the bookends of a logical 'decision involving correct subsumption under legal categories' (Damaška, 1981: 125). In practice, the law seldom functions so smoothly, as external forces influence prosecutorial decision-making. While distance from an investigation may enhance a prosecutor's objectivity, close cooperation with the police may lead to a form of agency capture. In my observation of German prosecution offices, I observed more of a conviction mentality in the drug crimes departments, where prosecutors work closely with the police to initiate investigations using extraordinary measures such as wiretaps. Given that the police in both systems may not function as truly disinterested investigators, a German prosecutor's commitment to objectivity may function as a more effective check on the sufficiency of the investigation.

3.3.2 Prosecutors and police

The investigation process commences when the police or a prosecution office receive a report of suspected criminal activity (StPO § 160(1)). Consistent with the German view that fact-gathering is part of a larger scientific process, German procedure law has traditionally entrusted the decision to supervise the investigation and charge a suspect to prosecutors rather than the police (StPO § 161(1)). However, consistent with the increasing professionalization of the police forces and the changing nature of crime, the relationship between police and prosecutors continues to evolve. Although the statutory responsibility for case investigation remains vested in the prosecution service, the distribution of investigative work between prosecutors and police varies by office, department, and individual prosecutor. These variations run the gamut, from issuing written instructions to police officers to working hand in hand with the police to plan an investigation.

Although the law aims to prevent police officers from dismissing cases without approval from a prosecutor, law enforcement officers may circumvent this oversight by not disclosing all investigative activities to prosecutors. In practice, because the growth of police department budgets has outstripped the resources of prosecution offices, it is often the police themselves who make crucial decisions during the investigative stage in cases of minor criminality (Appellate Judge Interview [22FE], July 22, 2004). Indeed, in most minor crime cases, police officers conduct the bulk of the investigation before turning the case over to the prosecution office. While 80 percent of the initial reports of crime originate with the police department (Siegismund, 2001: 61), during the course of my research in Germany, I observed many prosecutors in major crime departments actively investigate cases.

3.3.3 Prosecutors as investigators

The degree of prosecutorial involvement in the investigation stage depends upon local routines of practice, expediency, and the type of crime involved. In cases such as rape or economic crimes, which require investigative follow-up and expert testimony, the police officer leading the investigation would likely coordinate the follow-up investigation with the prosecutor. In these cases, the prosecutor will decide whether the police should interview additional witnesses and, if necessary, whether to seek a search warrant (Senior Prosecutor Interview [13OI], June 10, 2004).

In cases where search warrants are required, by law, the prosecutor, and ultimately a judge, must approve the warrant request (StPO § 103).

Where a delay in obtaining a warrant may compromise evidence collection, German procedure law permits prosecutors to approve a warrant without judicial oversight. In contrast to American criminal procedure, the level of suspicion required to obtain a warrant in Germany falls below the American probable cause requirement. The police may search a home, apartment, or business, for the purpose of arresting a suspect or if 'it may be presumed that such search will lead to the discovery of evidence' (Bradley, 1983: 1038).

In complex cases, the nature of the investigation and the complexity of the law mandate prosecutorial involvement. For example, because drug cases typically require the use of informants and search warrants, prosecutors routinely work hand in hand with the police on those cases, as prosecutors must approve such tactics in advance. Complex economic crime investigations require a similar partnership between police and prosecutors throughout the investigation, especially if the suspects have transferred capital across national boundaries. The nature of the police–prosecutor interaction in complex cases varies. In one prosecution office that I visited, an inter-agency economic crime investigative team worked with the lead prosecutor to map out a criminal syndicate's complex organizational structure and plan the investigation's future stages using software that facilitated this team-oriented approach. In another office, prosecutors complained that economic crime investigations were time-consuming and that the police department lacked the expertise to investigate accounting offenses (Lead Office Prosecutor [19BN], May 14, 2008). As a result, prosecutors in that office often investigated their own cases.

In better staffed offices with an anti-bureaucratic outlook, prosecutors working in the economic crimes department often chose to work those cases so that they could work closely with the police. As one prosecutor reported to me, 'we do not sit behind our desks all day as we go out and execute search warrants and play an active role in the investigation' (Prosecutor Interview [5XW], January 19, 2006). While some prosecutors are content to issue written directions and wait for a response from the police, more proactive prosecutors meet personally with the police on a regular basis, formulate a joint investigation plan, and often pick up the phone to communicate with members of the investigation team.

3.3.4   Cutting short the search for truth

Because of caseload pressures, in most cases, the first step that a prosecutor will seek to take with a case will not be to order additional investigation, but rather to determine whether or not she can find a way to dismiss the case with a fine or diversion (Justice Ministry interview

[9CK], May 4, 2006). As the German legislature continued to widen the range of prosecutors' discretion in minor crime cases, prosecutors began to search for ways to close cases in their early stages. Even in cases of more serious criminality, German prosecutors also possess the authority to dismiss cases with the court's consent by using penal orders which mandate a minimum sanction such as a fine and a suspended sentence (StPO §§ 407–412).

In contrast with the tendency of some American prosecutors to over-charge cases to gain leverage in the negotiation process, the initial instinct of German prosecutors, in all but the most serious cases, is to find a way to close the file using one of these pre-trial procedures. Instead of stretching the facts to support more charges, many German prosecutors prefer to dismiss cases or to impose minimal sanctions. As a result of this case-closing mindset, decision-making routines become a search for options to transfer cases out of the in-box. As one Appellate Court Judge commented, 'in the majority of low-level crime cases, prosecutors do the work of administration and not of justice – they get their papers signed and that is that' (Appellate Judge Interview [13MU], April 10, 2004).

Despite the fact that prosecutors across Germany are charged with implementing the same law, case screening and disposition practices vary widely. Local attitudes towards crime, resource levels, office norms, and practice routines determine the degree of leniency offered by prosecutors. Liberal Schleswig-Holstein led the way with case dismissal and diversion rates close to 63 percent (Heinz, 2014: 85). Consistent with their long-standing strict attitudes towards crime, prosecutors in Bavaria dismiss or defer the lowest percentage of cases, with close to 63 percent of cases proceeding to a main hearing (Heinz, 2014).

3.3.5 Organizational controls

Organizational controls also play a role in shaping pre-trial practice. Although the political independence of prosecution offices in the United States, taken in conjunction with differences between state penal codes, makes it difficult to isolate the impact of organizational controls on American offices, it is easier to draw comparisons across German offices. The existence of a common code and the fact that German prosecutors are part of a hierarchically ordered civil service make it easier to identify differences at the Land and office levels. Although key differences in personnel policies and charging practices exist throughout Germany, in recent decades, all prosecution offices now use organizational metrics to evaluate case-handling practices. Most notably, as resource constraints have intensified, the land-level Ministries of Justice have increasingly employed statistical indices to monitor productivity and staffing rates. The standards attempt to establish performance baselines for practices such as the average investigation length in a department. Within individual prosecution offices, the office leadership may use the data to identify prosecutors who 'process' their cases less efficiently than their peers. While the metrics attempt to gauge differences in the investigation requirements between different types of crimes, there is little doubt that the use of the metrics as a management tool privileges efficiency. For example, to meet productivity guidelines, one general crimes department calculated that prosecutors in the department had to screen and close each low-level crime case in under three minutes (Leading Office Prosecutor [16PP], May 11, 2006). Still, it is important to note that the introduction of computers has not only made it possible to track efficiency-related metrics but has also sped up the work process. One senior prosecutor (Senior Prosecutor [25IFG], April 16, 2008) related to me that:

> Through the use of technology, we have the possibility [of working] faster and more rationally. When I started in the general crimes department, we closed about 75 cases per month. Now they close 130 cases per month. But on the other side, we must do more work. We do more work on the computer now and less through writing.

3.3.6   The logic of documentation

Though technology has increased prosecutors' productivity, other traditional aspects of a German prosecutor's pre-trial routine are more archaic and idiosyncratic. The time that German prosecutors devote to documenting each individual decision, as well as 'issuing instructions', stand out when juxtaposed against American practice. Indeed, a significant part of a German prosecutor's initial training involves one-on-one instruction in the art of documenting actions taken on a case file. Not only does this one-on-one training ensure that prosecutors accurately and consistently document the history of a case in the case file; the training systematically conveys the routines of organizational practice to newcomers entering the organization. This unique aspect of German prosecutorial practice stems from the role that case files play in both systems. While American judges never review the prosecutor's file, German judges use the file not only to determine whether charges should proceed, but also to determine how to present the evidence at trial. A common system of nomenclature encourages prosecutors to handle cases in a consistent manner. In theory, any prosecutor could pick up another prosecutor's file and be able to immediately determine what has happened so far in the case. In contrast to American case files, the German file is a near-complete record of the investigation and the prosecutor's notes. Prosecutors' use of a common nomenclature increases the transparency of the pre-trial process.[6] Key criminal procedure obligations are based on the state of the evidence at any given point in a criminal inquiry. This makes it important for the case file to be transparent in disclosing what was done, and for prosecutors to be consistent in how they record the progress of an investigation. In some ways, the attempt to standardize practice reinforces an individual prosecutor's lack of identity and agency and reduces the opportunity for individual prosecutors to develop idiosyncratic case-handling practices.

During my observation studies of German prosecution offices, I observed many prosecutors use this time-consuming written bureaucratic practice of issuing instructions. In more traditional offices, after a prosecutor reviews a new file which requires more investigative work, he or she will then literally write an order in the file that directs the police to interview a particular witness or to take another action on the case. The prosecutor may also send the file to an administrative agency to determine whether the suspect's actions violated an environmental law, for example. The file is then physically transported to the police or another office. The prosecutor will also write an instruction in the file asking the department's administrative secretary to return the file to them in 'X' amount of time for follow up. While this method ensures that each step of the investigation is documented, it also takes time.

The German system's allegiance to the principle of legality is reflected not only in the transparency of case files, but also in the organization of responsibilities within individual offices. While a District Attorney or a US Attorney might steer certain cases to particular prosecutors to ensure that a case is handled in a particular way, German prosecution offices use annual organizational plans in an attempt to minimize political influence over case-handling practices. Each plan specifically details what prosecutor is responsible for which case files according to the type of crime(s) involved and the defendant's last name. For example, a prosecutor might be assigned to handle general crime cases where the suspect's last name begins with A through K for that year. Absent an order from their superior, that prosecutor will not jump in and handle other cases. The combination of this plan and the file documentation procedures allow supervisors to monitor whether prosecutors follow the correct procedures in handling particular cases (Senior Office Prosecutor [1ZU], March 15, 2006).

A key downside to this heavily routinized system of practice is that it requires prosecutors to devote significant time to following bureacratic procedures which, on their own, do not ensure that the prosecutor has conducted a neutral investigation designed to find the truth. As I spent time conducting interviews in over a dozen prosecution offices, I noticed a distinct difference in the 'life' of each office. In some offices, doors were closed and halls were quiet. In others, doors were open as a constant stream of police officers and witnesses flowed through the offices.

One must be careful to not to assign too much significance to subjective appraisals of the 'life' of each office. However, at key points in the criminal justice process, a prosecutor's reluctance to interact personally with witnesses, police officers, and other players in the process may narrow a prosecutor's understanding of the case. A prosecutor may indeed spend the day at her desk working the files by issuing written instructions and not meet with witnesses, police officers, and other agency officials. In some cases, a supervisor may simply look at the file's documentation procedures and conclude that the prosecutor is doing his or her job. Indeed, the system's dedication to bureaucratic documentation practices may privilege prosecutors who dot their 'i's' but fail to establish personal relationships with law enforcement officers, witnesses, and other interlocutors. On the other hand, prosecutors who establish personal connections and treat the police and other agencies as team members may benefit from more buy-in from other team members. While compliance with the documentation procedures guarantees a certain level of conformity and transparency, it does not by itself guarantee that a prosecutor has conducted a thorough and objective investigation. As one department leader in an economic crimes department related:

> Many department leaders are too bureaucratic. It is safer [for some] just to issue written orders. In order to resolve cases quickly, everything [in an investigation] must come together – the defense attorney, the judge, [and] the police. This does not always happen. We have changed a lot in this department. It is now less bureaucratic than most departments. [When I took over] the police were doing all the investigating and I changed the system so that the prosecutors started doing more investigative work. (Leading Office Prosecutor Interview [2BN], July 16, 2004)

Police investigations may also stall when the crime is a complex one and police investigators lack sufficient training to investigate the case. In rural areas, the lack of specialized law enforcement expertise may force prosecutors to investigate cases themselves or settle cases short of a full investigation (Leading Office Prosecutor [19BN], May 14, 2008).

In well-staffed regions, the prosecutor screening the investigation file may order the police to continue the investigation if the quantum of proof fails to satisfy the prosecutor's evaluation of the court's screening standards (Senior Prosecutor [13AS], June 10, 2004).

In all regions, complex cases such as organized crime investigations require the prosecutor to do more than simply function as office-bound bureaucrats. According to one department supervisor (Prosecutor [13BR], November 18, 2005), a model prosecutor would not be content with simply moving paper:

> One must be able to intuitively determine what investigation measures are possible. In the investigation, one must have knowledge of special measures in organized crime, for example, that comes with experience ... One must know how to work with people. I believe that the ideal prosecutor knows how to work with the police. [She must decide whether] the police [should] interview the suspect or a witness. [She must contemplate] how one should compile the file [by completing the investigation]. [She must decide] what technical investigation tools are available to [gather evidence on] the suspect?

3.3.7 Efficiency and the truth

A critical question regarding German pre-trial procedures is whether prosecutors have the time, dedication, and independence to fulfill their duty to look at cases with an objective eye. While the question of whether or not the suspect committed a crime may be easy to answer in most cases, one key test of the fairness of a criminal justice system is how it handles cases where a suspect's guilt is unclear. While it is apparent that most German prosecutors are not consumed with a desire to 'win' cases by securing convictions, the system's emphasis on efficiency and the use of archaic procedures also do not guarantee that prosecutors are sufficiently motivated to pursue every facet of a case that may enrich the court's understanding of the 'truth'. While I observed a large number of dedicated and hard-working prosecutors, I also observed a number of prosecutors who seemed content simply to 'work the file' and empty their in-box each day. When working the file merely means that the prosecutor has issued a few 'instructions' to other authorities, a 'closed case' may simply mean that the prosecutor has supervised a minimum level of investigation.

Unlike in the US, where victims have limited options for challenging a prosecutor's decision to close a case, in Germany a number of statutory and bureaucratic controls limit prosecutors' ability to dismiss or lightly investigate cases (StPO, §§ 171–175, 395(1)). Where a case involves a victim, German law gives the victim the right to appeal to the General Prosecutor's Office in that jurisdiction a prosecutor's decision to dismiss.

If that office refuses to take action, a victim may file an appeal with the regional appellate court. In addition, depending on the internal protocols of a particular prosecution office, prosecutors who are assigned to handle important or other high-profile cases must pen regular reports for their superiors describing the progress made on the case. While the purpose of the reporting process is to keep the authorities up to date on the status of a case that may appear in the media, the reports also impose subtle pressure on the prosecutor to handle the case according to the formal and informal guidelines of the office.

The structure of the German proceedings undercuts a defense attorney's ability to challenge the state's case. The nature of the defense role in Germany is different from that of its American counterpart in large part because a judicial panel rather than a jury will ultimately decide whether a suspect is guilty. Thus German judges are less likely to be swayed by defense strategies that hinge on sowing doubt in jurors' minds. In the pre-trial stages, the law permits counsel to petition the state to investigate leads that point away from the defendant's guilt (StPO § 163(a)). However, a prosecutor may decline to do so if she believes that the evidence is unimportant or the lead unpromising. In one case that a defense counsel recounted to me, the prosecutor refused to interview additional witnesses suggested by the defense (Defense Counsel Interview [20GU], February 6, 2006). When I queried one former defense attorney and current professor about a prosecutor's commitment to finding the truth, the attorney replied:

> [T]he problem is, they normally don't have any interest in only looking [beyond the] charges. The problem is that they often have a hypothesis about what has happened and then they don't question [that hypothesis]. And I often experienced [situations in which] I [would] say: 'Just go and look, I have proof which discharges my client's guilt'. Then the judges and the prosecutors would both suspect that you are sabotaging the procedure. So they are not willing to look at it. (Defense Counsel Interview [20GU], February 6, 2006)

If a defendant hires counsel while a prosecutor is still reviewing the case file, a defense lawyer may also seek to convince the prosecutor handling the case to defer prosecution or to dismiss the case altogether. In larger cases, defense counsel may initiate a conversation regarding the terms of a confession agreement. When office guidelines permit, prosecutors, who are facing a particularly heavy case load, may welcome these overtures – especially given the fact that most German prosecutors are not motivated to 'win' cases.

3.3.8 Prosecutors and judges

The final arbiter of the sufficiency of the evidence is not the defense, but the court. The case files in all but the most minor prosecutions end up on a judge's desk. Initially, the decision to send the case file to the court lies solely with the prosecutor and not with the police. Once the file arrives on a judge's desk, the court is obligated to review the facts in the file and determine whether there is sufficient evidence to open the 'preliminary proceedings' (StPO § 199). The necessary level of suspicion is '*Anfangs-verdacht*', which means that there are sufficient grounds to believe that the suspect has committed a criminal offense (StPO § 203). Although some judges interpret that requirement strictly, one senior prosecutor stated to me that, in his experience, judges had failed to open the preliminary proceedings only an appallingly low 1 percent of the time (Senior Prosecutor Interview [5BC], January 16, 2006). One reason why a judge will refuse to issue an order to open a main proceeding is that the nature of the judge–prosecutor relationship is strikingly different than the equivalent relationship in the US. Because the prosecutor functions not as a party, but rather as part of the administration of justice, a German judge may simply pick up the phone and discuss the case with the prosecutor and tell the prosecutor to gather more evidence (Leading Office Prosecutor [2BN], July 16, 2004). Similarly, a judge may pick up the phone and initiate a plea discussion with the defense without the prosecutor's participation (StPO § 202(a)). The judge may also decide to order further investigation on a case before making a decision to open the main proceeding (StPO § 173(3)).

Another intriguing aspect of German pre-trial practice is that, even before a prosecutor deposits a case file with the court, the prosecutor and the presiding judge may talk about the case. This communication may continue through the trial, as the judge and the prosecutor may engage in a joint decision-making dance as the evidence unfolds. Such communication is not unethical as it is an integral element of a criminal justice process that relies on close cooperation between prosecutors and judges. This institutional cooperation between the prosecutor's office and the judicial branch results in a pre-trial process that, on paper, is fundamentally different from the adversarial pre-trial process. Although American prosecutors must avoid engaging a judge in an *ex-parte* discussion about a pending case, German prosecutors face no similar prohibition, because they function as 'second judges'. However, just because prosecutors and judges may discuss cases pre-trial, does not mean that they are bound to present a united front. According to one prosecutor whom I interviewed, when a judge's suggestions conflict with office policy, prosecutors are not bound to agree with the bench (Prosecutor Interview [13BC],

December 8, 2005). However, lacking an adversarial perspective, German prosecutors may lack the incentive to contradict the court. Thus, rather than serve as a counterweight or an additional set of eyes to view the evidence, prosecutors and judges in Germany enjoy a more symbiotic relationship. Indeed, as one prosecutor explained to me, '[p]ersonally, I believe that I co-manage the proceedings before the court' (Prosecutor Interview [16AG], June 9, 2008). The most effective constraint on a prosecutor's decision-making is not the court, but the internal ethos of the prosecution service itself. To the extent that a prosecutor adheres to internalized group decision-making norms, a desire to conform to those norms may guide their decision-making.

3.3.9　Legal controls

There are two other notable pre-trial practice differences between Germany and the United States. American police are free to use a variety of psychological tools and deceptive practices to secure a confession, including lying to a suspect (*Frazier v. Cupp*). In Germany, statutory provisions and interrogation norms prohibit the police from lying to suspects or from misleading interrogation tactics which may produce a false confession (Ross, 2008: 443). In contrast to American criminal procedure, this prohibition extends even to cases where the police have not arrested the suspect or the suspect is not otherwise in custody. Another striking difference is that the German conception of 'voluntariness' is much stronger than its American counterpart, as Germany's exclusionary rules require that a presiding judge exclude from consideration any statement obtained through a prohibited interrogation technique (Ross, 2008: 447). In fact, even leading questions can lead to suppression of an answer.

A second, clear divergence from American practice is that German prosecutors cannot meet with witnesses to 'prep' them for trial. The need for such preparation is diminished because cross-examination of witnesses considerably more restrained. And since it is the judge or the judging panel that conducts most of the questioning during the main proceeding, prosecutors play only a secondary role in eliciting evidence. Prosecutors are not expected to use leading questions to advance their own theory of the case. Finally, the act of preparing witnesses for trial contradicts the German conception of a prosecutor as a neutral fact-finder. If new or slightly different facts are disclosed during the trial, it is expected that a prosecutor will adjust their closing argument to reflect those changes. Consistent with a German prosecutor's duty to weigh facts for and against an accused, a prosecutor may even recommend that the court acquit the defendant or dismiss some of the charges at the conclusion of the main proceeding.

One significant and pervasive control on discretion in the German system is the continuing role played by legal science. While one may challenge the extent to which day-to-day decision-making conforms to rigid models of scientific thinking, at key points in the process decision-makers must explain how the facts of a case and the legal reasoning support their decision-making. Although the file documentation processes do not guarantee that prosecutors will conduct an objective investigation, they must leave a paper trail that makes their decision-making process transparent to their supervisors. The bill of indictment must detail the evidence and witnesses against the accused (StPO § 200). When judges refuse to open a main proceeding, they must detail whether their decision is based on factual or legal grounds (StPO § 204). Finally, court judgments must detail how the court weighed the evidence presented in court and reconciled it with the law. Critically, the absence of an adversarial structure and the institutional ethos of the prosecution service cut against a prosecutor's potential desire to stretch the facts to fit a particular version of the truth. The legal training that all lawyers receive in law school teaches attorneys to believe that there is one legally correct answer to any legal problem. The desire to twist the facts of a case to 'win' a conviction is largely absent from prosecution offices. Finally, in the system as a whole, the players respect and, in many cases, privilege systematic legal thinking over the simple application of statutory provisions (Weigend, 2006b: 221).

At the same time, workload pressures may challenge a prosecutor's ability to ensure that the case investigation is thorough and comprehensive enough to satisfy the requirements of the law. The simple fact that a prosecutor documents the trajectory of their decision-making in a case file does not guarantee that she has fulfilled her duty of objective investigation. Facing pressures to 'move' files, a prosecutor may look first for ways to dismiss or defer a prosecution rather than to take the initiative to build a case. Although the formal requirements of the law ultimately require the court to reconcile the facts and law of a case, the mindset of many prosecutors who handle low-level crime cases is simply to move folders from the in-box to the out-box. In the mass of low-level criminal cases, a prosecutor performs their job simply by reading the file, checking off forms, and finding grounds to dismiss the case. That function appears to fall far short of the ideal of ensuring that a suspect's level of guilt is correctly identified and adjudicated. The danger exists that prosecutors who have adopted the mindset of low-level crimes practice and its privileging of efficient case-handling practices will not jettison that mindset when they turn their attention to major crimes cases. Indeed, several department supervisors complained to me that too many of their colleagues prefer to sit at their desks rather than take the initiative to speak with the police and witnesses to build a case (Prosecutor [5BC], January 16, 2006).

4.   DISCRETIONARY DECISION-MAKING IN PRE-TRIAL PRACTICE: POINTS OF COMPARISON

4.1   From Suspicion to Judgment

Traditionally, the goal of pre-trial practice in rule-of-law states has been to determine whether there is sufficient evidence to believe that a suspect has violated the law to justify convening a public proceeding. The legal goal at this stage of the process in both systems can be stated simply. In the United States, an investigation travels a course from reasonable suspicion to probable cause. In Germany, prosecutors will investigate a complaint when 'simple' suspicion (*Anfangsverdacht*) exists. Though mere suppositions of guilt are insufficient and some factual proof is required, the legal requirements necessary to open an investigation are ill defined (StPO § 152(2)).

At this stage, there is only the possibility that the investigation will yield sufficient evidence to file a charge. As a point of comparison, the American standard of reasonable suspicion has been defined as something 'more than a hunch', which must be based on 'specific and articulable facts taken together with inferences from those facts' (*Ybarra v. Illinois*). In Germany, at the end of the investigation, a prosecutor will only send a file to the court to convene proceedings if sufficient facts exist to warrant a finding of sufficient or aggravated suspicion (StPO § 170). This standard is satisfied when the investigation confirms the original suspicion of the accused.

It is evident, however, that the trajectory of the pre-trial process can no longer be defined solely in terms of the quantum of evidence collected and whether that evidence satisfies the legal standards necessary to proceed to trial. Traditionally, the pre-trial stage functioned primarily as a procedural safeguard. It allowed judicial officers or grand juries to assess the evidence to ensure that the prospective burden that would be imposed by the process was justifiable. Thus, before American prosecutors could proceed to try serious charges in the courtroom and before German judges 'opened' the main proceeding, a neutral decision-maker would ensure that the charges were grounded in sufficient evidence.

In both systems today, in many cases, the pre-trial process has become a case's end-stage. That change has profound implications for the construction of truth. In America's adversarial system, the parties play a dominant role, but the full battle between the parties settled by a jury is a rare occurrence. While there is no guarantee that a trial will lead a jury to the 'truth', resolving a case prior to trial assuredly results in a thinner presentation of evidence. In Germany, the judge, through her role in the main proceeding, functions as a final objective arbiter of the evidence. Although the new 'confession agreements' have not completely eliminated the presentation of evidence, they have certainly shortened the presentation of evidence in the courtroom. In complex fraud and tax cases in particular, the prospect of a confession agreement may drastically short-circuit a necessarily complex investigation. Thus, in both systems, when cases are resolved at an earlier procedural stage, the truth-finding process is less robust.

Indeed, this chapter questions the extent to which both systems remain committed to the normative goal of finding the 'truth'. Given that pre-trial practice in both countries now often ends in a consensual 'solution', a critical question is what kind of 'truth' do these short-circuited truth-finding processes produce?

Although pre-trial agreements cut short the truth-finding process, they do not completely sever the process from its truth-seeking orientation. One might posit that the goal in shortened proceedings is to find a consensual solution that has 'some' tie to the truth. When we explore the nature of that 'tie', it is evident that the level of truth required, as well as the role that truth plays in both systems' shortened processes, differs.

In the US, the defendant produces the 'truth' through her factual allocution at the time of the plea. Depending on a particular state's penal code, defendants must typically admit to a set of facts that satisfy the elements of the crime(s) to which the defendant pleads guilty. Alternatively, defense counsel may stipulate a set of facts which satisfies the same objective. However, the purpose of this factual allocution is not to determine the 'truth', but to ensure that the defendant understands the consequences of the change of plea process (*State v. Smullen*). The primary purpose of the 'factual basis' requirement is to ensure that the plea is 'voluntarily and understandingly tendered'.[7] In determining whether the allocation is sufficient, a court will not require a level of factual detail sufficient to meet the 'guilt beyond a reasonable doubt' standard. For example, in *People v. Calderon*, the California Court of Appeals held that the admission or stipulation need only establish a prima facie factual basis for the charges. Thus, US courts require a low threshold of proof to support the plea and the primary purpose of that threshold is to ensure that the defendant is aware that the court will find her guilty and impose punishment.

Despite the fact that similar efficiency-driven concerns motivate German courts to facilitate confession agreements, the level of evidence required to support such agreements is higher than in the US. A defendant's confession, by itself, is insufficient to support a finding of guilt, as the court must take evidence during the main trial (Mosbacher, 2014: 8). The evidence discovered during the investigation process must substantiate the level of guilt detailed in the confession agreement (BGHSt [Federal Court of Justice] Mar. 03, 2005). Because Germany's inquisitorial judges function as fact-finders and not mere gate-keepers, an agreement between the prosecutor and the defense does not obviate the court's judicial fact-finding role (Mosbacher, 2014: 8). While a confession agreement will reduce the length of the main proceeding, it does not eliminate the court's fact-finding and adjudicatory functions. One must acknowledge, however, that when German judges, like their American counterparts, face case-load pressures, judges may be more motivated to dispose of cases than to ensure accuracy.

One way to compare these differences between plea bargaining and confession bargaining is by using the concept of an 'equilibrium point'. The equilibrium point in each system is the point in the fact-finding process where the state has gathered enough facts to dispose of the case short of a full-fledged trial. In Figure 6.1, the equilibrium point in the German system is represented by the number '18'. Although the value of that number is artificial, it is further to the right on the x-axis than the US equilibrium point reached during the change of plea proceeding (number value 10). The reason for this placement is the fact that, although German law permits confession agreements, those agreements do not eliminate the court's need to hear evidence. Rather, they merely shorten the presentation of evidence. In the US system, the standard of evidence required during the factual allocution may be low enough to be satisfied by a rote recitation of the facts necessary to meet a *prima facie* standard of proof. Although the quantum of evidence required in the German system is tied to the Court's fact-finding role, the primary purpose of the US standard is to ensure that the defendant is aware of the consequences of the change of plea proceeding. The differences that exist between the roles of the institutional actors in both systems also influence the location of the equilibrium points. In the US system, the agreement is negotiated between the parties and is sanctioned by the court. In Germany, the court itself may facilitate the discussion and agreement. In addition, the agreement in the US system settles the dispute over the facts between the parties. In the German system, although the defendant's 'confession' may facilitate an abbreviated main proceeding, the defendant's confession must be corroborated by other evidence and the court must be convinced that the evidence substantiates the defendant's level of guilt.

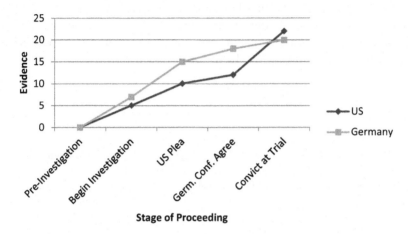

Figure 6.1 The impact of pre-trial bargaining on evidence collection

4.2 Structural Considerations

When cases do proceed beyond the pre-trial process, the shape of the pre-trial process may continue to influence a case's final outcome. While the trajectory and resolution of each criminal case reflects its own unique facts, this chapter has identified four structural factors that influence the case investigation and disposition processes at the pre-trial stage in both systems. The interaction of those factors sets the stage on a structural level for how cases proceed through the pre-trial process. By examining how these factors interact, one can begin to understand the differences between both systems' pre-trial processes. Given that practice on the ground in both systems no longer fulfills each system's normative aspirations, these macro-level factors are a useful starting point for comparison and include:

1. The defined role of the prosecutor and judge;
2. Institutional norms and constraints;
3. Legal checks on prosecutorial power;
4. Defense role at pre-trial stage.

In addition, three factors that have a more case-specific impact on outcomes include: resource constraints, the mindset of the particular prosecutor handling the case, and the evidentiary strength of the case. It is possible to fine tune the analysis even further by evaluating the nature of police–prosecutor relationships, courtroom dynamics, and so forth. At some point however, adding further variables to a comparative model undercuts the model's strength. One might compare the macro-level variables in table form – see Table 6.1.

Table 6.1   Structural comparison

	Germany	United States
Defined role of prosecutor and judge	Informal limits on power	Few formal or informal limits
Institutional norms	Efficiency/objectivity	Adversarial in major cases Dispute resolution model in low-level cases
Legal checks on prosecutorial discretion	Weakening	Few
Defense role at pre-trial stage	Minimal. May petition to supplement investigation	Weak in indigent cases

How do these structural variables help us to understand the differences between both systems in the pre-trial stage? To begin with, these factors capture not only the degree of discretion that prosecutors possess but also the institutional mindset of the prosecution service. The potential sources of constraint in both systems stem from the nature of the judicial power in the pre-trial stage and binding legal limits on prosecutorial decision-making, as well as the constraining impact of defense counsel. When we consider these factors together, a more interesting picture emerges.

In the case of Germany, the nominal source of constraint is the role played by the judiciary. Behind the scenes, judges may steer prosecutors acting outside the norm through phone calls and informal conversations. By law, the prosecutor and judge function as members of the same team to find the truth. While the law permits a judge to refuse to open a case filed by a prosecutor and to conduct his own investigation, open disagreement between prosecutors and judges is rare. Because the law presumes that a prosecutor will not act as a party, but will instead conduct an objective investigation, judges lack overt control to deter misconduct by excluding evidence. Although German judges may exclude evidence, they do so rarely. Because the rule is designed to remedy severe abuses, rather than to shape incentives, the seriousness of the violation must outweigh the significance of the evidence (Weigend, 2007: 251–252).

The more robust source of control stems from the fact that prosecutors are members of a hierarchically organized bureaucratic organization that privileges conformity. German prosecutors disavow the role of gun-slingers. Critically, they do not view convictions as notches in their belt. In an era of tight resources, however, I have detailed how the organization's use of performance metrics may be steering prosecutors away from their role as 'guardians of the law' who dispassionately seek to uncover the facts for and against a defendant. On the other hand, the hierarchical structure of the prosecution office, combined with comprehensive file documentation procedures, permit managers to review a prosecutor's decision-making.

While the combination of institutional and judicial controls paints a portrait of limited decision-making discretion in Germany, the German legislature has granted prosecutors more decision-making room during the past three decades. Although the principle of mandatory prosecution dictates that prosecutors file charges in all cases where sufficient suspicion of criminal behavior exists, in many cases, caseload pressures force prosecutors to turn to the plethora of disposition options to resolve cases. The traditional vision of the prosecutor as the chief of the investigation process who marshals the resources of the state to find the truth today applies to a narrower range of cases. The actual practice of the law has deviated from the system's core prescription of finding the truth through a full-fledged public trial (Weigend, 2006a: 214). The trial may remain, however it is no longer a process in which all parties attempt to fully flesh out the facts so that the decision-maker may evaluate them through the lens of the applicable law.

No modern inquisitorial system is structured to produce 'truth' at any price (Weigend, 2003: 167). In Germany, the search for truth is tempered by procedural rules that guarantee a defendant's right to remain silent, protect the sanctity of privileged relationships, and encourage courts to resolve cases in a manner that is 'speedy, efficient, and within the limits of reasonable expenditure' (Weigend, 2003: 163). Although it once was true that prosecutorial decisions were guided by their fidelity to the law, today pragmatic concerns about costs and limited resources often short-circuit the full search for truth.

With the explosion of plea bargaining in the United States, a key constraint on prosecutorial decision-making, namely the jury's verdict, has been lost. The loss of that constraint may have consequences for the objectivity of the investigation itself. If we assume that law enforcement officers in both countries lose their objectivity during the case investigation process, then it is important that prosecutors in both systems review that evidence with a neutral eye. As a consequence of the rise of plea bargaining in the US, prosecutors have acquired more leverage during the pre-trial process. Given that it is unlikely that a prosecutor's case will be tested in front of a jury, an American prosecutor's 'party' mentality may compound, rather than counter, the lack of objectivity by the police. In contrast, a German prosecutor is more likely to search for ways to dismiss a case.

The weakening of due process constraints in an age of heightened security, coupled with judges' historical deference towards prosecutorial decisions in the pre-trial stage, offer prosecutors an open playing field. Although the institutional structure and operating procedures of German prosecution offices is remarkably similar across Germany, those institutional similarities do not apply to the United States. As a result, one must be careful in making grand claims that prosecutors possess a conviction mentality that is unrestrained by their superiors. What can be said is that, in many prosecution offices, prosecutors are rewarded, not for pursuing justice, but for 'earning' high conviction rates and stiff sentences. This predilection not only stems from the model of trials as contests between parties, but is also fueled by the fact that district attorneys on the state level are elected representatives. While district attorneys' re-election campaigns do not often capture spirited public interest, a district attorney's failure to earn convictions in high-profile cases may end their public career.

The defense role during the pre-trial stage in both systems often varies with the defendant's financial status. In the United States, indigent defendants are oftentimes at the mercy of police investigation practices and a prosecutor's adversarial mindset. Defendants who lack counsel during the pre-trial investigation process may waive their constitutional right to remain silent and safeguard their privacy without truly understanding the consequences of those waivers. As a result, their appointed counsel may enter the scene only after the defendant has confessed and is facing a lengthy list of charges designed to drive him to a plea.

In the German system, prosecutors who are seeking ways to dismiss or defer prosecution often work with defense counsel to resolve cases as soon as possible. In cases where counsel has not yet been appointed, a prosecutor's desire to close files quickly may work in the defendant's favor. In any case, because the consequences of violating German law are less severe than in the United States, the stakes of the game are lower in German courts.

Turning away from the level of structural factors to case-level factors, in both systems, differences in the resource levels that prosecutors face when a particular case is ripe for adjudication may affect case dispositions. In addition, the particular personality of the prosecutor handling a case shapes the pre-trial process. Even in Germany, more punitive minded prosecutors often find themselves working on certain types of cases, most notably drug cases, where a hard-nosed attitude towards crime weighs against high dismissal rates and lenient sentencing recommendations. In the United States, prosecutors who see trial outcomes as victories may be more likely to pursue a case to trial rather than engage in pre-trial bargaining.

5. CONCLUSION

The trajectory of pre-trial practice in both systems is contingent on both structural and case-specific variables. As a result, it is apparent that the simplistic comparisons of the criminal justice systems that depend on normative truisms hold less weight than ever before. In particular, scholarship that compared both systems and praised the German system for its success in containing prosecutorial discretion oversimplifies case investigation practices (Langbein, 1979). In addition, the picture of the American system painted by scholars who have categorized the system as dominated by prosecutorial discretion, bargained justice, and widely varying sentencing outcomes may also be incomplete. Although it is true that prosecutors often possess leverage over the defendant when the defendant faces a long mandatory minimum sentence, it is also true that prosecutors lack the time to take every case to trial. When confronted with tight deadlines and high case volumes, a prosecutor's willingness to accept a plea may increase. Moreover, although prosecutors often face off against over-burdened public defenders, a prosecutor may find that a well-financed defense may undercut a prosecutor's typical negotiating advantage in the plea bargaining process.

The reality is that prosecutorial practice in both systems has diverged from each system's normative design. Pre-trial practice is not necessarily a truth-discovery exercise in either state. Both structural reforms and decision-making constraints on the local level must be implemented to ensure that, if the law cannot structure the process to find the 'truth', criminal justice systems should, at minimum, avoid injustice.

NOTES

1. Joy states: 'In an early study of the first sixty-two DNA exonerations, twenty-six (41.9%) cases involved prosecutorial misconduct. Of the DNA exonerations involving prosecutorial misconduct, the suppression of exculpatory evidence – *Brady/Giglio* violations – occurred forty-three percent of the time' (citing Dwyer et al., 2000: 263–265).
2. For a description of these models, please see Packer (1968) (conceptualizing 'two models of the criminal process').
3. During 2006–2014, I conducted over one hundred interviews of German prosecutors. To protect the anonymity of my interviewees, I assigned each prosecutor a unique code.
4. However, empirical data from US federal courts shows that rising caseloads did not lead to an increased declination rate in the period between 1994 and 2000. Bureau of Justice Statistics, U.S. Dep't of Justice, Federal Criminal Case Processing 2000, at 28–29 (2001), Appendix Tables A.3, A.6 (showing that, although the number of suspects in criminal matters increased from 94,980 in 1994 to 117,450 in 2000, the number of declined prosecutions over that time period decreased from 34,424 in 1994 to 30,444 in 2000).
5. For example, in *United States v. Williams*, 504 U.S. 36 (1992), the Supreme Court held that a trial court need not dismiss an indictment in cases where the prosecutor failed to present exculpatory evidence to the grand jury. In addition, to establish a due process violation, the defendant must show that: (1) the defense had requested the material, (2) the prosecutor's office suppressed the material, and (3) the evidence was both favorable to the defendant and material to the case.
6. The documentation would include: the date that a prosecutor received the file, the prosecutor's initial instructions to her secretary, orders to the police instructing them to interview certain witnesses, a request for information from a government agency such as the driver's driving history in the case of a traffic-related offense. (Prosecutor Interview [3TW], November 8, 2005).
7. Comment to the Pennsylvania Code, Rule 590 (A)(2).

BIBLIOGRAPHY

Alexander, Michelle. 2012. *The New Jim Crow: Mass Incarceration in the Age of Colorblindness* (2nd edn). New York: The New Press.

American Bar Association. 2004. *Gideon's Broken Promise: America's Continuing Quest for Equal Justice: A Report on the American Bar Association's Hearings on the Right to Counsel*. Chicago, IL: American Bar Association.

Ask, Karl, Anna Rebelius, and Pär Anders Granhag. 2008. 'The "Elasticity" of Criminal Evidence: A Moderator of Investigator Bias', 22 *Applied Cognitive Psychology* 1245–1259.

Barkow, Rachel E. 2006. 'Separation of Powers and the Criminal Law', 58 *Stanford Law Review* 989–1054.

Boyne, Shawn Marie. 2014. *The German Prosecutor Service: Guardians of the Law?* New York: Springer Publishing.

Bradley, Craig M. 1983. 'The Exclusionary Rule in Germany', 96 *Harvard Law Review* 1032–1066.

Brady v. Maryland, 373 U.S. 83 (1963).

Brewer v. Williams, 430 U.S. 387 (1977).

Brown, Darryl K. 2005. 'The Decline of Defense Counsel and the Rise of Accuracy in Criminal Adjudication', 93 *California Law Review* 1585–1645.

Bundesgerichtshof in Strafsachen [BGHSt] [Federal Court of Justice] Aug. 28, 1997.

Bundesgerichtshof in Strafsachen [BGHSt] [Federal Court of Justice] Mar. 03, 2005.

Bundesverfassungsgericht [BVerfG] [Federal Constitutional Court] Mar. 19, 2013, 2 BvR 2628/10.

Cappelletti, Mauro. 1989. *The Judicial Process in Comparative Perspective.* Oxford: Oxford University Press.

Damaška, Mirjan. 1981. 'The Reality of Prosecutorial Discretion: Comments on a German Monograph', 29 *American Journal of Comparative Law* 119–138.

Damaška, Mirjan. 1986. *The Faces of Justice and State Authority: A Comparative Approach to Legal Process.* New Haven: Yale University Press.

'Die Beschlüsse', 58 Deutscher Juristentag, 1990. *Neue Juristische Wochenschrift* 2991–2992.

Dwyer, Jim, Peter Neufeld, and Barry Scheck. 2000. *Actual Innocence: Five Days to Execution and Other Dispatches from the Wrongly Convicted.* New York: Doubleday.

Feeney, Floyd. 1998. 'German and American Prosecutions: An Approach to Statistical Comparison', Washington, D.C.: U.S. Department of Justice.

Feeney, Floyd and Joachim Hermann. 2005. *One Case – Two Systems: A Comparative View of American and German Criminal Justice Systems.* New York: Brill Academic Publishing.

Frazier v. Cupp, 394 U.S. 731 (1969).

Frederick, Bruce and Don Stemen. 2012. *The Anatomy of Discretion: An Analysis of Prosecutorial Decision Making.* New York: Vera Institute of Justice.

Goldstein, Abraham S. 1974. 'Reflections on Two Models: Inquisitorial Themes in American Criminal Procedure', 26 *Stanford Law Review* 1009–1025.

Goldstein, Abraham S. and Martin Marcus. 1977. 'The Myth of Judicial Supervision in Three "Inquisitorial" Systems: France, Italy, and Germany', 87 *Yale Law Journal* 240–283.

Heinz, Wolfgang. 2014. Entwicklung und Stand der freiheitsentziehenden Maßregeln der Besserung und Sicherung. Werkstattbericht auf der Grundlage der Strafrechtspflegestatistiken (Berichtsstand 2012/2013). Konstanz, Germany: Universität Konstanz.

Hermann, Joachim. 1992. 'Bargaining Justice: A Bargain for German Criminal Justice?', 53 *University of Pittsburgh Law Review* 755–776.

Jescheck, Hans-Heinrich. 1970. 'The Discretionary Powers of the Prosecuting Attorney in West Germany', 18 *American Journal of Criminal Law* 508–517.

Joy, Peter A. 2006. 'The Relationship between Prosecutorial Misconduct and Wrongful Convictions: Shaping Remedies for a Broken System', 84 *Wisconsin Law Review* 399–427.

Joy, Peter A. 2013. 'The Criminal Discovery Problem: Is Legislation a Solution?', 52 *Washburn Law Journal* 37–57.

Kassin, Saul M., Steven A. Drizin, Thomas Grisso, Gisli H. Gudjonsson, Richard A. Leo, and Allison Redlich. 2009. 'Police-Induced Confessions: Risk Factors and Recommendations', 34(1) *Law and Human Behavior* 1–37.

Keenan, David, Deborah Jane Cooper, David Lebowitz, and Tamar Lerer. 2011. 'The Myth of Prosecutorial Accountability After Connick v. Thompson: Why Existing Professional Responsibility Measures Cannot Protect Against Prosecutorial Misconduct', 121 *Yale Law Journal Online* 203–265.

Krug, Peter. 2002. 'Prosecutorial Discretion and its Limits', 50 *American Journal of Comparative Law Supplement: American Law in a Time of Global Interdependence.* U.S. National Reports to the 16th International Congress of Comparative Law 643–664.

Langbein, John. 1979. 'Land Without Plea Bargaining: How the Germans Do It', 78(2) *Michigan Law Review* 204–225.

Langer, Máximo. 2014. 'The Long Shadow of the Inquisitorial and Adversarial Categories', in Markus D. Dubber and Tatjana Höernle, eds., *The Oxford Handbook of Criminal Law*, Oxford: Oxford University Press, 887–912.

Liu, Sida and Terrence C. Halliday. 2009. 'Recursivity and Legal Change: Lawyers and Reforms of Chinese Criminal Procedure Law', 34 *Law & Social Inquiry* 911–950.

Massie, Alana. 2015. 'Press Release: Facts on Post-Conviction DNA Exonerations', New York: The Innocence Project.

Meares, Tracey L. 1995. 'Rewards for Good Behavior: Influencing Prosecutorial Discretion and Conduct with Financial Incentives', 64 *Fordham Law Review* 851–919.

Merryman, John Henry and Rogel Perez-Perdomo. 2007. *The Civil Law Tradition*. Palo Alto: Stanford University Press.

Missouri v. Seibert, 542 U.S. 600 (2004).

Mosbacher, Andreas. 2014. 'The Decision of the Federal Constitutional Court of 19 March 2013 on Plea Agreements', 15 *German Law Journal* 5–14.

Mosteller, Robert P. 2011. 'Failures of the American Adversarial System to Protect the Innocent and Conceptual Advantages in the Inquisitorial Design for Investigative Fairness', 36 *North Carolina Journal of International Law and Commercial Regulation* 319–363.

Nagel, Illene H. and Stephen J. Schulhofer. 1992. 'A Tale of Three Cities: An Empirical Study of Charging and Bargaining Practices Under the Federal Sentencing Guidelines', 66 *Southern California Law Review* 501–561.

New York Lawyer's Code of Professional Responsibility. 2013. Ethical Consideration 7–13.

Oberwittler, Dietrich and Sven Höfer. 2005. 'Crime and Justice in Germany: An Analysis of Recent Trends and Research', 2 *European Journal of Criminology* 465–508.

Opel, Richard. 2011. 'Sentencing Shift Gives New Leverage to Prosecutors', *New York Times* 25 September, A1.

Örücü, A. Esin. 2006. 'Methodology in Comparative Law', in Jan M. Smits, ed., *Elgar Encyclopedia of Comparative Law*. Cheltenham, UK: Edward Elgar Publishing.

Packer, Herbert L. 1968. *The Limits of the Criminal Sanction*. Palo Alto: Stanford University Press.

People v. Calderon, 232 Cal. App. 3d 930 (1991).

Rapping, Jonathan A. 2012. 'Who's Guarding the Henhouse? How the American Prosecutor Came to Devour Those He is Sworn to Protect', 51 *Washburn Law Journal* 513–569.

Roberts, Jenny. 2013. 'Crashing the Misdemeanor System', 70 *Washington & Lee Law Review* 1089–1131.

Ross, Jacqueline. 2008. 'Do Rules of Evidence Apply (Only) in the Courtroom: Deceptive Interrogation Practices in the United States and Germany', 28 *Oxford Journal of Legal Studies*, 443–473.

Schemmel, Alexander, Christian Corell, and Natalie Richter. 2014. 'Plea Bargaining in Criminal Proceedings: Changes to Criminal Defense Counsel Practice as a Result of the German Constitutional Court Verdict of 19 March 2013?', 15 *German Law Journal* 43–64.

Secunda, Paul M. 1997. 'Note: Cleaning Up the Chicken Coop of Sentencing Uniformity: Guiding the Discretion of Federal Prosecutors Through the Use of the Model Rules of Professional Conduct', 34 *American Criminal Law Review* 1267–1292.

Siegismund, Eberhard. 2001. 'The Public Prosecution Office in Germany: Legal Status, Functions, and Organization', United Nations Asia and Far East Institute for the Prevention of Crime and the Treatment of Offenders (UNAFEI) 120th International Senior Seminar Visiting Experts' Papers 58–76.

Slobogin, Christopher. 2013. 'The Exclusionary Rule: Is It on Its Way Out? Should It Be?' 10(2) *Ohio State Journal of Criminal Law* 341–355.

State v. Smullen, 118 N.J. 408, 571 A.2d 1305 (1990).

Stuckenberg, Carl-Friedrich. 2013. 'Commentary', in Volker Erb et al., eds., *Löwe-Rosenberg: Die Strafprozessordnung und Das Gerichtsverfassungsgesetz*, vol. 6(2). Berlin: DeGruyter. §§ 256ff.

Twinning, William. 1990. *Rethinking Evidence: Exploratory Essays*. Chicago, IL: Northwestern University Press.

United States v. Williams, 504 U.S. 36 (1992).

Uphoff, Rodney. 2010. 'Broke and Broken: Can We Fix Our State Indigent Defense System?', 75 *Missouri Law Review* 667–681.

U.S. Department of Justice, Bureau of Justice Statistics. Criminal Case Processing 2000.

Van Koppen, Peter J. and Steven D. Penrod. 2003. 'Adversarial or Inquisitorial: Comparing Systems', in Peter J. van Koppen and Steven D. Penrod, eds., *Adversarial Versus Inquisitorial Justice: Psychological Perspectives on Criminal Justice Systems*. New York: Kluwer Academic/Plenum Publishers.

Weigend, Thomas. 1990. 'Abgesprochene Gerechtigkeit: Effizienz durch Kooperation im Strafverfahren?' 45(2) *Juristenzeitung* 774–782.

Weigend, Thomas. 2003. 'Is the Criminal Process about Truth? A German Perspective', 26 *Harvard Journal of Law & Public Policy* 157–174.

Weigend, Thomas. 2006a. 'Why Have a Trial When You Can Have a Bargain', in R.A. Duff, Lindsay Farmer, Sandra Marshall and Victor Tadros, eds., *The Trial on Trial: Judgment and Calling to Account* (Vol. 2). Portland, OR: Hart Publishing, 207–222.

Weigend, Thomas. 2006b. 'Criminal Law and Criminal Procedure', in Jan Smits, ed., *Elgar Encyclopedia of Comparative Law*. Cheltenham, UK: Edward Elgar Publishing.

Weigend, Thomas. 2007. 'Germany', in Craig Bradley, ed., *Criminal Procedure: A World Wide Study*. Durham, NC: Carolina Academic Press.

Weisbord, Noah and Matthew A. Smith. 2001. 'The Reason Behind the Rules: From Description to Normativity in International Criminal Procedure', XXXVI *North Carolina Journal of International and Commercial Regulation* 255–274.

Ybarra v. Illinois, 444 U.S. 85 (1979).

7. From the domestic to the European: an empirical approach to comparative custodial legal advice

Jacqueline S. Hodgson

1. INTRODUCTION

Comparative criminal justice has much to teach us, not only in our relative understanding of the criminal procedures of national juris-dictions, but also in the critical analysis of wider European norms of the European Convention on Human Rights (ECHR) and most recently, the European Union (EU). Drawing on the findings of an empirical and comparative study of the suspect's right to legal counsel, together with earlier empirical research, this chapter analyses the scope and effect-iveness of the standards set by the European Court of Human Rights (ECtHR) in its interpretation of the ECHR and the recent EU provisions setting out procedural safeguards for suspects detained and interrogated in EU countries.

The chapter begins by setting out the recent changes in the European legal landscape relating to suspects' access to legal counsel whilst detained for questioning in police custody. Starting with the landmark ECtHR case *Salduz v Turkey* (36391/02 [2008] ECHR 1542), it identifies the more robust protection provided to suspects through Article 6 of the ECHR in relation to the right to legal counsel, but also the limitations of the Convention approach in terms of practical application and enforce-ment. It then examines recent EU legislative measures for the procedural protection of suspects. In contrast to the more serendipitous case-by-case nature of the ECtHR jurisprudence, the EU provisions have been produced after several years of discussion and negotiation, including detailed studies on the likely impact of the new measures in Member States. They include greater levels of detail on how legal assistance should be provided, and all Member States are required to transpose the protections into national law.

However, legislating for the criminal processes of 28 different juris-dictions is not without its problems. The different procedural traditions in place pose a real challenge to the idea of a single piece of legislation fitting into, and working effectively within, all European jurisdictions. Using the findings from a recent empirical study (Blackstock et al., 2014), funded by the European Commission and carried out with colleagues in the UK and the Netherlands, this chapter goes on to examine comparatively the suspect's right to legal counsel as understood through the practices of police detention and interrogation of suspects in four European countries.[1] By placing researchers alongside police and lawyers as they go about their daily work, we were able to understand the functioning of custodial legal advice in practice and to identify both good practices and the kinds of factors that inhibited effective legal counsel. As well as having different provisions in place for the detention and questioning of suspects, the four jurisdictions were at different stages in the protections they offered suspects, allowing us to compare the reception of defence rights across time as well as procedures. When applied to the jurisprudence of the ECtHR and the recent EU provisions, the empirical data highlights some of the limitations of these pan-European protections and suggests important ways in which they might be made more effective.

2. CUSTODIAL LEGAL ADVICE AND THE EUROPEAN CONVENTION ON HUMAN RIGHTS

The right to counsel for those accused of criminal offenses is enshrined within Article 6 of the ECHR, which guarantees the right to a fair trial to accused persons.[2] The Convention applies to all 47 member countries of the Council of Europe and so covers a range of criminal legal procedural traditions. The right to counsel is necessarily set out in very broad terms in the Convention, leaving the mode of implementation to individual states. This is known as the margin of appreciation doctrine and allows for a range of different practices and arrangements in different jurisdictions, provided that overall, the accused's Convention rights have been respected.[3] In this way the Convention is not a 'one size fits all' model.

Ensuring that Convention rights are implemented, and implemented effectively, is policed to a large extent by the ECtHR in Strasbourg. Citizens of a signatory state who believe that a Convention right has been breached may bring their case before the ECtHR. The Court's approach is a practical one. In determining whether the applicant's rights under the Convention have been breached, the Court has made clear that the ECHR is designed to guarantee not rights that are 'theoretical and illusory' but rights that are 'practical and effective' (*Artico v* Italy, No. 6694/74, para

33). The existence of rights on paper, but which are routinely denied or are unenforceable, will not satisfy the Court.

However, there are also limitations in the Court's approach. Whilst the margin of appreciation doctrine is designed to enable Convention rights to be applied in appropriate and effective ways across a wide variety of criminal procedures, it can also have the effect of undermining Convention safeguards and creating broad differences between the protections provided in different countries. This is further compounded by the holistic approach taken by the ECtHR in evaluating Convention breaches. When determining whether an applicant has received a fair trial under Article 6 ECHR, a breach of the Convention early on in the procedure will not necessarily amount to a breach of Article 6, if the application of subsequent safeguards has resulted in a fair trial overall. This is because the right to a fair trial consists of a bundle of rights, but these constituent rights are not freestanding; the breach of one may in effect be remedied by subsequent procedures and guarantees and so will not necessarily result in a finding that the applicant has been denied their right to a fair trial overall.

Although expressed as the right to a fair trial, the scope of Article 6 ECHR covers the investigation phase as well as court proceedings; the guarantees, including the right to legal counsel, therefore apply to pre-trial procedure as well as to the trial itself. The ECtHR has reasoned that the fairness of the trial is likely to be prejudiced by a pre-trial failure to comply with the provisions of Article 6 (for example, *Imbrioscia v Switzerland* 13972/88 [1993] ECHR 56, para 36). The right to counsel in particular, or in the language of European instruments, the right to legal assistance, is important not only in the preparation of the accused's case, but also in the effective assertion and enforcement of her other legal rights. This is especially true for suspects held in police custody for interrogation, who may not know or understand the nature of the charges in connection with which they are being held, how long they can be detained, the consequences of consenting to certain investigative measures or of failing to co-operate with the police. In England and Wales, for example, if a suspect is silent under police questioning, adverse evidential inferences may be drawn from this at trial (Section 34, Criminal Justice and Public Order Act 1994). The ECtHR has recognised the value of the lawyer at this early stage and has held that the right to legal assistance arises immediately upon arrest (*John Murray v United Kingdom* 18731/91 [1996] ECHR 3), and where the suspect's decisions during police interrogation may be decisive in future proceedings, she must be allowed to consult with a lawyer prior to police interrogation.[4]

3. THE DECISION IN *SALDUZ V TURKEY*

The landmark case of *Salduz v Turkey* went further than earlier case law and Article 6 was held to guarantee the suspect the right to have a lawyer present during her police interrogation as well as beforehand; before this, the Court had stopped short of saying that Article 6 required that the suspect must be permitted to have her lawyer present during questioning (*Brennan v United Kingdom* 39846/98 [2001] ECHR), even though this right had been recognised elsewhere as a fundamental safeguard against the ill treatment of detainees.[5] *Salduz* was an important case, guaranteeing in the strongest terms the suspect's right to custodial legal advice before and during police interrogation.

> ... the Court finds that in order for the right to a fair trial to remain sufficiently 'practical and effective' ... Article 6 § 1 requires that, as a rule, access to a lawyer should be provided as from the first interrogation of a suspect by the police ... The rights of the defence will in principle be irretrievably prejudiced when incriminating statements made during police interrogation without access to a lawyer are used for a conviction.

Some countries, such as the Netherlands, denied that this required lawyers to be present during interrogation, but subsequent cases have made it quite clear that compliance with Article 6 requires the suspect to be permitted to have her lawyer physically present during the police interrogation (see *Mader v Croatia* 56185/07 [2011] ECHR; *Sebalj v Croatia* 4429/09 [2011] ECHR).

The *Salduz* decision is also significant in making it clear that depriving suspects of access to custodial legal advice is not something that can be remedied by later measures: 'Neither the assistance provided subsequently by a lawyer nor the adversarial nature of the ensuing proceedings could cure the defects which had occurred during police custody' (para 58). If no lawyer is permitted, the rights of the defence will be 'irretrievably prejudiced' (para 55). *Salduz* places particular emphasis on the danger of admissions made in the absence of a lawyer, but it is not limited to the exclusion of confession evidence. Article 6 was breached in the same way in subsequent cases where there were no admissions and where the accused had remained silent (*Dayanan v Turkey* 7377/03 [2009] ECHR).

The decisions of the ECtHR apply to 47 countries, and so the level of prescriptive detail that can be set out in its judgments is necessarily limited. On the other hand, the Court does not wish to set standards that are too broad and open to interpretation. When considering the appropriate role of the criminal defence lawyer, this can be controversial. Historically, systems rooted in a more inquisitorial model have assigned a relatively restricted role to the defence, especially during the police investigation stage, which was considered to be preliminary and of little evidentiary significance (Hodgson, 2005). In France, for example, the defence lawyer has been able to participate in the investigation carried out by the *juge d'instruction*, including having access to the case file and being present during the questioning of the accused, since 1897. But during the police phase of the investigation, when the suspect is very much more vulnerable, lawyers have only been present since 1993 – and then for 30 minutes, 20 hours into detention. In 2000 suspects were permitted a half-hour consultation from the start of detention, and from 2011, as a result of *Salduz*, lawyers have been allowed into the interrogation room.

However, the role that lawyers can play in practice remains restricted. Lawyers are now present in the police interrogation in France, but they are not permitted to interrupt, to challenge police questions, or to ask questions or seek clarifications until the end of the interrogation. They do not have access to the case file and are provided with minimal information concerning the charges against the suspect, but no material concerning any substantive evidence. This contrasts with the position during the *instruction* phase, when those accused of the most serious offences are investigated under the authority of the *juge d'instruction*, during which time the accused and her lawyer have access to the case file. When cases are likely to go before the *juge d'instruction*, the lawyer may well advise silence, knowing that more information will be available within the next day or so and there is nothing to be gained by speaking at this early point. In other cases – which constitute the overwhelming majority – silence is rarely advised. Lawyers are still growing accustomed to their role and coupled with the poor light in which failure to co-operate is viewed in court (this is a process in which even simple witnesses may be detained in custody for up to four hours to provide information to the investigation), this makes silence an unlikely strategy.

In the Netherlands, lawyers were not present during the police detention and interrogation of suspects at the time of *Salduz*, and post-*Salduz* they are permitted only a 30-minute consultation with the suspect, prior to interrogation. They also receive only a scant outline of the charges against the suspect. This is typical of the response to *Salduz* by many countries: to allow the suspect the minimum opportunity for legal assistance that (they believe) the law allows, and, where lawyers are permitted to be present during the police interrogation, to restrict their role. Here too, silence is not a strategy with which lawyers are comfortable. They are relative newcomers to the investigation phase and have yet to develop the more adversarial reflexes of a profession that is confident in challenging the investigation and in asserting the rights of the accused.

This contrasts with the case law of the ECtHR, which sets out a more proactive role than that allowed for in many jurisdictions. Whilst assistance during interrogation is important, there are many other ways in which the lawyer can assist the suspect and ensure the lawfulness of her detention. Finding a clear breach of Article 6 ECHR, the Court in *Dayanan v Turkey* (7377/03 [2009] ECHR) stated:

> ... an accused person is entitled, as soon as he or she is taken into custody, to be assisted by a lawyer, and not only while being questioned ... Indeed the fairness of the proceedings requires that an accused be able to obtain the whole range of services specifically associated with legal counsel. In this regard, counsel has to be able to secure without restriction the fundamental aspects of that person's defence: discussion of the case, organisation of the defence, collection of evidence favourable to the accused, preparation for questioning, support of an accused in distress and checking of their conditions of detention. (Para 32)

As we will see in the subsequent discussion of custodial legal advice in practice, there are a number of obstacles preventing lawyers from providing this level of assistance.

4. CUSTODIAL LEGAL ADVICE AND EUROPEAN UNION LEGISLATION

In addition to the important developments that have taken place through the case law of the ECtHR, the procedural rights of suspects have also been the focus of attention in the EU. Over the last decade, a range of EU co-operation measures have been introduced, the most prominent being the European Arrest Warrant – a fast-track judicial (rather than political) extradition procedure. Until recently, the focus of these measures has tended to be on the promotion of mechanisms of co-operation in the investigation, prosecution and sentencing of crime, with no real attention paid to the need for corresponding safeguards for those subject to these measures (Hodgson, 2011). The first attempt to introduce procedural safeguards was the European Commission's Green Paper in 2003,[6] followed by a draft Framework Decision setting out key safeguards for suspects in a single measure in 2004.[7] These attempts were, ultimately, unsuccessful. In July 2009, the Swedish Presidency of the EU presented a 'roadmap' for strengthening procedural safeguards for suspects and accused persons. These protections were explained as being necessary in the context of increased cross-border criminality, as well as the activities of the EU itself in legislating measures for police and judicial co-operation. The idea was to adopt a step-by-step approach, rather than trying to agree on all of the safeguards in a single measure as before.

The first, and perhaps the least controversial measure to be agreed was that on the right to interpretation and translation in criminal proceedings, which was adopted by the European Parliament in October 2010, to be implemented in all Member States by October 2013 (Directive 2010/64/EU). The second measure, on the right to information in criminal proceedings was adopted in May 2012 and must be implemented at the national level by June 2014.[8] Both of these measures are important in enabling suspects to access and rely upon their defence rights, by providing them with information about the charges, about their rights (including to a lawyer) and ensuring that they can understand the proceedings if conducted in a language that the suspect does not understand. The most recent measure to be adopted is the Directive on the right of access to a lawyer (Directive 2013/48 EU).

In the light of the ECtHR case law described above, in which the suspect's rights to custodial legal advice are guaranteed in some detail, it may not be immediately obvious why the EU has also considered it necessary to legislate in this area. With 28 Member States, membership of the EU is smaller than that of the Council of Europe. The answer is that EU measures are more normative, prescriptive and enforceable. Whilst states have considerable latitude in how they implement the judgments of the ECtHR, and there are few sanctions for non-compliance, the position regarding EU legislation is very different.

First, Directives are transposed into national law by states themselves, but if they fail to do this, or if they are not faithful to the original instrument, in most instances an EU citizen can rely directly on the EU instrument to enforce a right in the national court. For example, Article 4 of the Directive on translation and interpretation makes clear that these services must be provided free of charge in all cases. If a Member State of the EU did not transpose this provision into national law and charged a suspect for an interpreter, the suspect (provided they were an EU citizen) could rely directly on the provisions of the Directive. Second, the jurisprudence of the ECtHR is the result of cases brought before it, alleging breaches of the ECHR. EU instruments, in contrast, are negotiated by representatives of the Member States and are not a minimum threshold below which states should not fall, but positive standards to apply in uniform and consistent ways. Third, the Directives contain much more detail on how the measures will work in practice and are preceded by impact assessments in order to ensure that the measures are workable. Finally, whilst the ECtHR reviews whether there has been a breach of a Convention right post conviction, EU standards must be built into criminal procedures and so have a much wider impact.

The Directive on legal assistance was always going to be the most challenging piece of legislation on which to reach agreement. It took more than 28 months and a record number of eight trilogue discussions before agreement was finally reached.[9] The Directive sets out the extent of the accused's right to legal assistance and is preceded by a detailed 'recital' explaining the articles of the Directive in more detail. Its provisions are consistent with ECtHR decisions emphasising the suspect's right to legal assistance from the point at which there is any curtailment of the suspect's freedom of action. But it also goes further in making provision for access to a lawyer during other investigative acts, such as house searches, and setting out the importance of enabling suspects to make contact with a lawyer.

In relation to the suspect's right to legal advice (whether or not they are detained by the police for questioning), Article 3 states that the suspect is entitled to a private consultation with a lawyer prior to any police or judicial questioning; and that the suspect has the right for a lawyer to be present and to participate effectively during questioning. The lawyer's participation is in accordance with national law, but must not prevent the suspect from exercising their rights of defence practically and effectively. Paragraph 25 of the recital explains that the lawyer 'may, inter alia, in accordance with such procedures, ask questions, request clarification and make statements'. Although the reference to national law risks maintaining national differences and so undermining the strength of the provision as a universal norm, arguably the Directive goes further than *Salduz* in its more detailed emphasis on practical and effective defence participation. If the suspect is permitted or required to be present at identity parades, confrontations or reconstructions of the scene of the crime, they may also have a lawyer present during these actions. Paragraph 4 requires that information be made available to the suspect to enable them to obtain the services of a lawyer. This may be through a website or leaflet available at the police station (Recital 27). Suspects may only be denied access to a lawyer in exceptional circumstances, as set out in paragraph 6: 'where there is an urgent need to avert serious adverse consequences for the life, liberty or physical integrity of a person' or 'where immediate action by the investigating authorities is imperative to prevent substantial jeopardy to criminal proceedings'.

5. COMPARING DOMESTIC LEGAL REGIMES

Although several jurisdictions have now made provision for custodial legal assistance following the ECtHR decisions, this has not been an easy path. Reform has generally been precipitated by the judgments of the appellate and constitutional courts, the result of concerted strategies of litigation.[10] This has been effective in bringing about change, but the speed of reform has meant that there has been little or no training of police and lawyers, proper financial arrangements have not been put in place, and the full implications of an expanded defence role in many procedures are not yet fully understood. The EU Directive now requires countries to ensure that their reforms are not simply a sticking plaster to appease any potential litigants to the ECtHR, but that they make full and proper provision for suspects detained and interrogated by the police to have access to effective legal counsel. As set out above, the EU Directive contains a greater level of detail setting out how the right to counsel should be provided.

The legal provisions currently in place vary across European jurisdictions, as one would expect given their different legal histories and traditions (Blackstock et al., 2014: chapter 3), and significant differences remain even after *Salduz*-driven reforms have been instituted. England and Wales, as an adversarially rooted procedure, has a fairly well established defence role. The defence is, after all, responsible not only for representing the interests of the accused, but, by investigating, selecting and presenting evidence for the defence case, she is also responsible for bringing relevant evidence before the court. Custodial legal advice has been on a statutory footing since the Police and Criminal Evidence Act 1984 (PACE), which provides for custodial legal advice for all suspects throughout their period of detention. This means that suspects may consult privately with their lawyer at any time (and no specific time limitation is placed on this), as well as having them present during police interrogation. The suspect is told of the reason for arrest, has information provided on the range of rights available during the period of police custody (for example, to call a lawyer, to remain silent, to have a third party informed of their detention, to have reasonable access to food, drink and rest, as well as information on the standards of conduct of police interrogation that might be expected). Detention is generally for a maximum of 36 hours.[11] Juveniles and those who are especially vulnerable through mental illness or learning disability must also have an appropriate adult present before and during interrogation.[12] There is no provision for access to the police case file. Although advice is free for all suspects, at least half of all suspects do not request a lawyer (Pleasence et al., 2011; Skinns, 2011 and research discussed therein).

Scotland is a mixed system with influences from both England and Wales and its more ancient alliance with France. Until the recent reform, suspects could be detained for only six hours and were permitted to have a lawyer informed of their detention (the so-called right of intimation), in order that the lawyer could be present when the suspect was later brought before the court. Following the Supreme Court decision in *Cadder*, those arrested and detained for questioning are now permitted to consult with a lawyer in private and to have a lawyer present during the police interrogation, but the period of detention has doubled, to twelve hours. They are also told that they may have a third party, rather than a lawyer, informed of their detention. Like England and Wales, vulnerable suspects are entitled to an appropriate adult.

In France, the picture is rather different. As part of an inquisitorially rooted criminal procedure, the defence has historically occupied a different space within the criminal process. Procedures such as those found in France, Belgium and the Netherlands are, in theory, character-ised by a centralised and broad-based judicial enquiry into the offence, rather than into an individual accused. In contrast to England and Wales' reliance on two opposing parties to bring all the relevant evidence before the court, the prosecution case is understood as the product of a judicial enquiry that encompasses both inculpating and exculpating evidence. And as judicial officers, those responsible for the investigation also have a role in protecting the rights and freedoms of the accused.

The defence role has evolved over time and is beginning to catch up with the reality of police-centred investigations, in which judicial super-vision is extremely light touch and largely retrospective, carried out by the public prosecutor rather than through the prolonged investigation by the *juge d'instruction* (Hodgson, 2005, 2013). Those held in police custody may be detained for 48 hours[13] and must be informed of the reasons for detention and of their basic rights during detention. There is no access to the case file. As noted above, in 1993, suspects detained for police questioning were first permitted a half-hour private consultation with a lawyer, 20 hours into the detention period. Since 2011, following *Salduz* and a challenge in the Constitutional Council, the adviser may be present throughout the period of detention and interrogation, though private consultation remains limited to 30 minutes and the lawyer is not permitted to take a proactive or interventionist role during the interroga-tion. In the Netherlands, also an inquisitorially rooted procedure, the so-called '*Salduz* reform' allows the suspect a half-hour consultation with a lawyer, but counsel is still not permitted to be present during interrogation, save in the case of juveniles and the most serious offenses.[14] The public prosecutor is in charge of the investigation and prosecution of suspects, who may be detained for up to 72 hours.

The different approaches to provision for legal counsel to suspects in police custody arise in part because of the very different roles of legal personnel across jurisdictions and, in particular, differences in the balance of power and responsibility between legal actors. In France and the Netherlands, the prosecutor is responsible for the supervision of the detention of suspects as part of her pre-trial judicial oversight role, and this is considered an important additional protection and form of police accountability. In England and Wales, the public prosecutor has no responsibility for either the investigation or the conduct of the detention period: responsibility for the detention of suspects, including access to key defence rights such as legal counsel, rests with the custody officer. The defence is an important guarantor of due process rights as well as being responsible for investigating the defence case.[15] One of the barriers to the acceptance of some ECtHR Article 6 jurisprudence and to the new EU provisions, is the fact that the safeguards are regarded by many countries, such as France, as more reflective of adversarial (often described as Anglo-Saxon) procedures.

The interaction of different rights and procedures is also an important factor in comparative evaluations of custodial legal advice: we are comparing the same right, but that right operates in a different context. There may be different structures of detention supervision or different weight attached to pre-trial evidence; there may be different rights available to suspects and these rights may be administered in quite different ways; there may be different police custody time limits. So, for example, the suspect in Scotland may have a lawyer present before and during police interrogation, and detention may last a maximum of 12 hours. In the Netherlands, suspects are permitted only a 30-minute consultation, but detention may be very much longer than in Scotland – lasting up to 72 hours.

In all four jurisdictions, suspects must be informed of their right to silence and their right to consult with a lawyer free of charge, prior to the first interrogation by the police. However, the point at which suspects are informed of these rights is not the same, and so their likelihood of exercising these rights will vary. In France, when she arrives at the police station, the suspect will be told of her right to speak, be silent or make a written statement, along with her other rights. She will not be informed of this right again – this is seen as inappropriate and to risk encouraging the suspect to exercise her right to silence. In England and Wales, this 'caution' must be repeated at the start of every interrogation. Without this, the evidence obtained will not be admissible. The manner in which suspects are informed of their rights also varies. For example, England and Wales was the only one of the four jurisdictions to require that information on rights be provided to suspects in a standardised written format (Blackstock et al., 2014: chapter 5). Aside from the core function of the protection of the suspect's interests and deciding on a strategy in response to interrogation, the defence has an important role in explaining procedure (in some instances making good the gap in police information) and the wider context in which the suspect must determine whether and how to exercise her rights.

6. THE EMPIRICAL STUDY

In our recently completed empirical study of England and Wales, France, the Netherlands and Scotland, we were able to observe first-hand the daily practices of police and lawyers in different sites in each jurisdiction. The study consisted of some 78 weeks of observation of police and lawyers, together with 84 interviews, and the collection of information on 384 case records (Blackstock et al., 2014: chapter 2 and the related annexes). For the police observation phase, researchers were based at police stations to observe the police as they 'booked in' suspects, informed them of their rights and interrogated them. This also enabled them to chat with officers and to observe their interactions with other personnel such as lawyers, prosecutors and interpreters.

Lawyer observations were organised in two principal ways, reflecting the different arrangements in place for the provision of custodial legal advice. In England and Wales, there are specialist firms of lawyers handling criminal work, and the tendering process for public legal aid funding also requires specialisation and a certain degree of economy of scale. This means that firms specialising in criminal work will have a high number of police station call outs and so the researcher was able to gather a sufficient case sample by being stationed with one or two firms of lawyers and accompanying them to the police station as the calls came in to the office. In France and the Netherlands, there is much less specialism in criminal work; being attached to a single firm would not generate sufficient cases. So, researchers contacted the lawyers on the duty rota and arranged to be called by whichever lawyer was called out to the police station. This generated a good case sample and also involved a wider cross-section of lawyers. In Scotland, lawyers were reluctant to co-operate and we observed very few cases. In addition, their overwhelming preference for the provision of telephone, rather than face-to-face advice, also made observations difficult.

Police station observations were more straightforward, with researchers being based in the custody area and gaining access to interrogations in many instances. The exception was France, where the police hierarchy refused us permission to be based at police stations. We were not, therefore, able to observe the French police informing the suspect of her rights on arrival at the police station – though we did attend interrogations and private consultations when accompanying French lawyers.

7. COMPARING THE PROVISION OF CUSTODIAL LEGAL ADVICE

Having explored some of the challenges in legislating rights across jurisdictions, and some broad differences in domestic arrangements, I want to focus on the ways in which empirical findings can help us to understand the key features of a universal and effective right to legal counsel for suspects held in police custody for questioning. By examining practices across jurisdictions, we can identify drivers of success and good practice, as well as the kinds of factors that inhibit the effectiveness of rights in practice. The *Inside Police Custody* study had the advantage of allowing us to draw on the differences in legal procedural tradition, as well as to examine the right to custodial legal advice at different stages in its development. This allows for comparison of the reception of the newly expanded right to counsel for suspects in police custody in Scotland, the Netherlands and France, with the more established procedure in England and Wales, examining in particular whether the behaviour of police, prosecutors and lawyers is jurisdiction-specific or indicative of broader organisational features.

The right to legal counsel for suspects held for questioning in police custody is not provided for in the same way in each country: the legal space assigned to the defence lawyer differs between jurisdictions, as set out above. These differences in legislative provision reflect broader differences in understanding of the defence role – whether the defence is the primary guarantor of defence rights, as in England and Wales, or plays a more diminished part, complementing that of the judicial officer responsible for the investigation, as in France and the Netherlands. These differences are reflected in the readiness of countries to embrace a new or expanded defence function.

The lawyer is permitted to be present during the police interrogation of the suspect in England and Wales, France and Scotland, but not the

Netherlands. But even where present, the lawyer does not participate in the same way in each jurisdiction. In England and Wales and in Scotland, the lawyer may seek clarification of questions, object to inappropriate or overbearing questions and, if necessary, stop the interview. In France, however, the lawyer is present, but must remain passive. She may not interrupt the police interrogation – only once it is finished may she pose questions or seek clarifications. As one lawyer explained: 'We're just allowed to breathe and that's it ... in terms of defence rights, it's useless: we are just decorative, like a vase on the table' (iFranCityLaw3 – interview with lawyer in large field site in France, see Blackstock et al., 2014: 50). French lawyers understand the role that has been assigned to them as providing minimal benefit to the suspect, whilst serving to legitimate the police investigation procedure: 'We are defenders but mostly we guarantee the integrity of the process' (iFranCityLaw2).

The arrangements in place for legal assistance prior to questioning are also very much more restrictive in France and the Netherlands, where consultation is limited to 30 minutes. This does not anticipate detailed preparation for interview or the possibility of engaging in the kinds of defence tasks set out in *Dayanan v Turkey*. The expectation is that the lawyer will ascertain some basic case facts from the suspect (there is little disclosure to the suspect or lawyer of the evidence held by the police) and provide largely generic advice on rights and procedure – there simply is not the time or the information to allow for much more than this. It should also be remembered that, in part because of lower levels of specialisation, most suspects in France and the Netherlands are seen by a duty lawyer, rather than their 'own' lawyer; there is no existing professional relationship. In addition to getting the suspect's version of events therefore, the lawyer must also gather some basic biographical information and establish a degree of professional trust – all within half an hour.

However, it is not only different legal provisions that reflect different understandings of the lawyer's role. The ways in which lawyers organise the provision of legal assistance – from the local bar down to the individuals on duty rotas – also reflect different conceptions of the lawyer's role. In the first years following the introduction of a statutory right to custodial legal advice in England and Wales, lawyers were found to delegate this work routinely and systematically to untrained, unqualified and often inexperienced staff (McConville and Hodgson, 1993; McConville et al., 1994). Quite simply, they failed to grasp the opportunity presented by this new role, preferring instead to regard it as a way to maximise their income by delegating tasks to lower paid staff whilst

claiming full solicitor legal aid rates. This resulted in a national programme of training and accreditation, ensuring that solicitors and their
representatives are fully trained and qualified in the provision of advice
to suspects in police custody.

In our recent empirical study, we observed some lawyers providing the
best quality advice that they could manage within the constraints of little
time and case-related information. However, these lawyers were in the
minority. In Scotland, lawyers preferred to speak to suspects by telephone, rather than attending the police station in person. Lawyers told us
that they would nearly always advise silence and this could be done as
well by telephone as in person.[16] Most significantly, this meant that they
were routinely absent from the interrogation of the suspect, but advising
a person by telephone rather than face-to-face is unsatisfactory in many
ways. Apart from issues of privacy and confidentiality, it is much harder
to assess the state of the suspect and their ability to withstand police
questioning.

In France and the Netherlands, there is less criminal specialism within
the local bar. As a result, duty lawyer schemes employed lawyers from all
areas of practice in order to have sufficient numbers to meet demand.
This is perhaps a pragmatic solution to a practical problem. However, this
resulted in suspects being advised by lawyers working in family or
commercial practice, with little experience or knowledge of criminal
procedure. Training was minimal or non-existent and the profession was
effectively allowing those with little or no knowledge of criminal
procedure to fulfil a key role in advising an accused person when they
are most vulnerable and most in need of informed explanation in order to
respond properly to police questions.

Another consequence of the relatively low numbers of specialist
criminal lawyers is that duty lawyers provide the bulk of both police
station and court work. There is no professional continuity in these cases.
The advice and representation provided at each phase is a one-off
transaction; the lawyer attending the suspect at the police station is
unlikely to represent her at court. This defines the suspect–lawyer
encounter differently from a private consultation attended by the suspect's 'own' lawyer: it means that there is little investment in the case or
in an ongoing professional lawyer–client relationship. This contrasts
sharply with England and Wales, where the expectation is that the firm
attending the suspect at the police station will go on to represent her at
court – incentivising lawyers to follow cases through, negotiate on bail
and charges, and so on.

8. POLICE ADMINISTRATION OF SUSPECTS' RIGHTS

Those who believe that reforms are likely to operate against their interests perhaps have the greatest incentive to try to undermine them. The police often regard the presence of lawyers as likely to undermine the investigation and to reduce the likelihood of suspects co-operating during interrogation. This argument has been put forward time and again – from the introduction of the lawyer during the French *instruction* in 1897, to the 30-minute consultation 20 hours into detention in France in 1993, and the introduction of a statutory right to custodial legal advice under s. 58 PACE in 1985 in England and Wales. In all of these cases, police fears have proved to be unfounded – indeed research shows that defence lawyers are often co-operative and insufficiently adversarial, rather than hindering the investigation (Field and West, 2003; Hodgson, 2005; McConville et al., 1994). But it is clear that the professional ideologies and occupational cultures of all legal actors have the potential to enhance or constrain the effectiveness of legal reform.

The police varied in their response to lawyers' presence at the police station. More experienced officers were more accepting of the lawyer's role, understanding that defence rights have a place in criminal procedure. These officers had also seen that suspects who received legal advice were not necessarily more obstructive or more likely to remain silent. The police in England and Wales had the most experience of lawyers assisting suspects before and during interrogation and, interestingly, across the four jurisdictions, they were the most accepting of the lawyer's role. Some officers were still resentful of the suspect's right to a lawyer and others thought that having a lawyer there complicated their work. French police were not enthusiastic about having lawyers present during the detention period, but they recognised that there was little that the lawyer could do and therefore little impact that they would have on the investigation. Whilst lawyers in the Netherlands have the most limited role during the suspect's detention, Dutch officers were the most hostile to the presence of the lawyer. They felt that lawyers delayed investigations, complicated cases and made suspects less likely to co-operate. The arrival of defence counsel is a very recent phenomenon in the Netherlands and it may be that once officers become accustomed to the lawyer's presence, as they have in England and Wales and to an extent in France, they will become less hostile to the idea. In Scotland, the position was rather different. It was not the presence of lawyers that officers found difficult (probably because most do not attend), but, rather, the process of informing suspects of their right to a lawyer, which required the police to administer a long, poorly worded and repetitive form (Blackstock et al., 2014: 230–234).

An aspect of police occupational culture that we observed across all jurisdictions was the practice of implementing due process or defence rights in ways that served police interests rather than those of the suspect. For example, in France and the Netherlands, the decision to appoint an interpreter was often not based on the suspect's need, but on the police's view of whether they could progress the investigation sufficiently without an interpreter. For example, in order to avoid calling in a professional interpreter, police officers themselves would act as interpreters if they had some knowledge of the relevant language; or they would reformulate questions in very simple terms so that they might be better understood by the suspect. This ignored the suspect's impaired understanding of the process and the charges, and took no account of the desirability of having an interpreter during the lawyer–client consultation.

This illustrates the wider point that where the police perceived due process rights to hinder or to be of no benefit to their own investigation, they were more likely to engage in rights avoidance strategies. This was often the case with the right to legal counsel, which was generally regarded as assisting the suspect and potentially delaying or obstructing the police enquiry. This view appears to be almost universal and has been observed across different criminal procedures: by researchers in England and Wales after the implementation of PACE (Sanders and Bridges, 1990); in France in my own earlier empirical studies (Hodgson, 2005); and in *Inside Police Custody*, in particular in the Netherlands, where the right has most recently been introduced. It appears to be most pronounced when the right to legal counsel for suspects is first introduced.

The police employ a range of strategies. The primary concern of most suspects is to get out of the police station as soon as possible, making the most effective ploy that of suggesting that contacting a lawyer would delay things and prolong the period of detention. Sometimes this is done overtly and directly, other times it is more subtle, with officers failing to disabuse suspects who fear that a lawyer will delay things, or that the charges are insufficiently serious to merit calling a lawyer. Given that more suspects waive their right to counsel during police custody than ask to see a lawyer, it is important to ensure that procedures are in place to ensure that any waiver is voluntary and fully informed. Typically, on arrival at the police station, as part of the 'booking-in' process, the suspect is asked whether she would like to take up her right to legal assistance. At this point, she has very little to go on. She may know that she has been arrested for theft, assault or a public order offence, but she is unlikely to know the precise extent and gravity of the charges, or of the evidence against her. It may seem unnecessary to call a lawyer at the outset of detention, but very much more desirable once the police case is revealed during interrogation. Of the four jurisdictions in our study, only in England and Wales were suspects told that the right to a lawyer was a continuing right and that the suspect could change her mind at any point. In the other three jurisdictions, once the decision to waive the right to counsel had been made, suspects were unaware of their continuing right and so unlikely to change their mind. This is an important gap in legal provision.

The availability of legal aid is another key factor in the suspect's decision-making process. Repeat players in the system know what they are entitled to and how to get it, but for those experiencing the process for the first time the situation is very different. Both police and lawyers in all four jurisdictions made this distinction to us, explaining that they would tend to be more thorough with someone who was being arrested and detained for the first time. If a first-time suspect is informed of her right to counsel, she may be concerned that she cannot afford a lawyer and so decline legal assistance on grounds of cost. In England and Wales, shortly after the right to custodial legal advice was introduced, research found that officers frequently omitted to tell suspects that legal assistance was free at the point of delivery. Many worried that they could not afford a lawyer and so waived their right to counsel. This resulted in changes to the Code of Practice, and the custody officer, who is responsible for the suspect's welfare, must now tell the suspect that she has the right to a lawyer and that this is available free of charge. In France, when legislation was first passed permitting the lawyer access to the police station (for a 30-minute consultation with the suspect, 20 hours into detention), the first things that lawyers did was to go on strike! Unfortunately, no provision for legal aid had been made, leaving lawyers unable to claim any state funding for custodial legal advice work. Proper provision for payment was then put in place, but this serves as a useful reminder of the importance of making rights effective in practice.

9. CONCLUSION: MAKING DEFENCE RIGHTS UNIVERSAL AND EFFECTIVE

The ECtHR and the EU have made important advances in setting out universal standards of legal assistance for suspects detained and questioned by the police. From a comparative law perspective, it is interesting to investigate the extent to which these kinds of pan-European measures are able to result in a degree of consensus over fair trial standards, which reaches across different procedural traditions. There are limitations on the extent to which the ECHR and the jurisprudence of the ECtHR can or should exact uniformity of standards. This is a model that sets broad standards of the requirements of a fair trial, leaving states with a margin of appreciation in how this might be achieved. It is also clear that ECHR standards are diluted through different interpretations at the national level, and through uneven modes of transposition into domestic legislation. The EU regime is more normative and demands higher levels of uniformity. Member States that do not comply can be challenged by defendants directly in national courts and ultimately in the Court of Justice of the European Union. In this way, an EU Directive sets a clearer standard that must be complied with in the same way across all Member States. However, the legal measures themselves allow variations in line with existing provisions within Member States, building in layers of difference in implementation.

An empirical examination of the daily practices of police and lawyers as they implement the right to legal counsel demonstrates the depth of difference that exists in legal provisions across jurisdictions, but also the very different perceptions that legal actors have of the role of lawyers in police custody. Some of these differences can be attributed to different criminal procedural traditions and the place that the lawyer has come to occupy in the criminal process; others reflect practical arrangements such as levels of legal aid.[17] But it is important that we recognise the agency of police and lawyers even within the legal and practical constraints within which they work. Their views of the value of legal assistance are often crucial in the success or otherwise of legal reform. Police officers who regard the presence of the lawyer as antithetical to the interests of an effective investigation will engage in a range of rights avoidance strategies: encouraging the suspect not to exercise their right to counsel, claiming that they will have to wait a long time for the lawyer to arrive and that this will delay the case and so the suspect's release from custody; failing to inform the suspect that the lawyer is free of charge; and allowing the suspect to think that the case is very straightforward and so no lawyer is necessary. It was clear in our own observations that for some suspects, this served to dissuade them from taking up the right to counsel.

For their part, lawyers must also value the opportunity that custodial legal advice represents – an opportunity to influence the case at the most crucial stage of the investigation, when suspects are at their most vulnerable. This requires adequate training in practical skills as well as law and procedure. Police station advice is not like court work or proof taking in the office. It is often tense and even confrontational; the lawyer must be able to think on her feet, assessing law and welfare issues and making representations where necessary – not to a judge in the public setting of a courtroom, but to a senior police officer in the closed environment of the police station.

Much of what we observed across the three jurisdictions where custodial legal advice has only recently been introduced or strengthened, was similar to my own findings in England and Wales in the early post-PACE years and my French empirical study published in 2005 (Hodgson, 2005; McConville and Hodgson, 1993; McConville et al., 1994). This is of particular interest to the comparativist as it suggests institutional and process drivers that cut across legal procedural differences. It underlines, in particular, the need for a more comprehensive understanding of the role of legal counsel for suspects, of the benefits in terms of procedural fairness and so evidential reliability, and the importance of equality of arms. This understanding is lacking not only from those whose interests might be seen as in opposition to those of the suspects, but also from lawyers themselves, who fail to grasp the significant influence that their assistance might have. Scottish lawyers, for example, remain content to provide telephone advice, perhaps not realising the importance of face-to-face meetings in assessing the suspect's ability to deal with police interrogation, and the difficulties of remaining silent when facing the police alone. What we observe is that it is less the procedural tradition of a criminal process that determines the lawyer's response than the way lawyers acclimatise to their new role. The law alone can be a blunt instrument of change. If police and lawyers are to 'buy in' to these legal reforms, they also need training to understand their value beyond the narrow interests of police, prosecutors or defense lawyers, to the good functioning of the wider criminal justice process.

NOTES

1. The study 'Procedural rights of suspects in police detention in the EU: empirical investigation and promoting best practice' JUST/2010/JPEN/AG/1578 was funded by the European Commission. Alongside the right to legal assistance at the police station, the study also examines the suspect's right to information, to interpretation and translation, and to silence.
2. See also *Poitrimol v France* (1993) A 277-A, 18 EHRR 130.
3. As the ECtHR explained in *Imbrioscia v Switzerland* 13972/88 [1993] ECHR 56, para 38: 'While it confers on everyone charged with a criminal offence the right to "defend himself in person or through legal assistance ...", Article 6 para. 3 (c) (art. 6-3-c) does not specify the manner of exercising this right. It thus leaves to the Contracting States the choice of the means of ensuring that it is secured in their

judicial systems, the Court's task being only to ascertain whether the method they have chosen is consistent with the requirements of a fair trial'.

4. *Averill v United Kingdom* 36408/97 [2000] ECHR, which involved inferences from silence under the 1988 Order in place in Northern Ireland at that time: '... an accused is confronted at the beginning of police interrogation with a fundamental dilemma relating to his defence. If he chooses to remain silent, adverse inferences may be drawn against him in accordance with the provisions of the Order. On the other hand, if the accused opts to break his silence during the course of interrogation, he runs the risk of prejudicing his defence without necessarily removing the possibility of inferences being drawn against him. Under such conditions the concept of fairness enshrined in Article 6 requires that the accused have the benefit of the assistance of a lawyer already at the initial stages of police interrogation ... The situation in which the accused finds himself during that 24 hour period is one where the rights of the defence may well be irretrievably prejudiced ...' (paras 59–60).

5. E.g. International Criminal Tribunal for the former Yugoslavia; European Committee for the Prevention of Torture and Inhuman or Degrading Treatment or Punishment.

6. Recognised as a 'necessary counterbalance to judicial co-operation measures that [have] enhanced the powers of prosecutors, courts and investigating officers', Brussels, 19.2.2003, COM(2003) 75f para 1.4.

7. COM/2004/0328 final. These included: legal advice and assistance; the provision of interpreters; special protection for vulnerable suspects; consular assistance; and knowledge of the existence of rights.

8. Directive 2012/13/EU. This requires Member States to inform suspects and accused persons of their right to legal assistance, including the conditions under which it is available free of charge; the right to be informed of the accusation; the right to interpretation and translation; and the right to remain silent. On arrest, it requires suspects to be provided with a Letter of Rights, setting out the right to access case materials; to have consular authorities and one person informed of their detention; to be given access to urgent medical assistance; to know how long you can be detained before being brought before a judge; and information on challenging the lawfulness of arrest, reviewing detention and requesting release.

9. Trilogues refer to discussion between members of the three EU institutions: Parliament, Council and the Commission.

10. For example in France, the *Conseil Constitutionnel* Decision 2010-14/22 QPC of 30 July 2010 and the *Cour de Cassation* Cass. ass. plén., 15 April 2011, Nos. 10-30.316, 10-30.313, 10-30.242 and 10-17.049; for the Netherlands, see the HR 30 June 2009, *NJ* 2009, 349; and for Scotland, see the UK Supreme Court decision in *Cadder v HM Advocate* [2010] UKSC 43. Most recently, see the Irish Supreme Court Decision *DPP v Gormley; DPP v White* [2014] IESC 17.

11. This can be extended on application to the court, or in terrorism cases.

12. PACE COP C. The appropriate adult role is to act as an additional safeguard for vulnerable individuals and to assist communication. The appropriate adult role is not to provide legal advice.

13. This can be extended by a judge in cases of terrorism, serious organised crime and drug trafficking.

14. In juvenile cases, the suspect may choose to have either an appropriate adult or a lawyer present – but not both.

15. This is a senior police officer who is wholly unconnected with the investigation.

16. Silence was the preferred advice because any confession must be corroborated by other evidence in Scotland.

17. For information on rates and mechanisms of payment for 'own' and duty lawyers, see Blackstock et al. (2014) pp. 82–83 (England and Wales); p. 98 (France); pp. 116–118 (Netherlands); pp. 135–136 (Scotland); and more generally pp. 388–389.

REFERENCES

Blackstock, Jodie, Ed Cape, Jacqueline Hodgson, Anna Ogorodova and Taru Spronken. 2014. *Inside Police Custody*. Cambridge, Antwerp, Portland: Intersentia.

Field, Stewart and Andrew West. 2003. 'Dialogue and the Inquisitorial Tradition: French Defence Lawyers in the Pre-Trial Criminal Process', 14 *Criminal Law Forum* 261–316.

Hodgson, Jacqueline. 2005. *French Criminal Justice: A Comparative Account of the Investigation and Prosecution of Crime in France*. Oxford: Hart Publishing.

Hodgson, Jacqueline. 2011. 'Safeguarding Suspects' Rights in Europe: A Comparative Perspective', 14 *New Criminal Law Review* 611–665.

Hodgson, Jacqueline. 2013. 'The Impact of *Salduz* in France: Making Custodial Legal Advice More Effective', 92 *Criminal Justice Matters* 14–15.

McConville, Mike and Jacqueline Hodgson. 1993. *Custodial Legal Advice and the Right to Silence*. London: HMSO.

McConville, Mike, Jacqueline Hodgson, Lee Bridges and Anita Pavlovic. 1994. *Standing Accused: The Organisation and Practices of Criminal Defence Lawyers in Britain*. Oxford: Clarendon Press.

Pleasence, Pascoe, Vicky Kemp and Nigel Balmer. 2011. 'The Justice Lottery? Police Station Advice 25 Years on from PACE', 1 *Criminal Law Review* 3–18.

Sanders, Andrew and Lee Bridges. 1990. 'Access to Legal Advice and Police Malpractice', *Criminal Law Review* 494–509.

Skinns, Layla. 2011. 'The Right to Legal Advice in the Police Station: Past, Present and Future', 1 *Criminal Law Review* 19–39.

8. A comparative perspective on the exclusionary rule in search and seizure cases

Christopher Slobogin

Judicial exclusion of evidence obtained during an illegal search or seizure is controversial because the evidence is almost always reliable proof of guilt, and thus suppression might well prevent conviction of an obvious criminal. Nonetheless, exclusion of such evidence occurs relatively frequently in the United States, and, over the past several decades, has become more prevalent in a number of other countries as well. At bottom, these various exclusion regimes rely on one of three rationales: deterrence of police misconduct; promotion of systemic integrity; or vindication of fundamental rights.

Since the 1970s, the United States Supreme Court has viewed the exclusionary rule primarily as a means of deterring police conduct that unduly infringes privacy, liberty or autonomy interests. But in years past the Court also proffered two other reasons for exclusion: the importance of ensuring the integrity of the legal system (primarily by avoiding judicial complicity with police illegality) and the need to vindicate constitutional guarantees. Some version of one or both of the latter two rationales also appears to be the primary motivation behind the exclusionary rules in other countries. In contrast to the United States, however, in most other countries exclusion is not very common. Those countries that focus on systemic integrity take into account not only the de-legitimizing impact of failing to exclude illegally seized evidence but also the truth-denigrating effect of excluding evidence. Those countries that focus on vindicating fundamental rights tend to define those rights narrowly, or undercut the vindication rationale in various other ways.

This chapter begins, in section 1, by describing the development of the exclusionary rule in the United States, the country which has adhered to some version of the rule over the longest period of time and that, partly as a result, provides the richest jurisprudence on the subject. The description of U.S. law is relatively elaborate because it provides a number of different rationales for and nuances on the exclusionary idea, many of which have parallels in other countries. Section 2 then surveys the exclusionary regimes in other nations, categorized under the two competing approaches to the deterrence model endorsed in the United States: the systemic integrity model and the rights vindication model. Section 3 examines, from both empirical and theoretical perspectives, the difficulties that arise in analyzing the various considerations identified in sections 1 and 2. Section 4 concludes with thoughts about the possible alternatives to exclusion, the ways in which the exclusionary remedy can be refined, and the interaction of the exclusionary rule with substantive search and seizure law.

1. THE EXCLUSIONARY RULE IN THE UNITED STATES: THE DETERRENCE OF POLICE MISCONDUCT MODEL[1]

The Fourth Amendment to the United States Constitution prohibits 'unreasonable searches and seizures' of 'persons, houses, papers and effects', and requires that warrants be based on 'probable cause' and describe with 'particularity' the person or place to be searched and the item to be seized. But the Amendment does not specify any remedy for its breach. At the time the Constitution was drafted, the principal means of seeking redress for an illegal search or seizure was a damages action against the government official who carried out the search (Wilson, 1986: 9–33). Exclusion, if it occurred at all, was rare (Roots, 2009–10: 14–20).

By the mid-nineteenth century, however, some state courts were dismissing cases because of illegal searches (Oliver, 2010: 504). And in 1886 the United States Supreme Court itself recognized that exclusion could be an appropriate remedy for a Fourth Amendment violation, although it did so somewhat circuitously. In *Boyd v. United States* (1886), the Court held that use at trial of private papers obtained from the accused through a subpoena ordering their production violated the *Fifth* Amendment to the U.S. Constitution, which states in part that 'no person ... shall be compelled in any criminal case to be a witness against himself'; this unconstitutional compulsion, in turn, made the seizure unreasonable under the Fourth Amendment (p. 663). The Court's reliance on the Fifth Amendment as well as the Fourth suggested that if the evidence seized could not be characterized as testimony from a 'witness' it would not be excluded even if the search and seizure was unreasonable. That rationale made the exclusionary remedy a relatively narrow one: while the papers seized in *Boyd* could be said to be 'testimonial', the type of evidence typically obtained during a search and seizure – contraband, stolen property and instrumentalities of crime such as weapons – do not fit in this category.

Three decades later, in *Weeks v. United States* (1914), the Court untethered exclusion from the Fifth Amendment. In an analysis that did not even mention the latter constitutional provision, the Court ordered exclusion simply on the ground that the government must return (prior to adjudication) any illegally seized property over which the accused had a superior property interest. This property-based approach avoided the testimony limitation of the Fifth Amendment.

But *Weeks* only applied to property legitimately owned by the accused, so exclusion still did not occur under this theory if the illegally seized evidence was contraband or the fruits of crime (over which the government clearly has a superior possessory interest). Furthermore, at the time these cases were decided, the Bill of Rights – the first ten amendments to the U.S. Constitution – was thought to apply solely to the federal government (*Barron v. City of Baltimore*, 1833, p. 247). Thus, *Boyd* and *Weeks* only affected federal prosecutions; they did not require exclusion in state court trials, where the lion's share of crime is adjudicated (*Stefanelli v. Minard*, 1951, p. 120).

The first obstacle to exclusion – based on the nature of the evidence seized – was fairly quickly removed in *Silverthorne v. United States* (1920) and other cases decided by the Court in the 1920s. According to Justice Holmes in *Silverthorne*, unless the exclusionary remedy applies in every criminal case, including those involving contraband and the like, the Fourth Amendment would be 'a form of words' (p. 392). Seven years later, Justice Brandeis declared that 'the government itself would become a lawbreaker' unless all illegally seized evidence were excluded (*Olmstead v. United States*, 1928, p. 438).[2] These types of statements introduced the notion that defendants are constitutionally entitled to exclusion of *every* type of evidence seized in violation of the Fourth Amendment, both to ensure vindication of their rights and to protect the integrity of the criminal justice system.

The second obstacle to exclusion – its limitation to federal cases – took longer to overcome. The Fourteenth Amendment to the U.S. Constitution, ratified after the Civil War in 1868, guarantees all citizens 'due process of law' (U.S. Const., 1789). If the Fourth Amendment right to be secure against unreasonable searches and seizures and the accompanying exclusionary remedy are aspects of due process, then the Fourteenth Amendment requires that they apply to state as well as federal cases. But despite the high-sounding language of Justices Holmes and Brandeis to the effect that the exclusionary rule is a fundamental right, the Court resisted applying it to state cases for almost half a century after *Weeks*, except when the police action was so egregious that it 'shocked the conscience'. At the Supreme Court level, this perilous state of affairs was discovered only once, in *Rochin v. California* (1954, p. 172), where police used a stomach pump to flush out drugs swallowed by a suspect.

In contrast, run-of-the-mill illegalities, the Court declared in *Wolf v. Colorado* (1949), did not require exclusion as a constitutional matter. The primary reason *Wolf* gave for this holding was a comparative one: it noted that very few countries in the Western world contemplated exclusion as a remedy and that fewer than half the states in the U.S. had adopted the rule on their own, instead relying on alternative methods of dealing with illegal searches and seizures (p. 29). To the Court, these facts demonstrated that suppression of illegally seized evidence was not 'essential' to the 'ordered liberty' and 'due process' guaranteed to state citizens by the Fourteenth Amendment (pp. 27–29).

It was only after another seven states had decided exclusion was necessary as a Fourth Amendment remedy – giving the rule a bare majority of state adherents – that the Court reversed *Wolf* and applied the rule nationwide. The Court's opinion in *Mapp v. Ohio*, decided in 1961, stated that 'the plain and unequivocal language of *Weeks* – and its later paraphrase in *Wolf* – to the effect that the *Weeks* rule is of constitutional origin, remains entirely undisturbed' (p. 641). This language appeared to endorse Justice Holmes' assertion that without exclusion, the Fourth Amendment was a 'form of words', and thus required suppression of any illegally seized evidence regardless of its effect on the police.

Mapp also discussed the efficacy of the rule, however. While 'not basically relevant to a decision that the exclusionary rule is an essential ingredient of the Fourth Amendment', the fact that other remedies for illegal searches and seizures had proven 'worthless and futile' was important enough to be noted by the majority (pp. 651–662). Later in the opinion, the Court went even further down the pragmatic road, stating that 'the purpose of the exclusionary rule "is to deter – to compel respect for the constitutional guaranty in the only effectively available way – by removing the incentive to disregard it"' (p. 656).

In subsequent cases, this latter language, far from remaining 'basically irrelevant', became the focal point of the Court's analysis. Twelve years after *Mapp*, the Court's decision in *United States v. Calandra* (1974) declared that 'the rule's prime purpose is to deter future unlawful police conduct and thereby effectuate the guarantee of the Fourth Amendment against unreasonable searches and seizures' (p. 347). By the time of *United States v. Leon* (1984) a majority of the Court was willing to respond to Justice Brandeis' assertion that the rule is meant to assure judicial clean hands with the statement: 'Our cases establish that the question whether the use of illegally obtained evidence in judicial proceedings represents judicial participation in a Fourth Amendment violation and offends the integrity of the courts "is essentially the same as the inquiry into whether exclusion would serve a deterrent purpose'" (p. 921). In other words, *Leon* asserted that if application of the rule in a given situation does not deter, it is not needed to enhance the legitimacy of the criminal justice system and might in fact undermine it.

Relying on this deterrence purpose, the Court has reduced significantly the situations in which the rule applies, in three different contexts: (1) secondary process cases; (2) good faith cases; and (3) attenuated fruit cases. First, the Court has reasoned that exclusion in the prosecution's case-in-chief is all that is necessary to deter violations of the Fourth Amendment; any additional disincentive that might result from preventing use of illegally seized evidence in *other* settings is so minimal that it does not justify suppression. Thus, exclusion of illegally seized evidence is not required in grand jury proceedings, post-conviction proceedings, parole revocation hearings, civil tax proceedings, civil deportation proceedings, or even at the criminal trial itself when the sole purpose for introducing the evidence is impeachment of the defendant (*United States v. Calandra*, 1974; *Stone v. Powell*, 1976; *Pennsylvania v. Scott*, 1998; *United States v. Janis*, 1976; *Immigration and Naturalization Service v. Lopez-Mendoza*, 1984; *United States v. Havens*, 1980).

Second, the Court has concluded that exclusion is also unnecessary when the police reasonably rely on an assertion by an authorized third party that a particular search or seizure is permissible. In these circumstances, the Court reasons, the officer will be undeterred by *any* remedy, because he or she will not realize the Constitution is being violated. This 'good faith exception' applies, according to the Court, when police reasonably rely on a warrant issued by a neutral and detached magistrate, on an assertion by a court or police clerk that such a warrant exists, or on a statute or court ruling later declared to be unconstitutional (*United States v. Leon*, 1984; *Arizona v. Evans*, 1995; *Herring v. United States*, 2009; *Michigan v. DeFillippo*, 1979; *Illinois v. Krull*, 1987; *Davis v. United States*, 2011).

Finally, the Court has held that when the connection between evidence and the illegal search or seizure that led to its discovery is so attenuated that the illegality probably was not perpetrated in order to obtain the evidentiary fruit, the deterrent effect of the rule is unlikely to operate.[3] Thus, while a confession obtained at the police station soon after an illegal arrest will usually be excluded, a later confession that appears to be a spontaneous exercise of will may be admissible, even though, but for the arrest, the confession would not have occurred (*Wong Sun v. United*

States, 1963). Similarly, a witness identified as a result of an illegal search usually will not be 'suppressed', on the theory that most searches are not carried out to discover witnesses (*United States v. Ceccolini*, 1978).

While the Court's analysis of the rule has focused on deterrence, it has also reduced the scope of the exclusionary rule in three other ways, none of which are tied to the deterrence rationale. First, exclusion is not permitted when the illegality did not infringe the defendant's own Fourth Amendment interests. If the purpose of exclusion is to deter police misconduct, one would think that a defendant could contest any illegal search or seizure, even if it is directed at a third party. But the Court has instead opted for an 'individual rights' approach to standing that does not allow challenges to searches and seizures of other individuals or their property (*Rakas v. Illinois*, 1978, pp. 133–138). It has adhered to this stance even when the police violate the third party's rights knowing and intending that the Court's standing rule will operate to prevent a challenge to their actions (*United States v. Payner*, 1980, p. 735).

Second, if the government can show that illegally seized evidence would eventually have been discovered through legal means, exclusion is not necessary, even if the police acted in bad faith. The idea here is that suppression of evidence that inevitably would have been found legally would put the police in a worse position than if the illegality had not occurred (*Nix v. Williams*, 1984). Although this rationale would seem to require strong proof that the evidence would have been found legally, the Court has held that 'inevitability' need only be proven by a preponderance of the evidence (p. 444 n. 5).

Third, exclusion is inapposite when it would not serve the interest protected by the constitutional guarantee, even if the police intentionally violate the guarantee to secure evidence. This last exception to the rule appears to be the best explanation for the Court's holding that exclusion need not occur when the police violate the Fourth Amendment requirement that they knock and announce their presence before non-exigent home entries; according to the Court, the primary purpose of the knock-and-announce rule is to protect against violence and property destruction, not illegal seizure of evidence (*Hudson v. Michigan*, 2006). The Court relied on a similar rationale in holding that an illegal warrantless home arrest of an individual who subsequently confesses at the stationhouse does not require exclusion of the confession; the rule that non-exigent arrests in the home require a warrant, the Court stated, is meant to protect against improper home invasions, not police conduct outside the home (*New York v. Harris*, 1990, p. 20; *United States v. Ramirez*, 1998, p. 72 n. 3).

These six exceptions have made the Fourth Amendment exclusionary rule a mockery of the original version of the rule established in the early twentieth century. It may be true that, as Justice Kennedy insisted in the recent decision of *Hudson v. Michigan* (2006), 'the continued operation of the exclusionary rule, as settled and defined by our precedents, is not in doubt' (p. 602). But the version of the rule that exists today is a far cry from the rule after *Silverthorne*, and at least five justices appear willing to increase that distance further (*Herring v. United States*, 2009).

Nonetheless, the American exclusionary rule still has teeth. Evidence that is the immediate result of an unconstitutional search or seizure of the defendant's person, house, papers or effects is usually inadmissible in the prosecution's case-in-chief unless obtained pursuant to a warrant, and even then is excluded if bad faith in procuring the warrant can be shown. When the defense can make a colorable argument that these circumstances exist, prosecutors are more likely to dismiss charges or make generous plea offers. Moreover, a number of state courts disagree with the Supreme Court's approach to exclusion and, based on their own constitutions, have adopted a more expansive rule (Clancy, 2013: 383–388).

Also important to note is the fact that, despite the reduction in its scope over the decades since *Mapp*, the American exclusionary rule has a comparatively significant effect because of the breadth of substantive Fourth Amendment law. In the United States, police act unconstitutionally if they enter a house without a warrant unless truly exigent circumstances or voluntary consent exist (*Payton v. New York*, 1980). They also violate the Fourth Amendment if, without individualized suspicion, they search a car (even when the occupants have just been arrested), detain an unwilling person longer than a few moments, or move a stereo set a few inches (*Arizona v. Gant*, 2009; *Florida v. Bostick*, 1991; *Arizona v. Hicks*, 1987). In many countries, these actions would not be deemed illegal.[4] As one study of American law indicated, most search and seizure violations are relatively technical (Gould and Mastrofski, 2004). It is the *combination* of the exclusionary remedy and significant restrictions on police search and seizure powers that, in the past half-century, has made the United States the country most likely to suppress probative evidence because of police investigative misconduct.

2. EXCLUSION IN OTHER COUNTRIES

While other countries resort to exclusion of illegally seized evidence more sparingly than the United States, the clear trend in some European, Latin American, Middle Eastern and Asian countries is toward greater use of this sanction. In contrast to the United States, in none of these countries is deterrence viewed as the primary goal of the rule. In these other nations the exclusion decision instead focuses either on the need to ensure the integrity of the criminal justice system or to vindicate important individual interests. There are a number of variations on these two themes, and in some countries it is difficult to decipher which approach is dominant, but the systemic integrity and vindication of rights models are sufficiently distinct from each other and from the deterrence model to provide meaningful categorizations.[5]

The following description of the law in other countries is both brief and tentative. It is brief because of space limitations and the number of countries discussed. It is tentative because of the difficulty of accessing the relevant sources, particularly those from non-English-speaking countries.

2.1 The Systemic Integrity Model

A number of countries reserve exclusion for significant violations of important rights in cases where dismissal of charges will not significantly undermine the state's interest in convicting those who have committed serious crimes. An example of this approach is found in Canada, where the exclusion principle is embedded in the Constitution:

> Where ... a court finds that evidence was obtained in a manner that infringed or denied any of the rights or freedoms guaranteed by this Charter, the evidence shall be excluded if it is established that, having regard to all the circumstances, the admission of it in the proceedings would bring the administration of justice into disrepute. (Canadian Charter of Rights and Freedoms, 1982, § 24(2))

As this language has been applied to illegal searches and seizures, Canadian courts have looked to the seriousness of the violation, the impact of the illegal action on the rights of the accused, and the societal interest in the adjudication of the case (*R. v. Grant*, 2009; Pizzi, 2011: 720–721). Unlike exclusion in the United States, deterrence of the police is not the primary goal; rather individual and state interests are balanced against one another.

Several other countries adopt a version of this multi-factor balancing analysis. In the United Kingdom, the relevant statute provides that the court may exclude evidence if 'the admission of the evidence would have such an adverse effect on the fairness of the proceedings that the court ought not to admit it', after considering: (1) the legality of the police action; (2) the seriousness of the offense; (3) the extent to which investigators acted in good or bad faith; (4) the type of evidence and its potential reliability; (5) the existence of other evidence; (6) the opportunity to challenge the evidence at trial; (7) the type of impropriety involved; and (8) the type of right or protection infringed (Police and Criminal Evidence Act, 1984, § 78; Ormerod, 2003). Along the same lines, in New Zealand the exclusion decision is based on the weighing of six factors: (1) the nature of the right and the nature of the breach; (2) whether the breach was done in bad faith, recklessly, negligently or due to a genuine misunderstanding of the law; (3) whether other investigatory techniques were available to the police but had not been used; (4) the reliability, cogency and probative value of the evidence at stake; (5) the seriousness of the crime; and (6) the importance and centrality of the evidence to the government's case (*R. v. Shaheed*, 2002).

The German version of the balancing test depends on the grievousness of the violation, the importance of the individual interest involved, the relevance of the evidence, and the seriousness of the offense (Weigend, 2007: 251–252; see also Gless, 2013: 121–126). Similarly, in the Netherlands, exclusion depends on the interests served by the infringed rule, the seriousness and intentionality of the violation, the effect of the violation on the accused, and the seriousness of the suspected criminal offense (Gruber et al., 2012). In an apparently explicit nod to the Canadian formulation, South African courts require exclusion if admission of the evidence would be 'detrimental to the administration of justice' (Schwikkard and van der Merwe, 2007). Israel, Scotland, Belgium, Ireland, Taiwan and Australia all also appear to have adopted the systemic integrity approach to exclusion (Beernaert and Traest, 2013: 165, 170; Bradley, 2001: 380; Duff, 2004: 153; Kitai-Sangero, 2007; Lewis, 2011: 649).

In most of these countries exclusion of evidence obtained through an illegal search and/or seizure is an unusual event. Take first what is known about the operation of the rule in countries outside of Europe. In South Africa and Israel, courts have made a distinction between real evidence and incriminating statements. Echoing the U.S. Supreme Court's opinion in *Boyd* interpreting the Fifth Amendment, the courts in these countries reason that since the former type of evidence 'pre-exists' the illegality (in contrast to confessions, which are created by the government), illegality connected with its seizure rarely rises to the level needed to mandate exclusion (Kitai-Sangero, 2007: 280; Schwikkard and van der Merwe, 2007: 488). In Australia, suppression is rare because '[o]rdinarily ... any unfairness to the particular accused will be of no more than peripheral importance' in deciding whether to exclude (*Ridgeway v. The Queen*, 1995). In Taiwan, the rule is still a 'work in progress' (Lewis, 2011: 650).

The story is not much different in Europe. In England and Scotland, the illegality must be particularly egregious to warrant suppression, especially if the crime is a felony (Ma, 2012: 314; Stark and Leverick, 2013: 80–81; Zander, 1990: 202–205);[6] in England, even illegal electronic eavesdropping does not require exclusion when the crime is serious (Feldman, 2007: 163). In Belgium, evidence obtained through illegal searches and seizures is almost always admitted (Beernaert and Traest, 2013: 171, 179). In the Netherlands, significant and bad faith infringements of privacy may result in exclusion, but generally a court will not dismiss a case when the police 'merely' violate the right to privacy, even when the violation involves invasive surveillance; furthermore, in lieu of exclusion, Dutch courts have the authority to reduce the sentence, an option they are more likely to take (Gruber et al., 2012: 224, 225).

Exclusion in Germany might be somewhat more frequent, at least when the police action is considered to be very intrusive. In one famous case, for instance, the contents of a diary were deemed inadmissible even though the diary was *legally* seized, because the interest in protecting intimate thoughts was 'more weighty' than prosecution of the relatively minor nature of the crime involved (*BGHSt*, 1964, cited in Thaman, 2008). However, the German Supreme Court's decision in that case also stated that exclusion would not have occurred had the criminal prosecution involved 'a serious attack on life' or 'other serious attacks on the legal order'; in these situations, 'the protection of the private life-sphere must give way' (p. 113). The German courts also commonly refuse to exclude evidence seized without a warrant if the police have justification for the search, on the ground that a warrant would have been issued had the police conducting the search sought one; thus, for purposes of inevitable discovery analysis, which American courts have sometimes called hypothetical independent source analysis (*Nix v. Williams*, 1984), the hypothetical source in Germany need not be 'independent' of the illegal source (Gless, 2013: 125; Thaman, 2011: 725).

Finally, as a general matter, in none of these European countries is tangible 'indirect' or 'derivative' evidence excluded. In other words, when the fruit of a poisonous tree is contraband or fruits of crime, it is admissible (Gruber et al., 2012: 224–225; Thaman, 2008). The European Court of Human Rights, which has been an aggressive protector of human rights in a number of other areas, has acquiesced in, if not affirmatively supported, these relatively weak exclusionary rules in European countries by holding that the European Convention of Human rights does not require suppression of evidence obtained through an illegal search and seizure (*Khan v. United Kingdom*, 2001).

To date, the major exceptions to this resistance to exclusion in countries that adopt the systemic integrity model of exclusion are Canada and Ireland. Initially, the Supreme Court of Canada seemed content to reserve exclusion for cases where the police used the suspect as a means of obtaining evidence (as in interrogations) and where police acted in bad faith to obtain evidence of minor crimes not crucial to the state's case (Roach, 2007: 70–73). In recent years, however, especially after the Court's decision in *R. v. Grant* (2009) refocused exclusion analysis *solely* on systemic integrity (rather than also looking at whether the police 'used' the suspect), Canadian courts have routinely excluded drugs even when they are essential for conviction (Madden, 2011: 244, 245). Furthermore, Canadian courts are now willing to exclude not only in cases of bad faith but also in cases involving mere negligence, at least in theory (*Grant*, 2009, para. 75). One survey of 2010 case law in Canada found that the exclusion rate at the trial court level is close to 70 percent for cases in which real evidence is obtained illegally and close to 65 percent even when a serious crime is involved (Madden, 2011: 243).

The same study found, however, that the exclusion rate at the appellate level is below 35 percent (Madden, 2011: 248).[7] Moreover, of course, the comparable rate in the United States at both the trial and appellate levels is much closer to 100 percent (discounting for those few cases where the police rely in good faith on a warrant or the inevitable discovery argument succeeds). Comments about the Canadian exclusionary rule made in 2007 are still apposite: 'exclusion of unconstitutionally obtained evidence is far from automatic, and will generally only occur in response to a very serious violation and after [consideration of] the adverse consequences to the reputation of the administration of justice of excluding the evidence' (Roach, 2007: 73).

The exclusionary rule saga in Ireland is somewhat different. For a time, Irish courts focused on whether the violation was deliberate (*People v. O'Brien*, 1964). In 1990, the Irish Supreme Court appeared to expand the exclusionary rule considerably, stating that

> evidence obtained by invasion of the constitutional personal rights of a citizen must be excluded unless a court is satisfied that the act constituting the breach of constitutional rights was committed unintentionally or accidentally, or is satisfied that there are extraordinary excusing circumstances which justify the admission of the evidence in its (the court's) discretion. (*People v. Kenny*, 1990, p. 134)

Twenty years later, however, the Court held that any evidence that is derivative of an illegal search or seizure is nonetheless admissible if it is obtained or discovered in conformity with the law; thus, for instance, an uncoerced confession, or a witness or tangible evidence discovered under proper procedures is admissible even if the result of an illegal arrest (*Director of Public Prosecutions v. Cash*, 2010, paras 41–42).

2.2 The Rights Vindication Model

The main competing approach to the deterrence model found in the United States and the systemic integrity model found in many other countries is a regime that requires exclusion if police infringe a fundamental or substantial right. In theory, in this type of regime exclusion's effect on police behavior is a secondary consideration and the good faith of the police and the nature of the offense are irrelevant. In practice, however, most countries that adopt this model routinely exclude only statements obtained through coercive practices. With a few exceptions, they rarely suppress evidence obtained through an illegal search and seizure.

Most countries that purport to follow the rights vindication model have a strong inquisitorial tradition or have experienced totalitarian governments in the recent past. The criminal code of Colombia provides for exclusion of '[a]ll evidence obtained in violation of fundamental guarantees', including derivative evidence (Thaman, 2011: 705). Similarly, the criminal code of Spain provides that 'evidence obtained, directly or indirectly in violation of fundamental rights and liberties is without effect' (Thaman, 2011: 705). Other countries appear to mandate exclusion not only of evidence obtained in violation of constitutional or fundamental guarantees but also when lesser prohibitions are infringed. For instance, the Italian code states that evidence is not 'usable' if 'acquired in violation of prohibitions established by law' (Thaman, 2011: 704). Both the Brazilian and Turkish constitutions state that evidence obtained by 'illegal means' is inadmissible (Thaman, 2011: 704). The constitution of Russia and many of the former Soviet republics likewise require exclusion of any evidence 'gathered in violation of federal law' (Thaman, 2011: 704; see also Newcombe, 2007). Serbia and Slovenia are even more explicit, banning the use both of evidence obtained in violation of the Constitution and ratified treaties and of evidence obtained in violation of the codes, as well as of evidence derived from those violations (Thaman, 2011: 704–705).

While these types of provisions imply that exclusion should be a frequent occurrence, in practice that does not appear to be the case. Countries undermine the rule-as-vindication in various ways. In 1993, the Supreme Court of Spain stated that '[o]ur case law has established an absolute prohibition of the use of evidence obtained in violation of fundamental rights' (Decision No. 49 of March 26, 1996, translated in Thaman, 2008: 116). But five years later the Court appeared to adopt the systemic integrity model, or at least a good faith exception (Thaman, 2011: 722). Italian courts, like the courts of South Africa and Israel, reason that even if the search for fruits, instrumentalities and contraband is not based on probable cause, their *seizure* is legal (Thaman, 2011: 735). In Russia, when an acquittal results from exclusion of evidence the prosecutor is able to obtain reversal on the unusual ground that the prosecutor's right to equality of arms was violated (Thaman, 2007: 409–410).

A variant of the fundamental rights model is the nullity principle, the idea that certain types of illegal acts are legally non-cognizable, and thus any evidence thereby acquired is inadmissible. Nullity provisions are not always of constitutional stature, but their violation is, at the least, prohibited by statute, and is considered a serious matter. Many of the countries discussed above recognize nullities, but have added an American-style exclusionary rule to the nullity scheme (Thaman, 2011: 726).[8] Other countries appear to rely entirely on the nullity concept when excluding evidence. The criminal code of Argentina declares, for instance, that 'the nullity of an act, once it has been declared, shall result in the nullity of all other acts deriving therefrom', language which some courts have held is compelled by the country's constitution (Carrió and Garro, 2007: 21). The nullity principle also governs in France, Egypt, Mexico and Greece. In France, exclusion – or sometimes dismissal of the entire case – automatically occurs if there is 'textual nullity' or a violation of a 'substantial' procedural rule (Frase, 2007: 212–213). In Egypt, courts have 'firmly established exclusion as a standard consequence of a finding of nullity', which occurs when a fundamental right is violated (Reza, 2007: 123). Mexico also declares certain illegal acts connected with searches and seizures null and void (Sarré and Perlin, 2007: 360). Greece recognizes both nullities and an independent exclusionary rule; the twist here is that illegal searches are criminal acts, which trigger exclusion under a statute that provides that evidence obtained through criminal acts may not be used in evidence (Triantafyllou, 2013: 267, 277).

In most of the countries that adopt the fundamental rights-nullity model, however, only evidence discovered as a direct result of the violation is excluded. Despite the constitutional language quoted above, for instance, courts in Spain, Argentina and Turkey admit evidence that inevitably would have been discovered through legal means (Carrió and Garro, 2007: 25; Sözüer and Sevdiren, 2013: 293, 313). France at least occasionally admits derivative evidence, as do Egypt and Mexico (Frase,

2007: 213; Reza, 2007: 123), while in Greece the courts have yet to directly address the issue (Triantafyllou, 2013: 279). Apparently, the reasoning is that rights are sufficiently vindicated if direct evidence from their violation is suppressed.

Under the fundamental rights model much depends, of course, on which rights are considered fundamental. In Mexico, nullities are virtually never declared, even in cases involving illegal arrests and searches of homes (Sarré and Perlin, 2007: 362). In Italy, only torture and illegal wiretapping appear to be considered a violation of fundamental rights (Van Cleave, 2007: 322), although of course evidence might be excluded on hearsay or other grounds. In Greece, the courts are inconsistent, with one Supreme Court case holding that even violation of wiretap rules does not require exclusion (Triantafyllou, 2013: 281). In France, nullities tend to be considered technical violations or are recognized only when the defendant can show that an interest other than avoiding state acquisition of incriminating evidence was harmed (Frase, 2007: 212–213, n. 83; see also Ma, 2012: 316, describing the defendant's burden in these cases as 'daunting'). In Spain, Argentina and Egypt, the definition of fundamental rights appears to be broader, and certainly includes unauthorized, non-exigent searches of homes. But even in these latter three countries the scope of particular rights is narrower than in the United States. For instance, in the first two countries warrants may be based on a lesser standard than probable cause and are not likely to be invalidated on what American courts would call particularity grounds, and in Egypt warrants are usually issued by prosecutors (Carrió and Garro, 2007: 13; Reza, 2007: 120; Thaman, 2008: 58). In contrast, Serbian courts tend to take a strong stand toward exclusion, although the fact that court decisions in that country lack significant precedential effect makes assessment of exclusion's prevalence difficult (Brkić, 2013: 324–325, 333).

3.   AN ANALYSIS OF THE FACTORS THAT MIGHT BE RELEVANT TO THE EXCLUSION DECISION

The foregoing survey of the law governing exclusion in search and seizure cases suggests several factors that might be considered in deciding whether exclusion should occur. These include: (1) its deterrent effect; (2) the impact of exclusion or admission on the reputation of the criminal justice system; (3) the seriousness of the target offense and the importance of the seized evidence to its successful prosecution; (4) the investigators' awareness of potential illegality and of alternative methods of obtaining the evidence; and (5) the nature of the right that has been violated. Each of these factors raises difficult analytical issues.

3.1 Deterrence

Deterrence of police misconduct is the sole rationale for exclusion in the United States. In other countries, deterrence is not the primary goal but is almost certainly a secondary reason for exclusion. A key empirical question, then, is how effective exclusion is at preventing illegal searches and seizures.

Presumably the rule does have a significant impact on the police in important cases involving prolonged investigations, especially where prosecutors are monitoring their actions. But in the average, quickly developing case, research suggests that the police are not particularly concerned about exclusion (Van Duizend et al., 1985: 17). Sociological studies in the United States indicate that police are much more interested in making an arrest and removing drugs and weapons from the streets than in ensuring conviction occurs, which they perceive as the prosecutor's job, not theirs; the incentive structure of the police is shaped largely by institutional pressures, which tend to focus on arrest quotas, not convictions. Police also know that suppression of evidence usually depends on their testimony, which can be slanted, and that their colleagues will usually back up their story (Slobogin, 1996: 1041–1048). Moreover, because exclusion, on those rare occasions when it does occur, is often announced well after the search or seizure or the suppression hearing, it may not provide much of a lesson to the miscreant officer (Hyman, 1979: 42).[9]

Other research confirms that the impact of these institutional arrangements is often stronger than the fear of exclusion. One survey found that, by their own admission, police in two modest-sized American police departments collectively committed acts they knew or suspected were violations of the Fourth Amendment approximately 600 times a month (Akers and Lanza-Kaduce, 1986: 4; Gould and Mastrofski, 2004: 331). Another survey of American police found that they preferred exclusion over any other response to illegality, including more training – a result that suggests that the exclusion remedy is less burdensome to police than attending classes (Perrin et al., 1999: 733). And the oft-repeated surmise that the rule at least provides an incentive for prosecutors to pressure police departments to provide better training on search and seizure issues is belied by several studies that show American police have at most a rudimentary understanding of the Fourth Amendment (Heffernan and Lovely, 1991: 333; Hyman, 1979: 47; Perrin et al., 1999: 727).

If the exclusionary rule were a good deterrent in the United States, one would expect that searches of cars, which require probable cause, would be successful about 50 percent of the time, and that stop and frisks, which require the lesser justification of reasonable suspicion, would produce evidence of crime somewhere around 30 percent of the time (Dripps, 2011: 772). In fact, the data from several American jurisdictions indicates that the 'hit rates' for car searches are between 10 and 40 percent and the hit rates for stops are well below 10 percent (Ridgeway, 2007: 43). The success rate for searches of houses in non-exigent circumstances appears to be much higher than 50 percent, but that could well be because police are required to get warrants for those types of searches (Benner and Samarkos, 2000: 249–250).

Much more could be said about the deterrent effect of the rule. But for present purposes it suffices to emphasize that exclusion is probably at best a weak deterrent in many investigative situations.

3.2 The Legitimacy of the Criminal Justice System

A second rationale for the exclusionary rule, at one time paramount in the United States and still important in many other countries, is the need to protect the integrity of the criminal justice system. As conceptualized and implemented in early American cases, this rationale requires exclusion of *all* illegally seized evidence, whether obtained in good faith or bad and regardless of the type of offense or the importance of the state's interest, on the ground that otherwise the courts are accomplices to the police misconduct. As Justice Holmes put it, courts and prosecutors should not be involved in the 'dirty business' of using illegally seized evidence (*Olmstead v. United States*, 1928, p. 470).

The primary problem with this rationale, of course, is that the legitimacy and reputation of the criminal justice system can also be sullied by a failure to convict clearly guilty people, which is often the result of exclusion. Some empirical evidence suggests that a failure to exclude illegally seized evidence can taint public perceptions of the courts (Bilz, 2012: 149; Lock, 1999: 45). But a significant amount of empirical evidence also indicates that a failure to convict the guilty can undermine faith in the criminal justice system, and perhaps even compromise compliance with it (Bilz, 2012: 166; Nadler, 2005: 1424).

The reputational rationale taken to extremes requires a choice between maintaining absolute procedural integrity (a goal that requires exclusion) and upholding the integrity of the substantive criminal law (in which case exclusion is not warranted). As the countries that have adopted the systemic integrity approach recognize, neither extreme is satisfactory.

Courts in these countries have decided that the choice as to whether procedural or substantive integrity is favored in a given case depends on additional factors, such as the seriousness of the state's interest, the culpability of the police, and the importance of the individual interest affected.

3.3   The Importance of the Government's Interest

If the charged crime is serious and the illegally seized evidence is crucial for conviction, exclusion rarely occurs in countries that follow the systemic integrity model. The courts in these countries reason that the administration of justice would be called into serious disrepute if a murderer, rapist or armed robber were allowed to walk free because 'the constable has blundered' (*People v. Defore*, 1926, p. 587). While this reasoning makes some sense, it also raises serious practical and theoretical problems.

First, if the seriousness of the suspected crime is to trump other factors, what level of crime is the tipping point?[10] One can imagine various thresholds, ranging from the relatively pro-prosecution misdemeanor-felony divide to the much more pro-exclusion distinction between non-violent and violent crimes. If instead, other factors can trump even serious crimes under the right circumstances, how does the balancing analysis work? The typical illegal search is likely to result in seizure of drugs or weapons, and the typical crime associated with these seizures will be drug distribution, or possession of drugs or weapons. These latter crimes are usually only mid-level felonies. Should exclusion in these cases therefore be common or, at the least, required whenever police *know* the search is illegal or whenever the illegality results in *particularly* significant infringement? Or might even these crimes be too important to countenance exclusion, especially in light of the fact that suppression of the drugs or weapons in such cases would almost certainly end the prosecution?

This latter question raises another: to what extent should the importance of the evidence to the prosecution's case affect the analysis? When this factor is given significant weight, a Catch-22 arises. If the evidence is crucial it is admitted, but if it is not crucial exclusion does not provide much benefit to the defendant, who thus may even forego an exclusion motion. In any event, this factor, if taken seriously, suggests that clean judicial hands are a concern only when they cost the system nothing.

Even assuming these conundra are resolved, an argument can be made that application of the exclusionary rule should not depend on the crime or the importance of the evidence. Otherwise, the message police hear might be that investigation of serious crime is not subject to significant regulation (Kamisar, 1987: 17). For this reason, Canadian courts have de-emphasized this factor (*R. v. Harrison*, 2009, para. 40). Although one can explain this de-emphasis as a matter of deterrence, it can also be justified on the ground that the administration of justice is called into question if citizens' remedies vary depending on the crime involved. At the least, this factor should probably be tempered by other factors such as the culpability of the police and the nature of the violation.

3.4 Culpability of the Police

The U.S. Supreme Court has slowly been moving toward the position that only intentional or reckless illegalities should lead to exclusion (*Herring v. United States*, 2009). In contrast, as noted earlier, the Supreme Courts of Canada and Ireland have moved in the opposite direction, albeit as part of a balancing analysis. On the one hand, a mistaken officer may not be deterrable and usually will not be acting egregiously. On the other hand, too much emphasis on this factor could mean that the relevant search and seizure law devolves into those rules the typical officer thinks exist, not the rules that the courts or statutes provide. If this factor is to play any role in exclusionary rule analysis, it should be based on what a reasonably well trained officer would know at the time of the search and seizure. When this definition is met, admission of the evidence could be said to be consistent with both a deterrent rationale –a reasonably well trained officer who does not realize he is committing an illegality is arguably undeterrable – and with the systemic integrity rationale, at least in the sense that police mistakes are easier to ignore if they are understandable.

A related factor that might be considered part of the culpability analysis is whether and to what extent police could have obtained the evidence through independent, legal means. Many countries endorse the rule that evidence that was discovered illegally nonetheless is admissible if it inevitably would have been discovered legally. But one could also make the argument that, given the existence of the legal option, the police are even more culpable for acting illegally, at least if they should have known of the legal option.[11] Ultimately, this factor is simply one aspect of what a reasonably well trained officer would have known at the time of the search.

In theory, the importance of the culpability factor could also vary depending upon the egregiousness of the violation. If the police illegality involves intrusion into a particularly private enclave, for example, per-haps even a 'reasonable' violation of a rule should result in exclusion, as

German law contemplates when the crime is not serious. This notion leads to the final factor – the nature of the individual interest infringed by the illegal search and seizure.

3.5   The Nature of the Individual Interest Infringed

In many countries, this issue is supposedly the sole inquiry in determining whether exclusion should occur. In those countries that take the fundamental right approach, deterrence, protecting the reputation of the system, sustaining important government interests, and sanctioning culpable police conduct are, in theory, irrelevant considerations, although realization of these goals might be a by-product of the exclusion decision. The key question, as noted earlier, is how courts should go about gauging the importance of this interest.

Perhaps it is enough to say, as Spanish courts do, that the right is ensconced in the Constitution, or, as French courts do, that violation would be a 'textual nullity'. But the indeterminacy of law means these formalistic statements are not very satisfying and are often not very helpful. For instance, a warrantless search of a house might normally trench on fundamental rights in non-exigent circumstances. But how does one define exigent circumstances (compare *Dorman v. United States*, 1970, with *Minnesota v. Olson*, 1990, p. 100)? And if the search is not of the bedroom or living room but of the curtilage, the garage or the basement, has a fundamental right been infringed (*Nikolas v. City of Omaha*, 2010)?

A separate concern relates to the commensurability of exclusion with certain types of illegalities. A failure to knock and announce under appropriate circumstances might be a violation of a fundamental right, but does that mean that exclusion is the correct remedy? Perhaps the U.S. Supreme Court is on to something when it suggests that exclusion does not seem to fit the 'crime' in such a case; rather the property damage and indignity that come from an abrupt police entry might best be handled through compensation, especially if, as could often be the case, no evidence is found.

The alternative to an approach that excludes evidence obtained as a result of *all* constitutional illegalities requires establishing a hierarchy of constitutional rights. But this too is a daunting task. Consider Justice Frankfurter's attempt to develop such a hierarchy in the years before *Mapp* required exclusion in all cases of illegal searches and seizures. In the *Rochin* case (1954), mentioned earlier, Justice Frankfurter wrote the majority opinion finding that evidence obtained via a stomach pump must be excluded because the technique shocked the conscience. Two years later, in a case involving the installation of a microphone in the defendant's home, he arrived at the same conclusion, albeit this time in dissent (*Irvine v. California*, 1954, pp. 145–146). In contrast, in a case in which the illegality consisted of police taking two day-books off the defendant's desk without probable cause, Justice Frankfurter wrote for the majority that exclusion was not required, even though he admitted that the right violated was 'basic to a free society' (*Wolf v. Colorado*, 1949, p. 27). As Professor Allen (1961) stated, '[t]o label a right as "basic to a free society" is to say about as much as one can say of a constitutional protection' (p. 252). Thus, Professor Allen continued drily, Frankfurter's position 'seems almost to involve a comparison of super-latives, which, whatever may be said for its logic, presents some difficulties of grammar' (p. 252).

4. CONCLUSION: SYSTEMIC INTEGRITY SHOULD BE THE PRIMARY GOAL

Whether the deterrence, systemic integrity, or fundamental rights model is adopted, determining when exclusion should occur in connection with an illegal search and seizure is not an easy chore. This fact, combined with the fact that dismissal of clearly worthy charges can be the result of the rule, suggests that alternatives to exclusion should at least be considered. These alternatives range from various types of damages actions and administrative penalties to criminal prosecutions of the miscreant officers and, as occurs in the Netherlands, mitigation of the offender's sentence.

The U.S. Supreme Court declared in 1961 that alternatives to the rule were 'worthless and futile', and many American commentators continue to agree with that assessment.[12] In contrast, I have argued that good alternatives are available, and have proposed a liquidated damages remedy that would impose non-indemnified personal liability on police who act in bad faith and on the police department when the police in the field make a mistake that is reasonable (Slobogin, 1999: 442). If such an alternative existed, I contended that violations would be deterred, sys-temic integrity would be maintained and fundamental rights would be vindicated. Police fearful of individual liability would avoid bad faith actions, and departments wanting to avoid liability for negligent actions would improve training programs. Procedural integrity would be main-tained because the 'dirty business' perpetrated by the police would be sanctioned, not condoned, by the courts, and substantive integrity would be protected because the guilty would be denied the windfall of exclusion. Finally, fundamental rights would be vindicated because violation of them would be directly condemned (via the damages action).

On the assumption, however, that legislatures will not enact this proposal or any other effective alternative remedy, judicial exclusion may be the only method of ensuring some deterrence and providing some measure of systemic integrity and rights vindication. The extent to which exclusion should occur will depend on which rationale or combination thereof is sought to be achieved.

If deterrence is the main goal, the rule should probably be mandatory except in those situations where a reasonably well trained officer would be unaware of a substantial risk that search and seizure rules were violated. As noted above, any deterrent effect from exclusion is likely to be minimal in the latter situation, but in all other situations the threat of exclusion could have some impact, at least in theory. In practice, this approach would recognize narrow versions of the U.S. Supreme Court's secondary process, good faith and attenuation exceptions to exclusion. However, that Court's standing, inevitable discovery, and non-commensurability exceptions would not be permitted.

If instead the goal is assuring vindication of fundamental rights, none of these exceptions would be permissible. The only issue would be whether the right violated was 'fundamental' or 'substantial' rather than run-of-the-mill. As indicated earlier, this differentiation can be very difficult, and in practice is likely to result in a fairly narrow definition of what is fundamental. Even academic advocates of this model have trouble subscribing to a pristine version of it (Ashworth, 1977: 725, 729).

Finally, if the goal is systemic integrity, courts would have to balance the nature of the right violated against a number of factors, which could include the extent to which the reputation of the criminal justice system would be enhanced or undermined by exclusion, the seriousness of the offense, the ability to convict the defendant without the evidence, and the culpability of the police. Intentional infringements of the most important rights would likely lead to exclusion in all but the most serious criminal cases, while non-negligent violations of technical rules would not, except perhaps in the most minor criminal cases. Cases in between these extremes would be more difficult to resolve. This model is the least definitive, and the most likely to produce disparate results.

Nonetheless, the systemic integrity model is probably the best approach to exclusion. That model is focused on optimizing the legitimacy of the criminal justice system by fostering a direct inquiry into both the procedural and substantive implications of exclusion. Under this model, exclusion could be reserved for cases involving egregious police misconduct that is incommensurate with the strength of the government's interests.[13] More specifically, this model might mandate that in cases involving lesser crimes, exclusion should occur only when police engage in a deliberate or grossly negligent infringement of the core constitutional guarantees accorded houses and persons, which might include situations in which, under United States law, a warrant or probable-cause-plus-exigency is required (for example, situations involving searches of homes and electronic surveillance.)[14] For more serious crimes (say, those with a maximum penalty of ten years or more) the police conduct would have to be particularly outrageous for exclusion to occur.

The fear that this regime will signal to police that it is open season on people suspected of major crime should be taken seriously. But four considerations should mitigate this concern. First, precisely because the systemic integrity approach focuses on the totality of the circumstances, police cannot be sure when exclusion will occur, which could actually enhance deterrence (Kahan, 1997: 137–141); one of the drawbacks of the relatively bright-line American rule is that police have learned to work around it (see, for example, *Payner v. United States*, 1980; *Murray v. United States*, 1989; *Immigration and Naturalization Service v. Lopez-Mendoza*, 1984). Second, if a court finds that police have, in fact, attempted to take advantage of the crime-seriousness factor, that in itself would suggest egregious misconduct, as would repetition of the same type of violation. Third, for reasons expressed earlier, exclusion should not depend on whether the illegally seized evidence is 'crucial' to the government's case, which should remove the incentive for police to violate a suspect's rights in serious cases simply because the evidence sought is important. Fourth, while it was assumed above that other remedies are 'futile', in fact most countries have parallel sanctions (Frase, 2007: 213–214; Reza, 2007: 123–124). Those options plus the fact that, even when exclusion does not occur, courts should still be required to pronounce that police have violated the law, can act as a further deterrent in serious cases.[15]

An analogy to the systemic integrity approach advocated here can be found in entrapment doctrine as it has developed in the United States. The entrapment defense is generally unavailable even when the government induced the defendant's crime, so long as the defendant was already predisposed to commit it (*United States v. Russell*, 1973). However, if the court considers the government's inducement 'outrageous' in relation to the government's objectives, dismissal of charges might be warranted under the due process clause even where the defendant was predisposed to engage in criminal conduct (*United States v. Russell*, 1973, pp. 431–432; *Hampton v. United States*, 1976; *Sorrells v. United States*, 1932).

Likewise, under a systemic integrity approach, dismissal of charges for an illegal search and seizure will occur only when the illegality is outrageous.

In contrast to the systemic integrity model, the deterrence model requires exclusion for every violation that is considered unreasonable, even when the violation is not significant and a serious and dangerous criminal might be freed, while the vindication of fundamental rights model not only ignores these systemic costs but also requires exclusion even if the violation is one a reasonable officer would have committed. Exclusion in these situations not only undermines public respect for the system, but is also deeply disproportionate to the harm caused by illegal searches and seizures. Imagine, for instance, that no evidence is found during an illegal search, meaning that the only recourse for the victim is a civil action. Presumably the plaintiff's compensation would be based on the extent of the privacy invasion, not on the prison time he or she would have received had evidence of crime been found. Yet exclusion dictates the equivalent of the latter relief.

Whatever model of exclusion is chosen, the deterrence, vindication and integrity goals should also be kept in mind when constructing the substantive law of search and seizure. This law should neither be too slack (as is apparently the case in countries like France and Mexico) or too fine-tuned and nuanced (as is arguably the case in the United States). Both extremes can detract from deterrence, by either failing to regulate the police or by creating disdain among police who feel over-regulated (cf. Orfield, 1987: 1044–1045). These extremes can also undermine respect for the legal system and demean the concept of rights, either by giving the government too much leeway or by handcuffing reasonable investigatory practices. The effects of the exclusionary rule cannot be analyzed without taking into account the types of violations it is meant to remedy.

NOTES

1. Parts of this section are taken from Slobogin (2013).
2. Although these statements came in dissents, the majority in these cases did not dispute them and they heavily influenced later cases.
3. As originally formulated, attenuation doctrine relied on much more than deterrence (see *Brown v. Illinois*, 1975). But its later manifestations are consistent with a deterrence rationale (see *United States v. Crews*, 1980).
4. For instance, in Germany, only a 'vague suspicion' is required to search a house and 'danger in delay' is defined broadly (Weigend, 2007: 249–250). In France warrants 'need not meet any degree of suspicion, or specify the parties or places to be searched, or things to be seized', and identity checks allowing detention for up to

four hours may take place 'regardless of the comportment of the person' or when any person is found within 20 kilometers of certain borders or in designated public areas (Frase, 2007: 208 (identity checks), 211 (warrants)).

5. Although I developed them independently, these categories are similar to those described in Duff (2004: 159) (describing the 'disciplinary', 'moral legitimacy', and 'vindicatory' models of exclusion), which in turn are taken from Ashworth (1977: 723).

6. Ma (2012), for instance, notes that English courts rarely exclude evidence in cases involving serious crimes, and Zander (1990) notes that most exclusions that do occur involve confessions.

7. The cited page indicates that the exclusion rate at the Supreme Court level is 33% and at the appellate court level 25%, which I assume means that the appellate courts refused to affirm a number of cases in which lower courts excluded illegally seized evidence.

8. In Spain and Italy, for instance, nullities refer to technical, as opposed to fundamental-rights violations, and thus many do not require exclusion (Thaman, 2011: 726).

9. For plea-bargained cases, which comprise the bulk of adjudications, the lines of communication are even worse (Barnett, 1983: 956 n. 46).

10. For a tripartite division of crime seriousness (grave, serious and minor), see Bellin (2011).

11. This argument has been successful in Canada (Roach and Friedland, 1996: 346) (stating that in Canada 'A conclusion that the police could have obtained the evidence through constitutional means, far from precluding exclusion ... actually makes exclusion more likely.').

12. For instance, in a recent seven-author symposium on the exclusionary rule, five of the authors argued or assumed that alternatives to the rule are ineffective, with several arguing that damages and administrative penalty schemes as currently constituted are toothless. See Symposium (2013: 341 et seq.).

13. At the same time, because systemic integrity, not rights vindication, is at stake, exclusion could be sought by *anyone*, not just those whose rights were violated.

14. In other work I have suggested that the exclusionary rule might also be apposite in potentially pretextual situations. See Slobogin (2010: 142). For instance, when police stop a person for a traffic offense or a pedestrian for loitering and 'inadvertently' find evidence of drug possession, the drugs might be excluded. One could base this approach on a deterrence rationale (if it reduced the motivation to engage in pretextual stops) or a rights vindication model (if one could prove pretext). Such a rule is probably best justified on systemic integrity grounds, however, because the target crime is trivial and the police behavior, although not always in bad faith, is often so. More importantly, it is often *perceived* to be carried out with a hidden, harassment-oriented agenda, thus undermining systemic legitimacy. See generally, Schulhofer, Tyler and Huq (2011: 349–356) (exploring the de-legitimizing impact of stops).

15. In the Netherlands, the Supreme Court regards acknowledgment of the violation as 'a form of redress in itself' (Gruber et al., 2012: 225 n. 69).

BIBLIOGRAPHY

Akers, Ron L. and Lonn Lanza-Kaduce. 1986. 'The Exclusionary Rule: Legal Doctrine and Social Research on Constitutional Norms', 2 *Sam Houston State University Criminal Justice Center Research Bulletin*, 1–6.

Allen, Francis A. 1961. 'The Exclusionary Rule in the American Law of Search and Seizure', 52 *Journal of Criminal Law & Criminology* 246.

Amos v. United States, 255 U.S. 313 (1921).

Arizona v. Evans, 514 U.S 1 (1995).

Arizona v. Gant, 556 U.S. 332 (2009).

Arizona v. Hicks, 480 U.S. 321 (1987).

Ashworth, Andrew. 1977. 'Excluding Evidence as Protecting Rights', 3 *Criminal Law Review* 723–735.

Barnett, Randy. 1983. 'Resolving the Dilemma of the Exclusionary Rule: An Application of Restitutive Principles of Justice', 32 *Emory Law Journal* 936.

Barron v. City of Baltimore, 32 U.S. 243 (1833).

Beernaert, Marie-Aude and Philip Traest. 2013. 'Belgium: From Categorical Nullities to a Judicially-Created Balancing Test', in Stephen C. Thaman, ed., *Exclusionary Rules in Comparative Law*. Dordrecht: Springer Science & Business Media.

Bellin, Jeffrey. 2011. 'Crime Severity Distinctions and the Fourth Amendment: Reassessing Reasonableness in a Changing World', 97 *Iowa Law Review* 1.

Benner, Laurence A. and Charles T. Samarkos. 2000. 'Searching for Narcotics in San Diego: Preliminary Findings from the San Diego Search Warrant Project', 36 *California Western Law Review* 221.

Bilz, Kenworthey. 2012. 'Dirty Hands or Deterrence? An Experimental Examination of the Exclusionary Rule', 9 *Journal of Empirical Legal Studies* 149–171.

Boyd v. United States, 116 U.S. 616 (1886).

Bradley, Craig. 2001. '*Mapp* Goes Abroad', 52 *Case Western Reserve Law Review* 375.

Brkić, Snežana. 2013. 'Serbia: Courts Struggle with a New Categorical Exclusionary Rule', in Craig Bradley, ed., *Criminal Procedure: A Worldwide Study*. Durham, NC: Carolina Academic Press.

Brown v. Illinois, 422 U.S. 590 (1975).

Canadian Charter of Rights and Freedoms, § 24(2) (1982).

Carrió, Alejandro D. and Alejandro M. Garro. 2007. 'Argentina', in Craig Bradley, ed., *Criminal Procedure: A Worldwide Study*. Durham, NC: Carolina Academic Press.

Clancy, Thomas. 2013. 'The Fourth Amendment's Exclusionary Rule as a Constitutional Right', 10 *Ohio State Journal of Criminal Law* 357.

Davis v. United States, 131 S. Ct. 2419 (2011).

Director of Public Prosecutions v. Cash [2010] 1 I.L.R.M. 389 (Ir.).

Dorman v. United States, 435 F.2d 385 (D.C. Cir. 1970).

Dorsey v. State, 761 A.2d 807 (Del. 2000).

Dripps, Donald A. 2011. 'The New Exclusionary Rule Debate: From "Still Preoccupied with 1985" to "Virtual Deterrence"', 37 *Fordham Urban Law Journal* 743.

Duff, Peter. 2004. 'Admissibility of Improperly Obtained Physical Evidence in the Scottish Criminal Trial: The Search for Principle', 8 *Edinburgh Law Review* 152–176.

Elkins v. United States, 364 U.S. 206 (1960).

Feldman, David J. 2007. 'England', in Craig Bradley, ed., *Criminal Procedure: A Worldwide Study*. Durham, NC: Carolina Academic Press.

Florida v. Bostick, 501 U.S. 429 (1991).

Frase, Richard. 2007. 'France', in Craig Bradley, ed., *Criminal Procedure: A Worldwide Study*. Durham, NC: Carolina Academic Press.

Gless, Sabine. 2013. 'Germany: Balancing Truth Against Protected Constitutional Interests', in Stephen C. Thaman, ed., *Exclusionary Rules in Comparative Law*. Dordrecht: Springer Science & Business Media.

Gould, Jon B. and Stephen D. Mastrofski. 2004. 'Suspect Searches: Assessing Police Behavior Under the U.S. Constitution', 3 *Criminology and Public Policy* 315–362.

Gouled v. United States, 255 U.S. 298 (1921).

Gruber, Aya, Vincente de Palacios and Piet Hein van Kempen. 2012. *Practical Global Criminal Procedure: United States, Argentina, and the Netherlands.* Durham, NC: Carolina Academic Press.

Hampton v. United States, 425 U.S. 484 (1976).

Heffernan, William C. and Lovely, Richard W. 1991. 'Evaluating the Fourth Amendment Exclusionary Rule: The Problem of Police Compliance with the Law', 24 *University of Michigan Journal of Law Reform* 311–370.

Herring v. United States, 555 U.S. 135 (2009).

Hudson v. Michigan, 547 U.S. 586 (2006).

Hyman, Eugene M. 1979. 'In Pursuit of a More Workable Exclusionary Rule: A Police Officer's Perspective', 10 *Pacific Law Journal* 33.

Illinois v. Krull, 480 U.S. 340 (1987).

Immigration and Naturalization Service v. Lopez-Mendoza, 468 U.S. 1032 (1984).

Irvine v. California, 347 U.S. 128 (1954).

Kahan, Dan M. 1997. 'Ignorance of Law Is an Excuse – But Only for the Virtuous', 96 *Michigan Law Review* 127.

Kamisar, Yale. 1987. '"Comparative Reprehensibility" and the Fourth Amendment Exclusionary Rule', 86 *Michigan Law Review* 1.

Khan v. United Kingdom, 31 Eur. Ct. H.R. 45 (2001).

Kitai-Sangero, Rinat. 2007. 'Israel', in Craig Bradley, ed., *Criminal Procedure: A Worldwide Study.* Durham, NC: Carolina Academic Press.

Lambert, John C. 2003. *Racial Profiling Data Analysis Study: Final Report for the San Antonio Police Department.* Chadds Ford, PA: Lambert Consulting.

Lewis, Margaret K. 2011. 'Controlling Abuse to Maintain Control: The Exclusionary Rule in China', 43 *New York University of International Law and Politics* 629.

Lock, Shmuel. 1999. *Crime, Public Opinion, and Civil Liberties: The Tolerant Public.* Westport, CT: Praeger Publishers.

Ma, Tue. 2012. 'The American Exclusionary Rule: Is There a Lesson to Learn from Others?' 22 *International Criminal Justice Review* 309.

Madden, Mike. 2011. 'Marshaling the Data: An Empirical Analysis of Canada's Section 24(2) Case Law in the Wake of *R. v. Grant*', 15 *Canadian Criminal Law Review* 229.

Mapp v. Ohio, 367 U.S. 643 (1961).

Massachusetts v. Sheppard, 468 U.S. 981 (1984).

Michigan v. DeFillippo, 443 U.S. 31 (1979).

Minnesota v. Olson, 495 U.S. 91 (1990).

Murray v. United States, 487 U.S. 433 (1989).

Nadler, Janice. 2005. 'Flouting the Law', 83 *Texas Law Review* 1399.

New York v. Harris, 495 U.S. 14 (1990).

Newcombe, Catherine. 2007. 'Russia', in Craig Bradley, ed., *Criminal Procedure: A Worldwide Study.* Durham, NC: Carolina Academic Press.

Nikolas v. City of Omaha, 605 F.3d 539 (8th Cir. 2010).

Nix v. Williams, 467 U.S. 431 (1984).

Oliver, Wesley. 2010. 'The Neglected History of Criminal Procedure, 1850–1940', 62 *Rutgers Law Review* 442.

Olmstead v. United States, 277 U.S. 438 (1928).

Orfield, Myron W. 1987. 'The Exclusionary Rule and Deterrence: An Empirical Study of Chicago Narcotics Officers', 54 *The University of Chicago Law Review* 1016–1069.

Ormerod, David. 2003. 'ECHR and the Exclusion of Evide–nce: Trial Remedies for Article 8 Breaches?' *Criminal Law Review* 61.

Payner v. United States, 447 U.S. 727 (1980).

Payton v. New York, 445 U.S. 573 (1980).

Pennsylvania v. Scott, 524 U.S. 357 (1998).

People v. Defore, 150 N.E. 585 (N.Y. 1926).

People v. Kenny [1990] 2 I.R. 110 (Ir.).
People v. O'Brien [1964] 1 I.R. 142 (Ir.).
Perrin, L. Timothy, Harry M. Caldwell, Carol A. Chase and Roland Fagan. 1999. 'If It's Broken, Fix It: Moving Beyond the Exclusionary Rule', 83 *Iowa Law Review* 669.
Pillay v. S 2004 (2) BCLR 158 (SCA) at para 97 (S. Afr.).
Pizzi, William T. 2011. 'The Need to Overrule *Mapp v. Ohio*', 82 *University of Colorado Law Review* 679.
Police and Criminal Evidence Act, 1984, c.60 § 78 (Eng.).
R. v. Grant [2009] 2 S.C.R. 353.
R. v. Harrison [2009] 2 S.C.R. 494.
R. v Shaheed [2002] 2 NZLR 377 (CA).
Rakas v. Illinois, 439 U.S. 128 (1978).
Reza, Sadiz. 2007. 'Egypt', in Craig Bradley, ed., *Criminal Procedure: A Worldwide Study*. Durham, NC: Carolina Academic Press.
Ridgeway v. The Queen (1995) 184 C.L.R. 19.
Ridgeway, Greg. 2007. *Analysis of Racial Disparities in the New York Police Department's Stop, Question, and Frisk Practices*. Santa Monica, CA: Rand Corporation.
Roach, Kent. 2007. 'Canada', in Craig Bradley, ed., *Criminal Procedure: A Worldwide Study*. Durham, NC: Carolina Academic Press.
Roach, Kent and M.L. Friedland. 1996. 'Borderline Justice: Policing in the Two Niagaras', *American Journal of Criminal Law* 241.
Rochin v. California, 342 U.S. 165, 172 (1954).
Roots, Roger. 2009–10. 'The Originalist Case for the Fourth Amendment Exclusionary Rule', 45 *Gonzaga Law Review* 1.
Rubinstein, Jonathan. 1973. *City Police*. New York, NY: Farrar, Straus and Giroux.
Sarré, Miguel and Jan Perlin. 2007. 'Mexico', in Craig Bradley, ed., *Criminal Procedure: A Worldwide Study*. Durham, NC: Carolina Academic Press.
Schulhofer, Stephen, Tom R. Tyler and Aziz Z. Huq. 2011. 'American Policing at a Crossroads: Unsustainable Policies and the Procedural Justice Alternative', 101 *Journal of Criminal Law & Criminology* 335–374.
Schwikkard, P.J. and S.E. van der Merwe. 2007. 'South Africa', in Craig Bradley, ed., *Criminal Procedure: A Worldwide Study*. Durham, NC: Carolina Academic Press.
Silverthorne v. United States, 251 U.S. 385 (1920).
Skolnick, Jerome H. 1975. *Justice Without Trial: Law Enforcement in Democratic Society*. New York, NY: Wiley.
Slobogin, Christopher. 1996. 'Testilying: Police Perjury and What to Do About It', 67 *University of Colorado Law Review* 1037.
Slobogin, Christopher. 1999. 'Why Liberals Should Chuck the Exclusionary Rule', 1999 *Illinois Law Review* 363.
Slobogin, Christopher. 2010. 'Government Dragnets', 73 *Law and Contemporary Problems* 107–143.
Slobogin, Christopher. 2013. 'The Exclusionary Rule: Is It on Its Way Out? Should It Be?' 10 *Ohio State Journal of Criminal Law* 341.
Sorrells v. United States, 287 U.S. 435 (1932).
Sözüer, Adem and Öznur Sevdiren. 2013. 'Turkey: The Move to Categorical Exclusion of Illegally Gathered Evidence', in Stephen C. Thaman, ed., *Exclusionary Rules in Comparative Law*. Dordrecht: Springer Science & Business Media.
Stark, Findlay and Fiona Leverick. 2013. 'Scotland: A Plea for Consistency', in Stephen C. Thaman, ed., *Exclusionary Rules in Comparative Law*. Dordrecht: Springer Science & Business Media.
State v. Cline, 617 N.W.2d 277 (Iowa 2000).
State v. Guzman, 842 P.2d 660 (Idaho 1992).
Stefanelli v. Minard, 342 U.S. 117 (1951).

Stone v. Powell, 428 U.S. 465 (1976).

Symposium (2013). 'The Exclusionary Rule: Is It on Its Way Out? Should It Be?', 10 *Ohio State Journal of Criminal Law* 341.

Thaman, Stephen C. 2007. 'The Nullification of the Russian Jury: Lessons for Jury-Inspired Reform in Eurasia and Beyond', 40 *Cornell International Law Journal* 355.

Thaman, Stephen C. 2008. *Comparative Criminal Procedure: A Casebook Approach*. Durham, NC: Carolina Academic Press.

Thaman, Stephen C. 2011. 'Constitutional Rights in the Balance: Modern Exclusionary Rules and the Toleration of Police Lawlessness in the Search for Truth', 61 *University of Toronto Law Journal* 691–735.

Triantafyllou, Georgios. 2013. 'Greece: From Statutory Nullities to a Categorical Statutory Exclusionary Rule', in Stephen C. Thaman, ed., *Exclusionary Rules in Comparative Law*. Dordrecht: Springer Science & Business Media.

United States v. Calandra, 414 U.S. 338 (1974).

United States v. Ceccolini, 435 U.S. 268 (1978).

United States v. Crews, 445 U.S. 463 (1980).

United States v. Havens, 446 U.S. 620 (1980).

United States v. Hernandez-Vasques, 513 F.3d 908 (9th Cir. 2008).

United States v. Janis, 428 U.S. 533 (1976).

United States v. Leon, 468 U.S. 897 (1984).

United States v. Payner, 447 U.S. 727 (1980).

United States v. Ramirez, 523 U.S. 65 (1998).

United States v. Russell, 411 U.S. 423 (1973).

U.S. Const., 1789, amend. XIV.

Van Cleave, Rachel A. 2007. 'Italy', in Craig Bradley, ed., *Criminal Procedure: A Worldwide Study*. Durham, NC: Carolina Academic Press.

Van Duizend, Richard, L. Paul Sutton and Charlotte A. Carter. 1985. *The Search Warrant Process: Preconceptions, Perceptions and Practices*. Williamsburg, VA: National Center for State Courts.

Weeks v. United States, 232 U.S. 383 (1914).

Weigend, Thomas. 2007. 'Germany', in Craig Bradley, ed., *Criminal Procedure: A Worldwide Study*. Durham, NC: Carolina Academic Press.

Whren v. United States, 517 U.S. 806 (1996).

Wilson, Bradford P. 1986. *Enforcing the Fourth Amendment: A Jurisprudential History*. Florence, KY: Taylor & Francis.

Wolf v. Colorado, 338 U.S. 25 (1949).

Wong Sun v. United States, 371 U.S. 471 (1963).

Zander, Michael. 1990. *The Police and Criminal Evidence Act 1984*. London: Sweet & Maxwell.

9. Silence, self-incrimination, and hazards of globalization
Jason Mazzone

1. INTRODUCTION

Criminal prosecutions are easier for the government if, rather than the government having to prove its case, the accused confesses to the charges and the only issue that remains is the sentence to be imposed. However, when criminal cases are resolved on the basis of the accused's own words, significant risks emerge. Most seriously, there is the risk that the accused has confessed falsely in order to avoid physical pain at the hands of his inquisitors. Or, perhaps, the accused was tricked into confessing after many rounds of clever questioning. Aside from these and related issues of the treatment of suspects and the reliability of resulting confessions, the government's capacity to send people to prison vastly increases if it need not be burdened with investigating a case, compiling an evidentiary record, and proving its account in court. Conviction by confession also circumvents the role of the public – in the jury box and beyond – in monitoring the government's uses and abuses of its prosecutorial tools.

For more than four centuries adversarial systems of criminal justice have protected against these risks by recognizing two rights for those accused of crimes: the right to remain silent and the right (or privilege) against self-incrimination. These rights are distinct: the first protects the ability of the accused to say nothing when questioned during the course of criminal proceedings, while the second protects the accused from having his words used as evidence in the government's case against him. The two rights are also closely related: the ability to say nothing reduces the risk of saying something that points to guilt. In recent years, these rights have spread beyond their origins and have found a place also in inquisitorial systems of justice. As the rights have spread, their form has also changed. This chapter traces the spread and evolution of the right to silence and the right against self-incrimination by examining the two rights from a comparative perspective. As the chapter demonstrates, numerous complexities surround the nature and scope of these two rights in their contemporary forms. Legislatures and courts have crafted detailed rules about the circumstances in which the rights apply and the ways in which they lawfully may be burdened or overridden. Many of these contemporary rules have resulted from a kind of cross-pollination: in shaping the two rights, jurisdictions have been influenced by experiences and developments elsewhere.

From one perspective, the overall trajectory has been one of increasing protections for criminal defendants: jurisdictions that did not traditionally protect the right to silence or the right against self-incrimination have incorporated and strengthened these rights. As the chapter shows, however, this march forward is just one side of the overall story. For globalization has a downside. At the same time that the two rights have spread, they have also been curtailed in new and significant ways. In particular, dialogue among jurisdictions has ended up weakening these rights by comparison with their strong adversarial origins.

The chapter examines developments in five jurisdictions: the United States, the United Kingdom, France, Germany, and the European Union. Following a brief discussion of common law origins, the chapter begins with an overview of the right to silence and the privilege against self-incrimination under the Constitution of the United States. The U.S. constitutional regime provides the framework for assessing, in the remainder of the chapter, developments in the other four jurisdictions. This approach is chosen because the two rights at issue have received their most extensive treatment in the case law of the U.S. Supreme Court and, compared to the other jurisdictions the chapter examines, the scope of the rights in the U.S. remains relatively stable.

As we will see, the interplay among the other four jurisdictions has resulted in considerable movement, with important questions on the table as to the future of the right to silence and the right against self-incrimination. In addition, there exist striking differences among the jurisdictions examined with respect to the values recognized at stake and the proper scope of the rights. In the United Kingdom, statutory reforms have curtailed common law protections, such that in some respects – for instance, whether at trial an adverse inference may be drawn from a defendant's silence – these rights are stronger in the United States, where they are constitutionally based. Germany and France, while neighbors, have very different approaches to silence and self-incrimination. In Germany, a robust commitment to individual dignity has produced very strong safeguards for these two rights throughout the criminal process – with the acceptance that solving and prosecuting crimes may be rendered more difficult as a result. France has traditionally given very little significance to the rights to silence and against self-incrimination, focusing instead on the public interest in crime control. Thus, the French regime has traditionally been structured to permit investigators unfettered access to suspects who may hold useful information. Under pressure from the European Court of Human Rights (ECtHR), France has recently strengthened protections for suspects and defendants to remain silent, but those reforms fall far short of the robust German approach. As for the ECtHR itself, it has read a right to silence and a privilege against self-incrimination into the fair trial requirements of Article 6 of the European Convention on Human Rights (ECHR) and has issued a series of decisions on the significance and scope of those rights. But it would be wrong to understand the ECtHR as simply an engine of progressive reform. Significantly, the Court has had to accommodate differences among signatory states. It has thus wisely avoided insisting on singular models. Here, the issue of remedies carries special significance. The U.S. Supreme Court has been able to back up its decisions on silence and self-incrimination with exclusionary rules prohibiting (where applicable) uses at trial of evidence obtained in violation of a defendant's rights. Exclusion, however, is a controversial remedy, and so far the ECtHR has declined to embrace an exclusionary regime – with the result that there remains significant leeway for states to decide how to structure their criminal processes and thus significant variation when it comes to the strength of protections for the rights to silence and against self-incrimination.

The chapter ends with some predictions about the future scope of the right to silence and the privilege against self-incrimination and some words of caution about efforts to pursue universal conceptions of those rights on a global scale.

2. COMMON LAW ORIGINS

The right to silence and the privilege against self-incrimination originate in the common law. The common law recognized these rights by the early seventeenth century. Most accounts trace the rights as emerging in response to the inquisitorial practices of ecclesiastical courts and the English Court of Star Chamber in which an individual was questioned under oath *ex officio*. That oath put the suspect in the position of having to choose whether to commit a sin (by lying), incriminate himself, or face punishment for refusing to answer. The Long Parliament that followed the Cromwellian Revolution outlawed the *ex officio* oath in 1641. The subsequent process by which opposition to self-incrimination migrated to the common law courts – where defendants were not even permitted to testify – and became also a part of the American tradition has been a subject of recent scholarly debate. The traditional account, by evidence scholar John H. Wigmore, is that beginning in the mid-seventeenth century the distinction between ecclesiastical and common law court procedures became blurred and a general hostility to forcing an accused to incriminate himself took hold (Wigmore, 1940: § 2250). Thus, by the time of the Philadelphia Convention, the right to silence and the privilege against self-incrimination were widely accepted as fundamental. Legal historian John Langbein instead focuses on the rise in an adversarial system of criminal justice in the eighteenth century as the origin of the modern right to silence and the privilege against self-incrimination. According to Langbein's (1994) account, in the sixteenth century and the early part of the seventeenth century, criminal defendants appeared in court without counsel to answer charges against them. An innocent defendant would readily explain away the accusations; a guilty defendant, under oath, would be unable to avoid the truth. When, beginning in the 1730s, criminal defendants were permitted to be accompanied by lawyers, the focus of the trial shifted from a proceeding centered around a defendant speaking to one in which lawyers challenged prosecutors at every step, including by refusing to allow their clients to provide evidence favorable to the government. In this context, Langbein argues, the right to silence and the privilege against self-incrimination became central components of the adversarial trial.

3. VALUES

Courts and commentators have offered a wide range of opinions about the values the right to silence and the privilege against self-incrimination promote in an adversarial system. A common argument is that the rights avoid subjecting the accused to the 'cruel trilemma of self-accusation, perjury or contempt'.[1] At the police station, the rights reduce the risk of false confessions made under pressure. At trial, they protect the innocent from tricky prosecutorial questioning that might make even an innocent person speak and act in a way that suggests guilt and, more generally, they promote the reliability of criminal trials. The rights are also said to serve to safeguard moral dignity in that the 'government disrespects a person when it uses him as the means of his own destruction' (Amar and Lettow, 1995: 896) and to protect individual privacy.[2] Finally, the rights require the government to bear the entire burden of proof in criminal cases, and thus are an essential component of an adversarial system of justice.[3] Not surprisingly, the right to silence and the privilege against self-incrimination have also come under significant criticism for, among other things, protecting the guilty (Amar, 1997: 48).

4. BASELINES: PROTECTIONS UNDER THE UNITED STATES CONSTITUTION

The scope of the right to silence and the privilege against self-incrimination in the United States provides a useful baseline for examining the approaches of other jurisdictions. Invoking the Fifth Amendment to the U.S. Constitution, the U.S. Supreme Court has been at the forefront of protecting these rights, including through the adoption of the *Miranda* warnings – known throughout the world – and exclusionary rules to deter rights violations.

4.1 Voluntariness

American courts traditionally relied upon the common law test of voluntariness to determine whether a defendant's confession was admissible as evidence.[4] Beginning in the late nineteenth century, constitutional rules displaced common law protections. The Fifth Amendment to the U.S. Constitution contains an explicit protection for the privilege against self-incrimination: no person, the Fifth Amendment provision says, 'shall be compelled in any criminal case to be a witness against himself'.[5] The most obvious application of this provision is that the government cannot force a defendant to take the stand and provide testimony that then sends the defendant to prison or the gallows. But the Court has understood the privilege to sweep more broadly than the courtroom, and much of the action under the Fifth Amendment occurs well before a trial even begins.

In early decisions, the Supreme Court understood this provision simply to have constitutionalized the common law rule of voluntariness.[6] As with the rest of the 1791 Bill of Rights, the Fifth Amendment initially constrained only the federal government. The Supreme Court did not hold the Fifth Amendment privilege applicable to the states, in whose courts most criminal prosecutions occur, until 1964.[7] Nonetheless, state court defendants were not without federal constitutional protections. Since 1868, the states have been subject to requirements of due process under the Fourteenth Amendment. For many years before applying the Fifth Amendment privilege to the states, the Court invoked Fourteenth Amendment due process to impose a voluntariness test on state court uses of incriminating statements by defendants, thereby giving state court defendants roughly the same rights as defendants in federal court.[8]

Today, with the Fifth Amendment privilege fully applicable to the states, most of the activity around self-incrimination is under the rubric of that provision. Nonetheless, due process remains a background principle. In particular, due process continues to prohibit the use of involuntary statements. The Supreme Court has held fast to the rule that due process prohibits use at a criminal trial of statements obtained involuntarily by law enforcement personnel, and coercive police conduct may also give rise to claims in a civil action even when an obtained statement is not used at trial.[9] Voluntariness, whether as a matter of due process or an aspect of the Fifth Amendment privilege against self-incrimination, is determined based on the 'totality of all the surrounding circumstances'.[10] Under this approach, the Court has held statements inadmissible when they are the product of threatened violence[11] or extreme psychological pressure.[12] In these kinds of cases, the Court has been concerned with much more than the reliability of the statements at issue: an insistence on voluntariness is meant to deter abusive police practices, whether they result in truthful statements or not. As the Justices have explained: 'In cases involving involuntary confessions, this Court enforces the strongly felt attitude of our society that important human values are sacrificed where an agency of the government, in the course of securing a conviction, wrings a confession out of an accused against his will'.[13]

4.2 Text and Doctrine

The text of the Fifth Amendment set outs the scope of the privilege against self-incrimination and provides also some important limits. The text is thus a useful way of delving into the applicable rules, although some Supreme Court interpretations are easier to square with the text than others. The Fifth Amendment provision applies to 'persons'. Consistent with this language, the Supreme Court has held that the privilege does not protect corporations and other non-persons.[14]

The provision protects against being 'compelled'. As we will see below, safeguarding accused individuals from compulsion, particularly in the context of custodial police interrogations, motivates some of the key judicial decisions in this area. For now, it is sufficient to note that while some government actions are clearly barred as entailing unlawful compulsion – use of physical force, for example, or imposition of a fine or a prison sentence for refusing to speak – not every pressure is impermissible. In one case, for example, the Supreme Court held that threatening to cancel a public contract and revoke eligibility for future public contracts for five years should the contractor refuse to testify before a grand jury concerning his transactions with the state constituted compulsion under the Fifth Amendment.[15] The Court has also held that prosecutors may not comment to a jury on a defendant's refusal to testify, because doing so is a form of compulsion to testify.[16] On the other hand, that a defendant may face a greater risk of being convicted if he does not take the stand and explain his side of the story does not give rise to compulsion under the Fifth Amendment.[17]

The text of the Fifth Amendment would appear to limit the privilege to criminal cases. However, the Supreme Court has read the privilege more broadly to protect individuals from compelled answers 'in any ... proceeding, civil or criminal, formal or informal' in which 'answers might incriminate ... [the individual] in future criminal proceedings'.[18] In other words, the privilege sweeps broadly because even though an individual might not be under criminal investigation today, he might well be tomorrow. In addition, the Court has explained that the risk that a statement will be used in a criminal prosecution must be 'substantial',[19] so that if there is no 'reasonable danger of incrimination' in a criminal prosecution the privilege does not apply to non-criminal contexts.[20] Accordingly, if the government grants an individual immunity from prosecution, the privilege disappears.[21]

Not every statement turns the person who makes it into a 'witness'. The Supreme Court has explained that the Fifth Amendment privilege is limited to communications that are 'testimonial' in nature. 'In order to be testimonial, an accused's communication must itself, explicitly or implicitly, relate a factual assertion or disclose information. Only then is a person compelled to be a "witness" against himself'.[22] Several important rules follow. One is that the privilege does not prohibit use of physical evidence obtained from the defendant such as when the government uses a blood sample to demonstrate the defendant's alcohol level in a drunk-driving prosecution.[23] Even though the taking of physical evidence may well be compelled and is certainly incriminating, and even though the defendant is the source of the evidence used against him, physical evidence is not testimonial.[24] Indeed, not all words are even testimonial. For example, the Court has held that a handwriting sample[25] and a voice sample are not testimonial when they are used to identify a suspect.[26]

Documents can of course be incriminating. Yet the Supreme Court has held that when the government compels the production of documents that were prepared voluntarily there is no Fifth Amendment privilege because the only thing that is actually compelled is turning over the documents themselves.[27] (On the other hand, if the very act of turning over the documents does have a testimonial component – such as by showing that the documents were in control of the suspect and this is a relevant element of the prosecution – there may be a Fifth Amendment privilege even against production.)[28]

With respect to required documents maintained pursuant to a government administrative requirement, however – such as records a business must keep as a matter of law – there is no Fifth Amendment privilege that covers either the content of the documents or the act of production.[29] In other contexts, the Court has held that routine government reporting requirements do not violate the Fifth Amendment even if the information reported might lead to a subsequent prosecution. For example, individuals can be required to file tax returns even though the return might contain information that will trigger a criminal investigation and prosecution.[30] In *California v. Byers*,[31] the Court upheld enforcement of California's statutory requirement that drivers of cars involved in accidents stop and provide their names and addresses.[32] The Court plurality reasoned that the statute did not work a Fifth Amendment violation because it 'was not intended to facilitate criminal convictions but to promote the satisfaction of civil liabilities arising from automobile accidents',[33] was 'directed at the public at large' rather than a disfavored group, and required no disclosure of inherently illegal activity.

4.3   The *Miranda* Revolution

In *Miranda v. Arizona* (1966), in response to abusive police practices, particularly at the state level, the Court significantly strengthened the rights of defendants with a set of a prophylactic measures derived from the self-incrimination clause of the Fifth Amendment and backed up by an exclusionary rule.[34] *Miranda* was revolutionary compared both to then-existing approaches in the United States and to the protections afforded suspects in the rest of the world.

Miranda is among the Supreme Court's most successful jurisprudential exports (see generally, Thaman, 2001). Since the *Miranda* decision, other countries have adopted similar measures to protect the interests of suspects subjected to police interrogation. Indeed, in some respects *Miranda*-style rights are stronger abroad than they are in the United States, where (as discussed below) the Supreme Court has trimmed some of the most far-reaching aspects of its own 1966 ruling.[35]

In *Miranda*, the Court held that given the inherently coercive nature of custodial questioning, the government may not at trial use statements, either inculpatory or exculpatory, stemming from a custodial interrogation unless the government demonstrates the use of procedural safeguards effective to protect the suspect's privilege against self-incrimination.[36] In other words, an exclusionary rule applies if the *Miranda* requirements are not satisfied. Thus, according to the Court:

> [U]nless other fully effective means are devised to inform accused persons of their right of silence and to assure a continuous opportunity to exercise it, the following measures are required. Prior to any questioning, the person must be warned that he has a right to remain silent, that any statement he does make may be used as evidence against him, and that he has a right to the presence of an attorney, either retained or appointed. The defendant may waive effectuation of these rights, provided the waiver is made voluntarily and intelligently. If, however, he indicates in any manner and at any stage of the process that he wishes to consult with an attorney before speaking there can be no questioning. Likewise, if the individual … indicates in any manner that he does not wish to be interrogated, the police may not question him.[37]

Although the language in *Miranda* suggested that interrogation without giving a suspect the requisite warnings and the opportunity to have a lawyer present itself violated the Fifth Amendment, the Court subsequently held that because the *Miranda* requirements are prophylactic measures to protect the Fifth Amendment privilege, a constitutional violation occurs only when a statement obtained in violation of the *Miranda* rules is used against the defendant at trial.[38] More generally, the *Miranda* rules are a creation of the Court (though it has described the rules as constitutionally based)[39] in order to safeguard the Fifth Amendment privilege – which is concerned with criminal liability. For that reason, the Court itself retains control over the scope of the rules and the remedies if they are violated. For instance, the Court has held that while a violation of the *Miranda* rules results in exclusion of a suspect's statements in order to deter police abuses, the violation does not generally require suppression of the fruits of the statement (e.g. physical evidence the statement leads to) because, the Court has reasoned, further exclusion serves no additional deterrent measure.[40]

Several additional aspects to *Miranda* bear emphasis. First, under the Court's approach in *Miranda*, all statements made during custodial interrogations are presumptively involuntary. Hence the need for safeguards (that is, the *Miranda* warnings) before those statements may legitimately be used against the suspect.

Second, the procedural protections apply in a specific context: custodial interrogation. The *Miranda* Court stated that a custodial interrogation occurs when 'an individual is taken into custody or otherwise deprived of his freedom by the authorities in any significant way and is subjected to questioning'.[41] Hence, the interrogation need not take place at the police station for the *Miranda* rules to be triggered.[42]

Third, *Miranda* provides the suspect with the right to have a lawyer present during the custodial interrogation – and to have the government pay for the attorney if he cannot otherwise afford one.[43] As the Court explained in *Miranda*, because '[t]he circumstances surrounding in-custody interrogation can operate very quickly to overbear the will of one merely made aware of his privilege by his interrogators ... the right to have counsel present at the interrogation is indispensable to the protection of the Fifth Amendment privilege'.[44]

Fourth, a suspect may waive his right to remain silent and the accompanying right to counsel. The *Miranda* Court explained, however, that 'a heavy burden rests on the government to demonstrate that the defendant knowingly and intelligently waived his privilege'.[45] Specifically:

> [a]n express statement that the individual is willing to make a statement and does not want an attorney followed closely by a statement could constitute a waiver. But a valid waiver will not be presumed simply from the silence of the accused after warnings are given or simply from the fact that a confession was in fact eventually obtained.[46]

The *Miranda* Court recognized that police might seek to wear down a silent suspect or deploy other methods to persuade the suspect to give up the privilege and speak. Thus, the Court explained:

> [T]he fact of lengthy interrogation or incommunicado incarceration before a statement is made is strong evidence that the accused did not validly waive his rights ... Moreover, any evidence that the accused was threatened, tricked, or cajoled into a waiver will, of course, show that the defendant did not voluntarily waive his privilege.[47]

Miranda did not explain precisely what constitutes interrogation, such that the requirement of safeguards is triggered. Subsequent Supreme Court decisions have held, however, that interrogation includes both express questioning as well as 'any words or actions on the part of the police (other than those normally attendant to arrest and custody) that the police should know are reasonably likely to elicit an incriminating response from the suspect'.[48]

4.4 Exceptions and New Limits

The Supreme Court has also developed a set of exceptions to the *Miranda* rules. One is a public safety exception, announced in *New York v. Quarles*.[49] The case involved police asking a suspect about the location of a gun in a supermarket; the Court held *Miranda* warnings were not required because of the need to locate the gun.[50] *Miranda* warnings are also not required, the Court has held, if the suspect makes a voluntary statement to somebody he does not know is a police officer. In *Illinois v. Perkins*, the Court held there was no *Miranda* violation when an undercover officer was placed in a defendant's cellblock (posing as an inmate) and, during casual conversation, the defendant made incriminating statements; those statements could be used against the defendant at trial.[51] The Court's rationale was that in such circumstances the element of compulsion that motivates *Miranda* is lacking.[52] *Miranda* also does not preclude police asking routine booking questions, such as an individual's name and address.[53]

While the Court has held firm to *Miranda*'s basic requirements, subsequent cases have trimmed back some of the broader reaches of the *Miranda* decision itself. For example, while *Miranda* indicated that once the suspect invokes the right to silence questioning must cease, the Court later held that this did not mean the police could never resume questioning. In *Michigan v. Mosley*,[54] a defendant invoked his *Miranda* rights, questioning stopped and then later that same day a different police officer gave the *Miranda* warnings again and obtained a waiver from the defendant who then made a confession.[55] The Court held that because the police had 'scrupulously honored' the initial invocation of the right to silence, the second round of questioning was permissible.[56] The Court has also relaxed the requirements for a showing of waiver of the right to silence. In *Berghuis v. Thompkins*,[57] the Court held that so long as the suspect was given and understood the warnings, a subsequent statement – without any specific waiver – is sufficient to presume the suspect has foregone the *Miranda* protection to remain silent.[58]

4.5 Summary

Although the Supreme Court has retreated from some of its earlier broader holdings on the scope of the Fifth Amendment privilege against self-incrimination, that right and the accompanying right to silence receive strong protection in the United States. Notably, the *Miranda* regime, based on the Court's recognition of the inherently coercive nature of custodial interrogation, provides significant safeguards to suspects in criminal cases – along with a strong remedy, the exclusionary rule, in order to deter police misconduct. This is not to say that suspects do not speak to their interrogators. Many do – to their detriment (see generally, Leo, 2008). Police also at times engage in coercive practices to extract confessions, some of which are false (see generally, Garrett, 2010). But as a legal matter, the Court, through its rulings, has taken a path to give the Fifth Amendment privilege considerable teeth.

5. THE UNITED KINGDOM: DIMINISHING PROTECTIONS

The constitutional rules developed in the United States have their origins in the English common law. Across the Atlantic, however, the common law has been under siege: statutory requirements have displaced long-standing common law protections for the right to silence and the privilege against self-incrimination. While these rights continue to receive protection, Parliament has imposed significant limitations upon them, in ways that weaken the rights by comparison with their common law origins.

5.1 PACE: Codification of Rights

First, the good news for criminal suspects: following recommendations of the Royal Commission on Criminal Procedure, Parliament enacted the Police and Criminal Evidence Act (1984) ('PACE'), which codified rules governing the powers of the police and the rights of criminal suspects and defendants. PACE and the accompanying Code of Practice for the Detention, Treatment and Questioning of Persons by Police Officers ('Code C') impose limits on the extent to which the police may question suspects and on the government's right to use a suspect's statements in subsequent criminal prosecutions.[59] Prior to a custodial interrogation, the police are required to warn suspects that they have a right to remain silent[60] and the right to consult with an attorney (including by obtaining free legal advice)[61] and to have the attorney present during questioning.[62] In addition, the police must inform an arrested suspect that he has a right to have a friend or family member notified that he has been detained and of his location.[63] Once a suspect requests counsel, questioning should cease until the suspect has consulted with a lawyer.[64] However, the police may delay access to counsel and may postpone notice to family members for up to 36 hours if there are reasonable grounds for concluding that evidence may be destroyed or other suspects alerted, that injury to other individuals may result, or that the recovery of property that resulted from the offense may be hindered.[65] In addition, as a result of the Terrorism Act of 2000, when the police detain suspected terrorists, access to counsel may be denied for up to 48 hours for a broad set of reasons, including to prevent future acts of terrorism.[66] Code C specifies that '[n]o interviewer may try to obtain answers or elicit a statement by the use of oppression',[67] and if during an interrogation the officer determines that there is sufficient evidence for a prosecution to succeed, questioning must cease.[68] Ordinarily, detainees must be allowed an eight-hour break from questioning each 24-hour period.[69] Apart from these statutory protections, under longstanding common law, defendants cannot be required to testify at trial (Wigmore, 1961: 269–270).

5.2   CJPOA: Diminished Protections

Now, the bad news for those accused of crimes: Under the common law, no adverse inference could be drawn from a defendant's silence. Reflecting that common law standard, the U.S. Supreme Court has long held that the privilege against self-incrimination prohibits drawing any inference from silence.[70] The approach avoids putting the guilty individual in the position of having to choose between confessing and committing perjury on the stand; it also guards against hostile or tricky prosecutorial questioning that might make even innocent defendants stumble, misspeak or otherwise appear guilty.

However, the U.K. Criminal Justice and Public Order Act (1994) ('CJPOA') did away with the common law rule and permits judges and juries, in reaching a verdict, to take account of a defendant's failure to answer questions during a police interrogation or to testify at trial.[71] This change, a marked departure from hundreds of years of common law protection, resulted from a vigorous challenge by conservative politicians to the traditional right to silence on the ground that it permitted criminals to avoid being held accountable (Doak and McGourlay, 2009: 99).

Section 34 of CJPOA provides that if, prior to being charged, an individual under questioning fails to mention a fact later relied upon in his defense or, on being charged, fails to mention a fact he could reasonably have been expected to mention under the circumstances, the trial judge or jury 'may draw such inferences from the failure as appear proper'.[72] Courts have identified conditions under which drawing the (adverse) inference is proper.[73] In addition to section 34, other provisions of CJPOA provide that if a suspect fails to offer a satisfactory account of his presence at a crime scene or of physical evidence recovered from him, the trial court may likewise draw an adverse inference from that failure.[74]

At trial, if a defendant refuses to answer questions, section 35 governs. It states that 'the court or jury, in determining whether the accused is guilty of the offence charged, may draw such inferences as appear proper from the failure of the accused to give evidence or his refusal, without good cause, to answer any question'.[75] The courts have identified required instructions to juries under section 35, including that an inference from the defendant's failure to give evidence cannot alone prove guilt.[76]

The CJPOA reforms altered the warning given to suspects prior to questioning. Suspects are now cautioned that, while there is a right to silence, a failure to speak can result in a negative inference later being drawn.[77] The required language is now as follows: 'You do not have to say anything. But it may harm your defence if you do not mention when questioned something which you later rely on in Court. Anything you do say may be given in evidence'.[78] This warning obviously puts a suspect in a difficult position – for *either* silence *or* making a statement can be detrimental. In this respect, access to counsel takes on special importance. A lawyer is almost certainly in a better position than a lay defendant to determine whether it is better to remain silent or answer police questions. For this reason, an exception to the adverse inference provision applies when suspects have not been able to consult with an attorney: '[w]hen a suspect detained at a police station is interviewed during any period for which access to legal advice has been delayed ... the court or jury may not draw adverse inferences from their silence'.[79]

5.3 Exclusion – and its Limits

As in the United States, an exclusionary rule serves as the remedy for a violation of the defendant's rights to silence and against self-incrimination. Two provisions of PACE govern. Section 76(2) mandates exclusion of involuntary confessions, defined as those obtained (i) through 'oppression' or (ii) in consequence of anything said or done by the police which is likely to render the confession 'unreliable'.[80] If the defendant challenges a confession under section 76(2), it is the prosecution's burden to prove beyond a reasonable doubt that the procedure that produced the confession did not run afoul of this provision.[81] Courts have invoked section 76(2) to exclude confessions made when police officers 'bullied and hectored' a suspect so that they 'were not questioning him so much as shouting at him what they wanted him to say'; falsely told the suspect his fingerprints had been found at the crime scene;[82] and told a suspect (interrogated for 13 hours) that questioning would continue until he 'got it right'.[83] Under section 76(2), however, there is no exclusion of any subsequent 'fruits' of the excluded confession.[84]

5.4   Oppression as Unique

A key difference within the above language of section 76(2) bears emphasis. With respect to the first category, oppression – defined to 'include[] torture, inhuman or degrading treatment, and the use or threat of violence (whether or not amounting to torture)'[85] – exclusion is automatic. In other words, even if the confession is actually reliable, it is still excluded when obtained through oppression. Courts have explained that this rule – under which even otherwise reliable evidence is excluded – reflects a moral condemnation of torture and related abuses.[86] The second category within 76(2), by contrast, focuses specifically on reliability: exclusion is required because of 'anything said or done by the police which is likely to render the confession unreliable'. This provision requires courts to determine whether the police conduct at issue had the effect of rendering a statement unreliable – and only then is exclusion mandated. Here, then, section 76(2) is concerned with a different value: accuracy. In making the reliability determination, courts engage in a fact-intensive inquiry attentive to all of the circumstances of the interrogation.[87]

5.5   Discretionary Exclusion

PACE also gives courts a general discretionary power to exclude statements. Section 78(1) permits – but does not require – courts to exclude evidence, including testimonial evidence, if admission would have an 'adverse effect on the fairness of the proceedings' in light of 'all the circumstances, including the circumstances in which the evidence was obtained'.[88] Here, fairness is the touchstone of exclusion: the approach thus differs from that in the United States, where exclusion is directed at deterring police misconduct. This difference has important implications. In contrast to the *Miranda* regime, under section 78(1), a confession obtained in violation of a defendant's right to silence is not necessarily excluded from evidence. Instead, a court will make an overall assessment of fairness if the confession is allowed to be admitted. The case law on the exclusion of statements under section 78 is notoriously devoid of general principles – and deliberately so. As one court has explained: 'It is undesirable to attempt any general guidance as to the way in which a judge's discretion under section 78 … should be exercised. Circumstances vary infinitely'.[89] Section 78 broadly empowers courts to exclude evidence on grounds of unfairness, and so lends itself to exclusion also of evidentiary fruits – physical or testimonial – that the excluded statement produced. Again, courts have reached mixed results in such cases, emphasizing that the determination is fact specific and eschewing generalizable rules.[90]

5.6 Summary

In the United Kingdom, recent parliamentary reform has undercut common law protections. On the one hand, individuals interrogated by the police do benefit from statutory provisions protecting a right to silence and a privilege against self-incrimination. On the other hand, Parliament has imposed significant burdens on the exercise of those rights. In particular, a suspect subject to interrogation must choose between incriminating himself by responding to police questions or risking an adverse inference drawn on the basis of his silence. Likewise, at trial, a defendant has a right not to testify, but failure to testify can be understood by the judge or jury as evidence of guilt. Moreover, these weakened rights exist in a context with only a weak exclusionary rule: the only instance in which the U.K. rules of exclusion track the robust exclusionary regime of the United States is with respect to statements obtained by torture or other forms of oppression.

By way of preview, the incursions in the U.K. on the right to silence and the privilege against self-incrimination have come at the same time that the ECtHR has read these two rights into the European Convention and developed mechanisms for protecting them. As discussed further below, there has occurred significant interplay between the European Court and the courts of the United Kingdom with respect to silence and self-incrimination. While the U.K. courts have made some minor adjustments to strengthen the interests of defendants, the overall result, so far, has been a willingness on the part of the European Court to accept the weakened rights that Parliament has produced. Before turning to that dynamic, the chapter takes up silence and self-incrimination in two neighboring European countries, France and Germany, where quite different approaches have developed.

6. FRANCE: INCREASING RIGHTS

While the United Kingdom has decreased protections for criminal defendants, France has pursued the opposite course. The French Constitution does not provide specifically for a right to silence or against self-incrimination and the Code of Criminal Procedure also did not traditionally protect those rights. Instead, until recent changes to the Code, police had a period in which to question suspects, in a process known as *garde à vue,* with very few restrictions. However, decisions from the European Court recognizing the rights of defendants under the European Convention have prompted significant reform to the traditional French approach.

6.1 Traditional Practices and Initial Reforms

The *garde à vue* permits police to detain a suspect for questioning for 24 hours.[91] With approval of the public prosecutor (*procureur*), the detention may be increased to 48 hours;[92] the prosecutor may also apply to the *juge des libertés et de la détention* or to the *juge d'instruction* for a further 48-hour period of detention in cases involving crimes listed in the Code;[93] the list includes drug trafficking, organized criminal activity, and terrorism.[94] (In addition, where there is an actual risk of a terrorist attack, detention may last up to six days.)[95] Traditionally, suspects had very limited rights in the context of the *garde à vue.* Prior to 1993, a year of reform, the whole point of the process was to maximize the ability of the police to obtain information from the suspect. Hence, the suspect had no right to legal assistance and was otherwise held incommunicado. Instead, the *procureur* was charged, as a judicial officer, with ensuring the lawful treatment of the detained suspect.

In January 1993, Parliament revised the Code of Criminal Procedure to provide suspects with some basic protections.[96] Suspects were granted the right to contact family members and employers to notify them of the detention.[97] In addition, the reforms required police to inform suspects of the nature of the offense for which they were being questioned and the length of time for which they could be detained.[98] Suspects were also given a right to be examined by a doctor.[99] In addition, for the first time a limited right to counsel was provided: a suspect could consult with an attorney for a 30-minute period at the beginning of the *garde à vue.*[100] Although this reform was quite modest, it soon proved too generous for the French: in August of 1993, with the election of a new government, the right to consult with counsel was amended to a 30-minute meeting available only after 20 hours of detention and questioning (and after 72 hours in the case of terrorism, drug offenses, and other specified crimes).[101] Significantly, under the 1993 reforms, there was no right to have an attorney actually present during the interrogation and the attorney had no access to the case file until formal charges had been filed. In addition, the 1993 reforms did not require the police to notify the suspect that he had any right to remain silent during questioning.

In June of 2000, with the French approach increasingly an outlier among European nations, Parliament again modified the Code of Criminal Procedure, this time to allow suspects to consult with an attorney for 30 minutes at the beginning of the *garde à vue* and then again 20 hours into the *garde à vue*.[102] As before, however, this law did not permit the suspect's attorney to be present during questioning. Nonetheless, the 2000 law required, for the first time, that the police inform the suspect specifically that he had a right not to respond to questions.[103] Once more, however, the increased right produced unease: in March 2002 the required caution was amended so as to inform the suspect that he had a right to make a statement, to answer questions or to remain silent;[104] and then a year later, the caution requirement was eliminated entirely.[105] Thus, in the space of three years, France adopted a caution similar to that given in other jurisdictions, watered it down by making it one of three available options, and then abandoned it. A further reduction in rights occurred in March 2004, with the second consultation with counsel pushed back to the beginning of any extension of the *garde à vue* beyond 24 hours, such that only if the detention period was extended would the suspect be able to access counsel a second time. In cases of terrorism, drug offenses, and other specified crimes, the second consultation with counsel was available only after 72 hours.[106]

6.2 External Pressures

By comparison with the pre-1993 system, these changes to the French Code conferred new protections on criminal defendants. Nonetheless, they lagged well behind the scope of protections the European Court was reading into the European Convention. As measured by that case law, discussed in greater detail below, the rights protected in France appeared stingy, and it seemed inevitable that the European Court would sooner or later force stronger reform.

In 2008, the Grand Chamber of the ECtHR issued its opinion in *Salduz v. Turkey*,[107] in which it held that by failing to give a detained suspect access to a lawyer, Turkey was in breach of Article 6 of the Convention.[108] At the time of *Salduz*, France did not deny counsel entirely. Nonetheless, it was far from clear whether allowing, as France did, only a 30-minute consultation at the outset of the interrogation, was sufficient to satisfy Convention rights. In *Salduz*, the Grand Chamber spoke broadly about the basic significance of the right to counsel in the context of a custodial interrogation:

in order for the right to a fair trial to remain sufficiently practical and effective
... access to a lawyer should be provided ... from the first interrogation of a
suspect by the police, unless it is demonstrated in the light of the particular
circumstances of each case that there are compelling reasons to restrict this
right.[109]

Without the ability to consult immediately with counsel, the Grand
Chamber pronounced, '[t]he rights of the defence will ... be irretrievably
prejudiced when incriminating statements made during police interrogation without access to a lawyer are used for a conviction'.[110] A year after
its ruling in *Salduz*, the European court issued another decision, this time
rejecting an argument by Turkey that where a custodial defendant had
exercised his right to silence, access to counsel was not necessary to
comply with Article 6.[111] Again, the court emphasized the importance of
counsel in the custodial setting and it cited several aspects to this right:
'[c]ounsel has to be able to secure without restriction the fundamental
aspects of that person's defence: discussion of the case, organisation of
the defence, collection of evidence favourable to the accused, preparation
for questioning, support of an accused in distress and checking of the
conditions of detention'.[112] Measured against this language, the French
regime, offering a short consultation with an attorney – lacking access to
any government evidence – appeared to fall short of Convention requirements.

6.3 Enhanced Rights

France took the hint, and over a two-year period the judiciary and the
legislature acted to strengthen significantly the rights of defendants in
custodial interrogation settings. The courts took the first step. On July 30,
2010, the *Conseil constitutionnel* ruled that the provision of the French
Code of Criminal Procedure, under which a suspect's access to an
attorney was limited to a 30-minute consultation prior to police interrogation, violated the French Constitution.[113] In its ruling, the *Conseil
constitutionnel* observed that although the government had strengthened
protections for detained suspects, beginning with the statutory reforms of
1993, there had also been since that time far greater reliance in criminal
cases upon the *garde à vue*, which was now 'commonplace' even for
minor offenses.[114] Hence, evidence obtained through the *garde à vue* had
become the basis for the prosecutor's case in most instances.[115] While the
garde à vue was a permissible investigatory tool, the court reasoned, the
needs of the police had to be balanced by safeguards for the interests of
defendants.[116] Among other problems, limiting access to counsel to a

30-minute consultation violated the presumption of innocence provision of the 1789 Declaration of the Rights of Man and was therefore unconstitutional.[117] The *Conseil's* principal problem was one of imbalance: the restriction on access to counsel 'is imposed without any consideration of particular circumstances likely to justify the same, in order to collect or conserve evidence or ensure the protection of persons'.[118] The imbalance was compounded by the fact that suspects were not informed of a right to silence.[119] Rather than effect an immediate repeal of the challenged provision, the *Conseil* postponed the implementation of its decision until July 1, 2011, in order to give Parliament time to remedy the law.[120]

Before Parliament had acted, a further judicial push occurred. On October 14, 2010, the European Court issued its decision in *Brusco v. France*.[121] In that case, the police had detained Claude Brusco and prior to interrogating him had administered an oath requiring him to tell the truth – thus triggering the possibility of a perjury prosecution should Brusco lie.[122] In accordance with the provisions of the French Code of Criminal Procedure then in effect, Brusco was not informed of any right to remain silent and was not given access to counsel until 20 hours after the start of the interrogation.[123] Brusco made incriminating statements and he was ultimately convicted on criminal charges.[124] The European Court held that without a warning and lacking the benefit of counsel to advise him as to whether to answer police questions, Brusco's right under Article 6 of the Convention to remain silent and to not incriminate himself had been violated and the court ordered a monetary remedy.[125]

Five days after the *Brusco* decision, the *Cour de cassation* issued three dramatic rulings, also based on Article 6. That Court held that Article 6 prohibited questioning a suspect in custody in the absence of counsel;[126] it required informing suspects of the right to silence and to the assistance of counsel from the outset of the *garde à vue* unless there were compelling reasons to restrict that right or the suspect waived the right;[127] and it prohibited restricting access to counsel based solely on the category of offense at issue.[128] The Court gave Parliament until July 1 of the following year to remedy the interrogation law – but within a few months the Court itself was holding that statements obtained in custodial interrogations without the benefit of counsel were inadmissible at trial.[129] In short order, the existing French regime was under judicial attack domestically and at the European level, on the basis of the French Constitution and the European Convention on Human Rights.

Parliament responded with the Act of April 14, 2011. That law amended the Code of Criminal Procedure in significant ways to provide enhanced protections for suspects, including safeguards for the right to

silence and access to counsel during the course of custodial interrogations. At the same time, Parliament limited the scope of those amendments such that the revised Code still falls far short of the procedural
rights available in other jurisdictions.

On the positive side for those who face custodial interrogation, as a
result of the 2011 reforms to the Code, a suspect must be informed, at the
outset of the *garde à vue*, that he has the right 'to make statements, to
answer questions asked of him, or to remain silent'.[130] (Note that this
language offers the defendant the 2010 menu of options rather than a
straight-up warning of the right to silence.) The suspect must also be
informed at the outset that he has the right 'to be assisted by an
attorney',[131] including the right to appointed counsel.[132] If the suspect
requests the assistance of counsel, the interrogation must be delayed for
two hours in order to allow time for the lawyer to arrive.[133] If the lawyer
arrives more than two hours after the suspect's request and, in the
interim, the interrogation has resumed, the suspect has the right to stop
the interrogation to allow for a 30-minute meeting with his attorney.[134]

On the negative side of the ledger, the 2011 law is riddled with
exceptions to the right to counsel. At the request of the police, the
procureur may allow interrogation to begin prior to the close of the
two-hour window if there are exigencies requiring immediate questioning.[135] The *procureuer* can also delay access to counsel entirely for a
period up to 12 hours – again on the basis of exigencies – and, in cases
punishable by a minimum of five years' incarceration, can request a
judicial order deferring access to counsel for a further 12 hours, in each
instance while questioning proceeds.[136] In addition to these options, the
2011 law provides that for a series of enumerated offenses (including
organized crime),[137] if warranted in particular cases, access to counsel
may be delayed for up to 48 hours – and up to 72 hours in cases of
terrorism or drug trafficking.[138]

Additional provisions of the 2011 law serve also to limit the right to
counsel ostensibly protected by the reforms to the Code. On the one
hand, a suspect's lawyer is given the right to view the police report of the
interrogation of the suspect,[139] but that right can also be delayed in
exigent circumstances.[140] A lawyer's role during the interrogation is also
deemed limited: the lawyer may take notes during the interrogation[141] but
may not ask questions until the very end of the interrogation[142] and even
the right to ask questions can be curtailed if doing so would undermine
the police investigation.[143] The right to counsel thus secured by the 2011
law appears on its face robust. But the wide range of exceptions and
limitations sap the right of much of its force.

6.4 Remedies

On the remedial side, French law has long empowered judges to declare a 'nullity' where there has been a procedural violation[144] and to refuse use at trial of the evidence obtained as a result of the violation as well as any subsequent fruits.[145] While the U.S. exclusionary rule is based on the principle of deterring unlawful government action – 'to prevent, not to repair'[146] – the French law of nullities is based largely on a concern with the integrity of the criminal process, including by ensuring fairness to the defendant. Hence, a nullity in violation of a procedural rule generally requires that the violation has 'damage[ed] the interests' of the defendant.[147] Given this focus, the defendant, in the presence of counsel, may waive any objection to the violation and 'regularize' the procedure (and thus the use of the evidence obtained).[148] Significantly, prejudice to the defendant must concern something other than merely having unfavorable evidence admitted.[149]

With respect to the right to counsel, the 2011 law created an additional remedy: the Code now prohibits convicting a defendant solely on the basis of statements the defendant made without the assistance of counsel.[150] As with much of the 2011 law, this provision, too, might not have much bite. While it will be significant in cases where there is absolutely no other evidence besides the uncounseled admission of the defendant, so long as the government has other evidence – physical evidence, say, or statements from other witnesses – the provision will not prevent a conviction.

6.5 Beyond the *Garde à Vue*

Beyond these reforms to the *garde à vue*, separate rules protect the rights of the accused in other contexts. An accused individual may be examined under oath by the investigating judge (*juge d'instruction*) assigned to the case. During this process, known as the *mis en examen*, the investigating judge must inform the accused at his first appearance of the charges against him and advise him that he has a right to remain silent and a right to an attorney (including to appointed counsel).[151] Questioning may then only proceed with the consent of the accused and such consent is only valid if given in the presence of the lawyer for the accused.[152] Statements that result from the interview by the judge are recorded in written form and signed by the accused.[153] If a case subsequently goes to trial, such statements make up part of the case dossier made available to the trial judge.

At trial, the defendant is required to submit to questioning by the trial judge – there is no right comparable to that in the United States simply to invoke the Fifth Amendment and end questioning – but may elect to remain silent in response.[154] An additional distinction between France and the United States also bears mentioning. In the United States, most convictions are a result of a guilty plea, often pursuant to a plea bargain, in which the defendant gives up the right to remain silent and the privilege against self-incrimination, by confessing to the charged offense.[155] While French courts do not permit American-style plea bargaining, in cases with a maximum sentence of five years' imprisonment there is the possibility of a truncated resolution: the defendant appears in court following an admission of guilt, entered with the assistance of counsel; the presiding judge reviews the charges and underlying facts; and if satisfied (a French court must always independently determine the guilt of the defendant: a confession is not conclusive), the judge can either accept or reject (but not alter) the penalty suggested by the *procureur* (see generally, Saas, 2004). The U.S. approach takes for granted that a robust conception of the right to silence and the privilege against self-incrimination necessarily means that an individual who possesses those rights can both exercise and waive them (or use them as negotiating chips). The French approach is more skeptical of waiver as a component of the two rights and thus France has not adopted the regime of pleas and bargaining that exists in the U.S. justice system.

6.6 Summary

Under pressure from the European Court of Human Rights, France has significantly enhanced the rights of suspects subjected to custodial interrogation. The traditional *garde à vue*, in which police freely questioned suspects, has been overhauled, in particular, by providing for suspects to have the assistance of an attorney during questioning and notifying suspects of the right not to answer questions. Nonetheless, in light of built-in exceptions to the reforms, most notably by allowing deferral of access to counsel, the new French protections fall short of those available to suspects in the United States and other jurisdictions. It remains to be seen whether additional pressures from the European Court will nudge France further along the path of reform. France need not look far for a different model: its neighbor, Germany, has in place very strong rights to silence and against self-incrimination, derived from a distinct understanding of the values at stake in protecting those rights.

7. GERMANY: THE ROLE OF DIGNITY

Across the border, Germany has long had more robust protections for the right to silence and the privilege against self-incrimination. These rights exist as statutory and constitutional protections. As a constitutional matter, they are grounded in notions of individual dignity – a broad concept that, as discussed below, includes concerns of privacy and individual personality.

7.1 Statutory Protections

Interlocking provisions of the German Code of Criminal Procedure (*Strafprozeßordnung*) ('StPO') protect the right to silence and the privilege against self-incrimination. Prior to the first interrogation – whether by the police, the prosecutor, or the judge – a suspect must be informed that he has the right to remain silent and the right to consult with an attorney at any stage of the proceedings.[156] These warnings must be repeated prior to subsequent interrogations.[157] An individual who is arrested must also be given notice of his rights, including the right to remain silent and to consult with a lawyer.[158] German law provides for a right to appointed counsel in felony and other serious cases but only once an individual is actually arrested[159] and an indictment has been secured[160] (though prosecutors have the power to request appointment of counsel at an earlier stage of proceedings).[161] As a result, a suspect brought in for interrogation may consult with retained counsel but there is no right at that stage to have counsel provided by the government. In addition, while there is a right to have counsel present during an interrogation by the prosecutor or judge, there is no right to have even retained counsel present during a police interrogation – even though there is the right to consult with counsel prior to the interrogation.[162]

The Code of Criminal Procedure backs up these rules with a mandatory exclusionary provision, in section 136a, that prohibits use of statements obtained as a result of coercive measures, defined very broadly to include 'fatigue, physical interference, administration of drugs, torment, deception or hypnosis' and '[t]hreatening the accused ... or holding out the prospect of an advantage not envisaged by statute'.[163] Cases in which this provision has been held violated – and thus statements automatically excluded – include: police showing the accused the corpse of his son to provoke a murder confession;[164] promising a suspect he will not be punished if he implicates an accomplice;[165] and depriving a suspect of sleep while interrogation continues.[166] Perhaps most striking is that section 136a applies if the police lie to a suspect or otherwise provide him with misleading information. Thus, for example, where the police falsely told a suspect they already had overwhelming evidence of his guilt, the suspect's ensuing statement was deemed inadmissible as produced by police deception.[167] The German rule thus stands in sharp contrast to the U.S. approach under which police may (and do) engage in a wide range of deceptive techniques in order to obtain a confession.[168]

7.2 Constitutional Grounding

German protections for the right to silence and the privilege against self-incrimination begin in statute but they do not end there. German constitutional law serves as a robust source of additional safeguards. The Basic Law does not provide for a specific right to remain silent or for a privilege against self-incrimination. Nonetheless, German courts have read these rights into the first article of the Basic Law. It provides that '[h]uman dignity shall be inviolable'[169] and mandates that '[t]o respect and protect ... [human dignity] shall be the duty of all state authority'.[170] The German courts have cast the provisions of the Code of Criminal Procedure discussed above as reflecting – and putting into effect – the Basic Law's dignitary provisions. Thus, the High Court (*Bundesgerichtshof*) ('BGH') has said that the procedural protections contained in the Code 'are not isolated rules for their own sake, but rather they express the constitutional stance of a criminal procedure which does not permit degrading proceedings against the defendant'.[171] In a 1954 decision holding the use of polygraphs illegal under section 136a, the BGH explained that dignitary concerns required recognizing that a defendant is 'a participant in' rather than 'the object of' a criminal proceeding.[172] As such, while the law may properly limit the defendant's physical freedom, his 'freedom of decision' is 'inviolable at every stage of the proceeding' such that in a criminal matter he 'need not respond to the charge nor contribute to the resolution of the matter'.[173] In other words, respecting the dignity of a defendant prohibited turning him into the means to his own conviction.

While the German approach robustly protects the rights of suspects, the focus on dignity does not mean the police must simply leave a suspect alone. Thus, German courts do not prohibit resumption of questioning after a defendant has invoked his rights. Instead, 'the interrogation may ... be continued after a certain period for reflection'.[174] On this approach, the dignity of the defendant is enhanced – rather than diminished – when after a respectful period an opportunity is provided to answer questions.

At times, the focus on dignitary interests produces rules that correspond to those in the United States. One example is that in Germany no adverse inference may be drawn from an accused's invocation of his right to silence (see Thaman, 2001: 613–615). In many instances, however, dignitary concerns impose considerably stronger limits on police practices than exist in the United States. For example, the BGH has held it illegal for the police to place informants in cells to elicit incriminating statements because doing so takes advantage of the suspects' 'psychological compulsion to unburden themselves'[175] and thus offends dignitary interests. This approach contrasts starkly with that of the U.S. Supreme Court, which, on similar facts, held in *Illinois v. Perkins*[176] that because the detained suspect did not actually know he was speaking to a police agent in his cell the coercive atmosphere of the interrogation room was absent and therefore there was no Fifth Amendment problem.[177]

7.3   Exclusion and its Limits

The scope of exclusion in the German context has also produced extensive case law. While section 136a contains a mandatory exclusionary rule with respect to an illegally obtained confession, an important question has been whether the subsequent fruits (e.g. physical evidence) of an interrogation that violates section 136a must also be excluded. Given the text of section 136a, limited to the exclusion of statements, courts have mostly permitted the use of fruits. For example, in the *Gäfgen* case, discussed below, the German courts rejected the argument that a violation of section 136a required exclusion of the defendant's subsequent confession at trial; the European Court of Human Rights held also that there was no Convention violation under the circumstances.

Courts have also produced rules of exclusion with respect to violations of section 136(1), which specify procedures for the initial examination of a suspect, including the requirement to inform the accused of the rights to silence and to consult with counsel.[178] By its text, section 136(1) does not require exclusion of statements when police fail to adhere to the specified procedures. In early case law, the BGH refused to require exclusion under this section.[179] However, in more recent cases, the BGH has deemed the section 136(1) requirements mandatory[180] and has relied upon exclusion as the remedy for violations. The general approach is for German courts to engage in a balancing of interests to determine if evidence obtained in violation of the defendant's rights should be excluded.[181] Under this approach, courts assess the significance to the defendant's interests of the right that has been violated: '[a] prohibition on use is appropriate when the violated procedural provision is designed to secure the foundations of the procedural position of the accused or defendant in a criminal prosecution'.[182] Courts also consider the seriousness of the violation in the context of the particular case. For example, a failure to warn a suspect of the right to silence prior to interrogation generally results in exclusion of any resulting statement.[183] On the other hand, if the suspect clearly knew already of the right to silence (and there is no evidence of police deception within the scope of section 136a), an inadvertent failure to warn the suspect of the right does not require exclusion.[184]

As for the fruits of section 136(1) violations, those are not excluded (see Weigend, 2007: 261). Here, too, the German approach ends up coinciding with that of the United States. While a *Miranda* violation prohibits use of the resulting statement, in general, additional fruits are not excluded at trial because the broader remedy is not needed to promote police compliance with the *Miranda* rules.[185] So, too, on a dignitary rationale, exclusion of the confession is adequate to protect the defendant's interests: physical or other evidence that is generated down the road does not implicate the same dignitary concerns.

7.4 Beyond Police Interrogation

Beyond the interrogation room, the right to silence and the privilege against self-incrimination are protected also at trial. The defendant has a right to remain silent during trial and must be informed of that right.[186] This right is exercised by refusing to answer questions put by the presiding judge. The defendant is also given an opportunity at the end of the trial to make a statement but need not do so.[187] No adverse inference may attach to the defendant's refusal to speak.[188] In a criminal trial, the court must determine whether the defendant is guilty.[189] '[T]he common law instrument of the guilty plea is unknown' (Rauxloh, 2011: 296) in the Germany system and even 'an admission of guilt is not sufficient to convict the defendant'.[190] The government may, however, reach a deal with the defendant under which the defendant admits his guilt in exchange for a lesser sentence.[191] Nonetheless, the trial court remains bound to determine independently whether the evidence – including any confession – actually supports a guilty verdict.[192]

7.5 Summary

While in the United Kingdom and in France the right to silence and the privilege against self-incrimination have been in flux in recent years, in Germany these rights have remained quite steady. By grounding these rights early on in notions of human dignity, Germany has created statutory and constitutional laws that provide broad protections to criminal suspects subject to interrogation and to defendants who are put on trial. The German approach provides an important backdrop to that of the European Court of Human Rights, the topic of the next section.

8. THE EUROPEAN COURT: ENGINE OF CHANGE?

The European Convention on Human Rights contains no specific provisions protecting a right to silence or a privilege against self-incrimination. The European Court of Human Rights has, however, inferred those rights from Article 6 of the Convention. Article 6 protects the right to a fair trial. In addition to its enumerated protections, such as the presumption of innocence, Article 6 has served as the basis for the Court to read into the Convention a series of rights for criminal defendants. In invoking Article 6 as the basis for inferring a right to silence and privilege against self-incrimination, the Court is in the process of creating a set of rules that specify the scope of those protections. In so doing, the Court has produced reform in domestic states – such as France, discussed above – with traditionally weak protections for these rights.

In some respects, the decisions of the European Court mirror those of the U.S. Supreme Court. For example, the European Court has followed the rule that questioning must cease once a defendant asks for counsel.[193] On occasion, the Court has adopted stronger protections than those recognized by the U.S. Supreme Court. For example, in contrast to the Supreme Court's decision in *Berghuis*, the European Court has held that a waiver cannot be presumed from answers the suspect gives following his acknowledgment that he understands he has the right to remain silent.[194] In important respects, however, the European Court has stopped short of recognizing all of the same rights of defendants under the U.S. constitutional regime. The European Court has, for instance, been slow to insist upon *Miranda*-style warnings, beyond an opaque suggestion that at least where a suspect is interrogated in a police station, the police should warn the suspect he has a right to remain silent.[195]

The right to silence and against self-incrimination under the European Convention remains a work in progress at the hands of the Court. An important question going forward is whether the European Court will be satisfied simply with raising the level of protections in outlier signatory states – those with the weakest protections – or work to produce stronger rights across the board. In identifying and securing rights protected by the Convention, the Court faces an unusual challenge: it confronts national systems that vary significantly in terms of the mechanisms of criminal prosecution, the traditional scope of rights, and the values deemed to be at stake. The Court thus constantly faces the question of whether it should insist upon a single specific rule across the board or leave instead room for national differences and, in the latter case, how much variation is compatible with the Court's understanding of Convention rights. In sum, the Court must aim for some degree of harmonization – for that is what belonging to a Convention means – but the challenge of difference shapes the nature and scope of rights that the Court can insist upon.

8.1   Origins

The development of rights to silence and against self-incrimination in the European Union began quite recently. The starting point is an otherwise dull 1993 decision involving not a defendant forced to confess under brutal police practices but bank records. In *Funke v. France* (1993),[196] the applicant was fined by a Strasbourg police court for refusing to provide bank statements to French customs authorities in connection with their investigation into violations of customs regulations. Reviewing the applicant's claim, the European Court invoked the provision of Article 6, ¶ 1 of the Convention, providing for 'a fair and public hearing', to hold, without further explication, that the applicant's 'right ... to remain silent and not to contribute to incriminating himself' had been violated.[197] With *Funke*, the ball was rolling.

Three years later, in *John Murray v. United Kingdom*,[198] the Grand Chamber invoked international standards as the basis for finding a right to silence and against self-incrimination embedded in Article 6.[199] 'Although not specifically mentioned in Article 6 of the Convention', the Court wrote:

> [T]here can be no doubt that the right to remain silent under police questioning and the privilege against self-incrimination are generally recognised international standards which lie at the heart of the notion of a fair procedure under Article 6. By providing the accused with protection against improper compulsion by the authorities these immunities contribute to avoiding miscarriages of justice and to securing the aims of Article 6.[200]

The facts of the case were more suited to making the point than was *Funke*. John Murray was arrested in Northern Ireland on terrorism charges and interviewed for 21 hours.[201] In accordance with the law of Northern Ireland, the police warned Murray that he had a right to silence but that anything he said could be used against him at trial and that an adverse inference could be drawn at trial if he failed to mention a fact that he later relied upon as part of his defense.[202] Murray steadfastly refused to answer any questions.[203] The police thereafter asked Murray to account for his presence at the crime scene, warning him that a failure to do so could result in an adverse inference being drawn at trial.[204] Again, Murray refused to answer.[205] Subsequently, Murray also refused to testify at trial, despite the judge's warning that under domestic law an adverse inference may result from silence; he also did not put up any evidence in his own support.[206] In accordance with domestic law, the trial judge drew an adverse inference against Murray on the basis of his refusal to account during the interrogation for his presence at the crime scene and refusal to testify at trial and found him guilty.[207] Supported by a submission from Amnesty International, Murray argued to the European Court that the incriminating inferences violated his right to silence and therefore he was automatically deprived of a fair trial under Article 6.

The Grand Chamber rejected Murray's broad claim but in so doing affirmed the importance of the right to silence and the privilege against self-incrimination under the Convention. In the Court's view, these rights were clearly implicated in the case, but they were not, as Murray argued, absolute in the sense that an adverse inference from a defendant's silence was always impermissible.[208] Surveying national practices, the Court observed that there was no uniform rule against a fact finder drawing an adverse inference from a defendant's refusal to speak.[209] Hence:

> Whether the drawing of adverse inferences from an accused's silence infringes Article 6 … is a matter to be determined in the light of all the circumstances of the case, having particular regard to the situations where inferences may be drawn, the weight attached to them by the national courts in their assessment of the evidence and the degree of compulsion inherent in the situation.[210]

Out of this vague pronouncement, one clear rule emerged: 'it is incompatible with the immunities under consideration to base a conviction *solely or mainly* on the accused's silence or on a refusal to answer questions or to give evidence himself'.[211] That rule was sufficient to reject Murray's application because in his prosecution other evidence amply supported the guilty verdict and thus there was no Article 6 violation.[212] Significantly, while the U.S. Supreme Court has prohibited an adverse inference on the ground that it compels a defendant to speak, the European Court saw things differently. While recognizing that the risk of an adverse inference creates 'a certain level of indirect compulsion', the *Murray* Court reasoned that because a defendant nonetheless remains free not to speak, drawing an adverse inference did not in and of itself run afoul of the right inferred from Article 6.[213]

8.2   A Maturing Approach

In *Saunders v. United Kingdom* (1997),[214] a case involving corporate fraud, the European Court held that the government violated the defendant's right to remain silent and the privilege against self-incrimination under Article 6 by reading to a criminal jury statements he had been required to make – under threat of contempt – about financial transactions in the course of an administrative investigation by the U.K. Department of Trade and Industry.[215] In its decision, the Court teased out a firmer rationale for recognizing these rights under the Convention. For one thing, the Court stated, '[t]he right not to incriminate oneself ... presupposes that the prosecution in a criminal case seek to prove their case against the accused without resort to evidence obtained through methods of coercion or oppression in defiance of the will of the accused'.[216] As such, the Court explained, 'the right is closely linked to the presumption of innocence contained in Article 6 para[graph] 2 of the Convention'.[217] That said, a more basic principle was paramount: '[t]he right not to incriminate oneself is primarily concerned ... with respecting the will of an accused person to remain silent'.[218] Although the Court did not say so, this notion brings to mind the German idea of human dignity. The European Court went on to reject the argument by the United Kingdom for a balancing test in which the rights at issue were to be weighed against the severity of the offense – such that the government's interest in prosecuting corporate fraud was sufficiently important to overcome the defendant's rights.[219] The Court also rejected the government's argument that procedural aspects of the investigation – the inspectors were acting under court supervision; plus the defendant was represented by counsel and had an opportunity to review and correct the transcript of the interview – justified overcoming the defendant's rights.[220]

Despite broad language in *Saunders*, the European Court has rejected claims of Article 6 violations in other compelled reporting contexts where penalties do not take the form of criminal liability or are otherwise minimal. For example, in *Allen v. United Kingdom* (2002)[221] the Court rejected a claim of a violation of Article 6 where the petitioner was required to provide regulatory information upon threat of a maximum fine of £300.[222] The Court explained that the right against self-incrimination 'is primarily concerned ... with respecting the will of an accused person to remain silent *in the context of criminal proceedings*' and that '[i]t does not per se prohibit the use of compulsory powers to require persons to provide information about their financial or company affairs'.[223]

Saunders rejected a balancing approach – in which the defendant's rights could be outweighed by public interests in prosecuting the most serious criminal cases (or by procedural protections). The Court again confronted a balancing argument in *Heaney and McGuinness v. Ireland* (2001).[224] That case involved an explosive attack on a British Army checkpoint and the deaths of five soldiers and one civilian.[225] The defendants were convicted under the Offences Against the State Act of 1939 for failing to account for their movements at the time of the attack: when taken into custody, the defendants had refused to answer all police questions.[226] Rejecting the government's argument for loosened protections for suspects in terrorism case, the European Court held that there was a violation of the right to silence and the privilege against self-incrimination under Article 6.[227] Here, however, is what the Court wrote: '[T]he security and public order concerns relied on by the Government cannot justify a provision which extinguishes the very essence of the applicants' rights to silence and against self-incrimination guaranteed by Article 6 § 1 of the Convention'.[228] On the one hand, then, the rights to silence and against self-incrimination applied even in cases of terrorism and there was to be no balancing away of the rights even in such serious circumstances. On the other hand, what was actually protected was 'the very essence' of the rights. The door was therefore opened to allowing governments to impose burdens on the right to silence and the privilege against self-incrimination – so long as those burdens did not undermine what lay at the essence of the rights.

8.3   A Retreat to Balancing

In *Allan v. United Kingdom* (2003), the Court provided additional analysis of the 'very essence' of the rights to silence and against self-incrimination.[229] *Allan* involved a police informant placed in the defendant's cell for the purpose of eliciting incriminating statements.[230] Those statements, some of which were recorded, were admitted at trial as the government's principal evidence, and the defendant was convicted of murder.[231] After reiterating the significance of the rights to silence and against self-incrimination to safeguarding the Article 6 guarantee of fair proceedings, the Court framed the relevant inquiry as follows: 'In examining whether a procedure has extinguished the very essence of the privilege against self-incrimination, the Court will examine the nature and degree of the compulsion, the existence of any relevant safeguards in the procedures and the use to which any material so obtained is put'.[232] The Court held there was indeed a violation of Article 6 in the circumstances of the case,[233] but the larger significance of the decision lay in its firming up of an approach to permit future incursions upon the right to silence and the privilege against self-incrimination.

In reaching its decision, the Court steered a middle path between the U.S. approach – focused on the absence of coercion when speaking to a perceived cellmate – and the German approach – focused on the essential indignity of deception. The European Court explained that 'the right to silence and the privilege against self-incrimination are primarily designed to protect against improper compulsion by the authorities and the obtaining of evidence through methods of coercion or oppression in defiance of the will of the accused' but that at the same time 'the right is not confined to cases where duress has been brought to bear on the accused or where the will of the accused has been directly overborne in some way'.[234] At issue, the Court found, is the 'freedom of a suspected person to choose whether to speak or to remain silent when questioned by the police'.[235] This freedom, the Court concluded, is 'effectively undermined' if, after a suspect has elected not to answer police questioning, 'the authorities use subterfuge to elicit ... statements of an incriminatory nature'.[236] In other words, and in contrast to the U.S. approach, what counts is that a police agent is doing the questioning – whether the defendant knows it or not. Unlike in Germany, however, deploying 'subterfuge' does not automatically constitute a violation of the defendant's rights. Instead, it was necessary to ask also '[w]hether the right to silence is undermined to such an extent as to give rise to a violation of Article 6' and this inquiry 'depends on all the circumstances of the individual case'.[237] Here, the issue came down to whether the informer was indeed 'acting as an agent of the State at the time the accused made the statement and ... it was the informer who caused the accused to make the statement'.[238] On the facts of the case, the individual placed in the cell with the defendant was a 'long-standing police informer' who was 'instructed [by the police] ... to "push him for what you can"'.[239] Given these facts, the incriminating statements were 'obtained in defiance of the [defendant's] will'[240] and it was this act that constituted the basis for the Article 6 violation of the right to silence and the privilege against self-incrimination.

8.4   Physical Evidence Reconsidered

The European Court's balancing approach marked a significant change in its consideration of the right to silence and the privilege against self-incrimination. Striking evidence of that change comes from the Court's current approach to physical evidence. In *Saunders*, the ECtHR, like the U.S. Supreme Court, flatly rejected any application of the privilege against self-incrimination to physical evidence:

> As commonly understood in the legal systems of the Contracting Parties to the Convention and elsewhere, ... [the privilege against compelled self-incrimination] does not extend to the use in criminal proceedings of material which may be obtained from the accused through the use of compulsory powers but which has an existence independent of the will of the suspect such as ... documents acquired pursuant to a warrant, breath, blood and urine samples and bodily tissue for the purpose of DNA testing.[241]

In *Jalloh v. Germany* (2006),[242] however, the European Court adopted a different approach. In *Jalloh*, police officers had restrained the defendant while a doctor administered an emetic by way of a tube through the defendant's nose to his stomach in order to force him to regurgitate a plastic bag he had swallowed that contained drugs.[243] The Grand Chamber held that this highly invasive procedure constituted inhumane and degrading treatment in violation of Article 3 of the Convention and that use of the evidence rendered the trial unfair.[244]

The conclusion that Article 3 had been violated might have ended the matter but the Grand Chamber went on to consider whether the right against self-incrimination had also been violated.[245] The obvious impediment to such a claim was that the evidence was obtained from the defendant's body: he was not in any way compelled to speak and no words of his were used at trial. The categorical rule of *Saunders* seemed to govern. But after *Allan*, balancing of interests was the order of the day – and balancing now applied even with respect to physical evidence and claims of self-incrimination. The *Jalloh* Court held that the privilege against compelled self-incrimination was indeed implicated under the circumstances of the case – and that the straightforward rule announced in *Saunders* did not therefore govern.[246] While recognizing that '[t]he evidence in issue ... could be considered to fall into the category of material having an existence independent of the will of the suspect', in this instance, the Court reasoned, 'several elements ... distinguish the present case from the examples listed in *Saunders*'.[247] First, the Court said, whereas 'the bodily material listed in *Saunders* concerned material obtained by coercion for forensic examination with a view to detecting, for example, the presence of alcohol or drugs', here 'the administration of emetics was used to retrieve real evidence in defiance of the applicant's will'.[248]

Second, the Court viewed it significant that the means by which the evidence was obtained was extraordinarily intrusive: the defendant was required to withstand 'the forcible introduction of a tube through his nose and the administration of a substance so as to provoke a pathological reaction in his body'.[249] Third, the Court reiterated, the procedure by which the evidence was obtained itself violated Article 3 of the Convention.[250] The Court did not explain why precisely these factors mattered for purposes of silence and self-incrimination (as apart from the Article 3 analysis): after all, nothing about the procedures the defendant underwent was directed at getting him to speak. Nonetheless, the Court concluded that the circumstances of the case set it apart from *Saunders* and the privilege against self-incrimination was implicated.[251] That said, further analysis was needed to determine whether the right was actually violated. On that issue, the Court set out the test as follows: 'In order to determine whether the applicant's right not to incriminate himself has been violated, the Court will have regard, in turn, to the following factors: the nature and degree of compulsion used to obtain the evidence; the weight of the public interest in the investigation and punishment of the offence in issue; the existence of any relevant safeguards in the procedure; and the use to which any material so obtained is put'.[252] Applying these four factors, the Court ruled there was indeed a violation of Article 6. The degree of compulsion was plainly severe; the crime was a minimal drug offense; there were inadequate safeguards for the defendant's health; and the evidence was decisive at trial.[253]

While in both *Allan* and *Jalloh* the Court held there was a violation of the Convention, these decisions marked a retreat from the Court's earlier approach to silence and self-incrimination. In *Saunders*, the Court rejected the government's argument that the right to silence and privilege against self-incrimination should be weighed against the public interest in prosecuting the offense at issue and measured also in light of procedural safeguards in place. In *Jalloh*, by contrast, the Court specifically invoked these same two factors as aspects of its four-part test. Although, as with any multi-part test, a single factor might not be decisive, the Court now permits consideration of the public interest (based on the severity of the crime) and the scope of procedural safeguards in determining whether a defendant's rights have been violated. That the European Court would rely on the balancing of multiple factors rather than categorical rules makes considerable sense. Balancing is a tool for accommodating variations among different jurisdictions – and a device also for avoiding a commitment to a hard rule that might well prove unsuited to the circumstances of particular signatory states.

8.5 Permissible Incursions

With the European Court having adopted a balancing approach, it was only a matter of time before the balance would tilt in the government's favor. The approach of *Allan* and *Jalloh* soon produced decisions that rejected claims of violations of the right to silence and the privilege against self-incrimination.

In *O'Halloran and Francis v. United Kingdom* (2007),[254] the Grand Chamber held there was no violation of Article 6 when the government required, upon threat of a fine, the owner of a vehicle to identify the driver at the time the vehicle was determined by a traffic camera to be speeding.[255] The Court rejected the applicants' argument that the rights at issue were immune to balancing against other interests. The Court explained that while 'in all the cases to date in which direct compulsion was applied to require an actual or potential suspect to provide information which contributed ... to his conviction, the Court has found a violation of the ... privilege against self-incrimination', it did not 'follow that any direct compulsion will automatically result in a violation' because 'what constitutes a fair trial cannot be the subject of a single unvarying rule but must depend on the circumstances of the particular case'.[256] The rejection of categorical rules was thus complete: the right to silence and the privilege against self-incrimination depended upon the circumstances of individual cases. In turn, that analysis demanded application of a multi-factor test. Ignoring (without explanation) the *Jalloh* Court's consideration of the public interest in the particular crime at issue, the Grand Chamber reduced the matter to three factors:

> [I]n order to determine whether the essence of the applicants' right to remain silent and privilege against self-incrimination was infringed, the Court will focus on the nature and degree of compulsion used to obtain the evidence, the existence of any relevant safeguards in the procedure, and the use to which any material so obtained was put.[257]

Applying this test, the Court found that although there was indeed 'direct compulsion' in that failure to provide the requested information triggered a criminal prosecution and fine, the Court observed that 'the compulsion was imposed in the context of ... the Road Traffic Act, which imposes a specific duty on the registered keeper of a vehicle to give information about the driver of the vehicle in certain circumstances'.[258] In other words, the compulsion only arose as part of a regulatory regime to which the owner of the vehicle had essentially consented.[259] In addition, the Court observed, the compelled information was limited to the identity of the driver.[260] Moreover, the regulatory regime included adequate procedural safeguards in that there is no criminal liability (for failure to disclose) if the owner of the vehicle reasonably lacks knowledge of the identity of the driver.[261] As to the use of the statements – the real concern of the applicants – the government was still required to prove the underlying offense (speeding) beyond reasonable doubt and the identity of the driver was only one element of the offense.[262] In this sense, the European Court's approach echoed that of the U.S. Supreme Court in *California v. Byers*: no self-incrimination problem arises just because information that is required to be disclosed might, in some instances, ultimately lead to criminal liability. In light of these factors, the European Court concluded, there was no violation of Article 6.

8.6   Adverse Inferences

If a defendant remains silent – either during questioning or by refusing to take the stand – may an adverse inference be drawn against that silence? A blanket decision by the European Court against adverse inferences – similar to that in the U.S. – would impose a common rule upon signatory nations, including by dismantling a key component of the recent reforms in the United Kingdom. The European Court has avoided such an outcome. Instead, in cases involving the United Kingdom, the Court has crafted rules that permit drawing adverse inferences while insisting upon certain safeguards for defendants subject to such inferences.

One such safeguard is access to counsel. In *John Murray v. United Kingdom*,[263] the defendant was arrested in Northern Ireland and, prior to interrogation, was advised that while he had a right to remain silent the law permitted adverse inferences to be drawn should he fail to answer questions.[264] The defendant refused to answer questions and asked to speak with his lawyer. Interrogation continued, however, and access to counsel was not provided for 48 hours. When the defendant was able to consult with his lawyer, the lawyer advised him to remain silent and the defendant thus continued to refuse to answer any questions. The defendant also refused to testify at his subsequent trial.[265] The trial judge drew an adverse inference against the defendant based on his silence at the interrogation and at trial.[266] The Grand Chamber held that the drawing of adverse inferences did not in and of itself render the trial unfair within the meaning of Article 6 of the Convention.[267] The Grand Chamber noted that, in accordance with the requirements of the domestic statutory scheme for drawing adverse inferences, the trial judge had ascertained that the defendant understood the consequences of choosing to remain silent and that there existed other evidence against the defendant.[268]

That determination did not, however, end the matter because the defendant had for 48 hours also been denied access to counsel. While recognizing that the right to counsel is not absolute, the Grand Chamber held that there was an Article 6 violation where the defendant *both* lacked counsel for a prolonged period *and* was subject to the adverse inference from his silence during the course of the ensuing interrogation.[269] The Grand Chamber explained that while '[n]ational laws may attach consequences to the attitude of an accused at the initial stages of police interrogation', when such consequences exist, 'it is of paramount importance for the rights of the defence that an accused has [immediate] access to a lawyer'.[270] In the Court's view, the reason for ensuring access to counsel when silence can be the basis for an adverse inference was obvious:

> [a]t the beginning of police interrogation, an accused is confronted with a fundamental dilemma relating to his defence. If he chooses to remain silent, adverse inferences may be drawn against him ... On the other hand, if the accused opts to break his silence during the course of interrogation, he runs the risk of prejudicing his defence without necessarily removing the possibility of inferences being drawn against him.[271]

Without the ability to consult with a lawyer, in other words, the suspect may well make the wrong choice – and there is no way to remedy the error. In sum, the *combination* of an adverse inference from silence and the denial of counsel before the choice to remain silent was made rendered the proceeding unfair in violation of Article 6.[272] The Court has affirmed this approach in subsequent cases.[273]

The threat of an adverse inference may lead a suspect to speak – and in so doing to make incriminating statements. The Court has also addressed the issue of counsel in that scenario. It has found a Convention violation where a suspect, denied access to counsel, was warned of the potential adverse effect of remaining silent and then issued an incriminating statement: the problem was that the suspect 'should have been given access to a solicitor at the initial stages of the interrogation as a counterweight to the intimidating atmosphere specifically devised to sap his will and make him confess to his interrogators'.[274]

The above discussion also indicates a second safeguard: quite apart from the issue of access to counsel, a conviction may not be based solely or mainly on an adverse inference drawn from the defendant's silence. As the Court in *John Murray* stated: '[I]t is incompatible with ... [the right to remain silent and the privilege against self-incrimination] to base a conviction solely or mainly on the accused's silence or on a refusal to answer questions or to give evidence himself'.[275] The European Court has reiterated this rule on multiple occasions.[276]

As a third safeguard, the European Court has insisted that juries be properly cautioned before drawing an adverse inference from silence. In *Condron v. United Kingdom* (2000),[277] the defendants, arrested and taken to police interrogation, were cautioned: "'You do not have to say anything but it may harm your defence if you do not mention when questioned something which you later rely on in court. Anything you say may be given in evidence'".[278] The defendants' lawyer, present during interrogation, advised his clients to remain silent because he believed they were suffering from drug withdrawal and thus were in no position to answer questions (the attending medical personnel disagreed with this assessment).[279] The trial judge gave the jury the following instruction with respect to the defendants' failure during the interrogation to mention facts they later relied upon in their defense at trial:

> You do not have to hold it against him or her. It is for you to decide whether it is proper to do so. Failure to mention the points in interview cannot on its own prove guilt but depending on the circumstances you may hold it against him or her when deciding whether he or she is guilty. You should decide whether in the circumstances which existed at the time of the interview the matters were ones which the defendant concerned could reasonably be expected then to mention.[280]

The European Court held that this instruction was deficient under Article 6 because it 'left the jury at liberty to draw an adverse inference notwithstanding that it may have been satisfied as to the plausibility of the explanation' the defendants gave at trial.[281]

A remarkable extension of this approach came in *Beckles v. United Kingdom* (2002).[282] In that case, the defendant's lawyer had instructed his client to remain silent during a police interrogation and the lawyer informed the police that he had given his client this advice.[283] At trial, the defendant testified as to facts to explain his innocence and when asked why he had not supplied those facts during the police interrogation he stated that he had been following the advice of his lawyer to remain silent.[284] As to whether the jury could draw an adverse inference from the defendant's refusal to answer questions during the police interrogation, the trial judge told the jury:

> [W]e have ... no independent evidence of what was said by the solicitor, but if simply saying 'Oh my solicitor advised me not to answer questions' was by itself a good and final answer, any competent solicitor and a defendant would have the power to strangle at birth any interview and that would make, you

may think, a mockery of the Act of Parliament which allows a jury, if they think it is right and proper, to make an adverse inference.[285]

The European Court found this instruction deficient because, again, the jury could have been satisfied by the defendant's explanation.[286] While the trial judge thought the defense was engaged in a ploy to evade the U.K. reforms permitting adverse inferences, the European Court saw things differently. The Court observed that 'the case-law of the domestic [that is, U.K.] courts in this area has steadily evolved ... [to recognize] the importance of giving due weight to an accused's reliance on legal advice to explain his failure to respond to police questioning' and it noted that model jury instructions from the U.K. actually comport with such an understanding.[287]

In light of these and similar decisions by the European Court, U.K. courts themselves have held that a trial judge must instruct the jury that it should not draw an adverse inference from silence where it is persuaded that the defendant reasonably relied upon the advice of his or her lawyer.[288] With respect to the issue of adverse inferences, the ECtHR and the U.K. courts have thus engaged in a dialogue. The European Court has understood the Convention to permit an adverse inference (thus under-scoring the legitimacy of the U.K. reforms), but it has insisted upon some safeguards for defendants – and these safeguards have, in turn, been adopted by the U.K. courts. Without the CJPOA, the European Court might have taken a less permissive approach to adverse inferences. For had the stronger common law protections for silence held fast in the United Kingdom, the European Court might have been less willing to allow Convention states to burden the right to silence via a negative inference at trial.

Nonetheless, the European Court's overall approach continues to eschew hard and fast rules, making outcomes in new cases difficult to predict. In *Ibrahim v. United Kingdom* (2014),[289] for example, a case involving acts of terrorism on the London transportation system, the Court held that admission of uncounseled statements at the trial of four defendants did not violate Article 6.[290] In reaching that result, the Court stated that the right to counsel can be 'subject to restrictions for good cause'[291] and referenced five factors: the applicable domestic legislative framework in place and its safeguards for defendants; the reliability of the evidence; whether the statement was retracted once legal advice became available; the procedural safeguards to allow the defendant to challenge the evidence; and the strength of the other evidence in the case.[292]

8.7 Exclusion

Aware of the differing approaches to admission of evidence among signatory states (and likely attentive also to criticisms of broad U.S.-style exclusionary rules), the European Court has avoided creating mandatory rules of exclusion in order to protect Convention rights. Instead, the Court emphasizes that its function is to determine only whether a proceeding has been fair.[293] As the cases discussed above demonstrate, use of evidence obtained in violation of the right to silence or the privilege against self-incrimination (or another Convention right) might, in particular circumstances, render a trial outcome unfair in the Court's judgment. But this is quite different from ruling as a general matter that the Convention itself requires exclusion of certain kinds of evidence – an approach the Court has taken (as discussed below) only with respect to evidence derived by torture. Besides the need to harmonize national differences, the European Court's refusal to embrace a robust exclusionary regime makes sense in light of the limited remedial powers of the Court. While the Court can impose monetary judgments against offending states, it lacks the power to overturn criminal convictions or to issue injunctions against uses of evidence. Instead, it depends upon signatory states to implement measures that will ensure compliance with Convention rights. Those measures, the Court understands, may well take different forms in different member states. Exclusion of evidence is one option, but other options – such as disciplining the police – exist as well.[294] Wholesale rules of exclusion could well prove poorly matched to protecting Convention rights under these circumstances.

Gäfgen v. Germany (2010)[295] demonstrates the Court's approach to exclusion of evidence and is therefore a useful case with which to end. In *Gäfgen*, the police threatened a student with physical violence if he did not reveal the location of a kidnapped child.[296] Within a few minutes of those threats, the student made incriminating statements and led the police to a lake where the child's body was located.[297] Writing that 'the real and immediate threats of deliberate and imminent ill-treatment to which the applicant was subjected during his interrogation must be regarded as having caused him considerable fear, anguish and mental suffering',[298] the Grand Chamber held that the police threats constituted inhumane and degrading treatment in violation of Article 3 of the Convention.[299] The Grand Chamber then turned to the question of whether the body and other physical evidence, discovered as a result of the confession, could be used at trial. The defendant argued that in order to deter future violations of Article 3, the Court should rule that all evidence obtained in violation of Article 3 must be excluded.[300] In addition, the defendant argued, the use of evidence obtained in violation of Article 3 independently violated his privilege against self-incrimination and rendered the trial unfair in violation of Article 6.[301]

The Court began its analysis with a statement of broad principles. 'While Article 6 guarantees the right to a fair hearing', the Court said, 'it does not lay down any rules on the admissibility of evidence as such, which is primarily a matter for regulation under national law'.[302] Accordingly, the question before the Court was 'whether the proceedings as a whole, including the way in which the evidence was obtained, were fair'.[303] That issue required examining 'the unlawfulness in question and, where the violation of another Convention right is concerned, the nature of the violation found'; 'whether the rights of the defence have been respected' by providing the defendant an 'opportunity to challenge the authenticity of the evidence and to oppose its use'; the 'quality of the evidence' at issue; 'where the evidence was obtained and whether these circumstances cast doubts on its reliability'; and whether the evidence was 'decisive ... for the outcome of the proceeding'.[304]

Having listed these factors, however, when the Court turned to the Article 3 issue, it simply announced that, 'particular considerations apply in respect of the use in criminal proceedings of evidence obtained in breach of Article 3' because '[t]he use of such evidence, secured as a result of a violation of one of the core and absolute rights guaranteed by the Convention, always raises serious issues as to the fairness of the proceedings, even if the admission of such evidence was not decisive in securing a conviction'.[305] The Court thus explained that in prior cases it had held that use of any evidence obtained through torture automatically rendered the trial unfair.[306]

Here, however, while the physical evidence was discovered as a result of a violation of Article 3, those violations did not rise to the level of torture – and there was an open question (unresolved by *Jalloh*) as to whether the rule that applied in cases of torture should govern all Article 3 cases – or whether instead, when Article 3 abuses did not rise to the level of torture, the list of multiple factors the Court had identified came into play.[307] Canvassing the approaches of other jurisdictions provided no guidance because there was 'no clear consensus ... about the exact scope of application of the exclusionary rule'.[308] Rather than decide the question, though, the Court simply concluded that no decision was needed because 'a criminal trial's fairness and the effective protection of the absolute prohibition under Article 3 ... are only at stake if ... the breach of Article 3 had a bearing on the outcome of the proceedings against the defendant'.[309] Here, the defendant had confessed at trial, that confession was the basis for the conviction, and the confession was freely given in court and was independent of the police misconduct at issue and of the resulting physical evidence the police had obtained in the case.[310] As such, '[t]he impugned real evidence was not necessary, and was not used to prove ... [the defendant] guilty or to determine his sentence. ... [T]here was a break in the causal chain'.[311]

Given that break, the larger question of whether use of evidence obtained as a result of inhumane treatment necessarily renders a trial unfair could be postponed to another day because the disputed physical evidence made no difference to the outcome. With that analysis resolving the Article 3 question, the self-incrimination claim could be quickly dispatched with also. The privilege against self-incrimination, the Court explained, prohibits the government from 'resort[ing] to evidence obtained through methods of coercion or oppression in defiance of the ... [defendant's] will'.[312] Here there was no violation because the defendant voluntarily confessed at trial and that confession was the basis for his conviction.[313]

Gäfgen's convoluted route to an ultimately simplistic holding comports with the European Court's overall approach to the right to silence and the privilege against self-incrimination. The Court recognizes the multiple interests that are at stake. It understands that different jurisdictions have different approaches. It is exceedingly cautious about adopting a single rule that would apply without room for variation among signatory states. It thus puts considerable stock in flexible tests and it focuses on the specific facts of cases in order to reach satisfactory resolutions in a way that allows for fluidity and accommodation in the future.

8.8 Summary

The European Court's recognition of a right to silence and a privilege against self-incrimination under the Convention is a recent development and a work in progress. Nonetheless, the Court has developed a set of basic protections for those rights that influence the practice of signatory states. It remains to be seen just how far the Court's rulings will extend in the future. On the one hand, the Court has been willing to produce significant reform in outlying states where the rights to silence and against self-incrimination have traditionally received little if any protection. On the other hand, the Court's decisions allow signatory states a good deal of leeway to structure their criminal justice systems on their own, including in ways that limit the scope of defendants' rights in significant ways.

The big issue going forward is whether the Court will settle for a minimal conception of the right to silence and the privilege against self-incrimination and leave it to individual states to develop, if they choose, stronger safeguards – or, instead, push reluctant states toward even stronger reforms. Put differently, the question is whether the Court will be satisfied with the modest changes that it has helped produce in France (and other states) or instead ambitiously seek to push for more robust protections of the kind already in place in Germany. Perhaps the best that the Court will achieve is a middling course: one that continues to nudge states with the weakest protections to enhance rights domestically, but that avoids the difficult task of imposing throughout the entire system a common set of rights that track those of states where criminal defendants receive the strongest protections.

9. CONCLUSION: HAZARDS OF GLOBALIZATION

As states and courts continue to develop the contours of the right to silence and the privilege against self-incrimination – and, in particular, as those rights develop further under the European Convention (and other international treaties) – a caution is warranted. In an age of globalization, human rights are increasingly conceived of in universal terms – such that there is a set of common rights that protect (or should protect) individuals throughout the entire world. Yet globalization and rights universalism carry a significant hazard. Defining and protecting rights through supranational institutions comes with an important cost. Treaties (like the European Convention on Human Rights) and other international compacts can serve to keep abusive governmental practices in line. But they can also operate to limit the expansion of rights. In nations with strong pre-commitments to individual rights, an international treaty can act as a ceiling – rather than a floor. That is, the treaty that is designed as the minimum level of protection a signatory nation must provide to individuals can end up as setting the maximum level of protection that is viewed as necessary or desirable. Domestic measures to augment rights beyond those mandated by the treaty can easily be seen as extravagant. If, after all, the nation already meets all of its obligations under the international agreement, why, domestic actors will ask, is it necessary to go further? Indeed, the stronger the focus on provisions of international treaties (and other sources of global standards), the harder it may become even to imagine that other kinds of rights, beyond those the treaty expresses, could exist.

The problem, from a human rights perspective, is that international agreements and other mechanisms of globalization are often insufficiently ambitious or end up being interpreted narrowly. Their goal is to provide a reachable standard for the largest possible set of signatory nations. While those standards might be difficult for the small number of nations with the poorest history of human rights protections or the greatest inclination to abuse human rights, the standards are nonetheless attainable for all, with some degree of effort. In order to be achievable, the treaty's demands must represent a middle course – something between the practices of the worst offenders and the practices of those nations with the highest capacity and inclination to protect human rights. Therein lies the risk: while poor performers can be reformed to raise their standards, the best performers might end up slouching. Left to their own devices, without the shadow cast by international agreements and the bright light of globalization, the best performing nations might well adopt stronger protections for rights. Once brought into the common system, however, ambitions can easily drop.

Like standardized educational requirements in a vast and diverse school system, human rights treaties and attendant mechanisms of globalization can produce, perversely, a uniform mediocrity. Even worse, globalization and universality can provide cover to local reformers interested in cutting back on pre-existing protections for individual rights. Such reformers can pursue this agenda by shifting attention away from their own traditions to less stringent standards required at the international level. In an age of universality, an appeal to localized traditions can easily seem provincial. Reformers who speak the language of globalization can impose changes that actually leave localized rights worse off. In this regard, the recent diminishment in the United Kingdom of common law protections for the right to silence and the privilege against self-incrimination serves as a striking example. Those changes enjoy legitimacy because they comport with the demands of the European Convention (as interpreted by the European Court) – even though as measured by the U.K.'s own past traditions they appear a radical diminishment in defendants' rights.

The risk of diminishing rights may be particularly great when a court is responsible for deciding the scope of protections signatory nations must accept. When a court sitting at the top interprets the meaning of a universal right it must do so with a view to the effects on the system as a whole – taking into account variations among signatory states. In performing this role, there are strong institutional pressures for the court to act with caution: to read rights modestly, avoid undue disruption, minimize the costs of compliance, and avoid public backlash (or worse disobedience). Giving enforcement to a top-level court can thus also water down rights. Here, the cautious approach of the European Court of Human Rights with respect to silence and self-incrimination is a prime example of the trend – a necessary product of the reach of that Court's interpretations of Convention protections. Finally, there may be a feedback effect: when rights diminish locally, universal requirements may themselves come to be understood more narrowly or to be ratcheted down in response. In this regard, the dialogue between the U.K. courts and the European Court on adverse inferences from silence is instructive: the end result of that dialogue was that the European Court accepted the compatibility of adverse inferences with the fair trial rights required by the Convention.

To be sure, there can be countervailing trends. Nation states might fully understand that global rules are merely a floor, and so stick to or pursue stronger rights domestically based upon their own more robust commitments and traditions. Here, the German approach to silence and self-incrimination is a good example. In addition, rights generated from above might provide the tools for domestic courts and other institutions to implement reforms that would otherwise be impossible. In France, for example, pressures from the European Court led to new statutory protections for the right to silence and the privilege against self-incrimination.

Nonetheless, long-term trends might prove less satisfying. In this regard, the longer experience of the United States sheds light. In the U.S. system, the federal Constitution ensures a minimum level of rights around the country, but states (and localities) remain free to provide their own citizens with stronger protections. Yet state constitutions, interpreted by state courts, have not proven a particularly robust alternative source of individual rights. Rather than decide independently what provisions of state constitutions mean, modern state courts have tended to hew to the Supreme Court's understandings of analogous provisions in the federal Constitution. While the trend is not entirely in one direction, 'systematic studies demonstrate that most state courts, when presented with the opportunity, have chosen not to depart from federal precedents when interpreting the rights-granting provisions of state constitutions' (Solimine, 2002: 338). Reasons for this phenomenon may include that because state courts spend so much energy adhering closely to Supreme Court precedent when resolving federal constitutional issues, they have lost capacity for independent analysis that could be brought to state constitutional questions; litigants tend to press claims in terms of federal rather than state rights; and judges and their staff members are trained in nationally oriented law schools that devote little attention to issues of state rights. Whatever the explanation, the federal floor has to a large degree capped the development of rights at the state level. The future ability of Germany (and other high-performing states) to continue, in an age of significant pressures of globalization, to focus on home-grown approaches to silence and self-incrimination, will likely be key to maintaining strong domestic protections for those rights. The U.S. experience suggests the task is far from easy.

Judged by their own past practices, nations that have newly adopted protections for the right to silence and the privilege against self-incrimination have enhanced individual liberties. Measured, however, against states with the strongest versions of those rights, such enhancements are less remarkable. Future increases in rights are possible – but there are significant hazards in pursuing such increases through a simple idea of universal conceptions and globalized mechanisms.

NOTES

1. *Pennsylvania v. Muniz*, 496 U.S. 582, 596 (1990) (internal quotation marks omitted).
2. *Murphy v. Waterfront Comm'n*, 378 U.S. 52, 55 (1964).
3. Ibid. at 55.
4. *Hopt v. Utah*, 110 U.S. 574 (1884).
5. U.S. Const. amend. V.
6. See, for example, *Bram v. United States*, 168 U.S. 532, 548 (1897).
7. See *Malloy v. Hogan*, 378 U.S. 1, 8 (1964).
8. See, for example, *Brown v. Mississippi*, 297 U.S. 278, 286 (1936).
9. *Chavez v. Martinez*, 538 U.S. 760, 780 (2003).
10. *Dickerson v. United States*, 530 U.S. 428, 434 (2000).
11. *Arizona v. Fulminante*, 499 U.S. 279, 283 (1991) (undercover agent offered to protect suspect from other inmates in exchange for his confession); *Beecher v. Alabama*, 389 U.S. 35, 36 (1967) (per curiam) (officer held gun held to suspect's head and threatened to kill him unless he confessed); *Ward v. Texas*, 316 U.S. 547, 555 (1942) (police interrogators warned suspect of threat of mob violence).
12. *Haynes v. Washington*, 373 U.S. 503, 513–515 (1963) (suspect told he could not contact anybody outside police station until he signed a written confession); *Ashcraft v. Tennessee*, 322 U.S. 143, 152 (1944) (suspect interrogated for 36 hours without rest).
13. *Blackburn v. Alabama*, 361 U.S. 199, 206–207 (1960).
14. *Hale v. Henkel*, 201 U.S. 43, 70 (1906).
15. *Lefkowitz v. Turley*, 414 U.S. 70, 82–83 (1973).
16. *Griffin v. California*, 380 U.S. 609, 615 (1965).
17. *McGautha v. California*, 402 U.S. 183, 213 (1971).
18. *Lefkowitz v. Turley*, 414 U.S. at 76.
19. *Marchetti v. United States*, 390 U.S. 39, 53 (1968).
20. *Hiibel v. Sixth Judicial District Court of Nevada*, 542 U.S. 177, 189 (2004).
21. *Kastigar v. United States*, 406 U.S. 441, 453 (1972).
22. *Doe v. United States*, 487 U.S. 201, 210 (1988).
23. *Schmerber v. California*, 384 U.S. 757, 764 (1996).
24. Ibid. at 763.
25. *Gilbert v. California*, 388 U.S. 263, 266–267 (1967).

26. *United States v. Dioniso*, 410 U.S. 1, 7 (1972); *United States v. Wade*, 388 U.S. 218, 222 (1967).
27. *Fisher v. United States*, 425 U.S. 391, 414 (1976).
28. See *United States v. Hubbell*, 530 U.S. 27, 40 (2000); *United States v. Doe*, 465 U.S. 605, 613 (1984).
29. *Shapiro v. United States*, 355 U.S. 1, 33 (1948).
30. *United States v. Sullivan*, 274 U.S. 259, 262–263 (1927).
31. 402 U.S. 424 (1971).
32. Ibid. at 425–426, 434.
33. Ibid. at 430–431.
34. *Miranda v. Arizona*, 384 U.S. 436 (1966).
35. For example, some jurisdictions require that police interrogations be transcribed or recorded. See, for example, Police and Criminal Evidence Act 1984 (U.K.) § 60 and Code E; Codice di Procedura Penale (Italy) art. 357, §2(b).
36. *Miranda v. Arizona*, 384 U.S. at 467–472.
37. Ibid. at 478–479.
38. See *United States v. Patane*, 542 U.S. 630, 641 (2004) (Thomas, J., plurality opinion, joined by Rehnquist, C.J. and Scalia, J.) ('Our cases ... make clear ... that a mere failure to give *Miranda* warnings does not, by itself, violate a suspect's constitutional rights or even the *Miranda* rule').
39. *Dickerson v. United States*, 530 U.S. 428, 438–439 (2000).
40. *United States v. Patane*, 542 U.S. at 636 (physical evidence not excluded as a fruit); *Michigan v. Tucker*, 417 U.S. 433, 447 (1974) (subsequent witness statement not excluded as a fruit). The 'no fruits' rule assumes that the statements in question, though unwarned, were nonetheless voluntary. See *Patane*, 542 U.S. at 636 ('The Self–Incrimination Clause ... is not implicated by the admission into evidence of the physical fruit of a voluntary statement'). See also *Oregon v. Elstad*, 470 U.S. 298, 317–318 (1985) (noting that a second *Mirandized* confession must be excluded if it or the first confession was actually involuntary such that a due process violation occurred); *Missouri v. Seibert*, 542 U.S. 600, 616–617 (2004) (holding that where the police deliberately bypassed *Miranda* in order to elicit a confession, then gave *Miranda* warnings and obtained the confession again, the post-warning confession was inadmissible).
41. *Miranda v. Arizona*, 384 U.S. at 478.
42. See, for example, *Orozco v. Texas*, 394 U.S. 324, 325 (1969) (suspect was in custody for purposes of *Miranda* when held in his bedroom by four police officers).
43. *Miranda v. Arizona*, 384 U.S. at 479. This right is separate from the Sixth Amendment right '[i]n all criminal prosecutions' of 'the accused' to 'have the assistance of counsel for his defense', U.S. Const. amend. VI.
44. *Miranda v. Arizona*, 384 U.S. at 470.
45. Ibid. at 475.
46. Ibid.
47. Ibid. at 476.
48. *Rhode Island v. Innis*, 446 U.S. 291, 301 (1980).
49. 467 U.S. 649 (1984).
50. Ibid. at 655–657.
51. 496 U.S. 292, 294 (1990).
52. Ibid. at 296.
53. *Pennsylvania v. Muniz*, 496 U.S. 582, 600 (1990).
54. 423 U.S. 96 (1975).
55. Ibid. at 97–98.
56. Ibid. at 102–103 (1975).
57. 560 U.S. 370 (2010).

58. Ibid. at 388–389.
59. PACE and Code C have undergone multiple revisions: the discussion that follows refers to the versions in place in 2014.
60. Revised Code of Practice for the Detention, Treatment and Questioning of Persons by Police Officers, Police and Criminal Evidence Act 1984 Code C (2014) ('Code C') ¶ 3.2(iv).
61. PACE § 58(1); Code C ¶ 3.1(a)(i).
62. Code C ¶ 6.8.
63. PACE § 56(1); Code C ¶ 3.1(a)(ii).
64. PACE § 58(4); Code C ¶ 6.6.
65. PACE §§ 56(5) and 58(8).
66. Terrorism Act 2000 (U.K.) § 8(1); Revised Code of Practice in Connection With: The Detention, Treatment and Questioning by Police Officers of Persons in Police Detention Under Section 41 of, and Schedule 8 to, the Terrorism Act 2000, Police and Criminal Evidence Act 1984 Code H ¶ 6.7(a) and Annex B ¶ A.
67. Code C ¶ 11.5.
68. Code C ¶11.6(c).
69. Code C ¶ 12.2.
70. *Griffin v. California*, 380 U.S. 609, 614–615 (1965).
71. Criminal Justice and Public Order ACT 1994 (U.K.) ('CJPOA') § 34.
72. CJPOA § 34.
73. See, for example, *R v. Argent* [1996] EWCA Crim 1728.
74. CJPOA §§ 36 and 37.
75. CJPOA § 35 (3).
76. *R v. Cowan* [1996] Q.B. 373, 381.
77. See Code C § 10.1 ('A person whom there are grounds to suspect of an offence … must be cautioned before any questions about an offence … are put to them if either the suspect's answers or silence … may be given as evidence to a court in prosecution').
78. Ibid. § 10.5
79. Code C Annex B § 15.
80. PACE § 76(2).
81. PACE, § 76(2).
82. *R v. Mason* [1988] 1 WLR 139.
83. *R v. Paris* [1993] 97 Cr. App. R. 99.
84. PACE § 76(4)(a).
85. PACE § 76(8).
86. See, for example, *A v. Secretary of State for the Home Department* [2004] EWCA Civ 1123, ¶ 92.
87. See, for example, *R v Delaney* [1989] 88 Cr App R 388.
88. PACE § 78.
89. *R v. Samuel* [1988] Q.B. 615, 630.
90. See, for example, *R v. Singleton* [2002] EWCA (Crim) 459.
91. Code of Criminal Procedure (France) ('CCP'), art. 63.
92. Ibid.
93. CCP art. 706-88.
94. See CCP art. 706-88 (referring to certain offenses listed in CCP, art. 706-73).
95. CCP art. 706-88-1.
96. Act no. 93-2 (Jan. 4, 1993).
97. CCP art. 63-2.
98. CCP art. 63-1.
99. CCP art. 63-3.
100. Act no. 93-2 (Jan. 4, 1993).

101. Act no. 93-1013 (Aug. 24, 1993).
102. Act no. 2000-516, art. 11 (June 15, 2000).
103. Ibid.
104. Act no. 2002-307 (March 4, 2002).
105. Act no. 2003-239 (March 18, 2003).
106. Act no. 2004-204 (March 9, 2004).
107. *Salduz v. Turkey*, 49 EHRR 421 (2008).
108. Ibid. ¶ 63.
109. Ibid. ¶ 55.
110. Ibid. ¶ 52.
111. *Dayanan v. Turkey*, ECHR 2278 (2009).
112. Ibid. ¶ 32.
113. Decision no. 2010-14/22 QPC, ¶ 29 (July 30, 2010).
114. Ibid. ¶ 18.
115. Ibid.
116. Ibid. ¶ 25.
117. Ibid. ¶ 29.
118. Ibid. ¶ 28.
119. Ibid. ¶¶ 28–29.
120. Ibid. ¶ 30.
121. 1466/07 (ECtHR) (Oct. 14, 2010).
122. Ibid. ¶ 14.
123. Ibid. ¶ 15.
124. Ibid. ¶ 23.
125. Ibid. ¶ 55.
126. Cour de cassation, Chambre criminelle, Bulletin criminel no. 163 (Oct. 19. 2010).
127. Cour de cassation, Chambre criminelle, Bulletin criminel no. 164 (Oct. 19. 2010).
128. Cour de cassation, Chambre criminelle, Bulletin criminel no. 165 (Oct. 19. 2010).
129. See, for example, Cour de cassation, Chambre criminelle, no. 10-85.520 (Jan. 4, 2011).
130. CCP art. 63-1.
131. CCP arts. 63-1 and 63-4-2.
132. CCP art. 63-3-1.
133. CCP art. 63-4-2.
134. CCP art. 63-4-2.
135. CCP art. 63-4-2.
136. CCP art. 63-4-2.
137. CCP art. 706-88 (referring to specified offenses in CCP, art. 706-73).
138. CCO art. 706-88.
139. CCP art. 63-4-1.
140. CCP art. 63-4-2.
141. CCP art. 63-4-2.
142. CCP art. 63-4-3.
143. CCP art. 63-4-3.
144. There exist two general categories of nullities. First, there exist textual nullities, established by the legislature as the penalty for a violation of a specific provision of the Code: 'a violation of formalities prescribed by law under penalty of nullity', CCP, art. 802. Second, there is the possibility of a court declaring a nullity where there has been a violation of some other procedural rule: 'a non-observance of substantial formalities', ibid.
145. CCP art. 206.
146. *Elkins v. United States*, 364 U.S. 206, 217 (1960).

147. CCP art. 802. In certain instances where a violation concerns an important public interest, French courts have not required a showing of prejudice to the defendant. See Tricot (2013: 222, 254).
148. CCP art. 172.
149. See Ma (2012: 316) (describing meeting the prejudice requirement as 'a daunting task').
150. CCP Article Préliminaire III.
151. CCP art. 116
152. CCP art. 116.
153. CCP art. 106.
154. CCP art. 328.
155. Stuntz (2011: 302) ('[G]uilty pleas and the quick bargains that precede them have become the primary means of judging criminal defendants' guilt or innocence').
156. German Code of Criminal Procedure (*Strafprozeßordnung*) ('StPO') § 136; see also ibid. § 163a.
157. See ibid. § 163a(3) (prosecutor interrogation); ibid. § 163a(4) (police interrogation).
158. StPO § 114b(1).
159. StPO §§ 114b(1) and 140.
160. StPO § 141 (1).
161. StPO § 141(3)
162. StPO 168c(1) and 163a(3).
163. StPO § 136a.
164. BGHSt 15, 187 (1960).
165. OLG Hamm StV 1984, 456.
166. BGHSt 13, 60 (1959).
167. BGHSt 35, 328 (1988).
168. See, for example, *Frazier v. Cupp,* 394 U.S. 731, 739 (1969); *Ledbetter v. Edwards,* 35 F.3d 1062, 1066, 1070, 1071 (6th Cir. 1994).
169. Basic Law for the Federal Republic of Germany, art. 1.
170. Ibid.
171. BGHSt 14, 358, 364 (1960).
172. BGHSt 5, 332 (1954), translated in Thaman (2008: 97).
173. Ibid.
174. BGHSt 42, 170, 173–174 (1996), translated in Thaman (2008: 87).
175. BGHSt 34, 362 (1987), cited in Ross (2007: 563).
176. 496 U.S. 292 (1990).
177. Ibid. at 296–298.
178. StPO § 136(1).
179. BGHSt 22, 129 (1968).
180. BGHSt 38, 372 (1992).
181. BGHSt 38, 214, translated in Thaman (2001: 607–608).
182. Ibid.
183. BGHSt 39, 352 (1993).
184. BGHSt 47, 172 (2001).
185. See supra note 40 and accompanying text.
186. StPO § 243(5).
187. StPO § 257.
188. BGHSt 38, 214, 218 (1992).
189. StPO § 244(2).
190. Ibid. at 297.
191. StPO § 257(c). On the increasing role of negotiated agreements in the German system as a way to resolve the growing docket of criminal cases, see Rauxloh (2011).

192. StPO § 257c(1); BGHSt 43, 195 (1997), translated in Thaman (2001: 151, 152–153).
193. *Pishchalnikov v. Russia* [2009] ECHR 1357.
194. Ibid. ¶ 77.
195. *Zaichenko v. Russia*, 39660/02 (2010), ¶ 52.
196. 16 EHRR 297 (1993).
197. Ibid. ¶ 44.
198. 22 EHRR 29 (1996).
199. Ibid. ¶ 45.
200. Ibid.
201. Ibid. ¶ 15.
202. Ibid. ¶ 11.
203. Ibid. ¶¶ 11, 13, 16.
204. Ibid. ¶ 13.
205. Ibid.
206. Ibid. ¶¶ 20–21.
207. Ibid. ¶¶ 22, 25.
208. Ibid. ¶ 47.
209. Ibid.
210. Ibid. ¶ 47.
211. Ibid. ¶ 47 (emphasis added).
212. Ibid. ¶ 52.
213. Ibid. ¶ 50.
214. 23 EHRR 313 (1997).
215. Ibid. ¶¶ 60, 81.
216. Ibid. ¶ 68.
217. Ibid.
218. Ibid. ¶ 69.
219. Ibid. ¶ 74.
220. Ibid. ¶¶ 63, 75.
221. 35 EHRR CD289 (2002).
222. Ibid.
223. Ibid. (emphasis added).
224. 33 EHRR 264 (2001)
225. Ibid. ¶ 8.
226. Ibid. ¶¶ 10, 12.
227. Ibid. ¶ 59.
228. Ibid. ¶ 58.
229. 36 EHRR 143 (2003).
230. Ibid. ¶ 13.
231. Ibid. ¶¶ 16, 21, 45.
232. Ibid. ¶ 44.
233. Ibid. ¶ 53.
234. Ibid. ¶ 50.
235. Ibid. ¶ 50.
236. Ibid. ¶ 50.
237. Ibid. ¶ 51.
238. Ibid. ¶ 51.
239. Ibid. ¶ 52.
240. Ibid. ¶ 52.
241. *Saunders v. United Kingdom*, 23 EHRR 313 (1997) ¶ 69.
242. 44 EHRR 32 (2007).
243. Ibid. ¶ 13.

244. Ibid. ¶ 108.
245. Ibid. ¶ 87.
246. Ibid. ¶ 116.
247. Ibid. ¶ 113.
248. Ibid. ¶ 113.
249. Ibid.
250. Ibid. ¶ 115.
251. Ibid. ¶ 116.
252. Ibid. ¶ 117.
253. Ibid. ¶¶ 118–121
254. 46 EHRR 21 (2008).
255. Ibid. ¶¶ 25, 63.
256. Ibid. ¶ 53.
257. Ibid. ¶ 54.
258. Ibid. ¶ 57.
259. Ibid. ¶ 57.
260. Ibid. ¶ 58.
261. Ibid. ¶ 59.
262. Ibid. ¶ 60.
263. *John Murray v. United Kingdom*, 22 EHRR 29 (1996).
264. Ibid. ¶ 11.The relevant law of Northern Ireland at the time of the defendant's arrest (in 1990) and trial (1991) provided for cautions and adverse inferences. Ibid. ¶ 27.
265. Ibid. ¶¶ 11–16, 21.
266. Ibid. ¶ 25.
267. Ibid. ¶ 58.
268. Ibid. ¶ 51.
269. Ibid. ¶¶ 63, 70.
270. Ibid. ¶¶ 63, 66.
271. Ibid. ¶ 66.
272. Ibid. ¶ 70.
273. See, for example, *Averill v. United Kingdom*, 31 EHRR 3, ¶ 60 (2001).
274. *Magee v. United Kingdom*, 31 EHRR 35, ¶ 43 (2001).
275. *John Murray, United Kingdom*, 22 EHRR 29 (1996) ¶ 47.
276. See, for example, *Averill v. United Kingdom*, 31 EHRR 3, ¶ 45 ('[I]t would be incompatible with the right to silence to base a conviction solely or mainly on the accused's silence or on a refusal to answer questions or to give evidence himself.')
277. 31 EHRR 1, ¶ 15 (2001).
278. Ibid. ¶ 15.
279. Ibid. ¶ 13.
280. Ibid. ¶ 22.
281. Ibid.
282. 36 EHRR 13 (2002).
283. Ibid. ¶ 16.
284. Ibid. ¶ 22.
285. Ibid. ¶ 24.
286. Ibid. ¶ 64.
287. Ibid. ¶ 64.
288. See *R v. Beckles*, ECWA Crim 2766 (2004).
289. *Ibrahim and Others v. United Kingdom*, 50541/08, 50571/08, 50573/08 and 40351/09 (Dec. 16, 2014).
290. Ibid. ¶ 224.
291. Ibid. ¶ 193.
292. Ibid. ¶ 196.

293. See, for example, *Schenk v. Switzerland*, 13 EHRR 1342 ¶ 46 (1991) ('While Article 6 guarantees the right to a fair hearing, it does not lay down any rules on the admissibility of evidence as such, which is primarily a matter for regulation under national law').
294. *Camdereli v. Turkey*, 28433/02, ¶ 37 (2008) ('[T]he rights enshrined in the Convention are practical and effective, and not theoretical and illusory. Therefore, in ... cases [of alleged violations], an effective investigation must be able to lead to the identification and punishment of those responsible'); *Scordino v. Italy*, 45 EHRR 7, ¶ 94 (2006) ('[T]he State enjoys a wide margin of appreciation with regard ... to choosing the means of enforcement [of a Convention right]').
295. 52 EHRR 1 (2011).
296. Ibid. ¶ 20.
297. Ibid. ¶ 16.
298. Ibid. ¶ 103.
299. Ibid. ¶ 132.
300. Ibid. ¶ 153.
301. Ibid. ¶ 150.
302. Ibid. ¶ 162.
303. Ibid. ¶ 163.
304. Ibid. ¶¶ 163–164.
305. Ibid. ¶¶ 165–166.
306. Ibid. ¶ 167.
307. Ibid. ¶ 167.
308. Ibid. ¶ 173
309. Ibid. ¶ 178.
310. Ibid. ¶ 179.
311. Ibid. ¶ 180.
312. Ibid. ¶ 186.
313. Ibid.

BIBLIOGRAPHY

Amar, Akhil Reed. 1997. *The Constitution and Criminal Procedure: First Principles*. New Haven, CT: Yale University Press.

Amar, Akhil Reed and Renée Lettow. 1995. 'Fifth Amendment First Principles: The Self-Incrimination Clause', 93 *Michigan Law Review* 857.

Doak, Jonathan and Claire McGourlay. 2009. *Criminal Evidence in Context*. Abingdon: Routledge-Cavendish.

Forsyth, William. 1994. *History of Trial by Jury* (2nd edn). Union, NJ: Lawbook Exchange.

Garrett, Brandon L. 2010. 'The Substance of False Confessions', 62 *Stanford Law Review* 1051.

Langbein, John H. 1974. *Prosecuting Crime in the Renaissance: England, Germany, France*. Cambridge, MA: Harvard University Press.

Langbein, John H. 1994. 'The Historical Origins of the Privilege Against Self-Incrimination at Common Law', 92 *Michigan Law Review* 1047.

Leo, Richard A. 2008. *Police Interrogation and American Justice*. Cambridge, MA: Harvard University Press.

Ma, Yue. 2012. 'The American Exclusionary Rule: Is There a Lesson to Learn from Others?', 22 *Int'l Crim. Justice Rev.* 309.

Rauxloh, Regina E. 2011. 'Formalization of Plea Bargaining in Germany: Will the New Legislation be Able to Square the Circle?', 34 *Fordham Int'l L.J.* 296.

Ross, Jacqueline E. 2007. 'The Place of Covert Surveillance in Democratic Societies: A Comparative Study of the United States and Germany', 55 *American Journal of Comparative Law* 493.

Saas, Claire. 2004. 'De la composition pénale au plaider-coupable: le pouvoir de sanction du procureur', *Revue de Science Criminelle et de Droit Pénal Comparé* 827.

Solimine, Michael E. 2002. 'Supreme Court Monitoring of State Courts in the Twenty First Century', 35 Ind. L. Rev. 335.

Stuntz, William J. 2011. *The Collapse of American Criminal Justice.* Cambridge, MA: Harvard University Press.

Thaman, Stephen C. 2001. '*Miranda* in Comparative Law', 45 *St Louis University Law Journal* 581.

Thaman, Stephen C. 2008. *Comparative Criminal Procedure: A Casebook Approach.* Durham, NC: Carolina Academic Press.

Tricot, Juliette. 2013. 'France', in Katalin Ligeti, ed., *Toward a Prosecutor for the European Union: A Comparative Analysis*, Vol. 1. Oxford: Hart Publishing.

Van Caenegem, R.C. 1973. *The Birth of the English Common Law.* New York: Cambridge University Press.

Weigend, Thomas. 2007. 'Germany', in Craig M. Bradley, ed., *Criminal Procedure: A Worldwide Study.* Durham, NC: Carolina Academic Press.

Wigmore, John H. 1940. *A Treatise on the Anglo-American System of Evidence in Trials at Common Law*, Vol. 8 (3rd edn). Boston: Little, Brown and Company.

Wigmore, John H. 1961. *Evidence in Trials at Common Law*, Vol. 8 (revised by John T. McNaughton). Boston: Little, Brown.

Williams, Glanville. 1963. *The Proof of Guilt: A Study of the English Criminal Trial.* London: Stevens.

C. Adjudication: jury trials

10. Rumba justice and the Spanish jury trial
*Elisabetta Grande**

1. INTRODUCTION

It is the aim of this chapter to provide a tentative description and explanation for what some scholars have described as the ongoing Americanization of the Continental European criminal process.[1] I will examine the Spanish jury trial as a special case of a more general phenomenon. During the last few decades, European criminal procedures underwent extensive reforms and in Continental Europe the American adversary system often became the reference model for the overhaul.[2] Legal institutions like hearsay prohibition, cross-examination, jury trial, or a governmental pre-trial investigation conducted by the police and the public prosecutor as opposed to a judicial pre-trial investigation conducted by the investigating magistrate, traveled from the American criminal procedure system to its European counterparts. Commentators often insist that American influence has made European criminal procedure more 'adversarial'.[3]

Did this diffusion of legal institutions from the American system really end up making European criminal procedure systems more adversarial?[4] Is it plausible that, to the contrary, embedded in the new context, American legal arrangements lost their resemblance to the original model? I will argue that the American import did not alter the non-adversary structure of the recipient European criminal procedure but instead melded with and even strengthened the non-adversarial Continental way of searching for the truth. The present chapter tries to trace the influence of American criminal procedure on European legal institutions through a case study of the Spanish jury system, which was loosely modeled on that of the United States. What kind of changes did this legal transplant bring about? Far from diffusing American practices and making the Spanish system more adversarial, I contend, the American import actually strengthened the non-adversarial structure of Spanish civil law. In identifying the dynamics by which Spain absorbed and adapted the American paradigm, I would like to suggest further inquiry into the hypothesis that similar patterns of transformation may characterize other 'adversarial' law reforms in Continental Europe.

In section 2, I will recapitulate my view of how adversarial and non-adversarial legal institutions differ (see Grande, 2008).[5] Section 3 argues that Spain's adoption of the jury system did not in fact transform its criminal procedure along adversarial lines and instead reinforced non-adversarial features of Spain's legal system. Section 4 will suggest ways in which this insight should transform inquiry into the impact of other American transplants on the European civil law systems that adopted them.

2.   GRASPING THE INTIMATE ESSENCE OF TWO MODELS OF CRIMINAL PROCEDURE: TANGO JUSTICE V. RUMBA JUSTICE

In order to assess the impact of the American jury trial on Spanish criminal procedure, one needs to bring the difference between adversarial and non-adversarial models into sharper focus.[6] This preliminary juxtaposition should lay the foundation for future work exploring American influences on other aspects of European criminal procedure, including the abolition of the investigating magistrate, the expansion of exclusionary rules, and the introduction of cross-examination.

Following Professor Damaška's application of Weberian ideal-typical models to the comparative study of criminal procedure more than forty years ago, the two rival procedural models can be fruitfully organized around the contrast between features distinguishing a party-controlled contest, on the one hand, from an officially-controlled inquiry, on the other.[7] (Damaška, 1973, 2001; Grande, 2000) The key difference between common law and Continental criminal procedure, in his view, resides in the distinct roles that parties and judges play in the fact-finding process. In a common law model, two contestants shape the expression of their dispute and manage the presentation of the evidence. In a Continental model, fact-finding responsibilities are assigned to court officials.

These differences between the respective roles of parties and judges reflect contrasting approaches to the search for truth. Starting from the idea that the truth is accessible to third parties, the Continental approach pursues the discovery of an objective truth. This reflects the 'revered civilian concept of substantive truth' (Damaška, 1973: 581 n. 199), which I have elsewhere called *ontological truth*, based as it is on the Continental system's commitment to the notion that an objective reconstruction of reality can actually be closely approached. For this purpose, non-partisan officials who are committed to the completeness of the evidentiary data-base and to the accuracy of factual findings are responsible for the investigation. In this sense, the discovery of the ontological truth follows the ordinary patterns of everyday life.[8] Consequently, the non-adversary model maintains that the pursuit of justice requires judges to seek as close as possible the *objective, substantive, ontological* truth in adjudicating criminal liability.

By way of contrast, the adversary system rests on the assumption that the ontological truth can't be known. Neutrality is deemed impossible to achieve. Even genuinely disinterested third parties inevitably form early hypotheses of the facts they seek to reconstruct. 'Because people assimilate information selectively' (Damaška, 1997: 95), their initial hypothesis makes them more receptive to evidence confirming it. These cognitive limitations lead fact-finders to interpret information in an unconsciously biased way, to fit with their assumptions. Concern about these cognitive limitations leads proponents of the adversarial model to deem any third party reconstruction of the facts to be biased and non-objective; a truly non-partisan search for the truth is viewed as unachievable. The search for the truth in a legal process therefore needs to depart from ordinary cognitive practices and to be pursued through a fair confrontation of two parties, each one promoting her side of the story in front of a passive adjudicator.[9] What results is a different notion of truth, which, short of being 'ontological', is indeed the product of a contest between two interpretations of reality.[10] I define it as *interpretive truth* to point to its skepticism about an objective reconstruction of reality. In this perspective, the only realistically discoverable truth is a 'second-best' one, if compared with the ideal of the ontological truth pursued by non-adversary systems. This 'interpretive' truth emerges from the parties' opposing views of reality, provided – of course – that fair rules are established and respected. The adversary model strictly equates justice and fairness, because only a fair contest can bring about just results.[11]

The 'relational' nature of the truth-discovering enterprise in an adversary system produces what I have elsewhere called a 'tango' idea of justice (Grande, 2008). As in tango, where it takes two – and only two – to dance, in an adversarial conception it takes two to produce a reconstruction of reality that can be equated with truth. By contrast (and I address the point in more depth later on), the alternative notion of justice of the non-adversary system can be associated with the metaphor of a (Cuban) rumba dance. As in the dance, in 'rumba justice' a variety of dancers (the defendant, her lawyer, the prosecutor, the victim, sometimes the public complainants or the civil third party defendants,[12] the judges and the lay assessors or jurors) perform together in a collective search for the 'ontological' truth.

2.1   Some Historical Background: The Emergence of the Adversarial Style

The divergence between non-adversary and adversary models outlined above, in other words, between non-partisan and dialectical searches for the truth in the criminal process, does not reach far back into the history of legal systems. On the contrary, as with many relevant systemic differences, it is relatively recent. According to John Langbein, it originates at the end of the eighteenth and the beginning of the nineteenth centuries.[13]

Until then, common law and Continental proceedings shared very much the same non-adversarial commitment to searching for the ontological truth. Common law criminal procedure – featuring a judge who examined the witnesses and the accused, and who deeply affected the adjudication of the jury and dominated the proceedings – could not yet be described as a *party-controlled contest*, to distinguish it from the *officially-controlled inquest* so characteristic of Continental procedure (Langbein, 1978, 1983, 1987, 1994, 1996). Both forms of procedure nevertheless bore a number of characteristic features. Many of the distinctive aspects of Continental procedure can be traced to the repressive arrangements of Continental criminal procedure prior to the French Revolution.[14]

More than one factor accounts for the revolutionary change that made the common law system depart from the Continental one, bringing about the modern polarization between non-adversary and adversary models.[15] Among them was the strong impact of *laissez-faire* Lockean values on English institutional arrangements in general and, for the purpose of the present argument, on procedural choices in particular.[16] The narrowing of judicial functions was indeed germane to the ambition of classic English liberalism to limit state intervention. The government was to be kept out of the citizen's life as much as possible and the role of the judge was to be limited in the criminal process. The classic liberal urge to keep the state at arm's length[17] required the restructuring of the criminal process as a dispute between two sides – the prosecution and the defense (very much conceived of as private parties) pursuing their opposing interests in front of a passive state official who had virtually no involvement in the investigation of the underlying facts.

In the classic liberal framework, any intervention of the judge in shaping the proceedings – by raising matters, adducing or supplementing parties' evidence, examining or cross-examining witnesses, raising *ex officio* questions of admissibility or inadmissibility, rejecting parties' stipulations, and so forth – was perceived as an unacceptable government invasion of individual freedom (Damaška, 1975: 535f.). The upshot was the removal of any official control over fact-finding. Henceforth, the truth was to emerge from a battle between adversaries. The development of the law of evidence, only applicable on request by the parties, could make such battle a fair contest.[18] Underlying the new procedural style was a general attitude of skepticism toward objectivity: 'Since no belief or idea regarding human affairs' was considered 'exclusively or demonstrably true' (Damaška, 1975: 532), a third party factual enquiry was regarded as an imposition upon the parties of an arbitrary single-sided reconstruction of reality. Thus, according to classical liberal ideology, neutrality and objectivity, viewed as unattainable in the human world, were even more suspect if vested in highly distrusted government officials. The new order substituted for the previous reliance upon a third party factual enquiry. An 'interpretive' truth, stemming from an equitably balanced confrontation between two one-sided accounts of reality (neither one of them possessing the complete truth), took the place of 'ontological' truth as ascertained through neutral enquiry. In light of this transformation, fairness became the proxy for justice, replacing the 'impossible' discovery of the 'objective' truth.[19]

2.2 The Restructuring of the Non-adversary Style

To be sure, the attack launched by the classic liberal credo against the very idea of a 'neutral' enquiry in the search for the truth did not spare the Continent. Over time, changes in Continental procedural arrangements show the desire of Continental systems to cope with the 'impossibility of neutrality'. Nevertheless, they never went so far as to provoke the Copernican revolution that occurred in the common law world. Continental lawyers refused in fact to renounce the idea of searching for a 'substantive' (or 'objective' or 'ontological') truth in the criminal process.

Starting from the beginning of the nineteenth century, the secret, unilateral, and official enquiry that had dominated previous Continental criminal proceedings for more than half of a millennium came increasingly under attack. Over the next 200 years, Continental systems relentlessly modified their criminal procedures in order to make its features compatible with the changed political and social climate that followed the French Revolution. Seeking to protect defendants against governmental oppression, Continental procedures eliminated for good negative inquisitorial features like the absence of specific charges, unlimited pre-trial detention, the presumption of guilt, coerced and unreliable confessions, unbridled searches and the absence of a right to defense

counsel. Continental systems also made changes in procedural arrangements aimed at coping with the possible lack of neutrality of the official
truth seeker. It became clear that the more unilateral the enquiry, the
higher the risk of undermining the truth seeker's impartiality. From this
perspective, the introduction in the French *Code d'Instruction Criminelle*
of 1808 of two additional figures – the prosecutor and the defense
counsel – into the new, so-called 'mixed' system of criminal procedure,
was the first step in making the official enquiry more collective,
pluralistic and unbiased.[20] The prosecutor assumed the novel function of
limiting the power of the investigative judge to set the boundaries of his
inquiries. Defense counsel became entitled to participate in proof-taking
and to offer a contrasting point of view through argument and debate at
trial (see Cordero, 1998: 64; Damaška, 1975: 535).

After World War II, many changes aimed at increasing the official truth
seeker's neutrality occurred in the various Continental criminal procedures. These changes were also prompted by the intense work of the then
new-born European Court of Human Rights, whose case law gave rise
over time to a European criminal procedure model characterized by
greater opportunity for judicial activism and by enhanced protection of
the procedural rights for all participants, including victims and defendants.[21] Continental systems everywhere in Europe abandoned the traditional investigative monopoly of state officials in favor of a multilateral
approach. In this spirit, defense attorneys were granted a role in the
pre-trial investigative phase of the proceeding, acquiring the right not
only to inspect the dossier freely but often also to be present when many
procedural activities were taking place and sometimes even to offer
counter-proof and counter-arguments.[22] Moreover, in many countries the
defense and in some countries – including Spain, France and Italy –
victims, too, were allowed to ask for pre-trial investigative steps to be
taken and in case of refusal were entitled to a formal reply subject to
appellate review.[23] By granting the defense and the victim greater input
into officially conducted investigations, European systems transformed
the search for the truth from a unilateral inquiry into a sort of collective
enterprise. The active participation of a plurality of actors in the
investigation provided for a plurality of external perspectives on the
investigation, increasing the impartiality of the official in charge of
the enquiry. In Germany, the lawyer for the defense is nowadays entitled
to undertake investigations himself (BGHSt 46,1: see Huber, 2008: 329,
fn. 218).[24] Italy went even further. After December 2000, it legitimated a
system of two parallel (but interrelated) pre-trial investigations, one
official and the other privately conducted by the defense.[25]

Everywhere in Continental systems, including Spain's, the enhanced right of the defense to be present and to present arguments and evidence at trial also provided for a more serious pluralistic approach to the overall official search for the truth.[26]

The efforts to increase the neutrality of the official search for truth took also a different route. In Spain as in France, Italy, and Portugal, the exclusion of the investigative judge from the trial court panel (before this institutional figure was eliminated in some of these countries) helped to fragment government authority over the investigation[27] and led to a plurality of perspectives within the decision-making process, as a kind of *internal* check on the process, in contrast to the *external* constraints provided by the participation of defense lawyers and victims.

The same rationale underlies the establishment in France, in 2000, of a *juge des libertés et de la detention* with power to decide over detention instead of the examining magistrate (Vogler, 2008: 209); or the separation in Italy of the authorities in charge of the pre-trial phase. Italy now vests judicial authority over the pre-trial investigation in the judge of the pre-trial investigation, or *gip (giudice dell'indagine preliminare)*, rather than the one in charge of the preliminary hearing, *gup (giudice dell'udienza preliminare)*, who decides whether the defendant has to stand trial or whether her case has to be dismissed.[28]

Again, the internal pluralistic rationale explains why different members of the trial court do not have equal access to the pre-trial investigative dossier. In France, for example, only the presiding trial judge has full previous access to the dossier as opposed to other components of the bench or lay assessors (Vogler, 2008: 251). In Germany, lay judges – *Schöffen* – have no knowledge of the investigation files (Gleß, 2010: 675, fn. 26). Other reforms likewise fostered diversity of perspectives among fact-finders, by limiting the use at trial of evidence from the official file of pre-trial investigative activities, therefore encouraging the trial court to develop a fresh understanding of the facts, untainted as much as possible by the views of any public official involved in a previous stage of the proceeding.[29]

In Continental systems, moreover, the old tradition of appellate supervision of criminal trial courts further fragments official authority over the investigation, particularly when *de novo* appellate review with a second trial on the merits is possible, multiplying the number of decision-makers and thereby enhancing the internal plurality of perspectives.[30]

Multiplying external and internal perspectives on criminal cases effectively transformed Continental procedure from an official unilateral inquiry into a pluralistic investigation, making Continental justice – in a dancing metaphor – resemble the (Cuban) 'rumba' dance, in which many dancers in different capacities dance together in the common enterprise of discovering the truth.[31] This was the reply to the 'impossibility of neutrality' problem raised from the end of the seventeenth century by English classic liberalism. Therefore, the Continental world still considers neutrality attainable in the criminal process. It never replaced the search for an 'objective' truth with a search for an 'interpretive' truth. Officials, made as impartial as possible, are still in charge of searching for it, as carefully as they can. In the Continental criminal process, justice – never equated with fairness – continues to be associated with the neutral search for a substantive, 'ontological' truth.[32]

Does this remain true even after some very typical legal features of the adversary system, like a police/prosecutor's investigation replacing the examining magistrate's inquest, cross-examination of witnesses, exclusionary rules, and the jury system found their way into the Continental systems? Or, to the contrary, as it is often contended, has the transplant of these classical American legal arrangements into European soil made Continental systems more adversarial? I'd like to question this frequent claim by specifically addressing the case of the jury trial in Spain, which has been patterned after the Anglo-American model.[33]

3. FROM 'TANGO JUSTICE' TO 'RUMBA JUSTICE': THE CASE OF JURY TRIALS IN SPAIN AND THE IMPACT OF AN AMERICAN TRANSPLANT

Different ideas about justice convey disparate images that I would like to capture through a dancing metaphor. The adversary system can be associated with the idea of a 'tango justice'; the non-adversary one with that of a 'rumba justice'. 'Tango' justice, like the dance, is performed by two dancers and only by those two, acting together – yet against each other – in the venture of establishing the adversarial truth. (Cuban) 'rumba' justice, to the contrary, is performed by a variable number of dancers, occasionally alone and occasionally in groups, with many shifts and continuous substitutions of dancers and roles.[34] It is a genuinely communal performance in the collective search of an objective truth.

On May 22, 1995, the Spanish Parliament passed legislation, effective as of November 24, 1995, reviving trial by jury in criminal cases.[35] The jury court in Spain has jurisdiction over only a select number of crimes. These include homicide, threats, failure to comply with a legal duty to provide assistance, burglary, arson in forestland, and several kinds of crimes against the Public Administration, such as mishandling official documents, bribery, influence peddling, embezzlement of public funds, fraud and illegal levies demanded by public officials, prohibited negotiations by public officials, and mistreatment of prisoners.[36] On May 27, 1996, Spanish juries began to try the first cases under the new law. Since then, jury trials have developed many shortcomings and practical problems.[37] Spanish practice has curtailed in different ways the actual operation of the jury trial, with a consequent limited application of the law.[38]

My question remains, however: did the 'Anglo-American jury format',[39] introduced in Spain by the Trial by Jury Organic Law 1995, produce an Americanization of the Spanish criminal procedure when criminal proceedings with juries are deployed? Did it transform, at least in part, the Spanish system from rumba justice into a tango justice procedure?

Though it has often been celebrated as an Anglo-American import, the jury trial – as opposed to the mixed panel trial[40] typical of the Continental tradition[41] – operates quite differently in Spain than it does in the United States.

The new jury system does not transform the Spanish criminal trial from a third party search for the truth into a contest between two and only two parties in complete control of the fact-finding enterprise. Nor does it carry with it the same message of individual freedom from the state as the American jury does. Rather than having made Spanish criminal procedure more adversarial, the introduction of the jury trial seems to fortify the non-adversarial features of a rumba justice. It adds a new actor in the participatory fact-finding process enterprise, thereby providing for a more dynamic and pluralistic effort to make the third party search for the truth more impartial.

3.1 The American Jury in the US Jury Trial

Anglo-American folklore celebrates the autonomous and independent power of laypeople to assess guilt or innocence, viewing this power as the ultimate protection against the government and possible abuses of government powers. In American law, the jury symbolizes the ultimate freedom from government because it truly takes away from state officials the crucial function of determining guilt, allowing the accused to benefit from a reserved, independent, and autonomous sphere of decision-making authority. The jury in the American trial is genuinely independent because of the exclusion of any judicial involvement in its deliberations (except of course in the case of a directed verdict of acquittal). Moreover, it is in its power to deliver largely inscrutable general verdicts, which are difficult to challenge on appeal from a conviction and impossible to challenge in case of acquittal.[42] This power demonstrates the extent of jury autonomy from state authority and conveys the message that the jury is the champion of the individual against the state. Allowing the jury to render a truly final verdict of acquittal gives substance to the aspiration of the defendant to be free from state oppression, since no state official has the power to second guess the jury finding. The extreme version of this rationale is the jury power of nullification. Here, the peers make a final determination of acquittal even in the face of uncontroverted evidence proving the defendant guilty and even in defiance of clear judicial instruction. This feature of the American jury system allows the jury to express its disagreement with the law the defendant has been charged with breaking, or the jury's belief that the law should not be applied in that particular case.[43]

Historically, moreover, the Anglo-American jury contributed to the increasingly adversarial character of the criminal trial. Indeed, the late eighteenth-century emergence of the Anglo-American adversary system, characterized by the novel posture of the trial judge as a mere umpire of the forensic contest, was certainly made easier by the very fact of the existence of the jury as a separate fact-finder. Released from the ultimate decision on the issue of guilt or innocence – a task now entrusted exclusively to the jury – the trial judge could easily divest himself of authority over the fact-finding process. To be sure, however, the transition to the adversarial style could not have come about but for the similarly passive role that the Anglo-American jury has played in the fact-finding process since the sixteenth century, when it gradually ceased informing itself through its own investigative efforts.[44]

3.2 The Spanish Jury in the Spanish Jury Trial

The Spanish jury, by contrast, is not designed as a passive adjudicator, nor is the Spanish trial judge (i.e. the *magistrado-presidente*) merely an umpire of a forensic contest between the prosecutor and the defendant in a party-controlled process for developing the evidence.

As in the Spanish non-jury trial,[45] the presiding magistrate must exclude illegally obtained evidence on her own initiative.[46] On her own motion, she can alter the order in which the evidence proposed by the parties is heard, whenever she deems it useful for a more accurate factual determination or for greater certainty about the underlying facts.[47] She can intervene in the cross-examination of the witnesses[48] and of the accused.[49] *Ex officio*, she can bring out evidence not presented by the parties whenever she deems it necessary to help prove or test the allegations,[50] and in the event of contradiction between the testimony of various witnesses or between the testimony of the accused and other witnesses, she may order a 'confrontation' (*careo*) in order to decide who deserves to be believed.[51] She can, *sua sponte* or upon a party's request, render the equivalent of what American criminal procedure calls a directed verdict of acquittal (or judgment of acquittal), dissolving the jury and acquitting the defendant whenever she 'considers that there is insufficient evidence to justify the accused being found guilty'.[52] Expert witnesses, moreover, are always judicially appointed, and they are required to be scrupulously impartial.

Contrast the role of the Spanish judge with her American counterpart. In most American jurisdictions, judges are not permitted to comment on the evidence and even when their intervention in proof-taking is permitted, judges who substantially intervene in proof-taking risk reversal on appeal, since their activism cannot but be perceived as a deviation from the adversary search for truth.[53] According to Rule 614 of the Federal Rules of Evidence, for example, a judge at a trial may call witnesses *sua sponte* and may also question witnesses at trial. Yet, as has been observed (Pizzi and Montagna, 2004: 447):

> Rule 614 is not problematic in the United States because judges sparingly use the power to call a witness and because appellate courts have always strongly cautioned trial judges about asking too many questions at trial lest they appear to the jury to have abandoned their neutral role and to have endorsed one side.

Even when both systems assign judges similar roles, like the power to direct a verdict of acquittal, these apparently congruent institutional powers belie important differences between the system-participants' orientation towards the circumstances in which it is appropriate for judges to exercise this power. This deeper difference reflects the systems' disparate conception of the kind of truth that one has to pursue throughout the criminal trial.

In the Spanish jury system – unlike its American counterpart – the need to search for ontological truth in a pluralistic way translates into the power of the appellate court to review the judgment of acquittal that a trial judge may direct before the case is submitted to the jury. The appellate court will indeed reverse that judgment if it was improperly ordered.[54] In order to protect the search for the truth, the Spanish jury system also enhances procedural safeguards designed to prevent false convictions. If the evidence produced at trial does not provide any reasonable ground for conviction, appellate courts review and reverse judgments, even if the defendant failed to move for a judgment of acquittal at trial, thereby 'contributing' to his own unjust conviction.[55] This applies to appeals by the prosecution as well as the defense.[56]

By contrast, in the United States, an interpretive notion of truth and the principle that a defendant must be allowed to make his own strategic choices, 'no matter how strange or even foolish they may seem to others' (Damaška, 1975: 532–3), mean that his failure to move for a judgment of acquittal within the proper time at trial (or immediately after it)[57] forecloses appellate review for sufficiency of the evidence. Since the plain error remedy is perceived as an inappropriately activist judicial intervention, and is therefore rarely applied,[58] it is possible in the United States (but less so in Spain) for a conviction to stand although unsupported by even minimally sufficient evidence.[59]

In the Spanish trial, the jury itself is an active participant in the fact-finding enterprise and not merely a passive audience for evidence developed by others. Jurors may intervene by asking questions of witnesses, experts, and defendants.[60] On their own initiative, they may examine documents and visit the scene of the crime, together with the presiding magistrate, in order to gain a first-hand impression.[61] Contrast this active truth-seeking role of the Spanish jury with the passive stance of the American jury, which sees what the parties want it to see. As lucidly sketched by Professor Damaška (1997: 90):

> ... when it comes to the jury, its passivity in the course of proof-taking is necessarily complete: jurors have no proof initiative and are usually not even permitted to ask question of witnesses. While evidence is being adduced, they sit silent, cast – one might say – into the role of potted courtroom plants.[62]

In the Spanish jury trial's collective search for the truth, even the prosecutor can – and sometimes does – intervene in favor of the defendant, to ask for an acquittal.[63]

Rather than a contest between two litigants shaping their own dispute according to their own interests in front of a passive adjudicator, the Spanish jury trial far more resembles a plural inquest in which many actors participate. These include the prosecutor, the defendant, the victim (i.e. the private prosecutor), the public complainant (or popular prosecutor, in other words, private third parties unconnected to the offense who are allowed to participate provided they comply with a series of requirements), any civil third party defendants (in other words, persons that are liable for damages in lieu of the defendant should the latter be insolvent), the presiding judge and the jurors. All assume an active and fluid role and share in the search for the substantive truth.[64]

In the Spanish jury trial the court (i.e. the presiding magistrate and the jury) – like its American counterpart – is given no access to the investigative case file, therefore it approaches the case as a *tabula rasa*.[65] The aim of eliminating the investigative dossier from the trial court was to prevent a court's *ex officio* examination of investigative documents. This avoids pre-determination of the judgment and reinforces immediacy by requiring the presentation of live testimony, which helps the jury to develop a fresh understanding of the evidence, in line not with a tango ideal of justice as in the United States, but with a rumba ideal of it that distributes roles to multiple participants in the fact-finding process in order to overcome the 'neutrality problem' of a third party search for the truth.[66]

During the pre-trial investigation, the limited powers of the investigating judge[67] combined with an active role of the many parties therein,[68] do not transform the pre-trial phase into a contest between the parties either. Instead, these features anticipate the participatory scheme that will unfold at the trial. It is indeed an impartial official with a residual power of *ex officio* investigation,[69] in other words, the investigative judge, who performs pre-trial investigative measures, although they are mainly requested by the 'parties'. In contrast with the American adversary system, moreover, the prosecutor is not vested with a truly partisan role, as she is in charge of promoting the 'activities of justice in defense of lawfulness, the rights of the citizens, and the public interest as protected by the law'.[70]

3.2.1   Giving reasons for the verdict

Consistent with a third party quest for substantive truth and with a rumba justice that always requires the logic and rationality of the third party findings to be checked, the Spanish jury has to give reasons for its conclusions.[71] If the reasons given by juries are determined to be inadequate,[72] their verdicts are either returned to the jurors by the supervising magistrate-president according to Art. 63(1)(d) or (e) LOTJ, or reversed on appeal by the Regional Supreme Court.[73] This holds true even for verdicts of acquittal, thereby preventing jury nullification.[74]

In the United States, the trial is supposed to serve as a fair contest between two adversaries. On this view, it is the application of fair rules that makes the outcome just, and there is no need to assess the substance of the jury's reasoning, nor any way of officially inquiring into jury deliberations. As with appeals of felonies in the medieval era, when a fair battle is over, *rien ne va plus*. This is why the American jury need not explain their factual determinations,[75] which consequently are extremely difficult to challenge. Appeals therefore focus largely on the fairness of the rules that have been applied at trial, as their application is the province of the judge, not of the jury. Asymmetrical rights of appeal, moreover, maximize defendants' freedom from the government in that jury verdicts of acquittal escape all official supervision and cannot be appealed on any ground.

By contrast, equating justice with the discovery of the substantive truth makes it necessary to facilitate reconsideration of the fact-finder's conclusions.[76] This concern helps to explain why some Continental countries, like Italy, always provide for a second trial on the merits on direct appeal from the initial judgment, and why a (further) opportunity for both sides to challenge the reasons given by the trier of the fact is generally allowed everywhere in Continental Europe. Thus appellate review contributes to 'rumba justice'.[77] In this vein, in Spain, appellate review requires higher courts to control the ways evidentiary materials are used at trial and the rationality of the jury inquiry into the facts. This supervision is necessary in order to ensure that the decision maker respects neutrality – according to the norms by which non-adversarial systems give content to that requirement – so that the substantive truth can emerge.[78]

Embedded therefore in a non-adversarial 'rumba justice' context, the Spanish jury does not enjoy the same level of autonomy from state power as its American counterpart. This prevents the Spanish jury from taking on the same role of champion of the defendant's right to be free from the state authority that legitimates the American jury system (whose nullification powers Mortimer Kadish and Sanford Kadish (1973) have described as 'discretion to disobey' the commands of the law.) While the American jury stands for the *defendant*'s right to a peer judgment, Spanish jury trials 'invoke a different legal notion: the *citizens*' right *to participate* in the administration of justice' (Vargas, 1999: 198). The defendant, as a consequence, does not have the right to waive it (Thaman, 1998: 256).

3.2.2   The Spanish jury verdict as a 'collective product'

Nor do Spanish jurors enjoy the same level of independence from state involvement in their decision-making that protects American jurors. Again, in a participatory scheme largely inconceivable in the American system, the jury verdict is a sort of collaborative product involving, in different roles and capacities, all the dancers who participate in rumba justice.

After arguments and the defendant's last word, the American jury enters a general verdict of 'guilty' or 'not guilty'; the Spanish jury does not. Consistent with Continental European precedents,[79] the Spanish jury has to return a special verdict shedding light on how it decided the case. It is the task of the presiding magistrate to prepare a verdict form (*objeto del veredicto*) in the form of a list of propositions or questions formulated in factual terms.[80] The propositions relate to the facts presented by the various parties during the trial and concern the elements of the crimes charged, the conditions which modify or exclude guilt, and the aggravating and mitigating circumstances of the crime. Varying from judge to judge, the propositions may differ significantly in number and length, and, in some instances, juries have been provided with nearly one hundred to assess.[81] Jurors are handed a copy of the question list while receiving instruction on how to deliberate and vote.[82] They must then vote on whether the list of factual propositions formulated in the verdict form were proved at trial. Afterwards, they are asked to affirm or deny proof of the defendant's guilt as to the 'criminal acts' alleged in the indictment.[83]

However, the jury's power to determine guilt does not require them to make a legal evaluation of the facts: that is left to the professional judge in her final judgment, which incorporates the jury verdict.[84] As already mentioned, jurors have also to give a 'succinct explanation of the reasons why they have declared, or refused to declare, certain facts as having been proved',[85] which means that the jury must always indicate fact by fact the evidence on which they based their finding. Moreover, if the court adopts a demanding approach the jurors have to explain why they relied on the mentioned evidence, though juries may be spared this task by a court that follows a minimalist approach to explanation. Proponents of the minimalist approach take the position that a well-executed question list can adequately justify a verdict of guilt even if the additional reasons are very bare-boned. To them, 'the reasoning or logic behind a verdict can be interpreted by the trial and appellate judges based on the jury's answers to the propositions in the question list and in light of the quality of the evidence adduced at trial' (Thaman, 2011: 634–5 and quoted literature at fn. 127).

The role of the written question list (or verdict form) in guiding and leading the jury in its fact-finding and adjudicating task is therefore evident. By formulating the factual propositions that the jurors have to answer and give reasons for, the Spanish trial judge clearly complements their efforts to assess the facts and to justify the verdict. This endeavor has absolutely no counterpart in the instructions given to the jury by the American judge. In a non-adversary search for the truth, the crucial role of the question list for the ultimate verdict involves all the dancers of the rumba justice system in its drafting. While normally based on the parties' pleadings, the judge may in fact *ex officio* add additional facts or inject issues which resulted from the taking of evidence, as long as they do not worsen the position of the defendant.[86] In exercising this power he may, for instance, add a defense theory of necessity or a question the answer to which may mitigate guilt and punishment by establishing a less culpable *mens rea*. Judges can supplement the list with other inquiries absent from the parties' pleadings.[87] The necessity of involving all the dancers then requires that, before the question list is finalized, the parties move to add questions not included by the judge in the draft verdict form, or exclude or reformulate those the judge has articulated. If any of the parties disagree with the final formulation, they can object in order to preserve the issue for appeal. Finally, if the jurors cannot achieve the required majority on a particular question,[88] it is their turn to amend the verdict form's phrasing, making the changes that correspond to their own appraisal of the facts. They can include a new or unsuggested paragraph as long as 'it does not involve not putting to a vote part of the points of fact proposed by the trial judge' and as long as the amendment does not substantially alter or aggravate the defendant's liability.[89]

After receiving the verdict from the jury, the presiding magistrate, who cannot participate in the jury's deliberation and interfere in their fact-finding, has the power to return a defective verdict form to the jury to correct omissions, contradictions between the verdict and factual findings, or other defects,[90] including – according to judicial interpretation of Art. 63(1)(e) LOTJ – the insufficiency of verdict reasons. If the judge goes back to the jury three times to repair defects in the verdict, and they fail to do so, the judge may dissolve the jury and retry the case before a new jury. If the new jury also fails to reach a verdict due to similar problems, the judge must *sua sponte* enter a verdict of acquittal.[91]

If the presiding magistrate accepts the jury's verdict, she will incorporate the jury's conclusions into her written judgment, which fleshes out the jurors' reasoning and determines the legal qualification of the facts that they found to be true.[92] The judgment itself is subject to a two-tier system of appeal (*apelación* – which, despite the rubric, does not include a re-evaluation of the facts or trial de novo – and *casación*).

All these features together both show a remarkable judicial control over how the jury assesses the facts that has no counterpart in the American system and suggest the complementary roles of jurors, judges, and parties in constructing the Spanish jury verdict (and the judicial judgment) as a 'collective product' of multiple system participants that again goes far beyond the light interplay between judge and jury which goes on in the American jury instruction phase and during deliberations, if jurors have a question.[93]

4. CONCLUSIONS

Fifteen years ago, I discussed the reception of the American model of criminal procedure in Italy, and I claimed that the transplant actually failed because of the absence of an infrastructure such as the jury, which is necessary for the adversary system to function (Grande, 2000: 251). Almost twenty years after Spain has provided itself with such an infrastructure, we have evidence that even this is not enough to overcome the 'Latin resistance' to the US adversary model. In its transplant from the American system to the Spanish one, the jury system ends up being highly modified by the new context, changing its original function and nature.[94] It has lost its original adversarial rationale as well as its autonomous and independent character, which symbolizes the ultimate protection against government over-reaching and abuse and which therefore legitimates the American jury.[95]

Though arguably resisted, the 'transplant' had very real repercussions. Unlike the original US model, it did not delegate most of the power and control over the process to the parties, rejecting the very notion of an impartial and official search for the truth, or help shield defendants against government activism. Yet, the 'transplant' served as an irritant that, by adding a new actor in the fact-finding enterprise, made the official search for the truth more pluralistic, participatory and dynamic – and consequently more impartial. Instead of creating 'tango justice' and making Continental procedure more adversarial, the introduction of the jury system into Spain therefore strengthened the tenets of a non-adversarial model of 'rumba justice'. In fact, the 'imported' feature, modified by the Latin *mentalité*, further contaminated the recipient system with a liberal ideology in criminal procedure that by increasing the impartiality of a third party search for the truth helps protect the individual against a monopolistic, therefore authoritarian, official search for the truth. In sum, the context of reception became more liberal but not more adversarial.

By incorporating a supposedly US-inspired jury into its criminal procedure (even if somewhat modified), the Spanish system managed moreover to reinforce the Spanish legal system's worldwide legitimacy as a progressive and liberal model of criminal justice.[96] In front of a still persistent rhetoric assigning to the non-adversary process the image of an oppressive process reminiscent of the inquisitorial era,[97] the 'import' of the jury trial – together with other 'American' legal features[98] – helped in fact to remove the ignominious inquisitorial look from the Spanish process. It thereby reduced the felt need to adopt a radically new adversary model in order for the Spanish criminal justice to be portrayed (especially by common law countries) as sufficiently protective of individual liberties and human rights.

The Spanish system, like that of other European countries that 'import' American procedural arrangements, succeeded in developing its own mechanisms to protect individuals against state abuses, without embracing an adversarial 'tango justice'. Arguably, mere 'acoustic imitation' of the adversary model enabled Spain (and other European countries importing different American procedural features besides) to improve its rumba way of protecting defendants against an authoritarian state, while adhering to the spirit of a non-adversarial search for the truth.

NOTES

*   I wish to thank Professor Mar Jimeno-Bulnes for her precious help in facilitating my understanding of the Spanish system. Mistakes of course are only mine.

1.   See Jimeno-Bulnes (2012–2013: 436), pointing out that: 'The increasing influence of the U.S. legal system in Europe in recent years must be taken into account'. For a classic analysis, pointing to a broad Americanization of European legal systems in general, see Wiegand (1991).

2.   See for the 1988 Italian reform, Pizzi and Montagna (2004: 430): '... the new Code purported to introduce an adversarial system based on the Anglo-American model into a country that previously had a strongly inquisitorial system'; or del Duca (1991: 74): 'A new Criminal Procedure Code became effective in Italy on October 24, 1989. It makes many significant changes in Italian criminal procedure by incorporating some basic features of the "adversarial" system on which the United States and other common law criminal justice systems are based'. For the Spanish jury trial reform, among many others, see: Gascón Inchausti and Villamarín López (2008: 628): 'A jury was introduced on the Anglo-American model'. See also Thaman (1998: 242), discussing whether the reintroduction of trial by jury in Spain upon an Anglo-American model 'can again be a catalyst in a move to a more adversarial criminal procedure on the European Continent as it was in the nineteenth century in the wake of the French Revolution'.

3.   Almost twenty years ago Craig Bradley noticed that European Continental systems were becoming more adversarial: 'In recent years, however, it would seem that the closure of the gap between the two models [i.e. inquisitorial and the common law systems] has been accelerating. Defense lawyers now play a more prominent role in civil law trials, and suspects have more rights for those lawyers to protect. Though jury trials remain in disfavor on the Continent, they are newly available in Spain and parts of Russia. A right against self-incrimination at trial, and against involuntary confessions, is now generally enforced, and the use of an exclusionary rule to force police to obey rules governing searches and interrogations is increasingly being used in most of the countries discussed in this book. *Miranda-type* warnings are also widely required. ... inquisitorial systems have become more adversarial': Bradley (1999: xix; now in the 2007 2nd edition, p. xxi), referring also to Bradley (1993: 95–143) (discussing how various common law and civil law countries are moving toward a US style, rights-oriented approach to rules governing criminal investigation). However, on the harmonizing effect of the European Court of Human Rights

decisions upon European criminal procedure systems and on the meaning assigned by this Court to the notion of 'adversarial' proceedings in connection with Art. 6 of European Convention on Human Rights, which does not necessarily correspond with the meaning assigned to it in common law countries, see extensively Jackson (2005: 747ff.).

4. 'Is the Inquisitorial Process on the Retreat?' is the question raised by Weigend (2011: 404). Professor Weigend notices indeed: '... there exists a clear trend toward an expansion of adversarial elements at the expense of "pure" inquisitorial systems. Several countries of the Continental tradition have opened up to adversariness and have embraced active party involvement at the trial stage, whereas no similar inroads of inquisitorial ideas in the common law world have been documented. One might be led to assume that this switchover movement finally proves the inherent superiority of the adversarial system, but there may be alternative explanation available'. The alternative explanation Professor Weigend offers is that a hybrid, cooperative or compromise procedural model is under construction, which 'may reflect the work of an invisible hand guiding the criminal process toward optimal conditions' (2011: 407ff.). In my understanding, this model is indeed nothing other than the old non-adversary model that has been constantly evolving since the nineteenth century.

5. Readers familiar with it can skip this section and start reading from section 3.

6. The analysis of the non-adversary/adversary or inquisitorial/accusatorial dichotomy has been at the core of the comparative criminal procedure studies and has been therefore extensively and deeply explored in a vast literature. For some quick reference to it see, Grande (2012: 199ff.). For one of the most recent investigations on the subject see Langer (2014).

7. I explored the implications of Damaška's move beyond the old accusatorial v. inquisitorial dichotomy, in Grande (2008).

8. As Damaška (1997: 90) explains: 'In their personal and business affairs, people are in the habit of actively taking part in obtaining knowledge about facts on which their decisions turn. As students, they ask questions in wrestling with ideas expressed in professional lectures. And in specialized fields of inquiry – such as history – they cherish their freedom actively to inform themselves about the subject of their study'.

9. To be sure, the defense has the advantage over the prosecutor that she does not always need to present an alternative truth to the one offered by the prosecutor in order to win her case. In fact, since the defendant does not bear the burden of proving her innocence, rather it is the prosecutor who bears the burden of proving her guilt and therefore of proving the crime elements beyond any reasonable doubt, the defense can strategically renounce providing her own reconstruction of the reality. She can simply claim that her adversary did not meet the evidentiary or the persuasive burden of proof, and is still able to get an acquittal. However, in so doing she takes the risk that the opponent's partisan and only available truth wins the mind of the passive adjudicator. Yet, in the adversary system, as long as the rules of the contest are fair and the defendant makes choices that are deemed to be free, the result is considered fair and the 'interpretive' truth (see *infra* in the text) ascertained.

10. For a more nuanced view on the search for the truth in the two systems, see Weigend (2003).

11. For a philosophical point of view on the subject, see Rawls (1999).

12. For the explanation of these terms see *infra* 3.2.

13. 'Adversary procedure cannot be defended as part of our historic common law bequest' (Langbein, 1978: 316). Professor Langbein's thoughts on the origins of the adversarial style in criminal matters are to be found in Langbein (2003). Even before John Langbein's research, conducted on the Old Bailey Session Papers, produced strong evidence of it, Professor Damaška pointed out that common law criminal proceedings before the nineteenth century were fundamentally non-adversary. 'The

adversarial style of processing criminal matters is largely a product of the early 19th century. Until the middle of that century, the pretrial phase of the process was essentially a type of judicial investigation along inquisitorial lines conducted by justices of the peace. Nor was the trial an adversary battle of counsel. Lawyers would seldom appear for the prosecution and defense counsel were not admitted in ordinary felony cases until 1837. In this situation the judge called witnesses and examined them, and in the century prior, had also interrogated the defendant' (Damaška, 1975: 542, fn. 156).

14. Continental criminal procedure included torture as a means of obtaining a defendant's confession as well as reliance on secret, written proceedings, in contrast to the open and oral English trial. These stereotypical images of Continental criminal procedure hold true in American minds still today: 'Americans tend to equate inquisitorial systems with coercive interrogation, unbridled search, and unduly efficient crime-control', notices Abraham Goldstein (1974: 1018). For a compelling discussion about the role that anti-inquisitorialism plays in shaping American criminal process today, see Sklansky (2009).

15. Certainly, the advent of an era in which lawyers both for the prosecution and the defense became the main actors in the common law criminal process can be held accountable for the rise of the new style. See Langbein (2003).

16. On the impact of *laissez-faire* Lockean values on English institutional arrangements, see extensively Damaška (1975: *passim* but especially 532 ff.; 1986). The present part relies heavily on these two masterpieces by Mirjan Damaška.

17. As it is very well known this expression was used by Karl Llewellyn (1962: 444–50) with regard to the adversary model, as opposed to a 'parental model', by which Llewellyn meant the inquisitorial one. For a further exploration of these models, labelled by the author 'battle' and 'family' models, see Griffiths (1970).

18. According to Langbein's (1994, 1996) reconstruction, the rise of the modern common law of evidence was contemporary with the advent of the adversary procedure in England, which originated at the turn of the nineteenth century. In the adversary system, the law of evidence plays the key role of establishing the rules that provide for a fair contest, allowing the tango to be successful in its production of the 'interpretive' truth. Evidence law evens the playing field of the dispute by assuring the balancing of advantages between litigants in the proof-taking activity, thereby giving the parties (whether or not they actually take advantage of it) equal opportunities to present their view of reality.

19. Then, to borrow Damaška's words (1975: 542): 'Transplanted to America, the classic liberal ethos fell upon fertile soil ... such circumstances as the frontier society, the natural abundance of resources, and the religious legacies of 17th century Protestantism, facilitated the introduction of liberal dispositions toward authority into the American political culture to an extent astonishing even to English 19th century liberals'.

20. On the *Code d'Instruction Criminelle* and the so-called 'mixed model' see, Jimeno-Bulnes (2012–2013: 423ff. and herein quoted literature).

21. For the increasing role of the ECtHR in influencing domestic Continental European courts to enhance defense participation as well as victim participation in the development, presentation, and testing of live testimony that, like the introduction of the jury system, challenge the judicial monopoly over the official inquiry at all phases of the criminal process, including the pre-trial investigation, the trial, and the appeal, see Jackson and Summers (2012).

22. In Italy that was also the outcome of a vast array of Constitutional Court decisions delivered when the 1930 Code of Criminal Procedure was still in effect: see Cordero (1982: 584–8). For an analysis of the changes that these 'participatory principles' produced in French pre-trial procedure, see Hodgson (2002).

23. See generally, Delmas-Marty and Spencer (2002). Regarding France, see Deriveux (2002: 242) and Vogler and Huber (2008: 185–7), explaining the increased role of the victims in criminal proceedings in France over the years since 1981; regarding Italy, see Vannini and Cocciardi (1986: 368). For Spain see Vogler (1999: 383) or Gascón Inchausti and Villamarín López (2008: 608). For the improved legal position of the victim in Germany in the last decades, see Huber (2008: 335).

24. Though in France a defense lawyer who attempts to take an active role in the collection of evidence still risks prosecution for improperly influencing witnesses or suborning perjury (Vogler and Huber, 2008: 233, quoting Hodgson 2005: 123–4).

25. See Law of December 7, 2000 'Disposizioni in materia di indagini difensive', *Gazzetta Ufficiale* n 2, January 3, 2001, now Art. 391 bis of the Italian Code of Criminal procedure (hereinafter 'CPP'). The defense, conducting its own investigation, is still allowed to be present when most prosecutorial activities are under way. Freely permitted to contact 'her own' witnesses in the pre-trial phase, the defense attorney may make the prosecutor interview potentially favorable witnesses on the defendant's behalf (Art. 391 bis 10 CPP) or seize materials in the defendant's interest (Art. 368 CPP), thus obtaining the prosecutor's help in conducting the defendant's own investigation. In the same vein, the defense can also ask the prosecutor, at the end of the prosecutor's investigation, to gather new exculpatory evidence (Art. 415 bis 4 CPP). Both parties, moreover, are allowed to freely inspect each other's dossiers before the trial begins (Arts 391 octies 3 and 433 CPP, 415 bis 2; 419.2 and 3; 430.2 CPP).

26. As John Jackson (2005: 753) observes, noticing the great influence the European Court on Human Rights had on the mentioned Continental European criminal procedure's reforms: 'The [Human Rights] Commission and Court sought to "translate" the defense rights prescribed in Article 6 into a vision of adversarialism that was as compatible with the Continental notion of *une procédure contradictoire* as with the common law adversary trial. Defendants have to be guaranteed rights to legal representation, a right to be informed of all information relevant to the proceedings, a right to be present and to present arguments and evidence at trial. But this does not rule out considerable participation by judges in asking questions or even calling witnesses'. See now also Jackson and Summers (2012: 86–7 and *passim*).

27. For France see Deriveux (2002: 232); see also art. 61 of the previous Italian Criminal Procedure Code (1930) and, for the reform that took place in Portugal in 1988, see de Souto de Moura (1995: 48). For the implementation of the principle of a fresh judge in Spain, see Gascón Inchausti and Villamarín López (2008: 562–3).

28. The differentiation took place (following a vast array of Constitutional Court decisions) on a pluralistic rationality base, ten years after the new code of criminal procedure was enacted in 1988, in order to avoid a decision-making concentration upon a single judge on issues related both to the investigation supervision and to the sufficiency of evidence for trial committal. See Art. 171 D. L.vo February 19, 1998, n. 51.

29. For the general rule in Spain that only evidence called at the oral hearing is considered probative, see Gascón Inchausti and Villamarín López, (2008: 615) and Vogler (1999: 388). The Italian system in 1988 accomplished the strongest severance between pre-trial investigation and adjudication in order to safeguard the truth seeker's impartiality. The then brand-new Italian Code eliminated every and all contact of the trial court with the file of the pre-trial investigation, organizing a 'double file' system which gives the trial court access only to the trial dossier but not to the pre-trial investigation dossier (for the working aspects of the double dossier system see Panzavolta (2005: 586)). By so doing it insulated the trial judge completely from the approach taken by public officials (public prosecutor, judge of

the pre-trial investigation, judge of the preliminary hearing) during the pre-trial phase, preventing the results of the pre-trial investigation from prejudicing the trial court before the trial even starts. The Italian trial judge today approaches the case as a *tabula rasa*. For a very similar solution in the Spanish jury trial, see infra section 3.2.

30. Contrast the strong Continental tradition of appellate supervision of criminal trial courts with the one level adjudication typical of the English common law process until 'well into the nineteenth century' (Langbein, 1987: 37). It is a contrast that still carries its legacy in present times. 'Quite naturally, then, the entire criminal process became identified with the trial, and the conclusion of this stage signaled the end of the criminal proceedings. This conception of the criminal process ... has not disappeared even now from Anglo-American law. ... Because the notion has not been entirely discarded that the decision of the trial court terminates the criminal proceeding, appellate review seems to conflict with the guarantee against double jeopardy: review appears as a "new jeopardy" rather than the continuation of the original one. ... The lasting vitality of the notion of trial adjudication as final also accounts for the relatively limited scope of appeal' (see Damaška, 1975: 514–15).

31. Jackson (2005) argues for the rise of a unique European 'participatory model' that transcends the contest/inquest divide and that is rooted in a philosophical and political tradition common to both sides of the English Channel. He ascribes this development to a realignment of European criminal procedures along the lines indicated by the European Court of Human Rights (ECtHR). On this same line of thought see also, Summers (2007), now also in Jackson and Summers (2012); Amann, (2000: 818–20, 870); Delmas-Marty (1995).

32. For more on the import of this fundamental divide, see Grande (2008: 155ff.).

33. The Anglo-American derivation of the Spanish jury system is indeed emphasized both by Spanish and foreign scholars, cf. *supra* n. 2.

34. In the pre-trial phase, for example, the victim can take the place of the prosecutor, as in Spain, where, as a truly private prosecutor, she can maintain the indictment against the public prosecutor's desire to dismiss the case, thereby giving the judge in the intermediate stage the chance to set the case for trial. In Portugal a similar role is performed by the *assistente* in front of the *juiz de instrucao*, while in Italy, with or without the victim's opposition to the prosecutor's decision to dismiss, the judge of the investigation can compel the prosecutor to charge the defendant. Therefore the prosecutor, the victim and the judge bring different points of view and interests to the proceedings, sometimes moving in the same direction and sometimes not. The victim in many systems, like in Spain, Portugal, or Germany, can appeal against the acquittal even when the prosecutor decides not to do so, and at trial, of course, the court, in searching for the truth, can adduce evidence for or against the defendant, sometimes dovetailing with the prosecutor's evidence and sometimes contradicting it, and the prosecutor at trial can even request acquittal or appeal the defendant's conviction, which may put the prosecutor at odds with the victim's own legal motions (for some interesting cases of public and private prosecutors' contrasting strategies see Thaman (1998: 397–400)).

35. Ley Orgánica del Tribunal del Jurado [L.O.T.J.], B.O.E. n. 122, May 22, 1995 (Spain). Spanish text available at https://www.boe.es/buscar/act.php?id=BOE-A-1995-12095 [hereinafter 'LOTJ']. For a detailed description of the jury trial institution in Spain and its history see Thaman (1998). See also Gleadow (2000, 2001–2002).

36. 'The Spanish legislature opted to condition the jurisdiction of the jury court only on the nature of the charged crimes, and specified the following categories of crimes when it first enacted the Jury Law in May of 1995: "(a) crimes against human life; (b) crimes committed by public officials in the exercise of their duties; (c) crimes

against honor; (d) crimes of failing to render aid; (e) crimes against privacy and the home; (f) crimes against liberty; and (g) crimes against the environment." When the Jury Law was amended in November of 1995, the phrase "crimes against human life" was replaced by "crimes against persons" and subsections (d) through (f) were replaced by "crimes against liberty and security" and "arson." Each version of the law also included specified articles of the Penal Code ("CP") which would fall under the general rubrics. The law had to be amended with the passage of the 1995 CP in November 1995 to conform to the numbering and organization of the new Penal Code' (Thaman, 1998: 259–60).

37. 'On the one hand, jury trials are very expensive, especially in proportion to the number of cases decided every year, while on the other, the introduction of the jury has not resulted in a wider social acceptance of the function of the jury, which continues to raise concerns amongst citizens, who have no desire to be called on jury service. Jury proceedings are slower than ordinary proceedings, and furthermore the appeal of judgments is almost inevitable, which means it takes longer to reach a final decision': Gascón Inchausti and Villamarín López (2008: 645). On the reluctance of the public to act as jurors see Jimeno-Bulnes (2011: 610ff.). For the many problems connected with the adequacy of jurors' reasoning, see *infra* 3.2.1 and 3.2.2.

38. '[T]he officials involved in the proceedings (judges and state prosecutors) tend to avoid jury trials by classifying the facts in different legal terms so that they do not qualify to be tried by this special process. Likewise, the enormous lack of faith that the defendants tend to have in the jury leads to a very high number of guilty pleas in jury trials, precisely in order to avoid the verdict of the jury' (Gascón Inchausti and Villamarín López, 2008: 645). The practice of avoiding the jury trial through an intense and possibly illegal use of the 'conformity institution' or 'plea bargaining', which takes place before the jury is selected and the trial begins, is thoroughly illustrated and discussed by Jimeno-Bulnes (2011: 606ff.). The author (Jimeno-Bulnes, 2011: 602ff.) also illustrates a different device used to limit the scope of offenses adjudicated by jury trial: namely, the Spanish Supreme Court's restrictive interpretation of the competence of the juries to adjudicate so-called 'related crimes', addressed in Article 5 of the LOTJ. 'The impact of jury proceedings in Spain is still more limited and symbolic than it should be according to legal rules', concludes Jimeno-Bulnes (2011: 609), providing the data for the small amount of cases tried by jury in Spain.

39. Gascón Inchausti and Villamarín López (2008: 645).

40. In which professional judges and lay assessors collegially decide all questions of fact, law and sentence.

41. On the spread of the English adapted jury trial throughout the Continent in nineteenth-century Europe following the French example, before the mixed panel trial of German origins took over from it in Russia, Germany, Italy, and France, see Thaman (2011: 616ff.) See also Padoa Schioppa (1987).

42. On the pressures and difficulties in making common law juries accountable, see Jackson (2002). Professor Jackson concludes: 'It has been argued that so long as the common law jury continues to derive its raison d'être from having to operate within a coordinate structure of authority, there will be limits to the extent to which juries can be made accountable in a hard sense for the decisions which they take. Despite the demands for greater accountability, the jury still derives its essential legitimacy from its independence from the legal system and from its ties to the community, with the result that accountability mechanisms will continue to be weaker than when decision makers are officials answerable to a hierarchy above' (2002: 528).

43. On jury nullification history, on the recent attempts to eliminate it and on its persistent value in coordinate models of justice, see Jackson (2002: 494ff., 503ff., 515ff.).

44. The medieval jury was self-informing, not necessarily in the sense of having first-hand knowledge of events (since jurors often lived too far away from the scene of the crime), but rather in the sense that jurors gathered the evidence. See Jackson (2002: 490 and the literature cited). 'In the thirteenth century "it is the duty of the jurors, so soon as they have been summoned, to make inquiries about the facts of which they will have to speak when they come before the court. They must collect testimony; they must weigh it and state the net result in a verdict." Medieval juries came to court more to speak than to listen', writes Langbein (1973: 314, quoting Pollock and Maitland, 1898: 624–5). For the sixteenth century as the moment in which jurors' role changed, from one of active fact-finding to a more passive role, see Jackson (2002: 490 and quoted literature).

45. In fact, non-jury trials rules work as default rules in jury trials according to Arts 24 (2) AND 42 (1) LOTJ. See Jimeno-Bulnes (2011: 598 and therein quoted literature).

46. Gascón Inchausti and Villamarín López (2008: 614).

47. Art. 701 (6) Ley de Enjuiciamiento Criminal (hereinafter 'LECrim').

48. Art. 708 (2) LECrim.

49. Art. 700 (2) LECrim.

50. Art. 729 (2) LECrim. For the restrictions imposed by case law on the reading of this article, allowing *ex officio* evidence only to test the reliability of the evidence put forward by the parties, see Gascón Inchausti and Villamarín López (2008: 561, 607, 613) and the literature cited therein.

51. Art. 729 (1) LECrim.

52. Article 49 LOTJ. The trial judge can dissolve the jury and acquit the defendant 'if he holds that the trial did not result in the existence of inculpatory evidence which could be the basis of a condemnation of the accused': (Thaman, 2011: 643), noticing how the article was patterned after the American Federal Rule of Criminal Procedure 29(a).

53. In Damaška's words (1997: 90, quoting Frankel, 1975: 1042): 'Note ... how risky it is for the judge to ask meaningful questions in a fact-finding process orchestrated by partisan lawyers: innocent as the judge is of the details of their cases, he may easily turn into a "blind and blundering intruder"'.

54. Art. 846 bis (c) lett. (d) LOTJ. In the US, by contrast, once the judgment of acquittal is entered, the government's right of appeal is effectively blocked by the Double Jeopardy Clause of the US Constitution, as the only remedy available to the Court of Appeals would be to order a retrial. This is why only the judgment of acquittal entered after a jury returns a guilty verdict can be challenged on appeal, since its reversal would simply reinstate the jury verdict with no need for a new trial. On that see the critical considerations moved by Sauber and Waldman (1994).

55. Art. 846 bis (c) lett. (e) LOTJ and last paragraph. In Spain the same need to protect the defendant's constitutionally guaranteed presumption of innocence also requires the trial judge, even if she did not rule on a motion for a judgment of acquittal before the jury retires, to assess the minimal sufficiency of the evidence the jury found proved. See Art. 70.2 LOTJ. By contrast, in the United States, after the jury verdict, the trial judge can no longer *sua sponte* enter a judgment of acquittal: see Federal Rules of Criminal Procedure, Rule 29(c). However, on the less stringent criteria applied in Spain in assessing the amount of evidence sufficient for a guilty verdict to stand, see Thaman (2011: 644–5 and fn. 151).

56. The public prosecutor can indeed appeal a conviction according to the principles of legality and impartiality ruling her activity, such as provided by Arts. 3, 4 and 6 of the Estatuto Orgánico del Ministerio Fiscal. See Todolí Gómez (2009) and case law ivi quoted at fn. 20.

57. According to Rule 29(a), (b) and (c) of the Federal Rules of Criminal Procedure.

58. According to the plain error doctrine, incorporated in rule 103(e) of the Federal Rules of Evidence, in spite of the fact that a proper objection was not made, an appellate court *may in its discretion* notice a forfeited error and reject the result at trial whenever the error 'seriously affects the fairness, integrity, or public reputation of judicial proceedings'. Yet, not only does it represent an appellate court's discretionary power, but since 'the adversary system, based on party responsibility, is deeply engrained in our jurisprudence, particularly in the field of evidence' (Graham, 2012: 695) the plain error doctrine is very rarely applied: 'The infrequency with which the doctrine is generally applied precludes deliberate reliance upon it during the trial of a case' (Graham, 2012: 696).

59. See Federal Rules of Criminal Procedure, Rule 29 and Phillips (1997), who criticizes *Carlisle v. United States*, 116 S.Ct. 1460 (1966) and suggests that a trial court should have discretionary power to enter a post-verdict judgment of acquittal *sua sponte* to remedy injustice stemming from the defendant's failure to (timely) move for it.

60. Art. 46(1) LOTJ. For a report of the active role played by jurors in directly questioning witnesses, experts, and defendants in the first years after the trial jury was introduced in Spain, see Thaman (1998: 305–6).

61. Art. 46(2) and (3) LOTJ.

62. For some experiments, involving a more active role for jurors in a number of states of the United States, see Jackson (2002: 493, fn. 70) and Damaška (1997: 90, fn. 32).

63. For concrete cases of acquittal request put forward by the prosecutor see Thaman (1998: 392–7). The (used) prerogative of the public prosecutor to ask for an acquittal could definitely be linked to the Spanish principle of compulsory prosecution, which can explain his counterintuitive move at trial. Yet, his role as representing the interests of society generally, therefore primarily to search for the substantive truth, provides a better rationale for it. It is the case, indeed, that the same prerogative is granted, and sometimes – though rarely – used also in France, where prosecutors have a wide discretion whether or not to initiate proceedings (principle of opportunity of prosecution). For a recent and renowned case (involving to be sure contrasting viewpoints between the investigating magistrate and the prosecutor) of a French prosecutor asking at trial for the defendant's acquittal, see the case of the former IMF chief, Dominique Strauss-Kahn, charged of aggravated pimping and acquitted on June 2015.

64. Thus, for example, if the defense does not participate in the search for the truth (bearing no duty in that regard) other actors can take her place, searching for the truth in her favor. In fact, the roles are so fluid that, in a dancing move that could definitely be considered surprising, even the private prosecutor can ask for the defendant's acquittal. For a concrete case in which that happened, see Thaman (1998, Appendix I, case LP-1 González case).

65. Unlike what happens in a non-jury trial. See LOTJ III: *Exposición de Motivos*; Art. 34(1) LOTJ; and Thaman (1998: 271ff., 281f.).

66. It should be noticed that the trial court's *tabula rasa* approach (adopted also in Italy in 1988, see *supra* n. 29) represents a further move toward improving the pluralistic rumba way of justice, since Continental systems have traditionally been much less adamant than the American tango's one in keeping the various stages of the process separate, because they have generally regarded the trial as the crucial passage of a continuous effort at determining the truth. 'Is it possible to have a presumption of innocence and an independent fact/guilt finder simultaneously in the form of a single professional judge, who has studied the investigative file and determined, before the trial, that sufficient evidence for a finding of guilt exists?' asks, indeed, quite rhetorically Thaman (1998: 244), tackling the usual Continental weak severance between the pre-trial and the trial.

67. Judges may investigate only in response to motions by parties. They may only investigate topics that bear on probable cause to charge the offense (LOTJ Art. 27). See Thaman (1998: 273): 'If interpreted literally, the LOTJ reduces the role of the investigative judge to that of a neutral evaluator of the existence of probable cause necessary to hold a suspect for trial, and neutral executor of the investigative requests of the parties in the criminal case, which should be limited to those items of evidence which cannot be repeated in court at the time of the jury trial'. See also Jimeno-Bulnes (2011: 598, fn. 65) for a detailed literature on the subject. Yet, for a residual power of *ex officio* investigation held by the investigative judge, see Art. 27(3) and 32(3) LOTJ, *infra* note 69.
68. Art. 29(4) LOTJ.
69. See Art. 27(3) LOTJ: 'Investigation Measures. ... If the judge were to consider that the requested measures' (that is, requested by the parties) 'are not necessary and *order none of his own motion* ...' (emphasis added) (see also the slightly different Spanish version of secs. (3) and (4)) and Art. 32 LOTJ: 'Decree of Dismissal or Opening of the Trial. Once the preliminary hearing has concluded ... 3. Before a resolution is adopted, the judge may also order additional measures to be carried out if he considers them necessary as a result of preliminary hearing' (official translation by the Ministry of Justice, retrievable at http://www.mjusticia.gob.es/cs/Satellite/ 1292426982029?blobheader=application%2Fpdf&blobheadername1=Content-Disposition &blobheadervalue1=attachment%3B+filename%3DOrganic_Act_5_1995__on_the_Jury_ %28Ley_Organica_del_Tribunal_del_Jurado%29.PDF).
70. Art. 124 of Spanish Constitution.
71. For the judicial implementation of the jury duty to give reasons in Spain and the different criteria applied by the Spanish courts for testing the sufficiency of the reasons given by juries for their verdicts, see Thaman (2011: 649ff.).
72. Studies have pointed out that 'more than approximately fifty percent of total verdicts were either poorly reasoned or unreasoned' (Jimeno-Bulnes, 2011: 602 quoting Serra Dominguez, 2001).
73. Art. 846 bis (c) (a) LECrim. See Jimeno-Bulnes (2011: 601).
74. A well-known instance in which an acquittal was reversed on appeal and a demanding test for reasons for acquittals was imposed by the Spanish Constitutional Court is that of Mikel Otegi. In the Otegi case the acquittal was reversed by the Superior Judicial Court of the Basque Country and the reversal was then upheld by the Supreme Court. The defendant appealed to the Constitutional Court, claiming that requiring the jury to provide reasons for an acquittal violated the presumption of innocence. The Constitutional Court upheld the reversal, holding that verdicts to acquit must also contain sufficient reasons for the decision. See Thaman (2011: 636).
75. 'A verdict of guilt in a murder case in the United States, for instance, might just indicate that: "the jury ... finds the defendant guilty of murder of the first degree." All one really knows, then, is that the jury found that the prosecutor had proved the elements of first degree murder in relation as charged in the indictment. It is not even necessary, in some states, for the jury to indicate whether a finding of murder in the first degree was based on a finding of "premeditation and deliberation," or whether the jury found the prosecution had only proved the defendant took part in a robbery which resulted in the unintended death of the victim – so-called felony murder', notices Thaman (2011: 646).
76. This explains why the Spanish Constitutional Court not only requires juries to give (quite extensive) reasons for their findings in their verdicts, whether they are of convictions or acquittals, but also held that where juries return inadequately reasoned verdicts the parties do not have to object the insufficiency of the verdict's reasoning in the post-verdict phase to preserve the issue for appeal. See the Otegi case, mentioned *supra*, at n. 74: S.T.C. Dec. 20, 2004, B.O.E., No. 1063, pp. 36, 40–1

available at http://www.boe.es/boe/dias/2005/01/21/pdfs/T00036-00043.pdf; see also the Moisés Macía Vega case: S.T.C., Oct. 6, 2004, B.O.E., No. 19069, p. 82, 90, available at http://www.boe.es/boe/dias/2004/11/09/pdfs/T00082-00092.pdf.

77. European case law requires that judgments in criminal cases be reasoned and based on a rational evaluation of evidence to ensure an effective right to appeal. See Thaman (2011: 633f.). In *Taxquet v. Belgium*, the European Court of Human Rights confirmed not only that professional judges must give reasons for their verdicts; jury verdicts, too, were subjected to the requirement of 'precise, unequivocal questions put to the jury by the judge, forming a framework on which the verdict is based or sufficiently offsetting the fact that no reasons are given for the jury's answers', in order for an appeal of the factual basis for a jury decision to be possible (*Taxquet v. Belgium*, GC, App. No. 926/05, Eur. Ct. H.R., Nov. 16, 2010, § 92 available at http://www.echr.coe.int).

78. In a non-adversary system in which the trier of the fact (whether judge or jury) is supposed to be an active participant in the fact-finding enterprise, a non-partisan reconstruction of the facts is strictly dependent on the removal of the third party's monopoly over the factual inquiry. On this view, neutrality and impartiality are only attainable when a serious pluralistic challenge to the third party fact reconstruction takes place. The review by a higher court of the reasoning and logic of the third party's factual assessment forms an essential part of this system. In the adversary system, by contrast, neutrality and impartiality are synonyms of passivity.

79. For more on this, see Thaman (2011: 615ff.).

80. Art. 52 LOTJ.

81. For example, in Otegi, *supra* n. 74, the verdict form included 91 factual questions. For more about this, see Thaman (1998: 329ff.).

82. Articles 53(3) and 54 LOTJ.

83. Section 2. Deliberation and Verdict, Art. 55ff. LOTJ. Since, as already pointed out, more than one prosecutor can be involved, different 'criminal acts' can likewise be alleged by different prosecutors.

84. Art. 70 LOTJ.

85. Art. 61(1)(d) LOTJ. How to interpret the notion of 'succinct explanation' – and where to position the threshold for a sufficiently reasoned verdict – has been hotly debated in Spain. The Spanish Supreme Court has provided a notable array of case law concerning the adequacy of a jury's reasons for their verdict. It announced three alternative theses by which the suitability of the reasoning in jury verdicts may be assessed: the demanding, the minimalist and the intermediate approach. See Jimeno-Bulnes (2007: 769–73; 2011: 601, fn. 84), Thaman (2011: 651–60), and Csere (2013: 422–4).

86. Art. 52(1)(g) LOTJ.

87. For examples from actual cases, see Thaman (1998: 349).

88. That is seven for unfavorable questions and five for favorable ones: Art. 59 (1) LOTJ.

89. Art. 59 last paragraph LOTJ (official translation).

90. Art. 63(1)(d) LOTJ.

91. Art. 65 LOTJ.

92. Art. 70 LOTJ.

93. This remains true even considering that many states allow the lawyers to request that certain instructions be given or that some jurisdictions (like Oklahoma, Tennessee or North Carolina) grant the judge the power to instruct *sua sponte* on lesser included counts.

94. In Inga Markovitz's (2004: 110) horticultural metaphor for legal transplants, the jury trial did not travel as a 'potted plant', nor did it find a fertile soil in the conflicting cultural values of the recipient systems. 'Reforms that carry with them their own surroundings ("potted plants") will do better, the more institutional support and

personnel they have and the less dependent they are on local cooperation and approval. Law reforms that are inconsistent with deeply held moral and political beliefs may work if they only slightly affect convictions at the periphery of the local value system. But their success is doubtful if they contradict fundamental cultural gut reactions. The more complex and multi-layered a particular environment, the greater the danger that legal imports will irritate local sensibilities. For this reason, procedural changes might be riskier than substantive reform because procedure is based on repetition, role-playing, and tradition ("we've always done it like this") and is saturated with unspoken assumptions and conditioned reflexes'.

95.   In this light, the reader could even legitimately wonder whether rather than a move toward the American model, the introduction of the trial by jury in Spain is actually a return to its own past. On the traits of the nineteenth century (and early twentieth) jury trial in Spain patterned after the French one, see Thaman (1998: 2011).

96.   In this sense, borrowing Jonathan Miller's (2003: 854) expression, it is possible to speak about a '*legitimacy-generating* transplant' (emphasis added). Or, following Inga Markovits's (2004:110) observations about the difficulties encountered by the American jury trial transplant in Russia, it is possible to speak about an image-generating or remake effect of the transplant. 'How did the Russian jury ever advance so far on the law reformer's drawing boards? In part, I think, because introducing the jury into Continental criminal procedure seemed like such a noble and romantic goal, conjuring up images of new world freedom; of self-confident citizens, walking tall; of twelve men good and true; maybe even of "Twelve Angry Men," because I see no reason to exclude film and television from the list of inspirations that drive a nation to remake itself'.

97.   For the persistent idea of the non-adversary process as an oppressive process that still 'evokes the image of hooded minions of the Spanish Inquisition' see Weigend (2011: 406 and fn. 82).

98.   These include cross-examination and the exclusionary rule, which I will further explore in relation to the Spanish as well as to other European systems in a forthcoming paper.

BIBLIOGRAPHY

Amann, Diane Marie 2000. 'Harmonic Convergence? Constitutional Criminal Procedure in an International Context', 75 *Indiana Law Journal* 809.

Bradley, Craig M. 1993. *The Failure of the Criminal Procedure Revolution*. Philadelphia: University of Philadelphia Press.

Bradley, Craig M. 1999. 'Overview', in Craig M. Bradley, ed., *Criminal Procedure: A Worldwide Study*. Durham, NC: Carolina Academic Press.

Cordero, Franco. 1982. *Procedura Penale*. Milano: Giuffrè Editore.

Cordero, Franco. 1998. *Procedura Penale*. Milano: Giuffrè Editore.

Csere, Michael. 2013. 'Reasoned Criminal Verdicts in the Netherlands and Spain: Implications for Juries in the United States', 12(2) *Connecticut Public Interest Law Journal* 415.

Damaška, Mirjan R. 1973. 'Evidentiary Barriers to Conviction and Two Models of Criminal Procedure: A Comparative Study', 121 *University of Pennsylvania Law Review* 506.

Damaška, Mirjan R. 1975. 'Structures of Authority and Comparative Criminal Procedure', 84 *Yale Law Journal* 480.

Damaška, Mirjan R. 1986. *The Faces of Justice and State Authority: A Comparative Approach to the Legal Process*. New Haven: Yale University Press.

Damaška, Mirjan R. 1997. *Evidence Law Adrift*. New Haven: Yale University Press.

Damaška, Mirjan R. 2001. 'Models of Criminal Procedure', 51 *Zbornik PFZ* (Collected Papers of Zagreb Law School) 477.

del Duca, Louis. 1991. 'An Historical Convergence of Civil and Common Law Systems – Italy's New "Adversarial" Criminal Procedure System', 10 *Dickinson Journal of International Law* 73.

Delmas-Marty, Mireille. 1995. 'Towards a European Model of the Criminal Trial', in Mirelle Delmas-Marty, ed., *The Criminal Process and Human Rights: Towards A European Consciousness*, Dordrecht, Boston, London: Martinus Nijhoff Publishers.

Delmas-Marty Mireille and J.R. Spencer, eds., 2002. *European Criminal Procedure*. Cambridge: Cambridge University Press.

Deriveux, Valérie. 2002. 'The French System', in Mireille Delmas-Marty and J.R. Spencer, eds., *European Criminal Procedure*, Cambridge: Cambridge University Press.

de Souto de Moura, José. 1995. 'The Criminal Process in Portugal', in Mireille Delmas-Marty, ed., *The Criminal Process and Human Rights: Toward A European Consciousness*. Dordrecht, Boston, London: Martinus Nijhoff Publishers.

Frankel, Marvin. 1975. 'The Search for the Truth: An Umpireal View', 123 *University Pennsylvania Law Review* 1031.

Gascón Inchausti, Fernando and María Luisa Villamarín López. 2008. 'Criminal Procedure in Spain', in Richard Vogler and Barbara Huber, eds., *Criminal Procedure in Europe*. Berlin: Duncker and Humblot.

Gleadow, Carmen. 2000. *History of Trial by Jury in the Spanish Legal System*. Lewiston, NY: Edwin Mellen Pr.

Gleadow, Carmen. 2001–2002. 'Spain's Return to Trial by Jury: Theoretical Foundations and Practical Results', *St. Louis-Warsaw Transatlantic Law Journal* 57.

Gleß, Sabine. 2010. 'Truth or Due Process? The Use of Illegally Gathered Evidence in Criminal Trial', 2010, retrievable at http://papers.ssrn.com/sol3/papers.cfm?abstract_id= 1743530.

Goldstein, Abraham. 1974. 'Reflections on Two Models: Inquisitorial Themes in American Criminal Procedure', 26 *Stanford Law Review* 1009.

Graham, Michael H. 2012. *Evidence. A Problem, Lecture and Discussion Approach* (3rd edn). St Paul, MN: West.

Grande, Elisabetta. 2000. 'Italian Criminal Justice: Borrowing and Resistance', 48 *American Journal of Comparative Law* 227.

Grande, Elisabetta. 2008. 'Dances of Criminal Justice: Thoughts on Systemic Differences and the Search for the Truth', in John Jackson, Máximo Langer, and Peter Tillers, eds., *Crime, Procedure and Evidence in a Comparative and International Context Essays in Honour of Professor Mirjan Damaška*. Oxford: Hart Publishing.

Grande, Elisabetta. 2012. 'Comparative Criminal Justice', in Mauro Bussani and Ugo Mattei, eds., *The Cambridge Companion to Comparative Law*. Cambridge: Cambridge University Press.

Griffiths, John. 1970. 'Ideology in Criminal Procedure or a Third "Model" of the Criminal Process', 79 *Yale Law Journal* 359.

Hodgson, Jacqueline. 2002. 'Constructing the Pre-trial Role of the Defense in French Criminal Procedure: An Adversarial Outsider in an Inquisitorial Process', 6 *International Journal of Evidence and Proof* 1.

Hodgson, Jacqueline. 2005. *French Criminal Justice: A Comparative Account of the Investigation and Prosecution of Crime in France*. Oxford: Oxford University Press.

Huber, Barbara. 2008. 'Criminal Procedure in Germany', in Richard Vogler and Barbara Huber, eds., *Criminal Procedure in Europe*. Berlin: Duncker and Humblot.

Jackson, John D. 2002. 'Making Juries Accountable', 50 *American Journal of Comparative Law* 477.

Jackson, John D. 2005. 'The Effect of Human Rights on Criminal Evidentiary Processes: Towards Convergence, Divergence or Realignment?' 68(5) *Modern Law Review* 737–64.

Jackson, John D. and Sarah J. Summers. 2012. *The Internationalisation of Criminal Evidence: Beyond the Common Law and Civil Law Traditions.* Cambridge: Cambridge University Press.

Jimeno-Bulnes, Mar. 2007. 'A Different Story Line for 12 Angry Men: Verdicts Reached by Majority Rule –The Spanish Perspective', 82 *Chicago-Kent Law Review* 759.

Jimeno-Bulnes, Mar. 2011. 'Jury Selection and Jury Trial in Spain: Between Theory and Practice', 86 *Chicago-Kent Law Review* 585.

Jimeno-Bulnes, Mar. 2012–2013. 'American Criminal Procedure in a European Context', 21 *Cardozo Journal of International and Comparative Law* 409.

Kadish, Mortimer R. and Sanford H. Kadish. 1973. *Discretion to Disobey: A Study of Lawful Departures from Legal Rules.* Stanford: Stanford University Press.

Langbein, John H. 1973. 'The Origins of Public Prosecution at Common Law', 17 *The American Journal of Legal History* 313.

Langbein, John H. 1978. 'The Criminal Trial before the Lawyers', 45 *University of Chicago Law Review* 263.

Langbein, John H. 1983. 'Shaping the Eighteenth-Century Criminal Trial: A View from the Ryder Sources', 50 *University of Chicago Law Review* 1.

Langbein, John H. 1987. 'The English Criminal Trial Jury on the Eve of the French Revolution', in Antonio Padoa Schioppa, ed., *The Trial Jury in England, France, Germany 1770–1900*, Berlin: Duncker and Humbolt.

Langbein, John H. 1994. 'The Historical Origins of the Privilege against Self Incrimination at Common Law', 92 *Michigan Law Review* 1047.

Langbein, John H. 1996. 'Historical Foundations of the Law of Evidence: A View from the Ryder Sources', 96 *Columbia Law Review* 1168.

Langbein, John H. 2003. *The Origins of Adversary Criminal Trial*, Oxford: Oxford University Press.

Langer, Máximo. 2014. 'The Long Shadow of the Adversarial And Inquisitorial Categories', in Markus D. Dubber and Tatjana Höernle, eds., *The Oxford Handbook of Criminal Law*. Oxford: Oxford University Press.

Llewellyn, Karl N. 1962. 'The Anthropology of Criminal Guilt', in *Jurisprudence: Realism in Theory and Practice*. Chicago: The University Press.

Markovitz, Inga. 2004. 'Exporting Law Reform: But Will It Travel?' 37 *Cornell International Law Journal* 95.

Miller, Jonathan M. 2003. 'A Typology of Legal Transplants: Using Sociology, Legal History and Argentine Examples to Explain the Transplant Process', 51 *American Journal of Comparative Law* 839.

Padoa Schioppa, Antonio, ed. 1987. *The Trial Jury in England, France, Germany, 1700–1900.* Berlin: Duncker and Humblot.

Panzavolta, Michele. 2005. 'Reforms and Counter-Reforms in the Italian Struggle for an Accusatorial Criminal Law System', 30 *North Carolina Journal of International Law & Commercial Regulation* 577.

Phillips, Dawn M. 1997. 'When Rules are More Important than Justice', 87 *Journal of Criminal Law and Criminology*, 1040.

Pizzi, William T. and Mariangela Montagna. 2004. 'The Battle to Establish an Adversarial Trial System in Italy', 25 *Michigan Journal of International Law* 429.

Pollock Frederick and Frederic William Maitland. 1898. *The History of English Law before the Time of Edward 1*, Vol. 2 (2nd edn). Cambridge: Cambridge University Press.

Rawls, John. 1999. *A Theory of Justice* (revised edn). Cambridge, MA: Harvard University Press.

Sauber Richard and Michael Waldman. 1994. 'Unlimited Power: Rule 29(a) and the Unreviewability of Directed Judgments of Acquittal', 44 *The American University Law Review* 433.

Serra Dominguez, Manuel. 2001. 'El Jurado: éxito o fracaso', in Joan Picó i Junoy, ed., *Problemas Actuales de la Justicia Penal*. Vallirana, Barcelona: J.M. Bosch Editor.

Sklansky, David A. 2009. 'Anti-Inquisitorialism', 122 *Harvard Law Review* 1634.

Summers, Sarah J. 2007. *Fair Trials: The European Criminal Procedural Tradition and the European Court of Human Rights*. Oxford and Portland: Hart Publishing.

Thaman, Stephen C. 1998. 'Spain Returns to Trial by Jury', 21 *Hastings International & Comparative Law Review* 241.

Thaman, Stephen C. 2011. 'Should Criminal Juries Give Reasons for Their Verdicts? The Spanish Experience and the Implications of the European Court of Human Rights Decision in *Taxquet v. Belgium*', 86 *Chicago-Kent Law Review* 613.

Todolí Gómez, Arturo. 2009. 'El recurso de apelación contra sentencia en el proceso ante el Tribunal del Jurado', retrievable at http://noticias.juridicas.com/articulos/65-Derecho-Procesal-Penal/252-el-recurso-de-apelacin-contra-la-sentencia-en-el-proceso-ante-el-tribunal-del-jurado.html.

Vannini, Ottorino and Giuseppe Cocciardi. 1986. *Manuale di Diritto Processuale Penale Italiano*. Milano: Giuffrè.

Vargas, Jorge A. 1999. 'Jury Trials in Spain: A Description and Analysis of the 1995 Organic Act and a Preliminary Appraisal of the Barcelona Trial', 18 *New York Law School Journal of International & Comparative Law* 181.

Vogler, Richard.1999. 'Spain', in Craig M. Bradley, ed., *Criminal Procedure: A Worldwide Study*. Durham, NC: Carolina Academic Press.

Vogler, Richard. 2008. 'Criminal Procedure in France', in Richard Vogler and Barbara Huber, eds., *Criminal Procedure in Europe*. Berlin: Duncker and Humblot.

Vogler, Richard and Barbara Huber, eds. 2008. *Criminal Procedure in Europe*. Berlin: Duncker and Humblot.

Weigend, Thomas. 2003. 'Is the Criminal Process about Truth? A German Perspective', 26 *Harvard Journal of Law & Public Policy* 157.

Weigend, Thomas. 2011. 'Should We Search for the Truth, and Who Should Do It?' 36 *North Carolina Journal of International Law & Commercial Regulation* 389.

Wiegand, Wolfgang. 1991. 'The Reception of American Law in Europe', 39 *American Journal of Comparative Law* 229.

11. Japan's lay judge system

David T. Johnson

For this institution [of the American jury] is not only important in itself as a part of our court procedures; it has exerted a mighty influence upon other elements of the court process. Like iron filings around a magnet, many features of our law arrange themselves around the jury.

(Benjamin Kaplan, 1961: 44)

After a 60-year moratorium on lay participation in Japanese criminal justice, the lay judge system has thrown a stone into the pond of Japanese society, and the ripples are gradually, and deeply, spreading.

(Satoru Shinomiya, 2010: 13)

In May 2009, Japan began a new trial system in which six lay persons sit with three professional judges to adjudicate guilt and determine the sentence in serious criminal cases. This 'lay judge system' (*saiban-in seido*) places citizen participation at the center of Japanese criminal trials – and Japanese criminal justice – for the first time since 1943, when Japan's original jury law was suspended after 15 years of fitful use (Johnson, 2002a: 42). At a time when adversarial trials in America are declining and perhaps even dying (Burns, 2009), Japan has implemented a trial reform that is so fundamental it could remake the country's criminal justice system in the years to come. But that is no sure thing, for the new form of civilian participation might also be marginalized by Japanese legal professionals – prosecutors and professional judges especially – who have vested interests in maintaining their standard operating procedures. This marginalization into obscurity and capture by legal experts has happened several times in the past when Japan has tried to make citizen participation a more central part of its criminal process (Anderson and Nolan, 2004: 970).

This chapter describes Japan's lay judge reform and explores how it is affecting the country's criminal justice system. Section 1 explains the political origins and jurisprudential justifications for this major change in criminal procedure. Section 2 describes the rules that govern the lay judge system and how it operated during its first three years. Section 3 examines how the lay judge system has influenced different aspects of

Japanese criminal justice, from interrogation and sentencing to defense lawyering and discovery. Section 4 concludes by considering the possibility that Japan's lay judge reform may be as important for what it does to the country's political culture as for the effects it has on criminal justice processes and outcomes.

1. RATIONALITY, POWER, AND REFORM

In May 2004, Japan enacted a lay judge law that gave courts and citizens five years to prepare for the advent of a new system of criminal trials. This reform was part of a much larger movement for 'justice system reform' (*shiho kaikaku undo*) that aimed to generate 'huge' and 'extensive' reforms in 'all aspects of Japan's justice system' (Anderson and Johnson, 2010: 372). Two main reasons were given to justify greater lay participation in Japan's criminal justice system. The first was the claim that lay participation would produce better criminal justice by ensuring that verdicts and sentences reflect citizens' experiences and common sense. Problems in Japanese criminal justice, such as the length, intensity, and intrusiveness of interrogations, procedural rules that favor state interests while providing few formal protections for suspects and defendants, wrongful convictions, and a serious shortage of transparency and accountability throughout the criminal process, also motivated the push for some form of lay participation. The second reason for the lay judge reform was a belief that civilian participation in trials would promote the development of Japanese democracy, a contention which took different forms. One version of this view held that when citizens are called for duty, they learn more about the judicial system and become more interested in it, and this translates into a legal system that is more responsive to society's needs. A variation on this view held that lay participation would ensure that the Japanese public shares ownership of criminal justice outcomes. On this view, a lay judge reform would also serve the judiciary's interest by insulating its decisions from criticism (Anderson and Johnson, 2010: 374).

The foregoing justifications might seem to suggest that Japan's lay judge reform was driven by reason. After all, rationality has been called the major means for making democracy work in modern societies (Flyvbjerg, 1998). But when it comes to reform, what counts as 'rational' frequently depends on context – and the most critical context of rationality is power. In Japan's justice system reform movement, power sometimes blurred the dividing line between rationality and rationalization by ensuring that some subjects that should have been reform imperatives – including the power and accountability of the police – were left off the reform agenda.

In Japan's justice system reform, the police were missing in action – and for no principled reason. Japanese police are extremely powerful, they misuse their power, and they are neither transparent nor accountable to external organs of authority. In these respects, the police constitute the primary impediment to the 'rule of law' that was aspired to in Japan's justice system reform movement. It would have been rational to place the police at the center of Japan's criminal justice reforms, but that did not happen because the police did not want it to. The police and their allies were able to limit the scope of the political process to consideration of only those issues that seemed innocuous to them. They thus succeeded in keeping key questions about police power, performance, and accountability outside public discussions. Their success at agenda-setting also illustrates the political truth that power has the capacity to define 'reality' by producing knowledge that is conducive to the policies it wants to pursue and by suppressing knowledge for which it has no use (Flyvbjerg, 1998).

Another truth about legal reform is that changes implemented in one part of a system inevitably stimulate changes elsewhere. As explained later in this chapter, lay judge trials in Japan are generating change in standard operating procedures in many parts of the pretrial process. In the long run, the net effect may be a shift in the balance of power in Japanese criminal justice – a balance that has long favored law enforcement's interest in obtaining confessions and convictions (Foote, 1992).

Perhaps the central puzzle about Japan's lay judge reform is how a new trial system got created even though powerful interests and institutions opposed it. Most notably, prosecutors profited from a trial system that was run solely by professional judges who were extraordinarily deferent to their demands and interests (Foote, 2010), and judges were hardly enthusiastic about sharing their decision-making powers with the public (Foote, 2007b). In legal systems generally, nothing is as deeply imbedded as the procedures for proof and trial (Langbein, 1978: 19), yet in the first decade of the 21st century, Japan designed a new trial system that changes many of the basic procedures for proof and trial. How did that happen?

Japan's lay judge reform rode a much larger wave of 'path-breaking change' that departed from the more 'gradualist' approach to reform that characterized the country in previous decades (Foote, 2008: 1). Several factors created momentum for an array of reforms that included the new trial system. First, Japan's long recession during the 'lost decade' of the 1990s undermined confidence in many aspects of the country's standard operating procedures, and this perception of failure created openness to new ways of doing things. Second, the impacts of internationalization generated demand for new legal services, especially among business elites who have come to appreciate the role that legal professionals play in an increasingly globalized world. Third, legal reform became a high priority among some key leaders, especially Prime Minister Koizumi Junichiro (2001–2006), one of the most effective reformers in Japan's post-war political history. Finally, the salience of justice system reform in Japanese political circles resulted in the creation of reform commissions and advisory committees that were *not* dominated by the branches of the legal profession – procuracy, judiciary, and bar – that had curtailed efforts at reform in previous years. Instead, Koizumi and other elites treated legal change as a matter of pressing public importance, and the persons they appointed to key committees and commissions included actors from outside the institutions who could be expected to resist significant reform. In the end, two key groups – politicians and business leaders – supported the general goals of legal reform, and once it became clear that justice system reform would be a subject of debate among a wide range of constituencies (not just among legal professionals), 'the door was opened for wide-reaching reforms' that included lay participation (Foote, 2008: 10).

As for what led to *this* form of lay participation in particular, Japan was the only developed nation that did not significantly involve the public in its judicial process at the time the Justice System Reform Council (JSRC) released its recommendations in 2001. The perception that Japan was an unjustifiable outlier in the developed world led the JSRC to recommend that citizens should become more involved in criminal trials while leaving open the precise form public participation should take. And this is where the three main legal professions made their preferences clear. The Japan Federation of Bar Associations favored a common law-style jury system in which lay persons would deliver verdicts independent of professional judges, as is the case in the United States. In contrast, the Japanese Supreme Court wanted to allow citizens to express their opinions to judges only in an 'advisory' manner. The Ministry of Justice, which is largely run by prosecutors and supervises their activities, took an intermediate position between the bar and bench, opposing a pure jury system but allowing citizens to discuss cases with judges and to decide verdicts and sentences together with them (as currently occurs in many European nations).[1] Eventually, prosecutors and judges came to see some kind of lay participation as all but inevitable, and they tried to avoid the outcome that seemed worst for them: a pure jury system. After considerable conflict between key stakeholders about what form the new trials would take, the lay judge system that emerged – three professional judges sitting with six citizens in serious criminal cases – can be considered a compromise between the more liberal position taken by the bar and the more conservative stances of the procuracy and the judiciary (Anderson and Johnson, 2010: 377).

2.   RULES AND REALITY

This section describes the new rules for criminal trials in Japan, and summarizes some of the main outcomes from the lay judge system's first three years of operation. The Act Concerning Participation of Lay Assessors in Criminal Trials (2004) and subsequent legislation establish the ground rules for this new system of adjudication. The rules can be organized around six central questions: What kinds of criminal cases do lay judges hear? How are lay judges selected? What is the composition of lay judge panels? What powers and duties do lay judges have? What protections and penalties govern citizens in their role as lay judges? And how are verdicts and sentences determined?

2.1   Cases

Japan's Lay Assessor Law states that lay judges shall hear two types of cases: those involving crimes that are punishable by death, by imprisonment for an indefinite period, or by imprisonment with hard labor; and those in which the victim has died due to an intentional criminal act. The Lay Assessor Law does not give defendants the right to waive a lay judge panel, but it does grant discretion to the court to find that a case that qualifies for a lay judge trial may nonetheless be heard by a panel of three professional judges if the court deems it in the public interest (as when the defendant is a gangster and there is reason to fear for the lay judges' safety). Based on crime statistics for 2007 and the definition of crimes that are justiciable by lay judges, the Ministry of Justice expected there to be about 3,600 lay judge trials in the first year of the new system's operation. In fact, however, there were only 1,142 new cases received for lay judge trial in the first year, and only 3,884 lay judge trials completed in the first three years (Supreme Court, 2012: 44). After the advent of the new trial system, Japanese prosecutors retained great discretion about whether and what to charge. They are the gatekeepers who determine how many cases proceed to lay judge trial, and in the first few years of the new system they adopted charging policies that are even more cautious and conservative than the 'trial sufficiency policy' that prevailed before the 2009 reform (Johnson, 2002a: 230).

In the three years between May 2009 and May 2012, lay judge trials were held most often for the crimes of robbery with injury (918), murder (873), burglary with arson (356), trafficking methamphetamines (353), and assault resulting in injury or death (339). These five crimes accounted for 73 percent of all completed lay judge trials, and the first two (robbery and murder) accounted for 46 percent of the total. But in broader perspective, lay judge trials accounted for only about 3 percent of all criminal trials during this period. The vast majority of criminal defendants in Japan continue to be adjudicated by one professional judge for less serious cases or by three professional judges in more serious ones (Supreme Court, 2012: 46). Except in very serious cases, criminal justice in Japan remains justice without any form of civilian participation.

2.2 Selection

The selection of lay judges in Japan is done by lot from electoral rolls within city and town jurisdictions. Hence, the main criterion for becoming a lay judge is eligibility to vote in Diet elections, for which Japanese citizens must be at least 20 years old. Permanent residents of Japan, including large numbers of Korean and Chinese descendants, are not eligible to serve as lay judges.

Japanese law also precludes some citizens from serving. First are those persons who have not completed compulsory education through year nine or who have been imprisoned. In addition, lawyers, quasi-lawyers such as tax attorneys and patent agents, and elected politicians are exempted from service. Currently enrolled students, persons 70 years or older, and persons who have served as a lay judge or alternate within the past five years may also decline to serve.

Besides these general exemptions, two more flexible exemptions are available. First, courts have broad discretion to disqualify persons deemed unable to act fairly at trial. This exemption is mainly for people who have conflicts of interest or relationships with participants in the trial. Second, courts can excuse persons with a serious illness or injury; family, childcare, or nursing responsibilities; important work obligations; or unavoidable social obligations such as attendance at a parent's funeral.

Prior to the new system's start, these broad categories raised concerns that lay judge panels would become unrepresentative if these exemptions were frequently used – as they are in many American jurisdictions (Adler, 1994: 48). And the first three years' experience suggests that such concerns may well be justified. Of the 328,967 Japanese citizens designated as lay judge candidates in the first three years after the new trials started, only 115,695 (35.1 percent) showed up for service on the day when lay judges were selected, and only 21,944 of those ended up serving as lay judges. In Japan, many people request to be excluded from service, and the vast majority of requests are granted. These striking 'I'd rather not' patterns have received little attention in the press so far, perhaps because they mesh with the widely shared assumption that lay judge service must not impose undue 'burdens' (*futan*) on Japanese citizens (Johnson, 2010).

2.3 Composition

Japan's Lay Assessor Law provides for two types of trial: by a panel of three judges and six lay judges, or a panel of one judge and four lay judges. The large panels are the default option, while the small ones may be deployed when factual issues are undisputed and when prosecutors, defense lawyers, and defendants do not object to its use.

In the first three years of Japan's lay judge system, the small panels were never used, despite rates of confession for defendants who go to trial that exceed 90 percent for all criminal cases and 60 percent for all lay judge cases (Supreme Court, 2012: 66). Concerns about efficiency are central to Japanese courts (Ramseyer and Rasmusen, 2003), and since the advent of the new system there has been much anxiety about the need to protect citizens who serve as lay judges from undue 'burdens' (*futan*). Hence, the non-use of the new system presents something of a puzzle. It is reasonable for professional judges to be prudent early in the life of the lay judge system, and large panels may have some advantages over small ones, including deeper deliberations and increased possibilities for dissent. But the most plausible explanation for the non-use of small panels is political. Many Japanese judges want to avoid sitting in judgment as the sole professional alongside four persons who have not been socialized in the judiciary. As one attorney explained in March 2013, 'Judges in Japan are insecure. They do not want to hold court only with lay people, and they want their professional colleagues' support during deliberations and decision-making' (interview with author, Tokyo, March 10, 2013). The non-use of the small panels apparently reflects the desire of Japan's professional judiciary to maintain as much control over trial proceedings as possible.

2.4 Powers and Duties

Japan's Lay Assessor Law stipulates that judges and lay judges must reach a verdict based on their recognition of the facts and application of the relevant laws and ordinances – and if they convict they must then sentence accordingly. Only professional judges are authorized to interpret the law and make decisions on litigation procedure, but lay judges are allowed to comment on such issues. Lay judges may also question witnesses, victims, and defendants during trial, but during and after trial 'information from the deliberations ... such as the particulars that lay judges are allowed to hear, the opinions and the number of both judges or lay judges who held these opinions (hereafter "deliberation secrets") shall not be revealed' (Article 70 of the Lay Assessor Law). If a person leaks a deliberation secret or 'other secrets learned' while serving as a lay judge, he or she is subject to a fine of up to ¥500,000 (about $5,000) or imprisonment for up to six months. In this way, former lay judges remain in eternal jeopardy of imprisonment if they reveal forbidden truths (such as opinions shared or votes cast during deliberation). Former lay judges are also barred from sharing what they thought the sentence should have been or what facts should have been found, and they may not even state whether they agreed or disagreed with the sentence actually imposed or the facts actually found by the court (Levin and Tice, 2009). This thoroughgoing 'duty of secrecy' (*shuhi gimu*) has been the subject of intense debate in Japan, with some people – including many citizens who have served as lay judges – arguing that it is unduly onerous and should be abolished or significantly relaxed.

Whatever its propriety, the lay judges' duty of secrecy performs several critical functions. It is meant to encourage candid conversation in the deliberation room, but the rule also prevents people from learning about how decisions that affect life, liberty, and reputation get made – and it prevents lay judges from writing or speaking about their experiences, as many former jurors have done in the United States.[2] The duty of secrecy in Japan also performs a protective function by insulating professional judges from external scrutiny and criticism. This may well be the most important function of all.

2.5 Protections and Penalties

Lay judges in Japan are protected from adverse treatment in their employment due to their service at or before trial; they are protected from disclosure (by reporters or others) of information about them; and they are protected from being contacted about the trial by third parties. Japan's

Lay Assessor Act also provides sanctions for people who threaten lay judges or solicit or leak information about them. Finally, lay judges can also be held criminally liable for making false statements during the selection process, failing to appear for service, or (as explained above) leaking secrets.

2.6 Decision Rules

Japan's Lay Assessor Law and its accompanying regulations leave one critical question – how professional and lay judges should work together to make decisions – unanswered. In principle, their views are to be accorded equal weight, they must provide reasons for whatever decision they reach (acquittal or conviction and sentence), and they are not required to reach consensus. Instead, decisions are based on the majority opinion of the members of the panel, so verdicts and sentencing decisions – including decisions to impose a sentence of death – can be made by a vote of 5–4, though at least one judge and one lay judge must agree with the majority view. The latter provision gives professional judges a veto of sorts over lay judges by precluding the possibility of a five- or six-person majority that is not joined by at least one professional judge. In sentencing, if a majority conclusion cannot be reached about the appropriate penalty, the minority opinion in favor of the harshest sentence is added to those opinions for the next harshest sentence until a majority is reached. All decisions reached by lay judge panels – acquittals, convictions, and sentences – can be appealed by the prosecution or the defense. One sign of the new system's success or failure will be how much appellate court judges defer to lay judge decisions. Japan's Supreme Court has declared that significant deference ought to be given, but several reversals of acquittals in the first few years suggest that this form of citizen participation could be 'marginalized' by legal professionals, as have similar reforms in Japan's past (Anderson and Nolan, 2004).

Japan's decision rules leave much room for disagreement and dissent, but because of the rule of secrecy, who dissented and about what are impossible to ascertain. Lay judges sometimes attend post-trial press conferences, especially for high-profile cases, but the questions they receive tend to be formulaic, and their answers reveal little about the deliberative process. Questions from the media are also screened by a clerk of the court who may cut off a question or answer in mid-sentence if it is deemed to raise concerns about lay judges' duty of secrecy.

In comparative perspective, Japan's lay judge system differs from America's jury system in several significant ways. The number of adjudicators differs: there are nine (or five) deciders in Japan versus 12 (usually) in the United States. Japan's lay judge panels are a mixture of lay persons and professional judges, whereas juries in America are composed entirely of non-professionals. Japan's lay judge panels are employed for a narrower range of criminal cases than are juries in America – though 'the triumph of plea bargaining' in the United States has made jury trials rare events there (Fisher, 2003).[3] Japan's lay judge panels use a mixed majority decision rule, whereas juries in the United States usually reach conclusions by consensus. Lay judges in Japan are more deeply involved in criminal trials than are jurors in the United States: they can ask questions of the witnesses during trial; they can discuss the trial proceedings with one another while the trial is still in progress; and they participate in decisions about both verdict *and* sentence, which in America typically occurs only in capital cases.[4] Their acquittals can also be appealed, in contrast to the United States where acquittals are final. And lay judges in Japan have much more significant restrictions on their ability to talk or write about their experiences at trial than do their juror counterparts in the United States.

Jury trials in America have been called the institution 'best designed to achieve truth-for-practical judgment' (Burns, 1999: 235). Although this view is contested (Adler, 1994; Langbein, 1978), most analysts praise the American jury for what it achieves and for what it symbolizes about American society (Abramson, 1994; Burns, 2009; Diamond and Rose, 2005; Kalven and Zeisel, 1966; Vidmar and Hans, 2007).[5] How has Japan's lay judge system performed so far? And how is it influencing the country's criminal process?

3. THE CONSEQUENCES OF REFORM

In his classic account of the parallels between torture in medieval Europe and the practice of plea bargaining in modern America, John Langbein (1978:19) observes that 'a legal system will do almost anything, tolerate almost anything, before it will admit the need for reform in its system of proof and trial'. In 2004, Japan passed a law which radically reformed its system of proof and trial. This section suggests *why* legal systems are reluctant to undertake fundamental reforms of this kind – because a trial system cannot be changed without changing other parts of the criminal process. Japan's lay judge system is transforming some aspects of Japanese criminal justice. There are striking continuities too, especially in case outcomes, but the changes being stimulated by the new trial system may be deeper and, in the long run, more important.

3.1   Continuity

If the proof is *only* in the pudding, one could claim that not much has changed in Japanese criminal justice. The three most striking continuities concern case outcomes: the conviction rate remains high in lay judge trials; the sentences imposed by lay judge panels have changed little for most categories of crime; and lay judges have been more willing to impose sentences of death than many observers expected.

3.1.1   Conviction rates

The first aspect of stasis in Japanese criminal justice concerns a conviction rate that seems, on the surface at least, to approach 100 percent. Analysts have said the country has 'the world's highest conviction rate', a 'dazzling' conviction rate, 'an extremely high conviction rate', and 'a conviction rate of close to 100%'. The point is also made conversely, as when it was said that Japan has an acquittal rate 'approaching absolute zero' (Johnson, 2002a: 215). But many commentators misread the significance of these numbers, especially when they contend that the high conviction rate reflects an 'iron hand' of criminal justice. At root, Japan's high conviction rate reflects the caution with which prosecutors exercise their discretion to charge cases. (There is no principle of compulsory prosecution.) This often benefits criminal suspects and offenders who do not get charged in Japan but who would get charged in similar circumstances in criminal justice systems with more aggressive charging policies. Many commentators also fail to compare apples with apples. Japan does not have an arraignment system, so defendants cannot plead guilty and thereby avoid going to trial. All criminal cases that prosecutors decide to charge go to trial, and the failure to take this fact into account has caused many analysts to overstate the 'gap' between trial conviction rates in the United States, where only 5–10 percent of charged cases go to trial in most jurisdictions, and conviction rates in Japan, where all charged cases do. Nonetheless, when apples are compared with apples and other appropriate controls are employed, Japan still has unusually high conviction rates and unusually low acquittal rates, although the gaps between its own rates and those in other systems do not yawn as widely as is often supposed (Johnson, 2002a: ch. 7).[6]

Japan's high conviction rate and the conservative charging policy that underlies it have mixed consequences. As suggested above, these patterns of practice protect many persons from criminal prosecution, which is a welcome effect to observers who believe in 'the limits of the criminal sanction' (Packer, 1968). Criminal penalties – and prison in particular – have a limited capacity to do good. They are always expensive, seldom effective, and often criminogenic. The Japanese patterns of practice also suggest that its criminal justice system may produce fewer wrongful convictions than do criminal justice systems in America that employ more aggressive charging policies (Huff and Killias, 2008: 296; Johnson, 2002a: 238). On the other hand, Japan's high conviction rate and its conservative charging policy generate unwelcome consequences as well. Many victims are never vindicated for the harms they have suffered because their cases never go to court. Some of the pedagogical functions that contested criminal trials perform are sacrificed on the altar of the high conviction rate. The extra general deterrence that would be generated by a more aggressive charging policy is never realized. The supply of vigorous and skilled defense lawyering is suppressed, because the likelihood of losing at trial dissuades many defense lawyers from doing all they can to win ('why bother?'), while other attorneys are discouraged from doing any defense work at all ('I have better things to do').

Japan's high conviction rate and conservative charging policy also link prosecutors and judges in a vicious circle – or perhaps two. Can judges remain neutral when they issue more than 99 convictions for every acquittal, or do these numbers numb their ability to detect reasonable doubt, thus driving the conviction rate even higher? Many informed observers believe Japanese judges have long been unduly deferential to prosecutors (Foote, 2010; Miyazawa, 1992). Conversely, the prosecutor's propensity to charge only clear winners may motivate some judges to expand the meaning of reasonable doubt. 'To a Japanese judge', one prosecutor has said, 'any doubt is reasonable. Prosecutors are being [careful] because judges require them to be' (quoted in Johnson, 2002a: 242). On this view, Japanese judges require proof beyond a reasonable doubt, and the fewer acquittals there are, the more attention each one receives – and the more cautious prosecutors become in the future.

Many Japanese insiders believe that, on balance, the costs of Japan's high conviction rate outweigh the benefits, and some of them expected that increased lay participation would significantly increase the number of acquittals, as was the case when Japan had a jury system in the prewar period. But that has not happened so far. In the three years before the lay judge system took effect, Japan's criminal trial conviction rate was 99.4 percent. By comparison, in the first three years after lay judge trials started, the conviction rate was 99.5 percent, and in the only crime category for which the conviction rate declined (trafficking methamphetamines), prosecutors appealed several of the acquittals and obtained reversals or retrials (Supreme Court of Japan, 2012: 46).

The main cause of stasis in Japan's conviction rate is prosecutor-gatekeepers, who are proceeding with extra caution in the shadow cast by the lay judge law. In the first several months after the new law took effect, prosecutors charged far fewer suspects than experts had predicted, and while their caution waned a little in subsequent months they remain more careful than they used to be about whether and what to charge. Japanese defense lawyers also note that prosecutors now use their discretion to charge less severely than they did in the past. The prosecutors' effort to avoid lay judge trials arises from a mixture of three motivations: a desire to avoid the uncertainties of the new trial system (prosecutors everywhere prefer predictability); the need to allocate resources efficiently (at the start of a new trial system, it is difficult to predict how much work a trial will take); and a commitment to maintaining the high conviction rate, which is considered by many prosecutors to be the leading indicator of their own prudence and professionalism. But some observers are less sanguine. In a blog entry that asked 'Are Japanese Prosecutors Pusillanimous?', Takashi Takano, the founder of Japan's Miranda Association and one of Tokyo's most prominent criminal defense attorneys, argued that Japanese prosecutors have become so selective about sending cases to lay judge trial that they are divesting citizens of their authority to decide questions of criminal responsibility and thereby undermining the integrity of the new trial system (Takano, 2009). Yet even Takano acknowledges that reality is complicated, for the effect of this change in practice on individual defendants – less severe punishment or no punishment at all – is welcomed by most criminal defendants and their attorneys (Johnson, 2009).

3.1.2 Criminal sentencing

There is also significant continuity in criminal sentencing in Japan before and after the 2009 reform. The most noticeable departures from a relatively lenient baseline of sentencing (Foote, 1992) can be seen in the increased severity of sentencing for rape with injury, sexual molestation, and assault with injury, though even for these crimes the heightened harshness must be called modest by American or British standards.[7] For other crimes such as homicide, attempted homicide, robbery, arson, and trafficking methamphetamines, Japan's pre-reform and post-reform sentencing patterns are so similar that when they are plotted on the same page they are often indistinguishable (Supreme Court of Japan, 2012: 83–90).[8] Lay judge panels are a little more inclined to use 'suspended sentences' (*shikko yuyo*) than panels of professional judges were, and when they use a suspended sentence they are much more inclined to impose 'probationary supervision' (*hogo kansatsu*) as one condition of the sentence – though how much such supervision helps reduce recidivism is impossible to say because rigorous studies have not been done (Supreme Court of Japan, 2012: 92). On the whole, however, there is much more continuity than change in criminal sentencing under Japan's new lay judge system,[9] and the same holds true for the ultimate sentence of death. The main proximate cause of this continuity is reliance on sentencing norms that are based on pre-reform sentencing practices, a back-to-the future policy that the judiciary pushed hard to implement in order to minimize the changes that would occur.

3.1.3 Death sentencing

Japan is, with the United States, one of only two developed democracies in the world that retain capital punishment and continue to carry out executions on a regular basis. In the United States, the number of death sentences declined by 75 percent between 1994 and 2012. This decline has several causes, including prosecution policies that have become more cautious in response to revelations of wrongful conviction, and juries that have become more reluctant to sentence convicted killers to death. In recent years, American juries have imposed a sentence of death less than half the time that prosecutors sought it: in Los Angeles County the death sentencing rate was 42 percent (Petersen and Lynch, 2012: 1262); in Washington state it was 38 percent (Kopta, 2008); and in the federal system it was 35 percent (Benac, 2006).

In Japan before the 2009 reform, panels of three professional judges imposed a sentence of death approximately two-thirds of the time that prosecutors sought it. Many advocates of the lay judge reform expected that citizen participation in sentencing would reduce the number of death sentences. In their view – which echoed the famous 'Marshall hypothesis' of a U.S. Supreme Court Justice – to learn more about capital punishment is to like it less (Steiker, 2009). Serving as a lay judge requires life-and-death decision-makers to learn more about a penalty that has long been shrouded by secrecy and silence in Japan (Johnson, 2006).

The expectation of increased capital caution in Japan has turned out to be partly right – but for the wrong reason. So far, lay judges in Japan have *not* been reluctant to impose sentences of death. In the first three and a half years of the new system, lay judge panels imposed a death sentence in 15 of the 21 cases where prosecutors asked for one, for a death sentencing rate of 71 percent (Yomiuri Shimbun Shakaibu, 2013: 274). But at the same time, the advent of Japan's lay judge system did prompt prosecutors to become more cautious about charging decisions generally and about death sentence demands in particular. In the three years between 2009 and 2011 (and while Japan's homicide rate remained flat), the country's 50 District Courts imposed a total of 22 first instance death sentences. In contrast, the number of death sentences for the three years before the reform (2006–2008) was 32, or nearly half again higher (Shikei Haishi Henshu Iinkai, 2012: 200).

Death sentences in Japan could drop more if some murder trials became truly capital. At present, however, the lay judge system operates on the premise that death is *not* a different form of punishment which calls for special procedures and protections. In most respects, murder trials in Japan look like other lay judge trials where the stakes are much lower. For example, Japanese prosecutors do not provide notice of their intent to seek a sentence of death until the penultimate day of trial. There are no special procedures for selecting lay judges. Trials are not bifurcated, leaving little room for defense attorneys to present mitigating evidence that might save a defendant's life. Death sentencing standards are little more than a laundry list of factors that judges and lay judges may consider, and little guidance is provided about how the various factors should be weighed. There is no automatic appellate review after a sentence of death has been imposed. Victims' demands for punishment are permitted during the fact-finding stages of contested trials – and hence can influence decisions about guilt. Prosecutors can appeal sentences less than death, and panels of three High Court judges may impose a capital sentence even if a lay judge panel acquitted (Johnson, 2011b). Most strikingly, lay judge panels in Japan can impose a sentence of death by a majority vote of 5 to 4. These conditions suggest that, much as in the pre-reform period, Japan has a system of capital punishment but does not have anything that can be called a 'capital trial' (Johnson, 2010). As long as these conditions continue, lay judge panels seem likely to continue delivering the decisions that prosecutors demand.

3.2   Change

Japan's new lay judge system has not generated significant change in conviction rates, criminal sentencing patterns generally, or death sentencing patterns in particular. These are important continuities. If politics is about who gets what, then the lay judge reform has not much changed the politics of criminal justice. But alongside these continuities changes are occurring. Most notably, prosecutors have become more cautious about what crimes they charge and the sentences they seek, and this helps explain the modest changes in aggregate guilty verdicts and sentences. At the same time, reform of Japan's system of proof and trial has stimulated a wide array of changes in Japan's standard operating procedures, and these may be slowly shifting a balance of advantage in criminal procedure that has long favored police and prosecutors.[10]

3.2.1 Changes in law

Three legal changes generated by the lay judge reform are altering Japan's criminal process. First, in anticipation of the new trial system, a new system of public defense for criminal suspects (*higisha kokusen bengo seido*) started operating in October 2006. Prior to that date, defense lawyers in Japan had long labored under major disadvantages compared with their adversaries in the procuracy (Feeley and Miyazawa, 2002). From arrest through investigation to indictment, trial, and sentence, defense lawyers were handicapped by three main factors: law, tradition, and the economics of criminal defense (Johnson, 2002a: 72). The first of those factors was especially formidable, especially in the pretrial stages, for law gave criminal suspects no right to bail before indictment, no permission to defense counsel to be present during interrogation, and no system of court-appointed counsel for indigent suspects before indictment. Suspects who could not afford an attorney often had to wait 23 days or more until one was appointed, and before the 2006 reform, fewer than 10 percent of criminal suspects secured lawyers during the crucial investigative stage (Johnson, 2002a: 74). After the reform, access to defense counsel increased dramatically, and it is expected to continue to increase as a central premise underlying the lay judge system – that Japan's criminal process should be more genuinely adversarial – takes deeper hold (Shinomiya, 2013b).

The second significant legal change stimulated by Japan's trial reform is the creation of a formal pretrial process (*kohan mae seiri tetsuzuki*) and the expansion of the defendant's discovery rights (*shoko kaiji*). The main purpose of these reforms, like the main purpose of the new system of public defense, is to invigorate criminal defense and thereby to shift the chief locus of decision-making authority away from police and prosecutors, who have long dominated Japan's criminal process, and toward the criminal trial. The new pretrial process requires the prosecution and defense to clarify the points in dispute and the evidence to be presented at trial so that trials can be run continuously, with minimal disruption to the lives of those citizens serving as lay judges. Similarly, the new system of discovery aims to put in the possession of the defense more of the case information that prosecutors have long monopolized with only limited obligations to disclose it to the defense. Many of the most egregious miscarriages of justice in post-war criminal justice in Japan occurred after prosecutors failed to disclose to the defense evidence of innocence or reasonable doubt. Under the new system, prosecutors' duty of disclosure expanded markedly, and even sharp critics of Japanese criminal justice acknowledge that there has been significant improvement in practice (Shinomiya, 2013a).

The third legal change is that lay judge trials are run continuously (*renjitsu teki kaitei*), unlike trials in front of professional judges, which proceed at a pace of one session every month or so, thereby leading to verdicts that come months or years after the first trial session was held (Shinomiya, 2013a). In judge-only trials between 2003 and 2005, the average uncontested case took 4.1 court sessions to complete while the average contested case took 9.4 court sessions – or about 9 months from first session to last. By contrast, in the first three years of the lay judge system, uncontested cases took an average of 3.5 court sessions while contested cases took an average of 4.9 sessions – or about 5 days (Supreme Court of Japan, 2012: 66). In an effort to reduce the 'burden' (*futan*) on lay judges, these trials have become more concentrated, with benefits to victims and defendants who receive speedier verdicts.

3.2.2   Changes in practice

While the foregoing changes in law were self-consciously sought by reformers aiming to place citizen participation in the center of Japan's criminal procedure, several other changes have occurred as side-effects of the lay judge reform. In the long run, these changes in practice may prove to be more profound than the changes in law.

The most important changes in practice concern criminal interrogation. If high conviction rates are the pride of Japan's procuracy, confessions are its cornerstone. When suspects confess, prosecutors file charges about two-thirds of the time, and when suspects do not confess they are seldom charged. In the years before the lay judge reform, only about one in 14 defendants contested the charges against them. Hence, a confession was a nearly necessary condition for indictment in Japan, and the procuracy's conservative charging policy – to charge only winners, and to gauge the probability of prevailing at trial by the quality of the confession – was the primary proximate cause of Japan's high conviction rate. It is often said that confessions lay at the heart of Japanese criminal justice. Though the syntactic difference is slight, it is more revealing to say that confessions *are* the heart – the pump that kept cases moving in the criminal justice system. This reliance on confessions has led to serious problems in the methods used to obtain them. The biggest problem occurred when a case was serious, the level of suspicion high, and the suspect refused to confess. In this thin but important slice of cases, extreme reliance on confessions can lead to extreme efforts to obtain them – through plea bargaining (which is not legal in Japan),[11] through the composition of 'prosecutor essays' (*kensatsukan no sakubun*) which synthesize and distort what suspects actually said in interrogation so as to make the recorded statements more helpful to the state, and through brutality and other high pressure tactics in the interrogation rooms where police and prosecutors try to obtain the all-important confession (Johnson, 2002a: ch. 8).

Japan's lay judge reform can be seen as an effort to shift the key locus of decision-making in criminal justice from the interrogation room to the courtroom. To make lay judges able to assess the voluntariness and reliability of confession evidence, interrogations needed to become more transparent – and they have. Although they are under no legal obligation to do so, police and prosecutors have started to video-record some interrogations in some cases. Their changes in practice are partial, and their resistance to a wholesale recording requirement remains strong, but because lay judges require more information about how confessions are obtained, the door to the most closed and secretive space in Japanese criminal justice is slowly being pried open – and the future seems likely to involve more openness still. Recording requirements are rapidly being established in criminal justice systems around the world, including those in the United States. In Japan, too, one does not need to be a weatherman to know which way this wind is blowing.

The practice of bail (*hoshaku*) is also changing in Japan. Criminal suspects in Japan have no right to bail before indictment, and, traditionally, suspects who asserted innocence were almost always denied bail (Johnson, 2002a: 74), leading critics to conclude that Japan had a system of 'kidnap justice' (*jinshitsu shiho*). But prompted by the premise that defendants should be allowed to assist in the preparation of their own defense, more and more defendants have been released by judges on bail since 2009, in contested and uncontested cases and for all categories of crime. The main mechanism of this change appears to be changing judicial sensibilities about the importance of adversarial contestation in open court (Shinomiya, 2013a).

A third major change in practice concerns 'the investigation of evidence' (*shoko shirabe*). In the pre-reform period, the most critical stages of the criminal process occurred before trial, and courtroom sessions were often called 'dossier trials' (*chosho saiban*) because of their heavy reliance on written statements composed by police and prosecutors during the pretrial investigation. For this reason, the dean of criminal justice studies in Japan famously concluded a quarter-century ago that Japanese criminal trials are merely 'empty rituals' for ratifying decisions already made by police and prosecutors (Hirano, 1989). Lay judge trials are significantly less reliant on dossier and significantly more aligned with the principles of 'trial-centeredness' (*kohanchushinshugi*) and 'directness' (*chokusetsushugi*) that were long dead letters in Japanese legal culture (Shinomiya, 2013a).

The practice of appeals (*joso*) also seems to be changing, in large part because of a decision by the Japanese Supreme Court in February 2012 which held that appellate courts should give acquittals by lay judge panels a high degree of deference. Although this decision is still fairly new at the time of this writing, it seems likely to reinforce the shifts in Japanese criminal justice toward the principles of 'trial-centeredness' and 'directness' mentioned in the preceding paragraph, and by some accounts it is causing legal professionals in Japan to reflect on their tendency to challenge the decisions reached in first-instance trials (Shinomiya, 2013a).

Finally, the most fundamental change in Japanese practice may be in the mindset of professional judges (*saibankan no maindosetto no henka*). Reform of institutions is widely regarded as the main means for developing democracy, but the idea that such reform alters actual practice 'is a hypothesis, not an axiom' (Flyvbjerg, 1998: 234). Research on 'making democracy work' warns that the 'designers of new institutions are often writing on water' (Putnam, 1993: 17). Culture and history condition the effectiveness of new institutions, and practices going back decades or centuries can limit the possibilities for implementing legal reform. Since culture counts, reformers must attend to this area as well. Invigorating Japan's '20% judiciary' (*niwari-shiho*)[12] will require more than adding law and lay judges to the traditional mix and stirring the ingredients thoroughly. The extraordinary passivity of Japanese judges vis-à-vis prosecutors must also be addressed (Foote, 2010) – and this is fundamentally a cultural challenge. One necessary step towards that end is improving the quality of public discussion about the role that judges *should* play in Japan's criminal justice system. This is starting to happen. As attorneys and analysts report, judicial attitudes in Japan are slowly starting to embrace principles of due process and adversarialism that have long been respected in the breach (Shinomiya, 2013a). The main reason for this change in judicial sensibilities appears to be the presence of lay judges. The fresh eyes of the amateur are important because, in law as in life, the more one looks at a thing, the less one sees it. As G. K. Chesterton (1909: 31) observed more than a century ago:

> It is a terrible business to mark a man out for the vengeance of men. But it is a thing to which a man can grow accustomed, as he can to other terrible things ... The horrible thing about all legal officials – even the best – about all judges, magistrates, barristers, detectives, and policemen, is not that they are

wicked (some of them are good), and not that they are stupid (several of them are quite intelligent). It is simply that they have got used to it. Strictly, they do not see the prisoner in the dock; all they see is the usual man in the usual place. They do not see the awful court of judgment; they only see their own workshop.

As one-shotters in the criminal process, lay judges do not see 'the usual man in the usual place', nor do they regard courtrooms as 'their own workshop'. In the long run, how much the lay judge system changes Japanese criminal justice may well depend on how widely this way of looking spreads.

4. CONCLUSION

When U.S. President Richard Nixon met Zhou Enlai on his historic visit to Beijing in 1972, he asked the Chinese leader what he thought the impacts of the French Revolution were on western civilization. Zhou reportedly said it was 'too early to tell'.

Japan's lay judge system is still in its infancy, and it is too early to tell what its long-term effects will be. So far the consequences are mixed, with significant changes in procedure and practice not yet producing major changes in trial verdicts or sentencing outcomes. The key link connecting continuity and change appears to be prosecutors, who continue to control the inputs into Japan's criminal justice system, and who have modified their charging policies in response to the risks raised by the new trial system. Changing prosecutors' practice may be the most difficult reform of all, for in Japan as in the United States, many of their most important decisions are 'totally discretionary and virtually unreviewable' (Davis, 2007: 5). Shortly after Japan's lay judge system started, a series of scandals exposed prosecutor misconduct, organizational cover-ups, and wrongful charges and convictions, but they led to little meaningful reform (Johnson, 2012).

The former foreman of an American jury wrote that 'If one learns anything from a criminal trial under the adversary system, it is that sincere folks can differ vehemently about events, and that there is seldom any easy way to figure out what actually went on' (Burnett, 2001: 14). Sincere folks also differ about what is presently occurring in Japanese criminal justice. In some assessments change looms large – while others see continuity. And in some accounts the changes seem positive – while others deem them negative (Kamiyama and Taoka, 2011). Similarly, there is no easy way to figure out 'what is actually going on' in Japan's lay judge system because the rules of confidentiality prevent citizen participants from describing what they have witnessed and experienced (Levin and Tice, 2009). In May 2013 – four years after the Lay Assessor Law took effect – a bipartisan panel of experts was considering what changes to recommend to Japan's lay judge system. Relaxing the rules of confidentiality was the most important proposal, and it met with much resistance from prosecutors, judges, and their allies.[13]

My conclusions about the consequences of Japan's lay judge reform – results are mixed, and it is hard to tell some things and too early to tell others – may seem drab, but they are at least rooted in a realistic assessment of the available evidence. And let us not miss the forest for the trees. Judging criminal trials solely in terms of their efficiency or effects on other parts of the criminal process makes no more sense than evaluating a wedding or funeral in terms of its accuracy (Kadri, 2005: 346). Trials pursue intangible goals that are critically important even though hard to measure (Burns, 2009: ch. 5). Every time a defendant is tried in front of a panel of lay judges in Tokyo or Takamatsu, a process unfolds that tests the precepts of Japanese democracy. Lay judge trials also enact the meaning of human dignity by demonstrating whether Japanese civilization treats its most despised enemies with respect, by presuming them innocent, and by giving them a champion to argue their cause. Courtrooms at their worst exemplify 'nothing more exalted than hypocrisy' (Kadri, 2005: 347). But at their best, criminal trials can reinvigorate the ideals of democracy and reinforce the importance of dignity and other human values. If lay judge trials in Japan are doing this too, it will be a major achievement.

NOTES

1. For a review of different forms of lay participation in legal systems around the world, see Vidmar (2000), and for an account of a new form of citizen participation in criminal trials in South Korea (where jury verdicts are not binding on professional judges), see Kim et al. (2013).
2. D. Graham Burnett served as jury foreman for a murder trial in Manhattan that ended in acquittal, and in his book-length account of that case he observed that 'Our enforced silence was *the most difficult thing*' – and this was said about a system in which jurors have much more liberty to talk than do lay judges in Japan (2001: 37, emphasis added).
3. In Japan, plea bargaining is illegal but does occur (Johnson, 2002a: 245–248; 2002b).
4. As for civilian controls on criminal prosecution, the United States has grand juries, which some American prosecutors believe are so thoroughly under their own control that they can get them to do their bidding, whatever it might be – including the indictment of ham sandwiches (Johnson, 2002a: 43). Japan does not have grand

juries to check prosecutors' decisions to charge, but it does have Prosecution Review Commissions (PRCs) (*kensatsu shinsakai*) to check their *non-charge* decisions. PRCs are lay advisory bodies composed of 11 private citizens who review prosecutors' exercise of discretion only after decisions have been made not to prosecute. They are a post-war creation, and there are about 200 of them in Japan at present (Johnson, 2002a: 222). Until 2009 their decisions did not bind prosecutors (and hence could be ignored), but in that year the law changed to make some PRC decisions binding, thus opening the door to criminal trial after prosecutors drop a case. Some analysts believe this new rule will help hold politically powerful offenders accountable and improve the quality of Japan's 'deliberative participatory democracy' (Fukurai, 2011), while others believe the new system is being abused and needs to be reformed (*Japan Times*, 2012).

5. For example, Shari Seidman Diamond and Mary Rose (2005: 278) reviewed real American juries in action and found 'little evidence that the jury fails to live up to the trust placed in it. Juries make mistakes and they display evidence of bias, but there is no convincing evidence that another decision maker would do better'. In contrast, Mark Twain (1962: 57–58) famously declared in 1872 that America's jury system 'puts a ban upon intelligence and honesty, and a premium upon ignorance, stupidity, and perjury'. His claims have been echoed and elaborated many times since.

6. For contested cases only, Japan's conviction rate usually hovers around 97 percent – significantly lower than the 99 percent-plus rates that are frequently cited for all cases (contested and uncontested), but still significantly higher than the trial conviction rates of 80 to 90 percent that prevail in many American jurisdictions (Johnson, 2002a: 240). In the Bronx jurisdiction of New York City in 2011, the trial conviction rate was only 46 percent, compared with a rate of about 77 percent for the rest of the city in the same year (Glaberson, 2013). When Japan had pure jury trials between 1928 and 1943, the conviction rate dropped dramatically, reaching 38 percent in the northern district of Sendai. Some observers believe Japan's jury disappeared at least partly because it returned verdicts that were unfavorable to prosecutors, judges, and other state officials (Johnson, 2002a: 43; Vanoverbeke, 2015). In South Korea's new trial system too, juries are more likely to acquit than professional judges are (Kim et al., 2013).

7. In addition to the lay judge system, a second reason for this increased severity in sentencing is new forms of victim participation in Japanese criminal justice (Saeki, 2010). More generally, the harshness of criminal penalties in Japan has been increasing since the 1990s (Johnson, 2012).

8. Another way to measure sentencing severity is by comparing the sentence prosecutors seek (*kyukei*) with the sentence actually imposed (*hanketsu*). When this is done, one sees only a small rise in the propensity of lay judge panels to match or exceed the severity of sentence prosecutors sought compared with what panels of three professional judges used to do (Supreme Court of Japan, 2012: 91).

9. There is less tolerance for inconsistency in criminal sentencing across jurisdictions in Japan than there is in the United States (Johnson, 2002a: 5), and this may help explain why most Japanese analysts stress the modest changes in sentencing that have occurred in recent years more than the many striking continuities.

10. In the United States and England, by contrast, recent criminal justice reforms have bolstered the powers of law enforcement to convict and punish offenders (Garland, 2001).

11. In England, too, plea bargaining has never been given legal recognition, but it occurs 'almost every day in almost every court of the land' (Kadri, 2005: 336).

12. The term '20% judiciary' (*niwari-shiho*) is used to express the view that Japanese courts are so passive that they do far less than the law permits and society requires (Sato, 2002).

13. The same bipartisan commission is considering three other proposals for the reform of Japan's lay judge system: (1) to make it easier for citizens affected by natural disaster to be excluded from lay judge service; (2) to have trials that are expected to last more than 100 days be adjudicated by panels of three professional judges (with no lay judge involvement); and (3) to remove sex crimes and capital crimes from the jurisdiction of lay judge panels. Proposals two and three arise from the premise that such cases impose too heavy a 'burden' (*futan*) on the citizens who try them. In my view, the first reform seems sound, the second unnecessary, and the third unwise. The Tohoku earthquake, tsunami, and nuclear disaster of 2011 caused havoc in the courts of that region, and some citizens were called to serve as lay judges despite severe hardships created by the triple catastrophe. By contrast, in the first 45 months of the new trial system, the longest lay judge trial lasted exactly 100 days (from selection of lay judges to final decision), and only four lay judge trials exceeded 50 days (*Asahi Shimbun*, 2013). Similarly, if the main point of lay participation is to make sure that important judgments about justice reflect citizens' common sense, why exclude those cases in which the human stakes are highest? A recurrent problem in domestic discussions of Japan's lay judge reform is the tendency to exaggerate the 'burdens' (*futan*) lay judges feel, while discounting the importance of more substantive concerns – such as whether a trial is thorough enough to produce clarity about the relevant facts and circumstances (Johnson, 2010).

BIBLIOGRAPHY

Abramson, Jeffrey. 1994. *We, the Jury: The Jury System and the Ideal of Democracy*. New York: Basic Books.

Adler, Stephan J. 1994. *The Jury: Trial and Error in the American Courtroom*. New York: Times Books.

Anderson, Kent and David T. Johnson. 2010. 'Japan's New Criminal Trials: Origins, Operations, and Implications', in Andrew Harding and Penelope (Pip) Nicholson, eds., *New Courts in Asia*. London and New York: Routledge, 371–390.

Anderson, Kent and Mark Nolan. 2004. 'Lay Participation in the Japanese Justice System: A Few Preliminary Thoughts Regarding the Lay Assessor System (saiban-in seido) from Domestic Historical and International Psychological Perspectives'. *Vanderbilt Journal of Transnational Law* 37: 935–992.

Asahi Shimbun. 2013. 'Choki Saiban Saibankan dake de: Homusho Kentokai Saibanin no Futan o Koryo', March 10, p. 1.

Bach, Amy. 2009. *Ordinary Injustice: How America Holds Court*. New York: Metropolitan Books.

Benac, Nancy. 2006. 'Death Penalty Trials a Painstaking Process', CBSNews.com. February 27.

Burnett, D. Graham. 2001. *A Trial by Jury*. New York: Vintage Books.

Burns, Robert P. 1999. *A Theory of the Trial*. Princeton: Princeton University Press.

Burns, Robert P. 2009. *The Death of the American Trial*. Chicago and London: The University of Chicago Press.

Chesterton, G. K. 1909. 'The Twelve Men', in *Tremendous Trifles* (republished in 2013 by Create Space Independent Publishing Platform).

Davis, Angela J. 2007. *Arbitrary Justice: The Power of the American Prosecutor*. New York: Oxford University Press.

Diamond, Shari Seidman and Mary R. Rose. 2005. 'Real Juries', in John Hagan, Kim Lane Scheppele, and Tom R. Tyler, eds., *Annual Review of Law and Social Science*. Palo Alto, CA: Annual Reviews, Vol. 1, 255–284.

Feeley, Malcolm M. and Setsuo Miyazawa, eds., 2002. *The Japanese Adversary System in Context: Controversies and Comparisons*. New York: Palgrave Macmillan.

Fisher, George. 2003. *Plea Bargaining's Triumph: A History of Plea Bargaining in America*. Stanford, CA: Stanford University Press.

Flyvbjerg, Bent. 1998. *Rationality and Power: Democracy in Practice*. Chicago, IL: The University of Chicago Press.

Foote, Daniel H. 1992. 'The Benevolent Paternalism of Japanese Criminal Justice', *California Law Review* 80(2) (March): 317–390.

Foote, Daniel H. 2007a. *Law in Japan: A Turning Point*. Seattle and London: University of Washington Press.

Foote, Daniel H. 2007b. *Na mo Kao mo Nai Shiho: Nihon no Saiban wa Kawaru no ka*. Tokyo: NTT.

Foote, Daniel H. 2008. 'Justice System Reform in Japan', available at http://www.reds.msh-paris.fr/communication/docs/foote.pdf (accessed May 8, 2013).

Foote, Daniel H. 2010. 'Policymaking by the Japanese Judiciary in the Criminal Justice Field', *Hoshakaigaku* 72: 6–45.

Fukurai, Hiroshi. 2011. 'Japan's Quasi-Jury and Grand Jury Systems as Deliberative Agents of Social Change: De-Colonial Strategies and Deliberative Participatory Democracy', *Chicago-Kent Law Review* 86(2): 789–829.

Garland, David. 2001. *The Culture of Control: Crime and Social Order in Contemporary Society*. Chicago: The University of Chicago Press.

Glaberson, William. 2013. 'Faltering Courts, Mired in Delays', *New York Times*. April 13, available at http://www.nytimes.com/2013/04/14/nyregion/justice-denied-bronx-court-system-mired-in-delays.html?_r=0 (accessed May 13, 2013).

Hirano, Ryuichi. 1989. 'Diagnosis of the Current Code of Criminal Procedure', translated by Daniel H. Foote. *Law in Japan*, Vol. 22, 129–142.

Huff, C. Ronald and Martin Killias, eds. 2008. *Wrongful Conviction: International Perspectives on Miscarriages of Justice*. Philadelphia: Temple University Press.

Japan Times. 2012. 'Overruling Doubt to Indict: Underbelly of Japan's Reform', May 28, available at http://www.japantimes.co.jp/opinion/2012/05/28/commentary/overruling-doubt-to-indict-underbelly-of-japans-reform/#.UYQeY8pLGIQ (accessed May 3, 2013).

Johnson, David T. 2002a. *The Japanese Way of Justice: Prosecuting Crime in Japan*. New York: Oxford University Press.

Johnson, David T. 2002b. 'Plea Bargaining in Japan', Malcolm M. Feeley and Setsuo Miyazawa, eds., *The Japanese Adversary System in Context: Controversies and Comparisons*. New York: Palgrave Macmillan, 140–172.

Johnson, David T. 2006. 'Where the State Kills in Secret: Capital Punishment in Japan', *Punishment & Society* 8(3) (July): 251–285.

Johnson, David T. 2009. 'Early Returns from Japan's New Criminal Trials', *The Asia-Pacific Journal* 36(3), September 7.

Johnson, David T. 2010. 'Capital Punishment without Capital Trials in Japan's Lay Judge System', *The Asia-Pacific Journal* 8(52), December 27.

Johnson, David T. 2011a. 'War in a Season of Slow Revolution: Defense Lawyers and Lay Judges in Japanese Criminal Justice', *The Asia-Pacific Journal* 9(26), June 27.

Johnson, David T. 2011b. 'Shikei wa Tokubetsu ka? Amerika no Shippai kara Erareru Kyokun' [Is Death Different? Capital Punishment in the United States and Japan]. Sekai. No. 823 (November), 280–291.

Johnson, David T. 2012. 'Japan's Prosecution System', in *Prosecutors and Politics: A Comparative Perspective* (Volume 41 of Crime and Justice: A Review of Research, edited by Michael Tonry). Chicago and London: The University of Chicago Press, 35–74.

Justice System Reform Council. 2001. 'Recommendations of the Justice System Reform Council – A Justice System to Support Japan in the 21st Century', available at http://www.kantei.go.jp/foreign/judiciary/2001/0612report.html (accessed May 8, 2013).

Kadri, Sadakat. 2005. *The Trial: Four Thousand Years of Courtroom Drama*. New York: Random House.

Kalven Jr, Harry and Hans Zeisel. 1966. *The American Jury*. Boston: Little, Brown.

Kamiyama, Hiroshi and Naohiro Taoka. 2011. 'Kisha wa Ko Miru Saibanin Saiban', *Niben Frontier* (3 parts) January–February, pp. 25–36; March, pp. 21–34; April, pp. 25–33.

Kaplan, Benjamin. 1961. 'Trial by Jury', in Harold J. Berman, ed., *Talks on American Law*. New York: Vintage Books, 44–54.

Kim, Sangjoon, Jaihyun Park, Kwangbai Park and Jin-Sup Eom. 2013. 'Judge-Jury Agreement in Criminal Cases: The First Three Years of the Korean Jury System', *Journal of Empirical Legal Studies* 10(1): 35–53.

Kopta, Chelsea. 2008. 'Success Rate Low in Death Penalty Cases', *keprtv.com*, July 3.

Langbein, John H. 1978. 'Torture and Plea Bargaining', *The University of Chicago Law Review* 46: 3–22.

Levin, Mark and Virginia Tice. 2009. 'Japan's New Citizen Judges: How Secrecy Imperils Judicial Reform', *The Asia-Pacific Journal* 19-6-09, available at http://www.japanfocus.org/-Virginia-Tice/3141 (accessed May 9, 2013).

Miyazawa, Setsuo. 1992. *Policing in Japan: A Study on Making Crime*. Albany: State University of New York Press.

Packer, Herbert L. 1968. *The Limits of the Criminal Sanction*. Stanford, CA: Stanford University Press.

Petersen, Nicholas and Mona Lynch. 2012. 'Prosecutorial Discretion, Hidden Costs, and the Death Penalty: The Case of Los Angeles County', *The Journal of Criminal Law & Criminology* 102(4): 1233–1274.

Putnam, Robert. 1993. *Making Democracy Work: Civic Traditions in Modern Italy*. Princeton, NJ: Princeton University Press.

Ramseyer, J. Mark and Eric B. Rasmusen. 2003. *Measuring Judicial Independence: The Political Economy of Judging in Japan*. Chicago and London: The University of Chicago Press.

Saeki, Masahiko. 2010. 'Victim Participation in Criminal Trials in Japan', *International Journal of Law, Crime and Justice* 38(4): 149–165.

Sato, Iwao. 2002. 'Judicial Reform in Japan in the 1990s: Increase of the Legal Profession, Reinforcement of Judicial Functions and Expansion of the Rule of Law', *Social Science Japan Journal* 5(1): 71–83.

Shikei Haishi Henshu Iinkai. 2012. *Shonen Jiken to Shikei: Nempo – Shikei Haishi 2012*. Tokyo: Impakuto.

Shinomiya, Satoru. 2010. 'Defying Experts' Predictions, Identifying Themselves as Sovereign: Citizens' Responses to Their Service as Lay Judges in Japan', *Social Science Japan* 43 (September): 8–13.

Shinomiya, Satoru. 2013a. 'Saibanin Saiban: Saibanin Seido wa Keiji Jitsumu o Dono yo ni Kaete Iru ka', unpublished paper, Kokugakuin University School of Law, Tokyo, March 13, pp. 1–13.

Shinomiya, Satoru. 2013b. 'Tetsuzuki Nibun no Kanosei to Bengo Jissen', unpublished paper, Kokugakuin University School of Law, Tokyo, March 13, pp. 1–16.

Simmel, Georg. 1950. *The Sociology of Georg Simmel* (translated, edited, and with an introduction by Kurt H. Wolff). Glencoe, IL: The Free Press.

Simon, Dan. 2012. *In Doubt: The Psychology of the Criminal Process*. Cambridge, MA: Harvard University Press.

Steiker, Carol. 2009. 'The Marshall Hypothesis Revisited', *Howard Law Journal* 52(3): 525–555.

Supreme Court of Japan. 2012. *Saibanin Saiban Jisshi Jokyo no Kensho Hokokusho*. Tokyo: Saikosaibansho Jimusokyoku. December, 1–122.

Takano, Takashi. 2009. 'Nihon no Kensatsu wa Hetare na no ka', in *Keiji Saiban o Kangaeru*. Takano Takashi@burogu, June 14 and June 23.

Twain, Mark. 1962. *Roughing It*. New York: Penguin Putnam.

Vanoverbeke, Dimitri. 2015. *Juries in the Japanese Legal System: The Continuing Struggle for Citizen Participation and Democracy*. London and New York: Routledge.

Vidmar, Neil, ed. 2000. *World Jury Systems*. New York: Oxford University Press.

Vidmar, Neil and Valerie P. Hans. 2007. *American Juries: The Verdict*. Amherst, NY: Prometheus Books.

Yomiuri Shimbun Shakaibu. 2013. *Shikei: Kyukoku no Batsu no Shinjitsu*. Tokyo: Chuokoron-Shinsha.

12. The French case for requiring juries to give reasons: safeguarding defendants or guarding the judges?

*Mathilde Cohen**

1. INTRODUCTION

The distinctive feature of adjudication by juries is that jurors usually do not explain their decisions. Common law jury verdicts are impenetrable. The decision-making processes and reasoning behind such jury verdicts are unknown. Juries in the United States and England return general verdicts, mere declarations of whether the defendant is 'guilty' or 'not guilty'.[1] An informal statement of the reasoning supporting the verdict is not merely *not* the practice, but positively illegal.[2] Far from decrying this black box characteristic of jury adjudication, observers (Fisher, 1997: 706) have identified it as a source of systemic legitimacy for the criminal justice system in protecting it from exposing its shortcomings publicly.

In contrast, in Europe, juries and reason-giving are not antinomic. Juries allowed to decide freely based on their inner conviction (the so-called French '*intime conviction*') have long coexisted with juries constrained by formal rules of evidence. This contrast partly reflects a split between jurisdictions relying on juries entirely comprised of lay participants and those using mixed courts where professional judges and lay assessors deliberate together. The former have traditionally been prohibited from disclosing their reasons while the latter have at times been required to substantiate their decisions, be it through special interrogatories or statements of reasons drafted by professional judges (Thaman, 2011: 615–17). In 2010, the tension between these distinct jury cultures came to a head with the European Court of Human Right's ('ECtHR') decision in *Taxquet v. Belgium*.[3] In its Grand Chamber decision, the Strasbourg court held that criminal defendants ought to be able to 'understand' jury verdicts. What this new behest means exactly is still disputed, but it has already led a number of European jurisdictions, including France, to overhaul their jury system by imposing a reason-giving requirement on criminal verdicts.[4]

422

This chapter argues that the goals for requiring jury reason-giving are manifold and sometimes conflicting. These goals matter because we cannot assess whether the turn to heightened reason-giving is a positive development unless, first, we know what it is trying to achieve and, second, assess whether it is working.

The ECtHR's interest in reason-giving can be described as a moral project. For the Strasbourg court, reason-giving appears to represent an individual human right, which can be linked to criminal law exceptionalism. Decision-makers ought to be particularly careful in their decision-making and explanations, the argument goes, because the potential deprivation of liberty is greatest in criminal cases. Defendants' interests in personal autonomy and even life might be at stake. A process compelling defendants to extrapolate the reasons for their conviction or sentence would be deficient. From that perspective, reason-giving is called for, not so much as a check on decision-makers to avoid high error costs, but mainly as a participatory and dignitary measure for defendants. Thus the ECtHR has held that as a matter of fundamental human rights, criminal defendants must be able to understand what they are charged with, and, if convicted, why.

In 2011, less than a year after *Taxquet*, France enacted a new statute mandating that its mixed juries provide reasons for their verdicts.[5] In addition to responding to the ECtHR, the reform was purportedly motivated by the objective of expanding defendants' rights and fixing a broken criminal justice system.[6] The *travaux préparatoires* show that legislators had two main concerns.

First, they wanted to remedy the 'incoherent' bifurcation of the criminal justice system.[7] In France, mixed juries try felonies punishable by a prison sentence of ten years or more in specialized criminal courts, the *'cours d'assises'*. Until the 2011 reform, these courts did not give reasons for their verdicts. Contrastingly, three-judge panels called *'tribunaux correctionnels'* try lesser offenses. Like all other professional French judges, judges of the *tribunal correctionnel* are statutorily obligated to provide written reasons for their decisions.[8] This split led to the paradoxical result that defendants charged with more serious offenses and risking the longest sentences were not entitled to reasons, while those charged with lesser offenses and liable to milder punishments were statutorily guaranteed access to the reasoning behind the adjudicators' decisions.

A second legislative concern was to facilitate appeals.[9] For most of their history, French jury verdicts could only be appealed to the *cour de cassation*, France's court of last resort for criminal and civil matters. The *cour de cassation* operates under an extremely deferential standard, strictly limiting its review to compliance with substantive and procedural law based on the records of the proceedings below. In 2000, in order to conform to the European Convention on Human Rights' principle of the right to appeal,[10] France introduced a new, intermediate appeals procedure.[11] Both defendants and prosecutors can now appeal as a matter of right a *cour d'assises* verdict before a second *cour d'assises*, which retries the case under a *de novo* standard.[12] By requiring the *cours d'assises* to give reasons for their verdicts, both at first instance and on appeal, French legislators hoped to strengthen this right to appeal.

While these two narratives are accurate to some extent, a closer look at the ECtHR's jurisprudence and at the French case reveals a more complicated story. The ECtHR's call for heightened reason-giving in jury trials is not a purely humanitarian position. As I will argue, it has been spurred in part by pragmatic considerations of administrability and the quest for stronger mechanisms of judicial accountability. Similarly, on the French side, the requirement that mixed juries explain their verdicts can be seen not only as a pro-defendant commitment, but also as a measure of administrative convenience and hierarchical control. Both for the Strasbourg court and the French reformers, the move toward reason-giving may have less to do with real or imagined qualities of the jury and the effect of reasons on the intelligibility of verdicts than with conceptions of the judicial role and the desire to keep judges in check.

The chapter proceeds in three parts. Section 2 examines the emergence of a right for criminal defendants to understand their conviction and sentence under the ECtHR's lead. Section 3 offers a case study of how the European shift toward reasoned jury verdicts has been implemented in France. Section 4 argues that despite a humanitarian rhetoric, neither the European nor the French demand for reasons is devoid of accountability considerations. In both legal orders, the push for reasons may come from similar motivations, with reason-giving conceived as a method to achieve fairness to defendants while monitoring legal actors who might otherwise enjoy great discretion. Reason-giving, I conclude, is not so much about ensuring that *defendants* understand their sentence, but rather about policing *judges*.

A note on methods: Because the French reform only began to be implemented in January of 2012, there is still very little case law or secondary literature addressing the sufficiency of *cours d'assises*' reasons. As a result, my analysis relies in part on informal conversations I had with a few French criminal lawyers and *cours d'assises* judges, who because of the sensitivity of the topic, have asked me not to quote them by name.

2. REASONS AND HUMAN RIGHTS IN THE COUNCIL OF EUROPE

According to the ECtHR, reason-giving is a human right. The European public in general and criminal defendants in particular have a fundamental right to understand court decisions that affect them. This approach is rooted in a general principle embodied in the European Convention on Human Rights, which protects individuals from arbitrariness. The Court inferred the reason-giving doctrine from the right to a fair trial, which is textually protected in Article 6(1) of the Convention.

Originally a Belgian case involving the murder of a politician, *Taxquet* challenged the compatibility of the Belgian jury, which did not provide reasons for its verdicts, with Article 6(1). That Article provides that '[i]n the determination of his civil rights and obligations or of any criminal charge against him, everyone is entitled to a fair and public hearing within a reasonable time by an independent and impartial tribunal established by law'. Since the 1990s, the Strasbourg Court had interpreted Article 6's right to a fair trial to require that 'judgments of courts and tribunals should adequately state the reasons on which they are based'.[13] National courts in the Council of Europe must explain their decisions, according to the Court, because reason-giving is a means to achieve access to justice and to show that parties' arguments have been heard.[14]

The ECtHR's doctrinal vocabulary – of fundamental rights, justice, and fairness – provides structure to its case law, which seems to endorse the view that the right to understand court decisions is a basic moral right. Implicit in the Court's jurisprudence is the liberal-democratic ideal that human beings should not be subjected to actions or institutional norms that cannot be justified to them. The liberal rationale is that it is part of what is owed to one as a citizen that one should be told what one is thought to have done and have an opportunity to respond. According to this view (Macedo, 1990; Nagel, 1987), reason-giving must be an essential activity of democratic states. More specifically, *reasoned* court decisions are fundamental to the political and moral legitimacy of a democracy (Rawls, 1993). Because people under conditions of freedom do not agree about values, public officials such as judges ought to justify the state's action with reasons that all citizens may reasonably accept, or at least understand. The Court seems to have extended this principle to juries. Just like professional judges, lay jurors – who become temporary agents of the state for the duration of a trial – ought to issue verdicts that defendants can comprehend.

Until the *Taxquet* decision, however, this reason-giving doctrine applied to professional judges only, not to juries.[15] In fact, before *Taxquet*, the bulk of the ECtHR's case law pertained to high courts, not trial courts or first instance judges, suggesting that juries were not on the Court's radar. The Strasbourg court was not even particularly concerned with criminal trials, as its jurisprudence focused on civil cases (Cunniberti, 2008: 28). The typical situation the Court had encountered was that of a domestic supreme court in one of the member states endorsing verbatim a lower court opinion without adding reasons of its own, raising the question whether it had adequately thought through its decision.[16] With *Taxquet*, however, the ECtHR specifically addresses reason-giving within the context of criminal procedure and the jury, declaring that 'for the requirements of a fair trial to be satisfied, the accused, and indeed the public, must be able to understand the verdict that has been given; this is a vital safeguard against arbitrariness'.[17] What is the meaning of this new duty for the jury system? Has the Strasbourg Court implied that common law criminal procedure, which traditionally relies on general jury verdicts, represents a violation of human rights?

The Grand Chamber decision does not impose on all European juries a hardline duty to give reasons, that much is clear, but the meaning of the new right to understand verdicts is ambiguous. On the one hand, the Court has emphasized that general jury verdicts do not provide specific legal and evidentiary justifications for a jury's decision. Even special verdict forms and special interrogatories might be insufficient to make up for the lack of explicit explanations issuing from the jury. In the underlying case, a Belgian jury had been required to answer no less than 32 questions posed by the presiding judge. But the Grand Chamber pinpointed the generality and vagueness of those questions as a major deficiency: 'the questions put in the present case did not enable the applicant to ascertain which of the items of evidence and factual circumstances discussed at the trial had ultimately caused the jury to answer the four questions concerning him in the affirmative'.[18]

On the other hand, the Court took pains to assert that, 'the Convention does not require jurors to give reasons for their decision', and 'that article 6 does not preclude a defendant from being tried by a lay jury even where reasons are not given for the verdict'.[19] This ambivalence suggests that the ECtHR, well aware that it is overseeing different models of lay adjudication within the Council of Europe countries, allows for the development of local conceptions of jury trial fairness. One major divide among member states differentiates countries following the common law jury[20] in which jurors deliberate and return their verdict without any professional judicial involvement from countries in which lay jurors sit with career judges in mixed panels, referred to as '*échevinage*'.[21] In such mixed courts, jurors decide both upon guilt and punishment together with professional judges (Hans, 2008; Jackson and Kovalev, 2006). The centuries-old British and Irish juries, exclusively composed of lay-persons, are arguably worlds apart from other continental juries, which are more recent additions and often use mixed panels. While a reason-giving requirement may be a plausible demand for mixed panels, there was a concern that, if applied to the classic common law jury, such a requirement might endanger rights protected in England since the Magna Carta. The Grand Chamber was therefore careful to say that it was not invalidating the institution of the common law jury system *per se*.

How then should juries go about delivering verdicts that are under-standable? The ECtHR, using its doctrine of margin of appreciation, declined to answer with a common, unified framework binding on all member states.[22] It merely declared that criminal defendants across Europe should be presented with a number of procedural guarantees enabling them to 'understand the reasons for [their] conviction'. While this new right could sometimes mean that an actual statement of reasons is required from the jury, this is not necessary in all contexts. To appease jurisdictions following the common law jury system, the Court recog-nized that other 'procedural safeguards' might contribute to the judg-ment's understanding, even where reasons are lacking. According to the Grand Chamber:

> [these] safeguards may include, for example, directions or guidance provided by the presiding judge to the jurors on the legal issues arising or the evidence adduced, and precise, unequivocal questions put to the jury by the judge, forming a framework on which the verdict is based or sufficiently offsetting the fact that no reasons are given for the jury's answers ... Lastly, regard must be had to any avenues of appeal open to the accused.[23]

In other words, the Grand Chamber acknowledged that there might be functional equivalents to reason-giving which accomplish the goal of producing understandable verdicts.

The first two mechanisms cited by the Court, judges' instructions and questions to the jury, arguably supply enough information about the crucial elements of the case for the accused to be able to understand what considerations may have swayed the jury.[24] When diligently prepared and presented, they provide defendants with a picture of the evidence against them and of the grounds for their conviction. The third substitute for reason-giving, the availability of an appeal, speaks to reason-giving only indirectly. In most jurisdictions, professional judges try appeals.[25] The Court's implicit argument is that defendants who have not had the opportunity to 'understand' their conviction in the first instance may be able to do so on appeal when appellate judges present them with a statement of reasons. Finally, the Court also seems to take into account as alternatives to reason-giving, albeit in a more limited way, the specificity of the indictment and the extent to which it contributes to the defendant's understanding of the verdict.[26] The more the indictment specifies the facts and the evidence, the better.

To sum up, the ECtHR has not declared a positive duty for juries to give reasons. In member states using common-law-style juries, the procedural safeguards described above may serve as functional equivalents to reason-giving. However, in mixed panel jurisdictions, more will be demanded. A presiding judge, for example, might be required to issue the jury a list of specific questions to which jurors must provide responses in delivering the verdict. But how does that work in practice? In what follows, I use France as a case study for the implications of the new right in a mixed court jurisdiction.

3. *TAXQUET*'S AFTERMATH IN FRANCE

France was quick to respond to the *Taxquet* ruling. In August of 2011, less than a year after the Grand Chamber decision, the French Parliament enacted a new statute mandating reason-giving for *cour d'assises* verdicts, thus breaking with a two-hundred-year tradition.[27] Who is responsible for articulating the jury's reasons? Are reasons given orally, from the bench, or in an opinion? In what follows, I map the contours of the new, unstable regime, pointing out the difficulties it raises.[28]

3.1 A New Reason-Giving Requirement

The *cours d'assises* are criminal trial courts with original and appellate jurisdiction to hear cases involving defendants accused of crimes defined as felonies punishable by a prison sentence of ten years or more. *Cours d'assises* use mixed panels comprised of three professional judges (a president and two associate judges) as well as six lay assessors in the first instance and nine on appeal. Judges and lay assessors decide together, adjudicating both guilt and punishment.[29]

What aspect of the decision must be justified? According to the new statute, only the *verdict* must be explained, not the sentence. This rule is sure to puzzle Anglo-American observers. The traditional common law principle is for juries to deliver unreasoned general verdicts, while professional judges, in charge of determining punishment, justify sentences. Exempting sentences from reason-giving hardly makes sense from a Gallic perspective either. At the *tribunaux correctionnels*, defendants are entitled to an explanation of both the verdict *and* the sentence.

Why should defendants charged with more serious offenses and exposed to harsher punishment lack the opportunity to know the reasons for their sentence? One would be hard pressed to find a principled justification for this disparity in the statute's legislative history. The issue was brought to the *cour de cassation*, which declined to impose a reason-giving requirement on sentencing decisions. The high court held that the discrepancy did not raise any 'serious concern' as sentences can 'be explained by the requirement of a majority vote or a majority of at least six out of eight votes when the maximum prison sentence is awarded'.[30] It is unclear whether legislators were persuaded by the argument that a supermajority vote compensates for unreasoned sentences. Other rationales, however, can be ventured. It could be that they legislated on the assumption that the primary decision, determinative of sentencing is the decision on guilt or innocence. On this view, justification for a sentence can be inferred from the explanations provided for the verdict as well as the jury's answers to the special interrogatory – particularly considering that special interrogatories must include questions on aggravating or mitigating circumstances. Another possibility is that legislators concluded that mandating reason-giving for verdicts was already such a revolution that they preferred to hold off – at least for the time being – on extending the injunction to sentencing.[31]

The next question is who is responsible for explaining verdicts? In Belgium, where a reason-giving requirement was enacted two years before France, jurors are responsible for reason-giving. Belgian jurors deliberate on their own, in the absence of professional judges, whom they summon to the deliberation room *ex post* to help them draft the statement of reasons (Jacobs, 2012: 566–567).[32] By contrast, French lay assessors deliberate together with professional judges who are the direct recipients of the duty to give reasons. The new article 365-1 of the French *Code of criminal procedure* provides that the president of the *cour d'assises* or one of the two professional associate judges sitting on the panel are tasked with 'drafting the judgment's reasons' and consigning them to a document called the 'reason-giving sheet'.[33]

In practice, the reason-giving sheet is a one-judge document, nearly always drafted by the president, who exerts a towering influence over the trial (Scharnitsky and Kalampalikis, 2007). The president is the sole specialized *cour d'assises* judge, recruited by the chief judge of the appellate court to serve for an undefined term.[34] The two associate judges are typically appellate or trial judges assigned to serve on the *cour d'assises* on rotation for one or two weeks each year on top of their regular assignments.[35] They may be specialized (for example, family court judges) or generalist judges with no specific expertise in criminal law. Their outsider status in tandem with the fact that they are often overwhelmed with their own caseload may explain why presidents monopolize reason-giving. It does not help that the president has not necessarily met her two colleagues before the trial begins; it would be hard to imagine a president delegating the drafting of reasons to a judge she hardly knows.

A *cour d'assises* president possesses a number of prerogatives allowing her to significantly weigh in on the proceedings and the final decision.[36] She only has one vote in the deliberation room, and is not supposed to divulge her opinion as to the defendant's culpability throughout the trial.[37] But unlike lay assessors and the two associate judges, who are to decide solely based on the oral evidence presented in open court, the president has access to the '*dossier d'instruction*', that is, the case file recording the investigation. Most importantly, the president has full control over the conduct of the hearings, being 'vested with a discretionary power by which he may … take any measure he believes useful for the discovery of the truth', which can include summoning people to testify without requiring that they take an oath.[38] She does the questioning herself – directly examining the defendant, the witnesses, the victim, and the experts. She has the ability to modify the order in which participants speak. She can, for example, call to the stand the witnesses, experts, and victims before or after examining the defendant. Further, she can interrupt the defendant's examination to call other trial participants to the stand. And, as if the president's command of the courtroom was not strong enough, it is matched by her vast powers in the deliberation room. Indeed, she drafts the special interrogatory on which jurors vote, instructs them on the law as well as the sentencing, and leads the discussion, deciding who gets to talk and in what order.[39]

In light of the great powers bestowed upon the president, it is not clear in practice whether the new reason-giving requirement helps or harms the '*intime conviction*' standard of proof, which was initially established as a way of protecting jurors' ability to decide free of undue influence.

3.2   Reasons Versus *Intime Conviction*

A new Code provision states that the mixed panel's reasons 'are those which are exposed during the court and the jury's deliberation … prior to voting on the questions'.[40] This language suggests that jurors are invited to state their views *before* voting on the defendant's guilt or innocence. The problem is that French jurors use secret ballots.[41] Even assuming that each participant expressed her views before proceeding to vote, the president does not have full knowledge of jurors' reasoning. When drafting the reasons sheet, how is she to discern which of the various arguments on the table persuaded jurors if she does not know who voted 'yes' or 'no' on a particular question? Truly collective reason-giving would seem to demand an open group discussion, including a discussion of each participant's vote. If individual jurors' votes remain undisclosed, the reasons extrapolated from the discussion are bound to remain speculative rather than reflective of their actual reasoning. When participants are divided, should the arguments raised against the prevailing outcome be revealed? Even if jurors agree on a verdict but each for slightly different reasons, which reasons should be disclosed? What about jurors who choose to remain silent during the deliberation – how is the president expected to convey their position?[42] Nothing in the Code addresses these issues. The maintained rule of secret ballot compels the president to reconstruct an *ex post* justification which accounts for the vote outcome, but not jurors' actual reasons. This problem is compounded by the French standard of proof.

The notion of *intime conviction*, which can be translated as 'inner' or 'deep-seated conviction', was initially introduced into French law as a rejection of artificially constrained and quantified Roman-canon systems of proof. In contrast to rules of formal evidence that prescribed exactly when the evidence amounted to proof, the *intime conviction* standard allows the court to hold against the defendant if the judge or jury are convinced that the facts brought forward by the prosecution are true. It became the standard of proof French jurors are instructed to follow. Since 2011, the revised Code of penal procedure's provision on *intime conviction* begins by a convoluted, arguably oxymoronic sentence:

> Subject to the reason-giving requirement, the law does not ask the judges and the jurors composing the *cour d'assises* to account for the means by which they convinced themselves; it does not charge them with any rule from which they shall specifically derive the fullness and adequacy of evidence.[43]

What does 'subject to the reason-giving requirement' mean? That the reason-giving requirement creates an exception to the *intime conviction* standard? Or that somehow the two seemingly antithetical aspirations must be reconciled? If the Code is indeed attempting to integrate reason-giving and *intime conviction*, the next question is what reasons should consist of if they exclude recounting the means by which decision-makers made up their minds. The Code responds, 'reasons consist in the statement of the principal elements of the charged offense, which for each charge against the accused, have convinced the *cour d'assises*'.[44]

The fact that only the panel's 'principal' reasons must be revealed suggests that there is no requirement for the reason-giving sheet to track the panel's decision process. It need not reveal all the considerations discussed in the deliberation room. Indeed, the sheets I have seen are short documents, running from a half page to three pages. In theory, lay assessors mostly interpret facts, not legal rules, even though there is no strict separation of questions of fact and law like in common law jurisdictions. We should therefore expect their reasons to be fact-intensive. Despite variations across presidents, reason-giving sheets tend to be written in a much more accessible style than standard French judicial opinions, sometimes even adopting a colloquial tone. The bulk of the reasoning is factual and descriptive of the evidence heard at trial, stated in plain language. Technical expressions only appear inasmuch as the statement mentions the qualifications of the crimes charged. Reason-giving sheets, however, retain elements of the French style in their relative terseness and formalized presentation. They tend to either be composed of a list of relevant factors, such as 'the defendant was positively identified by the victim', 'the defendant acknowledges to have delivered mortal blows, animated by a homicidal will and acting with premeditation', each introduced by dashes, or of short paragraphs associated by logical connectors such as 'consequently', 'however', 'hence', which echo the traditional 'whereas' used in French judicial opinions.

The combined constraints of secret ballot and *intime conviction* seem to have produced a highly factual form of reason-giving, departing from the French tradition of abstract and formulaic judicial opinions. By contrast with United States civil and criminal cases, the process of reason-giving focuses on uncontested issues and is not meant to draw the attention of the fact-finders to those issues about which the state and the defendant disagree. Plea-bargaining is still an exceptional process in France and is not (yet) available for serious offenses like those tried at the *cour d'assises*, so that many verdicts address fact-finding on uncontested issues in cases where the defendant essentially admits his guilt.[45] In such cases, reason-giving sheets may play the role of the factual basis in an American guilty plea, which is there essentially to document that all essential elements of a crime can be proven based on what transpired during the hearings, not to disclose the jury's deliberations as they unfolded behind closed doors.

Having described the French regime, the next section questions whether France's and the ECtHR's quest for reasons are really, or solely, prompted by humanitarian concerns. I argue that in addition to furthering defendants' rights, both the European and French regulatory frameworks are motivated by systemic accountability concerns.

4. SAFEGUARDING DEFENDANTS OR GUARDING THE JUDGES?

A close analysis of the ECtHR jurisprudence and the French reform shows that neither the Strasbourg court nor French legislators were exclusively motivated by a moral project when they extended the duty to give reasons. Significantly, both jurisdictions embraced reason-giving as an accountability mechanism bearing on *judges* rather than jurors. This focus suggests that what they viewed as the problem was not the existence of unreasoned verdicts *per se*, but rather the fact that *professional judges* were participating in the production of unreasoned verdicts.

4.1 Regimenting European Courts

With a few notable exceptions, such as the United Kingdom, most Council of Europe countries follow the civil legal tradition broadly defined (Damaška, 2010). In that tradition, bench trials represent the model of excellence in court decisions. In part this results from the fact that jury trials are a rare and comparatively new occurrence, while bench trials have an ancient history. This is also due to differing conceptions of the judicial office. Continental European judges are typically career bureaucrats embedded in tight hierarchical institutional and professional structures, rather than independent professionals elevated to the bench through lateral appointments (Damaška, 1986). On the continent, professional judges, unlike jurors, enjoy a steady institutional legitimacy verging on infallibility. For instance, French judicial opinions, which on account of their terseness and formalized language appear less than explanatory to the American reader, are nonetheless generally well received by litigants and the public (Wells, 1994). As Mitchell Lasser has argued (2004), the concision and obscurity of the French judicial opinion are partly compensated for by other aspects of a centralized and hierarchical judicial system, which carefully selects and rigidly trains its judges. French judges, like most of their continental counterparts, are considered inherently trustworthy because they are controlled by powerful educational and hierarchical means (Bell, 2010: 44–107).[46]

Jury trials, however, do not enjoy such an institutional legitimacy. Juries are a relatively recent innovation in civil legal systems. Lay participation in continental European courts, while common in older times, practically disappeared in the Middle Ages when the Fourth Lateran Council banned trial by ordeal in 1215 (Toulemon, 1930: 20–21). Professional judges took over the increasingly technical criminal proceedings and imposed written, inquisitorial procedures (Dawson, 1960: 94–110; Esmein, 1913: 32). The jury only reappeared in France during the Revolution and spread to neighboring countries conquered in the Napoleonic campaigns during the nineteenth century. To this day, in most continental jurisdictions, rather than representing the default in criminal proceedings, jury trials are reserved for the trial of only the most serious felonies.[47]

This history puts into perspective the ECtHR's jurisprudence on jury verdicts. While the European court's rhetoric may suggest that a human right for defendants to understand their conviction and sentence is in the making, in reality, that right can also be analyzed as a mechanism to monitor judges and administer the courts in line with the civil law tradition of a tightly monitored judiciary. Significantly, the Court is not concerned with the common law jury, entirely composed of laypeople. The Court is careful to emphasize that it is not creating a reason-giving requirement for jurisdictions like the UK, where professional judges take no part in jury deliberations and where a number of safeguards are in place to protect the jury's independence such as a very detailed indictment and impartial instructions. Instead, it focuses on jurisdictions where professional judges dominate the proceedings either because they use mixed panels or because, like Belgium, despite using pure juries, judges retain some measure of influence. This difference in treatment implies that the Court is indirectly targeting judges. Unreasoned verdicts only appear to raise the specter of arbitrary decision-making when professional judges have participated in their production. This indicates that the demand for reasons or alternative procedural guarantees is ultimately aimed at ensuring that the *judges* involved in jury trials – rather than lay jurors – structure the decision-making process according to the ECtHR's notion of a fair trial.

In fact, the importance of reason-giving in the Strasbourg jurisprudence partly stems from an interest in accountability. The Court's case law is worded in the language of human rights and morality, but it also reflects a managerial concern. The Court had previously held that the judicial duty to give reasons is 'linked to the proper administration of justice'[48] – not primarily attached to a moral project. The duty is as much about guaranteeing that litigants understand the judicial process as it is about policing judges. This accountability goal is most visible in the connection between reason-giving and the right to appeal. The right to appeal in criminal matters has been affirmed as a basic human right by a 1984 protocol added to the European Convention.[49] The effectiveness of a higher court's power to review is usually premised, at least in part, on the existence of a statement of reasons by the judge at first instance. This statement is key for verdicts to be understandable to *appellate judges* fulfilling their reviewing function. Reviewing courts need reasons to isolate correct and incorrect outcomes at the trial level. The Court embraced this argument in *Taxquet*: without a statement of reasons, it would be much harder for an appellate court to pin-point and correct possible errors, compromising its mission to ensure principled decision-making in the trial courts and diffusing accountability within the legal system.[50] The European pressure for juries to give reasons, therefore, may be a right against judges as much as it is a right for defendants.

4.2   Keeping French Judges in Check?

The French interest in reason-giving is just as ambivalent as the European – partly spurred by humanitarian concerns and partly prompted by a judicial accountability agenda. In imposing upon its juries a burden of explanation, French legislators have not only sought to advance defendants' rights, but also to keep professional judges in tighter check, and chief among them, the *cour d'assises* presidents.

4.2.1   Reasons by whom and for whom?

4.2.1.1   Reason-givers   The French reform has brought about a system whereby the jury's reasons are controlled by professional judges and primarily addressed to higher courts. At the *cour d'assises*, professional judges have the upper hand over the jury in the deliberation room because they enjoy a superior legal expertise and master the informal norms at work at the court (Jellab and Giglio-Jacquemot, 2012: 157–158). As discussed earlier, the president leads the trial and is seen as the bearer of objective knowledge. The president's prerogatives bestow on her such great legitimacy and influence over the two other judges as well as the lay assessors that a number of commentators (for example, Barraud, 2012: 399) have claimed that lay assessors' presence essentially serves as a façade of democratic legitimacy for judge-made, or even president-made decisions.

A glance at the way in which the reason-giving sheet is prepared reveals the extent of the president's ascendency. Following the typical

French judicial practice, presidents appear to draft the sheet *in advance* of jury deliberations (Cohen, 2014). The presidents I talked to acknowledged that they systematically write two drafts before the trial even begins: one supporting a conviction and one supporting an acquittal. Throughout the trial, during evenings and weekends, they 'refine' their drafts based on what happens in the courtroom. Reasons, therefore, are articulated well before any verdict has been reached.

There are considerable advantages from the point of view of the president's work organization in proceeding *ex ante*. To justify this method, one president mentioned that he 'explains to the jury that you can't draft collectively with nine or twelve people otherwise it would take the entire night'. He reported that once the panel reaches a decision, he immediately reads out loud whichever draft matches the verdict, soliciting feedback from participants sentence by sentence. He claims that he always asks the jurors in the minority if they want to consult the alternative draft which supports their view. According to him, they generally take him up on his offer so as to 'see for themselves that the system isn't rigged, that their position was also defensible'. By contrast, another president confided that she felt 'very uncomfortable' with this modus operandi. Even though she too writes two different drafts supporting contrary verdicts, she does not share that fact with the panel, for fear of disheartening jurors.

Case management and efficiency concerns seem to motivate this *ex ante* approach. For standard cases, deliberations run between three to six hours. As one president remarked, if he had to go back to his office to draft reasons after the deliberation, he would need to keep the jury waiting a couple of hours (assuming it were a relatively easy case) before returning to the deliberation room with a draft statement of reasons. Upon his return, the panel would need to debate the proposed reasoning, which could take an additional couple of hours. According to him, jurors would be reticent to stay at the court for such an extended period of time. Another option would be for the president to dismiss the jury once the panel has reached a verdict and determined the sentence so as to take a few days to write the statement of reasons. An obstacle to this solution is that the 2011 statute requires that the reason-giving sheet be signed by the jury foreperson.[51] The *travaux préparatoires* show that the Senate requested this signature 'in order to guarantee the jury's control over the reasons retained by the judge'.[52] If the president drafted the statement after dismissing the panel, however, she would need to summon the foreperson back to court to sign it. Given that the president operates under strict time limits – she must return the reason-giving sheet at the latest three days after the verdict – this callback procedure could prove dicey should the foreperson disagree with the reasoning. The statute, therefore, seems to have built-in incentives for presidents to follow the *ex ante* approach, which goes against the proclaimed goal of bolstering lay jurors' contribution to reason-giving. If reformers had been serious about promoting lay influence, the new regime would have been organized differently. Following the Spanish example, one or several lay jurors could draft a statement on their own, save for requesting a clerk's help if needed. Alternatively, the French could have adopted the scheme suggested by criminal lawyer François Saint-Pierre: each juror jots down on a piece of paper her reasons for or against a guilty verdict. Based on these notes, the president deduces a majority and a minority position and drafts an opinion reflecting both views (Saint-Pierre, 2013: 122).

4.2.1.2 Reason-recipients In sum, the reason-giving sheet appears to be a judge-made document rather than a lay juror document. But to whom is it addressed? In theory, its primary beneficiary should have been the criminal defendant. However, in practice, it seems that its main audience is the reviewing court, followed by the general public via the press. Retracing the *cour d'assises'* decision-making steps illustrates this. After deliberating, when the mixed jury returns to the courtroom, the Code prescribes that the president give a reading of the answers to the special interrogatory, stating only whether they are positive or negative.[53] Astonishingly for a reform aimed at making verdicts understandable to defendants, the statute does not require that the reason-giving sheet be read out loud publicly or communicated to the parties. Technically, the statement of reasons is a procedural, not a public document. Practices vary, with some presidents inclined to read it whenever they deem it feasible, in other words, when they think that the risk of disturbance in the courtroom is low. Others simply announce the verdict from the bench, keeping silent as to the reasons.

The judgment itself, that is, the official document stating the verdict ('guilty' or 'not guilty') and the sentence does not always include reasons. The statute leaves it up to judges to incorporate the reasons into the judgment or to keep them in a separate reason-giving sheet. In practice, this means that presidents have the choice between copy-pasting their reasons into the judgment or 'annexing' the reason-giving sheet to the judgment, that is, stapling the two hard copies before archiving them. A couple of presidents I talked to report that they prefer to annex the reason-giving sheet because it is easier and faster. One president noted that copy-pasting reasons into the judgment would be particularly time-consuming because it disturbs the formatting of the template. The difference between the two methods is far from trivial, however. When reasons appear in a separate document, defendants do not automatically get access to them, given that only judgments are sent to parties, not reason-giving sheets. Should they want copies for their clients, attorneys must specifically request reason-giving sheets from the court's registry.

This accessibility deficit, together with the predominant role of the president in the drafting, suggests that the reform is aimed as much at keeping presidents in check as at making verdicts understandable to defendants. Paradoxically, some *cours d'assises'* reasons are now more widely available to the general public through the press than they are to defendants. Before the reform, not only were *cours d'assises* not forthcoming with explanations; they were positively prohibited from giving reasons.[54] This prevented an important form of democratic accountability through the general public and the media; trial participants' indiscretions were often the only source of information available. One president thus applauded the reform in that the reason-giving requirement provided a new way for the court to 'communicate with the press'. He had adopted the practice of handing out a copy of the reason-giving sheet to journalists at the end of the proceedings and prided himself on the fact that 'the day after, I see the verbatim transcript of certain aspects of the reasoning in news reporting'.

Beyond the question of who holds the pen and who is the recipient of the reasons, another aspect of the reason-giving requirement indicates that it is meant as a check on judicial discretion as well as a protection for defendants: insufficient reasons are not protected against review by a harmless error doctrine.

4.2.2 A right with teeth

In the United States, as a general matter, a judge's failure to give reasons does not amount to reversible error (Mashaw, 2001: 20; Stack, 2007: 955).[55] Traditionally, no appeal lies on the sole grounds that a court gave inadequate or insufficient reasons.[56] The validity of a judgment is typically evaluated independently from the reasons given for it.[57] Unreasoned decisions are protected by the 'harmless error' doctrine.[58] The rationale behind this rule appears to be judicial economy: the courts' limited resources should be conserved for the correction of legal errors rather than failures to explain.

In France, reasons can be the basis for an appeal or for overturning the verdict in part because, as I argue below, reason-giving is one of the few ways in which reviewing courts can scrutinize lower court judges. Two tiers of appeals are successively available: the first runs from the *cour d'assises* (the first instance trial court) to the *cour d'assises d'appel* (which retries the case before a new mixed jury) and the second from the *cour d'assises d'appel* to the *cour de cassation*, the court of last resort for civil and criminal appeals.[59] Reasons play out differently for these two forms of appeal.

The first type of appeal transfers the entire matter to the *cour d'assises d'appel*, with respect to both questions of fact and law.[60] Both the defendant and the prosecution can appeal – meaning that the prosecution can appeal a verdict of acquittal. The *cour d'assises d'appel* empanels a new mixed jury to conduct new fact-finding under a *de novo* standard, rather than a critical review of the record developed at the first trial. It is debatable whether the quality and quantity of reasons given at first instance matter on appeal. On the one hand, neither defendants nor prosecutors need to explain why they wish to appeal in their notice of appeal. They enjoy an absolute right to a new trial, regardless of the cause for their dissatisfaction. In that sense, the reasons given at first instance are somewhat irrelevant. On the other hand, having access to the considerations that determined a finding of guilt or innocence at first instance might help both sides build a better case on appeal. The Code provides that the president of the *cour d'assises d'appel* must read the first instance reason-giving sheet in public at the opening of the second trial. This provides one of the only glimpses of information as to what happened at first instance, given that, until 2014, hearings were neither recorded nor transcribed.[61] By and large, but for what transpires in the statement of reasons, the new mixed panel does not know what was said or debated at first instance. Only the president has access to the dossier, and the dossier focuses on the pre-trial investigation. For example, if the defendant, witnesses, or experts completely change their testimony on appeal, the primary way for the panel to be aware of the turnaround and to confront witnesses with their inconsistent prior version of events would be through the statement of reasons.

As a criminal lawyer with a wide experience of the *cour d'assises* confided to me, 'until recently, the *cours d'assises* presidents did not allow [the witnesses'] testimonies to be included in the minutes and on appeal they did not want to know what had been said at first instance, invoking the sacrosanct principle of the orality of criminal proceedings'. To counteract this problem, since October 1, 2014 Article 308 of the *Code de procédure pénale* mandates the audio recording of the *cours d'assises*' hearings.[62] Implementation has been tumultuous so far. Several *cours d'assises* lack the equipment required to produce adequate recordings. Due to the burden involved in recording an entire trial, some presidents seem to restrict the recording to trials that are expected to stir controversy. It does not help that Article 308 provides that the failure to record the proceedings does not affect the legal validity of the trial and that transcriptions will not be issued automatically.[63] Without readily available transcripts, lawyers trying to verify a witness' account from a previous trial may need to listen to days and days of recordings. Given the time and expense required, in practice the reason-giving sheet remains the best available source of information on a previous trial. The new recording rule may put pressure on judges, prosecutors, and lawyers' courtroom behavior and statements, but so far it has fallen short of creating an accessible record.

Assuming an exhaustive record including a detailed statement of reasons were available to the *cour d'assises d'appel*, the defense team, and the prosecution, the question remains whether it would be of any use. The appellate court is in no way bound by the first instance court's fact-finding and reasoning. As a president stated, 'on appeal, we don't judge whether the case had been well or badly judged, we judge again'. The role of reasons given at first instance, therefore, remains ambiguous. They can help both the prosecution and the defense strategize their appellate battle plan. They may also be understood as a mechanism for creating a record or something that functions like a record to assist with cross-examination of witnesses and allow for a meaningful right to appeal. Beyond that, the reasons given at the first trial do not seem to influence what happens in the *de novo* trial on the merits on appeal.

Reasons given at the second trial matter considerably more for the second type of appeal, which is only open to defendants. Those convicted on appeal by a *cour d'assises d'appel* can file a second appeal, this time to the *cour de cassation*, a court of last resort which only reviews for legal or procedural errors under a highly deferential standard.[64] The notice of appeal must allege that specific substantive or procedural errors have been made during the trial, one of which could be the insufficiency of the *cour d'assises d'appel*'s reasons.[65] Controlling lower courts' reasoning has been one of the *cour de cassation*'s essential tasks since its creation in 1790, the same year French judges were first required to give reasons for their decisions.[66] Since then, French law has recognized the violations of the duty to give reasons as an independent cause to quash judicial decisions. The *cour de cassation* has a well-established jurisprudence according to which judgments that are unreasoned or badly reasoned will be vacated and/or remanded to lower courts for a new trial.[67] The court typically uses this mechanism to police trial and appellate judges, checking their exercise of discretion. Will the *cour de cassation* extend this approach to the jury, so that reasons can become a basis for overturning criminal verdicts?

French legislators were well aware of the *cour de cassation*'s jurisprudence on reason-giving when they prepared the 2011 reform, and one cannot help but assume that they were counting on its extension to juries. While it is too soon to draw positive conclusions, there has already been one instance in which the *cour de cassation* quashed a conviction because of insufficient reasons.[68] In that case, the defendant, Mekki Boughouas-Campagne, had been sentenced to 30 years of imprisonment for participating in a robbery. The robbery took place at the night club where he was employed as a doorman and resulted in the death of the club's 'artistic director'. The victim was found lying in a field behind the club, fatally stabbed. That night's earnings had disappeared from the club. Mekki Boughouas-Campagne was found guilty of murder and armed robbery at first instance and sentenced to 30 years' imprisonment. The *cour d'assises d'appel* convicted him on the lesser charge of 'armed robbery accompanied by violence leading to death', but concurred with the 30-year sentence. By way of explanation, it issued the following reason-giving sheet, here quoted in full:

> On the reasons: the elements of the case file do not permit to establish the identity of the author of the blows, the elements of the charged offense which have been gathered against the accused suggesting his presence on the premises rather than a homicidal act, the theft offense being uncontested.

According to the *cour de cassation*'s case law, adequate reasons should show the relationship between the facts of the case and the verdict. A reasoned explanation should enable the *cour de cassation* to determine whether irrelevant considerations have been taken into account or relevant considerations ignored. Here, the *cour de cassation* found that the *cour d'assises d'appel*'s cryptic explanation neither identified the elements of the charged offense nor the link between the defendant's presence on the crime scene and his implication in the victim's death. Following its own tradition of short and elliptical opinion writing, the *cour de cassation* did not say much about the type of reasoning it requires. Perhaps the *cour de cassation* expected more discussion of the defendant's role as distinct from that of his alleged accomplice, whom the first instance *cour d'assises* had found guilty of conspiracy to commit a crime and sentenced to four years' imprisonment. What is clear is that the *cour de cassation* concluded that the *cour d'assises d'appel* had 'enunciated confused and abstract reasons, which in no way distinguish the elements of the charged offense which have persuaded the courts regarding each of the facts attributed to the accused'. Rather than remanding to a different *cour d'assises* for a new trial as it usually does, the *cour de cassation* remanded to the same *cour d'assises* that had issued the deficient statement of reasons. This departure from standard procedure sends a strong signal to *cours d'assises*' presidents. It is almost as if the *cour de cassation* wanted to 'punish' the professional judges involved for unsatisfactory reason-giving and force them to do their homework by sending the case back to their court.

Based on this first precedent, the failure to give reasons of sufficient quality, clarity, or consistency for jury verdicts will not benefit from a harmless error analysis. The *cour de cassation* appears willing to apply the same standard of review for reason-giving to the *cours d'assises* as it does for regular courts. If the appellant can show that the defect is important enough, inadequate reasons will likely suffice to reverse the original decision and to warrant a new trial. The new reason-giving requirement, therefore, provides defendants a right with teeth, which can be the basis for overturning a verdict. By the same token, however, French legislators have provided the *cour de cassation* with a crucial instrument to facilitate its review of *cours d'assises*' decisions. Before the reform, the *cour de cassation* could hardly perform its error-correction mission given that there was neither a transcript of the oral argument to look over nor a statement of reasons explaining the verdict. The high court had to guess why the *cour d'assises* had decided the way it did, with very few clues as to whether procedural rules had been followed and what the mixed court's reasoning was for retaining a particular qualification of the crime or for finding particular elements of the crime to have been proved. This state of affairs left *cours d'assises* presidents with considerable discretion as to how to run their trials. The new regime establishes greater accountability for professional trial and appellate judges involved in mixed juries.

To be sure, this accountability effect is not necessarily at odds with the humanitarian premises behind the reason-giving requirement. Providing the *cour de cassation* with an instrument to facilitate review is also a way for legislators to reinforce defendants' rights. Based on the last publicly available statistics from 2008, only 43 percent of acquittals at first instance were confirmed by the *cours d'assises d'appel* when the prosecution appealed.[69] And that is the case even though on appeal there are nine lay jurors deciding together with the three professional judges – instead of six lay jurors and three professional judges at the first instance. It is therefore paramount for defendants to have access to the reasons underlying the second *cour d'assises* verdict. The absence of explanations could frustrate their right to appeal to the *cour de cassation* and their hope of reinstating their first instance acquittal.

5. CONCLUSION

The European approach to jury reason-giving is still somewhat in flux. The ECtHR has yet to announce its views on the revamped French reason-giving regime or on comparable efforts carried out in other jurisdictions. It will take a few more years for cases to percolate through the Council of Europe's member states' judicial systems before the Strasbourg court can decide them. So far, however, what we can observe is consistent with a theory that a global norm of reason-giving is gradually emerging, putting pressure on local decision-making contexts such as jury trials which historically developed without a reason-giving requirement. We live at a moment in time that is characterized by the profusion of reasons in all aspects of public life rather than by a shortage of reasons. Reason-giving is often brandished as a panacea to secure transparent governance. So much so that the continued existence of spheres of legal decision-making devoid of explanations seems unacceptable to the contemporary observer. This trend explains why reason-giving has been revitalized in criminal proceedings, where European judges and juries had long enjoyed considerable authority without the corresponding duty to justify their decisions. The most interesting question raised by *Taxquet* and its French reaction concerns the inextricable cluster of values underlying the imposition of stronger reason-giving. Both at the supranational, European level and at the domestic, French level, reason-giving seems to be about running a system *and* about fairness to defendants; about increasing judges' accountability *and* about moralizing the criminal trial. It could be that these values are complementary; after all, part of what it means to moralize a trial is for decision-makers to be accountable for their decisions.

NOTES

* For helpful conversations and comments on earlier drafts, I am deeply grateful to Timothy Everett, Julia Simon-Kerr, Thomas Morawetz, Jacqueline Ross, and Stephen Thaman. For research assistance, I thank the University of Connecticut law library staff as well as Jonathan Lamantia.

1. United States courts have mostly rejected special verdicts because they interfere with jury deliberations. But see Nepveu (2003) (arguing that juries increasingly rely on special verdict forms and special interrogatories so that they commonly return information beyond a simple 'guilty' or 'not guilty' in a wide range of criminal cases).
2. In Britain, it is illegal to interrogate jurors to gather information about the deliberation process. Contempt of Court Act, 1981, c. 49, § 8(1) ('It is a contempt of court to obtain, disclose or solicit any particulars of statements made, opinions

expressed, arguments advanced or votes cast by members of a jury in the course of their deliberation in any legal proceedings').

3. The ECtHR handed down two successive *Taxquet v. Belgium* decisions: the first judgment, in 2009, seemed to declare a new reason-giving requirement bearing on criminal juries; *Taxquet v. Belgium*, App. No., 926/05, (Eur. Ct. H.R. Jan. 13, 2009) [hereinafter *Taxquet I*], while the second, in 2010, retreated from that position and simply announced a broad right for criminal defendants to understand verdicts. *Taxquet v. Belgium*, App. No., 926/05, (Eur. Ct. H.R. Nov. 16, 2009) [hereinafter *Taxquet II*].

4. Belgium updated its reason-giving regime right after the ECtHR handed down its first section judgment in 2009. See *Loi relative à la réforme de la cour d'assises* [Law Concerning the Reform of the Court of Assizes] of Dec. 21, 2009, Moniteur Belge [M.B.] [Official Gazette of Belgium], Jan. 11, 2010, 751.

5. *Loi 2011-939 du 10 août 2011 sur la participation des citoyens au fonctionnement de la justice pénale et le jugement des mineurs* [Law 2011-939 of August 2011 on Citizen Participation in the Operation of the Justice System and the Trial of Minors], Journal Officiel de la République Française [J.O.], Aug. 11, 2011, p. 13744.

6. *Projet de loi sur la participation des citoyens au fonctionnement de la justice pénale et le jugement des mineurs. Étude d'impact* 30, 37 (Apr. 11, 2011) (author's translation). (Even though the auhtors of the study underlined that the reform was not 'imposed' by Strasbourg, a number of cases in the ECtHR's pipeline suggested that the European court might not review favorably the safeguards which existed in lieu of reason-giving, such as special interrogatories. In the case of *Papon v. France*, handed down on November 15, 2001 the ECtHR upheld an unreasoned verdict on account of the precision of the special interrogatory's questions, which, according to the court, 'adequately compensated the lack of reasons'. *Papon v. France (No. 2)*, 2001-XII Eur. Ct. H.R. This rationale indicated that, conversely, should a special interrogatory lack precision, the ECtHR would not find it sufficient to compensate for an unreasoned verdict, as was confirmed by France's condemnation in *Agnelet v. France*. See generally *Agnelet v. France*, App. No., 61198/08 (Eur. Ct. H.R. Jan. 10, 2013)).

7. *Projet de loi sur la participation des citoyens au fonctionnement de la justice pénale et le jugement des mineurs. Étude d'impact.* 31 (Apr. 11, 2011) (author's translation).

8. See Code de Procédure Pénale [C. pr. pén.] art. 485 (Fr.) ('Every judgment must include reasons and enacting terms. The reasons form the basis of the decision. The enacting terms state the offences for which the persons cited are declared guilty or liable, and also the penalty, the legal provisions implemented and the civil award'). It should be noted, however, that the quality of reason-giving by *tribunaux correctionnels* is often lagging, with judges occasionally copying and pasting the elements developed in the indictment (Guinchard, 2009: 940).

9. Jean-René Lecerf, Rapport au sénat no. 489 (2011) at 77 (Fr.).

10. Protcol 7, art. 2 of the Convention lays down the principle of a right to appeal ('*double degré de juridiction*'). The ECtHR had not condemned France, considering that the possibility of appealing a verdict to the *cour de cassation* satisfied the requirement, but many in France feared that it might if an extended right to appeal were not forthcoming.

11. *Loi 2000-516 du 15 juin 2000 renforçant la protection de la présomption d'innocence et les droits de la victime* [Law 2000-516 of June 2000 reinforcing the presumption of innocence and the rights of victims], Journal Officiel de la République Française [J.O.], Jun. 16, 2000, p. 9038.

12. The 2000 statute granted the right to appeal to defendants only. Less than two years later, however, a second statute extended the right to appeal to the prosecution. See *Loi 2002-307 du 4 mars 2002 complétant la loi 2000-516 du 15 juin* [Law 2002-307

of Mar. 4, 2002 supplementing the law 2000-516 of Jun. 15], Journal Officiel de la République Française [J.O.], Mar. 5, 2002.

13. *Hadjianastassiou v. Greece*, App. No., 12945/87, 16 Eur. H.R. Rep. 219, 237 (1993); *Hirvisaari v. Finland*, Judgment of 27 September 2001, No 49684/99, § 30; see also *Ruiz Torija v. Spain*, Judgment of 9 December 1994, série A nx 303-A, p. 12, § 29; *Higgins v. France*, Judgment of 19 February 1998, Reports of Judgments and Decisions 1998-I, p. 60, § 42.

14. *Nedzela v. France*, Judgment of 27 July 2006, §§ 45, 55.

15. In previous cases dealing with jury verdicts, the ECtHR had held that other features of the process, such as the right to waive a jury trial or directions provided by judges to jurors, sufficiently compensated for the absence of reasons. See, for example, *Saric v. Denmark*, App. No., 31913/96 (Eur. Ct. H.R. Feb. 2, 1999).

16. For example, *Jokela v. Finland*, App. No., 28856/95 (Eur. Ct. H.R. May 21, 2002) 73; see also *Nedzela v. France*, Judgment, App. No., 73695/01 (Eur. Ct. H.R. July 27, 2006) § 55; *Albina v. Romania*, App. No., 57808/00 (Eur. Ct. H.R. July 28, 2005) ¶ 34; *Garcia Ruiz v. Spain*, App. No., 30544/96 (Eur. Ct. H.R. January 21, 1999) § 26; *Helle v. Finland*, App. No., 157/1996/776/977 (Eur. Ct. H.R. Dec. 19, 1997) § 60.

17. *Taxquet II, supra* note 3, at § 90.

18. Ibid. § 97.

19. Ibid. § 90. The Court has more recently reaffirmed this position in *Agnelet v. France*. See generally *Agnelet v. France*, App. No., 61198/08 (Eur. Ct. H.R. Jan. 10, 2013); *Legillon v. France*, App. No., 53406/10 (Eur. Ct. H.R. Oct. 10, 2013).

20. Among its member states, the European court found that ten have adopted the 'traditional' jury system, defined as that in which 'professional judges are unable to take part in the jurors' deliberations on the verdict'. *Taxquet II, supra* note 3, §§ 43, 47. These states are: Austria, Belgium, Georgia, Ireland, Malta, Norway (for serious crimes and on appeal), the Russian Federation, Spain, Switzerland, and the United Kingdom (England, Wales, Scotland, and Northern Ireland). Ibid. § 47.

21. According to the Court, 24 states use the mixed form of jury: Bulgaria, Croatia, the Czech Republic, Denmark, Estonia, Finland, France, Germany, Greece, Hungary, Iceland, Italy, Liechtenstein, Monaco, Montenegro, Norway (for most cases), Poland, Portugal, Serbia, Slovakia, Slovenia, Sweden, 'the former Yugoslav Republic of Macedonia', and Ukraine. Ibid. § 46.

22. The majority emphasized that the notion of a fair trial is not univocal across member states: 'While the right of an accused to a fair trial should never be compromised, it could be attained in different ways in the Contracting States' criminal justice systems. States were to be afforded a margin of appreciation in arranging the judicial procedures through which the right to a fair trial was secured', *Taxquet II, supra* note 3, § 72.

23. Ibid. § 26.

24. Ibid. § 50.

25. There are notable exceptions, such as France and Norway, which employ lay assessors at the appellate level (Jackson and Kovalev, 2006: 118). Italy also uses mixed panels of judges and lay judges on appeal, in so-called *corte d'assise d'appello*.

26. *Taxquet II, supra* note 3, § 95.

27. See *Loi 2011-939 du 10 août 2011 sur la participation des citoyens au fonctionnement de la justice pénale et le jugement des mineurs* [Law 2011-939 of August 2011 on Citizen Participation in the Operation of the Justice System and the Trial of Minors], Journal Officiel de la République Française [J.O.], Aug. 11, 2011, p. 13744.

28. The statute went into effect in January of 2012 and is still in a state of experimentation.

29. Until the 1930s, similar to the common law jury, French jurors only decided on guilt. Since the passage of a 1932 statute, they also decide on punishment. See *Loi du 5 mars 1932 ayant pour objet d'associer le jury à la cour d'assises pour l'application de la peine* [Law of March 1932 associating the jury to the *cour d'assises* for the application of punishment] (author's translation).

30. Cour de cassation [Cass.] [supreme court for judicial matters] crim., Jun. 26, 2013, nos. 12-87.863, 12-87.637 (not published) and crim., Oct. 17, 2012, Bull No. 221 (Fr.) In the same decision, the *cour de cassation* refused to remand the issue to the constitutional court, the *Conseil constitutionnel*.

31. Of course, a number of legal decisions are insulated from the duty to give reasons, from supreme courts' denial of certiorari to summary dispositions to peremptory challenges to executive pardons, etc. I have shown elsewhere that the current trend toward increased reason-giving in the judicial context is a modern phenomenon. (Cohen, 2015). Mercy functions similarly to sentencing. It is a prerogative of the sovereign reminiscent of the baroque conception of power epitomized by the maxim *sic volo sic jubeo, stat pro ratione voluntas*, which can be translated as 'Thus I will, thus I command, my will shall stand for a reason'. In modern times, mercy has remained a matter of 'grace' rather than desert, thus closer to sentencing rather than adjudication of guilt or innocence. This may explain the relative unwillingness to require reason-giving at sentencing; though, ironically, it is where the United States system currently requires most reason giving. See 18 USC § 3553(c). I thank Jacqueline Ross for pressing me on this point.

32. See Code d'Instruction Criminelle [Cl.cr.] art. 334 (Belg.).

33. Code de Procédure Pénale [C. pr. pén.] art. 365-1 (Fr.) (mandating that 'reasons be memorialized in a document annexed to the questions sheet', called a 'reason-giving sheet' (*feuille de motivation*) (author's translation)).

34. See Code de Procédure Pénale [C. pr. pén.] arts 244–47 (Fr.).

35. Ibid. arts 248–50.

36. Ibid. arts 311, 328; see also Cour de cassation [Cass.] [supreme court for judicial matters] crim., Jun. 14, 1989, Bull. Crim. (Fr.).

37. Code de Procédure Pénale [C. pr. pén.] arts 328 (Fr.) (providing that the president 'has the duty not to disclose his opinion as to [the defendant's] guilt').

38. See ibid. art. 310 (providing that '[w]itnesses summoned in this way do not take an oath and their statements are only considered as a source of information').

39. See ibid. art. 309.

40. Ibid. art. 365-1 (author's translation).

41. See ibid. art. 357 (maintaining the rule according to which mixed courts must use secret ballots.)

42. A senate committee had underlined this possibility. See Lecerf, *supra* note 9, at 79.

43. See ibid. art. 353. The Belgian *Code d'instruction criminelle*, which used to contain similar language (at art. 342), was substantially revised in 2009 when the new Belgium reason-giving requirement was imposed upon juries to eliminate the reference to *intime conviction*. *See* Code d'Instruction Criminelle [C.I.cr.] arts 326(2), 327(2) (Belg.).

44. See ibid. art. 365-1 (author's translation).

45. Plea-bargaining was only introduced in France in 2004. It is strictly reserved for minor offenses, and so far talks of extending it to serious crimes have failed to elicit a legislative response. See *Loi 2004-204 du 9 mars 2004 portant adaptation de la justice aux évolutions de la criminalité* [Law 2004-204 of March 2004 Adapting Justice to Changes in Criminality], Journal Officiel de la République Française [J.O.], Mar. 10, 2004, p. 4565.

46. Continental judges are more analogous to American administrative officials in terms of education, recruitment, and career than to Article III judges. In France, a judicial

career begins with the post-law school, state-operated French national judge school and continues with yearly evaluations and reviews, sanctioned by promotions and transfers between courts (Bell, 2010: 44–107).

47. See Code de Procédure Pénale [C. pr. pén.] art. 231 (Fr.). As Stephen Thaman notes, for example, when Belgium became independent of the Netherlands, Article 98 of its 1831 Constitution proclaimed: 'The jury shall be constituted for all serious crimes and for political and press offences' (Thaman, 2011: 621).

48. *Hirvisaari v. Finland*, App. No 49684/99, Eur. Ct. H.R. at ¶ 30 (2001). See also *Rizos and Daskas v. Greece*, Judgment of Mai 27, 2004, No 65545/01, §7; *Alija v. Greece*, Judgment of April 7, 2005, No. 73717/01, § 21; *Dimitrellos v. Greece*, Judgment of April 16, 2005, No. 75483/01, § 16; *Nastos v. Greece*, Judgment of March 30, 2006, No. 35828/02, §26; *Benderskiy v. Ukraine*, Judgment of November 15, 2007, No. 22750/02, §42; *Velted-98 AD v. Bulgaria*, Judgment of December 11, 2008, No. 15239, §45.

49. See Protocol No. 7 of the Convention for the Protection of Human Rights and Fundamental Freedom, art. 2, Nov. 4, 1952, E.T.S. 117 (as amended by Protocol No. 11, Nov. 1, 1998, E.T.S. 155).

50. Thus, according to the ECtHR, in the first *Taxquet* case, because of the absence of reasons at the Belgian *cour d'assises*, 'the Court of Cassation was prevented from carrying out an effective review and from identifying, for example, any insufficiency or inconsistency in the reasoning', *Taxquet I, supra* note 3, at § 49.

51. Code de Procédure Pénale [C. pr. pén.] art. 364 (Fr.).

52. See Lecerf, *supra* note 9, at 79 ('[T]he reasons sheet [is] signed by the president and the jury foreperson in order to guarantee the jury's control over the reasoning retained by the professional judge' (author's translation)).

53. Code de Procédure Pénale [C. pr. pén.] art. 366 (Fr.).

54. The *cour de cassation* had struck down a *cour d'assises* judgment which contained explanations on the ground that giving reasons violated the *intime conviction* standard. In doing so, it reaffirmed its view that the mixed panel's responses to the special interrogatory form provided sufficient information as to the verdict's basis. Cour de cassation [Cass.] [supreme court for judicial matters] crim., Dec. 15, 1999, no. 99-84099, Bull No. 308 (Fr.).

55. Yet federal criminal law departs from this tradition. United States federal judges are under a statutory duty to provide a justification for their sentencing decisions. 18 U.S.C. § 3553(c)(2) (2006). Moreover, since the Supreme Court's *United States v. Booker* decision in 2005 and its progeny, district judges are subject to a judicially imposed requirement to 'adequately explain the chosen sentence to allow for a meaningful appellate review and to promote the perception of fair sentencing', *Gall v. United States*, 552 U.S. 38, 50 (2007).

56. See *People's Mojahedin Org. of Iran v. U.S. Dep't of State*, 182 F.3d 17, 23 (D.C. Cir. 1999) ('In cases on appeal from the district court, we are to review "judgments, not opinions." Orders issued by agencies are treated differently. In administrative law, we do not sustain a "right-result, wrong-reason" decision of an agency. We send the case back to the agency so that it may fix its reasoning or change its result') (citations omitted).

57. See *Helvering v. Gowran*, 302 U.S. 238, 245 (1937) ('In the review of judicial proceedings the rule is settled that, if the decision below is correct, it must be affirmed although the lower court relied upon a wrong ground or gave a wrong reason').

58. See Fed. R. Civ. P. 61 (requiring that federal courts 'disregard any error or defect in the proceedings which does not affect the substantial rights of the parties').

59. Every initial trial verdict must to go through a second *de novo* trial before it can reach the *cour de cassation*.

60. The *cour d'assises d'appel* is not hierarchically superior to the first instance *cour d'assises*. The only difference between the two courts is the number of decision-makers: on appeal, the number of lay assessors is increased from six to nine. See *Loi 2000-516 du 15 juin 2000 renforçant la protection de la présomption d'innocence et les droits de la victime* [Law 2000-516 of June 2000 reinforcing the presumption of innocence and the rights of victims], Journal Officiel de la République Française [J.O.], June 16, 2000, p. 9038.
61. This rule has been revised during the summer of 2014 by the *Loi n° 2014-640 du 20 juin 2014 relative à la réforme des procédures de révision et de réexamen d'une condamnation pénale définitive*. The revised Code of penal procedure now states that 'the *cour d'assises*' debates are audio recorded under the president's control. The president can also order, at the victim or the civil party's request, ... that their examination or deposition be video recorded' (author's translation). That same article also allows the president to audio or video record jury deliberations. Code de Procédure Pénale [C. pr. pén.], art. 308. (Fr.).
62. See Code de Procédure Pénale [C. pr. pén.], art. 308. (Fr.).
63. See Code de Procédure Pénale [C. pr. pén.], art. 308(6) and (7). (Fr.).
64. The prosecution's right to appeal verdicts of acquittals to the *cour de cassation* is limited to an appeal 'in the interests of law alone and without prejudice to the party acquitted', Code de Procédure Pénale [C. pr. pén.], art. 572. (Fr.).
65. The *cour de cassation* only reviews the reasons of the *cour d'assises d'appel*, not the first set of reasons from the first *cour d'assises* trial.
66. *Loi des 16 et 24 août 1790 sur l'organisation judiciaire*, art. 15 (codified in art. 485 and 543 of the Code of penal procedure.) In the name of consistent application of the law throughout the nation, that same statute established that the *cour de cassation* was empowered to overrule lower court decisions based on an erroneous application of the law.
67. Under the general category of '*défaut de motifs*' (which could be translated as defective reasons) the *cour de cassation* strikes down decisions on four different grounds: inexistent reasons, inconsistent reasons, non-response to a party's submissions, hypothetical or doubtful reasons.
68. Cour de cassation [Cass.] [supreme court for judicial matters] crim., Nov. 20, 2013, no. 12-86630, Bull No. 234 (Fr.).
69. See Pierre-Victor Tournier, 'Arpenter le champ pénal, nos. 85–86, April 14 2008', available at http://arpenter-champ-penal.blogspot.com/2008/04/toujours-plus-acp-85-86-supplment.html (Pierre-Victor Tournier is a demographer and social scientist at the French national research institute, the CNRS, who created a blog/newsletter which on many criminal justice topics is the only publicly available source of information).

REFERENCES

Barraud, Boris. 2012. 'La justice au hasard de quelques raisons juridiques de supprimer les jurys populaires', 83 *Revue internationale de droit pénal* 377–411.
Bell, John. 2010. *Judiciaries within Europe. A Comparative Review*. Cambridge: Cambridge University Press.
Cohen, Mathilde. 2014. 'Ex Ante Versus Ex Post Deliberations: Two Models of Judicial Deliberations in Courts of Last Resort', 62 *American Journal of Comparative Law* 401–457.
Cohen, Mathilde. 2015. 'When Judges Have Reasons Not to Give Reasons: A Comparative Law Approach', 72 *Washington & Lee Law Review* 483–571.

Cunniberti, Gilles. 2008. 'The Recognition of Foreign Judgments Lacking Reasons in Europe: Access to Justice, Foreign Court Avoidance, and Efficiency', 58 *International & Comparative Law Quarterly* 15–52.

Damaška, Mirjan. 1986. *The Faces of Justice and State Authority*. New Haven and London: Yale University Press.

Damaška, Mirjan. 2010. 'The Common Law/Civil Law Divide: Residual Truth of a Misleading Distinction', 49 *Supreme Court Review* (Canada) 3–21.

Dawson, John P. 1960. *A History of Lay Judges*. Cambridge, MA: Harvard University Press.

Esmein, Adhémar. 1913. *A History of Continental Criminal Procedure, with Special Reference to France*. Boston: Little Brown.

Fisher, George. 1997. 'The Jury's Rise as Lie Detector', 107 *Yale Law Journal* 575–713.

Guinchard, Serge, et al. 2009. *Droit processuel, droit commun et droit comparé du procès équitable*. Paris: Dalloz.

Hans, Valerie P. 2008. 'Jury Systems Around the World', 4 *Annual Review of Law & Social Science* 275–297.

Jackson, John D. and Nikolay P. Kovalev. 2006 'Lay Adjudication and Human Rights in Europe', 13 *Columbia Journal of European Law* 83–123.

Jacobs, Ann. 2012. 'Les spécificités de la procédure d'assises belge', *Revue pénitentiaire et de droit pénal* 559–573.

Jellab, Aziz and Armelle Giglio-Jacquemot. 2012. 'Les jurés populaires et les épreuves de la cour d'assises: entre légitimité d'un regard profane et interpellation du pouvoir des juges', 62 *L'année sociologique* 143–193.

Lasser, Mitchel de S.-O.-L'E. 2004. *Judicial Deliberations. A Comparative Analysis of Judicial Transparency and Legitimacy*. Oxford: Oxford University Press.

Macedo, Stephen. 1990. 'The Politics of Justification', 18 *Political Theory* 280–304.

Mashaw, Jerry L. 2001. 'Small Things Like Reasons Are Put in a Jar: Reason and Legitimacy in the Administrative State', 70 *Fordham Law Review* 17–35.

Nagel, Thomas. 1987. 'Moral Conflict and Political Legitimacy', 16 *Philosophy & Public Affairs* 215–240.

Nepveu, Kate H. 2003. 'Beyond "Guilty" or "Not Guilty": Giving Special Verdicts in Criminal Jury Trials', 21 *Yale Law & Policy Review* 263–300.

Rawls, John. 1993. *Political Liberalism*. New York: Columbia University Press.

Saint-Pierre, François. 2013. *Au nom du peuple français – Jury populaire ou juges professionnels?* Paris: Éditions Odile Jacob.

Scharnitsky Patrick and Nikos Kalampalikis. 2007. 'Analyse lexicale des sources d'influence dans les jurys d'assises', 60 *Bulletin de psychologie* 425–432.

Stack, Kevin. 2007. 'The Constitutional Foundations of *Chenery*', 116 *Yale Law Journal* 952–1021.

Thaman, Stephen C. 2011. 'Should Criminal Juries Give Reasons for Their Verdicts? The Spanish Experience and the Implications of the European Court of Human Rights Decision in *Taxquet v. Belgium*', 86 *Chicago-Kent Law Review* 613–668.

Toulemon, André. 1930. *La Question du jury*. Paris: Librairie du Recueil Sirey.

Wells, Michael L. 1994. 'French and American Judicial Opinions', 19 *Yale Journal of International Law* 81–133.

PART IV

SYNCHRONIC COMPARISONS: ALTERNATIVES TO TRIAL, TO CRIMINAL INVESTIGATIONS, AND TO THE CRIMINAL PROCESS ITSELF

13. Special investigative techniques in post-Soviet states: the divide between preventive policing and criminal investigation

Nikolai Kovalev and Stephen C. Thaman

1. INTRODUCTION

The fifteen independent republics which arose following the 1991 collapse of the Soviet Union are fascinating subjects of research in the transition from non-democratic, authoritarian legal norms to those compatible with democracy, international human rights norms, and due process. In the past, we have explored the developments in this realm in the area of lay participation in the criminal trial in the form of juries or mixed courts (Kovalev, 2010; Thaman, 2007), plea bargaining and the turn to adversary procedure (Kovalev, 2010; Thaman, 2008b).

In this chapter we focus on the approach taken by twelve of the post-Soviet republics, Armenia, Azerbaijan, Belarus, Georgia, Kazakhstan, Kyrgyzstan, Moldova, Russia, Tajikistan, Turkmenistan, Ukraine and Uzbekistan[1] in regulating secret investigative measures, such as wiretapping, bugging, use of undercover operatives, sting operations, etc., which impact on protected human rights of the citizenry, especially the right to privacy. These measures, which we will call 'special investigative techniques' (SITs)[2] have a long history in Russia and the Soviet Union, where they were and are still mostly known as 'operative-investigative measures' (*operativno-rozysknye meropriiatiia*). The Soviet approach also borrowed from the pre-revolutionary practices of the Russian Imperial criminal police (*sysknaia politsiia*) and political police (*okhranka*) (Zharov, 2010; Zharov and Sprishevskii, 2012: 9–12).

The relationship between preventive, proactive secret information-gathering by police and the reactive official criminal investigation seeking to identify suspects responsible for a past crime and prove their guilt is one of the most sensitive and critical issues facing societies and criminal justice systems today, due to the impact on the constitutionally protected human rights of privacy and human dignity inherent in secret state prying into the lives of its citizens, or even inducing them to commit crimes. The revelations of Edward Snowden as to the activities of the U.S. National Security Agency and the intelligence agencies of the United Kingdom and other countries have reawakened the discussion of this critical intersection between intelligence-gathering and targeted criminal investigation and prosecution.[3]

The specter of the Soviet police state should still haunt the countries which are the focus of this inquiry. Soviet legal theory and practice traditionally distinguished SITs, which were not regulated by law, from the pretrial criminal investigation, which was bound by the rules of the Code of Criminal Procedure (CCP). Investigators (*sledovateli*) conducted the preliminary criminal investigation, whereas undercover police detectives (*operativniki*) carried out the SITs. The planning and execution of SITs were considered to be state secrets (for example, Art. 17 Law on SITs-Belarus (1999); Art. 12(9) Law on SITs-Kazakhstan; Art. 7 Law on SITs-Kyrgyzstan; Art. 12(para.1) Law on SITs-Russia (1995)), whereas the results of the preliminary investigation were collected in the investigative dossier and revealed to the defendant at its completion before trial. SITs were not considered to be 'criminal procedure' and were not taught at Soviet law schools, but only in the specialized academies for police and the KGB (Sysalov, 2006: 9).

In Tsarist Russia, the government classified not only the methods of SITs, but also the very existence of the agencies which conducted the secret investigations. The organs that carried out the SITs did so based on classified guidelines and orders issued by the same agencies for which they worked (Vazehnin and Lugovich, 2014: 216). SITs, in Soviet times, especially wiretapping, were subject neither to judicial nor prosecutorial control and were used to gather information not only related to national security (that is, spying, etc.), but also to root out real or perceived regime opponents. If evidence derived from secret wiretapping made its way into a criminal prosecution, it did so deviously, without the fact of the secret eavesdropping ever being revealed. Before warrantless wiretapping was deemed to constitute a violation of the Fourth Amendment of the U.S. Constitution and was subject to regulation in 1968, the practice of U.S. law enforcement authorities bore a close resemblance to their Soviet counterparts.[4]

Post-Soviet law has come a long way since the collapse of the U.S.S.R. in 1991, and all post-Soviet republics have enacted a special statute regulating the use of SITs. We will describe in this chapter the kinds of activities regulated by a typical post-Soviet statute regulating Laws on SITs and analyze the extent to which these statutes, when read in conjunction with the respective country's constitution and CCP, adequately correspond to the requirements of modern human rights norms. We will concentrate on those SITs which clearly impact on important constitutional rights, such as wiretapping, bugging, gathering of communications metadata, long-term secret surveillance and the use of undercover operatives to enter private spaces, or arrange the preconditions for the commission of a crime, such as through sting operations, controlled buys and the like.

We will discuss the extent to which judicial authorization is required for the implementation of these SITs, the level of suspicion required to authorize them, the types of crimes which can be investigated using SITs, the length of time SITs may be employed, the proportionality of the measures and whether there is adequate judicial supervision of their implementation. We will analyze these aspects of the SITs statutes to see if they comport with internationally accepted minimal standards. Armenia, Azerbaijan, Georgia, Moldova, Russia and Ukraine have ratified the European Convention on Human Rights (ECHR) and are bound by the jurisprudence of the European Court of Human Rights (ECtHR). All of the countries discussed have ratified the U.N. International Covenant on Civil and Political Rights (ICCPR) and are thus bound by the decisions of the U.N. Human Rights Committee as well.

2. THE APPROACH TO SPECIAL INVESTIGATION TECHNIQUES IN THE FORMER SOVIET REPUBLICS

2.1 Introduction

SITs in the post-Soviet sphere are limited to secret preventive, proactive measures aimed at detection of crime, and this chapter will focus solely on these. We will not deal with the regulation of foreign intelligence and national security operations unrelated to typical law enforcement, which are governed by special statutes governing security agencies, foreign intelligence and state secrets.

2.2 Post-Soviet Legislation on Special Investigation Techniques

The first post-Soviet Laws on SITs were adopted in 1992 by Ukraine, Russia and Belarus, followed by Tajikistan in 1993, Turkmenistan, Moldova and Kazakhstan in 1994, Kyrgyzstan in 1998, Azerbaijan and Georgia in 1999, Armenia, in 2007, and Uzbekistan in 2012. The initial laws were replaced by reform legislation in Russia in 1995, in Belarus in

1999 and in Moldova in 2012. Tajikistan replaced its initial Law on SITs twice, once 1998 and again in 2011.

Russia quickly issued a new SITs law in 1995 because Art. 23 of the Russian Constitution, enacted in 1993, required judicial authorization for wiretapping and intrusions into private spaces. The reformed laws in Belarus, Georgia, Azerbaijan, Kyrgyzstan and Tajikistan were likely influenced by the adoption of the Model Law on SITs passed by the Interparliamentary Assembly of Member Nations of the Commonwealth of Independent States (CIS-IPA) in 1997. This model law was drafted by the Belarusian Parliament and approved by parliamentary delegations from nine countries: Armenia, Azerbaijan, Belarus, Georgia, Kazakhstan, Kyrgyzstan, Moldova, Russia and Tajikistan (Aleksandrov and Fedorov, 1999). A new version of the CIS Model Law on SITs was passed by the CIS-IPA in 2006.

The main purpose of CIS model laws, including the Model Law on SITs, has been to harmonize legislation in the CIS states. Although model laws are not mandatory for member states, participation of member-state representatives in the drafting and approval of the model laws by the Interparliamentary Assembly has fostered their adoption, in whole or in part, by several member states.

While some post-Soviet states, notably Moldova, Ukraine and Kazakhstan, have incorporated legal provisions regulating SITs into their CCPs (in particular in sections defining the powers of the prosecutor and the investigative bodies), the CCPs of most of the states make no mention of SITs. Pending draft laws in Armenia and Kyrgyzstan, however, perhaps indicate a trend towards incorporating rules governing SITs into the CCP, though there is still vigorous opposition from their law enforcement agencies.

2.3   Definition and Classification of SITs

The Model Law on SITs and national statutes define what constitutes a SIT. There are three main elements which can be found in almost any law on SITs across the post-Soviet states.

First, SITs are a type of investigative police activity with secrecy at its core. This means that they are carried out without the knowledge of their target, unlike ordinary overt investigative techniques such as police questioning, arrests, pretrial detentions and searches. In the words of an expert committee of the Council of Europe, they are 'techniques for gathering information systematically in such a way as *not to alert the target person(s)*, applied by law enforcement officials for the purpose of detecting and investigating crimes and suspects' (emphasis added) (Council of Europe, 2005: 13).

Second, this activity is carried out only by the law enforcement agencies authorized to do so by the statute regulating SITs and only within the scope of their powers. For instance, Art. 13 Law on SITs-Russia (1995) lists organs of the Ministry of the Interior, the Federal Security Agency (former KGB), and special organs dealing with state protection, customs, foreign intelligence and narcotics enforcement. Some statutes include other specialized organs, such as the financial police (Art. 12(1) Law on SITs-Georgia; Art. 16(4) Law on SITs-Kyrgyzstan). In some countries the prosecutor's office may also carry out SITs (Art. 12(1) Law on SITs-Georgia).

Third, the purpose of carrying out SITs is, according to the statutes, to protect the life, health, rights and freedom of individuals, and the security of society and the state from crime (Art. 1 Law on SITs-Russia (1995)).

Article 6 Model Law on SITs (2006) provides a list of seventeen different types of SITs. Many of these do not necessarily impinge on any protected constitutional rights of citizens and would not, in the U.S., even require the approval of a prosecutor, much less a judge: (1) interviews with citizens; (2) inquiries; (3) identification of individuals or other objects; (4) collection of samples for comparative studies; (5) undercover purchases; (6) covert examination of objects and documents or (7) covert investigative experiments or sting operations. Other CIS measures might require judicial authorization depending on whether they involve penetration into private spaces; (8) visual and other types of surveillance;[5] (9) investigative infiltration; (10) undercover controlled deliveries; and (11) covert inspections of premises, buildings, structures, terrain and vehicles. A third category clearly requires judicial authorization in the U.S. to the extent that it intrudes into the content of private communications (and requires judicial authorization in many European countries even if it only accesses telecommunications metadata or 'envelope information');[6] (12) monitoring of postal, telegraph and other communications; (13) interception of telephone communications; (14) acoustic control or interception of audio communication in private and public places (bugging); (15) collection of information from technical communication channels; (16) monitoring telecommunication networks and systems; and (17) monitoring the radio spectrum.

The lists in the individual countries' codes include more or less the same types of activity (cf. Art. 10 Law on SITs-Azerbaijan; Art. 11 Law on SITs-Belarus (1999); Art. 7 Law on SITs-Kyrgyzstan; Art. 6 Law on SITs-Russia (1995); Art. 6 Law on SITs-Tajikistan (2011); Art. 14 Law on SITs-Uzbekistan). The lists are exclusive: legislation is required to expand the list of SITs (Art. 6(para.1) Law on SITs-Russia (1995)).

According to Article 2 Model Law on SITs-CIS (2006), SITs are carried out to achieve the following objectives: (1) the detection, prevention, suppression and investigation of crimes, and identification of persons who are preparing, committing or have committed criminal offences; (2) searching for fugitives and missing persons; (3) obtaining information about events or actions that threaten the national security of the state or society or the rights and freedoms of citizens; (4) mutual assistance in the fight against crime in accordance with international treaties. Similar provisions can be found in the national statutes (cf. Art. 2 Law on SITs-Russia (1995), which was amended in 2008 to include, as a task of SITs, the discovery of property subject to confiscation and forfeiture).

In addition to the seventeen measures listed above legislators have introduced a number of other SITs such as feigned bribery (Art. 14(1)(16) Law on SITs-Armenia), monitoring of financial transactions (Art. 14(1)(16) Law on SITs-Armenia; 18(1)(1)(f) Law on SITs-Moldova (2012)), organization of undercover companies (storefront operations) (Art. 10(1)(17) Law on SITs-Azerbaijan; Art. 7(2) Law on SITs-Georgia; Art. 7(12) Law on SITs-Kyrgyzstan; Art. 11(2)(5) Law on SITs-Kazakhstan; Art. 6(1)(16) Law on SITs-Tajikistan (2011)), and censorship of prisoners' correspondence (Art. 7(2) Law on SITs-Georgia; Art. 9(1) Law on SITs-Turkmenistan).

3. CONFORMITY OF THE LAWS ON SITS WITH INTERNATIONAL HUMAN RIGHTS STANDARDS

3.1 In General

Article 17 of the ICCPR and Art. 8 ECHR prohibit arbitrary or unlawful interference with one's privacy, family, home or correspondence. In paragraph 8 of the General Comment No. 16, the UN Committee on Human Rights has noted that 'relevant legislation must specify in detail the precise circumstances in which such interferences may be permitted'. The UN Committee on Human Rights in its reports has also repeatedly criticized the governments of several post-Soviet states because their legislation dealing with wiretapping and other SITs has been insufficiently precise to comport with the terms of Art. 17 ICCPR. For example, in its concluding observations on the Russian Federation in 1995, the Committee expressed concern 'that the mechanisms to intrude into private telephone communication continue to exist, without clear legislation setting out the conditions of legitimate interferences with privacy and providing for safeguards against unlawful interferences' ((1995) UN doc. CCPR/C/79/Add.54, para. 19).

Article 8(2) ECHR, however, does provide for exceptions when the rights guaranteed under Article 8(1) may be encumbered: 'There shall be no interference by a public authority with the exercise of this right except such as is in accordance with the law and is necessary in a democratic society in the interests of national security, public safety or the economic well-being of the country, for the prevention of disorder or crime, for the protection of health or morals, or for the protection of the rights and freedoms of others.

The ECtHR has laid out some basic benchmarks for SITs which impact upon the right to privacy protected by Article 8 ECHR, and more particularly on wiretapping, arguably the SIT which constitutes the most drastic invasion of this kind. Several decisions have addressed the laws on SITs of post-Soviet republics. In general, the ECtHR has said that

> when it comes to the interception of communications for the purpose of a police investigation, the law must be sufficiently clear in its terms to give citizens an adequate indication as to the circumstances in which and the conditions on which public authorities are empowered to resort to this secret and potentially dangerous interference with the right to respect for private life and correspondence. (*Bykov v. Russia* (G.C.), No. 4378/02, 10 March 2009, para. 78)

We will now go through some of the most important aspects of the SITs and discuss the extent to which they comport with these international human rights standards.

3.2 The Extent to which Judicial Authorization is Required

Under Soviet law, the prosecutor and even the investigator, subject to supervision of the prosecutor, were authorized to issue search warrants for dwellings and other private spaces and to intercept private communications. The judge only played a role at the trial stage of criminal proceedings. After the collapse of the Soviet Union, however, the post-Soviet republics began to require judicial authorization for these measures in their constitutions and CCPs. But the transition was slow. Although judicial authorization was required by Articles 23 and 24 of the 1993 Russian constitution, and by amendments to the CCP of 1961 and the Law on SITs (Thaman, 2002) it didn't actually become a reality until the passage of the CCP in 2001.

Today the trend in the post-Soviet republics is to require judicial authorization for wiretaps, bugging and searches, and inspections of private spaces, whether conducted before or after initiation of criminal proceedings. The constitutions of at least six of the twelve post-Soviet republics under discussion here require judicial authorization before a non-consented entry into the dwelling is permitted (Art. 21(2) Const.-Armenia; Art. 33 Const.-Azerbaijan; Art. 18 Const.-Georgia; Art. 30(2) Const.-Kyrgyzstan; Art. 29(2)(1) Const.-Moldova; Art. 25 Const.-Russia; Art. 30 Const.-Ukraine). The same holds when it comes to issuance of an order to wiretap or bug a private space (Art. 20(3) Const.-Armenia; Art. 16(2) Const.-Azerbaijan; Art. 20 Const.-Georgia; Art. 29(2) Const.-Kyrgyzstan; Art. 14(2) Const.-Moldova; Art. 23 Const.- Russia; Art. 31 Const.-Ukraine). Of course, Art. 8 ECHR and all democratic systems provide for a narrow exception in cases of emergencies, danger in delay, or exigent circumstances, where the prosecutor or police may proceed with a search or wiretap. Normally, however, judicial authorization must be acquired *post factum* within 24 or 48 hours. Although the U.S. wiretap statute gives the prosecutor 48 hours to get retrospective judicial authorization, there is, unusually, no such requirement for dwelling searches conducted under exigent circumstances (Thaman, 2013: 419–420).

Even where the constitution does not explicitly mention judicial authorization, some former Soviet republics have included such protection in their CCPs (cf. Art. 192(1), 196(1) CCP-Tajikistan). Some of the Laws on SITs also expressly require judicial authorization for measures that impact on the right to privacy in the home or in one's conversations (Art. 18(1)(1) Law on SITs-Moldova (2012); Art. 9 Law on SITs-Russia (1995); Art. 9 Law on SITs-Tajikistan (2011)).

The influence of the ECtHR has certainly been instrumental in the development of the law in this area in some of the European post-Soviet republics. In condemning Moldova's overall Law on SITs in *Iordachi and Others v. Moldova* (no. 25198/02, ECHR 10 Feb. 2009) for being in violation of Art. 8 ECHR, the ECtHR noted that the 1994 Law on SITs, which did not require judicial authorization for wiretaps had been replaced by the 2003 Law on SITs, which, through a reference to the 2003 CCP, now required judicial authorization. After the *Iordachi* decision, the CCP was amended to add a list of SITs (Art. 132-1-138-3 CCP-Moldova) and the most recent version of Moldova's SITs law clearly places SITs into three different groups. The first, which requires judicial authorization, includes: covert examination of a dwelling and installation of audio and video surveillance equipment; surveillance of the dwelling using technical recording devices; interception and registration of messages and images; monitoring, examination and seizure of postal communications; monitoring of telegraphic and electronic communications; monitoring of financial transactions and access to financial information; localization and surveillance using GPS and other tracking devices; and collection of information from Internet providers. A second group of SITs requires authorization only by the prosecutor and includes such measures as cross-border supervision; visual surveillance; controlled deliveries and undercover purchases. The third group, including only interviews with citizens, collection of information about individuals and identification procedures, requires solely an endorsement from a chief of the investigative unit conducting the investigation (Art. 18(1)(1)(1-3) Law on SITs-Moldova (2012)).

This doubling of the lists of SITs in the CCP and the separate SITs Law also exists in Ukraine. As in Moldova, the investigative control judge must authorize any SIT under the provisions of the new code (Art. 247-48 CCP-Ukraine (2012)). Judicial authorization in Ukraine is also required for some activities that do not require it in the U.S., such as controlled deliveries, sting operations and infiltration of organizations (Art. 246(2), 271, 272, 274 CCP-Ukraine).[7] A Draft CCP from Kyrgyzstan also follows the Ukrainian model by listing SITs, which are called 'special investigative acts' in the code. Judicial authorization will, as in Ukraine, be required for the implementation of all of the SITs. As in Ukraine, the list includes controlled deliveries, sting operations but also the acquisition of telecommunications metadata, all not protected by the Fourth Amendment in the U.S. (Art. 234(2), 235 Draft-CCP-Kyrgyzstan (May 28, 2014)).

On the other hand, neither the CCP of Kazakhstan, which has recently included a list of SITs (Art. 234 CCP-Kazakhstan) nor its separate Law of SITs, with a similar list (Art. 11, 12(4) Law on SITs-Kazakhstan), requires judicial authorization, even when the privacy of the home or the confidentiality of communications is impacted. House searches are also still exempt from a requirement of a judicial warrant (Art. 220(13), 254(5) CCP-Kazakhstan). The only other countries which have remained with the Soviet procedure of allowing the prosecutor or investigator to authorize dwelling searches and SITs, such as wiretapping, which impact on the right to privacy are: Belarus (Art. 13 Law on SITs-Belarus (1999); Art. 204(7); 214(1) CCP-Belarus); Turkmenistan (Art. 11 Law on SITs-Turkmenistan; Art. 273, 282(1) CCP-Turkmenistan); and Uzbekistan (Art. 16 Law on SITs-Uzbekistan; Art. 161, 170 CCP-Uzbekistan).

'Doubling' of the list of SITs in the CCP and the Law on SITs only gives rise to problems if, for instance, the Law on SITs retains its Soviet paternity by allowing the conduct of SITs which impact upon the right to privacy in the home or correspondence without judicial authorization, yet the country's constitution and/or CCP have progressed and now require judicial authorization for such measures. In Belarus, Kazakhstan, Turkmenistan and Uzbekistan, which still have not progressed beyond the Soviet practice of allowing the prosecutor or investigator to issue search or wiretap warrants, there is no contradiction between the Law on SITs and the CCP.

Where the constitution or the CCP has developed beyond the language in the Law on SITs, such as in Kyrgyzstan, Moldova, Russia, Tajikistan and Ukraine, the Law on SITs has usually been amended to require judicial authorization. In May of 2014, the Georgian Ombudsman or 'public defender' brought a complaint before the Constitutional Court alleging that the Georgian Law on SITs violated the constitution by not requiring judicial authorization for the direct interception of conversations or direct access to on-line servers.[8]

The SITs involving use of undercover police officers and informants to infiltrate criminal organizations, make controlled narcotics buys, or set up sting operations will not necessarily require entry of private spaces or interception of confidential communications, but there is growing support for the view that judicial authorization should be needed to target a particular individual using such secret measures, and that there should be a showing that the person targeted has engaged in the suspected criminal activity in the past. The use of such undercover operatives not surprisingly leads to claims of entrapment by the persons targeted. Although U.S. law does not require judicial authorization to target a suspect with undercover measures such as those included in many SITs laws, it provides a limited excuse for entrapped defendants charged with crimes who can prove they were not criminally predisposed to commit the crime prior to the involvement of the undercover operatives (*Unites States v. Jacobson*, 503 U.S. 540 (1992)).

The ECtHR has identified a number of criteria in alleged entrapment cases which could lead, not to a substantive criminal defense, but to a violation of the Art. 6 ECHR right to fair proceedings and arguably to an exclusion of the evidence of the induced crime. These criteria include: (1) the absence of reasonable grounds to suspect the person which can be shown by pointing to the absence of any previous criminal activity; (2) in drug cases, the target's lack of immediate access to contraband, which can be shown by the fact that he or she had to procure it from a third party; (3) the absence of evidence that a target was subjectively predisposed to commit a crime; (4) the active role of the police in convincing a target to commit an offense (*Teixeira de Castro v. Portugal,* no. 25829/94, ECHR, 9 June 1998, para. 38).

In several judgments in cases against Russia which found entrapment, and thus a violation of Art. 6 ECHR, the ECtHR has emphasized that neither the law governing SITs nor any other legislation provides sufficient guarantees in relation to undercover purchases of contraband. For this reason, the Court called for independent judicial supervision of undercover operations. (Most recently paras 61–63 *Nosko & Nefedov v. Russia*, nos. 5753/09, 11789/10, ECHR, 30 Oct. 2014, citing, *Bannikova v. Russia*, no. 18757/06, ECHR 4 November 2010; *Khudobin v. Russia*, no. 59696/00, ECHR, 26 October 2006, *Veselov v. Russia,* nos. 23200/10, 24009/07 and 556/10, 2 January 2013, *inter alia*). Although the Presidium of the Russian Supreme Court found no violation of the Law on SITs in a case involving undercover narcotics purchases, it did find that a second undercover buy, after a previously successful one, violated Art. 2 Law on SITs-Russia (1995), because it was no longer conducted for the purpose of 'identification, prevention, interdiction and uncovering of crimes and the identification and discovery of persons who prepared or committed them'. Basically, it increased the level of criminality. The court then applied the general exclusionary rule of Article 75 CCP-Russia to exclude the evidence of the subsequent buy (No. 131-P12 (July 20, 2012), Biulleten' Verkhovnogo Suda Rossiyskoy Federatsii, Vol. 12, 2012).

In Germany, judicial authorization is required to use undercover officers to target a particular suspect, or when the covert operative intends to enter a private dwelling (§ 110b(2) CCP-Germany). In Denmark, as well, judicial authorization is required, and the court must be satisfied that: (1) the police have a well-corroborated basis for suspecting that a particular crime is presently being committed or that it will be committed; (2) other means of investigation are inadequate to advance the investigation (principle of subsidiarity); and (3) the suspected crime carries a maximum prison term of more than six years or is a second drug offense (principle of proportionality) (Slobogin, 2012: 515).

Unfortunately, the SITs laws of several post-Soviet republics are still unclear as to when judicial authorization is needed to conduct a SIT which impacts on human rights protected either under the constitution or international treaties, even where their CCPs more clearly lay this out. This could leave a loophole for police to exploit in conducting secret surveillance or interception of conversations without judicial authorization or sufficient probable cause.

The existence of separate laws for national security, terrorism or organized crime investigations, which, under the rubric of 'prevention' as opposed to criminal enforcement, allow wiretaps and other intrusions of privacy without judicial authorization are not limited to the post-Soviet space. In Italy, for instance, the prosecutor may conduct a wiretap for up to 40 days without judicial authorization (the CCP only allows wiretapping for 15 days with judicial approval) if it is 'necessary to acquire information concerning the prevention of [certain serious] crimes' (the CCP requires 'grave indicia of crime' for a wiretap, on the other hand) (Art. 226(1-2) Transitional Provisions, CCP-Italy). The U.S. Foreign Intelligence Surveillance Act also allows for wiretaps and secret searches of foreign agents and suspected foreign terrorists without judicial authorization for long periods (50 U.S.C. § 1802(a)(1)).

But how do the Laws on SITs of the twelve post-Soviet republics comport with other requirements laid down by the ECtHR and other international bodies in relation to secret investigation activities? We will examine the principle of proportionality to the extent that it limits use of these methods to the investigation of serious crimes, and only when the information cannot be gathered using less-intrusive means. Thereafter we will discuss whether a heightened level of suspicion is required before these intrusive measures may be employed and temporal limitations placed on their implementation.

3.3   The Principle of Proportionality: Seriousness of Suspected Crime and Last Resort

3.3.1   Wiretapping and other serious intrusions into privacy only in relation to serious crimes

The ECtHR noted that Article 6 Law on SITS-Moldova (2007) permitted use of SITS in the investigation of 'serious, very serious and especially serious crimes', and noted that this constituted nearly 59 percent of all the crimes in the Moldovan criminal code (para. 14 *Iordachi v. Moldova*). This rendered the law too imprecise to comport with Art. 8 ECHR (para. 44 *Iordachi v. Moldova*). The ECtHR further held that the Moldovan wiretap SIT was also deficient because it does 'not elaborate on the degree of reasonableness of the suspicion against a person for the purpose of authorising an interception' (para. 52 *Iordachi v. Moldova*).

The Russian law is even broader, allowing for wiretaps and investigative experiments in cases involving crimes of 'average, great or exceptional gravity' (Art. 8 Law on SITs-Russia (1995)). Art. 9 of the Law on SITs-Kyrgyzstan imposes similar limits. The Law on SITs-Armenia was found deficient by the ECtHR, among other things, while it contained no limitation of any kind for the types of crime subject to wiretapping (*Sefilyan v. Armenia*, No. 22491/08, ECHR, 2 Oct. 2012, para. 130).

In comparison, German legislation, for example, limits wiretaps to the investigation of a catalogue of serious offenses, such as murder, high treason, extortion, arson, drug offenses and money laundering (Art. 100a(2) CCP-Germany). In some countries, however, the catalogues of specific offenses for which a wiretap can be sought can be quite lengthy. This is true in the U.S. wiretap law (18 U.S.C. § 2516(1, 2)) as well as in the SITs section of Croatia's code (Art. 334 CCP-Croatia).

3.3.2 A showing that less intrusive methods have not been, or will not be successful

The prosecutor in both the U.S. (18 U.S. Code § 2518(1)(b)) and Canadian (s. 186(1)(2) CC-Canada) law must show why alternative less intrusive methods have not been tried, or would be unlikely to be successful or would be impractical before a wiretap order will be issued by the judge. Although Art. 333 CCP-Croatia clearly requires that SITs can only be employed 'if the investigation cannot be carried out in any other way or would be accompanied by great difficulties', and most European countries also require a similar showing of necessity, the Laws on SITs of the twelve post-Soviet republics are largely silent on this issue. An exception can perhaps be seen in the language of Art. 246(2) CCP-Ukraine which allows SITs only 'if information on the criminal offense and its perpetrator cannot be found otherwise'.

3.4 Level of Suspicion Needed to Approve a SIT

The ECtHR noted that Armenia's law not only did not 'specify the circumstances in which, or the grounds on which, such a measure could be ordered', but it added that 'the lack of such details was capable of leading to particularly serious consequences, given that this measure could be authorized in the absence of any criminal proceedings' (*Sefilyan v. Armenia*, para. 130).

The Kyrgyz law, like the version of the Moldovan law before the ECtHR in *Iordachi* and the Armenian law in *Sefilyan*, also gives no indication of what level of suspicion is required before a SIT which impacts on the right to privacy may be authorized. The law only states that 'SITs involving legally protected confidentiality of correspondence, telephone and other conversations', etc. 'are only permitted to collect information about individuals who are preparing or attempting to commit grave and especially grave crimes or have committed grave and especially grave crimes'.

The U.S. wiretap statute uses the language of the Fourth Amendment in requiring 'probable cause' that a serious crime has been committed, or is in the process of being committed, and that the measure will evidence going to prove the commission of such a crime. Thus, there is no difference between the suspicion needed to authorize the search of a dwelling or car, as opposed to a wiretap. Article 266 CCP-Italy requires a higher standard, 'grave indicia', than it does for a normal search, where Article 247 CCP-Italy requires 'reasonable grounds' (*fondato motivo*) (Thaman, 2008a: 64–65). Swedish law requires the showing of 'substantial grounds' to suspect a person of criminal activity (ch. 27, Art. 20 CCP-Sweden). Article 332 CCP-Croatia requires 'grounds for suspicion' for the imposition of SITs.

The wiretap statutes of Germany, France and Spain, however, also use vague formulations like those in the post-Soviet SITs statutes. In France wiretaps may be issued by the investigating magistrate 'when the necessities of the investigation require it' (Art. 100(para.1) CCP-France). Germany requires only a 'suspicion' (Art. 100a(para.1) and in Spain it only has to be shown that evidence of an 'important fact or circumstance in the case' can be discovered through the measure (Art. 579(1) CCP-Spain) (Thaman, 2008a: 65).

3.5   Length of Time Allowed for SITs

The ECtHR has found violations of Art. 8 ECHR in post-Soviet statutes for allowing use of SITs for up to six months with additional extensions (Art. 45 *Iordachi v. Moldova*; Art. 131 *Sefilyan v. Armenia*). Article 9 Law on SITs-Russia also allows SITs to run for up to six months, with the possibility of extension. The same is true for the Kyrgyz law. The SITs provision of the new Ukrainian CCP, however, limits their implementation to a maximum time of two months, with the possibility of extension (Art. 249(1) CCP-Ukraine) and wiretaps may only be authorized for up to 30 days according to Art. 135(4) CCP-Moldova.

The period of validity of a judge-ordered wiretap is, in comparison, up to 15 days in Italy, up to 30 days in Sweden (ch. 17, Art. 21 CCP-Sweden) and the U.S., up to 60 days in Canada (s. 196 CC-Canada), up to 90 days in Germany and Spain, and up to 120 days in France (Thaman, 2008a: 66; United Nations Office on Drugs and Crime, 2014: 36). Of course, the period of, say, a wiretap, can be extended upon a renewed petition to the judge in all of these countries.

3.6   Judicial Control of Implementation

The ECtHR in its settled case law has also required that serious intrusions into the right to privacy protected by Art. 8 ECHR be subjected to adequate judicial review in their execution, finding the Armenian provisions on wiretapping to be in violation due to the complete absence of any such provisions (para. 132 *Sefilyan v. Armenia*). The post-Soviet laws are still generally deficient in this area.

4. CONCLUSION

Since the collapse of the Soviet Union in 1991, the theretofore secret, unregulated and oppressive use of SITs has given way to their legislative regulation in both Laws on SITs and gradually in CCPs as well. The trend is clearly to require judicial authorization for the SITs which seriously impact on the right to privacy, such as wiretapping, bugging and interception of electronic communications and gradually to incorporate more precise regulations of SITs in the CCPs.

The Soviet inheritance of a strong prosecutor's office, the *prokuratura*, served to block and slow down the introduction of judicial authorization in this area, and the legislation of some of the former Soviet Asian republics, and Belarus, which is not a member of the Council of Europe, still follow the Soviet model in which the *prokuror* performs what should normally be judicial functions.

The influence of the ECtHR on the European former Soviet republics, as well as significant influence from the United Nations, the Organization for Security and Cooperation in Europe and from European and North American technical assistance programs has also helped along reforms in some of the non-European countries.

There is also a demonstrable trend towards incorporation of the regulation of SITs into CCPs, either through references to the separate statutes in the CCPs or through an incorporation of a list of SITs in the CCP itself. Through this process, the use of SITs will be considered as normal 'criminal procedure' aimed at solving or preventing crimes, whether or not a formal criminal investigation has been initiated in relation to the person, or crime subject to the SITs measure. This should lead to a more transparent legal framework and the avoidance of confusion created by different standards in the Law on SITs and the CCP. It will also help to delineate between procedures aimed at criminal law enforcement and those aimed solely at gathering intelligence for larger national security purposes.

Finally, one must ask whether technically improved provisions for SITs, whether found in separate laws or in the CCP, will really stem the arbitrary use of secret investigative measures in these formerly totalitarian lands. Although torture and other coercive methods of interrogation have never been permitted in the codes of the post-Soviet republics, there is solid evidence that these practices are still used (Thaman, 2008b: 102; Kovalev, 2010: 154-158).

Since professional judges actually assumed responsibility for ordering pretrial detention in Russia in 2002, judges have ordered it in larger proportions than prosecutors did before the changes. From 2005 through 2007, Moldovan judges approved of anywhere from 97.93 percent to 99.24 percent of all requests for a wiretap – a figure that clearly unsettled the ECtHR (Art. 13, 51 *Iordachi v. Moldova*). Will post-Soviet judges, not known for their independence from political pressures, become compliant rubber-stamps for prosecutorial requests for SITs? Whatever the answer to this question, it must be noted here that U.S. federal and state courts from 1968 through 2011 issued 99.98 percent of all wiretap requests.[9]

But let us assume the worst, that is, that post-Soviet officials will circumvent the strict requirements imposed by the ECtHR and international law and engage in secret wiretapping or other SITs which impact on privacy without getting a judge's approval, or, say, without probable cause. What will be the consequence? Unfortunately, the ECtHR, while it has found the wiretap legislation of numerous member states, including several post-Soviet republics, to violate Art. 8 ECHR, it has never found a violation of the Art. 6 ECHR right to a fair trial when the evidence gathered in the illegal wiretap or bugging was used to convict its victim, much less the victim of any violation of the right to privacy (Ölçer, 2013: 394–396). One of the most egregious cases was from England and Wales, where the police had secretly bugged the petitioner's house without judicial authorization, in fact, without there even having been a statute regulating such practices. The recording was the only evidence of guilt in the case. The ECtHR, of course, found a violation of Art. 8 ECHR, but held that the issue of exclusion of the evidence was left to national law. No violation of Art. 6 ECHR was found (*Khan v. United Kingdom*, no. 35394/97, ECHR, 12 May 2000, Art. 35-40).

The most effective way to make sure that the increased protections of the right to privacy in the implementation of SITs become reality, is to prevent use of evidence gathered in blatant disregard of the law. Unfortunately, Western European law, perhaps with the exception of Spain, is woefully inadequate in this respect, especially when it comes to use of evidence derived from illegal wiretaps, in that the concept of 'fruit of the poisonous tree' has largely not been recognized. England and Wales has virtually never suppressed physical evidence no matter how egregious the human rights violation which led to its discovery, as long as it is otherwise reliable and relevant. Italian courts never suppress what they call the *corpus delicti* of an offense (contraband, fruits, instrumentalities of crime), even if it is gathered by a patently unconstitutional search or wiretap. The German balancing approach to exclusion also seldom leads to exclusion of physical evidence gathered in violation of the right to privacy (Thaman, 2013: 433–436).

Unlike the legislation in most Western European states, the U.S. wiretap law expressly applies to the 'fruits of the poisonous tree' (18 U.S.C. § 2515). Spain's statutory exclusionary rule also expressly extends to derivative evidence (Art. 11.01 Law on the Judicial Power-Spain).

Russia was also a pioneer, in this respect, when in Art. 50(2) Const.-Russia it recognized as a constitutional rule that evidence gathered in violation of the constitution or federal law was inadmissible in a criminal prosecution. Many of the post-Soviet constitutions followed suit, including those of Azerbaijan, Belarus, Georgia and Kazakhstan. Strong exclusionary rules using similar language can also be found in the CCPs of Russia (Art. 75(1) CCP), as well as in Belarus (Art. 105(4-5) CCP and Kyrgyzstan (Art. 6(3) CCP). Art. 72(1) CCP-Georgia even extends exclusion to the fruits of substantive violations of the provisions of the code. Armenia, Azerbaijan, Moldova and Turkmenistan, however, have limited their exclusionary rules to evidence which, due to the violation, is deemed to be untrustworthy (therefore limiting them in practice to improperly induced confessions) (Thaman, 2013: 438–439).

For the citizenry of the post-Soviet republics, use of SITs with inadequate safeguards will remain a concern, much as their use remains a concern in the U.S. and other countries with massive secret information-gathering practices. Rubber-stamp judges and toothless exclusionary rules will also be hindrances to charged criminal defendants when they attempt to show that SITs were illegally used against them.

But the ECtHR, while weak in its jurisprudence on exclusionary rules in relation to privacy violations, has given *uncharged* citizens the tools to challenge the use of SITs, even when they do not know for sure whether they have been the target of a secret information-gathering measure. Thus, the petitioners in *Iordachi v. Moldova* were lawyers in an organization called 'Lawyers for Human Rights' who successfully convinced the ECtHR that they had standing to challenge the law, even though they could not prove they had been wiretapped. The court held that the

[the] mere existence of the legislation entails, for all those who might fall within its reach, a menace of surveillance; this menace necessarily strikes at

freedom of communication between users of the postal and telecommunications services and thereby constitutes an 'interference by a public authority' with the exercise of the applicants' right to respect for correspondence. (Art. 7-10, 34)

A Bulgarian human rights group had earlier challenged a 1997 law dealing with 'special means of surveillance' and had prevailed on the same basis (*Association for European Integration and Human Rights and Ekimdzhiev v. Bulgaria*, No. 62540/00, ECHR 28 June 2007, Art. 5-8, 93). Potential victims of the National Security Agency's arguably unconstitutional widespread information-gathering practices have, in contrast, been denied any remedy by the U.S. Supreme Court unless they can show they *have* been victims of the secret dragnet (*Clapper v. Amnesty International*, 133 S.Ct. 1138 (2013)).

NOTES

1. Until recently, these twelve states were either members, participating states or associate states of the Commonwealth of Independent States (CIS). We will not deal with the three Baltic former Soviet republics, Estonia, Latvia and Lithuania, which have become members of the European Union.
2. The term 'special investigative (investigation) techniques' has been used recently by the Council of Europe (Council of Europe, 2005).
3. The chapter by Jacqueline Ross in this book compares the U.S. and German approaches to dealing with the intersection between information-gathering in the interests of national security and criminal investigations.
4. The U.S. Supreme Court held that warrantless wiretapping violated the Fourth Amendment in *Katz v. United States*, 389 U.S. 347 (1967). The Federal Wiretap Statute was promulgated a year later in 1968. On the wide use of secret illegal unregulated wiretapping theretofore, see Freiwald (2004: 10).
5. When it comes to long-term surveillance by GPS or cell-site location, some countries, like Germany, require judicial authorization. §§ 100i, 101 CCP-Germany.
6. On 'envelope information', whether addresses on letters or packages, or telephone numbers called or websites visited, see Kerr (2010: 1019). Judicial authorization is required to collect telecommunications metadata in Italy and Germany for instance, see Thaman (2008b: 69–70).
7. Article 332 CCP-Croatia (2009) also includes a very similar list to that in the CCP-Ukraine, although it also includes the tracking of individuals in public spaces. Judicial authorization is, of course, required. See Art. 336 CCP-Croatia.
8. Gruziia on-line. 'Ombudsmen prosit KC priznat' nezakonnymi otdel'nye polozheniia zakona 'Ob operativno-rozysknoj deiatel'nosti'', available at http://www.apsny.ge/2014/pol/1401486307.php. The Law on SITs with changes up to August 18, 2014, still does not require judicial authorization. Presumably, it will be amended to conform with the constitution and CCP.
9. http://epic.org/privacy/wiretap/stats/wiretap_stats.html.

BIBLIOGRAPHY

Literature

Aleksandrov, A.I. and A.V. Fedorov. 1999. 'Model'nyi zakon "Ob operativno-rozysknoi deiatel'nosti dlia gosudarstv – uchastnikov SNG', *Pravovedenie* 1: 173–180.

Council of Europe. 2005. *Terrorism: Special Investigation Techniques*. Strasbourg: Council of Europe Publishing.

Freiwald, Susan. 2004. 'Online Surveillance: Remembering the Lessons of the Wiretap Act', 56 *Alabama Law Review* 9–84.

Kerr, Orin S. 2010. 'Applying the Fourth Amendment to the Internet: A General Approach', (2010) 62 *Stanford Law Review* 1005–1049.

Kovalev, Nikolai. 2010. *Criminal Justice Reform in Russia, Ukraine and the Former Republics of the Soviet Union*. Lewiston, NY: Edwin Mellen Press.

Ölçer, F. Pinar, 2013. 'The European Court of Human Rights: The Fair Trial Analysis Under Article 6 of the European Convention of Human Rights', in Stephen C. Thaman, ed., *Exclusionary Rules in Comparative Law*. Dordrecht, Heidelberg, New York, London: Springer.

Slobogin, Christopher. 2012. *Criminal Procedure: Regulation of Police Investigation: Legal, Historical, Empirical and Comparative Materials* (5th edn). New Providence, NJ: LexisNexis.

Sysalov, M.P. 2006. *Osnovy operativno-rozysknoi deiatel'nosti*: Almaty: Iuridicheskaia Literatura.

Thaman, Stephen C. 2002, 'Comparative Criminal Enforcement: Russia', in Joshua C. Dressler, eds., *Encyclopedia of Crime and Justice*. New York: Macmillan Reference, Vol. 1. 207–218.

Thaman, Stephen C. 2007. 'The Nullification of the Russian Jury: Lessons for Jury-Inspired Reforms in Eurasia and Beyond', 40 *Cornell International Law Journal* 357–428.

Thaman, Stephen C. 2008a. *Comparative Criminal Procedure: A Casebook Approach* (2nd edn). Durham, NC: Carolina Academic Press.

Thaman, Stephen C. 2008b. 'The Two Faces of Justice in the Post-Soviet Legal Sphere: Adversarial Procedure, Jury Trial, Plea Bargaining and the Inquisitorial Legacy', in John Jackson, Máximo Langer and Peter Tillers, eds., *Crime, Procedure and Evidence in a Comparative and International Context: Essays in Honour of Professor Mirjan Damaška*. Oxford: Hart Publishing, 99–118.

Thaman, Stephen C. 2013. 'Balancing Truth Against Human Rights: A Theory of Modern Exclusionary Rules', in Stephen C. Thaman, ed., *Exclusionary Rules in Comparative Law*. Dordrecht, Heidelberg, New York, London: Springer.

United Nations Office on Drugs and Crime. 2014. *Analysis of the Legislation of the Kyrgyz Republic on Special Investigative Measures*. Analytical report prepared by Nikolai Kovalev. Bishkek: UNODC.

Vazhenin V.V. and S.M. Lugovich. 2014, 'Nekotorye aspekty regulirovaniia pravovogo statusa dolzhnostnogo litsa, osushchestvliaiushchego operativno-rozysknuiu deiatel'nost', po zakonodatel'stvu stran dal'nego zarubezh'ia', *Obshchestvo i Pravo* 4(50): 216.

Zharov, S.N. 2010. Operativno-rozysknaia deiatel'nost' v Rossii: organizatsiia, metody, pravovoe regulirovanie (istoriko-iuridicheskoe issledovanie). Dissertatsiia na soiskanie uchenoi stepeni doktora iuridicheskikh nauk. Ekaterinburg: Ural'skaia gosudarstvennaia iuridicheskaia akademiia. Unpublished dissertation (on file with authors).

Zharov S.N. and N.S. Sprishevskii. 2012. 'O sozdanii sistemy pravovogo regulirovania politicheskogo i ugolovnogo syska Rossii v XIX-nachale XX vekov', *Vestnik IUUrGU* 20: 9–12.

Legal Norms

Laws on SITs

Federal'nyi Zakon 'Ob operativno-rozysknoi deiatel'nosti' ot 12 avgusta 1995 g. No. 144-FZ (Law on SITs-Russia (1995)).

Model'nyi Zakon 'Ob operativno-rozysknoi deiatel'nosti' (novaia redaktsiia) adopted by Resolution of the Interparliamentary Assembly of the CIS member states No. 27-6, 16 November 2006 (Model Law on SITs-CIS (2006)).

Model'nyi Zakon SNG 'Ob operativno-rozysknoi deiatel'nosti' adopted by Resolution of the Interparliamentary Assembly of CIS member states No. 10-12, 6 December 1997 (Model Law on SITS-CIS (1997)).

Zakon Azerbaidzhanskoi Respubliki 'Ob operativno-rozysknoi deiatel'nosti' ot 28 oktiabria 1999 g. No. 728-IG (Law on SITs-Azerbaijan).

Zakon Gruzii 'Ob operativno-rozysknoi deiatel'nosti' ot 30 aprelia 1999 g. No. 1933-IIs (Law on SITs-Georgia).

Zakon Kyrgyzskoi Respubliki 'Ob operativno-rozysknoi deitel'nosti' ot 16 oktiabria 1998 g. No. 131 (Law on SITs-Kyrgyzstan).

Zakon Ob operativno-rozysknoi deitel'nosti v Rossiiskoi Federatsii ot 13 marta 1992 g. No. 2506-1 (Law on SITs-Russia (1992)).

Zakon Respubliki Belarus ot 12 noiabria 1992 g. 'Ob operativno-rozysknoi deiatel'nosti' (Law on SITs-Belarus (1992)).

Zakon Respubliki Belarus 'Ob operativno-rozysknoi deiatel'nosti' ot 9 iiulia 1999 g. No. 289-3 (Law on SITs-Belarus (1999)).

Zakon Respubliki Kazakhstan 'Ob operativno-rozysknoi deiatel'nosti' ot 15 sentiabria 1994 g. No. 154-XIII (Law on SITs-Kazakhstan).

Zakon Respubliki Moldova 'Ob operativno-rozysknoi deiatel'nosti' ot 12 aprelia 1994 g. No. 45-XIII (Law on SITs-Moldova (1994)).

Zakon Respubliki Moldova 'O spetsial'noi rozysknoi deiatel'nosti' ot 29 marta 2012 No. 59 (Law on SITS-Moldova (2012)).

Zakon Respubliki Tajikistan 'Ob operativno-rozysknoi deiatel'nosti v Respublike Tajikistan' ot 28 dekabria 1993 g. (Law on SITs-Tajikistan (1993)).

Zakon Respubliki Tajikistan 'Ob operativno-rozysknoi deiatel'nosti' ot 23 maia 1998 g. No. 651 (Law on SITs-Tajikistan (1998)).

Zakon Respubliki Tajikistan 'Ob operativno-rozysknoi deiatel'nosti' ot 25 marta 2011 g. No. 687 (Law on SITs-Tajikistan (2011)).

Zakon Respubliki Uzbekistan 'Ob operativno-rozysknoi deiatel'nosti' ot 25 dekabria 2012 g. No. ZRU-344 (Law on SITs-Uzbekistan).

Zakon Turkmenistana 'Ob operativno-rozysknoi deiatel'nosti' ot 23 sentiabria 1994 g. No. 965-XII (Law on SITs-Turkmenistan).

Zakon Ukrainy 'Pro operativno-rozshukovu diial'nist'' 18 liutogo 1992 g. No. 2135-XII (Law on SITs-Ukraine).

Codes of Criminal Procedure

Criminal Code of Canada (CC-Canada) available at http://laws-lois.justice.gc.ca/eng/acts/C-46/FullText.html.

Croatian Criminal Procedure Code (Zakon o kaznennom postupku). 2009. NN 152/08; NN 76/09, available at https://www.google.de/?gws_rd=ssl#q=croatian+code+of+criminal+procedure (CCP-Croatia).

Swedish Code of Judicial Procedure, available at http://www.government.se/contentassets/a1be9e99a5c64d1bb93a96ce5d517e9c/the-swedish-code-of-judicial-procedure-ds-1998_65.pdf (CCP-Sweden).

Ugolovno-protsessual'nyy Kodeks Armenii. July 1, 1998, with amendments through June 19, 2015, available at http://www.parliament.am/legislation.php?sel=show&ID=1450&lang=rus (CCP-Armenia).

Ugolovno-protsessual'nyy Kodeks Azerbaydzhanskoy Respubliki. July 14, 2000. No. 907-IG. Amendments through Oct. 3, 2002, available at https://www.unodc.org/tldb/pdf/Azerbaijan_Code_of_Criminal_Procedure_in_Russian_Full_text.pdf (CCP-Azerbaijan).

Ugolovno-protsessual'nyy Kodeks Gruzii. Oct. 9, 2009. No. 1772-IIc. available at http://pravo.org.ua/files/Criminal%20justice/_-09_10_2009.pdf (CCP-Georgia).

'Ugolovno-protsessual'nyy Kodeks Kyrgyzskoy Respubliki'. 2010, in *Sbornik Ugolovno-protsessual'nykh kodeksov stran central'noy azii*. Almaty: OSCE-ODIHR, 301–486 (CCP-Kyrgyzstan).

Ugolovno-protsessual'nyy Kodeks Respubliki Belarus'. July 16, 1999. No. 295-3. With amendments through July 15, 2015, available at http://www.pravo.by/world_of_law/text.asp?RN=hk9900295 (CCP-Belarus).

'Ugolovno-protsessual'nyy Kodeks Respubliki Kazakhstan'. 2010, in *Sbornik Ugolovno-protsessual'nykh kodeksov stran central'noy azii*. Almaty: OSCE-ODIHR, 4-300 (CCP-Kazakhstan).

Ugolovno-protsessual'nyy Kodeks Respubliki Moldova. Published June 7, 2003. Monitorul Official No. 104-10. With amendments through Aug. 12, 2005, available at http://lex.justice.md/viewdoc.php?action=view&view=doc&id=326970&lang=2 (CCP-Moldova).

'Ugolovno-protsesual'nyy Kodeks Respubliki Tadzhikistan'. 2010, in *Sbornik Ugolovno-protsessual'nykh kodeksov stran central'noy azii*. Almaty: OSCE-ODIHR, 487–657 (CCP-Tajikistan).

'Ugolovno-protsessual'nyy Kodeks Respubliki Uzbekistan'. 2010, in *Sbornik Ugolovno-protsessual'nykh kodeksov stran central'noy azii*. Almaty: OSCE-ODIHR, 870–1080 (CCP-Uzbekistan).

Ugolovno-protsessual'nyy Kodeks Rossiyskoy Federatsii. 2014. Moscow: Omega-L. (CCP-Russia).

'Ugolovno-protsessual'nyy Kodeks Turkmenistana'. 2010 in *Sbornik Ugolovno-protsessual'nykh kodeksov stran central'noy azii*. Almaty: OSCE-ODIHR, 658–869 (CCP-Turkmenistan).

Ugolovno-protsessual'nyy Kodeks Ukraini. April 13, 2012, available at http://www.iuaj.net/node/1099 (CCP-Ukraine).

Constitutions

Constitution of Georgia. Aug. 24, 1995, amendments through Dec. 27, 2006, available at http://www.parliament.ge/files/68_1944_951190_CONSTIT_27_12.06.pdf (Const.-Georgia).

Konstitutsiia Azerbaydzhanskoy Respubliki. Nov. 12, 1995, with amendments through Sept. 19, 2002, available at http://ru.president.az/azerbaijan/constitution (Const.-Azerbaijan).

Konstitutsiia Respubliki Armenii. July 5, 1995, with amendments, available at http://www.parliament.am/parliament.php?id=constitution&lang=rus (Const.-Armenia).

Konstitutsiia Respubliki Belarus'. 1994. With amendments from Nov. 24, 1996 and Oct. 17, 2004, available at http://www.pravo.by/main.aspx?guid=6351 (Const.-Belarus).

Konstitutsiia Respubliki Kazakhstan. Aug. 30, 1995, with amendments through Feb. 2, 2011, available at http://www.constitution.kz/ (Const.-Kazakhstan).

Konstitutsiia Kyrgyzskoy Respubliki. June 27, 2010, available at http://base.spinform.ru/show_doc.fwx?rgn=31497 (CCP-Kyrgyzstan).

Konstitutsiia Respubliki Moldova. July 29, 1994, with amendments through July 19, 1996, available at http://lex.justice.md/viewdoc.php?id=311496&lang=2 (Const.-Moldova).

Konstitutsiia Respubliki Tadzhikistan. Nov. 6, 1994, with amendments through June 22, 2003, available at http://www.prezident.tj/ru/taxonomy/term/5/112 (Const.-Tajikistan).

Konstitutsiia Respubliki Uzbekistan. Dec. 15, 1992, with amendments through 2008, available at http://www.lex.uz/pages/getact.aspx?lact_id=35869.

Konstitutsiia Rossiyskoy Federatsii. Dec. 12, 1993, available at http://www.constitution.ru/ (Const.-Russia).

Konstitutsiia Turkmenistana. May 18, 1992 with amendments through Dec. 27, 1995, available at http://www.parliament.am/library/sahmanadrutyunner/turqmenistan.pdf.

Konstitutsiia Ukraini. June 28, 1996, with amendments through May 15, 2014, available at http://meget.kiev.ua/zakon/konstitutsia-ukraini/ (Const.-Ukraine).

Strafprozessordnung. Reissued Sept. 12, 1950, amendments through July 27, 2015, available at http://www.gesetze-im-internet.de/bundesrecht/stpo/gesamt.pdf.

Other normative Acts

UN Human Rights Committee, General Comment No. 16, available at http://ccprcentre.org/doc/ICCPR/General%20Comments/HRI.GEN.1.Rev.9%28Vol.I%29_%28GC16%29_en.pdf.

14. The emergence of foreign intelligence investigations as alternatives to the criminal process: a view of American counterterrorism surveillance through German lenses

Jacqueline E. Ross

1. INTRODUCTION

In the United States, as in Germany, efforts to counter terrorist threats make use of the government's intelligence-gathering powers alongside the criminal process. But the division of labor between the two differs across legal systems. Germany, unlike the United States, differentiates such powers according to whether they implicate the preventive or reactive prerogatives of the state. In contrast to the United States, Germany strictly separates intelligence operations from criminal investigations by assigning the former exclusively to its intelligence services and the latter exclusively to its state and federal police agencies. This division is constitutionally mandated by the principle of separation, which has been a cornerstone of Germany's post-war security architecture. In order to prevent dangerous concentrations of power in its executive branches, Germany's post-war constitutional design prohibits intelligence agencies from conducting interrogations, making arrests, or exercising other coercive powers, while the police may not gather or analyze intelligence outside the confines of their mandate to prevent and prosecute crimes.

A further distinction between the 'preventive' and 'repressive' prerogatives of the police themselves derives from constitutional norms that require judicial and prosecutorial oversight of police investigations that are used to generate evidence for criminal prosecutions and thus to justify deprivations of liberty through use of criminal sanctions. Germany's federal Code of Criminal Procedure defines the scope of the so-called 'repressive' authority of the police to investigate past or ongoing crimes, while the individual states' police laws define their 'preventive' prerogatives to anticipate and prevent future offenses.

This institutional division of labor translates into a temporal division of investigative prerogatives such that German intelligence services are assigned to the investigation of inchoate threats, while the police are responsible for intervening at later stages, when extremist discourse ripens into criminal plots. 'Preventive' prerogatives govern what the police may do to protect the public from harm once inchoate threats have ripened into the planning stages of a criminal offense, while 'repressive' powers govern the powers of the police to disrupt and prove offenses that have either been completed or that have at least reached the stage of a criminal attempt.

This temporal allocation of investigative responsibilities applies with equal force to terrorist plots and to ordinary criminal acts. Though German intelligence agencies focus on a narrower band of security concerns, such as espionage, terrorism, and political extremism, they have, in the past, been asked to monitor forms of criminal activity, such as organized crime, that are not ideologically motivated, but that were deemed sufficiently systemic and sufficiently successful at infiltrating public institutions to pose a threat to the 'democratic constitutional order' of the state. This potential area of overlap with police work made the temporal division of labor –based on the imminence of a security threat – a matter of continuing practical as well as theoretical relevance to the ways in which the respective responsibilities of police and intelligence agencies are demarcated from each other.

In the domain of police work, too, increased reliance on proactive investigative methods to fight organized crime, drug trafficking, cyber-crime, and terrorism have made the distinction between the public safety prerogatives of the police and their crime-fighting powers politically salient and highly contested. The legislatures of the 16 German *Laender* have enacted – and sometimes rejected – police laws that increasingly allow the police to anticipate future offenses using many of the same covert surveillance tactics in their purely preventive capacity that the federal Code of Criminal Procedure once reserved exclusively for criminal investigations of past and ongoing criminal activity. German regulation of counterterrorism investigations accords with the regulation of other types of investigations insofar as the prerogatives of investigators depend on the imminence of the perceived threat, with early-stage forms of surveillance seen as paving the way for an eventual prosecution, while, I will argue, American regulation of counterterrorism surveillance allows the government's surveillance prerogatives to turn on the government's willingness to bypass the criminal process altogether. I propose to view the temporal orientation of German security governance as a contrast case that highlights the distinctive way in which American security governance demarcates the investigation of terrorism from the regular criminal process. I will argue that these distinct national approaches shape the very different tolerance of the German and American legal systems for the collection and aggregation of bulk personal data, and that the American approach has led to the emergence of a new surveillance paradigm, and a two-track system of surveillance regulation, that the German regulatory approach disfavors.

In the United States, the temporal distance or proximity of national security threats plays no comparable regulatory role in distinguishing the prerogatives of intelligence agencies from those of the police. Instead, the division of labor between intelligence and law enforcement prerogatives tracks the limits of Fourth Amendment protections for privacy. Foreign intelligence investigations are subject to fewer Fourth Amendment strictures than regular criminal investigations. As a result, recent American efforts to develop new investigative and legal tools to fight terrorism have expanded the domain of foreign intelligence investigations to cover a great deal of surveillance and intelligence-gathering that was once regulated through ordinary criminal procedure. In the process, the United States has developed a new surveillance paradigm that de-emphasizes advance judicial approval based on individualized thresholds of suspicion in favor of executive self-regulation and *ex post facto* administrative controls such as reporting requirements and administrative audits. The new paradigm centers on the aggregation of large amounts of personal data, which provides new opportunities for predictive analysis of threats, but which also intensifies concerns about the over-collection of private data about innocent persons and about the reduction of judicial oversight over the collection and use of this data.

Section 2 of this chapter will contrast the regulatory paradigms by which Germany and the United States distinguish between intelligence-gathering and law enforcement prerogatives for the investigation of terrorism. Section 3 will identify five ways in which American efforts to counter terrorism seek to avoid statutory and constitutional constraints on the use of surveillance and the collection of personal data, and the effect that these trends have had in reducing judicial, congressional, and even executive oversight over government surveillance programs. Section 4 will describe the emergence of the new surveillance paradigm and its roles in encouraging new forms of predictive analysis both in the fight against terrorism and in other law-enforcement contexts. Section 5 will discuss some of the resulting concerns about over-collection of personal data. Section 6 explores the ways in which Germany's privacy protections and its use of time horizons to structure investigative prerogatives disfavor both the collection and aggregation of bulk data about persons not suspected of criminal offenses and the use of intelligence operations to circumvent constraints on the criminal process. As I will argue in conclusion, the new American surveillance paradigm calls for the creation of new regulatory mechanisms to monitor the use to which the growing volume of personal data can be put, and to provide new safeguards when such data feed into criminal and administrative processes that must make potentially momentous individualized findings on a reasoned, transparent, and case-by-case basis.

2. DIFFERENTIATING PREVENTIVE POLICING FROM LAW ENFORCEMENT: A CONTRAST BETWEEN AMERICAN AND GERMAN APPROACHES

In the United States, national security investigations take place in three separate investigative domains. The first of these is the ordinary domain of criminal investigations, targeting terrorism offenses. These must abide by Fourth Amendment constraints on searches and seizures, and by Congressional legislation that imposes significant constraints on electronic surveillance, the pursuit of bank records, and other investigative tactics that impinge on the privacy of personal data. Domestic intelligence operations occupy a second investigative sphere, in which litigation, consent decrees, and internal agency guidelines seek to take account of First Amendment concerns about police and FBI efforts to infiltrate mosques, civic groups, charities, and other political and religious organizations. Foreign counter-intelligence operations make up the third and fastest growing investigative sector. Because such investigations target foreign nationals and communications taking place at least partly on foreign soil (or between U.S. persons and foreign nationals), such operations are in many ways freed from Fourth Amendment constraints and, consequently, from external oversight, particularly by the judiciary.

This tripartite division of labor may puzzle German observers, who are used to distinguishing between terrorism-related investigations on the basis of an investigation's temporal relationship to the events under scrutiny. German criminal investigations are meant to illuminate past offenses, while preventive police investigations are supposed to anticipate and neutralize future threats to public safety (see for example, Dubber, 2007). German intelligence operations are said to intervene even earlier in the course of events, since they target extremist political groups, some of whose members the government fears may pose future risks to the democratic constitutional order. Government surveillance is meant to help intelligence agencies to identify the relevant players and threats *before* people and resources coalesce around particular unlawful projects.[1] Internal FBI regulations may pay lip-service to the temporal ordering of investigative stages, since FBI guidelines distinguish full-scale intelligence investigations from preliminary threat assessments, which permit FBI agents to pursue initial investigative leads before deciding whether to launch a full investigation. Nonetheless, the German distinction between 'preventive' (forward-looking) and so-called 'repressive' (backward-looking) operations is not very useful, in the American context, for distinguishing between ordinary criminal investigations and intelligence operations that concern themselves with threats to national security and with terrorism in particular.

There are two reasons for this. First, the structure of American criminal law makes it easy to charge inchoate crimes, permitting investigators to arrest plotters before criminal harms reach fruition. This permits the police to forestall many future offenses in the guise of punishing past infractions. Through possession offenses, conspiracy law, and statutes that prohibit 'material support' for terrorist organizations,[2] American criminal law makes it possible for police and federal agents to intervene at ever earlier stages of criminal plans. Second, and relatedly, American criminal law facilitates pretext prosecutions not only for inchoate offenses that threaten future harm but also for structuring,[3] money laundering,[4] false statement,[5] and non-reporting offenses[6] that enable police and federal agencies to charge provable second-order crimes in place of primary criminal conduct. Accordingly, prevention is no less the catchword for American criminal law and criminal investigations than it is for domestic intelligence or foreign counter-intelligence operations.

If German scholars distinguish terrorism operations from ordinary criminal investigations based on the timing of the government's intervention, this reflects institutional peculiarities of the German criminal process as well as separation of powers concerns that have no close American analogue. While a country-wide federal Code of Criminal Procedure governs the crime-solving, 'repressive' prerogatives of the police, state police laws regulate the preventive, public safety powers of the police that allow the police to conduct surveillance before a sufficient threshold of suspicion exists to justify similar action in their 'crime-solving' capacity (see Roewer, 1986). In addition, Germany's state and federal Agencies for the Protection of the Constitution ('*Verfassungs-schutz*') are responsible for domestic intelligence investigations of extremist political and religious groups; their tasks do not center on the investigation of criminal offenses, which remains the domain of the state and federal police.[7] Once latent risks turn into more immediate dangers, the police may investigate in their preventive capacity, until concrete evidence of a criminal offense allows the police to initiate a full-fledged criminal investigation. The so-called 'principle of separation' enforces this functional and institutional division by denying intelligence agencies coercive prerogatives (such as arrest powers), while prohibiting the police from gathering intelligence, as distinguished from evidence.[8] In the United States, by contrast, the FBI may pursue terrorist offenses either through regular criminal investigations, domestic intelligence operations, or foreign intelligence operations (even if some of these tasks are shared with state and local police, the National Security Agency, and other federal agencies).

Thus, American differentiation among anti-terrorism investigations does not reflect any fundamental divide between prevention and law enforcement or between the respective competencies of different institutional actors. The recent evolution of the three types of national security investigations does, however, reflect an executive determination to avoid constitutional, statutory, and administrative constraints on criminal investigations, such as those posed by the Fourth Amendment's Warrant Clause; by federal legislation regulating the use of electronic surveillance; and by internal undercover regulations of law enforcement agencies. Law enforcement agencies and intelligence services can avoid these constraints by conducting national security investigations under the less restrictive rules that govern foreign intelligence operations.

The principal reason why foreign intelligence operations can avoid the Fourth Amendment's Warrant Clause and its requirement of individualized showings of probable cause is that American courts have recognized an exception to that Clause modeled on the exception to the Warrant Clause for 'special needs' cases, that is, for cases in which government searches or seizures (in the form of random sobriety checkpoints, for example) serve some purpose beyond the routine enforcement of the criminal laws. The issue raised but ultimately reserved by *United States v. U.S. District Court (Keith)*[9] was 'whether the reasoning of the "special needs" cases[10] applies by analogy to justify a foreign intelligence exception to the warrant requirement for surveillance undertaken for national security purposes and directed at a foreign power or an agent of a foreign power reasonably believed to be located outside the United States'.[11] Federal courts eventually determined that it does.[12] The 'special needs' cases exempt the police from having to seek a warrant or demonstrate probable cause when the police act in their 'community caretaking' capacity rather than as enforcers of the criminal law.

But unlike the preventive powers of the German police, community caretaking powers are often unregulated by statute and need not be invoked prior to the initiation of a criminal investigation. Instead, this exception, which may apply to safety sweeps of a car or questioning of a suspect suspected of carrying a weapon, allows the police to opt out of Fourth Amendment or Fifth Amendment strictures temporarily, regardless of whether the police are already engaged in a criminal investigation. Application of the 'special needs' exception means that, although Congress has imposed a lesser warrant requirement for foreign intelligence operations (as further discussed below), the Supreme Court reads the Constitution to mandate no advance judicial authorization or showing of probable cause to suspect targets of criminal activity before the government may intercept electronic communications within the ambit of foreign intelligence operations. Thus, foreign intelligence interceptions escape constitutional and statutory constraints that apply to interceptions in the context of criminal investigations – even though foreign intelligence interceptions may capture the communications of many Americans alongside those of foreign powers or their agents. Foreign intelligence interceptions may be performed by the National Security Agency (NSA) or by federal agencies (like the FBI) that may act in either a law enforcement or intelligence capacity to investigate immediate dangers or reveal criminal offenses. They are not confined to early stage exploration of chatter about inchoate threats.

Under German law, by contrast, the police are prohibited from conducting intelligence operations and must initiate a criminal investigation as soon as their evidence reaches a sufficient threshold to trigger application of the principle of mandatory prosecution or investigation of a criminal offense. Once that occurs, the police may no longer resort to the state police laws that govern their preventive powers and may therefore not opt out of the procedural strictures and warrant requirements governing full-fledged criminal investigations.

Accordingly, what sets foreign intelligence investigations apart from criminal investigations is not their timing in relation to a risk or whether the investigators count as intelligence agents but the subject matter – terrorism – and the regulatory loophole created by the dearth of Fourth Amendment protections for 'special needs' operations.

3. HOW TERRORISM INVESTIGATIONS AVOID STATUTORY AND CONSTITUTIONAL WARRANT REQUIREMENTS

The Patriot Act increased the government's investigative powers in criminal cases, including those involving terrorism. Congress has amended the Federal Wiretap Statute, 18 U.S.C.S. § 2510 *et seq.*, to permit electronic surveillance of an expanded range of terrorism-related offenses[13] and ancillary crimes such as computer fraud.[14] The Patriot Act also simplified other investigative mechanisms by eliminating jurisdictional limitations on the issuance of pen registers and trap and trace orders (which disclose calls to and from particular telephones) and by permitting courts to issue nation-wide orders for telephone records, emails, and voicemails.[15] At the same time, however, American efforts to soften or avoid the strictures of ordinary criminal investigations are evident in five developments.

3.1 How Criminal Investigations Bypass the Statutory Warrant Requirement

Legal reforms have made it possible to conduct some types of surveillance through criminal procedure mechanisms that avoid the more cumbersome statutory warrant procedure. Amendments to the Omnibus Crime Control Act of 1968 (hereafter the 'Federal Wiretap Act')[16] removed the interception of voicemails that had been stored for more than 180 days from the category of 'electronic surveillance' to which the Act applies. A parallel amendment to 18 U.S.C. Section 2703 put these stored voicemails on a par with emails, which can now be obtained with ordinary search warrants. The change effectively bypassed the more exacting requirements of the federal wiretap statute.[17] Similarly, in Section 217, the Patriot Act authorizes the interception of computer communications[18] when the intercepted communications were those of computer trespassers (that is, hackers). Such interceptions were previously illegal unless authorized by a court order obtained pursuant to the federal wiretap statute.

These reforms are not specific to investigations of terrorism, however, and still invite the use of the criminal process, while allowing many forms of electronic surveillance to avoid the stringent requirements of the Federal Wiretap Act. At the same time, however, it has become easier for the executive branch to forego criminal investigations of terrorism in favor of foreign intelligence operations governed by the amended Foreign Intelligence Surveillance Act of 1978[19] (FISA), and to take greater advantage of the foreign intelligence exception to the Fourth Amendment's Warrant Clause.

3.2 How FISA Allows Investigators to Bypass the Criminal Process

FISA created special courts to review applications for warrants authorizing electronic surveillance of 'foreign powers and agents of foreign powers'. FISA's warrant procedure bypasses many of the constraints that the criminal process places on the government's electronic surveillance powers (such as the need to show probable cause to believe that the targets of surveillance are engaged in criminal activity and the need to show that less invasive tactics are not likely to suffice).

The Patriot Act expanded FISA powers, first, by amending FISA so that it now covers transnational terrorist investigations that have a domestic component. The amendments did this because terrorist acts 'transcending national boundaries' – the basis of FISA jurisdiction – now include conduct occurring in the United States as well as outside.[20] Second, the Patriot Act eliminated the requirement that obtaining foreign intelligence information be 'the [sole or primary] purpose' for the surveillance. The police may now bypass the Federal Wiretap Statute and use FISA instead whenever the pursuit of foreign intelligence is 'a significant purpose of surveillance', alongside other aims.[21] This permits the police to gather evidence for use in a criminal prosecution alongside foreign intelligence, effectively tearing down the wall that long existed between criminal and intelligence investigations of terrorism offenses.

The Patriot Act (Section 203) further facilitated the use of FISA intercepts for law enforcement purposes by making it easier for government agencies to share information relevant to criminal investigations.[22] Information gathered through FISA surveillance may now be used in criminal prosecutions, alleviating the need for prosecutors to resort to the more cumbersome procedure of the Federal Wiretap Statute (which required probable cause to believe that the government's targets are engaged in criminal violations). Instead, the government need only show that the targeted facility and location is being used by foreign agents or agents of a foreign power. Together with the amended language concerning the purpose of FISA intercepts, this reform allows such intercepts to feed back into the criminal process without the need to demonstrate the kind of individualized suspicion on which the Federal Wiretap Act conditions the use of electronic surveillance.

The so-called 'lone wolf' amendment[23] to FISA similarly expanded FISA's scope to cover suspected terrorists in the United States who neither belong to an international terrorist group nor act 'for or on behalf of a foreign power', as FISA used to require.[24] Though rarely used, the 'lone wolf' provision aims to extend FISA to unaffiliated individuals who self-radicalize on the Internet. As amended, FISA now defines an 'agent of a foreign power' as including any 'non-U.S. person' (meaning someone other than a U.S. citizen or permanent resident) who 'engages in international terrorism or activities in preparation therefor', even when that person lacks any nexus to a foreign government or terrorist organization. Accordingly, this provision has the potential to reach a great deal of domestic criminal activity that would once have been pursued through the criminal process. Defenders of this reform contend that 'criminal warrants are poor substitutes for FISA', because 'the criminal justice system has a very limited, and highly contingent, ability to protect classified information' (Woods, 2005). Critics argue that using the government's foreign intelligence powers to pursue individual suspected terrorists is not appropriate for purely domestic targets, and that investigators should instead pursue a criminal warrant, '[i]f it ultimately becomes clear that the target is acting alone' (Spaulding, 2005).

As amended, FISA now permits the government to bypass the ordinary criminal process not only when intercepting communications but also when obtaining other private data, including some with First Amendment significance. Section 215 of the Patriot Act allows the government to obtain court orders for the production of library circulation records, book sales records, book customer lists, and medical records, for example, without needing to establish probable cause linking these documents to the violation of any law. Though FISA is premised on a foreign intelligence exception to the Fourth Amendment's warrant requirement, these records need not relate to an identified 'foreign agent or foreign power' and may instead concern 'United States persons', so long as the government seeks these documents as part of an investigation 'to protect against international terrorism or clandestine intelligence activities'.[25]

The FBI may obtain other private financial data and records from banks, credit card companies, telephone companies and internet service providers through so-called 'national security letters', which the FBI is believed to have used to obtain data on individuals who are not themselves targets of either criminal or national security investigations but who belong to the 'community of interest' of such targets, in connection with a 'data mining' technique known as 'link analysis' (Hersh, 2006). Like Section 215 orders, national security letters bypass the ordinary criminal process. As with Section 215 orders, the FBI could obtain these records simply by asserting that these records are 'relevant to a terrorism investigation'. Unlike Section 215 orders, however, national security letters require no advance judicial approval. They require no individualized showing of suspicion and enjoy heightened protections for the secrecy of the government's investigation, which makes them more difficult to challenge in court.

Indeed, the Patriot Act provided for gag orders that prohibited recipients of national security letters from disclosing the government's request to anyone, including their attorneys, effectively precluding judicial review of the letters' legality. Subsequent amendments allowed disclosure to legal counsel along with opportunities to challenge national security letters in court, but a number of lower court and appellate decisions have questioned the constitutionality of the amended statute, insofar as it requires courts to accept as conclusive the government's *ex parte* submissions certifying that disclosure would harm national security or diplomatic relations.[26] According to Senator Feingold:

> What did the reauthorization legislation do with regard to NSLs [national security letters]? Well, primarily it created the illusion of judicial review, both for the letters themselves and for the accompanying gag rule. At a Judiciary Committee hearing this week, the FBI Director pointed to this after-the-fact judicial review provision as a privacy protection for NSLs. But if you look at the details, it was drafted in a way that makes that review virtually meaningless. With regard to the NSLs themselves, the reauthorization permits recipients to consult their lawyer and seek judicial review, but it also allows the Government to keep all of its submissions secret and not share them with the challenger, regardless of whether there are national security interests at stake.[27]

National security letters (which have been compared to administrative subpoenas) already existed before the Patriot Act, but Section 505 of the Patriot Act made national security letters available without any showing that the information sought pertained to a foreign power or agent of a foreign power, instead requiring only that the request for information be relevant to an investigation to protect against international terrorism or foreign espionage. The only other constraint on using national security letters against American targets is 'the caveat that no such investigation of an American ... be predicated exclusively on First Amendment protected activities'.[28] Information that was previously obtainable primarily through a court order or grand jury subpoena – which required a pending criminal investigation of specified criminal activity – could now be obtained not only about agents of foreign powers or members of terrorist organizations but also about individuals, including Americans, whose connections to foreign targets and terrorist investigations were more tenuous.

In line with fears that foreign intelligence powers would increasingly be used against American as well as foreign targets, the Inspector General for the Department of Justice has found that an increasing proportion of NSL requests concerned U.S. citizens and permanent residents – up from 39 percent in 2003 to 53 percent in 2005.[29] In 2008 the ACLU claimed that national security letters were being used to skirt legal restrictions on domestic surveillance, since national security letters made it possible to obtain the records of Americans by means of a statute premised on a constitutional exception for foreigners.[30]

Moreover, if national security letters themselves represented a national security preference for the use of foreign intelligence powers in lieu of the criminal process, there is some evidence that the FBI in fact circumvented even those constraints that national security letters imposed on the already broader powers of the executive in the foreign intelligence context. The Inspector General's report detailed numerous instances in which the FBI used an emergency procedure to obtain records without first issuing a national security letter, and that in many other instances it issued national security letters without first determining that the requested documents related to any authorized investigation, or that there was in fact any authorized investigation in progress at all to justify the request for information.[31]

3.3   How FISA Reforms Expand Electronic and Documentary Surveillance of Americans Outside the Criminal Process

As it became easier to conduct terrorism investigations under FISA, without resort to the ordinary criminal process, the Patriot Act and subsequent amendments to FISA also increased the government's surveillance powers when conducting foreign intelligence investigations. For example, Section 206 of the Patriot Act amended FISA to provide for roving surveillance authority 'in circumstances where the Court finds that the actions of the target of the application may have the effect of thwarting the identification of a particular person'.[32] The same court order could permit continued interception of wire communications if targets sought to evade interception by switching telephones frequently. Put differently, the 'roving wiretap' authority authorizes the government to intercept communications to and from all telephones that the target is using to thwart his identification.

This amendment seemingly provides investigators with the same powers when they pursue foreign intelligence that they already possess when they investigate crimes (under 18 U.S.C. section 2518(11)). However, the roving wiretap authority under FISA employs a much broader definition of the 'person' to be specified as a target; such a 'person' may be either a group or a foreign power.[33] Moreover, the order need not identify any particular provider and the facility to be monitored may be defined not as a particular telephone line but as any international gateway or switching station through which calls of a targeted organization, such as Al Qaeda, are believed to pass.[34] Commentators such as James X.

Dempsey, Executive Director of the Center for Democracy and Technology, criticized this new provision by claiming that it might authorize 'John Doe' roving wiretaps, that is, wiretap orders that identify neither the target, nor the location of the interception, nor the telephone number, nor the identity of the service provider, thus permitting investigators to use a single authorization to intercept any telephone used by any individual suspected of membership in a given terrorist organization (Dempsey, 2005).

Roving wiretaps are not the only example of amendments that purport to align the government's investigative powers in the foreign intelligence realm with those in ordinary criminal investigations while actually expanding such prerogatives well beyond those governing ordinary criminal investigations. Section 213 of the Patriot Act statutorily authorized so-called 'sneak and peek' search warrants, which allow the government to delay notification of the execution of a search warrant in cases where nothing was physically seized, in both ordinary criminal and terrorism cases. Sneak and peek warrants are designed to allow investigators to gain secret access to a place where there is a reasonable expectation of privacy; to observe evidence of criminal activity; and to leave without disturbing or seizing anything or providing contemporaneous notice of the search.

A limited version of this power has been available in ordinary criminal investigations since the 1980s, when courts interpreted 18 U.S.C. section 2705 to permit notification to be delayed by only a matter of days, and only on a particularized showing of need for the delay.[35] A robust version of the sneak and peek warrant was officially added to the FISA regime in 1994.[36] The foreign intelligence analogue permits notification of the search only if the Attorney General finds that no national security interest would be threatened by the disclosure, thus permitting notification to be suspended altogether in most cases and effectively eliminating the after-the-fact safeguard that was meant to compensate for the *ex parte* nature of the application for the order and for the secrecy with which it is executed.[37] Moreover, the sneak-and-peek warrant contemplated by FISA does not require any showing of criminal activity on the part of the target, but only that the premises were being used by a foreign power or agent of a foreign power, or that the property contains foreign intelligence information.[38] The Patriot Act (Sections 213 and 114) not only allows delay of notification for criminal and terrorism cases for 30 days with the possibility of successive 90-day extensions where good cause is shown, but also permits seizure of tangible property and communications where a court finds 'reasonable necessity' for the seizure.[39] The Patriot Act also indirectly expands the domestic reach of the government's power to conduct sneak and peek searches, because Section 218 now requires that the pursuit of foreign intelligence be only 'a significant purpose of surveillance', potentially alongside other purposes, rather than 'the [sole or primary] purpose'.[40]

3.4   How National Security Investigations Expand the Role of Undercover Agents Outside the Criminal Process

Legislative reforms have expanded the scope of national security investigations – and of domestic intelligence investigations, in particular – by facilitating interpersonal as well as electronic and documentary surveillance of groups identified along ethnic, religious, and political lines. These powers had been tightly cabined from the 1970s on. Following the Church Committee's disclosure of widespread misuses of domestic intelligence investigations to target civil rights leaders and members of the anti-war movements in the 1960s and 70s, Attorney General Edward Levi established new FBI guidelines designed to protect First Amendment rights of free speech and free association by restricting domestic intelligence operations to the investigation of individuals or groups whose activities 'involve or will involve the violation of federal law' as well as 'the use of force or violence'.[41]

In 1983, Attorney General William French Smith somewhat reduced the evidentiary threshold for initiating domestic intelligence investigations, no longer requiring 'specific and articulable facts' and instead demanding only 'facts or circumstances reasonably indicat[ing]' that the government's targets 'are engaged in an enterprise for the purpose of furthering political or social goals wholly or in part through [criminal] activities that involve force or violence'.[42] After the September 11 attacks, Attorney General John Ashcroft further untethered domestic intelligence operations from any requirement of suspected criminal activity, authorizing FBI agents to 'attend public events ... for the purpose of detecting or preventing terrorist activities, without the predication required to investigate leads or conduct a preliminary inquiry or full investigation'.[43] Nevertheless, domestic intelligence investigations retained their link to some version of the criminal standard until September, 2009, when Attorney General Mukasey abandoned it.

FBI Guidelines now permit investigators to pursue anonymous tips about terrorism by conducting pretext interviews, disguising the purpose of their questions, conducting 'undisclosed participation' in religious and political meetings, or otherwise investigating religious and political organizations without any reason to suspect the organization or its members of criminal activity.[44] Thus FBI agents may now conduct 'threat assessments' of particular individuals, groups and communities – for example, by planting informants in houses of worship – without any factual predicate or justification, so long as the initiative is not based on 'arbitrary or groundless speculation'.[45] The FBI is now explicitly permitted to take account of what Charlie Savage (2009) calls 'specific and relevant behavior' by ethnic groups and to identify locations of what he terms 'concentrated ethnic communities' in deciding whom to target for domestic intelligence investigations, so long as the FBI does not target any group or individual 'solely on the exercise of First Amendment protected activities or on [the] race, ethnicity, national origin, or religion of the subject'.[46]

In one sense, these reforms simply approximate powers that the FBI already possess when investigating ordinary criminal activity, since the Supreme Court has never interpreted the Fourth Amendment to require any threshold showing of suspicion before investigators and informants may go undercover to identify ordinary criminals. The Supreme Court has never treated interpersonal surveillance as an intrusion into constitutionally protected privacy interests[47] (though it reasons that the Sixth Amendment right to counsel prohibits the police from questioning criminal defendants undercover about crimes with which they have already been formally charged).[48]

At the same time, however, domestic intelligence investigations may implicate First Amendment interests that have no counterpart in ordinary criminal investigations.[49] These were the rights and concerns that prompted the creation of the Levi Guidelines and gave rise to a number of consent decrees. First Amendment litigation resulted in consent decrees that allowed city police departments to resolve class actions by political activists who challenged the activities of municipal 'red squads', or intelligence units that investigated left-wing activists in the 1970s and 80s. In the wake of the September 11 attacks, municipal police departments revived their dormant or non-existent intelligence units in order to identify terrorist cells, centers of radical Islam, and organizations that sought to recruit future terrorists.

In New York City, for example, a consent decree had established an administrative warrant procedure whereby the police had to obtain approval from a three-person panel (staffed by two police officials and one civilian) before the police could infiltrate a political or religious organization.[50] The warrant procedure required the police to make some advance determination about their targets' involvement in criminal activity. This procedure was in place from 1987 to 2002, when New York City started bypassing the warrant procedure altogether (Levitt, 2003). During legal action to enforce the consent decree, New York City insisted that the required showing of criminal activity was too restrictive; the court agreed to adopt the FBI's own version of the criminal standard as the new standard for the New York Police Department. The NYPD also instituted a new internal review procedure in place of the three-member review panel and created a new Intelligence Unit responsible, among other duties, for deploying undercover agents in mosques, bookstores, and other public venues and gatherings in Muslim communities to keep track of radical discourse and identify people and groups vulnerable to recruitment by terrorists.[51] The New York intelligence unit is particularly notable, among municipal intelligence units, for having an international presence, through police representatives and liaisons that the NYPD has posted to capital cities around the world.[52]

Similar, if smaller, intelligence units proliferated in municipal police departments around the country. The Chicago Police Department, in particular, formed its own human intelligence squad to do surveillance work in neighborhoods with large Arab populations or many Arab-owned businesses.[53] Freed from their law enforcement responsibilities, police officers were asked to develop relationships with students, educators, businessmen and clergy in order to 'take the pulse' of their neighborhoods and to build a degree of confidence that would encourage members of the targeted communities to come forward with investigative leads about transfers of funds or persons suspected of smuggling or dealing in dangerous chemicals or untaxed cigarettes (whose sale is believed to assist in the financing of terrorism). Through joint terrorism task forces with the FBI, municipal police departments linked these local intelligence initiatives to national databases and federal investigative networks.

But if the New York intelligence unit worked largely independently of the NYPD's law enforcement mission, the Chicago Police Department sought to harness some of the criminal intelligence developed by organized crime and narcotics detectives to its potential use against terrorists.[54] Narcotics units thus conduct surveillance of drug trafficking in front of stores owned by Arab immigrants, in order to learn whether drug traffickers are paying store owners for the privilege of selling drugs in front of their businesses, and whether the businesses use these revenues to fund terrorism abroad. The Chicago intelligence unit also sought to staff its human intelligence squad with officers who had extensive plainclothes and undercover experience from working on organized crime and drug trafficking investigations and who could bring their own networks of sources to the squad. Like New York, Chicago, until recently,[55] was subject to a consent decree that limited its ability to use undercover tactics against political and religious organizations; but to the extent its human intelligence unit does not target such organizations *per se* but focuses on building ties to individual community members and conducts surveillance of terrorist-related criminal activity, its undercover work falls largely outside First Amendment strictures.

3.5 How U.S. Intelligence Operations Bypass FISA

Despite the government's greater powers under FISA and increased ability to use FISA in place of the criminal process, the executive branch found ways of avoiding such strictures as FISA imposed, just as it had found ways of avoiding the criminal process by resort to foreign intelligence operations. In 2002, an executive order authorized the National Security Agency to bypass FISA in intercepting electronic communications between Americans and agents of foreign powers in the United States and abroad. News of this secret program only leaked in 2004; subsequently, Congress ratified this program by enacting the Protect America Act,[56] which was eventually superseded by the FISA Amendment Act of 2008.[57]

Ongoing discussion of FISA reform focuses on 'whether and to what extent the government will be subject to FISA's individualized warrant requirement'.[58] Proponents of FISA reform contend that FISA needs to be modernized because it now regulates many more communications than Congress had originally intended it to reach. Transoceanic communications now take place by fiber optic cable (which FISA regulates) far more than by satellite radio waves (to which FISA does not apply.) And many interceptions which took place in the Atlantic ocean (and to which FISA therefore did not apply) now take place within the United States, and thereby come within FISA's purview, simply because the government increasingly requires the assistance of telecommunications providers to conduct such interceptions. To the extent that many foreign-to-foreign email communications are now stored in the United States, FISA reaches those as well, even though FISA would not regulate foreign telephone communications between foreign locales. Reducing FISA's reach is difficult simply because the government may not be able to determine where the parties to email messages are located and whether the parties to such communications are foreign.

Scholars speculate that in order to avoid these technical difficulties, a FISA court order from 2007 gave wholesale permission to the government to intercept 'international communications into or out of the United States where there is probable cause to believe that one of the communicants is a member or agent of Al Qaeda or an associated terrorist organization', relieving the government of the need to apply for a separate order for every international communication linked to Al Qaeda and its affiliates.[59]

Under that interpretation of FISA, according to David Kris, one such order could cover all international communications to and from Al Qaeda members that went through a particular monitored facility; and David Kris notes that

> the government seem[ed] to have persuaded the FISA Court in 2007 that the international gateway switches ... between the United States and the rest of the world's telecommunications grids are reasonably particular FISA facilities and that al Qaeda is using them. Nothing more particular about the affected telephone numbers seemed to have been required.[60]

After a later FISA ruling disagreed with this broad interpretation of FISA's warrant requirement,[61] Congress enacted a new compromise bill that reintroduced the requirement that the government's targets be 'reasonably believed to be located outside the United States',[62] but which also made clear that the government did not need a separate warrant for each of the monitored places or facilities and needed to show no probable cause to believe that the target was a foreign power or agent of a foreign power.[63]

Thus the government's initial circumvention of FISA prompted legislative reforms designed to ratify the NSA program and its key component – the avoidance of an individualized warrant procedure – even though that procedure had never required probable cause or even reasonable suspicion of the targets' involvement in terrorism or other criminal activity.

Like the expanded statutory authority for the issuance of national security letters, sneak-and-peek warrants, and the new statutory treatment of computer trespassing and stored voicemails, the NSA wiretap program and the subsequent revisions to FISA had a tendency to avoid or dilute judicial oversight of executive surveillance programs. The new regulatory regime for surveillance of computer trespassers and stored voicemails relieved the executive of an obligation to seek a judicial warrant under the rigorous Electronic Communications Privacy Act of 1986. New statutory authority for the issuance of national security letters limited telecommunications providers' access to the courts, imposed extra layers of secrecy, due to the *ex parte* nature of the government's submissions, and, like the new sneak-and-peek revisions, required judicial deference to executive determinations of need both for these investigative methods and for the attendant secrecy and delays in notifying those whose privacy was affected.

Subsequent reforms to FISA removed judicial supervision of surveillance programs affecting U.S. persons from the purview of regular courts to FISA courts. The NSA wiretap program went farther still, as it allowed the government to avoid even the FISA courts altogether. Legislative ratification made it possible for the executive to forego individualized FISA warrants for identified targets, facilities, and locations in favor of warrants approving electronic interception on a wholesale basis for all users and communications passing through particular entry points.

But the NSA program not only avoided or reduced judicial oversight; in foregoing the FISA process, the program also allowed the executive to circumvent statutory constraints and congressional oversight, at least until news about the program leaked to the public in 2004.

Indeed, the NSA surveillance program even bypassed institutional constraints inside the executive branch. In 2009, a joint report of the Offices of Inspectors General of the Department of Defense, Department of Justice, CIA, NSA, and Office of National Intelligence revealed that the program had been misdescribed in authorizing opinions issued by the Department of Justice's Office of Legal Counsel and administered in secret by most of the supervisory personnel of the Department of Justice.[64] An opinion whose legal basis subsequently met with strong opposition from many of those who were privy to information about the NSA program authorized the avoidance of FISA courts.[65]

Disagreement among high-level officials about the legality of the NSA program led to a stand-off within the administration, during which high-level Department of Justice officials, including the Deputy Attorney General, as well as the Director of the FBI, threatened to resign unless the legal basis of the program was clarified or improved through Congressional notification and involvement.[66] When Attorney General Gonzalez subsequently testified before Congress about the program, the OIG concluded that the Attorney General gave misleading, confusing, and inaccurate testimony about the nature and scope of the program.

The OIG report concluded that the secrecy surrounding the program within the Department of Justice (DOJ) contributed to the lack of oversight that, in turn, made it possible for the NSA surveillance program to be approved on the basis of a factually and legally flawed legal opinion formulated by a single DOJ Attorney. Noting that the White House had denied the Attorney General's requests that his chief of staff and Deputy Attorney General be informed about the nature and scope of the program, the OIG report found that 'the White House's strict controls over DOJ access to the [NSA program] undermined DOJ's ability to perform its critical legal function during the [program's] early phase of operation.'[67]

4.   THE NEW SURVEILLANCE PARADIGM

These developments are emblematic of a gradually developing security paradigm that centers less on the development of individualized suspicion and the assembly of proof for individual prosecutions. Instead, this new paradigm emphasizes the aggregation of vast quantities of data about people who are not themselves suspected terrorists, for the purpose of making threat assessments, that is to say, predictive judgments about what kinds of patterns of activity may characterize incipient terrorist plots; what individuals may be particularly susceptible to recruitment as future terrorists; and what patterns of spending and communication tend to be associated with ongoing terrorist conspiracies. Samuel Rascoff (2010: 584) notes that:

> At different points in the last century, most notably in the wake of 1970s-era revelations of abusive practices within the intelligence community, American officials and commentators on domestic intelligence imported the tools and conceptual frameworks of criminal law to the universe of domestic intelligence. The intelligence process was assimilated to the investigation of crime, and the modalities of checking state power in this area were largely borrowed from criminal procedure. [Citation omitted.] Neither approach was a very good fit, but they nevertheless endured for a quarter-century of relative stability until they came under increased pressure from the post-9/11 counter-terrorism imperative and, specifically, the need to design an intelligence regime equipped to anticipate and help prevent certain high-impact, low-probability events.

Rascoff refers to the new security paradigm as the 'risk assessment model of counterterrorism intelligence', pointing out that the FISA Amendments Act of 2008 authorizes the Foreign Intelligence Surveillance Court ('FISC') to issue 'basket' warrants for entire intelligence-gathering programs rather than surveillance operations directed at individual targets.[68] Techniques such as data mining, in particular, require the amalgamation of vast and heterogeneous data sets about law-abiding persons along with suspects, in order to permit analysts to apply a variety of search tools designed to ferret out suspicious patterns of activity. According to NSA whistleblower Russell Tice, the National Security Agency 'combined information from phone wiretaps with data that was mined from credit card and other financial records. Once that information gets to the NSA, they start to put it through filters, and they start looking for word-recognition' (Zetter, 2009) (through keyword searches.)

Likewise, with telephone call data, 'The NSA programmed computers to map the connections between telephone numbers in the United States and suspect numbers abroad, sometimes focusing on a geographic area, rather than on a specific person – for example, a region of Pakistan. Such calls often triggered a process ("chaining") in which subsequent calls to and from the American number were monitored and linked taking the first number out to two, three or more levels of separation', to see if someone down the chain was also calling the original, suspect number (Hersh, 2006). Once such additional links between downstream callers and suspect overseas numbers were established, government officials could approach the FISA courts for warrants to intercept 'internal' call data, in other words, to listen in on the content of the calls themselves, though Seymour Hersh notes that the volume and ambiguity of such data made it impracticable for the administration to pursue individual warrants. ('There's too many calls and not enough judges in the world', according to a former senior intelligence official from the Bush administration, cited by Hersh (2006).)

In this way, the government not only collected 'external' data about domestic calling patterns, affording it an ability to conduct 'social network analysis', and to learn 'how terrorist networks contact each other and how they are tied together' (Cauley, 2006). The NSA also began, 'in some cases, to eavesdrop on callers (often using computers to listen for key words)', without first obtaining an FISA warrant (Hersh, 2006). According to Tice, 'if someone just talked about the daily news and mentioned something about the Middle East, they could ... hav[e] a little flag put by their name that says "potential terrorist"' (Zetter, 2009).

Edward Snowden's recent revelations, however, suggest an evolution in the opposite direction. Using powers granted by Section 215 of the Patriot Act, requiring the records sought to be 'relevant to an authorized investigation', the NSA has been collecting bulk metadata about domestic as well as international phone calls, based on FISA court orders requiring U.S. telecommunications service providers to make ongoing disclosures to the NSA of all telephone metadata, for domestic as well as foreign communications, over a five-year period.[69] This information includes the phone numbers dialed as well as the time and duration of each call, along with information about the cell phone towers used to make these calls, which allows the NSA to track the location of each cell phone at the time of each call. Although Section 215 orders are meant to authorize the collection of foreign intelligence about foreign powers and their agents, the vast bulk of the data concerned domestic calls by Americans.

NSA computers also appear to have listened to the content of calls, using keyword searches to identify communications for follow-up investigation (Miller and Perlroth, 2013). According to Edward Snowden's revelations to Glenn Greenwald of the Guardian, the NSA operated a clandestine government program code-named PRISM and used computer software known as XKeyScore, to 'collect and aggregate information from numerous service providers into a single searchable database'.[70] In an effort to gain access to communications on social media sites, PRISM collected 'audio and video chats, photographs, e-mails, documents, and connection logs' from service providers such as Microsoft, Yahoo!, Google, Facebook, and Skype, among others (Gellman and Poitras, 2013). 'This information, collected in real time, is indexed for analysis and searchability' Florek (2014: 572). Microsoft apparently provided the NSA with regularly updated access to customer data along with access to SkyDrive, its cloud storage service (Savage et al., 2013a). Verizon is claimed to have set up a dedicated fiber-optic line running from New Jersey to Quantico, Virginia, allowing government officials from multiple agencies to gain access to all communications flowing through the carrier's operations center (Risen and Lichtblau, 2013).

The new security paradigm is not unique to terrorism investigations; similar kinds of predictive analyses are going on right now in the criminal investigation of gang-related shootings and juvenile delinquency. In Chicago, for example, the police maintain databases on members of street gangs, which the police use to assist in the analysis of gang-related shootings, in order to monitor ongoing gang conflicts and thereby to identify the likely targets of retaliatory violence.[71] The relevant databases depend on a steady stream of fresh data from street stops of suspected gang members. For each police contact with suspected gang members and their associates, the police fill out a 'contact card' that describes the location and circumstances of the stop, and the people who were with the suspected gang member at the time of the stop, in order to update each gang member's 'community of interest' and to establish his relationships – whether friendly or antagonistic – with other known gangs or gang subunits in the area. Such information is used to prepare the response to gang-related shootings by allowing the police to pinpoint the likely location of retaliatory violence and to direct their resources to that area.

Likewise, the Chicago Public Schools (CPS) conduct statistical studies of violent incidents involving students in order to identify the students most at risk of falling victim to violence.[72] Statistical analyses makes use of information specific to each school and geographic area within the city, as well as demographic and personal data about students, including unexcused absences from school, disciplinary records, academic achievement, and whether a student has qualified for special support services. (The data were not, however, collected for the purpose of this predictive program; instead the program sought to capitalize on data already available to the school, though it aggregated and analyzed the data in new ways to yield predictions about students most at risk of becoming victims of gang violence.) The data that the CPS uses to identify potential victims are difficult to distinguish from the data the CPS would use to identify potential delinquents, as the CPS has indicated that many of the same risk factors apply to both; but by characterizing the targeted group as potential victims rather than potential offenders, the CPS has been able to legitimate a preventive approach that focuses on opportunities (such as help finding after-school jobs) and support services (such as tutoring and counseling) for at-risk youth.[73]

5. CONCERNS ABOUT THE NEW SECURITY PARADIGM: THE PROBLEM OF OVER-COLLECTION

Criticism of the new security paradigm and about data mining in particular centers on the tendency of government officials to accumulate a great deal of personal data about persons not suspected of criminal activity – including many Americans whose activities have scant bearing on national security and little value as foreign intelligence. Concerns about the indiscriminate use of this comparatively unconstrained investigative tool, and about the extent of its use against non-targets, have been fueled by reports by the Office of the Inspector General, which found a dramatic increase in the FBI's use of national security letters. In 2000, the FBI issued 8,500 national security letters; in 2003 it issued 39,000; in 2004 it issued 56,000; and it issued 47,000 in 2005, for a total of 143,074 requests over a three-year period.[74]

The problem of 'over-collection' came into focus in 2007, when the *New York Times* reported on the FBI's use of national security letters to obtain broader information for data mining purposes. 'In many cases, the target of a national security letter whose records are being sought is not necessarily the actual subject of a terrorism investigation and may not be suspected at all' (Lichtblau, 2007). In April 2009, the Obama administration disclosed further problems of over-collection (Lichtblau and Risen, 2009). A routine review of the NSA surveillance program revealed the continuing over-collection of private American communications as a byproduct of foreign intelligence investigations. According to NSA whistleblower Russell Tice, the NSA 'vacuumed in all domestic communications of Americans, including faxes, phone calls, and network traffic … the spy agency also combined information from phone wiretaps with data that was mined from credit card and other financial records' (Zetter, 2009).

American telephone metadata programs, too, had been criticized as overbroad even before Edward Snowden's revelations. In 2006, Lesley Cauley reported that the NSA had created a national call database providing

> access to records of billions of domestic calls. [In this way] the NSA has gained a secret window into the communication habits of millions of Americans. Customers' names, street addresses and other personal information are not being handed over as part of NSA's domestic program. But the phone numbers the NSA collects can easily be cross-checked with other databases to obtain that information. (Cauley, 2006)

The NSA did this by requesting 'call-detail records', in other words, a complete listing of the calling histories of their millions of customers, from many of the nation's biggest telecommunications companies, some of which seem to have backed away from their past practice of requiring a court order before such information could be disclosed to the government (Cauley, 2006).

Bryan Kreykes has argued that the telephone metadata programs produce a significant number of false positive identifications of potential terrorists and too much time and manpower is required to investigate such an over-inclusive set of positive identifications (2008: 449–450). Commentators such as Kreykes argue that '[t]raditional investigative tools that rely on particularized suspicion, as opposed to a wide dragnet of communications records and other data, present a more effective and more efficient means of investigating potential terrorists' (2008: 450). In Kreykes' opinion, 'the government should conserve resources by prioritizing suspects' (2008: 450).

The breadth of collection programs has also, at times, been evaluated according to the adequacy of the description the government provides to the courts assigned to assess the programs' legality. Two decisions of the FISA court, from 2009 and 2011, have rebuked the NSA for misleading the court about the data mining procedures it used to analyze the reservoir of call data (Shane and Perlroth, 2013; Savage et al. 2013b). Professor Laura K. Donohue has argued that 'telephony metadata lacks the particularization' required by FISA and that 'the statute rejects the wholesale collection of domestic information. It relies on the *prior* targeting of foreign intelligence targets to justify surveillance. It provides U.S. persons a heightened level of protection. And it seeks to minimize the acquisition (not just the retention and dissemination) of information' (Donohue, 2014: 803).

Like the metadata program, PRISM has been criticized for its overbreadth. The program was authorized under the 2008 Amendments to

Section 702 of the Foreign Intelligence Surveillance Act of 1974. Nonetheless, it seems to violate FISA restrictions that prohibit surveillance of U.S. citizens and that require such programs to target non-Americans outside the United States. The program may be found to violate Fourth Amendment protections of privacy, if it leads the Supreme Court to re-examine the third party doctrine, according to which people forfeit a reasonable expectation of privacy with regard to information that they voluntarily disclose to others (such as telecommunications service providers.)[75]

FISA surveillance of emails has posed particularly serious problems of over-inclusiveness, as the government decided not to intercept emails at trans-Atlantic cable heads but at domestic switching centers, where domestic and foreign emails proved very difficult to differentiate, so that 'some amount of Americans' e-mail would inevitably be captured by the N.S.A.' (Risen and Lichtblau, 2009: A1). Moreover, when the NSA obtained authorization to monitor an already large block of email addresses associated with a single corporate entity, the NSA often broadened the grant of authority in practice (Risen and Lichtblau, 2009: A1).

The debate about the legitimacy of the new surveillance paradigm brings together a number of different concerns. These include the nature of the privacy interests at stake. Is it reasonable to protect expectations of privacy that attach to personal data, including telecommunications meta-data and financial information, without reference to the purposes for which they are collected and the ways in which they are analyzed? Perhaps it should matter to the protections accorded such data that they are 'merely' searched for predictive purposes, to help identify unusual patterns characteristic of terrorists. If bulk data are instead combined in a targeted way to create a comprehensive profile of particular suspects, one could argue that this form of aggregation raises heightened privacy concerns that may require individualized, reasonable suspicion, or even probable cause, even if the suspects are not formally targets of criminal investigation. Likewise, criticisms of PRISM and of the protection accorded telephony metadata rarely distinguish between the privacy interests involved. Should communications receive greater protections than personal data that do not reveal the content of speech or thought? Are browsing habits more like telecommunications metadata, or more like communication, because they reveal one's thoughts and interests?

The debate about how much collection is too much turns on the question of when legal filters should come into play. Should privacy protections intervene at the point of collection, the point of analysis – or the later stage, when insights generated by analysis lead to concrete repercussions for suspects who are classified as security risks, or even prosecuted? In light of these concerns, the relevance of the distinction between U.S. persons and foreigners seems of questionable relevance and bears little relation to the 'special needs' exception that justifies the diminution of Fourth Amendment protections. Does it make sense to regulate the surveillance of 'foreign powers and their agents' differently from the surveillance of Americans, when surveillance of the former inevitably affects not just some Americans but – in the case of telephone metadata – all of them?

Quite aside from first questions about what the government should be permitted to do, and whether the current two-track system aligns with our sense of fairness, there remain unavoidable questions regarding what to do about the data that has already been collected. How long the data may be stored, or how they may be used, remains unclear – but may prove crucial to the legitimacy of the investigative tactics that produced them.

6.   LIMITATIONS ON BULK DATA COLLECTION AND DATA MINING IN GERMANY

In contrast to the United States, where Fourth Amendment privacy protections apply primarily to criminal investigations, German privacy protections, like those of the European Convention on Human Rights, apply to personal data directly, independently of the purpose for which they are collected. Germany's Basic Law has been held to protect so-called 'rights of personality', which protect 'the freedom to realize one's potential as an individual' or 'freedom in the creation of the self' (Degenhart, 1992: Kunig, 1993: 595). In 1984, Germany's Constitutional Court held that the government's collection and processing of census data had to respect a newly recognized constitutional right of 'informational self-determination', that is, a right of every citizen to know what information the government has collected about her and to limit the government's use, storage, and transmission of the data.[76] The new legal construct can be understood as an expression of what James Whitman (2004) has described as a continental conception of 'privacy as an aspect of [personal] dignity', as distinct from the U.S. conception of privacy as 'an aspect of liberty', Germany's Constitutional Court thus holds that government access to personal data burdens this constitutionally pro-tected interest, irrespective of whether such data is collected during the course of a criminal investigation or for some other governmental purpose. As a result, government programs that provide investigators with access to personal data require a showing of need; a showing that the collection program is narrowly tailored to satisfy the legitimating purpose; and a demonstration that the invasion of privacy represented by such a collection program and the scope of the information disclosed are not disproportionate to the purposes for which the data are gathered.

These legal requirements have limited German authorities' access to bulk personal data not only for law enforcement purposes but in all investigative contexts, including those that concern national security. On March 15, 2006, for example, the European Union enacted a guideline requiring member states to enact data retention legislation that would obligate telecommunication service providers to store call bulk metadata such as telephone numbers, email addresses, and IP connections, detail records and Internet transaction data for a minimum of somewhere between six months and two years, and to make such data available to government authorities upon request, though it was up to the legislatures of the member states to specify the showings government investigators had to make in order to obtain access to these data. In 2007, the German Bundestag enacted legislation to implement the requirements of this guideline, requiring telecommunications companies to preserve such data for at least six months.[77]

On March 2, 2010, however, Germany's Constitutional Court invalidated Germany's implementing legislation as inconsistent with Germany's Basic Law. Bulk data of this sort could provide investigators with extremely comprehensive information about the social network of telecommunications customers, without sufficient safeguards for misuse or sufficient legal strictures either on the purposes for which government agencies could obtain access to the data or on the showings the government would be required to make as a condition of access. The decision effectively limited government access to bulk telecommunications data regardless of the purpose for which the data were sought, by ordering telecommunications providers to erase the collected data sets immediately and by limiting future storage of telecommunications data to a period of no more than seven days. On April 8, 2014, the European Court of Justice likewise invalidated the underlying guideline for violating the privacy rights of telecommunications customers.[78] The guideline did not limit or tailor the data set to any particular subset of suspects or to the gravity of the crime being investigated, nor did the guideline specify what agencies could obtain access to the data, and what threshold showings were required for disclosure.

Despite these legal and practical restrictions, however, Edward Snowden's revelations about the NSA's close cooperation with Germany's foreign and spy agencies, the *Bundesnachrichtendienst* (BND) and the Agency for the Protection of the Constitution, suggest that

Germany may have shared bulk metadata of European citizens with the NSA[79] and that the NSA in turn supplied Germany's intelligence agencies with a software, known as XKeyScore, that permits intelligence analysts to monitor emails, online chats, and Internet browsing histories in real time.[80] Technical advances and international cooperation may thus enable Germany's intelligence agencies to access bulk metadata and monitor live Internet communications in ways that compensate intelligence services for the loss of access to the bulk metadata that telecommunications providers were ordered to destroy. The extent to which Germany's intelligence services have implemented the software for this purpose remains in dispute, and it remains unclear whether any data generated by such protocols have been integrated into Germany's joint anti-terrorism database, or would be available for consultation by the police.

Data protections aside, however, aggregation of bulk data sets, and the mining of such data sets for predictive purposes, are further limited, in Germany, by the very reforms that were intended to improve cooperation between police and intelligence agencies in matters of national security. Germany has sought to better coordinate efforts against international terrorism as well as domestic extremism by establishing a joint anti-terrorist database, as well as a database of right-wing extremists, to which both police and intelligence agencies will have access. Privacy protections mean that these databases may not contain personal data for persons not suspected of terrorist or extremist activity. But this limitation also follows from the temporal division of labor among investigators. If intelligence agencies are understood to focus on the earliest stages of subversive activity that may one day ripen into criminal activity, and criminal investigators are viewed as downstream investigators of some subset of these suspects, then anyone included in these databases is conceived of as someone who might eventually be prosecuted, at a later stage of the government's investigative activity. This means that there is no room for thinking about intelligence operations as aggregating bulk data about innocent transactions and communications of people who are not suspects with the transactions and communications of potential terrorists and extremists, even if the purpose of this aggregation is to analyze social networks and communications patterns that help investigators to profile and distinguish patterns typical of potential terrorists.

And though both intelligence services and the police have access to these databases, the principle of separation between police and intelligence agencies, along with differences between the 'preventive' and 'repressive' powers of the police, required the implementing statute to constrain access by police and intelligence agencies in ways that align with their distinct legal prerogatives, limiting the information they may share with each other. This, too, prevents any wholesale aggregation of databases to which police and intelligence agencies do not have equal access. Designed to alert agencies to information that other services may have about persons of interest, these databases are not meant to allow the police to circumvent legal constraints on their investigative activities by providing them with information from other agencies when that information was obtained by collection efforts – such as electronic interception – that are subject to less stringent standards.

These limitations on the data that may be included in the database, and the ways in which it may be shared across agencies, are written directly into the governing statute. The joint anti-terrorist database was first established in 2006, through legislation that was designed to allow police and intelligence agencies to expand the scope of available data about people already of interest to these services on independent grounds.[81] However, the Federal Constitutional Court subsequently invalidated it in part and remanded it to the federal legislature (Bundestag) for further revision to improve compliance with constitutional privacy protections.[82]

In April, 2014, the Bundestag introduced an amended version that still allowed police and intelligence agencies to access personal data such as nationality, religious affiliation, special skills, employment in security-relevant fields, locations a person has been known to visit, telephone numbers, IP addresses, and even the content ('phonetic data') of intercepted conversations and telecommunications, for the purpose of identifying terrorist plots.[83] The statute provided for these relatively broad categories to be further narrowed through administrative guidelines but did authorize a limited form of data mining, allowing participating agencies to extract personal data from multiple data sets to transform it into more complete profiles of persons of interest; to establish links between individuals, groups, institutions, tangible objects, and sensitive infrastructure; and to identify patterns of behavior that could indicate involvement in terrorist plots. But the statute also provided that data mining had to be undertaken as part of a coherent and sustained investigative 'project' which had to be approved, in advance, by a special four-member parliamentary commission known as the G10 commission (though exigent circumstances could permit the requesting service to access a source agency's sensitive information without advance authorization, so long as it sought subsequent ratification). 'Project data' could be accessed for only up to two years. The German federal police (known as *Bundeskriminalamt* [BKA]), which oversees the joint database, was required to report to the Bundestag every three years about how these powers had been used, and the federal data protection agency was authorized to conduct regular spot checks on how the data protection provisions of the law were being implemented.

Although it authorized a limited form of data mining, the original law had avoided bulk data collection by confining databases to personal data about persons suspected of participating in terrorist organizations, planning terrorist attacks, or advocating the use of violence for political ends, but the law had also permitted collection of such data about the mere associates of such individuals. The Constitutional Court decision required the Bundestag to further narrow the criteria for inclusion in the anti-terror database by insisting that the intelligence community and the police could not target someone solely on the basis of his opinions unless he directly advocated the use of violence, with the intent of supporting, preparing or instigating acts of violence.

The new law also prohibited targeting someone merely for associating with a suspected terrorist, absent some reason to think that the associate knew about and supported the target's terrorist plots. The decision of the Constitutional Court, which had partially invalidated the old law, had expressed concern, in particular, that support of communal organizations, such as kindergartens, should not be allowed to qualify someone for inclusion in the anti-terror database simply because the mosque that sponsored the kindergarten was suspected of secretly supporting terrorism.[84] Only limited personal data could be stored about mere associates of suspected terrorists.

Legal distinctions between intelligence work, preventive police operations, and full-fledged criminal investigations shaped the ways in which this information was coded, meaning that a requesting agency might see that certain information existed but not be able to access its content without directly contacting the investigators who had gathered it. For example, sensitive data derived from ambient surveillance or the interception of telephone and Internet communications could only be entered and accessed in a coded form that required the user to contact the source agency for further details. The intercepted contents could only be shared if the source agency determined that the requesting agency had a valid reason as well as legal authority for requesting it, and that access would not allow the requesting agency to circumvent legal constraints that might have prohibited the requesting agency from intercepting the relevant communications on its own. In this way, the drafters sought to ensure that intelligence work remained meaningfully different from police work and to discourage an end-run around the constitutional norms that limit electronic surveillance by the police.

In contrast to the amended FISA statute and NSA data collection initiatives, these reforms concerned only the ways in which data were used and shared, not the ways in which they were collected. Whether the personal data concerned foreign or domestic individuals did not enter into the design of the rules governing the information that could be stored or shared. With very limited exceptions for basic information about persons in direct contact with suspects, personal data on individuals who were not suspects or criminal associates of suspects could not be stored or accessed (though investigators were free to surf openly accessible websites proactively). The report submitting the amendments for approval expressly disallowed so-called 'inverse searches', in which keyword searches of multiple data sets allow investigators to query the names of previously unsuspected persons whose characteristics fit the profile of a potential terrorist. And the reform did not allow intelligence investigations to circumvent the rules of criminal procedure, as the law prohibited requesting agencies from using the database to circumvent constitutional protections by accessing electronic communications that they could not have collected under the statutes that governed their own interception activities.

This legal reform represents an effort to legalize *ad hoc* forms of data mining which Germany first instituted following the September 11 attacks, in an attempt to identify sleeper cells within Germany. Because the federal Code of Criminal Procedure at the time made no provision for data mining, the first efforts to implement a form of data mining were governed by state police laws, which govern the purely preventive prerogative of the police. Because state police laws do not apply to Germany's federal police, the BKA could not take the lead in these initiatives, though it could assist the state police in gathering personal data and connecting electronic databases. Nor was there already an anti-terror database that investigators could use for data mining. Instead, databases from a variety of government agencies were used and cross-checked against lists of suspects. It has been claimed in the German press that more than 13 million transactions data involving credit and debit cards were included in these databases, along with personal data about hotel stays and car rentals, though the German government denies that transaction data were either aggregated or mined.[85]

Unlike the anti-terror database that was eventually created by statute, early data mining efforts did not include only the names of suspected terrorists and their associates. Investigators were able to cross-check bulk data about ordinary members of the public using protocols that were designed to identify individuals who fit the profile of suspected terrorists. Data protection agencies were assigned the task of supervising these efforts, to ensure that the relevant data were used only for limited purposes over a limited period of time. For example, data monitors in

Bavaria scrutinized efforts by the Bavarian police, in the wake of the September 11 attacks, to compile data from universities, immigration bureaus, social welfare agencies, and pilot training facilities about Muslim students between the ages of 18 and 40 who were *not* recipients of welfare assistance (and therefore presumably had outside financing from unknown sources).[86] Data monitors insisted that that an independent data processing agency check social welfare databases against the lists of students forwarded by Bavarian universities, in order to identify only those students who were not listed as aid recipients in the social welfare databases. In this way, the police would not be able to gain access to the files of actual aid recipients. Bavarian data monitors sought to have the data set generated for data mining purposes destroyed once the names of students fitting the search parameters had been identified, to avoid the records' future availability for further data mining along other parameters.[87]

The anti-terror database institutionalized these ad hoc initiatives by creating a permanent database, but it also legalized a much narrower form of data mining, insofar as it was limited to personal data about people already identified as suspected terrorists and their associates. The statute represented an effort to improve information-sharing between intelligence and law enforcement agencies, while retaining the guiding principle that information obtained through searches and electronic interception had to be coded to indicate the nature of its source, and that the police could only use information in a criminal investigation if they would have been legally authorized to obtain the information under the federal Code of Criminal Procedure. In this way, the statutory reform sought to limit the use of data in ways that tracked not only the difference between intelligence work and policing, but also the distinction between the preventive and the law enforcement prerogatives of the police.

7. CONCLUSION

In the German legal context, concerns about the growth of the preventive powers of police and intelligence agencies presuppose a temporal distinction between the government's prerogative to investigate past events and its powers to avert future threats. The legal rules governing both domains are said to depend on the timing of the government's investigative interventions, so that different sets of rules govern the early detection of risks and threats, on the one hand, and the law enforcement response to past, present, or impending criminal violations on the other. In the United

States, by contrast, the criminal laws and rules of criminal procedure already pose few barriers to early intervention by law enforcement agencies. Instead, the choice among regulatory frameworks depends largely on whether the investigation is treated as an intelligence operation or a criminal investigation. While domestic intelligence operations were once subject to different rules concerning the use of informants and undercover agents, the functional distinction between domestic intelligence investigations and criminal investigations has been largely superseded by that between criminal and foreign intelligence investigations.

This distinction among regulatory frameworks is largely motivated by the reduced application of Fourth Amendment protections to foreign intelligence operations. Accordingly, recent efforts to increase the government's surveillance prerogatives in the war against terror have largely focused on increasing the powers and scope of foreign intelligence operations, which now reach many U.S. citizens and permanent residents, along with foreign nationals identified as agents of a foreign power.

The expansion of foreign intelligence investigations signals a shift towards a new surveillance paradigm that emphasizes the aggregation of vast quantities of personal data. In contrast to the German regulation of personal data, the American surveillance paradigm imposes far fewer constraints on the collection, aggregation, and dissemination of personal data among government agencies. The U.S. does not treat domestic or foreign intelligence programs as precursors but as alternatives to the criminal process, permitting investigators to bypass statutory and constitutional constraints on surveillance and on the collection of personal data. Intelligence programs combine data on innocent persons and suspected terrorists in ways that the criminal process prohibits. The federal Wiretap statute and the process of applying for search warrants, in particular, require the government to supply a level of individualized suspicion that intelligence programs are not designed to develop. At the same time, such intelligence programs are designed to generate patterns and predictions in ways in which criminal investigations cannot. Yet the intelligence generated through these alternatives to the criminal process is shared among agencies much more easily in the United States than in Germany, so that intelligence generated through foreign or domestic intelligence operations can now feed back into the American criminal process and be used as evidence for criminal prosecutions. Inevitably, American courts will have to determine whether the purposes for which information is generated should affect the ways in which that information is used.

In recent American debates about the accumulation of personal data and the risks of insulating this process from judicial or legislative oversight there has been relatively little consideration of the purposes for which data are collected and analyzed. Yet this may have some bearing on the appropriateness of a given regulatory mechanism, and specifically on the choice between individualized showings of suspicion and advance judicial oversight, on the one hand, and *ex post facto* controls such as reporting requirements or administrative audits, on the other.

To describe the purpose of data-gathering as predictive and its products as 'threat assessments' is too general. The use of gang databases to prevent retaliatory gang violence, the compilation of data to identify terrorist cells, and the use of personal data to predict school shootings all involve some form of risk assessment. Yet in the school context, this process may lead to extra tutoring for at-risk students; when fighting gang violence, it may lead to the deployment of extra police resources in high-crime areas; and in the anti-terrorism context, it may lead to travel restrictions, arrests, or extra-judicial killings. Regulation of how data are acquired, shared, and handled could perhaps be tailored to the nature of the interventions that risk assessments may be used to justify.

In addition, regulation could be tailored to the nature of the analytical use to which personal data are put. Thus, aggregate personal data *could* be used to narrow the government's investigative focus for the purpose of generating individualized suspicion, making intelligence-gathering a kind of precursor to a regular criminal investigation (which is very much akin to the German model of the purposes for which intelligence is gathered and analyzed). But such data could also be used in a number of other ways. For example, analysts may use such data to identify vulnerabilities in particular institutions, organizations, facilities, or data-processing systems and to develop safeguards against them; to create profiles of 'normal' patterns of consumption or communication, which makes it easier to spot aberrant patterns (such as suspicious financial transactions or purchasing patterns) associated with illicit activities such as terrorism or organized crime; to acquire quasi-anthropological information about particular groups or communities; to test the impact of the government's efforts to 'counter' terrorist activity; or to construct profiles of individuals susceptible to recruitment by terrorists.

Depending on how personal data are used, they may have more significance as aggregate data about behavioral patterns and regularities than as information prefiguring targeted investigations of identified individual and may accordingly present different types of threats to civil liberties, such as privacy, freedom of speech, and freedom of association. Courts, inspectors general, administrative agencies, and legislative committees differ in their characteristic expertise and institutional capabilities, and each may be better at supervising the acquisition, sharing, and use of information associated with some of these analytical functions than with others.

But regulatory decisions must take account not only of institutional competence but of the consequences that the collection and handling of such intelligence may have for its targets. Recent experience with the over-collection of intelligence intensifies concerns about the ways in which accumulated data stores may infringe not only privacy but liberty. Existing reporting requirements do not address what becomes of personal data, and the ways it may be used. There are as yet few provisions for the destruction of such data, including the many personal records that were over-collected in violation of the law. Given the increasing ease with which such data may be shared among government agencies, such data may well lead to the inclusion of new names on no-fly lists, or may be used to deny security clearances or visas, to exclude and deport aliens and permanent residents, or to generate evidence for criminal prosecutions, and may come to chill the exercise of First Amendment rights. The source and reliability of the threat assessments that underlie these government actions may be difficult to determine. The new security paradigm may be here to stay, but it must be adapted in ways that allow it to co-exist with highly individualized administrative and criminal procedures whose potential effects on liberty are momentous. The legitimacy of these procedures depends on the fact-finder's ability to make reliable, narrowly tailored and transparent decisions on a case-by-case basis.

NOTES

1. For more on the 'principle of separation' between German law enforcement and intelligence agencies see for example, Roewer (1986: 205).
2. 18 U.S.C.A. § 2339A(a) states: 'Whoever provides material support or resources or conceals or disguises the nature, location, source, or ownership of material support or resources, knowing or intending that they are to be used in preparation for, or in carrying out, a violation of [an underlying terrorism offense] ... shall be fined under this title, imprisoned not more than 15 years, or both, and, if the death of any person results, shall be imprisoned for any term of years or for life'.
3. 31 U.S.C.A. § 5324.
4. 18 U.S.C.A. § 1956.
5. 18 U.S.C.A. § 1001.
6. 26 U.S.C.A. § 7201 (creating a felony crime for failure to report taxable assets).
7. Ibid.
8. Ibid.
9. 407 U.S. 297, 308–309 (1972).

10. These permit randomized sobriety checkpoints, drug testing of high school athletes, and safety sweeps of stopped vehicles, insofar as these serve some safety purpose distinct from a law enforcement objective.
11. In re Directives Pursuant to Section 105b of the Foreign Intelligence Surveillance Act, 2008 U.S. App. LEXIS 27439 (U.S. Foreign Intell. Surveil. Ct. Rev. Aug 22, 2008).
12. Ibid.
13. These now include harboring terrorists, financing terrorism, receiving military-type training from foreign terrorist organizations, *per* Section 201 of the Patriot Act.
14. *Per* Section 202.
15. 18 U.S.C. §2703, Patriot Act §216, amending 18 U.S.C. §§3121, 3123 (permitting the use of pen registers and trap and trace devices for electronic communications); Patriot Act §216(c) amending 18 U.S.C. §§3123(b)(1)(C), 3127 (permitting 'roving' wiretaps not bound to any US jurisdiction).
16. Pub. L. No. 90-351, sections 801–804, 82 Stat. 197, 211–225 (codified as amended at 18 U.S.C. sections 2510–2522, as amended by Patriot Act §209).
17. Section 102(a) of the Improvement and Reauthorization Act made the change permanent.
18. *Per* 18 U.S.C. Section 2511.
19. P.L. 95-5.
20. See USA Patriot Act §808, amending 18 U.S.C. 2332b.
21. See USA Patriot Act §218, amending 18 U.S.C. 1804(a), 1823(a).
22. See USA Patriot Act §203, amending 50 U.S.C. 403-5d.
23. Section 6001 of the Intelligence Reform and Terrorism Prevention Act of 2004.
24. FISA Section 101(b)(2)(C).
25. 18 U.S.C. §2709(b).
26. See *Doe v. Ashcroft*, 334 F. Supp. 2d 471, 494–506 (S.D.N.Y., 2004) (invalidating section 2709 as unconstitutional under the Fourth Amendment because it authorized 'coercive searches effectively immune from any judicial process'), aff'd in part, rev'd in part sub nom. *John Doe, Inc. v. Mukasey*, 549 F.3d 861 (2d Cir., 2008) (upholding §2709(c) only after broadly construing the government's certification and burden of proof requirements).
27. 153 Cong. Rec. S.4039 (March 28, 2007), statement of Sen. Feingold, https://www.gpo.gov/fdsys/pkg/CREC-2007-03-28/pdf/CREC-2007-03-28-pt1-PgS4039.pdf.
28. Doyle (2001) (citing P.L. 107–156, § 203, 115 Stat. 365–366 (2001)).
29. Ibid.
30. 'ACLU: Military Using FBI to Skirt Restrictions', http://www.msnbc.msn.com/id/23908142.
31. Ibid. at S4,041.
32. Patriot Act §206, amending 50 U.S.C.S. §1805.
33. Patriot Act §206 amending 50 U.S.C.S §1805(c).
34. 50 U.S.C.S. 1805(c)(2)–(3).
35. See, for example, *United States v. Freitas*, 800 F.2d 1451, 1453 (9th Cir. 1986) (upholding the constitutionality of sneak and peek warrants but setting a hard deadline of 7 days for notification); but see *United States v. Villegas*, 899 F.2d 1324, 1338 (2d Cir. 1990) (upholding a 2-month delay in notification based on a series of 7-day extensions of the initial sneak and peek warrant where good cause for the extended delay was shown).
36. Intelligence Authorization Act for Fiscal Year 1995, P.L. 103-359.
37. 50 U.S.C. §1825.
38. 50 U.S.C. §1823(a).
39. See *USA Patriot Act §§114, 213*, amending 18 U.S.C. 3103a(b)(3).
40. See *USA Patriot Act §218*, amending 18 U.S.C. 1804(a), 1823(a).

41. Federal Bureau of Investigation Compliance with the Attorney General's Investigative Guidelines, Special Report, September 2005 at III.A, referring to Levi Guidelines for Domestic Security Investigations.

42. 1983 House Oversight Hearings on Domestic Security Guidelines, at 79 (Smith Guidelines Section II).

43. September 1, 2004 Guidelines of the Counterterrorism Division.

44. Federal Bureau of Investigation, Domestic Investigations and Operations Guidelines (2011).

45. Ibid.

46. Federal Bureau of Investigation, Domestic Investigations and Operations Guidelines (2011). These Guidelines authorize 'undercover participation in group activities', but provide that 'investigative activity that involves assemblies or associations of individuals in the United States, exercising their First Amendment rights must have an authorized purpose' under the Guidelines. The FBI may 'identify locations of concentrated ethnic communities if these locations will reasonably aid in the analysis of potential threats and vulnerabilities', ibid, Sections 4.2 and 4.3.

47. Instead, the U.S. Supreme Court holds that offenders assume the risk of betrayal by their associates, including the danger that such associates will turn out to be informants or undercover agents. *Hoffa v. United States*, 385 U.S. 293, 302 (1966); *Lewis v. United States*, 385 U.S. 206 (1966); *Illinois v. Perkins*, 496 U.S. 292, 300 (1990).

48. *Massiah v. United States*, 377 U.S. 201, 204–205, 84 S.Ct. 1199, 12 L.Ed.2d 246 (1964).

49. For a discussion of the ways in which government information gathering conflicts with First Amendment values, see Solove (2007); Berry (1982); Krelmer (2004); Lislager (2004).

50. For more on the so-called Handshu decree, *Handshu v. Special Services Division*, 787 F.2d 828 (2d Cir. 1986), see Chevigny (1984).

51. Note, however, that the NYPD has recently disbanded the Demographics Unit and abandoned its undercover activities in Muslim communities (Apuzzo and Goldstein, 2014).

52. Information about the NYPD Intelligence Unit is based on the author's interviews with members of the NYPD, with officials of the American Embassy in Paris, and with members of the French Police Nationale, as conducted in 2008–2010.

53. Information about the intelligence-gathering practices of the Chicago Police Department is based on the author's interviews with members of the Chicago Police Department in 2009.

54. Information about the intelligence-gathering practices of the Chicago Police Department is based on the author's interviews with members of the Chicago Police Department in 2009.

55. 'Red Squad Rules Get Tossed Out', *Sun Times*, June 9, 2009, available at https://www.highbeam.com/doc/1N1-128B99215DFD8168.html.

56. P.L. 110-55.

57. P.L. 110-261.

58. Posting of David Kris on Balkanization, http://balkin.blogspot.com/2008/06/guide-to-new-fisa-bill-part-i.html (June 21, 2008, 08:50 EST).

59. Ibid.

60. Ibid.

61. The FISA ruling itself is classified, but for evidence of the Bush Administration's reaction to the ruling, see 'Foreign Intelligence Surveillance Act', Times Topics, *New York Times*, April 16, 2009, available at http://topics.nytimes.com/topics/reference/timestopics/subjects/f/foreign_intelligence_surveillance_act_fisa/index.html; Hulse and Andrews (2007: A1).

62. FISA Act of 1978 Amendments Act, §101, amending 50 U.S.C. 1801.
63. FISA Act of 1978 Amendments Act, §702, amending 50 U.S.C. 1801 (permitting the Attorney General or the Director of National Intelligence to issue directives compelling information from telecommunications companies without a separate FISA warrant).
64. *Unclassified Report on the President's Surveillance Program*, 10 July 2009, prepared by the Offices of Inspectors General of the Department of Defense, Department of Justice, Central Intelligence Agency, National Security Agency, Office of the Director of National Intelligence (hereafter 'OIG report').
65. In the opinion of the memorandum's author, John Yoo, who was then Deputy Assistant Attorney General in the DOJ Office of Legal Counsel, 'FISA did not expressly apply to wartime operations, ... [which other officials believed] contradicted Yoo's assertion that Congress did not intend FISA to apply to wartime operations', though 'Yoo's memoranda omitted any reference to the FISA provision allowing the interception of electronic communications without a warrant for a period of 15 days following a congressional declaration of war' (OIG report at 20). Yoo also concluded that 'we do not believe that Congress may restrict the President's inherent constitutional powers, which allow him to gather intelligence necessary to defend the nation from direct attack' (Yoo memorandum as cited by OIG Report at 13).
66. OIG Report at 21–30.
67. OIG Report at 30.
68. Rascoff (2010), citing Council on Foreign Relations, Working Paper, The War Over Terror ('The new act does not require individual warrants from the FISA Court for each acquisition when the target is a non-U.S. person located outside the United States. In such cases, the FISA court no longer reviews each application. Instead, its oversight is more general and takes the form of what are known as basket warrants. These authorizations can last up to one year. The act does not specify the breadth of the surveillance they can approve, leading some to characterize the authorization as monitoring plans').
69. See, for example, *In re* Application of the Fed. Bureau of Investigation for an Order Requiring the Prod. of Tangible Things from [Telecommunications Providers] Relating to [REDACTED], Order, No. BR 0605 (FISA Ct. May 24, 2006), available at https://www.eff.org/sites/default/files/filenode/docket_06-05_1dec201_redacted.ex_-_ocr_0.pdf [http://perma.cc/MT9D-4W2Y] (released by court order as part of the Electronic Frontier Foundation's Freedom of Information Act (FOIA) litigation). See also, Savage and Wyatt (2013); Savage (2013).
70. Florek (2014: 571). Florek in turn cites Greenwald and MacAskill (2013).
71. This is based on the author's own interviews with members of the Chicago Police Department, in summer, 2009.
72. This is based on the author's interviews with officials in charge of the 2009 anti-violence initiative of the Chicago Public Schools.
73. This account is based on the author's interviews with officials in the Chicago Public School System who were responsible for designing the selection criteria. These interviews were conducted in 2009–2010.
74. 153 Cong. Rec. S.4039 (March 28, 2007), statement of Sen. Feingold, https://www.gpo.gov/fdsys/pkg/CREC-2007-03-28/pdf/CREC-2007-03-28-pt1-PgS4039.pdf.
75. *Smith v. Maryland*, 442 U.S. 735 (1979).
76. BVerfGE 65, 1, Neue Juristische Wochenschrift 1984, 419.
77. Neuregelung der Telekommunikationsüberwachung und anderer verdeckter Ermittlungsmaßnahmen sowie zur Umsetzung der Richtlinie 2006/24/EG vom 21. Dezember 2007 (BGBl I S. 3198).
78. ECJ 8. April, 2014-C-293/12 and C594/12.

79. According to the *Spiegel Online*, 'the BND confirmed that it does transmit connection data to the NSA. But it notes: "Before metadata relating to other countries is passed on, it is purged, in a multistep process, of any personal data about German citizens it may contain." According to the BND, its surveillance does not apply to German telecommunications and German citizens'. 'Transfers from Germany Aid US Surveillance', *Spiegel Online*, 08/05.2013.
80. *Spiegel Online*, 'Secret Links Between Germany and the NSA', 07/22/2014. According to the *Guardian*'s Glenn Greenwald, training materials for the software program boast that it 'covers "nearly everything a typical user does on the internet", including the content of emails, websites visited and searches, as well as their metadata. Analysts can also use XKeyscore and other NSA systems to obtain ongoing "real-time" interception of an individual's internet activity', *Guardian*, 31 July, 2013.
81. Antiterrordateigesetz vom 22. Dezember 2006 (BGBI. I S. 3409), further amended by Article 5, Gesetz vom 26. February 2008 (BGBI. I S. 215).
82. 1BvR 1215/07, decided 24 April, 2013.
83. Bundesrat, Gesetzentwurf 11. April, 2014, DS 153/14. The reform also provided for the parallel creation of a database of 'right wing extremists', to be governed by similar restrictions.
84. 1BvR 1215/07, decided 24 April, 2013.
85. Matthias Monroy, *Rasterfahndungen könnten polizeialltäglich werden, Gesetzentwurf nächste Woche in erster Lesung im Innenausschuss*, Netzpolitik (May 28, 2014, 4:31PM), https://netzpolitik.org/2014/rasterfahndungen-koennten-polizeialltaeglich-werden-gesetzentwurf-naechste-woche-in-erster-lesung-im-innenausschuss/
86. Taetigkeitsbericht 2002 des Bayerischen Landesbeauftragten fuer den Datenschutz, Section 6.11; see also Rasterfahndung: Ersuchen erfuellt, http://www.uni-protokolle.de/nachrichten/id/8367/
87. Ibid.

BIBLIOGRAPHY

Apuzzo, Mark and Joseph Goldstein, 'New York Drops Unit that Spied among Muslims', *New York Times*, April 15, 2014.
Berry, Dave. 1982. 'The First Amendment and Law Enforcement Infiltration of Political Groups', 56 *So. Cal. L. Rev.* 207.
Cauley, Leslie. 2006. 'NSA Has Massive Database of Americans' Phone Calls', *USA Today*, May 11, available at http://www.usatoday.com/news/washington/2006-05-10-nsa_x.htm.
Chevigny, Paul G. 1984. 'Politics and Law in the Control of Local Surveillance', 69 *Cornell L. Rev.* 735.
Degenhart, Christoph. 1992. 'Das Allgemeine Persönlichkeitsrecht, Art. 2 I i.V. mit Art. 1 I GG', *Juristische Schulung* 361.
Dempsey, James X. 2005. 'Why Section 206 Should be Modified', *Patriot Debates* (Stewart A. Baker and John Kavanagh, eds.), available at http://www.abanet.org/natsecurity/patriotdebates/section-206.
Doe v. Ashcroft, 334 F. Supp. 2d 471, 494-506 (S.D.N.Y., 2004) aff'd in part, rev'd in part sub nom. *John Doe, Inc. v. Mukasey*, 549 F.3d 861 (2d Cir., 2008).
Donohue, Laura K. 2014. 'Bulk Metadata Collection: Statutory and Constitutional Considerations', 37 *Harv. J. L. & Pub. Pol'y* 757.
Doyle, Charles. 2001. 'National Security Letters in Foreign Intelligence Investigations: Legal Background and Recent Amendments', CRS Report for Congress, September 8.
Dubber, Markus. 2007. *The Police Power*. New York: Columbia University Press.

Florek, Adam. 2014. 'The Problems with PRISM: How a Modern Definition of Privacy Necessarily Protects Privacy Interests in Digital Communications', 30 *J. Info. Tech. & Priv. L.* 571.

Gellman, Barton and Laura Poitras. 2013. 'U.S., British Intelligence Mining Data from Nine U.S. Internet Companies in Broad Secret Program', *Washington Post*, June 6.

Greenwald, Glenn and Ewen MacAskill. 2013. 'NSA Prism Program Taps in to User Data of Apple, Google and Others', *The Guardian*, 6 June.

Hersh, Seymour M. 2006. 'Listening In', *The New Yorker*, May 29, available at http://www.newyorker.com/archive/2006/05/29/060529ta_talk_hersh.

Hulse, Carl and Edmund L. Andrews. 2007. 'House Approves Changes in Eavesdropping', *New York Times*, August 5, available at http://query.nytimes.com/gst/fullpage.html?res=9B00E7D91530F936A3575BC0A9619C8B63&sec=&spon=&pagewanted=1.

Krelmer, Seth F. 2004. 'Watching the Watchers: Surveillance, Transparency, and Political Freedom in the War on Terror', 7 *U. Pa. J. Const. L.* 133.

Kreykes, Bryan D. 2008. 'Data Mining and Counter-Terrorism: The Use of Telephone Records as an Investigatory Tool in the "War on Terror"', 4 *Info. & Sec.* 431.

Kunig, Philip. 1993. *Der Grundsatz informationeller Selbstbestimmung*. JURA: Juristische Ausbildung.

Levitt, Leonard. 2003. 'NYPD Spying Power Widens: Investigative Limits are Lifted', *Newsday*, 12 February.

Lichtblau, Eric. 2007. 'F.B.I. Data Mining Reached Beyond Initial Targets', *New York Times*, September 9, available at http://www.nytimes.com/2007/09/09/washington/09fbi.html?pagewanted=print.

Lichtblau, Eric and James Risen. 2009. 'N.S.A.'s Intercepts Exceed Limits Set by Congress', *New York Times*, April 16.

Lislager, Tom. 2004. 'Sects, Lies, and Videotape: The Surveillance and Infiltration of Religious Groups', 89 *Iowa L. Rev.* 1201.

Miller, Claire Cain and Nicole Perlroth. 2013. 'Secret Security Court Identifies Yahoo in 2008 Case', *New York Times*, 29 June.

Rascoff, Samuel J. 2010. 'Domesticating Intelligence', 83(3) *Southern California Law Review* 575.

Risen, James and Eric Lichtblau. 2013. 'How the U.S. Uses Technology to Mine Data More Quickly', *New York Times*, 9 June.

Risen, James and Eric Lichtblau. 2009. 'E-Mail Surveillance Renews Concerns in Congress', *New York Times*, June 16, available at http://www.nytimes.com/2009/06/17/us/17nsa.html.

Roewer, Helmut. 1986. 'Trennung von Polizei und Verfassungsschutzbehörden', *Deutsches Verwaltungsblatt* 101:205–208.

Savage, Charlie. 2009. 'Loosening of F.B.I. Rules Stirs Privacy Concerns', *New York Times*, October 28, available at http://www.nytimes.com/2009/10/29/us/29manual.html.

Savage, Charlie. 2013. 'Extended Ruling by Secret Court Backs Collection of Phone Data', *New York Times*, 18 September.

Savage, Charlie and Edward Wyatt. 2013. 'U.S. Secretly Collecting Logs of Business Calls', *New York Times*, 6 June.

Savage, Charlie, Edward Wyatt, and Peter Baker. 2013a. 'U.S. Confirms Gathering of Web Data Overseas', *New York Times*, 7 June.

Scott Shane, Charlie Savage, Gerry Mullany, and John F. Burns. 2013b. 'Leaker Charged with Violating Espionage Act', *New York Times*, 22 August.

Scott Shane and Nicole Perlroth. 2013. 'N.S.A Violated Rules on Use of Phone Logs, Intelligence Court Found in 2009', *New York Times*, 11 September.

Solove, Daniel J. 2007. 'The First Amendment as Criminal Procedure', 82 *New York University Law Review* 112.

Spaulding, Suzanne. 2005. 'If it Ain't Broke, Don't Fix It', *Patriot Debates* (Stewart A. Baker and John Kavanagh, eds.), available at http://www.abanet.org/natsecurity/patriotdebates/lone-wolf.

Unclassified Report on the President's Surveillance Program, 10 July 2009, prepared by the Offices of Inspectors General of the Department of Defense, Department of Justice, Central Intelligence Agency, National Security Agency, Office of the Director of National Intelligence.

Whitman, James Q. 2004. 'The Two Western Cultures of Privacy: Dignity Versus Liberty', 113 *Yale L. J.* 1151.

Woods, Michael J. 2005. 'Targeting the Loosely-Affiliated Terrorist', *Patriot Debates* (Stewart A. Baker and John Kavanagh, eds.) available at http://www.abanet.org/natsecurity/patriotdebates/lone-wolf.

Zetter, Kim. 2009. 'Wiretaps Were Combined with Credit Card Records of U.S. Citizens', *Wired*, January 23, available at http://www.wired.com/threatlevel/2009/01/nsa-whistlebl-1.

PART V

EPILOGUE

15. Strength, weakness, or both? On the endurance of the adversarial-inquisitorial systems in comparative criminal procedure

*Máximo Langer**

1. INTRODUCTION

This book has gathered essays by a group of distinguished comparative criminal procedure scholars who are mostly based in Europe and the United States. Given that comparative criminal procedure is a small academic field, the 14 chapters by these 17 scholars can be considered representative of the main trends in comparative criminal procedure scholarship today. In addition, because a substantial number of these scholars have been in legal academia for less than twenty years, they not only represent the current generation of comparative criminal procedure scholars, but also indicate which directions this scholarship is likely to take in the upcoming years.

Writing the epilogue of this Handbook provides a unique opportunity to make a general reflection on comparative criminal procedure as a field of research, inquiry and policy-making. This chapter will concentrate on the opposition between adversarial and inquisitorial systems in particular and between civil law and common law more generally, distinctions that have been at the center of comparative criminal procedure for a very long time. Contrary to claims that comparative criminal procedure is a new field, my first argument in this epilogue is that this collection of essays shows that contemporary comparative criminal procedure is an heir of this adversarial-inquisitorial and common law-civil law tradition. Ten out of the 14 essays make the distinction between adversarial and inquisitorial systems central to their analysis (Boyne, 2016; Grande, 2016; Hodgson, 2016; Iontcheva Turner, 2016; Mazzone, 2016; Thaman, 2016; Wen and Leipold, 2016) or structure their analysis as a comparison between civil law jurisdictions like France or Germany and common law jurisdictions like England or the United States (Cohen, 2016; Ross, 2016; Vogler and Fouladvand, 2016). The four remaining essays also use the distinctions between adversarial and inquisitorial systems (Johnson, 2016; Kovalev and Thaman, 2016; Slobogin, 2016) or Anglo-American versus non Anglo-American jurisdictions (Khanna and Mahajan, 2016) in their analysis, even if these distinctions are less central.

I also argue that these essays show that the distinctions between adversarial and inquisitorial systems and common law and civil law still provide important insights for analysis of the criminal process from a comparative angle. I thus do not suggest that comparative criminal procedure should abandon the use of these categories. However, I also maintain that, in many contexts, the centrality of the adversarial-inquisitorial and common law-civil law distinctions have had blinding, blurring and distracting effects on comparative analysis of the criminal process. I illustrate these effects with examples taken from this collection's essays, as well as from other comparative criminal procedure contexts, such as the recent wave of Latin American adversarial criminal procedure reforms. Finally, I argue that in order to be an even richer field of research, judicial and legal analysis and inquiry and policy-making, comparative criminal procedure may have to transcend the adversarial-inquisitorial and common law-civil law dichotomies.

2. CONTEMPORARY COMPARATIVE CRIMINAL PROCEDURE AS AN HEIR OF THE ADVERSARIAL-INQUISITORIAL AND COMMON LAW-CIVIL LAW INTELLECTUAL TRADITION

Comparative criminal procedure has used the distinction between civil and common law for a long time. In the fifteenth century, the English judge and thinker Fortescue compared the criminal processes of common law and civil law (Fortescue, 1997) (on Fortescue's contributions to comparative criminal procedure, see Langer (forthcoming 2016)). In the eighteenth century, continental European commentators and policy-makers became deeply interested in English criminal procedure, discussed the differences between the criminal processes of England and the Continent, and considered the former as a model for reform (Schioppa, 1986).

At some point between the end of the eighteenth century and the first half of the nineteenth century, commentators started to use the expressions 'accusatorial system' and 'inquisitorial system' to refer to the Anglo-American and continental European criminal processes respectively (H., 1834; Hélie, 1853; Mittermaier, 1832, 1834). The accusatorial system was defined as a criminal process controlled by the parties, with the court as a passive umpire. The accusatorial process did not try to elicit the defendant's confession to prove the defendant's guilt, and adjudicated criminal cases in an oral, public trial by jury. Adjudicators had to evaluate the evidence freely, according to their impressions of the case, and their verdict could not be appealed. In contrast, the inquisitorial system consisted of a criminal process controlled by the court, in which the court acted on its own initiative in investigating and adjudicating cases. The inquisitorial process tried to elicit the defendant's confession as part of its investigation of the case, and adjudicated criminal cases in written, secret proceedings by professional judges. Adjudicators had to evaluate the evidence of the case according to a system of legal proof, and their verdict could be appealed (H., 1834; Hélie, 1853; Mittermaier, 1832, 1834).

Despite claims that comparative criminal procedure is a new field (Grande, 2012; Roberts, 2002),[1] the chapters in this collection show that today's scholarship is a continued reflection of the nineteenth-century conception of these comparative categories of accusatorial (later also referred to as 'adversarial') and inquisitorial. Like nineteenth-century commentators, the authors of these chapters associate the adversarial system with Anglo-American jurisdictions and the inquisitorial system with Continental Europe (Boyne, 2016; Hodgson, 2016; Johnson, 2016; Mazzone, 2016; Wen and Leipold, 2016). The scholars in this collection also associate the differences between an adversarial system and an inquisitorial system with: party-driven versus impartially-driven procedure (Boyne, 2016; Grande, 2016; Hodgson, 2016; Iontcheva Turner, 2016; Thaman, 2016); passive versus active tribunals (Grande, 2016; Wen and Leipold, 2016); strong versus weak right to counsel (Boyne, 2016; Johnson, 2016; Hodgson, 2016; Wen and Leipold, 2016); strong versus weak protections against coerced confessions (Hodgson, 2016; Mazzone, 2016); oral versus written proceedings (Iontcheva Turner, 2016; Thaman, 2016); trial by jury versus trial by professional judges (Cohen, 2016; Grande, 2016); and limited versus broad appealability of verdicts (Cohen, 2016; Iontcheva Turner, 2016).

Nineteenth-century commentators associated the accusatorial and inquisitorial systems with different conceptions of truth and different types of social and political systems. Thus, a number of commentators considered that each system had its own way of gathering, producing and evaluating evidence, and of determining the truth about a case. According to one scholarly account, the accusatorial system had a 'synthetic conception' of investigating the truth, since each of the parties had to present evidence that supported its assertions. The accusatorial system also assumed that proper evaluation of evidence only required the common sense, education and experience of any citizen. In contrast, the inquisitorial system had an 'analytical conception' of determining the truth, since each procedural step required clear indications that the defendant was guilty. In addition, the inquisitorial process required the government-appointed professional adjudicators to apply a system of legal proof assumed to be the product of scientific knowledge (Mitter-maier, 1834).

Like commentators in the nineteenth century, the authors of these essays also conceive of the accusatorial and inquisitorial processes as systems (Grande, 2016; Iontcheva Turner, 2016; Johnson, 2016; Maz-zone, 2016). One or more epistemological, social, or political principles underpin and connect the features of these processes.

For instance, in an elaboration of classical epistemological themes, Grande (2016) argues that at the core of the difference between adversary versus non-adversary proceedings would lie a very different attitude toward the search for the truth. The adversary system would embrace an interpretative conception of truth, capturing its skepticism about the possibility of an objective recontruction of reality and based on the belief that the only realistically discoverable truth is a 'second-best one'. In contrast, non-adversary proceedings would embrace an ontological con-ception of truth based on the belief that an objective reconstruction of reality is attainable (Grande, 2016).

Similarly, Professor Iontcheva Turner's argument that the adversarial and inquisitorial traditions can explain some of the different limits that competing policies impose on the search for truth in different legal systems can also be considered an elaboration on this traditional theme. One of the classic arguments she invokes is that the inquisitorial tradition has a stronger preference for procedures that enhance accuracy and ensure the consistent application of legal norms (Iontcheva Turner, 2016).

Commentators in the nineteenth century also associated the accusa-torial system with a democratic or people's conception of the state, aimed at protecting individual rights and liberties, and the inquisitorial system with an authoritarian or monarchical conception of the state, aimed at efficiently enforcing criminal law (Hélie, 1853; Mittermaier, 1834). Elaborating on this theme and relying on Mirjan Damaška's work, Elisabetta Grande (2016) argues in her chapter for this collection that there was a relationship between the development of adversarial proceed-ings and Lockean political liberalism in England. Jacqueline Hodgson (2016) might also be touching on this theme when she argues that the adversarially-rooted tradition of England and Wales provides a stronger right to counsel than the inquisitorially-rooted tradition of France and the

Netherlands. Relatedly, David Johnson (2016) argues in his essay that the introduction of lay adjudicators in Japanese criminal justice can re-invigorate the ideals of democracy in that country.

Finally, nineteenth-century commentators understood the adversarial-inquisitorial distinction as a way to explain the institutional differences between, and different rules of, the criminal processes in common law and civil law jurisdictions. Similarly, all the chapters in this collection concentrate on the rules and institutions of the criminal process rather than on other aspects, such as who are the adjudicators, prosecutors, defense attorneys, defendants and victims in the criminal processes of different jurisdictions.

3. THE ADVERSARIAL AND INQUISITORIAL CATEGORIES AS A STRENGTH

The chapters in this collection not only illustrate that the distinction between adversarial and inquisitorial systems is both old and alive, but also that it still has important explanatory and heuristic value for comparative analysis of criminal processes.

The first reason for the persisting utility of these categories is that many of the elements of the adversarial and inquisitorial systems help explain important differences between the criminal processes of different jurisdictions. The categories thus constitute helpful theoretical tools to analyze criminal proceedings synchronically and diachronically (Langer, 2004, 2005; Langer and Roach, 2013).

For instance, in her chapter, Hodgson (2016) employs these categories and analyzes how England and Wales, Scotland, France and the Nether-lands have reacted differently to the decision by the European Court of Human Rights in *Salduz v. Turkey* (36391/02 [2008] ECHR 1542), which held that a suspect has a right to have a lawyer present before and during police interrogation, and to European Union legislation establishing, among other things, the right of access to a lawyer.

Hodgson explains that England and Wales statutorily established the right to custodial legal advice in 1984, but that the other jurisdictions introduced reforms after *Salduz*. She describes important differences in the right to custodial legal advice in each of these jurisdictions, with England and Wales having the strongest conception of this right, fol-lowed by Scotland, and then by France and the Netherlands. In England, the lawyer is permitted to be present during the police interrogation of a suspect and may seek clarification of questions and object to inappropri-ate questions. In Scotland, those arrested and detained for questioning are permitted to consult with a lawyer in private and to have a lawyer present during the police interrogation, and the lawyer may seek clarification of questions and object to inappropriate questions. However, in Scotland, lawyers prefer to speak to suspects by telephone, rather than in person, and are routinely absent from the interrogation. In France, the lawyer may be present during the police interrogation but must remain passive, legal assistance prior to questioning is limited to 30 minutes, and the lawyer is a 'duty lawyer', rather than the suspect's own lawyer. In the Netherlands, the lawyer may not be present during the police interrogation, legal assistance prior to questioning is limited to 30 minutes, and the lawyer is a 'duty lawyer', rather than the suspect's own lawyer.

Hodgson argues that these differences in the regulation and practice of the right to counsel can be explained using the adversarial-inquisitorial categories. In an adversarially-rooted jurisdiction like England and Wales, criminal procedure is conceived of as a contest between two parties. This has led to a stronger conception of the role of the defense attorney. In addition, the police act on their own during interrogation and custody, which makes the role of the defense lawyer central to ensuring that due process is respected. In inquisitorially-rooted jurisdictions like France and the Netherlands, criminal procedure has been conceived of as an impartially-driven investigation, and the police act under the hierchical control of prosecutors who are, in theory, impartial officials. As a consequence, in these jurisdictions the role of the defense attorney would be more limited. As a mixed jurisdiction, Scotland falls somewhere in between the other three jurisdictions.

Hodgson's analysis is particularly persuasive because it indicates that these differences in the right to custodial counsel are present not only in the letter of the law but also in the implementation of the regulations. She also goes beyond a general invocation of the adversarial and inquisitorial systems and articulates specific reasons why party-driven versus impartiality-driven proceedings and less or more hierarchical administrations of criminal justice would lead to different conceptions of the role of the defense attorney. Her analysis illustrates the usefulness of the adversarial and inquisitorial categories to describe and explain persisting cultural and power-distribution differences among different actors and institutions across several contemporary criminal processes (Langer, 2004).

Another example of the persisting explanatory usefulness of the adversarial and inquisitorial categories comes from Professor Boyne's chapter, which she presents as an indictment of the current validity of the adversarial and inquisitorial categories as normative models in the United States and Germany. Boyne (2016) persuasively argues that caseload pressures have created incentives for prosecutors to dispose of criminal cases without full-fledged public trials and have thus led the American and German criminal proceedings to skew the structure and goals of their truth-finding processes and move away from their normative models.

But her analysis also illustrates that these systems' reactions to the pressures do reflect the social and institutional norms of the adversarial and inquisitorial conceptions of the criminal process (Langer, 2004). As Boyne acknowledges in her piece, in the U.S. system, in which the prosecutor is conceived of as a party and in which prosecutors have a 'conviction mentality', prosecutors are more likely to seek convictions through plea bargains. By contrast, in Germany, where the prosecutors are conceived of as objective officials and are isolated from politics by a bureaucratic apparatus, prosecutors do not view cases as an opportunity to 'win' in the courtroom. As a consequence, in response to caseload pressures, the initial instinct of German prosecutors is not to over-charge cases to gain leverage in the negotiating process as many American prosecutors do, but rather to find a way to close the file using one of the pretrial proceedings, in all except the most serious cases (Boyne, 2016).

Boyne also rightly acknowledges that other correlates of the adversarial and inquisitorial dichotomy, such as the strong versus weak right to counsel, of less versus more hierarchical organization of the prosecution service, and of an informal pretrial phase versus a written dossier, all help to explain differences between the U.S. and German pretrial phases in criminal proceedings, even when both jurisdictions experience similar caseload pressures (Boyne, 2016).

Grande (2016), too, shows the persisting usefulness of these categories, by arguing that, to this day, Anglo-American criminal proceedings are structured like a dispute between two parties, while Continental criminal procedures are structured as officially driven investigations. The adversarial/inquisitorial concepts enable her to analyze the extent to which Spanish criminal procedure changed with the introduction of the jury in 1995. Iontcheva Turner (2016) also shows how the adversarial and inquisitorial traditions may explain the ways in which different jurisdictions have regulated double jeopardy rules, plea agreements and other consensual arrangements, as well as trial verdicts.

A second reason why the adversarial and inquisitorial categories are useful tools is that they enable researchers to generate hypotheses to explain or account for differences between procedural regulations across jurisdictions. For example, based on the history of the hierarchical conception of the administration of justice in the inquisitorial systems of continental Europe, Professor Cohen (2016) hypothesizes that the European Court of Human Rights' decision in *Taxquet* establishes not (only) a defendant's human right to understand his convictions, but (also) a mechanism to monitor trial judges through appeals. The generation of this type of hypothesis is useful even when the hypothesis is proven wrong or cannot be fully proven.

A third reason why the adversarial and inquisitorial systems are still useful theoretical tools is because, if carefully used, they enable scholars to discuss a large number of jurisdictions at once, which can be helpful in analyzing specific topics from a global perspective. Professor Thaman's chapter is an example. Thaman (2016) argues that the current regulation and implementation of trials and appeals in both civil law and common law jurisdictions – including the requirement that convictions be based on a reasoned judgment reviewable on appeal – are insufficient to prevent wrongful convictions. Employing the distinction between civil law and common law criminal proceedings and giving specific examples from each type of jurisdiction, Thaman illustrates his argument about the insufficiency of current regulations in both traditions. This enables him to articulate a global argument for the introduction of formal rules of evidence in serious criminal cases directed at jurisdictions in both traditions. These rules would include, for example, a negative corroboration rule in 'witness against witness', 'eyewitness identification' and 'confession' cases.

4.   THE ADVERSARIAL AND INQUISITORIAL CATEGORIES AS A WEAKNESS: THEIR BLINDING, DISTRACTING AND BLURRING EFFECTS

Despite the continued utility of the distinction between adversarial and inquisitorial systems in particular and common law and civil law more generally, the centrality of these categories also has had negative effects on the comparative analysis of the criminal process.

The first of these negative effects is *blinding*. The centrality of the adversarial-inquisitorial distinction has made aspects of or perspectives on the criminal process invisible to comparative criminal procedure scholars (and judges and policy-makers). The second of these effects is *distracting*. Even when comparative criminal procedure scholars have been aware of unexplored issues around the criminal process, the centrality of the adversarial-inquisitorial categories has led scholars (and judges and policy-makers) to concentrate on certain topics, perspectives and methodologies to the detriment of others. The third of these effects is *blurring*. The centrality of these categories has, in some cases, impoverished the analysis by comparative criminal procedure scholars (and judges and policy-makers).

Let me illustrate these effects with a few concrete examples,[2] mostly from this collection, starting with the *blinding* and *distracting effects*.[3] First, comparative criminal procedure has been mostly interested in understanding and explaining the differences between Anglo-American and Continental European jurisdictions. While not its exclusive interest, this distinction has long been central to the discipline. The centrality of the association of the adversarial and inquisitorial categories with, respectively, Anglo-American and continental jurisdictions has likely contributed to the perpetuation of the geographical limitations of the field.

This association has conferred primacy on explaining England, the United States, France, Germany and Italy because the adversarial and inquisitorial systems were abstracted from these countries' criminal processes and/or because these jurisdictions are considered the most influential originators or adapters of adversarial and inquisitorial ideas and practices. This downplays the criminal processes of lower income countries and non-Western countries, making most comparative criminal procedure scholarship an enterprise to understand the developed West, rather than a truly global exercise.

This collection reflects this phenomenon, even if its first-rank editors have made a conscious effort to include chapters about India (Khanna and Mahajan, 2016), Japan (Johnson, 2016), Russia (Kovalev and Thaman, 2016), and Taiwan (Wen and Leipold, 2016), and even if two chapters use examples from around the world to discuss their topics (Iontcheva Turner, 2016; Slobogin, 2016). Still, eight of fourteen essays in this collection primarily analyze European jurisdictions and the United States (Boyne, 2016; Cohen, 2016; Grande, 2016; Hodgson, 2016; Mazzone, 2016; Ross, 2016; Thaman, 2016; Vogler and Fouladvand, 2016).

Another illustration of the blinding and distracting effects is that, though comparative criminal procedure has assumed that individual jurisdictions may be members of legal families and that jurisdictions may influence each other (Grande, 2016; Langer, 2004), it has been interested, almost exclusively, in a criminal process that investigates and prosecutes criminal cases within a single jurisdiction, most typically within a single nation-state. The prosecution of cases for which the crimes, persons or evidence are located outside the prosecuting jurisdiction has attracted the interest of transnational criminal law, international relations and international law scholars, but little attention from comparative criminal procedure quarters. This limited interest may relate to the shaping of the discipline of comparative criminal procedure by the adversarial and inquisitorial categories, which occurred before transnational crime became an important phenomenon. Within the traditional comparative criminal procedure paradigm, the goal has been to explain differences in the way civil and common law jurisdictions prosecute and adjudicate their own domestic crime, rather than to understand how jurisdictions may interact with each other in the prosecution and adjudication of individual cases.[4]

This collection of essays reflects this narrow focus as none of the essays (with the possible limited exception of Ross (2016)) concentrates on the transnational dimensions of prosecuting and adjudicating crime.

Another example of the blinding and distracting effects is that comparative criminal procedure has maintained its focus on doctrine, institutions and roles. The field has been mostly interested in explaining why civil and common law jurisdictions have different rules and institutions to prosecute and adjudicate crime, and why prosecutors, judges, defense attorneys and other actors are assigned different roles in each type of jurisdiction; in explaining the principles or rationales that may underlie these rules, institutional arrangements and roles; in using these doctrinal, institutional and role differences to analyze specific criminal procedure issues; and in evaluating which set of rules, institutional arrangements and roles is most appealing. These differences between rules, institutions, and professional roles are the salient features for observers interested in contrasting adversarial and inquisitorial systems.

All of the essays in this collection fit into this narrowly focused perspective. For instance, none of them gives us a sense of the class, educational background, gender, immigration status or race of the main players in the criminal processes across jurisdictions, such as defendants, victims, witnesses, judges, prosecutors, defense attorneys, and others.

A final illustration of the blinding and distracting effects is that, despite its fixation on institutions and roles, comparative criminal procedure scholarship has shown interest mostly in a limited set of criminal justice institutions and actors – those related to the formal process of prosecution and adjudication. Once again, the lingering influence of the adversarial and inquisitorial processes may result in highlighting differences in institutions and actors such as the office of the prosecutor, the courts, and the bar, rather than in other institutions and actors that play a role in the criminal process, such as the police, diversion/probation officers, post-conviction and post-appeal proceedings, and administrative agencies, just to mention a few.

As one example, comparative criminal procedure has arguably done little to explain the police as an institution. To be sure, the legal powers of the police and the rights of suspects during police investigation are often covered in comparative analyses of the criminal process (Bradley, 2007; Thaman, 2008), as Hodgson (2016), Ross (2016), Slogobin (2016) and Vogler and Fouladvand (2016) illustrate in this collection. Professor Ross has also done important work on covert policing (Ross, 2007, 2008). However, we know little about how different law enforcement agencies employ criminal process across disparate social groups, how police departments are structured as organizations, the demographics of police departments, or the array of functions police departments perform in different jurisdictions. The limited attention paid to the police may be a consequence of the police world-wide being, by definition, inquisitorial, in the sense that they investigate cases on their own initiative and in relative secrecy. The adversarial-inquisitorial opposition may fail to trigger interest in and study of the diverse configurations of these inquisitorial institutions.

Similarly, we know very little about what types of administrative agencies (other than police) play a role in the prevention, investigation and prosecution of crime in different jurisdictions, and how these administrative agencies perform these roles.

As for possible illustrations of the *blurring effect* of adversarial and inquisitorial systems, it is important to note that the adversarial and inquisitorial systems are multi-dimensional models. In other words, the adversarial and inquisitorial systems include many features, such as party-driven versus impartial procedure, passive versus active tribunals, strong versus weak right to counsel, strong versus weak protections against coerced confessions, oral versus written proceedings, trial by jury versus trial by professional judges, and limited versus broad appealability of verdicts. Even when these multiple dimensions are reduced to a few underlying variables, those variables themselves are often multiple. For instance, adversarial and inquisitorial features are often reduced to sets of opposing variables, such as dispute versus inquiry and day-in-court versus sequential process (Damaška, 1986; Langer, 2004).

My point is not to dismiss multi-dimensional models. Comparative criminal procedure has produced many positive insights through these models and should keep using them when they are appropriate to describe or analyze a phenomenon. For example, relying on multi-dimensional models can be a very helpful tool for identifying and analyzing interrelated features of a given social or institutional practice, such as a procedural culture or power arrangement (Langer, 2004, 2005).

However, multi-dimensional models can be problematic when used to analyze other types of social or institutional phenomena. For instance, in analyzing why different jurisdictions have different levels of pretrial detention, the adversarial and inquisitorial systems have been proposed as the main independent variable under the hypothesis that the more inquisitorial a jurisdiction, the higher the levels of pretrial detention (Binder, 1993). But even if there were a correlation between inquisitorial systems and levels of pretrial detention, the problem with this hypothesis is that the inquisitorial system may have multiple features that may affect the levels of pretrial detention, such as a weaker presumption of innocence, a more formalistic process with a written dossier that leads to longer time between arrest and conviction, investigating judges that may be conflicted between their prosecutorial and adjudicatory roles, and a secret pretrial phase. Using the inquisitorial and adversarial systems as independent variables would not enable us to tease these four elements apart to determine whether it is one of them, a combination of them or none of them that leads to higher levels of pretrial detention.

To use an example from this collection as further illustration, in her informative and thought-provoking chapter, Professor Cohen (2016) argues that the introduction in France of the requirement that juries give reasons may not be a way to safeguard defendants, but a tool to control trial judges by monitoring their decisions through appeals. She articulates this hypothesis based on the civil law and inquisitorial hierarchical conception of the administration of justice predominant in France, in which superior judges control lower-court judges through different mechanisms. But, relying on this same tradition, which not only established hierarchical controls of adjudicators but also distrusted lay adjudicators, could it not be true that the new requirement suggests instead a distrust of lay decision-makers, rather than an attempt to control lower professional judges? I am not saying that Professor Cohen's hypothesis has less explanatory power than this alternative one – she knows the French legal system better than I do. But if the basis for articulating her hypothesis is the French inquisitorial history and tradition, multiple features immediately come into play.

Another possible example of the *blurring effect* comes from the fact that comparative criminal procedure analyses based on the adversarial and inquisitorial systems have tended to emphasize certain factors, such as different types of political regimes, theories of truth and cultural factors, to explain why different jurisdictions have different criminal procedure rules and institutions, and assign different roles to the main actors in the criminal process. Using the adversarial and inquisitorial systems as central categories thus may lead to overvaluing the influence of these factors compared to the many other factors that may affect the criminal process.

In their important chapter discussing a jurisdiction under-studied by comparative criminal procedure, Professor Wen and Professor Leipold (2016) argue that Taiwan's Continental tradition, with its rule of mandatory prosecution, may help explain why prosecutors have brought weak cases, especially against politicians. But as I read their chapter, I wondered whether other factors, such as the strength of institutions, incentives for prosecutors or contemporary politics in Taiwan, may be more important in explaining why Taiwanese prosecutors brought those weak cases against politicians. Professor Wen and Professor Leipold know Taiwan's criminal justice and political systems much better than I do, so I am probably wrong about the explanatory power of these alternative variables. However, my questions still illustrate my broader point.

A final example of the *blurring effect* comes out of the normative use of the adversarial and inquisitorial categories. Many scholars and policy-makers have framed the choice between adversarial and inquisitorial systems as the central normative choice in criminal procedure. The wave of criminal procedure reforms in Latin America over the last twenty-five years provides an illustration of this phenomenon. Policy-makers and scholars argued that shifting Latin American criminal proceedings from an inquisitorial to an adversarial system was crucial to reducing corruption of the main actors in the criminal justice system and to improving due process standards as well as the efficiency of the criminal process in investigating and prosecuting crime (Langer, 2007).

For example, reformers argued that re-defining judges as passive umpires instead of active investigators would enable them to evaluate guilt, pretrial detention, arrests, and searches and seizures more impartially. However, it is unclear that defendants tried by passive judges feel that they are treated more fairly than those tried by investigating trial judges (Bergman and Langer, 2015). The fairness of proceedings may depend not only on factors associated with the adversarial-inquisitorial dichotomy, such as a judge's role at pretrial and trial, but also on other factors, such as the quality of indigent defense systems or the level of social and educational gap between criminal defendants and the professional actors of the criminal justice system. In addition, even if Latin American criminal procedure reforms have generally reduced the percentage of inmates in pretrial detention, this result seems to have been achieved mostly by introducing and implementing guilty pleas, with attendant reductions in the time it takes to adjudicate cases, rather than through more impartial decision-making by pretrial judges (Bergman and Langer, 2015).

Similarly, Latin American reformers claimed that separation between prosecutors and judges (an adversarial characteristic) combined with enhanced prosecutorial powers would improve the Latin American criminal justice systems' ability to lead complex criminal inquiries because prosecutors would be able to concentrate on their investigative and prosecuting functions (Binder, 1993). However, it is unclear that the reforms have made any substantial improvements in this respect (Barrera Nieto and Hernando, 2009: 261–263; CEJA, 2010, 2013). This may be unsurprising if we assume that the capacity of the criminal justice system to investigate complex crimes may depend not only, or not mainly, on features associated with the adversarial-inquisitorial dichotomy, such as the definition of the role of prosecutors, but also, or rather, on other features, such as the capacity of the police and other administrative agencies to investigate these crimes, and their institutional incentives and independence for doing so.

It is thus important that we distinguish between form and substance. The adversarial and inquisitorial systems are ways to implement the principles and goals of the criminal process, but they should not be confounded with the principles and goals themselves. Instead of starting by asking which system, adversarial or inquisitorial, is normatively superior, we should start by asking which principles and goals we value in the criminal process and then we should discuss the best ways to implement those principles and goals in specific jurisdictions (Langer, 2014).

5. CONCLUSION

This chapter has argued that contemporary comparative criminal procedure is descended from the adversarial-inquisitorial and common law-civil law tradition. These categories have been used to conceptualize the criminal process as a system of rules and institutional roles and practices that are connected by and to different conceptions of truth and different types of social and political arrangements.

These categories are still helpful tools for describing and analyzing certain aspects of the criminal process. However, this essay also argues that these categories have *blinding*, *distracting*, and *blurring* effects on comparative analysis of criminal procedure.

As I already explained, I am not advocating that comparative criminal procedure abandon the adversarial and inquisitorial systems and the common law-civil law categories. As several chapters in this collection demonstrate, these categories still can be used alone or in combination with other variables and perspectives to shed light on criminal process. I am also not 'trashing' any of these essays. Each of these essays includes insightful points for our comparative understanding of criminal process around the world. Similarly, I am not 'trashing' the Latin American criminal procedure reforms that I have used to illustrate the *blurring* effect of the adversarial and inquisitorial systems. These reforms brought some improvements to Latin American criminal justice systems in: transparency, by introducing oral and public trials and pretrial hearings; efficiency, by reducing the length of criminal proceedings; and due process standards, by strengthing defendants' rights.

Rather, my point is that comparative criminal procedure, like any other field, has operated within a certain intellectual tradition that has strengths and weaknesses. Being aware of this tradition and its strengths and weaknesses may enable comparative criminal procedure to become an even richer and stronger field of research, judicial and legal analysis and inquiry and policy-making.

NOTES

*   I would like to thank Jackie Ross for her feedback over an earlier version of this piece and Elyse Meyers for her edits on it.
1.   Grande (2012) (characterizing comparative law as being born and developed within the private law arena and paying almost no attention to criminal justice in its modern foundation); Roberts (2002) (arguing that by the 1990s, comparative legal scholarship was undergoing a third major transformation and fired a new (or at least reinvigorated) sociological imagination, while penal law joined the traditional canon of private and commercial law topics).
2.   Some of these examples are taken from Langer (2014).
3.   I analyze the *blinding* and *distracting effects* together because it would require more space than this piece allows to tell these effects apart in individual cases. This is because these two effects lead to similar consequences – the omission of certain perspectives and phenomena from analysis – though for different reasons. In the case of the *blinding effect*, the scholar, judge or policy-maker does not even see other perspectives and/or phenomena. In the case of the *distracting effect*, the scholar, judge or policy-maker is aware of the omitted perspectives and phenomena, but concentrates on the perspectives and phenomena that the adversarial-inquisitorial categories highlight instead.
4.   For recent exceptions, see Keitner (2011) and Langer (2011).

REFERENCES

Barreto Nieto and Luis Hernando. 2009. 'Valoración de la Gestión del Sistema Oral Penal Acusatorio entre Enero de 2005 y Mayo de 2008', in *Una mirada a la impunidad en el marco del Sistema Penal Oral Acusatorio en Colombia.* Bogotá: Ministerio del Interior y de Justicia, 211.

Bergman, Marcelo and Langer, Máximo. 2015. 'El Nuevo Código Procesal Penal Nacional Acusatorio: Aportes Empíricos para la Discusion en Base a la Experiencia en Provincia de Buenos Aires', 1 *Revista de Derecho Procesal Penal* 51.

Binder, Alberto. 1993. *Justicia Penal y Estado de Derecho*. Buenos Aires: Ad-Hoc.

Boyne, Shawn Marie. 2016. 'Procedural Economy in Pre-trial Procedure: Developments in Germany and the United States', in Jacqueline Ross and Stephen Thaman, eds., *Comparative Criminal Procedure*. Cheltenham, UK and Northampton, MA, USA: Edward Elgar.

Bradley, Craig M., ed. 2007. *Criminal Procedure: A Worldwide Study*. Durham, NC: Carolina Academic Press.

CEJA. 2010. *Persecución de Delitos Complejos: Capacidades de los Sistemas Penales en América Latina*. Santiago, Chile: CEJA.

CEJA. 2013. *Persecución de Delitos Complejos: Experiencias en la Investigación Criminal*. Santiago, Chile: CEJA.

Cohen, Mathilde. 2016. 'The French Case for Requiring Juries to Give Reasons: Safeguarding Defendants or Guarding the Judges?', in Jacqueline Ross and Stephen Thaman, eds., *Comparative Criminal Procedure*. Cheltenham, UK and Northampton, MA, USA: Edward Elgar.

Damaška, Mirjan. 1986. *The Faces of Justice and State Authority*. New Haven, CT: Yale University Press.

Fortescue, John. 1997. *In Praise of the Laws of England* (Shelley Lockwood ed.). Cambridge: University of Cambridge Press.

Grande, Elisabetta. 2012. 'Comparative Criminal Justice', in Mauro Busani and Ugo Mattei eds., *The Cambridge Companion to Comparative Law*. Cambridge: Cambridge University Press, 191.

Grande, Elisabetta. 2016. 'Rumba Justice and the Spanish Jury Trial', in Jacqueline Ross and Stephen Thaman, eds., *Comparative Criminal Procedure*. Cheltenham, UK and Northampton, MA, USA: Edward Elgar.

H. 1834. 'An Account of the Criminal Law, Criminal Courts, and Criminal Procedure of Germany; With Notices of the Principal Writers on Penal Jurisprudence, and the Principal Theories of Penal Legislation Prevailing There', 11 *Law Magazine Quarterly Review of Jurisprudence* 1.

Hélie, Faustin. 1853. *Traité de l'instruction criminelle*, Vol. 5.

Hodgson, Jacqueline S. 2016. 'From the Domestic to the European: An Empirical Approach to Comparative Custodial Legal Advice', in Jacqueline Ross and Stephen Thaman, eds., *Comparative Criminal Procedure*. Cheltenham, UK and Northampton, MA, USA: Edward Elgar.

Iontcheva Turner, Jenia. 2016. 'Limits on the Search for Truth in Criminal Procedure: A Comparative View', in Jacqueline Ross and Stephen Thaman, eds., *Comparative Criminal Procedure*. Cheltenham, UK and Northampton, MA, USA: Edward Elgar.

Johnson, David T. 2016. 'Japan's Lay Judge System', in Jacqueline Ross and Stephen Thaman, eds., *Comparative Criminal Procedure*. Cheltenham, UK and Northampton, MA, USA: Edward Elgar.

Keitner, Chimene. 2011. 'Rights Beyond Borders', 36 *Yale Journal of International Law* 55.

Khanna, Vikramaditya S. and Kartikey Mahajan. 2016. 'Anticipatory Bail in India: Addressing Misuse of the Criminal Justice Process?', in Jacqueline Ross and Stephen Thaman, eds., *Comparative Criminal Procedure*. Cheltenham, UK and Northampton, MA, USA: Edward Elgar.

Kovalev, Nikolai and Thaman, Steven. 2016. 'Special Investigative Techniques in Post-Soviet States: The Divide between Preventive Policing and Criminal Investigation', in Jacqueline Ross and Stephen Thaman, eds., *Comparative Criminal Procedure*. Cheltenham, UK and Northampton, MA, USA: Edward Elgar.

Langer, Máximo. 2004. 'From Legal Transplants to Legal Translations: The Globalization of Plea Bargaining and the Americanization Thesis in Criminal Procedure', 45 *Harvard International Law Journal* 1.

Langer, Máximo. 2005. 'The Rise of Managerial Judging in International Criminal Law', 53 *American Journal of Comparative Law* 835.

Langer, Máximo. 2007. 'Revolution in Latin American Criminal Procedure: Diffusion of Legal Ideas from the Periphery', 55 *American Journal of Comparative Law* 617.

Langer, Máximo. 2011. 'The Diplomacy of Universal Jurisdiction: The Political Branches and the Transnational Prosecution of International Crimes', 105 *American Journal of International Law* 1.

Langer, Máximo. 2014. 'The Long Shadow of the Adversarial and Inquisitorial Categories', in Markus D. Dubber and Tatjana Höernle, eds., *Handbook on Criminal Law.* Oxford: Oxford University Press, 887.

Langer, Máximo. Forthcoming 2016. 'In the Beginning Was Fortescue: On the Intellectual Origins of the Adversarial and Inquisitorial Systems', in *Liber Amicorum in Honor of Mirjan Damaška.* Berlin: Duncker & Humblot.

Langer, Máximo and Kent Roach. 2013. 'Rights in the Criminal Process: A Case Study of Convergence and Disclosure Rights', in Mark Tushnet, Thomas Fleiner and Cheryl Saunders, eds., *Routledge Handbook of Constitutional Law.* Abingdon: Routledge, 273.

Mazzone, Jason. 2016. 'Silence, Self-Incrimination, and Hazards of Globalization', in Jacqueline Ross and Stephen Thaman, eds., *Comparative Criminal Procedure.* Cheltenham, UK and Northampton, MA, USA: Edward Elgar.

Mittermaier, K.J.A. 1832. *Das deutsche Strafverfahren in der Fortbildung durch Gerichts-Gebrauch und Partikular-Gesetzbücher in genauer Vergleichung mit dem englischen und französischen Straf-Prozesse.*

Mittermaier, Karl J.A. 1834. *Die Lehre vom Beweise im deutschen Strafprozesse nach der Fortbildung durch richtsgebrauch und deutsche Gesetzbücher in Vergleichung mit den Ansichten des englischen und französischen Strafverfahrens.*

Roberts, Paul. 2002. 'On Method: The Ascent of Comparative Criminal Justice' (book review), 22 *Oxford Journal of Legal Studies* 539.

Ross, Jacqueline. 2007. 'The Place of Covert Policing in Democratic Societies: A Comparative Study of the United States and Germany', 55 *American Journal of Comparative Law* 493.

Ross, Jacqueline. 2008. 'Undercover Policing and the Shifting Terms of Scholarly Debate: The United States and Europe in Counterpoint', 4(1) *Annual Review of Law and the Social Sciences* 239–273.

Ross, Jacqueline. 2016. 'The Emergence of Foreign Intellegence Investigations as Alternatives to the Criminal Process: A View of American Counterterrorism Surveillance through German Lenses', in Jacqueline Ross and Stephen Thaman, eds., *Comparative Criminal Procedure.* Cheltenham, UK and Northampton, MA, USA: Edward Elgar.

Schioppa, Antonio Padoa. 1986. 'I Philosophes e la Giuria Penale', I-II *Nuova Rivista Storica* 107.

Slobogin, Christopher. 2016. 'A Comparative Perspective on the Exclusionary Rule in Search and Seizure Cases', in Jacqueline Ross and Stephen Thaman, eds., *Comparative Criminal Procedure.* Cheltenham, UK and Northampton, MA, USA: Edward Elgar.

Thaman, Stephen. 2008. *Comparative Criminal Procedure: A Casebook Approach* (2nd edn). Durham, NC: Carolina Academic Press.

Thaman, Stephen C. 2016. 'Ensuring the Factual Reliability of Criminal Convictions: Reasoned Judgements or a Return to Formal Rules of Evidence?', in Jacqueline Ross and Stephen Thaman, eds., *Research Handbook on Comparative Criminal Procedure.* Cheltenham, UK and Northampton, MA, USA: Edward Elgar.

Vogler, Richard and Shahrzad Fouladvand. 2016. 'Standard for Making Factual Determinations in Arrest and Pre-trial Detention: A Comparative Analysis of Law and Practice',

in Jacqueline Ross and Stephen Thaman, eds., *Comparative Criminal Procedure*. Cheltenham, UK and Northampton, MA, USA: Edward Elgar.

Wen, Tzu-te and Andrew D. Leipold. 2016. 'Mechanisms for Screening Prosecutorial Charging Decisions in the United States and Taiwan', in Jacqueline Ross and Stephen Thaman, eds., *Comparative Criminal Procedure*. Cheltenham, UK and Northampton, MA, USA: Edward Elgar.

Index